THE OXFORD ILLUSTRATED DICKENS

Charles John Huffham Dickens was born on 7 February 1812 at Landport near Portsmouth, where his father was a Navy pay clerk. His family moved to London in 1815 and in 1817 to Chatham, where Dickens spent the happiest time of his boyhood. This was followed by a period of misery during which his father was imprisoned for debt in the Marshalsea and Dickens was withdrawn from school and, at the age of 12, sent to work in a blacking warehouse. These experiences deeply affected him and his future work. He returned to school, and left at 15 to become a clerk, a shorthand reporter in the law courts, and a reporter of debates in the Commons. In 1833 he began contributing articles to periodicals, which were later reprinted as *Sketches by Boz* (1836–7); these led to an approach from publishers, resulting in the creation of Mr Pickwick and the publication in monthly numbers of *The Posthumous Papers of the Pickwick Club* (1836–7). In 1836 he married Catherine Hogarth; they had ten children over the next 16 years. Dickens began to publish *Oliver Twist* in 1837 in *Bentley's Miscellany*, a periodical of which he was the first editor. *Nicholas Nickleby* followed in 1838–9. *The Old Curiosity Shop* (1840–1) and *Barnaby Rudge* (1841) were intended for *Master Humphrey's Clock*, a weekly written by Dickens, but he eventually abandoned 'Master Humphrey'.

Dickens's visit to America in 1842 resulted in *American Notes* (1842) and an American section in *Martin Chuzzlewit* (1843–4). He lost readership with the latter but regained it with 'A Christmas Carol' (1843), the first of his five *Christmas Books*. In 1844 he visited Italy, and contributed 'Pictures from Italy' (1846) to the *Daily News*, a paper he founded. *Dombey and Son* appeared in 1846–8 and *David Copperfield* in 1849–50. In 1850 Dickens began the weekly journal *Household Words*, incorporated in 1859 into *All The Year Round*, which he edited until his death. In these appeared essays later issued as *Reprinted Pieces* (1858) and *The Uncommercial Traveller* (1861), and his *Christmas Stories*. *A Child's History of England* was published in 1851–3, *Bleak House* in 1852–3, *Hard Times* in 1854, *Little Dorrit* in 1855–7, *A Tale of Two Cities* in 1859, *Great Expectations* in 1860–1, and *Our Mutual Friend* in 1864–5. In 1856 Dickens bought a country house, Gad's Hill Place, near Rochester, and in 1858 he and his wife separated. He threw himself into public readings of his works, which were greatly successful but draining. His last work, *The Mystery of Edwin Drood*, was left unfinished when he died suddenly on 9 June 1870.

Tom Tiddler's Ground

CHRISTMAS STORIES

By
CHARLES DICKENS

With Thirteen Illustrations by E. G. Dalziel,
Townley Green, Charles Green and others
and an Introduction by
MARGARET LANE

OXFORD   NEW YORK   TORONTO   MELBOURNE
OXFORD UNIVERSITY PRESS

Oxford University Press, Walton Street, Oxford OX2 6DP

Oxford New York Toronto
Delhi Bombay Calcutta Madras Karachi
Petaling Jaya Singapore Hong Kong Tokyo
Nairobi Dar es Salaam Cape Town
Melbourne Auckland

and associated companies in
Berlin Ibadan

Oxford is a trade mark of Oxford University Press

The contents of *Christmas Stories* originally appeared in *Household Words* and *All the Year Round*, and the majority of the stories were first collected under this title in the Charles Dickens Edition of 1871. The present edition includes additional pieces written for the Christmas numbers of these magazines.

Dickens received assistance with several of the stories. In particular, he collaborated with Wilkie Collins in 'The Wreck of the Golden Mary', 'A Message from the Sea', 'No Thoroughfare', and 'The Lazy Tour of Two Idle Apprentices'. Following the 1871 edition, certain passages, known to be by other hands, have been omitted here.

The illustrations have been taken from the 1871 Charles Dickens Edition and from the Illustrated Library Edition of 1874.

In the Oxford Illustrated Dickens (known before 1966 as the New Oxford Illustrated Dickens) *Christmas Stories* was first published in 1956, and reprinted in 1959, 1964, 1968, 1971, 1975, 1979, 1987, 1989, 1989, 1990, 1991.

Published in the United States by Oxford University Press, USA

This volume: ISBN 0 19 254517 5
21-volume set: ISBN 0 19 254522 1

Printed in the United States of America

INTRODUCTION

by MARGARET LANE

THESE stories belong to Dickens's maturity and middle age, to the seventeen crowded years between *David Copperfield* and *Edwin Drood*. They are small beer, if you like; part of the overflow of that volcanic vitality which neither life nor works was able to exhaust; but all the same, on this modest level, rewarding.

It is a mistake to read the book straight through. It best serves the purpose of a bedside book, to be dipped into by degrees, as the stories were written, for the Dickens who wrote *A Christmas Tree* in 1850 was a vastly different man from the one who wrote *No Thoroughfare* in 1867. The *Christmas Stories* can, in fact, be taken as a reflection of significant developments in Dickens, and have most to offer when they are read against the background of his life.

Dickens was thirty-eight, at the height of his powers and in the midst of writing *David Copperfield*, when he launched his twopenny weekly, *Household Words*, as a means of putting himself into ever closer touch with his huge public. It was to be a platform for his views on current affairs, expressed with a directness hardly possible in the novels. It was also to be the perfect family entertainment, and the main Christmas attraction at the end of each year was to be a long short story written by Dickens himself.

The first few stories in the volume fall neatly enough into this conventional frame. They are the Dickens we were taught to expect at Christmas—light-hearted, tender, full of recollections of childhood and zest for the amusements of youth, for ghost stories and roast chestnuts and family theatricals, and for that 'Christmas spirit which is the spirit of active usefulness, perseverance, cheerful discharge of duty, kindness and forbearance'. They are sentimental here and there, but not mawkish; they are too high-spirited for that. They are stories written to be read in the family circle, to a mixed audience of old and young, eager to be amused and not too critical, and anyone who has put them to their proper use knows how admirably they still fulfil their purpose.

Before long, however, there is a dramatic change; the voice of the story-teller deepens. That complacent family circle, warm and well-fed and contented round the crackling fire, must be made to look beyond the plush curtains and the solid walls, and listen to another, this time a disagreeably radical voice. Dickens has been despised as a social reformer by those who know too little about his life. In fact he was a tireless campaigner against every form of social injustice, devoting an astounding proportion of his time and energy to a variety of progressive causes—enough, one would suppose, to have absorbed the whole creative energy of a lesser man. The comfortable reader, opening his *Household Words* for an instalment of Christmas cheer, must have been chilled and disappointed by *Nobody's Story*, for this is Dickens's angry voice, the voice of his private conviction, which believed that neglect of the poor in England was a certain invitation to revolution. 'The people will not bear for any length of time what they bear now', he wrote to Miss Burdett-Coutts in 1855. 'I see it written in every truthful indication that I am capable of discerning anywhere. And I want to interpose something between them and their wrath. For this reason solely I am a Reformer heart and soul. I have nothing to gain—everything to lose (for public quiet is my bread)—but I am in desperate earnest because I know it is a desperate case.' It is this same desperately earnest voice which speaks in *Nobody's Story*.

I have begun to understand a little [says the nameless dweller in the slums, when the filth of the rookeries has been blamed for a spreading pestilence] that most calamities will come from us, as this one did, and that none will stop at our poor doors. . . . We cannot live healthily and decently, unless those who undertook to manage us provide the means. We cannot be instructed unless they will teach us; we cannot be rationally amused, unless they will amuse us. . . . The evil consequences of pernicious neglect, the evil consequences of unnatural restraint and the denial of humanising enjoyments, will all come from us, and none of them will stop with us. They will spread far and wide. They always do; they always have done—just like the pestilence. I understand so much, I think, at last.

Dickens did not make the mistake, however, of turning his Christmas stories into sermons. He knew his business as an entertainer far too well, and when he had a pill to offer confected it expertly with spice and sugar. We laugh over the opening chapter of *The Seven Poor Travellers*, and absorb by the way the fact that the poor old men in the almshouse are scurvily treated. He took immense pains with his short stories; conscious, perhaps, that it was not the literary form which suited him best. His genius was too full, exuberant, and irrepressible to be confined easily in a small compass, and in story after story we find it breaking out untidily, running after an attractive hare of oddity or humour when it should have been drawing instead to a shapely conclusion. Yet it is these breaks with conventional story-teller's discipline which most often produce unexpected and delightful results. Christmas, as Dickens saw it, was a time for ghost stories, and he applied himself like a good journeyman to their manufacture; but his own scepticism keeps ridiculously breaking in, making a delicious mockery of the very goods he is pretending to sell. His *Haunted House* is no more genuinely haunted than Borley Rectory (unless, like some of the investigators of Borley, we can seriously accept an ''ooded woman with a howl' and other capital nonsense) and the spiritualist encountered in the train on the way there provides evidence worthy of the archives of a psychical research society.

'The conferences of the night began,' continued the gentleman, turning several leaves of his notebook, 'with this message: Evil communications corrupt good manners.'

'Sound,' I said, 'but, absolutely new?'

'New from spirits,' returned the gentleman.

I could only repeat my rather snappish 'O!' and ask if I might be favoured with the last communication.

'A bird in the hand,' said the gentleman, reading his last entry with great solemnity, 'is worth two in the Bosh.'

'Truly I am of the same opinion,' said I, 'but shouldn't it be Bush?'

'It came to me, Bosh,' returned the gentleman.

A number of the stories, both in *Household Words* and its successor *All the Year Round*, were written in collaboration with Wilkie Collins; a practical arrangement but not a happy one, for Dickens was not the man to run well in double harness. The elaborately contrived plot, at which Collins was adept, was cramping to the natural play of his fancy and humour; even those chapters which are known to have belonged to Dickens alone read as though they were written under constraint. The two men spared no pains over the collaboration, going down into the country together to gather material whenever it seemed necessary, enduring the miseries of bad hotels in a diligent search for a substitute for inspiration. 'We had stinking fish for dinner,' Dickens wrote from Bideford, where they had gone to seek local colour for *A Message from the Sea*, 'and have been able to drink nothing, though we have ordered wine, beer and brandy-and-water. There is nothing in the house but two tarts and a pair of snuffers.' These were not the conditions which suited him, though one has the impression that it was the presence of Collins rather than the stinking fish which spoiled the prospect. Left to himself, Dickens made brilliant capital out of the squalid vicissitudes of inns and travelling.

It is, of course, in those sudden bursts of nonsense, when Dickens's sense of the ridiculous gets the better of him and puts the plot out of countenance, that the modern reader most enjoys himself. There are fragments here and there which, if they had been embedded in *Dombey* or *Martin Chuzzlewit*, would long have been famous, but they have missed several generations through lying unread in the attic, where the *Christmas Stories* are most commonly found, and they come out with the freshness of discoveries. How did the Head Waiter in *Somebody's Luggage* escape from his proper place in one of the major novels? It is preposterous to regard him simply as an overflow, yet that is obviously what he is. He is so much a part of the Victorian coffee-room scene that he seems to breathe, not air, but a damp exhalation of sawdust and stale cruets.

We are not a general dining business, nor do we wish it. In consequence, when diners drop in, we know what to give 'em as will keep 'em away another time. We are a Private Room or Family Business also; but Coffee-room principal. Me and the Directory and the Writing Materials and cetrer occupy a place to ourselves—a place fended off up a step or two at the end of the Coffee-room, in what I call the good old-fashioned style. The good old-fashioned style is, that whatever you want, down to a wafer, you must be olely and solely dependent on the Head Waiter for. You must put yourself a new-born Child into his hands. There is no other way in which a business untinged with continental vice can be conducted.

Did the British catering trade, I wonder, ever take any notice of the merciless fun which Dickens occasionally poked

at it ? Of course not. The refreshment-room staff at Mugby
Junction would find themselves at home in almost any provincial railway station today, and Mrs. Sniff would have
even greater scope for her crushing talents.

She's the one! She's the one as you'll notice to be always
looking another way from you, when you look at her. She's the
one with the small waist buskled in tight in front, and with
the lace cuffs at her wrists, which she puts on the edge of the
counter before her, and stands a-smoothing while the public
foams. This smoothing the cuffs and looking another way while
the public foams is the last accomplishment taught to the young
ladies as come to Mugby to be finished by Our Missis; and it's
always taught by Mrs. Sniff.

To those readers who enjoy a man's work the more when
they can see it against the background of his life, there is a
special interest in Dickens's Christmas stories, for they reflect
something of the change that took place in himself during
their seventeen years. They begin with the Dickens most
familiar to the world—famous, still young, still happily married, bubbling over with creative energy and high spirits,
and they come to an end three years before his death, when
he had become a more sombre and complex character, hag-
ridden by restlessness, driving himself furiously to exhaustion in the public readings which he used as a drug to stifle
emotional unhappiness. The stories reflect none of this
clearly, it is true; but the change of tone is there, and a
falling-off in the old high-spirited love of absurdity, and a
preoccupation with darker, more sinister themes. It is worth
remembering, too, that one or two of the later stories were
used by Dickens himself in his public readings, when his
obscure dissatisfactions with life and fame were driving him
into ever more frenzied efforts to increase his hypnotic
emotional hold on the public. No very definite conclusions
can be reached, perhaps, by looking at the *Christmas Stories*
in this stereoscopic way, but it increases the depth, and
gives a finer edge to enjoyment and understanding.

LIST OF ILLUSTRATIONS

A CHRISTMAS TREE

[1850]

A CHRISTMAS TREE

I HAVE been looking on, this evening, at a merry company
of children assembled round that pretty German toy, a
Christmas Tree. The tree was planted in the middle of a
great round table, and towered high above their heads. It
was brilliantly lighted by a multitude of little tapers; and
everywhere sparkled and glittered with bright objects. There
were rosy-cheeked dolls, hiding behind the green leaves; and
there were real watches (with movable hands, at least, and
an endless capacity of being wound up) dangling from innumerable twigs; there were French-polished tables, chairs,
bedsteads, wardrobes, eight-day clocks, and various other
articles of domestic furniture (wonderfully made, in tin, at
Wolverhampton), perched among the boughs, as if in preparation for some fairy housekeeping; there were jolly, broad-
faced little men, much more agreeable in appearance than
many real men—and no wonder, for their heads took off,
and showed them to be full of sugar-plums; there were
fiddles and drums; there were tambourines, books, work-
boxes, paint-boxes, sweetmeat boxes, peep-show boxes, and
all kinds of boxes; there were trinkets for the elder girls,
far brighter than any grown-up gold and jewels; there were
baskets and pincushions in all devices; there were guns,
swords, and banners; there were witches standing in enchanted rings of pasteboard, to tell fortunes; there were tee-
totums, humming-tops, needle-cases, pen-wipers, smelling-
bottles, conversation-cards, bouquet-holders; real fruit, made
artificially dazzling with gold leaf; imitation apples, pears,
and walnuts, crammed with surprises; in short, as a pretty
child, before me, delightedly whispered to another pretty
child, her bosom friend, "There was everything, and more."
This motley collection of odd objects, clustering on the tree

like magic fruit, and flashing back the bright looks directed towards it from every side—some of the diamond-eyes admiring it were hardly on a level with the table, and a few were languishing in timid wonder on the bosoms of pretty mothers, aunts, and nurses—made a lively realisation of the fancies of childhood; and set me thinking how all the trees that grow and all the things that come into existence on the earth, have their wild adornments at that well-remembered time.

Being now at home again, and alone, the only person in the house awake, my thoughts are drawn back, by a fascination which I do not care to resist, to my own childhood. I begin to consider, what do we all remember best upon the branches of the Christmas Tree of our own young Christmas days, by which we climbed to real life.

Straight, in the middle of the room, cramped in the freedom of its growth by no encircling walls or soon-reached ceiling, a shadowy tree arises; and, looking up into the dreamy brightness of its top—for I observe in this tree the singular property that it appears to grow downward towards the earth—I look into my youngest Christmas recollections!

All toys at first, I find. Up yonder, among the green holly and red berries, is the Tumbler with his hands in his pockets, who wouldn't lie down, but whenever he was put upon the floor, persisted in rolling his fat body about, until he rolled himself still, and brought those lobster eyes of his to bear upon me—when I affected to laugh very much, but in my heart of hearts was extremely doubtful of him. Close beside him is that infernal snuff-box, out of which there sprang a demoniacal Counsellor in a black gown, with an obnoxious head of hair, and a red cloth mouth, wide open, who was not to be endured on any terms, but could not be put away either; for he used suddenly, in a highly magnified state, to fly out of Mammoth Snuff-boxes in dreams, when least expected. Nor is the frog with cobbler's wax on his tail, far off; for there was no knowing where he wouldn't jump; and when he flew over the candle, and came upon one's hand with that spotted back—red on a green ground—he was horrible. The cardboard lady in a blue-silk skirt, who was stood up against the candlestick to dance, and whom I see on the same branch, was milder, and was beautiful; but I can't say as much for the larger cardboard man, who used to be hung against the wall and pulled by a string; there an unreasonable disposition in the respectable Kelmar, and some others, to become faint in the legs, and double up, at exciting points of the drama), a teeming world of fancies so suggestive and all-embracing, that, far below it on my Christmas Tree, I see dark, dirty, real Theatres in the day-time, adorned with these associations as with the freshest garlands of the rarest flowers, and charming me yet.

But hark! The Waits are playing, and they break my childish sleep! What images do I associate with the Christmas music as I see them set forth on the Christmas Tree? Known before all the others, keeping far apart from all the others, they gather round my little bed. An angel, speaking to a group of shepherds in a field; some travellers, with eyes uplifted, following a star; a baby in a manger; a child in a spacious temple, talking with grave men; a solemn figure, with a mild and beautiful face, raising a dead girl by the hand; again. near a city gate, calling back the son of a widow, on his bier, to life; a crowd of people looking through the opened roof of a chamber where he sits, and letting down a sick person on a bed, with ropes; the same, in a tempest, walking on the water to a ship; again, on a sea-shore, teaching a great multitude; again, with a child upon his knee, and other children round; again, restoring sight to the blind, speech to the dumb, hearing to the deaf, health to the sick, strength to the lame, knowledge to the ignorant; again, dying upon a Cross, watched by armed soldiers, a thick darkness coming on, the earth beginning to shake, and only one voice heard, " Forgive them, for they know not what they do."

Still, on the lower and maturer branches of the Tree, Christmas associations cluster thick. School-books shut up; Ovid and Virgil silenced; the Rule of Three, with its cool impertinent inquiries, long disposed of; Terence and Plautus acted no more, in an arena of huddled desks and forms, all chipped, and notched, and inked; cricket-bats, stumps, and balls, left higher up, with the smell of trodden grass and the softened noise of shouts in the evening air; the tree is still fresh, still gay. If I no more come home at Christmas-time, there will be boys and girls (thank Heaven!) while the World lasts; and they do! Yonder they dance and play upon the branches of my Tree, God bless them, merrily, and my heart dances and plays too!

And I *do* come home at Christmas. We all do, or we all should. We all come home, or ought to come home, for

a short holiday—the longer, the better—from the great
boarding-school, where we are for ever working at our arithmetical slates, to take, and give a rest. As to going a visiting,
where can we not go, if we will; where have we not been,
when we would; starting our fancy from our Christmas Tree!

Away into the winter prospect. There are many such
upon the tree! On, by low-lying, misty grounds, through
fens and fogs, up long hills, winding dark as caverns between
thick plantations, almost shutting out the sparkling stars;
so, out on broad heights, until we stop at last, with sudden
silence, at an avenue. The gate-bell has a deep, half-awful
sound in the frosty air; the gate swings open on its hinges;
and, as we drive up to a great house, the glancing lights
grow larger in the windows, and the opposing rows of trees
seem to fall solemnly back on either side, to give us place.
At intervals, all day, a frightened hare has shot across this
whitened turf; or the distant clatter of a herd of deer tramp-
ling the hard frost, has, for the minute, crushed the silence
too. Their watchful eyes beneath the fern may be shining
now, if we could see them, like the icy dewdrops on the
leaves; but they are still, and all is still. And so, the lights
growing larger, and the trees falling back before us, and
closing up again behind us, as if to forbid retreat, we come
to the house.

There is probably a smell of roasted chestnuts and other
good comfortable things all the time, for we are telling
Winter Stories—Ghost Stories, or more shame for us—round
the Christmas fire; and we have never stirred, except to draw
a little nearer to it. But, no matter for that. We came to
the house, and it is an old house, full of great chimneys
where wood is burnt on ancient dogs upon the hearth, and
grim portraits (some of them with grim legends, too) lower
distrustfully from the oaken panels of the walls. We are
a middle-aged nobleman, and we make a generous supper
with our host and hostess and their guests—it being
Christmas-time, and the old house full of company—and
then we go to bed. Our room is a very old room. It is
hung with tapestry. We don't like the portrait of a cavalier
in green, over the fireplace. There are great black beams in
the ceiling, and there is a great black bedstead, supported at
the foot by two great black figures, who seem to have come
off a couple of tombs in the old baronial church in the park,
for our particular accommodation. But, we are not a super-

stitious nobleman, and we don't mind. Well! we dismiss
our servant, lock the door, and sit before the fire in our
dressing-gown, musing about a great many things. At length
we go to bed. Well! we can't sleep. We toss and tumble,
and can't sleep. The embers on the hearth burn fitfully and
make the room look ghostly. We can't help peeping out over
the counterpane, at the two black figures and the cavalier—
that wicked-looking cavalier—in green. In the flickering
light they seem to advance and retire: which, though we are
not by any means a superstitious nobleman, is not agreeable.
Well! we get nervous—more and more nervous. We say
"This is very foolish, but we can't stand this; we'll pretend to be ill, and knock up somebody." Well! we are just
going to do it, when the locked door opens, and there comes
in a young woman, deadly pale, and with long fair hair, who
glides to the fire, and sits down in the chair we have left
there, wringing her hands. Then, we notice that her clothes
are wet. Our tongue cleaves to the roof of our mouth, and
we can't speak; but, we observe her accurately. Her clothes
are wet; her long hair is dabbled with moist mud; she is
dressed in the fashion of two hundred years ago; and she
has at her girdle a bunch of rusty keys. Well! there she
sits, and we can't even faint, we are in such a state about it.
Presently she gets up, and tries all the locks in the room
with the rusty keys, which won't fit one of them; then, she
fixes her eyes on the portrait of the cavalier in green, and
says, in a low, terrible voice, "The stags know it!" After
that, she wrings her hands again, passes the bedside, and
goes out at the door. We hurry on our dressing-gown, seize
our pistols (we always travel with pistols), and are following.
when we find the door locked. We turn the key, look out
into the dark gallery; no one there. We wander away,
and try to find our servant. Can't be done. We pace the
gallery till daybreak; then return to our deserted room, fall
asleep, and are awakened by our servant (nothing ever haunts
him) and the shining sun. Well! we make a wretched breakfast, and all the company say we look queer. After breakfast,
we go over the house with our host, and then we take him to
the portrait of the cavalier in green, and then it all comes
out. He was false to a young housekeeper once attached to
that family, and famous for her beauty, who drowned herself
in a pond, and whose body was discovered, after a long time,
because the stags refused to drink of the water. Since which,

it has been whispered that she traverses the house at midnight (but goes especially to that room where the cavalier in green was wont to sleep), trying the old locks with the rusty keys. Well! we tell our host of what we have seen, and a shade comes over his features, and he begs it may be hushed up; and so it is. But, it's all true; and we said so, before we died (we are dead now) to many responsible people.

There is no end to the old houses, with resounding galleries, and dismal state-bedchambers, and haunted wings shut up for many years, through which we may ramble, with an agreeable creeping up our back, and encounter any number of ghosts, but (it is worthy of remark perhaps) reducible to a very few general types and classes; for, ghosts have little originality, and "walk" in a beaten track. Thus, it comes to pass, that a certain room in a certain old hall, where a certain bad lord, baronet, knight, or gentleman, shot himself, has certain planks in the floor from which the blood *will not* be taken out. You may scrape and scrape, as the present owner has done, or plane and plane, as his father did, or scrub and scrub, as his grandfather did, or burn and burn with strong acids, as his great-grandfather did, but, there the blood will still be—no redder and no paler—no more and no less—always just the same. Thus, in such another house there is a haunted door, that never will keep open; or another door that never will keep shut; or a haunted sound of a spinning-wheel, or a hammer, or a footstep, or a cry, or a sigh, or a horse's tramp, or the rattling of a chain. Or else, there is a turret-clock, which, at the midnight hour, strikes thirteen when the head of the family is going to die; or a shadowy, immovable black carriage which at such a time is always seen by somebody, waiting near the great gates in the stable-yard. Or thus, it came to pass how Lady Mary went to pay a visit at a large wild house in the Scottish Highlands, and, being fatigued with her long journey, retired to bed early, and innocently said, next morning, at the breakfast-table, "How odd, to have so late a party last night, in this remote place, and not to tell me of it, before I went to bed!" Then, every one asked Lady Mary what she meant? Then, Lady Mary replied, "Why, all night long, the carriages were driving round and round the terrace, underneath my window!" Then, the owner of the house turned pale, and so did his Lady, and Charles Macdoodle of Macdoodle signed to Lady Mary to say no more, and every one was silent. After breakfast, Charles Macdoodle told Lady Mary that it was a tradition in the family that those rumbling carriages on the terrace betokened death. And so it proved, for, two months afterwards, the Lady of the mansion died. And Lady Mary, who was a Maid of Honour at Court, often told this story to the old Queen Charlotte; by this token that the old King always said, "Eh, eh? What, what? Ghosts, ghosts? No such thing, no such thing!" And never left off saying so, until he went to bed.

Or, a friend of somebody's whom most of us know, when he was a young man at college, had a particular friend, with whom he made the compact that, if it were possible for the Spirit to return to this earth after its separation from the body, he of the twain who first died, should reappear to the other. In course of time, this compact was forgotten by our friend; the two young men having progressed in life, and taken diverging paths that were wide asunder. But, one night, many years afterwards, our friend being in the North of England, and staying for the night in an inn, on the Yorkshire Moors, happened to look out of bed; and there, in the moonlight, leaning on a bureau near the window, steadfastly regarding him, saw his old college friend! The appearance being solemnly addressed, replied, in a kind of whisper, but very audibly, "Do not come near me. I am dead. I am here to redeem my promise. I come from another world, but may not disclose its secrets!" Then, the whole form becoming paler, melted, as it were, into the moonlight, and faded away.

Or, there was the daughter of the first occupier of the picturesque Elizabethan house, só famous in our neighbourhood. You have heard about her? No! Why, *She* went out one summer evening at twilight, when she was a beautiful girl, just seventeen years of age, to gather flowers in the garden; and presently came running, terrified, into the hall to her father, saying, "Oh, dear father, I have met myself!" He took her in his arms, and told her it was fancy, but she said, "Oh no! I met myself in the broad walk, and I was pale and gathering withered flowers, and I turned my head, and held them up!" And, that night, she died; and a picture of her story was begun, though never finished, and they say it is somewhere in the house to this day, with its face to the wall.

Or, the uncle of my brother's wife was riding home on horseback, one mellow evening at sunset, when, in a green lane close to his own house, he saw a man standing before him, in the very centre of a narrow way. "Why does that man in the cloak stand there?" he thought. "Does he want me to ride over him?" But the figure never moved. He felt a strange sensation at seeing it so still, but slackened his trot and rode forward. When he was so close to it, as almost to touch it with his stirrup, his horse shied, and the figure glided up the bank, in a curious, unearthly manner— backward, and without seeming to use its feet—and was gone. The uncle of my brother's wife, exclaiming, "Good Heaven! It's my cousin Harry, from Bombay!" put spurs to his horse, which was suddenly in a profuse sweat, and, wondering at such strange behaviour, dashed round to the front of his house. There, he saw the same figure, just passing in at the long French window of the drawing-room, opening on the ground. He threw his bridle to a servant, and hastened in after it. His sister was sitting there, alone. "Alice, where's my cousin Harry?" "Your cousin Harry, John?" "Yes. From Bombay. I met him in the lane just now, and saw him enter here, this instant." Not a creature had been seen by any one; and in that hour and minute, as it afterwards appeared, this cousin died in India.

Or, it was a certain sensible old maiden lady, who died at ninety-nine, and retained her faculties to the last, who really did see the Orphan Boy; a story which has often been incorrectly told, but, of which the real truth is this—because it is, in fact, a story belonging to our family—and she was a connexion of our family. When she was about forty years of age, and still an uncommonly fine woman (her lover died young, which was the reason why she never married, though she had many offers), she went to stay at a place in Kent, which her brother, an Indian-Merchant, had newly bought. There was a story that this place had once been held in trust, by the guardian of a young boy; who was himself the next heir, and who killed the young boy by harsh and cruel treatment. She knew nothing of that. It has been said that there was a Cage in her bedroom in which the guardian used to put the boy. There was no such thing. There was only a closet. She went to bed, made no alarm whatever in the night, and in the morning said composedly to her maid when she came in, "Who is the pretty forlorn-looking child who has been peeping out of that closet all night?" The maid replied by giving a loud scream, and instantly decamping. She was surprised; but she was a woman of remarkable strength of mind, and she dressed herself and went downstairs, and closeted herself with her brother. "Now, Walter," she said, "I have been disturbed all night by a pretty, forlorn-looking boy, who has been constantly peeping out of that closet in my room, which I can't open. This is some trick." "I am afraid not, Charlotte," said he, "for it is the legend of the house. It is the Orphan Boy. What did he do?" "He opened the door softly," said she, "and peeped out. Sometimes, he came a step or two into the room. Then, I called to him, to encourage him, and he shrunk, and shuddered, and crept in again, and shut the door." "The closet has no communication, Charlotte," said her brother, "with any other part of the house, and it's nailed up." This was undeniably true, and it took two carpenters a whole forenoon to get it open, for examination. Then, she was satisfied that she had seen the Orphan Boy. But, the wild and terrible part of the story is, that he was also seen by three of her brother's sons, in succession, who all died young. On the occasion of each child being taken ill, he came home in a heat, twelve hours before, and said, Oh, mama, he had been playing under a particular oak-tree, in a certain meadow, with a strange boy—a pretty, forlorn-looking boy, who was very timid, and made signs! From fatal experience, the parents came to know that this was the Orphan Boy, and that the course of that child whom he chose for his little playmate was surely run.

Legion is the name of the German castles, where we sit up alone to wait for the Spectre—where we are shown into a room, made comparatively cheerful for our reception—where we glance round at the shadows, thrown on the blank walls by the crackling fire—where we feel very lonely when the village innkeeper and his pretty daughter have retired, after laying down a fresh store of wood upon the hearth, and setting forth on the small table such supper-cheer as a cold roast capon, bread, grapes, and a flask of old Rhine wine—where the reverberating doors close on their retreat, one after another. like so many peals of sullen thunder—and where, about the small hours of the night, we come into the knowledge of divers supernatural mysteries. Legion is the name of the haunted German students, in whose society we draw yet nearer to the fire, while the schoolboy in the corner opens his eyes wide and round, and flies off the footstool he has chosen for his seat, when the door accidentally blows open. Vast is the crop of such fruit, shining on our Christmas Tree ; in blossom, almost at the very top; ripening all down the boughs !

Among the later toys and fancies hanging there—as idle often and less pure—be the images once associated with the sweet old Waits, the softened music in the night, ever unalterable ! Encircled by the social thoughts of Christmas-time, still let the benignant figure of my childhood stand unchanged ! In every cheerful image and suggestion that the season brings, may the bright star that rested above the poor roof, be the star of all the Christian world ! A moment's pause, O vanishing tree, of which the lower boughs are dark to me as yet, and let me look once more ! I know there are blank spaces on thy branches, where eyes that I have loved, have shone and smiled ; from which they are departed. But, far above, I see the raiser of the dead girl, and the Widow's Son ; and God is good ! If Age be hiding for me in the unseen portion of thy downward growth, O may I, with a grey head, turn a child's heart to that figure yet, and a child's trustfulness and confidence !

Now, the tree is decorated with bright merriment, and song, and dance, and cheerfulness. And they are welcome. Innocent and welcome be they ever held, beneath the branches of the Christmas Tree, which cast no gloomy shadow ! But, as it sinks into the ground, I hear a whisper going through the leaves. " This, in commemoration of the law of love and kindness, mercy and compassion. This, in remembrance of Me ! "

WHAT CHRISTMAS IS AS WE GROW OLDER

[1851]

WHAT CHRISTMAS IS AS
WE GROW OLDER

TIME was, with most of us, when Christmas Day encircling all our limited world like a magic ring, left nothing out for us to miss or seek ; bound together all our home enjoyments, affections, and hopes; grouped everything and every one around the Christmas fire ; and made the little picture shining in our bright young eyes, complete.

Time came, perhaps, all too soon, when our thoughts overleaped that narrow boundary ; when there was some one (very dear, we thought then, very beautiful, and absolutely perfect) wanting to the fulness of our happiness ; when we were wanting too (or we thought so, which did just as well) at the Christmas hearth by which that some one sat ; and when we intertwined with every wreath and garland of our life that some one's name.

That was the time for the bright visionary Christmases which have long arisen from us to show faintly, after summer rain, in the palest edges of the rainbow ! That was the time for the beatified enjoyment of the things that were to be, and never were, and yet the things that were so real in our resolute hope that it would be hard to say, now, what realities achieved since, have been stronger !

What ! Did that Christmas never really come when we and the priceless pearl who was our young choice were received, after the happiest of totally impossible marriages, by the two united families previously at daggers-drawn on our account ? When brothers and sisters in law who had always been rather cool to us before our relationship was effected, perfectly doted on us, and when fathers and mothers overwhelmed us with unlimited incomes ? Was that Christmas dinner never really eaten, after which we arose, and generously and eloquently rendered honour to our late rival, present in the company, then and there exchanging friendship and forgiveness, and founding an attachment, not to be surpassed in Greek or Roman story, which subsisted until death? Has that same rival long ceased to care for that same priceless pearl, and married for money, and become usurious? Above all, do we really know, now, that we should probably have been miserable if we had won and worn the pearl, and that we are better without her?

That Christmas when we had recently achieved so much fame; when we had been carried in triumph somewhere, for doing something great and good; when we had won an honoured and ennobled name, and arrived and were received at home in a shower of tears of joy; is it possible that *that* Christmas has not come yet?

And is our life here, at the best, so constituted that, pausing as we advance at such a noticeable milestone in the track as this great birthday, we look back on the things that never were, as naturally and full as gravely as on the things that have been and are gone, or have been and still are? If it be so, and so it seems to be, must we come to the conclusion that life is little better than a dream, and little worth the loves and strivings that we crowd into it?

No! Far be such miscalled philosophy from us, dear Reader, on Christmas Day! Nearer and closer to our hearts be the Christmas spirit, which is the spirit of active usefulness, perseverance, cheerful discharge of duty, kindness and forbearance! It is in the last virtues especially, that we are, or should be, strengthened by the unaccomplished visions of our youth; for, who shall say that they are not our teachers to deal gently even with the impalpable nothings of the earth!

Therefore, as we grow older, let us be more thankful that the circle of our Christmas associations and of the lessons that they bring, expands! Let us welcome every one of them, and summon them to take their places by the Christmas hearth.

Welcome, old aspirations, glittering creatures of an ardent fancy, to your shelter underneath the holly! We know you, and have not outlived you yet. Welcome, old projects and old loves, however fleeting, to your nooks among the steadier lights that burn around us. Welcome, all that was ever real to our hearts; and for the earnestness that made you real, thanks to Heaven! Do we build no Christmas castles in the clouds now? Let our thoughts, fluttering like butter-flies among these flowers of children, bear witness! Before this boy, there stretches out a Future, brighter than we ever looked on in our old romantic time, but bright with honour and with truth. Around this little head on which the sunny curls lie heaped, the graces sport, as prettily, as airily, as when there was no scythe within the reach of Time to shear away the curls of our first-love. Upon another girl's face near it—placider but smiling bright—a quiet and contented little face, we see Home fairly written. Shining from the word, as rays shine from a star, we see how, when our graves are old, other hopes than ours are young, other hearts than ours are moved; how other ways are smoothed; how other happiness blooms, ripens, and decays—no, not decays, for other homes and other bands of children, not yet in being nor for ages yet to be, arise, and bloom and ripen to the end of all!

Welcome, everything! Welcome, alike what has been, and what never was, and what we hope may be, to your shelter underneath the holly, to your places round the Christmas fire, where what is sits open-hearted! In yonder shadow, do we see obtruding furtively upon the blaze, an enemy's face? By Christmas Day we do forgive him! If the injury he has done us may admit of such companionship, let him come here and take his place. If otherwise, unhappily, let him go hence, assured that we will never injure nor accuse him.

On this day we shut out Nothing!

"Pause," says a low voice. "Nothing? Think!"

"On Christmas Day, we will shut out from our fireside, Nothing."

"Not the shadow of a vast City where the withered leaves are lying deep?" the voice replies. "Not the shadow that darkens the whole globe? Not the shadow of the City of the Dead?"

Not even that. Of all days in the year, we will turn our faces towards that City upon Christmas Day, and from its silent hosts bring those we loved, among us. City of the Dead, in the blessed name wherein we are gathered together at this time, and in the Presence that is here among us according to the promise, we will receive, and not dismiss, the people who are dear to us!

Yes. We can look upon these children angels that alight, so solemnly, so beautifully among the living children by the fire, and can bear to think how they departed from us. Entertaining angels unawares, as the Patriarchs did, the playful children are unconscious of their guests; but we can see them—can see a radiant arm around one favourite neck, as if there were a tempting of that child away. Among the celestial figures there is one, a poor mis-shapen boy on earth, of a glorious beauty now, of whom his dying mother said it grieved her much to leave him here, alone, for so many years as it was likely would elapse before he came to her—being such a little child. But he went quickly, and was laid upon her breast, and in her hand she leads him.

There was a gallant boy, who fell, far away, upon a burning sand beneath a burning sun, and said, "Tell them at home, with my last love, how much I could have wished to kiss them once, but that I died contented and had done my duty!" Or there was another, over whom they read the words, "Therefore we commit his body to the deep," and so consigned him to the lonely ocean and sailed on. Or there was another, who lay down to his rest in the dark shadow of great forests, and, on earth, awoke no more. O shall they not, from sand and sea and forest, be brought home at such a time?

There was a dear girl—almost a woman—never to be one —who made a mourning Christmas in a house of joy, and went her trackless way to the silent City. Do we recollect her, worn out, faintly whispering what could not be heard, and falling into that last sleep for weariness? O look upon her now! O look upon her beauty, her serenity, her changeless youth, her happiness! The daughter of Jairus was recalled to life, to die; but she, more blest, has heard the same voice, saying unto her, "Arise for ever!"

We had a friend who was our friend from early days, with whom we often pictured the changes that were to come upon our lives, and merrily imagined how we would speak, and walk, and think, and talk, when we came to be old. His destined habitation in the City of the Dead received him in his prime. Shall he be shut out from our Christmas remembrance? Would his love have so excluded us? Lost friend, lost child, lost parent, sister, brother, husband, wife, we will not so discard you! You shall hold your cherished places in our Christmas hearts, and by our Christmas fires; and in the season of immortal hope, and on the birthday of immortal mercy, we will shut out Nothing!

The winter sun goes down over town and village; on the sea it makes a rosy path, as if the Sacred tread were fresh upon the water. A few more moments, and it sinks, and night comes on, and lights begin to sparkle in the prospect. On the hill-side beyond the shapelessly-diffused town, and in the quiet keeping of the trees that gird the village-steeple, remembrances are cut in stone, planted in common flowers, growing in grass, entwined with lowly brambles around many a mound of earth. In town and village, there are doors and windows closed against the weather, there are flaming logs heaped high, there are joyful faces, there is healthy music of voices. Be all ungentleness and harm excluded from the temples of the Household Gods, but be those remembrances admitted with tender encouragement! They are of the time and all its comforting and peaceful reassurances; and of the history that reunited even upon earth the living and the dead; and of the broad beneficence and goodness that too many men have tried to tear to narrow shreds.

CHARACTERS

UNCLE CHILL, *an avaricious, crabbed old man; uncle to Michael.*

CHRISTIANA, *an old sweetheart of Michael's.*

LITTLE FRANK, *a diffident boy; a cousin of Michael's.*

MICHAEL, *the 'poor relation', and narrator of the story.*

BETSY SNAP, *a withered old woman, Uncle Chill's servant.*

JOHN SPATTER, *Michael's clerk, afterwards his partner.*

THE
POOR RELATION'S STORY

HE was very reluctant to take precedence of so many respected members of the family, by beginning the round of stories they were to relate as they sat in a goodly circle by the Christmas fire; and he modestly suggested that it would be more correct if "John our esteemed host" (whose health he begged to drink) would have the kindness to begin. For as to himself, he said, he was so little used to lead the way that really—— But as they all cried out here, that he must begin, and agreed with one voice that he might, could, would, and should begin, he left off rubbing his hands, and took his legs out from under his armchair, and did begin.

I have no doubt (said the poor relation) that I shall surprise the assembled members of our family, and particularly John our esteemed host to whom we are so much indebted for the great hospitality with which he has this day entertained us, by the confession I am going to make. But, if you do me the honour to be surprised at anything that falls from a person so unimportant in the family as I am, I can only say that I shall be scrupulously accurate in all I relate.

I am not what I am supposed to be. I am quite another thing. Perhaps before I go further, I had better glance at what I *am* supposed to be.

It is supposed, unless I mistake—the assembled members of our family will correct me if I do, which is very likely (here the poor relation looked mildly about him for contradiction); that I am nobody's enemy but my own. That I never met with any particular success in anything. That I failed in business because I was unbusiness-like and credulous

—in not being prepared for the interested designs of my partner. That I failed in love, because I was ridiculously trustful—in thinking it impossible that Christiana could deceive me. That I failed in my expectations from my uncle Chill, on account of not being as sharp as he could have wished in worldly matters. That, through life, I have been rather put upon and disappointed in a general way. That I am at present a bachelor of between fifty-nine and sixty years of age, living on a limited income in the form of a quarterly allowance, to which I see that John our esteemed host wishes me to make no further allusion.

The supposition as to my present pursuits and habits is to the following effect.

I live in a lodging in the Clapham Road—a very clean back room, in a very respectable house—where I am expected not to be at home in the day-time, unless poorly; and which I usually leave in the morning at nine o'clock, on pretence of going to business. I take my breakfast—my roll and butter, and my half-pint of coffee—at the old-established coffee-shop near Westminster Bridge; and then I go into the City—I don't know why—and sit in Garraway's Coffee House, and on 'Change, and walk about, and look into a few offices and counting-houses where some of my relations or acquaintance are so good as to tolerate me, and where I stand by the fire if the weather happens to be cold. I get through the day in this way until five o'clock, and then I dine: at a cost, on the average, of one and threepence. Having still a little money to spend on my evening's entertainment, I look into the old-established coffee-shop as I go home, and take my cup of tea, and perhaps my bit of toast. So, as the large hand of the clock makes its way round to the morning hour again, I make my way round to the Clapham Road again, and go to bed when I get to my lodging—fire being expensive, and being objected to by the family on account of its giving trouble and making a dirt.

Sometimes, one of my relations or acquaintance is so obliging as to ask me to dinner. Those are holiday occasions, and then I generally walk in the Park. I am a solitary man, and seldom walk with anybody. Not that I am avoided because I am shabby; for I am not at all shabby, having always a very good suit of black on (or rather Oxford mixture, which has the appearance of black and wears much better); but I have got into a habit of speaking low, and being rather silent, and my spirits are not high, and I am sensible that I am not an attractive companion.

The only exception to this general rule is the child of my first cousin, Little Frank. I have a particular affection for that child, and he takes very kindly to me. He is a diffident boy by nature ; and in a crowd he is soon run over, as I may say, and forgotten. He and I, however, get on exceedingly well. I have a fancy that the poor child will in time succeed to my peculiar position in the family. We talk but little ; still, we understand each other. We walk about, hand in hand ; and without much speaking he knows what I mean, and I know what he means. When he was very little indeed, I used to take him to the windows of the toy-shops, and show him the toys inside. It is surprising how soon he found out that I would have made him a great many presents if I had been in circumstances to do it.

Little Frank and I go and look at the outside of the Monument—he is very fond of the Monument—and at the Bridges, and at all the sights that are free. On two of my birthdays, we have dined on à-la-mode beef, and gone at half-price to the play, and been deeply interested. I was once walking with him in Lombard Street, which we often visit on account of my having mentioned to him that there are great riches there—he is very fond of Lombard Street—when a gentleman said to me as he passed by, "Sir, your little son has dropped his glove." I assure you, if you will excuse my remarking on so trivial a circumstance, this accidental mention of the child as mine, quite touched my heart and brought the foolish tears into my eyes.

When Little Frank is sent to school in the country, I shall be very much at a loss what to do with myself, but I have the intention of walking down there once a month and seeing him on a half-holiday. I am told he will then be at play upon the Heath ; and if my visits should be objected to, as unsettling the child, I can see him from a distance without his seeing me, and walk back again. His mother comes of a highly genteel family, and rather disapproves, I am aware, of our being too much together. I know that I am not calculated to improve his retiring disposition ; but I think he would miss me beyond the feeling of the moment if we were wholly separated.

When I die in the Clapham Road, I shall not leave much more in this world than I shall take out of it ; but, I happen to have a miniature of a bright-faced boy, with a curling head, and an open shirt-frill waving down his bosom (my mother had it taken for me, but I can't believe that it was ever like), which will be worth nothing to sell, and which I shall beg may be given to Frank. I have written my dear boy a little letter with it, in which I have told him that I felt very sorry to part from him, though bound to confess that I knew no reason why I should remain here. I have given him some short advice, the best in my power, to take warning of the consequences of being nobody's enemy but his own; and I have endeavoured to comfort him for what I fear he will consider a bereavement, by pointing out to him, that I was only a superfluous something to every one but him; and that having by some means failed to find a place in this great assembly, I am better out of it.

Such (said the poor relation, clearing his throat and beginning to speak a little louder) is the general impression about me. Now, it is a remarkable circumstance which forms the aim and purpose of my story, that this is all wrong. This is not my life, and these are not my habits. I do not even live in the Clapham Road. Comparatively speaking, I am very seldom there. I reside, mostly, in a—I am almost ashamed to say the word, it sounds so full of pretension—in a Castle. I do not mean that it is an old baronial habitation, but still it is a building always known to every one by the name of a Castle. In it, I preserve the particulars of my history; they run thus:

It was when I first took John Spatter (who had been my clerk) into partnership, and when I was still a young man of not more than five-and-twenty, residing in the house of my uncle Chill, from whom I had considerable expectations, that I ventured to propose to Christiana. I had loved Christiana a long time. She was very beautiful, and very winning in all respects. I rather mistrusted her widowed mother, who I feared was of a plotting and mercenary turn of mind; but, I thought as well of her as I could, for Christiana's sake. I never had loved any one but Christiana, and she had been all the world, and O far more than all the world, to me, from our childhood!

Christiana accepted me with her mother's consent, and I was rendered very happy indeed. My life at my uncle Chill's was of a spare dull kind, and my garret chamber was as dull, and bare, and cold, as an upper prison room in some stern northern fortress. But, having Christiana's love, I wanted nothing upon earth. I would not have changed my lot with any human being.

Avarice was, unhappily, my uncle Chill's master-vice. Though he was rich, he pinched, and scraped, and clutched, and lived miserably. As Christiana had no fortune, I was for some time a little fearful of confessing our engagement to him ; but, at length I wrote him a letter, saying how it all truly was. I put it into his hand one night, on going to bed.

As I came downstairs next morning, shivering in the cold December air ; colder in my uncle's unwarmed house than in the street, where the winter sun did sometimes shine, and which was at all events enlivened by cheerful faces and voices passing along ; I carried a heavy heart towards the long, low breakfast-room in which my uncle sat. It was a large room with a small fire, and there was a great bay window in it which the rain had marked in the night as if with the tears of houseless people. It stared upon a raw yard, with a cracked stone pavement, and some rusted iron railings half uprooted, whence an ugly out-building that had once been a dissecting-room (in the time of the great surgeon who had mortgaged the house to my uncle), stared at it.

We rose so early always, that at that time of the year we breakfasted by candle-light. When I went into the room, my uncle was so contracted by the cold, and so huddled together in his chair behind the one dim candle, that I did not see him until I was close to the table.

As I held out my hand to him, he caught up his stick (being infirm, he always walked about the house with a stick), and made a blow at me, and said, " You fool ! "

"Uncle," I returned, "I didn't expect you to be so angry as this." Nor had I expected it, though he was a hard and angry old man.

"You didn't expect !" said he; "when did you ever expect? When did you ever calculate, or look forward, you contemptible dog ? "

"These are hard words, uncle ! "

"Hard words? Feathers, to pelt such an idiot as you with," said he. "Here! Betsy Snap! Look at him ! "

Betsy Snap was a withered, hard-favoured, yellow old woman—our only domestic—always employed, at this time of the morning, in rubbing my uncle's legs. As my uncle adjured her to look at me, he put his lean grip on the crown of her head, she kneeling beside him, and turned her face towards me. An involuntary thought connecting them both with the Dissecting Room, as it must often have been in the surgeon's time, passed across my mind in the midst of my anxiety.

"Look at the snivelling milksop!" said my uncle. "Look at the baby! This is the gentleman who, people say, is nobody's enemy but his own. This is the gentleman who can't say no. This is the gentleman who was making such large profits in his business that he must needs take a partner, t'other day. This is the gentleman who is going to marry a wife without a penny, and who falls into the hands of Jezebels who are speculating on my death!"

I knew, now, how great my uncle's rage was; for nothing short of his being almost beside himself would have induced him to utter that concluding word, which he held in such repugnance that it was never spoken or hinted at before him on any account.

"On my death," he repeated, as if he were defying me by defying his own abhorrence of the word. "On my death—death—Death! But I'll spoil the speculation. Eat your last under this roof, you feeble wretch, and may it choke you!"

You may suppose that I had not much appetite for the breakfast to which I was bidden in these terms; but, I took my accustomed seat. I saw that I was repudiated henceforth by my uncle; still I could bear that very well, possessing Christiana's heart.

He emptied his basin of bread and milk as usual, only that he took it on his knees with his chair turned away from the table where I sat. When he had done, he carefully snuffed out the candle; and the cold, slate-coloured, miserable day looked in upon us.

"Now, Mr. Michael," said he, "before we part, I should like to have a word with these ladies in your presence."

"As you will, Sir," I returned; "but you deceive yourself, and wrong us, cruelly, if you suppose that there is any feeling at stake in this contract but pure, disinterested, faithful love."

To this, he only replied, "You lie!" and not one other word.

We went, through half-thawed snow and half-frozen rain, to the house where Christiana and her mother lived. My uncle knew them very well. They were sitting at their breakfast, and were surprised to see us at that hour.

"Your servant, ma'am," said my uncle to the mother. "You divine the purpose of my visit, I dare say, ma'am. I understand there is a world of pure, disinterested, faithful love cooped up here. I am happy to bring it all it wants, to make it complete. I bring you your son-in-law, ma'am —and you, your husband, miss. The gentleman is a perfect stranger to me, but I wish him joy of his wise bargain."

He snarled at me as he went out, and I never saw him again.

It is altogether a mistake (continued the poor relation) to suppose that my dear Christiana, over-persuaded and influenced by her mother, married a rich man, the dirt from whose carriage-wheels is often, in these changed times, thrown upon me as she rides by. No, no. She married me.

The way we came to be married rather sooner than we intended, was this. I took a frugal lodging and was saving and planning for her sake, when, one day, she spoke to me with great earnestness, and said:

"My dear Michael, I have given you my heart. I have said that I loved you, and I have pledged myself to be your wife. I am as much yours through all changes of good and evil as if we had been married on the day when such words passed between us. I know you well, and know that if we should be separated and our union broken off, your whole life would be shadowed, and all that might, even now, be stronger in your character for the conflict with the world would then be weakened to the shadow of what it is!"

"God help me, Christiana!" said I. "You speak the truth."

"Michael!" said she, putting her hand in mine, in all maidenly devotion, "let us keep apart no longer. It is but for me to say that I can live contented upon such means as you have, and I well know you are happy. I say so from my heart. Strive no more alone; let us strive together. My dear Michael, it is not right that I should keep secret from you what you do not suspect, but what distresses my whole life. My mother: without considering that what you have lost, you have lost for me, and on the assurance of my faith: sets her heart on riches, and urges another suit upon me, to my misery. I cannot bear this, for to bear it is to be untrue to you. I would rather share your struggles than look on. I want no better home than you can give me. I know that you will aspire and labour with a higher courage if I am wholly yours, and let it be so when you will!"

I was blest indeed, that day, and a new world opened to me. We were married in a very little while, and I took my wife to our happy home. That was the beginning of the residence I have spoken of; the Castle we have ever since inhabited together, dates from that time. All our children have been born in it. Our first child—now married—was a little girl, whom we called Christiana. Her son is so like Little Frank, that I hardly know which is which.

The current impression as to my partner's dealings with me is also quite erroneous. He did not begin to treat me coldly, as a poor simpleton, when my uncle and I so fatally quarrelled; nor did he afterwards gradually possess himself of our business and edge me out. On the contrary, he behaved to me with the utmost good faith and honour.

Matters between us took this turn:—On the day of my separation from my uncle, and even before the arrival at our counting-house of my trunks (which he sent after me, *not* carriage paid), I went down to our room of business, on our little wharf, overlooking the river; and there I told John Spatter what had happened. John did not say, in reply, that rich old relatives were palpable facts, and that love and sentiment were moonshine and fiction. He addressed me thus:

"Michael," said John, "we were at school together, and I generally had the knack of getting on better than you, and making a higher reputation."

"You had, John," I returned.

"Although," said John, "I borrowed your books and lost them; borrowed your pocket-money, and never repaid it; got you to buy my damaged knives at a higher price than I had given for them new; and to own to the windows that I had broken."

"All not worth mentioning, John Spatter," said I, "but certainly true."

"When you were first established in this infant business, which promises to thrive so well," pursued John, "I came to you, in my search for almost any employment, and you made me your clerk."

"Still not worth mentioning, my dear John Spatter," said I; "still, equally true."

"And finding that I had a good head for business, and that I was really useful *to* the business, you did not like to retain me in that capacity, and thought it an act of justice soon to make me your partner."

"Still less worth mentioning than any of those other little circumstances you have recalled, John Spatter," said I; "for I was, and am, sensible of your merits and my deficiencies."

"Now, my good friend," said John, drawing my arm through his, as he had had a habit of doing at school; while two vessels outside the windows of our counting-house—which were shaped like the stern windows of a ship—went lightly down the river with the tide, as John and I might then be sailing away in company, and in trust and confidence, on our voyage of life; "let there, under these friendly circumstances, be a right understanding between us. You are too easy, Michael. You are nobody's enemy but your own. If I were to give you that damaging character among our connexion, with a shrug, and a shake of the head, and a sigh; and if I were further to abuse the trust you place in me——"

"But you never will abuse it at all, John," I observed.

"Never!" said he: "but I am putting a case—I say, and if I were further to abuse that trust by keeping this piece of our common affairs in the dark, and this other piece in the light, and again this other piece in the twilight, and so on, I should strengthen my strength, and weaken your weakness, day by day, until at last I found myself on the high road to fortune, and you left behind on some bare common, a hopeless number of miles out of the way."

"Exactly so," said I.

"To prevent this, Michael," said John Spatter, "or the remotest chance of this, there must be perfect openness between us. Nothing must be concealed, and we must have but one interest."

"My dear John Spatter," I assured him, "that is precisely what I mean."

"And when you are too easy," pursued John, his face glowing with friendship, "you must allow me to prevent that imperfection in your nature from being taken advantage of, by any one; you must not expect me to humour it——"

"My dear John Spatter," I interrupted, "I *don't* expect you to humour it. I want to correct it."

"And I, too," said John.

"Exactly so!" cried I. "We both have the same end in view; and, honourably seeking it, and fully trusting one another, and having but one interest, ours will be a prosperous and happy partnership."

"I am sure of it!" returned John Spatter. And we shook hands most affectionately.

I took John home to my Castle, and we had a very happy day. Our partnership throve well. My friend and partner supplied what I wanted, as I had foreseen that he would; and by improving both the business and myself, amply acknowledged any little rise in life to which I had helped him.

I am not (said the poor relation, looking at the fire as he slowly rubbed his hands) very rich, for I never cared to be that; but I have enough, and am above all moderate wants and anxieties. My Castle is not a splendid place, but it is very comfortable, and it has a warm and cheerful air, and is quite a picture of Home.

Our eldest girl, who is very like her mother, married John Spatter's eldest son. Our two families are closely united in other ties of attachment. It is very pleasant of an evening, when we are all assembled together—which frequently happens—and when John and I talk over old times, and the one interest there has always been between us.

I really do not know, in my Castle, what loneliness is. Some of our children or grandchildren are always about it, and the young voices of my descendants are delightful—O, how delightful!—to me to hear. My dearest and most devoted wife, ever faithful, ever loving, ever helpful and sustaining and consoling, is the priceless blessing of my house; from whom all its other blessings spring. We are rather a musical family, and when Christiana sees me, at any time, a little weary or depressed, she steals to the piano and sings a gentle air she used to sing when we were first betrothed. So weak a man am I, that I cannot bear to hear it from any other source. They played it once, at the Theatre, when I was there with Little Frank; and the child said wondering, "Cousin Michael, whose hot tears are these that have fallen on my hand?"

Such is my Castle, and such are the real particulars of my life therein preserved. I often take Little Frank home there. He is very welcome to my grandchildren, and they play together. At this time of the year—the Christmas and New Year time—I am seldom out of my Castle. For, the associations of the season seem to hold me there, and the precepts of the season seem to teach me that it is well to be there.

"And the Castle is——" observed a grave, kind voice among the company.

"Yes. My Castle," said the poor relation, shaking his head as he still looked at the fire, "is in the Air. John our esteemed host suggests its situation accurately. My Castle is in the Air! I have done. Will you be so good as to pass the story!"

THE CHILD'S STORY

[1852]

THE CHILD'S STORY

ONCE upon a time, a good many years ago, there was a traveller, and he set out upon a journey. It was a magic journey, and was to seem very long when he began it, and very short when he got half way through.

He travelled along a rather dark path for some little time, without meeting anything, until at last he came to a beautiful child. So he said to the child, "What do you do here?" And the child said, "I am always at play. Come and play with me!"

So, he played with that child, the whole day long, and they were very merry. The sky was so blue, the sun was so bright, the water was so sparkling, the leaves were so green, the flowers were so lovely, and they heard such singing-birds and saw so many butterflies, that everything was beautiful. This was in fine weather. When it rained, they loved to watch the falling drops, and to smell the fresh scents. When it blew, it was delightful to listen to the wind, and fancy what it said, as it came rushing from its home—where was that, they wondered!—whistling and howling, driving the clouds before it, bending the trees, rumbling in the chimneys, shaking the house, and making the sea roar in fury. But, when it snowed, that was best of all; for, they liked nothing so well as to look up at the white flakes falling fast and thick, like down from the breasts of millions of white birds; and to see how smooth and deep the drift was; and to listen to the hush upon the paths and roads.

They had plenty of the finest toys in the world, and the most astonishing picture-books: all about scimitars and slippers and turbans, and dwarfs and giants and genii and fairies, and blue-beards and bean-stalks and riches and caverns and forests and Valentines and Orsons: and all new and all true.

But, one day, of a sudden, the traveller lost the child. He

called to him over and over again, but got no answer. So, he went upon his road, and went on for a little while without meeting anything, until at last he came to a handsome boy. So, he said to the boy, "What do you do here?" And the boy said, "I am always learning. Come and learn with me."

So he learned with that boy about Jupiter and Juno, and the Greeks and the Romans, and I don't know what, and learned more than I could tell—or he either, for he soon forgot a great deal of it. But, they were not always learning; they had the merriest games that ever were played. They rowed upon the river in summer, and skated on the ice in winter; they were active afoot, and active on horseback; at cricket, and all games at ball; at prisoners' base, hare and hounds, follow my leader, and more sports than I can think of; nobody could beat them. They had holidays too, and Twelfth cakes, and parties where they danced till midnight, and real Theatres where they saw palaces of real gold and silver rise out of the real earth, and saw all the wonders of the world at once. As to friends, they had such dear friends and so many of them, that I want the time to reckon them up. They were all young, like the handsome boy, and were never to be strange to one another all their lives through.

Still, one day, in the midst of all these pleasures, the traveller lost the boy as he had lost the child, and, after calling to him in vain, went on upon his journey. So he went on for a little while without seeing anything, until at last he came to a young man. So, he said to the young man, "What do you do here?" And the young man said, "I am always in love. Come and love with me."

So, he went away with that young man, and presently they came to one of the prettiest girls that ever was seen— just like Fanny in the corner there—and she had eyes like Fanny, and hair like Fanny, and dimples like Fanny's, and she laughed and coloured just as Fanny does while I am talking about her. So, the young man fell in love directly —just as Somebody I won't mention, the first time he came here, did with Fanny. Well! he was teased sometimes—just as Somebody used to be by Fanny; and they quarrelled sometimes—just as Somebody and Fanny used to quarrel; and they made it up, and sat in the dark, and wrote letters every day, and never were happy asunder, and were always looking out for one another and pretending not to, and were engaged at Christmas-time, and sat close to one another by the fire, and were going to be married very soon—all exactly like Somebody I won't mention, and Fanny!

But, the traveller lost them one day, as he had lost the rest of his friends, and, after calling to them to come back, which they never did, went on upon his journey. So, he went on for a little while without seeing anything, until at last he came to a middle-aged gentleman. So, he said to the gentleman, "What are you doing here?" And his answer was, "I am always busy. Come and be busy with me!"

So, he began to be very busy with that gentleman, and they went on through the wood together. The whole journey was through a wood, only it had been open and green at first, like a wood in spring; and now began to be thick and dark, like a wood in summer; some of the little trees that had come out earliest, were even turning brown. The gentleman was not alone, but had a lady of about the same age with him, who was his Wife; and they had children, who were with them too. So, they all went on together through the wood, cutting down the trees, and making a path through the branches and the fallen leaves, and carrying burdens, and working hard.

Sometimes, they came to a long green avenue that opened into deeper woods. Then they would hear a very little distant voice crying, "Father, father, I am another child! Stop for me!" And presently they would see a very little figure, growing larger as it came along, running to join them. When it came up, they all crowded round it, and kissed and welcomed it; and then they all went on together.

Sometimes, they came to several avenues at once, and then they all stood still, and one of the children said, "Father, I am going to sea," and another said, "Father, I am going to India," and another, "Father, I am going to seek my fortune where I can," and another, "Father, I am going to Heaven!" So, with many tears at parting, they went, solitary, down those avenues, each child upon its way; and the child who went to Heaven, rose into the golden air and vanished.

Whenever these partings happened, the traveller looked at the gentleman, and saw him glance up at the sky above the trees, where the day was beginning to decline, and the sunset to come on. He saw, too, that his hair was turning grey. But, they never could rest long, for they had their journey to perform, and it was necessary for them to be always busy.

At last, there had been so many partings that there were no children left, and only the traveller, the gentleman, and the lady, went upon their way in company. And now the wood was yellow; and now brown; and the leaves, even of the forest trees, began to fall.

So, they came to an avenue that was darker than the rest, and were pressing forward on their journey without looking down it when the lady stopped.

"My husband," said the lady. "I am called."

They listened, and they heard a voice a long way down the avenue, say, "Mother, mother!"

It was the voice of the first child who had said, "I am going to Heaven!" and the father said, "I pray not yet. The sunset is very near. I pray not yet!"

But, the voice cried, "Mother, mother!" without minding him, though his hair was now quite white, and tears were on his face.

Then, the mother, who was already drawn into the shade of the dark avenue and moving away with her arms still round his neck, kissed him, and said, "My dearest, I am summoned, and I go!" And she was gone. And the traveller and he were left alone together.

And they went on and on together, until they came to very near the end of the wood: so near, that they could see the sunset shining red before them through the trees.

Yet, once more, while he broke his way among the branches, the traveller lost his friend. He called and called, but there was no reply, and when he passed out of the wood, and saw the peaceful sun going down upon a wide purple prospect, he came to an old man sitting on a fallen tree. So, he said to the old man, "What do you do here?" And the old man said with a calm smile, "I am always remembering. Come and remember with me!"

So the traveller sat down by the side of that old man, face to face with the serene sunset; and all his friends came softly back and stood around him. The beautiful child, the handsome boy, the young man in love, the father, mother, and children: every one of them was there, and he had lost nothing. So, he loved them all, and was kind and forbearing with them all, and was always pleased to watch them all, and they all honoured and loved him. And I think the traveller must be yourself, dear Grandfather, because this is what you do to us, and what we do to you.

THE SCHOOLBOY'S STORY

[1853]

CHARACTERS

OLD CHEESEMAN, *a poor boy at a boarding-school, afterwards second Latin Master.*

JANE PITT, *a kind of wardrobe-woman to the boys.*

BOB TARTER, *the 'first boy' in the school.*

THE SCHOOLBOY'S STORY

BEING rather young at present—I am getting on in years,
but still I am rather young—I have no particular adventures
of my own to fall back upon. It wouldn't much interest
anybody here, I suppose, to know what a screw the Reverend
is, or what a griffin *she* is, or how they do stick it into
parents—particularly hair-cutting, and medical attendance.
One of our fellows was charged in his half's account twelve
and sixpence for two pills—tolerably profitable at six and
threepence a-piece, I should think—and he never took them
either, but put them up the sleeve of his jacket.

As to the beef, it's shameful. It's *not* beef. Regular beef
isn't veins. You can chew regular beef. Besides which,
there's gravy to regular beef, and you never see a drop to
ours. Another of our fellows went home ill, and heard the
family doctor tell his father that he couldn't account for his
complaint unless it was the beer. Of course it was the beer,
and well it might be!

However, beef and Old Cheeseman are two different things.
So is beer. It was Old Cheeseman I meant to tell about;
not the manner in which our fellows get their constitutions
destroyed for the sake of profit.

Why, look at the pie-crust alone. There's no flakiness in
it. It's solid—like damp lead. Then our fellows get nightmares, and are bolstered for calling out and waking other
fellows. Who can wonder!

Old Cheeseman one night walked in his sleep, put his hat
on over his nightcap, got hold of a fishing-rod and a cricket-
bat, and went down into the parlour, where they naturally
thought from his appearance he was a Ghost. Why, he
never would have done that if his meals had been wholesome.
When we all begin to walk in our sleeps, I suppose they'll
be sorry for it.

Old Cheeseman wasn't second Latin Master then; he was a fellow himself. He was first brought there, very small, in a post-chaise, by a woman who was always taking snuff and shaking him—and that was the most he remembered about it. He never went home for the holidays. His accounts (he never learnt any extras) were sent to a Bank, and the Bank paid them; and he had a brown suit twice a-year, and went into boots at twelve. They were always too big for him, too.

In the Midsummer holidays, some of our fellows who lived within walking distance, used to come back and climb the trees outside the playground wall, on purpose to look at Old Cheeseman reading there by himself. He was always as mild as the tea—and *that's* pretty mild, I should hope!—so when they whistled to him, he looked up and nodded; and when they said, "Halloa, Old Cheeseman, what have you had for dinner?" he said, "Boiled mutton;" and when they said, "An't it solitary, Old Cheeseman?" he said, "It is a little dull sometimes:" and then they said, "Well, good-bye, Old Cheeseman!" and climbed down again. Of course it was imposing on Old Cheeseman to give him nothing but boiled mutton through a whole Vacation, but that was just like the system. When they didn't give him boiled mutton, they gave him rice pudding, pretending it was a treat. And saved the butcher.

So Old Cheeseman went on. The holidays brought him into other trouble besides the loneliness; because when the fellows began to come back, not wanting to, he was always glad to see them; which was aggravating when they were not at all glad to see him, and so he got his head knocked against walls, and that was the way his nose bled. But he was a favourite in general. Once a subscription was raised for him; and, to keep up his spirits, he was presented before the holidays with two white mice, a rabbit, a pigeon, and a beautiful puppy. Old Cheeseman cried about it—especially soon afterwards, when they all ate one another.

Of course Old Cheeseman used to be called by the names of all sorts of cheeses—Double Glo'sterman, Family Cheshireman, Dutchman, North Wiltshireman, and all that. But he never minded it. And I don't mean to say he was old in point of years—because he wasn't—only he was called from the first, Old Cheeseman.

At last, Old Cheeseman was made second Latin Master.

He was brought in one morning at the beginning of a new half, and presented to the school in that capacity as "Mr. Cheeseman." Then our fellows all agreed that Old Cheeseman was a spy, and a deserter, who had gone over to the enemy's camp, and sold himself for gold. It was no excuse for him that he had sold himself for very little gold—two pound ten a quarter and his washing, as was reported. It was decided by a Parliament which sat about it, that Old Cheeseman's mercenary motives could alone be taken into account, and that he had "coined our blood for drachmas." The Parliament took the expression out of the quarrel scene between Brutus and Cassius.

When it was settled in this strong way that Old Cheeseman was a tremendous traitor, who had wormed himself into our fellows' secrets on purpose to get himself into favour by giving up everything he knew, all courageous fellows were invited to come forward and enrol themselves in a Society for making a set against him. The President of the Society was First boy, named Bob Tarter. His father was in the West Indies, and he owned, himself, that his father was worth millions. He had great power among our fellows, and he wrote a parody, beginning—

> "Who made believe to be so meek
> That we could hardly hear him speak,
> Yet turned out an Informing Sneak?
> Old Cheeseman."

—and on in that way through more than a dozen verses, which he used to go and sing, every morning, close by the new master's desk. He trained one of the low boys, too, a rosy-cheeked little Brass who didn't care what he did, to go up to him with his Latin Grammar one morning, and say it so: *Nominativus pronominum*—Old Cheeseman, *raro exprimitur*— was never suspected, *nisi distinctionis*—of being an informer, *aut emphasis gratiâ*—until he proved one. *Ut*—for instance, *Vos damnastis*—when he sold the boys. *Quasi*—as though, *dicat*—he should say, *Præterea nemo*—I'm a Judas! All this produced a great effect on Old Cheeseman. He had never had much hair; but what he had, began to get thinner and thinner every day. He grew paler and more worn; and sometimes of an evening he was seen sitting at his desk with a precious long snuff to his candle, and his hands before his face, crying. But no member of the Society could pity him, even if he felt inclined, because the President said it was Old Cheeseman's conscience.

So Old Cheeseman went on, and didn't he lead a miserable life! Of course the Reverend turned up his nose at him, and of course *she* did—because both of them always do that at all the masters—but he suffered from the fellows most, and he suffered from them constantly. He never told about it, that the Society could find out; but he got no credit for that, because the President said it was Old Cheeseman's cowardice.

He had only one friend in the world, and that one was almost as powerless as he was, for it was only Jane. Jane was a sort of wardrobe-woman to our fellows, and took care of the boxes. She had come at first, I believe, as a kind of apprentice—some of our fellows say from a Charity, but *I* don't know—and after her time was out, had stopped at so much a year. So little a year, perhaps I ought to say, for it is far more likely. However, she had put some pounds in the Savings' Bank, and she was a very nice young woman. She was not quite pretty; but she had a very frank, honest, bright face, and all our fellows were fond of her. She was uncommonly neat and cheerful, and uncommonly comfortable and kind. And if anything was the matter with a fellow's mother, he always went and showed the letter to Jane.

Jane was Old Cheeseman's friend. The more the Society went against him, the more Jane stood by him. She used to give him a good-humoured look out of her still-room window, sometimes, that seemed to set him up for the day. She used to pass out of the orchard and the kitchen garden (always kept locked, I believe you!) through the playground, when she might have gone the other way, only to give a turn of her head, as much as to say, "Keep up your spirits!" to Old Cheeseman. His slip of a room was so fresh and orderly that it was well known who looked after it while he was at his desk; and when our fellows saw a smoking hot dumpling on his plate at dinner, they knew with indignation who had sent it up.

Under these circumstances, the Society resolved, after a quantity of meeting and debating, that Jane should be requested to cut Old Cheeseman dead; and that if she refused, she must be sent to Coventry herself. So a deputation, headed by the President, was appointed to wait on Jane, and inform her of the vote the Society had been under the

painful necessity of passing. She was very much respected
for all her good qualities, and there was a story about her
having once waylaid the Reverend in his own study, and
got a fellow off from severe punishment, of her own kind
comfortable heart. So the deputation didn't much like the
job. However, they went up, and the President told Jane
all about it. Upon which Jane turned very red, burst into
tears, informed the President and the deputation, in a way
not at all like her usual way, that they were a parcel of
malicious young savages, and turned the whole respected body
out of the room. Consequently it was entered in the Society's
book (kept in astronomical cypher for fear of detection),
that all communication with Jane was interdicted : and the
President addressed the members on this convincing instance
of Old Cheeseman's undermining.

But Jane was as true to Old Cheeseman as Old Cheeseman
was false to our fellows—in their opinion, at all events—and
steadily continued to be his only friend. It was a great
exasperation to the Society, because Jane was as much a
loss to them as she was a gain to him ; and being more
inveterate against him than ever, they treated him worse
than ever. At last, one morning, his desk stood empty,
his room was peeped into, and found to be vacant, and
a whisper went about among the pale faces of our fellows
that Old Cheeseman, unable to bear it any longer, had got
up early and drowned himself.

The mysterious looks of the other masters after breakfast,
and the evident fact that Old Cheeseman was not expected,
confirmed the Society in this opinion. Some began to
discuss whether the President was liable to hanging or only
transportation for life, and the President's face showed a
great anxiety to know which. However, he said that a jury
of his country should find him game; and that in his address
he should put it to them to lay their hands upon their hearts
and say whether they as Britons approved of informers, and
how they thought they would like it themselves. Some of
the Society considered that he had better run away until he
found a forest where he might change clothes with a wood-
cutter, and stain his face with blackberries; but the majority
believed that if he stood his ground, his father—belonging as
he did to the West Indies, and being worth millions—could
buy him off.

All our fellows' hearts beat fast when the Reverend came

in, and made a sort of a Roman, or a Field-Marshal, of himself with the ruler; as he always did before delivering an
address. But their fears were nothing to their astonishment
when he came out with the story that Old Cheeseman, "so
long our respected friend and fellow-pilgrim in the pleasant
plains of knowledge," he called him—O yes! I dare say! Much
of that!—was the orphan child of a disinherited young lady
who had married against her father's wish, and whose young
husband had died, and who had died of sorrow herself, and
whose unfortunate baby (Old Cheeseman) had been brought
up at the cost of a grandfather who would never consent to
see it, baby, boy, or man: which grandfather was now dead,
and serve him right—that's *my* putting in—and which grandfather's large property, there being no will, was now, and all
of a sudden and for ever, Old Cheeseman's! Our so long
respected friend and fellow-pilgrim in the pleasant plains of
knowledge, the Reverend wound up a lot of bothering quotations by saying, would "come among us once more" that
day fortnight, when he desired to take leave of us himself,
in a more particular manner. With these words, he stared
severely round at our fellows, and went solemnly out.

There was precious consternation among the members of
the Society, now. Lots of them wanted to resign, and lots
more began to try to make out that they had never belonged
to it. However, the President stuck up, and said that they
must stand or fall together, and that if a breach was made
it should be over his body—which was meant to encourage
the Society: but it didn't. The President further said, he
would consider the position in which they stood, and would
give them his best opinion and advice in a few days. This
was eagerly looked for, as he knew a good deal of the world
on account of his father's being in the West Indies.

After days and days of hard thinking, and drawing armies
all over his slate, the President called our fellows together,
and made the matter clear. He said it was plain that when
Old Cheeseman came on the appointed day, his first revenge
would be to impeach the Society, and have it flogged all
round. After witnessing with joy the torture of his enemies,
and gloating over the cries which agony would extort from
them, the probability was that he would invite the Reverend,
on pretence of conversation, into a private room—say the
parlour into which Parents were shown, where the two great
globes were which were never used—and would there re-

proach him with the various frauds and oppressions he had
endured at his hands. At the close of his observations he
would make a signal to a Prizefighter concealed in the passage, who would then appear and pitch into the Reverend,
till he was left insensible. Old Cheeseman would then make
Jane a present of from five to ten pounds, and would leave
the establishment in fiendish triumph.

The President explained that against the parlour part, or
the Jane part, of these arrangements he had nothing to say ;
but, on the part of the Society, he counselled deadly resistance. With this view he recommended that all available
desks should be filled with stones, and that the first word of
the complaint should be the signal to every fellow to let fly
at Old Cheeseman. The bold advice put the Society in better
spirits, and was unanimously taken. A post about Old
Cheeseman's size was put up in the playground, and all our
fellows practised at it till it was dinted all over.

When the day came, and Places were called, every fellow
sat down in a tremble. There had been much discussing
and disputing as to how Old Cheeseman would come ; but it
was the general opinion that he would appear in a sort of
triumphal car drawn by four horses, with two livery servants
in front, and the Prizefighter in disguise up behind. So, all
our fellows sat listening for the sound of wheels. But no
wheels were heard, for Old Cheeseman walked after all, and
came into the school without any preparation. Pretty much
as he used to be, only dressed in black.

"Gentlemen," said the Reverend, presenting him, "our
so long respected friend and fellow-pilgrim in the pleasant
plains of knowledge, is desirous to offer a word or two.
Attention, gentlemen, one and all !"

Every fellow stole his hand into his desk and looked at
the President. The President was all ready, and taking aim
at Old Cheeseman with his eyes.

What did Old Cheeseman then, but walk up to his old desk,
look round him with a queer smile as if there was a tear in
his eye, and begin in a quavering mild voice, "My dear companions and old friends !"

Every fellow's hand came out of his desk, and the President suddenly began to cry.

"My dear companions and old friends," said Old Cheeseman, "you have heard of my good fortune. I have passed
so many years under this roof—my entire life so far, I may

say—that I hope you have been glad to hear of it for my sake. I could never enjoy it without exchanging congratulations with you. If we have ever misunderstood one another at all, pray, my dear boys, let us forgive and forget. I have a great tenderness for you, and I am sure you return it. I want in the fulness of a grateful heart to shake hands with you every one. I have come back to do it, if you please, my dear boys."

Since the President had begun to cry, several other fellows had broken out here and there: but now, when Old Cheeseman began with him as first boy, laid his left hand affectionately on his shoulder and gave him his right; and when the President said " Indeed, I don't deserve it, sir; upon my honour I don't; " there was sobbing and crying all over the school. Every other fellow said he didn't deserve it, much in the same way; but Old Cheeseman, not minding that a bit, went cheerfully round to every boy, and wound up with every master—finishing off the Reverend last.

Then a snivelling little chap in a corner, who was always under some punishment or other, set up a shrill cry of "Success to Old Cheeseman! Hooray!" The Reverend glared upon him, and said, "*Mr.* Cheeseman, Sir." But, Old Cheeseman protesting that he liked his old name a great deal better than his new one, all our fellows took up the cry; and, for I don't know how many minutes, there was such a thundering of feet and hands, and such a roaring of Old Cheeseman, as never was heard.

After that, there was a spread in the dining-room of the most magnificent kind. Fowls, tongues, preserves, fruits, confectionaries, jellies, neguses, barley-sugar temples, trifles, crackers—eat all you can and pocket what you like—all at Old Cheeseman's expense. After that, speeches, whole holiday, double and treble sets of all manners of things for all manners of games, donkeys, pony-chaises and drive yourself, dinner for all the masters at the Seven Bells (twenty pounds a-head our fellows estimated it at), an annual holiday and feast fixed for that day every year, and another on Old Cheeseman's birthday—Reverend bound down before the fellows to allow it, so that he could never back out—all at Old Cheeseman's expense.

And didn't our fellows go down in a body and cheer outside the Seven Bells? O no!

But there's something else besides. Don't look at the

next story-teller, for there's more yet. Next day, it was
resolved that the Society should make it up with Jane, and
then be dissolved. What do you think of Jane being gone,
though? "What? Gone for ever?" said our fellows, with
long faces. "Yes, to be sure," was all the answer they could
get. None of the people about the house would say anything more. At length, the first boy took upon himself to
ask the Reverend whether our old friend Jane was really
gone? The Reverend (he has got a daughter at home—
turn-up nose, and red) replied severely, "Yes, Sir, Miss Pitt
is gone." The idea of calling Jane, Miss Pitt! Some said
she had been sent away in disgrace for taking money from
Old Cheeseman; others said she had gone into Old Cheeseman's service at a rise of ten pounds a year. All that our
fellows knew, was, she was gone.

It was two or three months afterwards, when, one afternoon, an open carriage stopped at the cricket field, just outside bounds, with a lady and gentleman in it, who looked at
the game a long time and stood up to see it played. Nobody
thought much about them, until the same little snivelling
chap came in, against all rules, from the post where he was
Scout, and said, "It's Jane!" Both Elevens forgot the game
directly, and ran crowding round the carriage. It *was* Jane!
In such a bonnet! And if you'll believe me, Jane was
married to Old Cheeseman.

It soon became quite a regular thing when our fellows
were hard at it in the playground, to see a carriage at the
low part of the wall where it joins the high part, and a
lady and gentleman standing up in it, looking over. The
gentleman was always Old Cheeseman, and the lady was
always Jane.

The first time I ever saw them, I saw them in that way.
There had been a good many changes among our fellows
then, and it had turned out that Bob Tarter's father wasn't
worth Millions! He wasn't worth anything. Bob had gone
for a soldier, and Old Cheeseman had purchased his discharge.
But that's not the carriage. The carriage stopped, and all
our fellows stopped as soon as it was seen.

"So you have never sent me to Coventry after all!" said
the lady, laughing, as our fellows swarmed up the wall to
shake hands with her. "Are you never going to do it?"

"Never! never! never!" on all sides.

I didn't understand what she meant then, but of course I

do now. I was very much pleased with her face though, and with her good way, and I couldn't help looking at her—and at him too—with all our fellows clustering so joyfully about them.

They soon took notice of me as a new boy, so I thought I might as well swarm up the wall myself, and shake hands with them as the rest did. I was quite as glad to see them as the rest were, and was quite as familiar with them in a moment.

"Only a fortnight now," said Old Cheeseman, "to the holidays. Who stops? Anybody?"

A good many fingers pointed at me, and a good many voices cried "He does!" For it was the year when you were all away; and rather low I was about it, I can tell you.

"Oh!" said Old Cheeseman. "But it's solitary here in the holiday time. He had better come to us."

So I went to their delightful house, and was as happy as I could possibly be. They understand how to conduct themselves towards boys, *they* do. When they take a boy to the play, for instance, they *do* take him. They don't go in after it's begun, or come out before it's over. They know how to bring a boy up, too. Look at their own! Though he is very little as yet, what a capital boy he is! Why, my next favourite to Mrs. Cheeseman and Old Cheeseman, is young Cheeseman.

So, now I have told you all I know about Old Cheeseman. And it's not much after all, I am afraid. Is it?

NOBODY'S STORY

NOBODY'S STORY

He lived on the bank of a mighty river, broad and deep, which was always silently rolling on to a vast undiscovered ocean. It had rolled on, ever since the world began. It had changed its course sometimes, and turned into new channels, leaving its old ways dry and barren; but it had ever been upon the flow, and ever was to flow until Time should be no more. Against its strong, unfathomable stream, nothing made head. No living creature, no flower, no leaf, no particle of animate or inanimate existence, ever strayed back from the undiscovered ocean. The tide of the river set resistlessly towards it; and the tide never stopped, any more than the earth stops in its circling round the sun.

He lived in a busy place, and he worked very hard to live. He had no hope of ever being rich enough to live a month without hard work, but he was quite content, God knows, to labour with a cheerful will. He was one of an immense family, all of whose sons and daughters gained their daily bread by daily work, prolonged from their rising up betimes until their lying down at night. Beyond this destiny he had no prospect, and he sought none.

There was over-much drumming, trumpeting, and speech-making, in the neighbourhood where he dwelt; but he had nothing to do with that. Such clash and uproar came from the Bigwig family, at the unaccountable proceedings of which race, he marvelled much. They set up the strangest statues, in iron, marble, bronze, and brass. before his door; and darkened his house with the legs and tails of uncouth images of horses. He wondered what it all meant, smiled in a rough good-humoured way he had, and kept at his hard work.

The Bigwig family (composed of all the stateliest people thereabouts, and all the noisiest) had undertaken to save him the trouble of thinking for himself, and to manage him and his affairs. "Why truly," said he, "I have little time upon my hands; and if you will be so good as to take care of me, in return for the money I pay over"—for the Bigwig family were not above his money—"I shall be relieved and much obliged, considering that you know best." Hence the drumming, trumpeting, and speech-making, and the ugly images of horses which he was expected to fall down and worship.

"I don't understand all this," said he, rubbing his furrowed brow confusedly. "But it *has* a meaning, maybe, if I could find it out."

"It means," returned the Bigwig family, suspecting something of what he said, "honour and glory in the highest, to the highest merit."

"Oh!" said he. And he was glad to hear that.

But, when he looked among the images in iron, marble, bronze, and brass, he failed to find a rather meritorious countryman of his, once the son of a Warwickshire wooldealer, or any single countryman whomsoever of that kind. He could find none of the men whose knowledge had rescued him and his children from terrific and disfiguring disease, whose boldness had raised his forefathers from the condition of serfs, whose wise fancy had opened a new and high existence to the humblest, whose skill had filled the working man's world with accumulated wonders. Whereas, he did find others whom he knew no good of, and even others whom he knew much ill of.

"Humph!" said he. "I don't quite understand it."

So, he went home, and sat down by his fireside to get it out of his mind.

Now, his fireside was a bare one, all hemmed in by blackened streets; but it was a precious place to him. The hands of his wife were hardened with toil, and she was old before her time; but she was dear to him. His children, stunted in their growth, bore traces of unwholesome nurture: but they had beauty in his sight. Above all other things, it was an earnest desire of this man's soul that his children should be taught. "If I am sometimes misled," said he, "for want of knowledge, at least let them know better, and avoid my mistakes. If it is hard to me to reap the harvest of pleasure and instruction that is stored in books, let it be easier to them."

But, the Bigwig family broke out into violent family quarrels concerning what it was lawful to teach to this man's children. Some of the family insisted on such a thing being primary and indispensable above all other things; and others of the family insisted on such another thing being primary and indispensable above all other things; and the Bigwig family, rent into factions, wrote pamphlets, held convocations, delivered charges, orations, and all varieties of discourses; impounded one another in courts Lay and courts Ecclesiastical; threw dirt, exchanged pummelings, and fell together by the ears in unintelligible animosity. Meanwhile, this man, in his short evening snatches at his fireside, saw the demon Ignorance arise there, and take his children to itself. He saw his daughter perverted into a heavy slatternly drudge; he saw his son go moping down the ways of low sensuality, to brutality and crime; he saw the dawning light of intelligence in the eyes of his babies so changing into cunning and suspicion, that he could have rather wished them idiots.

"I don't understand this any the better," said he; "but I think it cannot be right. Nay, by the clouded Heaven above me, I protest against this as my wrong!"

Becoming peaceable again (for his passion was usually short-lived, and his nature kind), he looked about him on his Sundays and holidays, and he saw how much monotony and weariness there was, and thence how drunkenness arose with all its train of ruin. Then he appealed to the Bigwig family, and said, "We are a labouring people, and I have a glimmering suspicion in me that labouring people of whatever condition were made—by a higher intelligence than yours, as I poorly understand it—to be in need of mental refreshment and recreation. See what we fall into, when we rest without it. Come! Amuse me harmlessly, show me something, give me an escape!"

But, here the Bigwig family fell into a state of uproar absolutely deafening. When some few voices were faintly heard, proposing to show him the wonders of the world, the greatness of creation, the mighty changes of time, the workings of nature and the beauties of art—to show him these things, that is to say, at any period of his life when he could look upon them—there arose among the Bigwigs such roaring and raving, such pulpiting and petitioning, such maundering and memorialising, such name-calling and dirt-throwing, such a shrill wind of parliamentary questioning and feeble replying—where "I dare not" waited on "I would"— that the poor fellow stood aghast, staring wildly around.

"Have I provoked all this," said he, with his hands to his affrighted ears, "by what was meant to be an innocent request, plainly arising out of my familiar experience, and the common knowledge of all men who choose to open their eyes? I don't understand, and I am not understood. What is to come of such a state of things?"

He was bending over his work, often asking himself the question, when the news began to spread that a pestilence had appeared among the labourers, and was slaying them by thousands. Going forth to look about him, he soon found this to be true. The dying and the dead were mingled in the close and tainted houses among which his life was passed. New poison was distilled into the always murky, always sickening air. The robust and the weak, old age and infancy, the father and the mother, all were stricken down alike.

What means of flight had he? He remained there, where he was, and saw those who were dearest to him die. A kind preacher came to him, and would have said some prayers to soften his heart in his gloom, but he replied:

"O what avails it, missionary, to come to me, a man condemned to residence in this fœtid place, where every sense bestowed upon me for my delight becomes a torment, and where every minute of my numbered days is new mire added to the heap under which I lie oppressed! But, give me my first glimpse of Heaven, through a little of its light and air; give me pure water; help me to be clean; lighten this heavy atmosphere and heavy life, in which our spirits sink, and we become the indifferent and callous creatures you too often see us; gently and kindly take the bodies of those who die among us, out of the small room where we grow to be so familiar with the awful change that even ITS sanctity is lost to us; and, Teacher, then I will hear—none know better than you, how willingly—of Him whose thoughts were so much with the poor, and who had compassion for all human sorrow!"

He was at work again, solitary and sad, when his Master came and stood near to him dressed in black. He, also, had suffered heavily. His young wife, his beautiful and good young wife, was dead; so, too, his only child.

"Master, 'tis hard to bear—I know it—but be comforted. I would give you comfort, if I could."

The Master thanked him from his heart, but, said he, "O you labouring men! The calamity began among you. If you had but lived more healthily and decently, I should not be the widowed and bereft mourner that I am this day."

"Master," returned the other, shaking his head, "I have begun to understand a little that most calamities will come from us, as this one did, and that none will stop at our poor doors, until we are united with that great squabbling family yonder, to do the things that are right. We cannot live healthily and decently, unless they who undertook to manage us provide the means. We cannot be instructed unless they will teach us; we cannot be rationally amused, unless they will amuse us; we cannot but have some false gods of our own, while they set up so many of theirs in all the public places. The evil consequences of imperfect instruction, the evil consequences of pernicious neglect, the evil consequences of unnatural restraint and the denial of humanising enjoyments, will all come from us, and none of them will stop with us. They will spread far and wide. They always do; they always have done—just like the pestilence. I understand so much, I think, at last."

But the Master said again, "O you labouring men! How seldom do we ever hear of you, except in connexion with some trouble!"

"Master," he replied, "I am Nobody, and little likely to be heard of (nor yet much wanted to be heard of, perhaps), except when there *is* some trouble. But it never begins with me, and it never can end with me. As sure as Death, it comes down to me, and it goes up from me."

There was so much reason in what he said, that the Bigwig family, getting wind of it, and being horribly frightened by the late desolation, resolved to unite with him to do the things that were right—at all events, so far as the said things were associated with the direct prevention, humanly speaking, of another pestilence. But, as their fear wore off, which it soon began to do, they resumed their falling out among themselves, and did nothing. Consequently the scourge appeared again—low down as before—and spread avengingly upward as before, and carried off vast numbers of the brawlers. But not a man among them ever admitted, if in the least degree he ever perceived, that he had anything to do with it.

So Nobody lived and died in the old, old, old way; and this, in the main, is the whole of Nobody's story.

Had he no name, you ask? Perhaps it was Legion. It matters little what his name was. Let us call him Legion.

If you were ever in the Belgian villages near the field of Waterloo, you will have seen, in some quiet little church, a monument erected by faithful companions in arms to the memory of Colonel A, Major B, Captains C, D and E, Lieutenants F and G, Ensigns H, I and J, seven non-commissioned officers, and one hundred and thirty rank and file, who fell in the discharge of their duty on the memorable day. The story of Nobody is the story of the rank and file of the earth. They bear their share of the battle; they have their part in the victory; they fall; they leave no name but in the mass. The march of the proudest of us, leads to the dusty way by which they go. O! Let us think of them this year at the Christmas fire, and not forget them when it is burnt out.

THE
SEVEN POOR TRAVELLERS

[1854]

CHARACTERS

BEN, *a waiter.*

RICHARD DOUBLEDICK, *a wild young man, who enlists in the army.*

MARY MARSHALL, *the betrothed of Richard Doubledick.*

CAPTAIN TAUNTON, *captain of the company in which Private Doubledick serves.*

MRS. TAUNTON, *mother of the preceding.*

THE

SEVEN POOR TRAVELLERS

IN THREE CHAPTERS

CHAPTER I

IN THE OLD CITY OF ROCHESTER

STRICTLY speaking, there were only six Poor Travellers; but,
being a Traveller myself, though an idle one, and being
withal as poor as I hope to be, I brought the number up to
seven. This word of explanation is due at once, for what
says the inscription over the quaint old door?

RICHARD WATTS, Esq.
by his Will, dated 22 Aug. 1579,
founded this Charity
for Six poor Travellers,
who not being ROGUES, or PROCTORS,
May receive gratis for one Night,
Lodging, Entertainment,
and Fourpence each.

It was in the ancient little city of Rochester in Kent, of
all the good days in the year upon a Christmas-eve, that
I stood reading this inscription over the quaint old door in
question. I had been wandering about the neighbouring
Cathedral, and had seen the tomb of Richard Watts, with
the effigy of worthy Master Richard starting out of it like
a ship's figure-head; and I had felt that I could do no less,
as I gave the Verger his fee, than inquire the way to Watts's
Charity. The way being very short and very plain, I had

come prosperously to the inscription and the quaint old door.

"Now," said I to myself, as I looked at the knocker, "I know I am not a Proctor; I wonder whether I am a Rogue!"

Upon the whole, though Conscience reproduced two or three pretty faces which might have had smaller attraction for a moral Goliath than they had had for me, who am but a Tom Thumb in that way, I came to the conclusion that I was not a Rogue. So, beginning to regard the establishment as in some sort my property, bequeathed to me and divers co-legatees, share and share alike, by the Worshipful Master Richard Watts, I stepped backward into the road to survey my inheritance.

I found it to be a clean white house, of a staid and venerable air, with the quaint old door already three times mentioned (an arched door), choice little long low lattice-windows, and a roof of three gables. The silent High-street of Rochester is full of gables, with old beams and timbers carved into strange faces. It is oddly garnished with a queer old clock that projects over the pavement out of a grave red-brick building, as if Time carried on business there, and hung out his sign. Sooth to say, he did an active stroke of work in Rochester, in the old days of the Romans, and the Saxons, and the Normans; and down to the times of King John, when the rugged castle—I will not undertake to say how many hundreds of years old then—was abandoned to the centuries of weather which have so defaced the dark apertures in its walls, that the ruin looks as if the rooks and daws had pecked its eyes out.

I was very well pleased, both with my property and its situation. While I was yet surveying it with growing content, I espied, at one of the upper lattices which stood open, a decent body, of a wholesome matronly appearance, whose eyes I caught inquiringly addressed to mine. They said so plainly, "Do you wish to see the house?" that I answered aloud, "Yes, if you please." And within a minute the old door opened, and I bent my head, and went down two steps into the entry.

"This," said the matronly presence, ushering me into a low room on the right, "is where the Travellers sit by the fire, and cook what bits of suppers they buy with their fourpences."

"O! Then they have no Entertainment?" said I. For
the inscription over the outer door was still running in my
head, and I was mentally repeating, in a kind of tune,
"Lodging, entertainment, and fourpence each."

"They have a fire provided for 'em," returned the matron,
—a mighty civil person, not, as I could make out, overpaid;
"and these cooking utensils. And this what's painted on
a board is the rules for their behaviour. They have their
fourpences when they get their tickets from the steward
over the way,—for I don't admit 'em myself, they must get
their tickets first,—and sometimes one buys a rasher of
bacon, and another a herring, and another a pound of potatoes, or what not. Sometimes two or three of 'em will club
their fourpences together, and make a supper that way.
But not much of anything is to be got for fourpence, at
present, when provisions is so dear."

"True indeed," I remarked. I had been looking about
the room, admiring its snug fireside at the upper end, its
glimpse of the street through the low mullioned window,
and its beams overhead. "It is very comfortable," said I.

"Ill-conwenient," observed the matronly presence.

I liked to hear her say so; for it showed a commendable
anxiety to execute in no niggardly spirit the intentions of
Master Richard Watts. But the room was really so well
adapted to its purpose that I protested, quite enthusiastically,
against her disparagement.

"Nay, ma'am," said I, "I am sure it is warm in winter
and cool in summer. It has a look of homely welcome and
soothing rest. It has a remarkably cosy fireside, the very
blink of which, gleaming out into the street upon a winter
night, is enough to warm all Rochester's heart. And as to
the convenience of the six Poor Travellers—— "

"I don't mean them," returned the presence. "I speak
of its being an ill-conwenience to myself and my daughter,
having no other room to sit in of a night."

This was true enough, but there was another quaint room
of corresponding dimensions on the opposite side of the
entry: so I stepped across to it, through the open doors of
both rooms, and asked what this chamber was for.

"This," returned the presence, "is the Board Room.
Where the gentlemen meet when they come here."

Let me see. I had counted from the street six upper
windows besides these on the ground-story. Making a per-

plexed calculation in my mind, I rejoined, "Then the six Poor Travellers sleep upstairs?"

My new friend shook her head. "They sleep," she answered, "in two little outer galleries at the back, where their beds has always been, ever since the Charity was founded. It being so very ill-convenient to me as things is at present, the gentlemen are going to take off a bit of the back yard, and make a slip of a room for 'em there, to sit in before they go to bed."

"And then the six Poor Travellers," said I, "will be entirely out of the house?"

"Entirely out of the house," assented the presence, comfortably smoothing her hands. "Which is considered much better for all parties, and much more convenient."

I had been a little startled, in the Cathedral, by the emphasis with which the effigy of Master Richard Watts was bursting out of his tomb; but I began to think, now, that it might be expected to come across the High-street some stormy night, and make a disturbance here.

Howbeit, I kept my thoughts to myself, and accompanied the presence to the little galleries at the back. I found them on a tiny scale, like the galleries in old inn-yards; and they were very clean. While I was looking at them, the matron gave me to understand that the prescribed number of Poor Travellers were forthcoming every night from year's end to year's end; and that the beds were always occupied. My questions upon this, and her replies, brought us back to the Board Room so essential to the dignity of "the gentlemen," where she showed me the printed accounts of the Charity hanging up by the window. From them I gathered that the greater part of the property bequeathed by the Worshipful Master Richard Watts for the maintenance of this foundation was, at the period of his death, mere marshland; but that, in course of time, it had been reclaimed and built upon, and was very considerably increased in value. I found, too, that about a thirtieth part of the annual revenue was now expended on the purposes commemorated in the inscription over the door; the rest being handsomely laid out in Chancery, law expenses, collectorship, receivership, poundage, and other appendages of management, highly complimentary to the importance of the six Poor Travellers. In short, I made the not entirely new discovery that it may be said of an establishment like this, in dear old England,

as of the fat oyster in the American story, that it takes a
good many men to swallow it whole.

"And pray, ma'am," said I, sensible that the blankness of
my face began to brighten as the thought occurred to me,
"could one see these Travellers?"

"Well!" she returned dubiously, "no!"

"Not to-night, for instance!" said I.

"Well!" she returned more positively, "no. Nobody
ever asked to see them, and nobody ever did see them."

As I am not easily baulked in a design when I am set
upon it, I urged to the good lady that this was Christmas-
eve; that Christmas comes but once a year,—which is unhappily too true, for when it begins to stay with us the whole
year round we shall make this earth a very different place;
that I was possessed by the desire to treat the Travellers to
a supper and a temperate glass of hot Wassail; that the voice
of Fame had been heard in that land, declaring my ability
to make hot Wassail; that if I were permitted to hold the
feast, I should be found conformable to reason, sobriety, and
good hours; in a word, that I could be merry and wise myself, and had been even known at a pinch to keep others so,
although I was decorated with no badge or medal, and was
not a Brother, Orator, Apostle, Saint, or Prophet of any
denomination whatever. In the end I prevailed, to my
great joy. It was settled that at nine o'clock that night a
Turkey and a piece of Roast Beef should smoke upon the
board; and that I, faint and unworthy minister for once of
Master Richard Watts, should preside as the Christmas-sup-
per host of the six Poor Travellers.

I went back to my inn to give the necessary directions for
the Turkey and Roast Beef, and, during the remainder of
the day, could settle to nothing for thinking of the Poor
Travellers. When the wind blew hard against the windows,
—it was a cold day, with dark gusts of sleet alternating
with periods of wild brightness, as if the year were dying
fitfully,—I pictured them advancing towards their resting-
place along various cold roads, and felt delighted to think
how little they foresaw the supper that awaited them. I
painted their portraits in my mind, and indulged in little
heightening touches. I made them footsore; I made them
weary; I made them carry packs and bundles; I made them
stop by finger-posts and milestones, leaning on their bent
sticks, and looking wistfully at what was written there; I

made them lose their way; and filled their five wits with apprehensions of lying out all night, and being frozen to death. I took up my hat, and went out, climbed to the top of the Old Castle, and looked over the windy hills that slope down to the Medway, almost believing that I could descry some of my Travellers in the distance. After it fell dark, and the Cathedral bell was heard in the invisible steeple— quite a bower of frosty rime when I had last seen it—strik- ing five, six, seven. I became so full of my Travellers that I could eat no dinner, and felt constrained to watch them still in the red coals of my fire. They were all arrived by this time, I thought, had got their tickets, and were gone in.— There my pleasure was dashed by the reflection that proba- bly some Travellers had come too late and were shut out.

After the Cathedral bell had struck eight, I could smell a delicious savour of Turkey and Roast Beef rising to the window of my adjoining bedroom, which looked down into the inn-yard just where the lights of the kitchen reddened a massive fragment of the Castle Wall. It was high time to make the Wassail now; therefore I had up the materials (which, together with their proportions and combinations, I must decline to impart, as the only secret of my own I was ever known to keep), and made a glorious jorum. Not in a bowl; for a bowl anywhere but on a shelf is a low supersti- tion, fraught with cooling and slopping; but in a brown earthenware pitcher, tenderly suffocated, when full, with a coarse cloth. It being now upon the stroke of nine, I set out for Watts's Charity, carrying my brown beauty in my arms. I would trust Ben, the waiter, with untold gold; but there are strings in the human heart which must never be sounded by another, and drinks that I make myself are those strings in mine.

The Travellers were all assembled, the cloth was laid, and Ben had brought a great billet of wood, and had laid it artfully on the top of the fire, so that a touch or two of the poker after supper should make a roaring blaze. Having deposited my brown beauty in a red nook of the hearth, inside the fender, where she soon began to sing like an ethereal cricket, diffusing at the same time odours as of ripe vineyards, spice forests, and orange groves,—I say, having stationed my beauty in a place of security and improvement, I introduced myself to my guests by shaking hands all round, and giving them a hearty welcome.

I found the party to be thus composed. Firstly, myself. Secondly, a very decent man indeed, with his right arm in a sling, who had a certain clean agreeable smell of wood about him, from which I judged him to have something to do with shipbuilding. Thirdly, a little sailor-boy, a mere child, with a profusion of rich dark brown hair, and deep womanly-looking eyes. Fourthly, a shabby-genteel personage in a threadbare black suit, and apparently in very bad circumstances, with a dry suspicious look; the absent buttons on his waistcoat eked out with red tape; and a bundle of extraordinarily tattered papers sticking out of an inner breast-pocket. Fifthly, a foreigner by birth, but an Englishman in speech, who carried his pipe in the band of his hat, and lost no time in telling me, in an easy, simple, engaging way, that he was a watchmaker from Geneva, and travelled all about the Continent, mostly on foot, working as a journeyman, and seeing new countries,—possibly (I thought) also smuggling a watch or so, now and then. Sixthly, a little widow, who had been very pretty and was still very young, but whose beauty had been wrecked in some great misfortune, and whose manner was remarkably timid, scared, and solitary. Seventhly and lastly, a Traveller of a kind familiar to my boyhood, but now almost obsolete,—a Book-Pedlar, who had a quantity of Pamphlets and Numbers with him, and who presently boasted that he could repeat more verses in an evening than he could sell in a twelvemonth.

All these I have mentioned in the order in which they sat at table. I presided, and the matronly presence faced me. We were not long in taking our places, for the supper had arrived with me, in the following procession:

Myself with the pitcher.
Ben with Beer.
Inattentive Boy with hot plates.   Inattentive Boy with hot plates.
THE TURKEY.
Female carrying sauces to be heated on the spot.
THE BEEF.
Man with Tray on his head, containing Vegetables and Sundries.
Volunteer Hostler from Hotel, grinning,
And rendering no assistance.

As we passed along the High-street, comet-like, we left a long tail of fragrance behind us which caused the public to stop, sniffing in wonder. We had previously left at the corner of the inn-yard a wall-eyed young man connected with the Fly department, and well accustomed to the sound of a railway whistle which Ben always carries in his pocket, whose instructions were, so soon as he should hear the whistle blown, to dash into the kitchen, seize the hot plum-pudding and mince-pies, and speed with them to Watts's Charity, where they would be received (he was further instructed) by the sauce-female, who would be provided with brandy in a blue state of combustion.

All these arrangements were executed in the most exact and punctual manner. I never saw a finer turkey, finer beef, or greater prodigality of sauce and gravy; and my Travellers did wonderful justice to everything set before them. It made my heart rejoice to observe how their wind and frost hardened faces softened in the clatter of plates and knives and forks, and mellowed in the fire and supper heat. While their hats and caps and wrappers, hanging up, a few small bundles on the ground in a corner, and in another corner three or four old walking-sticks, worn down at the end to mere fringe, linked this snug interior with the bleak outside in a golden chain.

When supper was done, and my brown beauty had been elevated on the table, there was a general requisition to me to "take the corner;" which suggested to me comfortably enough how much my friends here made of a fire,—for when had *I* ever thought so highly of the corner, since the days when I connected it with Jack Horner? However, as I declined, Ben, whose touch on all convivial instruments is perfect, drew the table apart, and instructing my Travellers to open right and left on either side of me, and form round the fire, closed up the centre with myself and my chair, and preserved the order we had kept at table. He had already, in a tranquil manner, boxed the ears of the inattentive boys until they had been by imperceptible degrees boxed out of the room; and he now rapidly skirmished the sauce-female into the High-street, disappeared, and softly closed the door.

This was the time for bringing the poker to bear on the billet of wood. I tapped it three times, like an enchanted talisman, and a brilliant host of merry-makers burst out of it, and sported off by the chimney,—rushing up the middle in a fiery country dance, and never coming down again. Meanwhile, by their sparkling light, which threw our lamp into the shade, I filled the glasses, and gave my Travellers, CHRISTMAS!—CHRISTMAS-EVE, my friends, when the shepherds, who were Poor Travellers, too, in their way, heard the Angels sing, "On earth, peace. Good-will towards men!"

I don't know who was the first among us to think that we ought to take hands as we sat, in deference to the toast, or whether any one of us anticipated the others, but at any rate we all did it. We then drank to the memory of the good Master Richard Watts. And I wish his Ghost may never have had worse usage under that roof than it had from us.

It was the witching time for Story-telling. "Our whole life, Travellers," said I, "is a story more or less intelligible, —generally less; but we shall read it by a clearer light when it is ended. I, for one, am so divided this night between fact and fiction, that I scarce know which is which. Shall I beguile the time by telling you a story as we sit here?"

They all answered, yes. I had little to tell them, but I was bound by my own proposal. Therefore, after looking for awhile at the spiral column of smoke wreathing up from my brown beauty, through which I could have almost sworn I saw the effigy of Master Richard Watts less startled than usual, I fired away.

CHAPTER II

THE STORY OF RICHARD DOUBLEDICK

IN the year one thousand seven hundred and ninety-nine, a relative of mine came limping down, on foot, to this town of Chatham. I call it this town, because if anybody present knows to a nicety where Rochester ends and Chatham begins, it is more than I do. He was a poor traveller, with not a farthing in his pocket. He sat by the fire in this very room, and he slept one night in a bed that will be occupied to-night by some one here.

My relative came down to Chatham to enlist in a cavalry regiment, if a cavalry regiment would have him; if not, to take King George's shilling from any corporal or sergeant who would put a bunch of ribbons in his hat. His object was to get shot; but he thought he might as well ride to death as be at the trouble of walking.

My relative's Christian name was Richard, but he was better known as Dick. He dropped his own surname on the road down, and took up that of Doubledick. He was passed as Richard Doubledick; age, twenty-two; height, five foot ten; native place, Exmouth, which he had never been near in his life. There was no cavalry in Chatham when he limped over the bridge here with half a shoe to his dusty feet, so he enlisted into a regiment of the line, and was glad to get drunk and forget all about it.

You are to know that this relative of mine had gone wrong, and run wild. His heart was in the right place, but it was sealed up. He had been betrothed to a good and beautiful girl, whom he had loved better than she—or perhaps even he—believed; but in an evil hour he had given her cause to say to him solemnly, "Richard, I will never marry another man. I will live single for your sake but Mary Marshall's lips"—her name was Mary Marshall—"never address another word to you on earth. Go, Richard! Heaven forgive you!" This finished him. This brought him down to Chatham. This made him Private Richard Doubledick, with a determination to be shot.

There was not a more dissipated and reckless soldier in Chatham barracks, in the year one thousand seven hundred and ninety-nine, than Private Richard Doubledick. He associated with the dregs of every regiment; he was as seldom sober as he could be, and was constantly under punishment. It became clear to the whole barracks that Private Richard Doubledick would very soon be flogged.

Now the Captain of Richard Doubledick's company was a young gentleman not above five years his senior, whose eyes had an expression in them which affected Private Richard Doubledick in a very remarkable way. They were bright, handsome, dark eyes,—what are called laughing eyes generally, and, when serious, rather steady than severe,—but they were the only eyes now left in his narrowed world that Private Richard Doubledick could not stand. Unabashed by evil report and punishment, defiant of everything else and everybody else, he had but to know that those eyes looked at him for a moment, and he felt ashamed. He could not

The Seven Poor Travellers

so much as salute Captain Taunton in the street like any other officer. He was reproached and confused,—troubled by the mere possibility of the captain's looking at him. In his worst moments, he would rather turn back, and go any distance out of his way, than encounter those two handsome, dark, bright eyes.

One day, when Private Richard Doubledick came out of the Black hole, where he had been passing the last eight-and-forty hours, and in which retreat he spent a good deal of his time, he was ordered to betake himself to Captain Taunton's quarters. In the stale and squalid state of a man just out of the Black hole, he had less fancy than ever for being seen by the Captain; but he was not so mad yet as to disobey orders, and consequently went up to the terrace overlooking the parade-ground, where the officers' quarters were; twisting and breaking in his hands, as he went along, a bit of the straw that had formed the decorative furniture of the Black hole.

"Come in!" cried the Captain, when he knocked with his knuckles at the door. Private Richard Doubledick pulled off his cap, took a stride forward, and felt very conscious that he stood in the light of the dark, bright eyes.

There was a silent pause. Private Richard Doubledick had put the straw in his mouth, and was gradually doubling it up into his windpipe and choking himself.

"Doubledick," said the Captain, "do you know where you are going to?"

"To the Devil, Sir?" faltered Doubledick.

"Yes," returned the Captain. "And very fast."

Private Richard Doubledick turned the straw of the Blac hole in his mouth, and made a miserable salute of acquiescenc

"Doubledick," said the Captain, "since I entered] Majesty's service, a boy of seventeen, I have been pained see many men of promise going that road; but I have ne been so pained to see a man determined to make the sham journey as I have been, ever since you joined the regin to see you."

Private Richard Doubledick began to find a film ste. over the floor at which he looked; also to find the legs of the Captain's breakfast-table turning crooked, as if he saw them through water.

"I am only a common soldier, Sir," said he. "It signifies very little what such a poor brute comes to."

"You are a man," returned the Captain, with grave indignation, "of education and superior advantages; and if you say that, meaning what you say, you have sunk lower than I had believed. How low that must be, I leave you to consider, knowing what I know of your disgrace, and seeing what I see."

"I hope to get shot soon, Sir," said Private Richard Doubledick; "and then the regiment and the world together will be rid of me."

The legs of the table were becoming very crooked. Doubledick, looking up to steady his vision, met the eyes that had so strong an influence over him. He put his hand before his own eyes, and the breast of his disgrace-jacket swelled as if it would fly asunder.

"I would rather," said the young Captain, "see this in you, Doubledick, than I would see five thousand guineas counted out upon this table for a gift to my good mother. Have you a mother?"

"I am thankful to say she is dead, Sir."

"If your praises," returned the Captain, "were sounded from mouth to mouth through the whole regiment, through the whole army, through the whole country, you would wish she had lived to say, with pride and joy, 'He is my son!'"

"Spare me, Sir," said Doubledick. "She would never have heard any good of me. She would never have had any pride and joy in owning herself my mother. Love and compassion she might have had, and would have always had, I know; but not—Spare me, Sir! I am a broken wretch, quite at your mercy!" And he turned his face to the wall, and stretched out his imploring hand.

"My friend——" began the Captain.

"God bless you, Sir!" sobbed Private Richard Doubledick.

"You are at the crisis of your fate. Hold your course unchanged a little longer, and you know what must happen. *I* know even better than you can imagine, that, after that has happened, you are lost. No man who could shed those tears could bear those marks."

"I fully believe it, Sir," in a low, shivering voice said Private Richard Doubledick.

"But a man in any station can do his duty," said the young Captain, "and, in doing it, can earn his own respect, even if his case should be so very unfortunate and so very rare that he can earn no other man's. A common soldier, poor brute though you called him just now, has this advantage in the stormy times we live in, that he always does his duty before a host of sympathising witnesses. Do you doubt that he may so do it as to be extolled through a whole regiment, through a whole army, through a whole country? Turn while you may yet retrieve the past, and try."

"I will! I ask for only one witness, Sir," cried Richard, with a bursting heart.

"I understand you. I will be a watchful and a faithful one."

I have heard from Private Richard Doubledick's own lips, that he dropped down upon his knee, kissed that officer's hand, arose, and went out of the light of the dark, bright eyes, an altered man.

In that year, one thousand seven hundred and ninety-nine, the French were in Egypt, in Italy, in Germany, where not? Napoleon Bonaparte had likewise begun to stir against us in India, and most men could read the signs of the great troubles that were coming on. In the very next year, when we formed an alliance with Austria against him, Captain Taunton's regiment was on service in India. And there was not a finer non-commissioned officer in it,—no, nor in the whole line—than Corporal Richard Doubledick.

In eighteen hundred and one, the Indian army were on the coast of Egypt. Next year was the year of the proclamation of the short peace, and they were recalled. It had then become well known to thousands of men, that wherever Captain Taunton, with the dark, bright eyes, led, there, close to him, ever at his side, firm as a rock, true as the sun. and brave as Mars, would be certain to be found, while life beat in their hearts, that famous soldier, Sergeant Richard Doubledick.

Eighteen hundred and five, besides being the great year of Trafalgar, was a year of hard fighting in India. That year saw such wonders done by a Sergeant-Major, who cut his way single-handed through a solid mass of men, recovered the colours of his regiment, which had been seized from the hand of a poor boy shot through the heart, and rescued his wounded Captain, who was down, and in a very jungle of horses' hoofs and sabres,—saw such wonders done, I say, by this brave Sergeant-Major, that he was specially made the bearer of the colours he had won; and Ensign Richard Doubledick had risen from the ranks.

Sorely cut up in every battle, but always reinforced by the

bravest of men,—for the fame of following the old colours, shot through and through, which Ensign Richard Doubledick had saved, inspired all breasts,—this regiment fought its way through the Peninsular war, up to the investment of Badajos in eighteen hundred and twelve. Again and again it had been cheered through the British ranks until the tears had sprung into men's eyes at the mere hearing of the mighty British voice, so exultant in their valour; and there was not a drummer-boy but knew the legend, that wherever the two friends, Major Taunton, with the dark, bright eyes, and Ensign Richard Doubledick, who was devoted to him, were seen to go, there the boldest spirits in the English army became wild to follow.

One day, at Badajos,—not in the great storming, but in repelling a hot sally of the besieged upon our men at work in the trenches, who had given way,—the two officers found themselves hurrying forward, face to face, against a party of French infantry, who made a stand. There was an officer at their head, encouraging his men,—a courageous, handsome, gallant officer of five-and-thirty, whom Doubledick saw hurriedly, almost momentarily, but saw well. He particularly noticed this officer waving his sword, and rallying his men with an eager and excited cry, when they fired in obedience to his gesture, and Major Taunton dropped.

It was over in ten minutes more, and Doubledick returned to the spot where he had laid the best friend man ever had on a coat spread upon the wet clay. Major Taunton's uniform was opened at the breast, and on his shirt were three little spots of blood.

"Dear Doubledick," said he, "I am dying."

"For the love of Heaven, no!" exclaimed the other, kneeling down beside him, and passing his arm round his neck to raise his head. "Taunton! My preserver, my guardian angel, my witness! Dearest, truest, kindest of human beings! Taunton! For God's sake!"

The bright, dark eyes—so very, very dark now, in the pale face—smiled upon him; and the hand he had kissed thirteen years ago laid itself fondly on his breast.

"Write to my mother. You will see Home again. Tell her how we became friends. It will comfort her, as it comforts me."

He spoke no more, but faintly signed for a moment towards his hair as it fluttered in the wind. The Ensign understood him. He smiled again when he saw that, and, gently turning his face over on the supporting arm as if for rest, died, with his hand upon the breast in which he had revived a soul.

No dry eye looked on Ensign Richard Doubledick that melancholy day. He buried his friend on the field, and became a lone, bereaved man. Beyond his duty he appeared to have but two remaining cares in life,—one, to preserve the little packet of hair he was to give to Taunton's mother; the other, to encounter that French officer who had rallied the men under whose fire Taunton fell. A new legend now began to circulate among our troops; and it was, that when he and the French officer came face to face once more, there would be weeping in France.

The war went on—and through it went the exact picture of the French officer on the one side, and the bodily reality upon the other—until the Battle of Toulouse was fought. In the returns sent home appeared these words: "Severely wounded, but not dangerously, Lieutenant Richard Doubledick."

At Midsummer-time, in the year eighteen hundred and fourteen, Lieutenant Richard Doubledick, now a browned soldier, seven-and-thirty years of age, came home to England invalided. He brought the hair with him, near his heart. Many a French officer had he seen since that day; many a dreadful night, in searching with men and lanterns for his wounded, had he relieved French officers lying disabled; but the mental picture and the reality had never come together.

Though he was weak and suffered pain, he lost not an hour in getting down to Frome in Somersetshire, where Taunton's mother lived. In the sweet, compassionate words that naturally present themselves to the mind to-night, "he was the only son of his mother, and she was a widow."

It was a Sunday evening, and the lady sat at her quiet garden-window, reading the Bible; reading to herself, in a trembling voice, that very passage in it, as I have heard him tell. He heard the words: "Young man, I say unto thee, arise!"

He had to pass the window; and the bright, dark eyes of his debased time seemed to look at him. Her heart told her who he was; she came to the door quickly, and fell upon his neck.

"He saved me from ruin, made me a human creature, won me from infamy and shame. O, God for ever bless him! As He will, He will!"

"He will!" the lady answered. "I know he is in Heaven!" Then she piteously cried, "But O, my darling boy, my darling boy!"

Never from the hour when Private Richard Doubledick enlisted at Chatham had the Private, Corporal, Sergeant, Sergeant-Major, Ensign, or Lieutenant breathed his right name, or the name of Mary Marshall, or a word of the story of his life, into any ear except his reclaimer's. That previous scene in his existence was closed. He had firmly resolved that his expiation should be to live unknown; to disturb no more the peace that had long grown over his old offences; to let it be revealed, when he was dead, that he had striven and suffered, and had never forgotten; and then, if they could forgive him and believe him—well, it would be time enough—time enough!

But that night, remembering the words he had cherished for two years, "Tell her how we became friends. It will comfort her, as it comforts me," he related everything. It gradually seemed to him as if in his maturity he had recovered a mother; it gradually seemed to her as if in her bereavement she had found a son. During his stay in England, the quiet garden into which he had slowly and painfully crept, a stranger, became the boundary of his home; when he was able to rejoin his regiment in the spring, he left the garden, thinking was this indeed the first time he had ever turned his face towards the old colours with a woman's blessing!

He followed them—so ragged, so scarred and pierced now, that they would scarcely hold together—to Quatre Bras and Ligny. He stood beside them, in an awful stillness of many men, shadowy through the mist and drizzle of a wet June forenoon, on the field of Waterloo. And down to that hour the picture in his mind of the French officer had never been compared with the reality.

The famous regiment was in action early in the battle, and received its first check in many an eventful year, when he was seen to fall. But it swept on to avenge him, and left behind it no such creature in the world of consciousness as Lieutenant Richard Doubledick.

Through pits of mire, and pools of rain; along deep ditches, once roads, that were pounded and ploughed to pieces by artillery, heavy waggons, tramp of men and horses, and the struggle of every wheeled thing that could carry wounded soldiers; jolted among the dying and the dead, so disfigured by blood and mud as to be hardly recognisable for humanity; undisturbed by the moaning of men and the shrieking of horses, which, newly taken from the peaceful pursuits of life, could not endure the sight of the stragglers lying by the wayside, never to resume their toilsome journey; dead, as to any sentient life that was in it, and yet alive,—the form that had been Lieutenant Richard Doubledick, with whose praises England rang, was conveyed to Brussels. There it was tenderly laid down in hospital; and there it lay, week after week, through the long bright summer days, until the harvest, spared by war, had ripened and was gathered in.

Over and over again the sun rose and set upon the crowded city; over and over again the moonlight nights were quiet on the plains of Waterloo: and all that time was a blank to what had been Lieutenant Richard Doubledick. Rejoicing troops marched into Brussels, and marched out; brothers and fathers, sisters, mothers, and wives, came thronging thither, drew their lots of joy or agony, and departed; so many times a day the bells rang; so many times the shadows of the great buildings changed; so many lights sprang up at dusk; so many feet passed here and there upon the pavements; so many hours of sleep and cooler air of night succeeded: indifferent to all, a marble face lay on a bed, like the face of a recumbent statue on the tomb of Lieutenant Richard Doubledick.

Slowly labouring, at last, through a long heavy dream of confused time and place, presenting faint glimpses of army surgeons whom he knew, and of faces that had been familiar to his youth,—dearest and kindest among them, Mary Marshall's, with a solicitude upon it more like reality than anything he could discern,—Lieutenant Richard Doubledick came back to life. To the beautiful life of a calm autumn evening sunset, to the peaceful life of a fresh quiet room with a large window standing open; a balcony beyond, in which were moving leaves and sweet-smelling flowers; beyond, again, the clear sky, with the sun full in his sight, pouring its golden radiance on his bed.

It was so tranquil and so lovely that he thought he had passed into another world. And he said in a faint voice, "Taunton, are you near me?"

A face bent over him. Not his, his mother's.

"I came to nurse you. We have nursed you many weeks. You were moved here long ago. Do you remember nothing?"

"Nothing."

The lady kissed his cheek, and held his hand, soothing him.

"Where is the regiment? What has happened? Let me call you mother. What has happened, mother?"

"A great victory, dear. The war is over, and the regiment was the bravest in the field."

His eyes kindled, his lips trembled, he sobbed, and the tears ran down his face. He was very weak, too weak to move his hand.

"Was it dark just now?" he asked presently.

"No."

"It was only dark to me? Something passed away, like a black shadow. But as it went, and the sun—O the blessed sun, how beautiful it is!—touched my face, I thought I saw a light white cloud pass out at the door. Was there nothing that went out?"

She shook her head, and in a little while he fell asleep, she still holding his hand, and soothing him.

From that time, he recovered. Slowly, for he had been desperately wounded in the head, and had been shot in the body, but making some little advance every day. When he had gained sufficient strength to converse as he lay in bed, he soon began to remark that Mrs. Taunton always brought him back to his own history. Then he recalled his preserver's dying words, and thought, "It comforts her."

One day he awoke out of a sleep, refreshed, and asked her to read to him. But the curtain of the bed, softening the light, which she always drew back when he awoke, that she might see him from her table at the bedside where she sat at work, was held undrawn ; and a woman's voice spoke, which was not hers.

"Can you bear to see a stranger?" it said softly. "Will you like to see a stranger?"

"Stranger!" he repeated. The voice awoke old memories, before the days of Private Richard Doubledick.

"A stranger now, but not a stranger once," it said in tones that thrilled him. "Richard, dear Richard, lost through so many years, my name——"

He cried out her name, "Mary," and she held him in her arms, and his head lay on her bosom.

"I am not breaking a rash vow, Richard. These are not Mary Marshall's lips that speak. I have another name."

She was married.

"I have another name, Richard. Did you ever hear it?"

"Never!"

He looked into her face, so pensively beautiful, and wondered at the smile upon it through her tears.

"Think again, Richard. Are you sure you never heard my altered name?"

"Never!"

"Don't move your head to look at me, dear Richard. Let it lie here, while I tell my story. I loved a generous, noble man; loved him with my whole heart; loved him for years and years; loved him faithfully, devotedly; loved him with no hope of return; loved him, knowing nothing of his highest qualities—not even knowing that he was alive. He was a brave soldier. He was honoured and beloved by thousands of thousands, when the mother of his dear friend found me, and showed me that in all his triumphs he had never forgotten me. He was wounded in a great battle. He was brought, dying, here, into Brussels. I came to watch and tend him, as I would have joyfully gone, with such a purpose, to the dreariest ends of the earth. When he knew no one else, he knew me. When he suffered most, he bore his sufferings barely murmuring, content to rest his head where yours rests now. When he lay at the point of death, he married me, that he might call me Wife before he died. And the name, my dear love, that I took on that forgotten night—— "

"I know it now!" he sobbed. "The shadowy remembrance strengthens. It is come back. I thank Heaven that my mind is quite restored! My Mary, kiss me; lull this weary head to rest, or I shall die of gratitude. His parting words were fulfilled. I see Home again!"

Well! They were happy. It was a long recovery, but they were happy through it all. The snow had melted on the ground, and the birds were singing in the leafless thickets of the early spring, when those three were first able to ride out together, and when people flocked about the open carriage to cheer and congratulate Captain Richard Doubledick.

But even then it became necessary for the Captain, instead of returning to England, to complete his recovery in the climate of Southern France. They found a spot upon the

Rhône, within a ride of the old town of Avignon, and within view of its broken bridge, which was all they could desire; they lived there, together, six months; then returned to England. Mrs. Taunton, growing old after three years—though not so old as that her bright, dark eyes were dimmed —and remembering that her strength had been benefited by the change, resolved to go back for a year to those parts. So she went with a faithful servant, who had often carried her son in his arms; and she was to be rejoined and escorted home, at the year's end, by Captain Richard Doubledick.

She wrote regularly to her children (as she called them now), and they to her. She went to the neighbourhood of Aix; and there, in their own château near the farmer's house she rented, she grew into intimacy with a family belonging to that part of France. The intimacy began in her often meeting among the vineyards a pretty child, a girl with a most compassionate heart, who was never tired of listening to the solitary English lady's stories of her poor son and the cruel wars. The family were as gentle as the child, and at length she came to know them so well that she accepted their invitation to pass the last month of her residence abroad under their roof. All this intelligence she wrote home, piecemeal as it came about, from time to time: and at last enclosed a polite note, from the head of the château, soliciting, on the occasion of his approaching mission to that neighbourhood, the honour of the company of cet homme si justement célèbre, Monsieur le Capitaine Richard Doubledick.

Captain Doubledick, now a hardy, handsome man in the full vigour of life, broader across the chest and shoulders than he had ever been before, dispatched a courteous reply, and followed it in person. Travelling through all that extent of country after three years of Peace, he blessed the better days on which the world had fallen. The corn was golden, not drenched in unnatural red; was bound in sheaves for food, not trodden underfoot by men in mortal fight. The smoke rose up from peaceful hearths, not blazing ruins. The carts were laden with the fair fruits of the earth, not with wounds and death. To him who had so often seen the terrible reverse, these things were beautiful indeed; and they brought him in a softened spirit to the old château near Aix upon a deep blue evening.

It was a large château of the genuine old ghostly kind, with round towers, and extinguishers, and a high leaden roof, and more windows than Aladdin's Palace. The lattice blinds were all thrown open after the heat of the day, and there were glimpses of rambling walls and corridors within. Then there were immense out-buildings fallen into partial decay, masses of dark trees, terrace-gardens, balustrades; tanks of water, too weak to play and too dirty to work; statues, weeds, and thickets of iron railing that seemed to have overgrown themselves like the shrubberies, and to have branched out in all manner of wild shapes. The entrance doors stood open, as doors often do in that country when the heat of the day is past; and the Captain saw no bell or knocker, and walked in.

He walked into a lofty stone hall, refreshingly cool and gloomy after the glare of a Southern day's travel. Extending along the four sides of this hall was a gallery, leading to suites of rooms; and it was lighted from the top. Still no bell was to be seen.

"Faith," said the Captain halting, ashamed of the clanking of his boots, "this is a ghostly beginning!"

He started back, and felt his face turn white. In the gallery, looking down at him, stood the French officer—the officer whose picture he had carried in his mind so long and so far. Compared with the original, at last—in every lineament how like it was!

He moved, and disappeared, and Captain Richard Doubledick heard his steps coming quickly down into the hall. He entered through an archway. There was a bright, sudden look upon his face, much such a look as it had worn in that fatal moment.

Monsieur le Capitaine Richard Doubledick? Enchanted to receive him! A thousand apologies! The servants were all out in the air. There was a little fête among them in the garden. In effect, it was the fête day of my daughter, the little cherished and protected of Madame Taunton.

He was so gracious and so frank that Monsieur le Capitaine Richard Doubledick could not withhold his hand. "It is the hand of a brave Englishman," said the French officer, retaining it while he spoke. "I could respect a brave Englishman, even as my foe, how much more as my friend! I also am a soldier."

"He has not remembered me, as I have remembered him;

he did not take such note of my face, that day, as I took of his," thought Captain Richard Doubledick. "How shall I tell him?"

The French officer conducted his guest into a garden and presented him to his wife, an engaging and beautiful woman, sitting with Mrs. Taunton in a whimsical old-fashioned pavilion. His daughter, her fair young face beaming with joy, came running to embrace him; and there was a boy-baby to tumble down among the orange trees on the broad steps, in making for his father's legs. A multitude of children visitors were dancing to sprightly music; and all the servants and peasants about the château were dancing too. It was a scene of innocent happiness that might have been invented for the climax of the scenes of peace which had soothed the Captain's journey.

He looked on, greatly troubled in his mind, until a resounding bell rang, and the French officer begged to show him his rooms. They went upstairs into the gallery from which the officer had looked down; and Monsieur le Capitaine Richard Doubledick was cordially welcomed to a grand outer chamber, and a smaller one within, all clocks and draperies, and hearths, and brazen dogs, and tiles, and cool devices, and elegance, and vastness.

"You were at Waterloo," said the French officer.

"I was," said Captain Richard Doubledick. "And at Badajos."

Left alone with the sound of his own stern voice in his ears, he sat down to consider, What shall I do, and how shall I tell him? At that time, unhappily, many deplorable duels had been fought between English and French officers, arising out of the recent war; and these duels, and how to avoid this officer's hospitality, were the uppermost thought in Captain Richard Doubledick's mind.

He was thinking, and letting the time run out in which he should have dressed for dinner, when Mrs. Taunton spoke to him outside the door, asking if he could give her the letter he had brought from Mary. "His mother, above all," the Captain thought. "How shall I tell her?"

"You will form a friendship with your host, I hope," said Mrs. Taunton, whom he hurriedly admitted, "that will last for life. He is so true-hearted and so generous, Richard, that you can hardly fail to esteem one another. If He had been spared," she kissed (not without tears) the locket in which she wore his hair, "he would have appreciated him with his own magnanimity, and would have been truly happy that the evil days were past which made such a man his enemy."

She left the room; and the Captain walked, first to one window, whence he could see the dancing in the garden, then to another window, whence he could see the smiling prospect and the peaceful vineyards.

"Spirit of my departed friend," said he, "is it through thee these better thoughts are rising in my mind? Is it thou who hast shown me, all the way I have been drawn to meet this man, the blessings of the altered time? Is it thou who hast sent thy stricken mother to me, to stay my angry hand? Is it from thee the whisper comes, that this man did his duty as thou didst,—and as I did, through thy guidance, which has wholly saved me here on earth,—and that he did no more?"

He sat down, with his head buried in his hands, and, when he rose up, made the second strong resolution of his life,— that neither to the French officer, nor to the mother of his departed friend, nor to any soul, while either of the two was living, would he breathe what only he knew. And when he touched that French officer's glass with his own, that day at dinner, he secretly forgave him in the name of the Divine Forgiver of injuries.

Here I ended my story as the first Poor Traveller. But, if I had told it now, I could have added that the time has since come when the son of Major Richard Doubledick, and the son of that French officer, friends as their fathers were before them, fought side by side in one cause, with their respective nations, like long-divided brothers whom the better times have brought together, fast united.

CHAPTER III

THE ROAD

My story being finished, and the Wassail too, we broke up as the Cathedral bell struck Twelve. I did not take leave of my travellers that night; for it had come into my head to reappear, in conjunction with some hot coffee, at seven in the morning.

As I passed along the High-street, I heard the Waits at a distance, and struck off to find them. They were playing near one of the old gates of the City, at the corner of a wonderfully quaint row of red-brick tenements, which the clarionet obligingly informed me were inhabited by the Minor-Canons. They had odd little porches over the doors, like sounding-boards over old pulpits; and I thought I should like to see one of the Minor-Canons come out upon his top step, and favour us with a little Christmas discourse about the poor scholars of Rochester; taking for his text the words of his Master relative to the devouring of Widows' houses.

The clarionet was so communicative, and my inclinations were (as they generally are) of so vagabond a tendency, that I accompanied the Waits across an open green called the Vines, and assisted—in the French sense—at the performance of two waltzes, two polkas, and three Irish melodies, before I thought of my inn any more. However, I returned to it then, and found a fiddle in the kitchen, and Ben, the wall-eyed young man, and two chambermaids, circling round the great deal table with the utmost animation.

I had a very bad night. It cannot have been owing to the turkey or the beef,—and the Wassail is out of the question, —but in every endeavour that I made to get to sleep I failed most dismally. I was never asleep; and in whatsoever unreasonable direction my mind rambled, the effigy of Master Richard Watts perpetually embarrassed it.

In a word, I only got out of the Worshipful Master Richard Watts's way by getting out of bed in the dark at six o'clock, and tumbling, as my custom is, into all the cold

water that could be accumulated for the purpose.   The outer
air was dull and cold enough in the street, when I came
down there; and the one candle in our supper-room at
Watts's Charity looked as pale in the burning as if it had
had a bad night too.   But my Travellers had all slept soundly,
and they took to the hot coffee, and the piles of bread-and-
butter, which Ben had arranged like deals in a timber-yard,
as kindly as I could desire.

While it was yet scarcely daylight, we all came out into
the street together, and there shook hands.   The widow took
the little sailor towards Chatham, where he was to find a
steamboat for Sheerness; the lawyer, with an extremely
knowing look, went his own way, without committing himself
by announcing his intentions; two more struck off by the
cathedral and old castle for Maidstone: and the book-pedlar
accompanied me over the bridge.   As for me, I was going to
walk by Cobham Woods, as far upon my way to London as
I fancied.

When I came to the stile and footpath by which I was to
diverge from the main road, I bade farewell to my last
remaining Poor Traveller, and pursued my way alone.   And
now the mists began to rise in the most beautiful manner,
and the sun to shine; and as I went on through the bracing
air, seeing the hoar-frost sparkle everywhere, I felt as if all
Nature shared in the joy of the great Birthday.

Going through the woods, the softness of my tread upon
the mossy ground and among the brown leaves enhanced the
Christmas sacredness by which I felt surrounded.   As the
whitened stems environed me, I thought how the Founder of
the time had never raised his benignant hand, save to bless
and heal, except in the case of one unconscious tree.   By
Cobham Hall, I came to the village, and the churchyard
where the dead had been quietly buried, "in the sure and
certain hope" which Christmas-time inspired.   What children
could I see at play, and not be loving of, recalling who had
loved them!   No garden that I passed was out of unison with
the day, for I remembered that the tomb was in a garden,
and that "she, supposing him to be the gardener," had
said, "Sir, if thou have borne him hence, tell me where thou
hast laid him, and I will take him away."   In time, the
distant river with the ships came full in view, and with it
pictures of the poor fishermen, mending their nets, who
arose and followed him,—of the teaching of the people from

THE HOLLY-TREE

[1855]

CHARACTERS

CHARLEY, *a guest at the Holly-Tree Inn.*

COBBS, *boots at the Holly-Tree Inn; formerly under-gardener to Mr. Walmers.*

EDWIN, *the supposed rival of Charley.*

EMMELINE, *cousin to Angela Leath.*

ANGELA LEATH, *the sweetheart, afterwards the wife, of Charley.*

NORAH, *a little girl, cousin to Master Harry Walmers.*

MASTER HARRY WALMERS, *a boy not quite eight years old, in love with his cousin Norah.*

MR. WALMERS, *the father of Master Harry.*

THE HOLLY-TREE

THREE BRANCHES

FIRST BRANCH

MYSELF

I HAVE kept one secret in the course of my life. I am a bashful man. Nobody would suppose it, nobody ever does suppose it, nobody ever did suppose it, but I am naturally a bashful man. This is the secret which I have never breathed until now.

I might greatly move the reader by some account of the innumerable places I have not been to, the innumerable people I have not called upon or received, the innumerable social evasions I have been guilty of, solely because I am by original constitution and character a bashful man. But I will leave the reader unmoved, and proceed with the object before me.

That object is to give a plain account of my travels and discoveries in the Holly-Tree Inn; in which place of good entertainment for man and beast I was once snowed up.

It happened in the memorable year when I parted for ever from Angela Leath, whom I was shortly to have married, on making the discovery that she preferred my bosom friend. From our school-days I had freely admitted Edwin, in my own mind, to be far superior to myself; and, though I was grievously wounded at heart, I felt the preference to be natural, and tried to forgive them both. It was under these circumstances that I resolved to go to America—on my way to the Devil.

Communicating my discovery neither to Angela nor to

Edwin, but resolving to write each of them an affecting letter conveying my blessing and forgiveness, which the steam-tender for shore should carry to the post when I myself should be bound for the New World, far beyond recall, —I say, locking up my grief in my own breast, and consoling myself as I could with the prospect of being generous, I quietly left all I held dear, and started on the desolate journey I have mentioned.

The dead winter-time was in full dreariness when I left my chambers for ever, at five o'clock in the morning. I had shaved by candle-light, of course, and was miserably cold, and experienced that general all-pervading sensation of getting up to be hanged which I have usually found inseparable from untimely rising under such circumstances.

How well I remember the forlorn aspect of Fleet-street when I came out of the Temple! The street-lamps flickering in the gusty north-east wind, as if the very gas were contorted with cold; the white-topped houses; the bleak, star-lighted sky; the market people and other early stragglers, trotting to circulate their almost frozen blood; the hospitable light and warmth of the few coffee-shops and public-houses that were open for such customers; the hard, dry, frosty rime with which the air was charged (the wind had already beaten it into every crevice), and which lashed my face like a steel whip.

It wanted nine days to the end of the month, and end of the year. The Post-office packet for the United States was to depart from Liverpool, weather permitting, on the first of the ensuing month, and I had the intervening time on my hands. I had taken this into consideration, and had resolved to make a visit to a certain spot (which I need not name) on the farther borders of Yorkshire. It was endeared to me by my having first seen Angela at a farmhouse in that place, and my melancholy was gratified by the idea of taking a wintry leave of it before my expatriation. I ought to explain, that, to avoid being sought out before my resolution should have been rendered irrevocable by being carried into full effect, I had written to Angela overnight, in my usual manner, lamenting that urgent business, of which she should know all particulars by-and-by—took me unexpectedly away from her for a week or ten days.

There was no Northern Railway at that time, and in its place there were stage-coaches; which I occasionally find myself, in common with some other people, affecting to lament now, but which everybody dreaded as a very serious penance then. I had secured the box-seat on the fastest of these, and my business in Fleet-street was to get into a cab with my portmanteau, so to make the best of my way to the Peacock at Islington, where I was to join this coach. But when one of our Temple watchmen, who carried my portmanteau into Fleet-street for me, told me about the huge blocks of ice that had for some days past been floating in the river, having closed up in the night, and made a walk from the Temple Gardens over to the Surrey shore, I began to ask myself the question, whether the box-seat would not be likely to put a sudden and a frosty end to my unhappiness. I was heart-broken, it is true, and yet I was not quite so far gone as to wish to be frozen to death.

When I got up to the Peacock,—where I found everybody drinking hot purl, in self-preservation,—I asked if there were an inside seat to spare. I then discovered that, inside or out, I was the only passenger. This gave me a still livelier idea of the great inclemency of the weather, since that coach always loaded particularly well. However, I took a little purl (which I found uncommonly good), and got into the coach. When I was seated, they built me up with straw to the waist, and, conscious of making a rather ridiculous appearance, I began my journey.

It was still dark when we left the Peacock. For a little while, pale, uncertain ghosts of houses and trees appeared and vanished, and then it was hard, black, frozen day. People were lighting their fires; smoke was mounting straight up high into the rarefied air; and we were rattling for Highgate Archway over the hardest ground I have ever heard the ring of iron shoes on. As we got into the country, everything seemed to have grown old and gray. The roads, the trees, thatched roofs of cottages and homesteads, the ricks in farmers' yards. Out-door work was abandoned, horse-troughs at roadside inns were frozen hard, no stragglers lounged about, doors were close shut, little turnpike houses had blazing fires inside, and children (even turnpike people have children, and seem to like them) rubbed the frost from the little panes of glass with their chubby arms, that their bright eyes might catch a glimpse of the solitary coach going by. I don't know when the snow began to set in; but I know that we were changing horses somewhere when I heard the guard remark, "That the old lady up in the sky was picking her geese pretty hard to-day." Then, indeed, I found the white down falling fast and thick.

The lonely day wore on, and I dozed it out, as a lonely traveller does. I was warm and valiant after eating and drinking,—particularly after dinner; cold and depressed at all other times. I was always bewildered as to time and place, and always more or less out of my senses. The coach and horses seemed to execute in chorus Auld Lang Syne, without a moment's intermission. They kept the time and tune with the greatest regularity, and rose into the swell at the beginning of the Refrain, with a precision that worried me to death. While we changed horses, the guard and coachman went stumping up and down the road, printing off their shoes in the snow, and poured so much liquid consolation into themselves without being any the worse for it, that I began to confound them, as it darkened again, with two great white casks standing on end. Our horses tumbled down in solitary places, and we got them up,—which was the pleasantest variety *I* had, for it warmed me. And it snowed and snowed, and still it snowed, and never left off snowing. All night long we went on in this manner. Thus we came round the clock, upon the Great North Road, to the performance of Auld Lang Syne all day again. And it snowed and snowed, and still it snowed, and never left off snowing.

I forget now where we were at noon on the second day, and where we ought to have been ; but I know that we were scores of miles behindhand, and that our case was growing worse every hour. The drift was becoming prodigiously deep ; landmarks were getting snowed out ; the road and the fields were all one ; instead of having fences and hedge-rows to guide us, we went crunching on over an unbroken surface of ghastly white that might sink beneath us at any moment and drop us down a whole hillside. Still the coachman and guard—who kept together on the box, always in council, and looking well about them—made out the track with astonishing sagacity.

When we came in sight of a town, it looked, to my fancy, like a large drawing on a slate, with abundance of slate-pencil expended on the churches and houses where the snow lay thickest. When we came within a town, and found the church clocks all stopped, the dial-faces choked with snow, and the inn-signs blotted out, it seemed as if the whole place were overgrown with white moss. As to the coach, it was a mere snowball; similarly, the men and boys who ran along beside us to the town's end, turning our clogged wheels and encouraging our horses, were men and boys of snow; and the bleak wild solitude to which they at last dismissed us was a snowy Sahara. One would have thought this enough : notwithstanding which, I pledge my word that it snowed and snowed, and still it snowed, and never left off snowing.

We performed Auld Lang Syne the whole day; seeing nothing, out of towns and villages, but the track of stoats, hares, and foxes, and sometimes of birds. At nine o'clock at night, on a Yorkshire moor, a cheerful burst from our horn, and a welcome sound of talking, with a glimmering and moving about of lanterns, roused me from my drowsy state. I found that we were going to change.

They helped me out, and I said to a waiter, whose bare head became as white as King Lear's in a single minute, "What Inn is this?"

"The Holly-Tree, Sir," said he.

"Upon my word, I believe," said I, apologetically, to the guard and coachman, "that I must stop here."

Now the landlord, and the landlady, and the ostler, and the postboy, and all the stable authorities, had already asked the coachman, to the wide-eyed interest of all the rest of the establishment, if he meant to go on. The coachman had already replied, "Yes, he'd take her through it,"—meaning by Her the coach,—"if so be as George would stand by him." George was the guard, and he had already sworn that he *would* stand by him. So the helpers were already getting the horses out.

My declaring myself beaten, after this parley, was not an announcement without preparation. Indeed, but for the way to the announcement being smoothed by the parley, I more than doubt whether, as an innately bashful man, I should have had the confidence to make it. As it was, it received the approval even of the guard and coachman. Therefore, with many confirmations of my inclining, and many remarks from one bystander to another, that the gentleman could go for'ard by the mail to-morrow, whereas to-night he would only be froze, and where was the good of a gentleman being froze,—ah, let alone buried alive (which latter clause was added by a humorous helper as a joke at my expense, and was extremely well received), I saw my portmanteau got out stiff, like a frozen body; did the handsome thing by the guard and coachman; wished them goodnight and a prosperous journey; and, a little ashamed of myself, after all, for leaving them to fight it out alone, followed the landlord, landlady, and waiter of the Holly-Tree upstairs.

I thought I had never seen such a large room as that into which they showed me. It had five windows, with dark red curtains that would have absorbed the light of a general illumination; and there were complications of drapery at the top of the curtains, that went wandering about the wall in a most extraordinary manner. I asked for a smaller room, and they told me there was no smaller room. They could screen me in, however, the landlord said. They brought a great old japanned screen, with natives (Japanese, I suppose) engaged in a variety of idiotic pursuits all over it; and left me roasting whole before an immense fire.

My bedroom was some quarter of a mile off, up a great staircase at the end of a long gallery; and nobody knows what a misery this is to a bashful man who would rather not meet people on the stairs. It was the grimmest room I have ever had the nightmare in; and all the furniture, from the four posts of the bed to the two old silver candlesticks, was tall, high-shouldered, and spindle-waisted. Below, in my sitting-room, if I looked round my screen, the wind rushed at me like a mad bull; if I stuck to my armchair, the fire scorched me to the colour of a new brick. The chimneypiece was very high, and there was a bad glass—what I may call a wavy glass—above it, which, when I stood up, just showed me my anterior phrenological developments, —and these never look well, in any subject, cut short off at the eyebrow. If I stood with my back to the fire, a gloomy vault of darkness above and beyond the screen insisted on being looked at; and, in its dim remoteness, the drapery of the ten curtains of the five windows went twisting and creeping about, like a nest of gigantic worms.

I suppose that what I observe in myself must be observed by some other men of similar character in *themselves*; therefore I am emboldened to mention, that, when I travel, I never arrive at a place but I immediately want to go away from it. Before I had finished my supper of broiled fowl and mulled port, I had impressed upon the waiter in detail my arrangements for departure in the morning. Breakfast and bill at eight. Fly at nine. Two horses, or, if needful, even four.

Tired though I was, the night appeared about a week long. In oases of nightmare, I thought of Angela, and felt more depressed than ever by the reflection that I was on the shortest road to Gretna Green. What had *I* to do with Gretna Green? I was not going *that* way to the Devil, but by the American route, I remarked in my bitterness.

In the morning I found that it was snowing still, that it had snowed all night, and that I was snowed up. Nothing could get out of that spot on the moor, or could come at it, until the road had been cut out by labourers from the market-town. When they might cut their way to the Holly-Tree nobody could tell me.

It was now Christmas-eve. I should have had a dismal Christmas-time of it anywhere, and consequently that did not so much matter; still, being snowed up was like dying of frost, a thing I had not bargained for. I felt very lonely. Yet I could no more have proposed to the landlord and landlady to admit me to their society (though I should have liked it very much) than I could have asked them to present me with a piece of plate. Here my great secret, the real bashfulness of my character, is to be observed. Like most bashful men, I judge of other people as if they were bashful too. Besides being far too shamefaced to make the proposal myself, I really had a delicate misgiving that it would be in the last degree disconcerting to them.

Trying to settle down, therefore, in my solitude, I first of all asked what books there were in the house. The waiter brought me a *Book of Roads*, two or three old Newspapers, a little Song-Book, terminating in a collection of Toasts and Sentiments, a little Jest-Book, an odd volume of *Peregrine Pickle*, and the *Sentimental Journey*. I knew every word of the two last already, but I read them through again, then tried to hum all the songs (Auld Lang Syne was among them); went entirely through the jokes,—in which I found a fund of melancholy adapted to my state of mind; proposed all the toasts, enunciated all the sentiments, and mastered the papers. The latter had nothing in them but stock advertisements, a meeting about a county rate, and a highway robbery. As I am a greedy reader, I could not make this supply hold out until night; it was exhausted by tea-time.

Being then entirely cast upon my own resources, I got through an hour in considering what to do next. Ultimately, it came into my head (from which I was anxious by any means to exclude Angela and Edwin), that I would endeavour to recall my experience of Inns, and would try how long it lasted me. I stirred the fire, moved my chair a little to one side of the screen,—not daring to go far, for I knew the wind was waiting to make a rush at me, I could hear it growling, —and began.

My first impressions of an Inn dated from the Nursery; consequently I went back to the Nursery for a starting-point, and found myself at the knee of a sallow woman with a fishy eye, an aquiline nose, and a green gown, whose specialty was a dismal narrative of a landlord by the roadside, whose visitors unaccountably disappeared for many years, until it was discovered that the pursuit of his life had been to convert them into pies. For the better devotion of himself to this branch of industry, he had constructed a secret door behind the head of the bed; and when the visitor (oppressed with pie) had fallen asleep, this wicked landlord would look softly in with a lamp in one hand and a knife in the other, would cut his throat, and would make him into pies; for which purpose he had coppers, underneath a trap-door, always boiling; and rolled out his pastry in the dead of the night. Yet even he was not insensible to the stings of conscience, for he never went to sleep without being heard to mutter, "Too much pepper!" which was eventually the cause of his being brought to justice. I had no sooner disposed of this criminal than there started up another of the same period, whose profession was originally housebreaking; in the pursuit of which art he had had his right ear chopped off one night, as he was burglariously getting in at a window, by a brave and lovely servant-maid (whom the aquiline-nosed woman, though not at all answering the description, always mysteriously implied to be herself). After several years, this brave and lovely servant-maid was married to the landlord of a country Inn; which landlord had this remarkable characteristic, that he always wore a silk nightcap, and never would on any consideration take it off. At last, one night, when he was fast asleep, the brave and lovely woman lifted up his silk nightcap on the right side, and found that he had no ear there; upon which she sagaciously perceived that he was the clipped housebreaker, who had married her with the intention of putting her to death. She immediately heated the poker and terminated his career, for which she was taken to King George upon his throne, and received the compliments of royalty on her great discretion and valour. This same narrator, who had a Ghoulish pleasure, I have long been persuaded, in terrifying me to the utmost confines of my reason, had another authentic anecdote within her own experience, founded, I now believe, upon *Raymond and Agnes, or the Bleeding Nun.* She said it happened to her brother-in-law, who was immensely rich,—which my father was not; and immensely tall,—which my father was not. It was always a point with this Ghoul to present my dearest relations and friends to my youthful mind under circumstances of disparaging contrast. The brother-in-law was riding once through a forest on a magnificent horse (we had no magnificent horse at our house), attended by a favourite and valuable Newfoundland dog (we had no dog), when he found himself benighted, and came to an Inn. A dark woman opened the door, and he asked her if he could have a bed there. She answered yes, and put his horse in the stable, and took him into a room where there were two dark men. While he was at supper, a parrot in the room began to talk, saying, "Blood, blood! Wipe up the blood!" Upon which one of the dark men wrung the parrot's neck, and said he was fond of roasted parrots, and he meant to have this one for breakfast in the morning. After eating and drinking heartily, the immensely rich, tall brother-in-law went up to bed; but he was rather vexed, because they had shut his dog in the stable, saying that they never allowed dogs in the house. He sat very quiet for more than an hour, thinking and thinking, when, just as his candle was burning out, he heard a scratch at the door. He opened the door, and there was the Newfoundland dog! The dog came softly in, smelt about him, went straight to some straw in the corner which the dark men had said covered apples, tore the straw away, and disclosed two sheets steeped in blood. Just at that moment the candle went out, and the brother-in-law, looking through a chink in the door, saw the two dark men stealing upstairs; one armed with a dagger that long (about five feet); the other carrying a chopper, a sack, and a spade. Having no remembrance of the close of this adventure, I suppose my faculties to have been always so frozen with terror at this stage of it, that the power of listening stagnated within me for some quarter of an hour.

These barbarous stories carried me, sitting there on the Holly-Tree hearth, to the Roadside Inn, renowned in my time in a sixpenny book with a folding plate, representing in a central compartment of oval form the portrait of Jonathan Bradford, and in four corner compartments four incidents of the tragedy with which the name is associated, —coloured with a hand at once so free and economical, that the bloom of Jonathan's complexion passed without any pause into the breeches of the ostler, and, smearing itself off into the next division, became rum in a bottle. Then I remembered how the landlord was found at the murdered traveller's bedside, with his own knife at his feet, and blood upon his hand ; how he was hanged for the murder, notwithstanding his protestation that he had indeed come there to kill the traveller for his saddle-bags, but had been stricken motionless on finding him already slain; and how the ostler, years afterwards, owned the deed. By this time I had made myself quite uncomfortable. I stirred the fire, and stood with my back to it as long as I could bear the heat, looking up at the darkness beyond the screen, and at the wormy curtains creeping in and creeping out. like the worms in the ballad of Alonzo the Brave and the Fair Imogene.

There was an Inn in the cathedral town where I went to school, which had pleasanter recollections about it than any of these. I took it next. It was the Inn where friends used to put up, and where we used to go to see parents, and to have salmon and fowls, and be tipped. It had an ecclesiastical sign,—the Mitre,—and a bar that seemed to be the next best thing to a bishopric, it was so snug. I loved the landlord's youngest daughter to distraction,—but let that pass. It was in this Inn that I was cried over by my rosy little sister, because I had acquired a black eye in a fight. And though she had been, that Holly-Tree night, for many a long year where all tears are dried, the Mitre softened me yet.

"To be continued to-morrow," said I, when I took my candle to go to bed. But my bed took it upon itself to continue the train of thought that night. It carried me away, like the enchanted carpet, to a distant place (though still in England), and there, alighting from a stage-coach at another Inn in the snow, as I had actually done some years before, I repeated in my sleep a curious experience I had really had here. More than a year before I made the journey in the course of which I put up at that Inn, I had lost a very near and dear friend by death. Every night since, at home or away from home, I had dreamed of that friend; sometimes as still living; sometimes as returning from the world of shadows to comfort me; always as being beautiful, placid, and happy, never in association with any approach to fear or distress. It was at a lonely Inn in a wide moorland place, that I halted to pass the night. When I had looked from my bedroom window over the waste of snow on which the moon was shining, I sat down by my fire to write a letter. I had always, until that hour, kept it within my own breast that I dreamed every night of the dear lost one. But in the letter that I wrote I recorded the circumstance, and added that I felt much interested in proving whether the subject of my dream would still be faithful to me, travel-tired, and in that remote place. No. I lost the beloved figure of my vision in parting with the secret. My sleep has never looked upon it since, in sixteen years, but once. I was in Italy, and awoke (or seemed to awake), the well-remembered voice distinctly in my ears, conversing with it. I entreated it, as it rose above my bed and soared up to the vaulted roof of the old room, to answer me a question I had asked touching the Future Life. My hands were still outstretched towards it as it vanished, when I heard a bell ringing by the garden wall, and a voice in the deep stillness of the night calling on all good Christians to pray for the souls of the dead; it being All Souls' Eve.

To return to the Holly-Tree. When I awoke next day, it was freezing hard, and the lowering sky threatened more snow. My breakfast cleared away, I drew my chair into its former place, and, with the fire getting so much the better of the landscape that I sat in twilight, resumed my Inn remembrances.

That was a good Inn down in Wiltshire where I put up once, in the days of the hard Wiltshire ale, and before all beer was bitterness. It was on the skirts of Salisbury Plain, and the midnight wind that rattled my lattice window came moaning at me from Stonehenge. There was a hanger-on at that establishment (a supernaturally preserved Druid I believe him to have been, and to be still), with long white hair, and a flinty blue eye always looking afar off; who claimed to have been a shepherd, and who seemed to be ever watching for the reappearance, on the verge of the horizon, of some ghostly flock of sheep that had been mutton for

many ages. He was a man with a weird belief in him that
no one could count the stones of Stonehenge twice, and make
the same number of them; likewise, that any one who
counted them three times nine times, and then stood in the
centre and said, "I dare!" would behold a tremendous
apparition, and be stricken dead. He pretended to have
seen a bustard (I suspect him to have been familiar with the
dodo), in manner following: He was out upon the plain at
the close of a late autumn day, when he dimly discerned,
going on before him at a curious fitfully bounding pace,
what he at first supposed to be a gig-umbrella that had been
blown from some conveyance, but what he presently believed
to be a lean dwarf man upon a little pony. Having followed
this object for some distance without gaining on it, and
having called to it many times without receiving any answer,
he pursued it for miles and miles, when, at length coming up
with it, he discovered it to be the last bustard in Great
Britain, degenerated into a wingless state, and running along
the ground. Resolved to capture him or perish in the
attempt, he closed with the bustard; but the bustard, who
had formed a counter-resolution that he should do neither,
threw him, stunned him, and was last seen making off due
west. This weird man, at that stage of metempsychosis, may
have been a sleep-walker or an enthusiast or a robber; but
I awoke one night to find him in the dark at my bedside,
repeating the Athanasian Creed in a terrific voice. I paid
my bill next day, and retired from the county with all
possible precipitation.

That was not a commonplace story which worked itself
out at a little Inn in Switzerland, while I was staying there.
It was a very homely place, in a village of one narrow zigzag
street, among mountains, and you went in at the main door
through the cow-house, and among the mules and the dogs
and the fowls, before ascending a great bare staircase to the
rooms; which were all of unpainted wood, without plastering
or papering,—like rough packing-cases. Outside there was
nothing but the straggling street, a little toy church with a
copper-coloured steeple, a pine forest, a torrent, mists, and
mountain-sides. A young man belonging to this Inn had
disappeared eight weeks before (it was winter-time), and was
supposed to have had some undiscovered love affair, and to
have gone for a soldier. He had got up in the night, and
dropped into the village street from the loft in which he

slept with another man; and he had done it so quietly, that
his companion and fellow-labourer had heard no movement
when he was awakened in the morning, and they said,
"Louis, where is Henri?" They looked for him high and
low, in vain, and gave him up. Now, outside this Inn, there
stood, as there stood outside every dwelling in the village, a
stack of firewood; but the stack belonging to the Inn was
higher than any of the rest, because the Inn was the richest
house, and burnt the most fuel. It began to be noticed,
while they were looking high and low, that a Bantam cock,
part of the live stock of the Inn, put himself wonderfully
out of his way to get to the top of this wood-stack; and
that he would stay there for hours and hours, crowing, until
he appeared in danger of splitting himself. Five weeks went
on,—six weeks,—and still this terrible Bantam, neglecting his
domestic affairs, was always on the top of the wood-stack,
crowing the very eyes out of his head. By this time it was
perceived that Louis had become inspired with a violent
animosity towards the terrible Bantam, and one morning he
was seen by a woman, who sat nursing her goître at a little
window in a gleam of sun, to catch up a rough billet of
wood, with a great oath, hurl it at the terrible Bantam
crowing on the wood-stack, and bring him down dead. Hereupon the woman, with a sudden light in her mind, stole
round to the back of the wood-stack, and, being a good
climber, as all those women are, climbed up, and soon was
seen upon the summit, screaming, looking down the hollow
within, and crying, "Seize Louis, the murderer! Ring the
church bell! Here is the body!" I saw the murderer that
day, and I saw him as I sat by my fire at the Holly-Tree
Inn, and I see him now, lying shackled with cords on the
stable litter, among the mild eyes and the smoking breath of
the cows, waiting to be taken away by the police, and stared
at by the fearful village. A heavy animal,—the dullest
animal in the stables,—with a stupid head, and a lumpish
face devoid of any trace of sensibility, who had been, within
the knowledge of the murdered youth, an embezzler of certain
small moneys belonging to his master, and who had taken
this hopeful mode of putting a possible accuser out of his way.
All of which he confessed next day, like a sulky wretch who
couldn't be troubled any more, now that they had got hold
of him, and meant to make an end of him. I saw him once
again, on the day of my departure from the Inn. In that

E

Canton the headsman still does his office with a sword; and I came upon this murderer sitting bound to a chair, with his eyes bandaged, on a scaffold in a little market-place. In that instant, a great sword (loaded with quicksilver in the thick part of the blade) swept round him like a gust of wind or fire, and there was no such creature in the world. My wonder was, not that he was so suddenly dispatched, but that any head was left unreaped, within a radius of fifty yards of that tremendous sickle.

That was a good Inn, too, with the kind, cheerful landlady and the honest landlord, where I lived in the shadow of Mont Blanc, and where one of the apartments has a zoological papering on the walls, not so accurately joined but that the elephant occasionally rejoices in a tiger's hind legs and tail, while the lion puts on a trunk and tusks, and the bear, moulting as it were, appears as to portions of himself like a leopard. I made several American friends at that Inn, who all called Mont Blanc Mount Blank,—except one good-humoured gentleman, of a very sociable nature, who became on such intimate terms with it that he spoke of it familiarly as "Blank;" observing, at breakfast, "Blank looks pretty tall this morning;" or considerably doubting in the courtyard in the evening, whether there warn't some go-ahead naters in our country, Sir, that would make out the top of Blank in a couple of hours from first start—now!

Once I passed a fortnight at an Inn in the North of England, where I was haunted by the ghost of a tremendous pie. It was a Yorkshire pie, like a fort,—an abandoned fort with nothing in it; but the waiter had a fixed idea that it was a point of ceremony at every meal to put the pie on the table. After some days I tried to hint, in several delicate ways, that I considered the pie done with; as, for example, by emptying fag-ends of glasses of wine into it; putting cheese-plates and spoons into it, as into a basket; putting wine-bottles into it, as into a cooler; but always in vain, the pie being invariably cleaned out again and brought up as before. At last, beginning to be doubtful whether I was not the victim of a spectral illusion, and whether my health and spirits might not sink under the horrors of an imaginary pie, I cut a triangle out of it, fully as large as the musical instrument of that name in a powerful orchestra. Human prevision could not have foreseen the result—but the waiter mended the pie. With some effectual species of cement, he adroitly fitted the triangle in again, and I paid my reckoning and fled.

The Holly-Tree was getting rather dismal. I made an overland expedition beyond the screen, and penetrated as far as the fourth window. Here I was driven back by stress of weather. Arrived at my winter-quarters once more, I made up the fire, and took another Inn.

It was in the remotest part of Cornwall. A great annual Miner's Feast was being holden at the Inn, when I and my travelling companions presented ourselves at night among the wild crowd that were dancing before it by torchlight. We had had a break-down in the dark, on a stony morass some miles away; and I had the honour of leading one of the unharnassed post-horses. If any lady or gentleman, on perusal of the present lines, will take any very tall post-horse with his traces hanging about his legs, and will conduct him by the bearing-rein into the heart of a country dance of a hundred and fifty couples, that lady or gentleman will then, and only then, form an adequate idea of the extent to which that post-horse will tread on his conductor's toes. Over and above which, the post-horse, finding three hundred people whirling about him, will probably rear, and also lash out with his hind legs, in a manner incompatible with dignity or self-respect on his conductor's part. With such little drawbacks on my usually impressive aspect, I appeared at this Cornish Inn, to the unutterable wonder of the Cornish Miners. It was full, and twenty times full, and nobody could be received but the post-horse,—though to get rid of that noble animal was something. While my fellow-travellers and I were discussing how to pass the night and so much of the next day as must intervene before the jovial blacksmith and the jovial wheelwright would be in a condition to go out on the morass and mend the coach, an honest man stepped forth from the crowd and proposed his unlet floor of two rooms, with supper of eggs and bacon, ale and punch. We joyfully accompanied him home to the strangest of clean houses, where we were well entertained to the satisfaction of all parties. But the novel feature of the entertainment was, that our host was a chairmaker, and that the chairs assigned to us were mere frames, altogether without bottoms of any sort; so that we passed the evening on perches. Nor was this the absurdest consequence; for when we unbent at supper, and any one of us gave way to laughter, he forgot the peculiarity of his position, and instantly disappeared. I myself, doubled up into an attitude from which self-extrication was impossible, was taken out of my frame, like a clown in a comic pantomime who has tumbled into a tub, five times by the taper's light during the eggs and bacon.

The Holly-Tree was fast reviving within me a sense of loneliness. I began to feel conscious that my subject would never carry on until I was dug out. I might be a week here,—weeks!

There was a story with a singular idea in it, connected with an Inn I once passed a night at in a picturesque old town on the Welsh border. In a large double-bedded room of this Inn there had been a suicide committed by poison, in one bed, while a tired traveller slept unconscious in the other. After that time, the suicide bed was never used, but the other constantly was; the disused bedstead remaining in the room empty, though as to all other respects in its old state. The story ran, that whosoever slept in this room, though never so entire a stranger, from never so far off, was invariably observed to come down in the morning with an impression that he smelt Laudanum, and that his mind always turned upon the subject of suicide; to which, whatever kind of man he might be, he was certain to make some reference if he conversed with any one. This went on for years, until it at length induced the landlord to take the disused bedstead down, and bodily burn it,—bed, hangings, and all. The strange influence (this was the story) now changed to a fainter one, but never changed afterwards. The occupant of that room, with occasional but very rare exceptions, would come down in the morning, trying to recall a forgotten dream he had had in the night. The landlord, on his mentioning his perplexity, would suggest various commonplace subjects, not one of which, as he very well knew, was the true subject. But the moment the landlord suggested "Poison," the traveller started, and cried, "Yes!" He never failed to accept that suggestion, and he never recalled any more of the dream.

This reminiscence brought the Welsh Inns in general before me; with the women in their round hats, and the harpers with their white beards (venerable, but humbugs, I am afraid), playing outside the door while I took my dinner. The transition was natural to the Highland Inns, with the

oatmeal bannocks, the honey, the venison steaks, the trout
from the loch, the whisky, and perhaps (having the
materials so temptingly at hand) the Athol brose.   Once
was I coming south from the Scottish Highlands in hot
haste, hoping to change quickly at the station at the
bottom of a certain wild historical glen, when these eyes did
with mortification see the landlord come out with a telescope
and sweep the whole prospect for the horses ; which horses
were away picking up their own living, and did not heave in
sight under four hours.   Having thought of the loch-trout,
I was taken by quick association to the Anglers' Inns of
England (I have assisted at innumerable feats of angling by
lying in the bottom of the boat, whole summer days, doing
nothing with the greatest perseverance ; which I have
generally found to be as effectual towards the taking of fish
as the finest tackle and the utmost science), and to the
pleasant white, clean, flower-pot-decorated bedrooms of those
inns, overlooking the river, and the ferry, and the green ait,
and the church-spire, and the country bridge ; and to the
peerless Emma with the bright eyes and the pretty smile,
who waited, bless her ! with a natural grace that would have
converted Blue-Beard.   Casting my eyes upon my Holly-Tree
fire, I next discerned among the glowing coals the pictures
of a score or more of those wonderful English posting-inns
which we are all so sorry to have lost, which were so large
and so comfortable, and which were such monuments of
British submission to rapacity and extortion.   He who
would see these houses pining away, let him walk from
Basingstoke, or even Windsor, to London, by way of
Hounslow, and moralise on their perishing remains ; the
stables crumbling to dust; unsettled labourers and wanderers
bivouacking in the outhouses ; grass growing in the yards ;
the rooms, where erst so many hundred beds of down were
made up, let off to Irish lodgers at eighteenpence a week ;
a little ill-looking beer-shop shrinking in the tap of former
days, burning coach-house gates for firewood, having one of
its two windows bunged up, as if it had received punishment
in a fight with the Railroad ; a low, bandy-legged, brick-
making bulldog standing in the doorway.   What could I
next see in my fire so naturally as the new railway-house of
these times near the dismal country station ; with nothing
particular on draught but cold air and damp, nothing
worth mentioning in the larder but new mortar, and no

business doing beyond a conceited affectation of luggage in
the hall? Then I came to the Inns of Paris, with the
pretty apartment of four pieces up one hundred and
seventy-five waxed stairs, the privilege of ringing the bell all
day long without influencing anybody's mind or body but
your own, and the not-too-much-for-dinner, considering the
price. Next to the provincial Inns of France, with the
great church-tower rising above the courtyard, the horse-bells
jingling merrily up and down the street beyond, and the
clocks of all descriptions in all the rooms, which are never
right, unless taken at the precise minute when, by getting
exactly twelve hours too fast or too slow, they unintentionally become so. Away I went, next, to the lesser roadside Inns of Italy; where all the dirty clothes in the house
(not in wear) are always lying in your anteroom; where the
mosquitoes make a raisin pudding of your face in summer,
and the cold bites it blue in winter; where you get what you
can, and forget what you can't; where I should again like to
be boiling my tea in a pocket-handkerchief dumpling, for
want of a teapot. So to the old palace Inns and old monastery
Inns, in towns and cities of the same bright country; with
their massive quadrangular staircases, whence you may look
from among clustering pillars high into the blue vault of
heaven; with their stately banqueting-rooms, and vast refec-
tories; with their labyrinths of ghostly bedchambers, and
their glimpses into gorgeous streets that have no appearance
of reality or possibility. So to the close little Inns of the
Malaria districts, with their pale attendants, and their
peculiar smell of never letting in the air. So to the immense
fantastic Inns of Venice, with the cry of the gondolier below,
as he skims the corner; the grip of the watery odours on one
particular little bit of the bridge of your nose (which is never
released while you stay there); and the great bell of St. Mark's
Cathedral tolling midnight. Next I put up for a minute
at the restless Inns upon the Rhine, where your going to bed,
no matter at what hour, appears to be the tocsin for everybody else's getting up; and where, in the table-d'hôte room
at the end of the long table (with several Towers of Babel
on it at the other end, all made of white plates), one knot of
stoutish men, entirely dressed in jewels and dirt, and having
nothing else upon them, *will* remain all night, clinking glasses,
and singing about the river that flows, and the grape that
grows, and Rhine wine that beguiles, and Rhine woman that

smiles and hi drink drink my friend and ho drink drink my
brother, and all the rest of it. I departed thence, as a matter
of course, to other German Inns, where all the eatables are
soddened down to the same flavour, and where the mind is
disturbed by the apparition of hot puddings, and boiled
cherries, sweet and slab, at awfully unexpected periods of the
repast.   After a draught of sparkling beer from a foaming
glass jug, and a glance of recognition through the windows
of the student beer-houses at Heidelberg and elsewhere, I
put out to sea for the Inns of America, with their four
hundred beds apiece, and their eight or nine hundred ladies
and gentlemen at dinner every day.   Again I stood in the
bar-rooms thereof, taking my evening cobbler, julep, sling,
or cocktail.   Again I listened to my friend the General,—
whom I had known for five minutes, in the course of which
period he had made me intimate for life with two Majors,
who again had made me intimate for life with three Colonels,
who again had made me brother to twenty-two civilians,—
again, I say, I listened to my friend the General, leisurely
expounding the resources of the establishment, as to gentlemen's morning-room, Sir; ladies' morning-room, Sir; gentlemen's evening-room, Sir; ladies' evening-room, Sir; ladies' and
gentlemen's evening reuniting-room, Sir; music-room, Sir;
reading-room, Sir; over four hundred sleeping-rooms, Sir; and
the entire planned and finished within twelve calendar months
from the first clearing off of the old encumbrances on the
plot, at a cost of five hundred thousand dollars, Sir.   Again
I found, as to my individual way of thinking, that the
greater, the more gorgeous, and the more dollarous the
establishment was, the less desirable it was.   Nevertheless,
again I drank my cobbler, julep, sling, or cocktail, in all
good-will, to my friend the General, and my friends the
Majors, Colonels, and civilians all; full well knowing that,
whatever little motes my beamy eyes may have descried in
theirs, they belong to a kind, generous, large-hearted, and
great people.

I had been going on lately at a quick pace to keep my
solitude out of my mind; but here I broke down for good,
and gave up the subject.   What was I to do?   What was to
become of me?   Into what extremity was I submissively to
sink?   Supposing that, like Baron Trenck, I looked out for
a mouse or spider, and found one, and beguiled my imprison-
ment by training it?   Even that might be dangerous with

a view to the future. I might be so far gone when the road did come to be cut through the snow, that, on my way forth, I might burst into tears, and beseech, like the prisoner who was released in his old age from the Bastille, to be taken back again to the five windows, the ten curtains, and the sinuous drapery.

A desperate idea came into my head. Under any other circumstances I should have rejected it; but, in the strait at which I was, I held it fast. Could I so far overcome the inherent bashfulness which withheld me from the landlord's table and the company I might find there, as to call up the Boots, and ask him to take a chair,—and something in a liquid form,—and talk to me? I could. I would. I did.

SECOND BRANCH

THE BOOTS

WHERE had he been in his time? he repeated, when I asked him the question. Lord, he had been everywhere! And what had he been? Bless you, he had been everything you could mention a'most!

Seen a good deal? Why, of course he had. I should say so, he could assure me, if I only knew about a twentieth part of what had come in *his* way. Why, it would be easier for him, he expected, to tell what he hadn't seen than what he had. Ah! A deal, it would.

What was the curiousest thing he had seen? Well! He didn't know. He couldn't momently name what was the curiousest thing he had seen,—unless it was a Unicorn,—and he see *him* once at a Fair. But supposing a young gentleman not eight year old was to run away with a fine young woman of seven, might I think *that* a queer start? Certainly. Then that was a start as he himself had had his blessed eyes on, and he had cleaned the shoes they run away in—and they was so little that he couldn't get his hand into 'em.

Master Harry Walmers' father, you see, he lived at the Elmses, down away by Shooter's Hill there, six or seven miles from Lunnon. He was a gentleman of spirit, and good-looking, and held his head up when he walked, and

had what you may call Fire about him. He wrote poetry,
and he rode, and he ran, and he cricketed, and he danced,
and he acted, and he done it all equally beautiful. He was
uncommon proud of Master Harry as was his only child;
but he didn't spoil him neither. He was a gentleman that
had a will of his own and a eye of his own, and that would
be minded. Consequently, though he made quite a companion
of the fine bright boy, and was delighted to see him so fond
of reading his fairy books, and was never tired of hearing
him say my name is Norval, or hearing him sing his songs
about Young May Moons is beaming love, and When he as
adores thee has left but the name, and that; still he kept
the command over the child, and the child *was* a child, and
it's to be wished more of 'em was!

How did Boots happen to know all this? Why, through
being under-gardener. Of course he couldn't be under-
gardener, and be always about, in the summer-time, near the
windows on the lawn, a mowing, and sweeping, and weeding,
and pruning, and this and that, without getting acquainted
with the ways of the family. Even supposing Master Harry
hadn't come to him one morning early, and said, "Cobbs,
how should you spell Norah, if you was asked?" and then
began cutting it in print all over the fence.

He couldn't say he had taken particular notice of children
before that; but really it was pretty to see them two mites
a going about the place together, deep in love. And the
courage of the boy! Bless your soul, he'd have throwed off
his little hat, and tucked up his little sleeves, and gone in
at a Lion, he would, if they had happened to meet one, and
she had been frightened of him. One day he stops, along
with her, where Boots was hoeing weeds in the gravel, and
says, speaking up, "Cobbs," he says, "I like *you*." "Do you,
Sir? I'm proud to hear it." "Yes, I do, Cobbs. Why do
I like you, do you think, Cobbs?" "Don't know, Master
Harry, I am sure." "Because Norah likes you, Cobbs."
"Indeed, Sir? That's very gratifying." "Gratifying, Cobbs?
It's better than millions of the brightest diamonds to be liked
by Norah." "Certainly, Sir." "You're going away, ain't you,
Cobbs?" "Yes, Sir." "Would you like another situation,
Cobbs?" "Well, Sir, I shouldn't object, if it was a good 'un."
"Then, Cobbs," says he, "you shall be our Head Gardener
when we are married." And he tucks her, in her little sky-
blue mantle, under his arm, and walks away.

Boots could assure me that it was better than a picter, and
equal to a play, to see them babies, with their long, bright
curling hair, their sparkling eyes, and their beautiful light
tread, a rambling about the garden, deep in love.   Boots
was of opinion that the birds believed they was birds, and
kept up with 'em, singing to please 'em.   Sometimes they
would creep under the Tulip-tree, and would sit there with
their arms round one another's necks, and their soft cheeks
touching, a reading about the Prince and the Dragon, and the
good and bad enchanters, and the king's fair daughter.
Sometimes he would hear them planning about having a
house in a forest, keeping bees and a cow, and living entirely
on milk and honey.   Once he came upon them by the pond,
and heard Master Harry say, "Adorable Norah, kiss me, and
say you love me to distraction, or I'll jump in head-foremost."
And Boots made no question he would have done it if she
hadn't complied.   On the whole, Boots said it had a tendency
to make him feel as if he was in love himself—only he didn't
exactly know who with.

"Cobbs," said Master Harry, one evening, when Cobbs was
watering the flowers, "I am going on a visit, this present
Midsummer, to my grandmamma's at York."

"Are you indeed, Sir? I hope you'll have a pleasant time.
I am going into Yorkshire, myself, when I leave here."

"Are you going to your grandmamma's, Cobbs?"

"No, Sir. I haven't got such a thing."

"Not as a grandmamma, Cobbs?"

"No, Sir."

The boy looked on at the watering of the flowers for a
little while, and then said, "I shall be very glad indeed to go,
Cobbs,—Norah's going."

"You'll be all right then, Sir," says Cobbs, "with your
beautiful sweetheart by your side."

"Cobbs," returned the boy, flushing, "I never let anybody
joke about it, when I can prevent them."

"It wasn't a joke, Sir," says Cobbs, with humility,—
"wasn't so meant."

"I am glad of that, Cobbs, because I like you, you know,
and you're going to live with us.—Cobbs!"

"Sir."

"What do you think my grandmamma gives me when I go
down there?"

"I couldn't so much as make a guess, Sir."

The Holly-Tree

"A Bank of England five-pound note, Cobbs."

"Whew!" says Cobbs, "that's a spanking sum of money, Master Harry."

"A person could do a good deal with such a sum of money as that,—couldn't a person, Cobbs?"

"I believe you, Sir!"

"Cobbs," said the boy, "I'll tell you a secret. At Norah's house, they have been joking her about me, and pretending to laugh at our being engaged,—pretending to make game of it, Cobbs!"

"Such, Sir," says Cobbs, "is the depravity of human natur."

The boy, looking exactly like his father, stood for a few minutes with his glowing face towards the sunset, and then departed with, "Good-night, Cobbs. I'm going in."

If I was to ask Boots how it happened that he was a going to leave that place just at that present time, well, he couldn't rightly answer me. He did suppose he might have stayed there till now if he had been anyways inclined. But, you see, he was younger then, and he wanted change. That's what he wanted,—change. Mr. Walmers, he said to him when he gave him notice of his intentions to leave, "Cobbs," he says, "have you anythink to complain of? I make the inquiry because if I find that any of my people really has anythink to complain of, I wish to make it right if I can." "No, Sir," says Cobbs; "thanking you, Sir, I find myself as well sitiwated here as I could hope to be anywheres. The truth is, Sir, that I'm a-going to seek my fortun'." "O, indeed, Cobbs!" he says; "I hope you may find it." And Boots could assure me—which he did, touching his hair with his bootjack, as a salute in the way of his present calling—that he hadn't found it yet.

Well, Sir! Boots left the Elmses when his time was up, and Master Harry, he went down to the old lady's at York, which old lady would have given that child the teeth out of her head (if she had had any), she was so wrapped up in him. What does that Infant do,—for Infant you may call him and be within the mark,—but cut away from that old lady's with his Norah, on a expedition to go to Gretna Green and be married!

Sir, Boots was at this identical Holly-Tree Inn (having left it several times since to better himself, but always come back through one thing or another), when, one summer afternoon, the coach drives up, and out of the coach gets them two children. The Guard says to our Governor, "I don't quite make out these little passengers, but the young gentleman's words was, that they was to be brought here." The young gentleman gets out; hands his lady out; gives the Guard something for himself; says to our Governor, "We're to stop here to-night, please. Sitting-room and two bedrooms will be required. Chops and cherry-pudding for two!" and tucks her, in her little sky-blue mantle, under his arm, and walks into the house much bolder than Brass.

Boots leaves me to judge what the amazement of that establishment was, when these two tiny creatures all alone by themselves was marched into the Angel,—much more so, when he, who had seen them without their seeing him, give the Governor his views of the expedition they was upon. "Cobbs," says the Governor, "if this is so, I must set off myself to York, and quiet their friends' minds. In which case you must keep your eye upon 'em, and humour 'em, till I come back. But before I take these measures, Cobbs, I should wish you to find from themselves whether your opinion is correct. "Sir, to you," says Cobbs, "that shall be done directly."

So Boots goes upstairs to the Angel, and there he finds Master Harry on a e-normous sofa,—immense at any time, but looking like the Great Bed of Ware, compared with him, —a drying the eyes of Miss Norah with his pocket-hankecher. Their little legs was entirely off the ground, of course, and it really is not possible for Boots to express to me how small them children looked.

"It's Cobbs! It's Cobbs!" cried Master Harry, and comes running to him, and catching hold of his hand. Miss Norah comes running to him on t'other side and catching hold of his t'other hand, and they both jump for joy.

"I see you a getting out, Sir," says Cobbs. "I thought it was you. I thought I couldn't be mistaken in your height and figure. What's the object of your journey, Sir?—Matrimonial?"

"We are going to be married, Cobbs, at Gretna Green," returned the boy. "We have run away on purpose. Norah has been in rather low spirits, Cobbs; but she'll be happy, now we have found you to be our friend."

"Thank you, Sir, and thank *you*, Miss," says Cobbs, "for your good opinion. *Did* you bring any luggage with you, Sir?"

If I will believe Boots when he gives me his word and honour upon it, the lady had got a parasol, a smelling-bottle, a round and a half of cold buttered toast, eight peppermint drops, and a hair-brush,—seemingly a doll's. The gentleman had got about half-a-dozen yards of string, a knife, three or four sheets of writing-paper folded up surprising small, a orange, and a Chaney mug with his name upon it.

"What may be the exact natur of your plans, Sir?" says Cobbs.

"To go on," replied the boy,—which the courage of that boy was something wonderful!—"in the morning, and be married to-morrow."

"Just so, Sir," says Cobbs. "Would it meet your views, Sir, if I was to accompany you?"

When Cobbs said this, they both jumped for joy again, and cried out, "Oh, yes, yes, Cobbs! Yes!"

"Well, Sir," says Cobbs. "If you will excuse my having the freedom to give an opinion, what I should recommend would be this. I'm acquainted with a pony, Sir, which, put in a pheayton that I could borrow, would take you and Mrs. Harry Walmers, Junior, (myself driving, if you approved,) to the end of your journey in a very short space of time. I am not altogether sure, Sir, that this pony will be at liberty to-morrow, but even if you had to wait over to-morrow for him, it might be worth your while. As to the small account here, Sir, in case you was to find yourself running at all short, that don't signify; because I'm a part proprietor of this inn, and it could stand over."

Boots assures me that when they clapped their hands, and jumped for joy again, and called him "Good Cobbs!" and "Dear Cobbs!" and bent across him to kiss one another in the delight of their confiding hearts, he felt himself the meanest rascal for deceiving 'em that ever was born.

"Is there anything you want just at present, Sir?" says Cobbs, mortally ashamed of himself.

"We should like some cakes after dinner," answered Master Harry, folding his arms, putting out one leg, and looking straight at him, "and two apples,—and jam. With dinner we should like to have toast-and-water. But Norah has always been accustomed to half a glass of currant wine at dessert. And so have I."

"It shall be ordered at the bar, Sir," says Cobbs; and away he went.

Boots has the feeling as fresh upon him at this minute of speaking as he had then, that he would far rather have had it out in half-a-dozen rounds with the Governor than have combined with him; and that he wished with all his heart there was any impossible place where those two babies could make an impossible marriage, and live impossibly happy ever afterwards. However, as it couldn't be, he went into the Governor's plans, and the Governor set off for York in half an hour.

The way in which the women of that house—without exception—every one of 'em—married *and* single—took to that boy when they heard the story, Boots considers surprising. It was as much as he could do to keep 'em from dashing into the room and kissing him. They climbed up all sorts of places, at the risk of their lives, to look at him through a pane of glass. They was seven deep at the keyhole. They was out of their minds about him and his bold spirit.

In the evening, Boots went into the room to see how the runaway couple was getting on. The gentleman was on the window-seat, supporting the lady in his arms. She had tears upon her face, and was lying, very tired and half asleep, with her head upon his shoulder.

"Mrs. Harry Walmers, Junior, fatigued, Sir?" says Cobbs.

"Yes, she is tired, Cobbs; but she is not used to be away from home, and she has been in low spirits again. Cobbs, do you think you could bring a biffin, please?"

"I ask your pardon, Sir," says Cobbs. "What was it you—— ?"

"I think a Norfolk biffin would rouse her, Cobbs. She is very fond of them."

Boots withdrew in search of the required, restorative, and, when he brought it in, the gentleman handed it to the lady, and fed her with a spoon, and took a little himself; the lady being heavy with sleep, and rather cross. "What should you think, Sir," says Cobbs, "of a chamber candle-stick?" The gentleman approved; the chambermaid went first, up the great staircase; the lady, in her sky-blue mantle, followed, gallantly escorted by the gentleman; the gentleman embraced her at her door, and retired to his own apartment, where Boots softly locked him up.

Boots couldn't but feel with increased acuteness what a base deceiver he was, when they consulted him at breakfast (they had ordered sweet milk-and-water, and toast and currant jelly, overnight) about the pony. It really was as much as he could do, he don't mind confessing to me, to look them two young things in the face, and think what a wicked old father of lies he had grown up to be. Howsomever, he went on a lying like a Trojan about the pony. He told 'em that it did so unfort'nately happen that the pony was half clipped, you see, and that he couldn't be taken out in that state, for fear it should strike to his inside. But that he'd be finished clipping in the course of the day, and that to-morrow morning at eight o'clock the pheayton would be ready. Boots's view of the whole case, looking back on it in my room, is, that Mrs. Harry Walmers, Junior, was beginning to give in. She hadn't had her hair curled when she went to bed, and she didn't seem quite up to brushing it herself, and its getting in her eyes put her out. But nothing put out Master Harry. He sat behind his breakfast-cup, a tearing away at the jelly, as if he had been his own father.

After breakfast, Boots is inclined to consider that they drawed soldiers,—at least, he knows that many such was found in the fireplace, all on horseback. In the course of the morning, Master Harry rang the bell,—it was surprising how that there boy did carry on,—and said, in a sprightly way, "Cobbs, is there any good walks in this neighbour-hood?"

"Yes, Sir," says Cobbs. "There's Love-lane."

"Get out with you, Cobbs!"—that was that there boy's expression,—"you're joking."

"Begging your pardon, Sir," says Cobbs, "there really is Love-lane. And a pleasant walk it is, and proud shall I be to show it to yourself and Mrs. Harry Walmers, Junior."

"Norah, dear," said Master Harry, "this is curious. We really ought to see Love-lane. Put on your bonnet, my sweetest darling, and we will go there with Cobbs."

Boots leaves me to judge what a Beast he felt himself to be, when that young pair told him, as they all three jogged along together, that they had made up their minds to give him two thousand guineas a year as head-gardener, on ac-counts of his being so true a friend to 'em. Boots could have wished at the moment that the earth would have opened and swallowed him up, he felt so mean, with their beaming eyes a looking at him, and believing him. Well, Sir, he turned the conversation as well as he could, and he took 'em down Love-lane to the water-meadows, and there

Master Harry would have drowned himself in half a moment more, a getting out a water-lily for her,—but nothing daunted that boy. Well, Sir, they was tired out. All being so new and strange to 'em, they was tired as tired could be. And they laid down on a bank of daisies, like the children in the wood, leastways meadows, and fell asleep.

Boots don't know—perhaps I do,—but never mind, it don't signify either way—why it made a man fit to make a fool of himself to see them two pretty babies a lying there in the clear still sunny day, not dreaming half so hard when they was asleep as they done when they was awake. But, Lord! when you come to think of yourself, you know, and what a game you have been up to ever since you was in your own cradle, and what a poor sort of a chap you are, and how it's always either Yesterday with you, or else To-morrow, and never To-day, that's where it is!

Well, Sir, they woke up at last, and then one thing was getting pretty clear to Boots, namely, that Mrs. Harry Walmerses, Junior's, temper was on the move. When Master Harry took her round the waist, she said he "teased her so;" and when he says, "Norah, my young May Moon, your Harry tease you?" she tells him, "Yes; and I want to go home!"

A biled fowl, and baked bread-and-butter pudding, brought Mrs. Walmers up a little; but Boots could have wished, he must privately own to me, to have seen her more sensible of the woice of love, and less abandoning of herself to currants. However, Master Harry, he kept up, and his noble heart was as fond as ever. Mrs. Walmers turned very sleepy about dusk, and began to cry. Therefore, Mrs. Walmers went off to bed as per yesterday; and Master Harry ditto repeated.

About eleven or twelve at night comes back the Governor in a chaise, along with Mr. Walmers and a elderly lady. Mr. Walmers looks amused and very serious, both at once, and says to our missis, "We are much indebted to you, ma'am, for your kind care of our little children, which we can never sufficiently acknowledge. Pray, ma'am, where is my boy?" Our missis says, "Cobbs has the dear child in charge, Sir. Cobbs, show Forty!" Then he says to Cobbs, "Ah, Cobbs, I am glad to see *you!* I understood you was here!" And Cobbs says, "Yes, Sir. Your most obedient, Sir."

I may be surprised to hear Boots say it, perhaps; but

Boots assures me that his heart beat like a hammer, going upstairs. "I beg your pardon, Sir," says he, while unlocking the door; "I hope you are not angry with Master Harry. For Master Harry is a fine boy, Sir, and will do you credit and honour." And Boots signifies to me, that, if the fine boy's father had contradicted him in the daring state of mind in which he then was, he thinks he should have "fetched him a crack," and taken the consequences.

But Mr. Walmers only says, "No, Cobbs. No, my good fellow. Thank you!" And, the door being opened, goes in.

Boots goes in too, holding the light, and he sees Mr. Walmers go up to the bedside, bend gently down, and kiss the little sleeping face. Then he stands looking at it for a minute, looking wonderfully like it (they do say he ran away with Mrs. Walmers); and then he gently shakes the little shoulder.

"Harry, my dear boy! Harry!"

Master Harry starts up and looks at him. Looks at Cobbs too. Such is the honour of that mite, that he looks at Cobbs, to see whether he has brought him into trouble.

"I am not angry, my child. I only want you to dress yourself and come home."

"Yes, pa."

Master Harry dresses himself quickly. His breast begins to swell when he has nearly finished, and it swells more and more as he stands, at last, a looking at his father: his father standing a looking at him, the quiet image of him.

"Please may I"—the spirit of that little creatur, and the way he kept his rising tears down!—"please, dear pa—may I—kiss Norah before I go?"

"You may, my child."

So he takes Master Harry in his hand, and Boots leads the way with the candle, and they come to that other bedroom, where the elderly lady is seated by the bed, and poor little Mrs. Harry Walmers, Junior, is fast asleep. There the father lifts the child up to the pillow, and he lays his little face down for an instant by the little warm face of poor unconscious little Mrs. Harry Walmers, Junior, and gently draws it to him,—a sight so touching to the chambermaids who are peeping through the door, that one of them calls out, "It's a shame to part 'em!" But this chambermaid was always, as Boots informs me, a soft-hearted one. Not that there was any harm in that girl. Far from it.

Finally, Boots says, that's all about it. Mr. Walmers drove away in the chaise, having hold of Master Harry's hand. The elderly lady and Mrs. Harry Walmers, Junior, that was never to be (she married a Captain long afterwards, and died in India), went off next day. In conclusion, Boots put it to me whether I hold with him in two opinions: firstly, that there are not many couples on their way to be married who are half as innocent of guile as those two children ; secondly, that it would be a jolly good thing for a great many couples on their way to be married, if they could only be stopped in time, and brought back separately.

THIRD BRANCH

THE BILL

I HAD been snowed up a whole week. The time had hung so lightly on my hands, that I should have been in great doubt of the fact but for a piece of documentary evidence that lay upon my table.

The road had been dug out of the snow on the previous day, and the document in question was my bill. It testified emphatically to my having eaten and drunk, and warmed myself, and slept among the sheltering branches of the Holly-Tree, seven days and nights.

I had yesterday allowed the road twenty-four hours to improve itself, finding that I required that additional margin of time for the completion of my task. I had ordered my bill to be upon the table, and a chaise to be at the door, "at eight o'clock to-morrow evening." It was eight o'clock to-morrow evening when I buckled up my travelling writing-desk in its leather case, paid my bill, and got on my warm coats and wrappers. Of course, no time now remained for my travelling on to add a frozen tear to the icicles which were doubtless hanging plentifully about the farmhouse where I had first seen Angela. What I had to do was to get across to Liverpool by the shortest open road, there to meet my heavy baggage and embark. It was quite enough to do, and I had not an hour too much time to do it in.

I had taken leave of all my Holly-Tree friends—almost,

for the time being, of my bashfulness too—and was standing for half a minute at the Inn door watching the ostler as he took another turn at the cord which tied my portmanteau on the chaise, when I saw lamps coming down towards the Holly-Tree. The road was so padded with snow that no wheels were audible; but all of us who were standing at the Inn door saw lamps coming on, and at a lively rate too, between the walls of snow that had been heaped up on either side of the track. The chambermaid instantly divined how the case stood, and called to the ostler, "Tom, this is a Gretna job!" The ostler, knowing that her sex instinctively scented a marriage, or anything in that direction, rushed up the yard bawling, "Next four out!" and in a moment the whole establishment was thrown into commotion.

I had a melancholy interest in seeing the happy man who loved and was beloved; and therefore, instead of driving off at once, I remained at the Inn door when the fugitives drove up. A bright-eyed fellow, muffled in a mantle, jumped out so briskly that he almost overthrew me. He turned to apologise, and, by Heaven, it was Edwin!

"Charley!" said he, recoiling. "Gracious powers, what do you do here?"

"Edwin," said I, recoiling, "gracious powers, what do *you* do here?" I struck my forehead as I said it, and an insupportable blaze of light seemed to shoot before my eyes.

He hurried me into the little parlour (always kept with a slow fire in it and no poker), where posting company waited while their horses were putting to, and, shutting the door, said:

"Charley, forgive me!"

"Edwin!" I returned. "Was this well? When I loved her so dearly! When I had garnered up my heart so long!" I could say no more.

He was shocked when he saw how moved I was, and made the cruel observation, that he had not thought I should have taken it so much to heart.

I looked at him. I reproached him no more. But I looked at him.

"My dear, dear Charley," said he, "don't think ill of me, I beseech you! I know you have a right to my utmost confidence, and, believe me, you have ever had it until now. I abhor secrecy. Its meanness is intolerable to me. But I and my dear girl have observed it for your sake."

He and his dear girl! It steeled me.

"You have observed it for my sake, Sir?" said I, wondering how his frank face could face it out so.

"Yes!—and Angela's," said he.

I found the room reeling round in an uncertain way, like a labouring humming-top. "Explain yourself," said I, holding on by one hand to an armchair.

"Dear old darling Charley!" returned Edwin, in his cordial manner, "consider! When you were going on so happily with Angela, why should I compromise you with the old gentleman by making you a party to our engagement, and (after he had declined my proposals) to our secret intention? Surely it was better that you should be able honourably to say, 'He never took counsel with me, never told me, never breathed a word of it.' If Angela suspected it, and showed me all the favour and support she could—God bless her for a precious creature and a priceless wife!—I couldn't help that. Neither I nor Emmeline ever told her, any more than we told you. And for the same good reason, Charley; trust me, for the same good reason, and no other upon earth!"

Emmeline was Angela's cousin. Lived with her. Had been brought up with her. Was her father's ward. Had property.

"Emmeline is in the chaise, my dear Edwin!" said I, embracing him with the greatest affection.

"My good fellow!" said he, "do you suppose I should be going to Gretna Green without her?"

I ran out with Edwin, I opened the chaise door, I took Emmeline in my arms, I folded her to my heart. She was wrapped in soft white fur, like the snowy landscape: but was warm, and young, and lovely. I put their leaders to with my own hands, I gave the boys a five-pound note apiece, I cheered them as they drove away, I drove the other way myself as hard as I could pelt.

I never went to Liverpool, I never went to America, I went straight back to London, and I married Angela. I have never until this time, even to her, disclosed the secret of my character, and the mistrust and the mistaken journey into which it led me. When she, and they, and our eight children and their seven—I mean Edwin's and Emmeline's, whose eldest girl is old enough now to wear white for herself, and to look very like her mother in it—come to read these pages, as of course they will, I shall hardly fail to be found out at last. Never mind! I can bear it. I began at the Holly-Tree, by idle accident, to associate the Christmas-time of year with human interest, and with some inquiry into, and some care for, the lives of those by whom I find myself surrounded. I hope that I am none the worse for it, and that no one near me or afar off is the worse for it. And I say, May the green Holly-Tree flourish, striking its roots deep into our English ground, and having its germinating qualities carried by the birds of Heaven all over the world!

THE WRECK OF THE
GOLDEN MARY

[1856]

[*Written in collaboration with* WILKIE COLLINS]

CHARACTERS

MRS. ATHERFIELD, *a young mother; a passenger on board the* Golden Mary.

LUCY ATHERFIELD ('The Golden Lucy'), *her child.*

MISS COLESHAW, *a passenger.*

JOHN MULLION, *a brave, devoted seaman.*

WILLIAM RAMES, *second mate.*

MR. RARX, *a passenger; a sordid and selfish old gentleman.*

WILLIAM GEORGE RAVENDER, *the heroic master of the vessel.*

SMITHICK AND WATERSBY, *a Liverpool shipping-firm.*

TOM SNOW, *a black steward.*

JOHN STEADIMAN, *chief mate.*

THE WRECK OF THE GOLDEN MARY

THE WRECK

I was apprenticed to the Sea when I was twelve years old, and I have encountered a great deal of rough weather, both literal and metaphorical. It has always been my opinion since I first possessed such a thing as an opinion, that the man who knows only one subject is next tiresome to the man who knows no subject. Therefore, in the course of my life I have taught myself whatever I could, and although I am not an educated man, I am able, I am thankful to say, to have an intelligent interest in most things.

A person might suppose, from reading the above, that I am in the habit of holding forth about number one. That is not the case. Just as if I was to come into a room among strangers, and must either be introduced or introduce myself, so I have taken the liberty of passing these few remarks, simply and plainly that it may be known who and what I am. I will add no more of the sort than that my name is William George Ravender, that I was born at Penrith half a year after my own father was drowned, and that I am on the second day of this present blessed Christmas week of one thousand eight hundred and fifty-six, fifty-six years of age.

When the rumour first went flying up and down that there was gold in California—which, as most people know, was before it was discovered in the British colony of Australia—I was in the West Indies, trading among the Islands. Being in command and likewise part-owner of a smart schooner, I had my work cut out for me, and I was doing it.   Consequently, gold in California was no business of mine.

But, by the time when I came home to England again, the thing was as clear as your hand held up before you at noonday.   There was Californian gold in the museums and in the goldsmiths' shops, and the very first time I went upon 'Change, I met a friend of mine (a seafaring man like myself), with a Californian nugget hanging to his watch-chain.   I handled it.   It was as like a peeled walnut with bits unevenly broken off here and there, and then electrotyped all over, as ever I saw anything in my life.

I am a single man (she was too good for this world and for me, and she died six weeks before our marriage-day), so when I am ashore, I live in my house at Poplar.   My house at Poplar is taken care of and kept ship-shape by an old lady who was my mother's maid before I was born.   She is as handsome and as upright as any old lady in the world. She is as fond of me as if she had ever had an only son, and I was he.   Well do I know wherever I sail that she never lays down her head at night without having said, " Merciful Lord! bless and preserve William George Ravender, and send him safe home, through Christ our Saviour!"   I have thought of it in many a dangerous moment, when it has done me no harm, I am sure.

In my house at Poplar, along with this old lady, I lived quiet for best part of a year : having had a long spell of it among the Islands, and having (which was very uncommon in me) taken the fever rather badly.   At last, being strong and hearty, and having read every book I could lay hold of, right out, I was walking down Leadenhall Street in the City of London, thinking of turning-to again, when I met what I call Smithick and Watersby of Liverpool.   I chanced to lift up my eyes from looking in at a ship's chronometer in a window, and I saw him bearing down upon me, head on.

It is, personally, neither Smithick, nor Watersby, that I here mention, nor was I ever acquainted with any man of either of those names, nor do I think that there has been any one of either of those names in that Liverpool House for years back.   But, it is in reality the House itself that I refer to ; and a wiser merchant or a truer gentleman never stepped.

"My dear Captain Ravender," says he.   "Of all the men

on earth, I wanted to see you most. I was on my way to you."

"Well!" says I. "That looks as if you *were* to see me, don't it?" With that I put my arm in his, and we walked on towards the Royal Exchange, and when we got there, walked up and down at the back of it where the Clock-Tower is. We walked an hour and more, for he had much to say to me. He had a scheme for chartering a new ship of their own to take out cargo to the diggers and emigrants in California, and to buy and bring back gold. Into the particulars of that scheme I will not enter, and I have no right to enter. All I say of it is, that it was a very original one, a very fine one, a very sound one, and a very lucrative one beyond doubt.

He imparted it to me as freely as if I had been a part of himself. After doing so, he made me the handsomest sharing offer that ever was made to me, boy or man—or I believe to any other captain in the Merchant Navy—and he took this round turn to finish with :

"Ravender, you are well aware that the lawlessness of that coast and country at present, is as special as the circumstances in which it is placed. Crews of vessels outward-bound, desert as soon as they make the land ; crews of vessels homeward-bound, ship at enormous wages, with the express intention of murdering the captain and seizing the gold freight ; no man can trust another, and the devil seems let loose. Now," says he, "you know my opinion of you, and you know I am only expressing it, and with no singularity, when I tell you that you are almost the only man on whose integrity, discretion, and energy—" &c., &c. For, I don't want to repeat what he said, though I was and am sensible of it.

Notwithstanding my being, as I have mentioned, quite ready for a voyage, still I´had some doubts of this voyage. Of course I knew, without being told, that there were peculiar difficulties and dangers in it, a long way over and above those which attend all voyages. It must not be supposed that I was afraid to face them ; but. in my opinion a man has no manly motive or sustainment in his own breast for facing dangers, unless he has well considered what they are, and is able quietly to say to himself, "None of these perils can now take me by surprise ; I shall know what to do for the best in any of them ; all the rest lies in the higher and greater hands to which I humbly commit myself." On this principle I have so attentively considered (regarding it as my duty) all the hazards I have ever been able to think of, in the ordinary way of storm, shipwreck, and fire at sea, that I hope I should be prepared to do, in any of those cases, whatever could be done, to save the lives intrusted to my charge.

As I was thoughtful, my good friend proposed that he should leave me to walk there as long as I liked, and that I should dine with him by-and-by at his club in Pall Mall. I accepted the invitation and I walked up and down there, quarter-deck fashion, a matter of a couple of hours; now and then looking up at the weathercock as I might have looked up aloft; and now and then taking a look into Cornhill. as I might have taken a look over the side.

All dinner-time, and all after dinner-time, we talked it over again. I gave him my views of his plan, and he very much approved of the same. I told him I had nearly decided, but not quite. "Well, well," says he, "come down to Liverpool to-morrow with me, and see the Golden Mary." I liked the name (her name was Mary, and she was golden, if golden stands for good), so I began to feel that it was almost done when I said I would go to Liverpool. On the next morning but one we were on board the Golden Mary. I might have known, from his asking me to come down and see her, what she was. I declare her to have been the completest and most exquisite Beauty that ever I set my eyes upon.

We had inspected every timber in her, and had come back to the gangway to go ashore from the dock-basin, when I put out my hand to my friend. "Touch upon it," says I, "and touch heartily. I take command of this ship, and I am hers and yours, if I can get John Steadiman for my chief mate."

John Steadiman had sailed with me four voyages. The first voyage John was third mate out to China, and came home second. The other three voyages he was my first officer. At this time of chartering the Golden Mary, he was aged thirty-two. A brisk, bright, blue-eyed fellow, a very neat figure and rather under the middle size, never out of the way and never in it, a face that pleased everybody and that all children took to, a habit of going about singing as cheerily as a blackbird, and a perfect sailor.

We were in one of those Liverpool hackney-coaches in less

than a minute, and we cruised about in her upwards of three hours, looking for John. John had come home from Van Diemen's Land barely a month before, and I had heard of him as taking a frisk in Liverpool. We asked after him, among many other places, at the two boarding-houses he was fondest of, and we found he had had a week's spell at each of them; but, he had gone here and gone there, and had set off "to lay out on the main-to'-gallant-yard of the highest Welsh mountain" (so he had told the people of the house), and where he might be then, or when he might come back, nobody could tell us. But it was surprising, to be sure, to see how every face brightened the moment there was mention made of the name of Mr. Steadiman.

We were taken aback at meeting with no better luck, and we had wore ship and put her head for my friends, when as we were jogging through the streets, I clap my eyes on John himself coming out of a toyshop! He was carrying a little boy, and conducting two uncommon pretty women to their coach, and he told me afterwards that he had never in his life seen one of the three before, but that he was so taken with them on looking in at the toyshop while they were buying the child a cranky Noah's Ark, very much down by the head, that he had gone in and asked the ladies' permission to treat him to a tolerably correct Cutter there was in the window, in order that such a handsome boy might not grow up with a lubberly idea of naval architecture.

We stood off and on until the ladies' coachman began to give way, and then we hailed John. On his coming aboard of us, I told him, very gravely, what I had said to my friend. It struck him, as he said himself, amidships. He was quite shaken by it. "Captain Ravender," were John Steadiman's words, "such an opinion from you is true commendation, and I'll sail round the world with you for twenty years if you hoist the signal, and stand by you for ever!" And now indeed I felt that it was done, and that the Golden Mary was afloat.

Grass never grew yet under the feet of Smithick and Watersby. The riggers were out of that ship in a fortnight's time, and we had begun taking in cargo. John was always aboard, seeing everything stowed with his own eyes; and whenever I went aboard myself early or late, whether he was below in the hold, or on deck at the hatchway, or overhauling his cabin, nailing up pictures in it of the Blush

Roses of England, the Blue Bells of Scotland, and the female Shamrock of Ireland: of a certainty I heard John singing like a blackbird.

We had room for twenty passengers. Our sailing advertisement was no sooner out, than we might have taken these twenty times over. In entering our men, I and John (both together) picked them, and we entered none but good hands —as good as were to be found in that port. And so, in a good ship of the best build, well owned, well arranged, well officered, well manned, well found in all respects, we parted with our pilot at a quarter past four o'clock in the afternoon of the seventh of March, one thousand eight hundred and fifty-one, and stood with a fair wind out to sea.

It may be easily believed that up to that time I had had no leisure to be intimate with my passengers. The most of them were then in their berths sea-sick; however, in going among them, telling them what was good for them, persuading them not to be there, but to come up on deck and feel the breeze, and in rousing them with a joke, or a comfortable word, I made acquaintance with them, perhaps, in a more friendly and confidential way from the first, than I might have done at the cabin table.

Of my passengers, I need only particularise, just at present, a bright-eyed blooming young wife who was going out to join her husband in California, taking with her their only child, a little girl of three years old, whom he had never seen; a sedate young woman in black, some five years older (about thirty as I should say), who was going out to join a brother; and an old gentleman, a good deal like a hawk if his eyes had been better and not so red, who was always talking, morning, noon, and night, about the gold discovery. But, whether he was making the voyage, thinking his old arms could dig for gold, or whether his speculation was to buy it, or to barter for it, or to cheat for it, or to snatch it anyhow from other people, was his secret. He kept his secret.

These three and the child were the soonest well. The child was a most engaging child, to be sure, and very fond of me: though I am bound to admit that John Steadiman and I were borne on her pretty little books in reverse order, and that he was captain there, and I was mate. It was beautiful to watch her with John, and it was beautiful to watch John with her. Few would have thought it possible, to see John playing at bo-peep round the mast, that he was the man who had caught up an iron bar and struck a Malay and a Maltese dead, as they were gliding with their knives down the cabin stair aboard the barque Old England, when the captain lay ill in his cot, off Saugar Point. But he was; and give him his back against a bulwark, he would have done the same by half-a-dozen of them. The name of the young mother was Mrs. Atherfield, the name of the young lady in black was Miss Coleshaw, and the name of the old gentleman was Mr. Rarx.

As the child had a quantity of shining fair hair, cluster-ing in curls all about her face, and as her name was Lucy, Steadiman gave her the name of the Golden Lucy. So, we had the Golden Lucy and the Golden Mary; and John kept up the idea to that extent as he and the child went playing about the decks, that I believe she used to think the ship was alive somehow—a sister or companion, going to the same place as herself. She liked to be by the wheel, and in fine weather, I have often stood by the man whose trick it was at the wheel, only to hear her, sitting near my feet, talking to the ship. Never had a child such a doll before, I suppose; but she made a doll of the Golden Mary, and used to dress her up by tying ribbons and little bits of finery to the belaying-pins; and nobody ever moved them, unless it was to save them from being blown away.

Of course I took charge of the two young women, and I called them "my dear," and they never minded, knowing that whatever I said was said in a fatherly and protecting spirit. I gave them their places on each side of me at dinner, Mrs. Atherfield on my right and Miss Coleshaw on my left; and I directed the unmarried lady to serve out the break-fast, and the married lady to serve out the tea. Likewise I said to my black steward in their presence, "Tom Snow, these two ladies are equally the mistresses of this house, and do you obey their orders equally;" at which Tom laughed, and they all laughed.

Old Mr. Rarx was not a pleasant man to look at, nor yet to talk to, or to be with, for no one could help seeing that he was a sordid and selfish character, and that he had warped further and further out of the straight with time. Not but what he was on his best behaviour with us, as everybody was; for we had no bickering among us, for'ard or aft. I only mean to say, he was not the man one would have chosen for a messmate. If choice there had been, one might even have gone a few points out of one's course, to say, "No! Not him!" But, there was one curious inconsistency in Mr. Rarx. That was, that he took an astonishing interest in the child. He looked, and I may add, he was, one of the last of men to care at all for a child, or to care much for any human creature. Still, he went so far as to be habitually uneasy, if the child was long on deck, out of his sight. He was always afraid of her falling overboard, or falling down a hatchway, or of a block or what not coming down upon her from the rigging in the working of the ship, or of her getting some hurt or other. He used to look at her and touch her, as if she was something precious to him. He was always solicitous about her not injuring her health, and constantly entreated her mother to be careful of it. This was so much the more curious, because the child did not like him, but used to shrink away from him, and would not even put out her hand to him without coaxing from others. I believe that every soul on board frequently noticed this, and not one of us understood it. However, it was such a plain fact, that John Steadiman said more than once when old Mr. Rarx was not within earshot, that if the Golden Mary felt a tenderness for the dear old gentleman she carried in her lap, she must be bitterly jealous of the Golden Lucy.

Before I go any further with this narrative, I will state that our ship was a barque of three hundred tons, carrying a crew of eighteen men, a second mate in addition to John, a carpenter, an armourer or smith, and two apprentices (one a Scotch boy, poor little fellow). We had three boats; the Long-boat, capable of carrying twenty-five men; the Cutter, capable of carrying fifteen; and the Surf-boat, capable of carrying ten. I put down the capacity of these boats according to the numbers they were really meant to hold.

We had tastes of bad weather and head-winds, of course; but, on the whole we had as fine a run as any reasonable man could expect, for sixty days. I then began to enter two remarks in the ship's Log and in my Journal; first, that there was an unusual and amazing quantity of ice; second, that the nights were most wonderfully dark, in spite of the ice.

For five days and a half, it seemed quite useless and hopeless to alter the ship's course so as to stand out of the way of this ice. I made what southing I could; but, all that time, we were beset by it. Mrs. Atherfield after standing by me on deck once, looking for some time in an awed manner at the great bergs that surrounded us, said in a whisper, "O! Captain Ravender, it looks as if the whole solid earth had changed into ice, and broken up!" I said to her, laughing, "I don't wonder that it does, to your inexperienced eyes, my dear." But I had never seen a twentieth part of the quantity, and, in reality, I was pretty much of her opinion.

However, at two P.M. on the afternoon of the sixth day, that is to say, when we were sixty-six days out, John Steadiman who had gone aloft, sang out from the top, that the sea was clear ahead. Before four P.M. a strong breeze springing up right astern, we were in open water at sunset. The breeze then freshening into half a gale of wind, and the Golden Mary being a very fast sailer, we went before the wind merrily, all night.

I had thought it impossible that it could be darker than it had been, until the sun, moon, and stars should fall out of the Heavens, and Time should be destroyed; but, it had been next to light, in comparison with what it was now. The darkness was so profound, that looking into it was painful and oppressive—like looking, without a ray of light, into a dense black bandage put as close before the eyes as it could be, without touching them. I doubled the look-out, and John and I stood in the bow side-by-side, never leaving it all night. Yet I should no more have known that he was near me when he was silent, without putting out my arm and touching him, than I should if he had turned in and been fast asleep below. We were not so much looking out, all of us, as listening to the utmost, both with our eyes and ears.

Next day, I found that the mercury in the barometer, which had risen steadily since we cleared the ice, remained steady. I had had very good observations, with now and then the interruption of a day or so, since our departure. I got the sun at noon, and found that we were in Lat. 58° S., Long. 60° W., off New South Shetland; in the neighbourhood of Cape Horn. We were sixty-seven days out, that day. The ship's reckoning was accurately worked and made up. The ship did her duty admirably, all on board were well, and all hands were as smart, efficient, and contented, as it was possible to be.

When the night came on again as dark as before, it was the eighth night I had been on deck. Nor had I taken more than a very little sleep in the daytime, my station being always near the helm, and often at it, while we were among the ice. Few but those who have tried it can imagine the difficulty and pain of only keeping the eyes open—physically open—under such circumstances, in such darkness. They get struck by the darkness, and blinded by the darkness. They make patterns in it, and they flash in it. as if they had gone out of your head to look at you. On the turn of midnight, John Steadiman, who was alert and fresh (for I had always made him turn in by day), said to me, "Captain Ravender, I entreat of you to go below. I am sure you can hardly stand, and your voice is getting weak, Sir. Go below, and take a little rest. I'll call you if a block chafes." I said to John in answer, "Well, well, John! Let us wait till the turn of one o'clock, before we talk about that." I had just had one of the ship's lanterns held up, that I might see how the night went by my watch, and it was then twenty minutes after twelve.

At five minutes before one, John sang out to the boy to bring the lantern again, and when I told him once more what the time was, entreated and prayed of me to go below. "Captain Ravender," says he, "all's well; we can't afford to have you laid up for a single hour; and I respectfully and earnestly beg of you to go below." The end of it was, that I agreed to do so, on the understanding that if I failed to come up of my own accord within three hours, I was to be punctually called. Having settled that, I left John in charge. But I called him to me once afterwards, to ask him a question. I had been to look at the barometer, and had seen the mercury still perfectly steady, and had come up the companion again to take a last look about me—if I can use such a word in reference to such darkness—when I thought that the waves, as the Golden Mary parted them and shook them off, had a hollow sound in them; something that I fancied was a rather unusual reverberation. I was standing by the quarter-deck rail on the starboard side, when I called John aft to me, and bade him listen. He did so with the greatest attention. Turning to me he then said, "Rely upon it, Captain Ravender, you have been without rest too long, and the novelty is only in the state of your sense of hearing." I thought so too by that time, and I think so now, though I can never know for absolute certain in this world, whether it was or not.

When I left John Steadiman in charge, the ship was still

going at a great rate through the water. The wind still blew right astern. Though she was making great way, she was under shortened sail, and had no more than she could easily carry. All was snug, and nothing complained. There was a pretty sea running, but not a very high sea neither, nor at all a confused one.

I turned in, as we seamen say, all standing. The meaning of that is, I did not pull my clothes off—no, not even so much as my coat: though I did my shoes, for my feet were badly swelled with the deck. There was a little swing-lamp alight in my cabin. I thought, as I looked at it before shutting my eyes, that I was so tired of darkness, and troubled by darkness, that I could have gone to sleep best in the midst of a million of flaming gas-lights. That was the last thought I had before I went off, except the prevailing thought that I should not be able to get to sleep at all.

I dreamed that I was back at Penrith again, and was trying to get round the church, which had altered its shape very much since I last saw it, and was cloven all down the middle of the steeple in a most singular manner. Why I wanted to get round the church I don't know; but I was as anxious to do it as if my life depended upon it. Indeed, I believe it did in the dream. For all that, I could not get round the church. I was still trying, when I came against it with a violent shock, and was flung out of my cot against the ship's side. Shrieks and a terrific outcry struck me far harder than the bruising timbers, and amidst sounds of grinding and crashing, and a heavy rushing and breaking of water—sounds I understood too well—I made my way on deck. It was not an easy thing to do, for the ship heeled over frightfully, and was beating in a furious manner.

I could not see the men as I went forward, but I could hear that they were hauling in sail, in disorder. I had my trumpet in my hand, and, after directing and encouraging them in this till it was done, I hailed first John Steadiman, and then my second mate, Mr. William Rames. Both answered clearly and steadily. Now, I had practised them and all my crew, as I have ever made it a custom to practise all who sail with me, to take certain stations and wait my orders, in case of any unexpected crisis. When my voice was heard hailing, and their voices were heard answering, I was aware, through all the noises of the ship and sea, and all the crying of the passengers below, that there was a pause. " Are you ready, Rames ? "—" Ay, ay, Sir ! "—"Then light up, for God's sake ! "   In a moment he and another were burning blue-lights, and the ship and all on board seemed to be enclosed in a mist of light, under a great black dome.

The light shone up so high that I could see the huge Iceberg upon which we had struck, cloven at the top and down the middle, exactly like Penrith Church in my dream. At the same moment I could see the watch last relieved, crowding up and down on deck ; I could see Mrs. Atherfield and Miss Coleshaw thrown about on the top of the companion as they struggled to bring the child up from below ; I could see that the masts were going with the shock and the beating of the ship ; I could see the frightful breach stove in on the starboard side, half the length of the vessel, and the sheathing and timbers spirting up ; I could see that the Cutter was disabled, in a wreck of broken fragments ; and I could see every eye turned upon me.   It is my belief that if there had been ten thousand eyes there, I should have seen them all, with their different looks.   And all this in a moment.   But you must consider what a moment.

I saw the men, as they looked at me, fall towards their appointed stations, like good men and true.   If she had not righted, they could have done very little there or anywhere but die—not that it is little for a man to die at his post—I mean they could have done nothing to save the passengers and themselves.   Happily, however, the violence of the shock with which we had so determinedly borne down direct on that fatal Iceberg, as if it had been our destination instead of our destruction, had so smashed and pounded the ship that she got off in this same instant and righted.   I did not want the carpenter to tell me she was filling and going down ; I could see and hear that.   I gave Rames the word to lower the Long-boat and the Surf-boat, and I myself told off the men for each duty.   Not one hung back, or came before the other.   I now whispered to John Steadiman, "John, I stand at the gangway here, to see every soul on board safe over the side.   You shall have the next post of honour, and shall be the last but one to leave the ship. Bring up the passengers, and range them behind me ; and put what provision and water you can get at, in the boats. Cast your eye for'ard, John, and you'll see you have not a moment to lose."

My noble fellows got the boats over the side as orderly as

I ever saw boats lowered with any sea running, and, when they were launched, two or three of the nearest men in them as they held on, rising and falling with the swell, called out, looking up at me, "Captain Ravender, if anything goes wrong with us, and you are saved, remember we stood by you!"—"We'll all stand by one another ashore, yet, please God, my lads!" says I. "Hold on bravely, and be tender with the women."

The women were an example to us. They trembled very much, but they were quiet and perfectly collected. "Kiss me, Captain Ravender," says Mrs. Atherfield, "and God in heaven bless you, you good man!" "My dear," says I, "those words are better for me than a lifeboat." I held her child in my arms till she was in the boat, and then kissed the child and handed her safe down. I now said to the people in her, "You have got your freight, my lads, all but me, and I am not coming yet awhile. Pull away from the ship, and keep off!"

That was the Long-boat. Old Mr. Rarx was one of her complement, and he was the only passenger who had greatly misbehaved since the ship struck. Others had been a little wild, which was not to be wondered at, and not very blamable; but, he had made a lamentation and uproar which it was dangerous for the people to hear, as there is always contagion in weakness and selfishness. His incessant cry had been that he must not be separated from the child, that he couldn't see the child, and that he and the child must go together. He had even tried to wrest the child out of my arms, that he might keep her in his. "Mr. Rarx," said I to him when it came to that, "I have a loaded pistol in my pocket; and if you don't stand out of the gangway, and keep perfectly quiet, I shall shoot you through the heart, if you have got one." Says he, "You won't do murder, Captain Ravender!" "No, Sir," says I, "I won't murder forty-four people to humour you, but I'll shoot you to save them." After that he was quiet, and stood shivering a little way off, until I named him to go over the side.

The Long-boat being cast off, the Surf-boat was soon filled. There only remained aboard the Golden Mary, John Mullion, the man who had kept on burning the blue-lights (and who had lighted every new one at every old one before it went out, as quietly as if he had been at an illumination); John Steadiman; and myself. I hurried those two into the Surf-boat, called to them to keep off, and waited with a

grateful and relieved heart for the Long-boat to come and
take me in, if she could.   I looked at my watch, and it
showed me, by the blue-light, ten minutes past two.   They
lost no time.   As soon as she was near enough, I swung
myself into her, and called to the men, "With a will, lads!
She's reeling!"   We were not an inch too far out of the
inner vortex of her going down, when, by the blue-light
which John Mullion still burnt in the bow of the Surf-boat,
we saw her lurch, and plunge to the bottom head-foremost.
The child cried, weeping wildly, "O the dear Golden Mary!
O look at her! Save her! Save the poor Golden Mary!"
And then the light burnt out, and the black dome seemed to
come down upon us.

I suppose if we had all stood a-top of a mountain, and
seen the whole remainder of the world sink away from under
us, we could hardly have felt more shocked and solitary than
we did when we knew we were alone on the wide ocean,
and that the beautiful ship in which most of us had been
securely asleep within half an hour was gone for ever.
There was an awful silence in our boat, and such a kind of
palsy on the rowers and the man at the rudder, that I felt
they were scarcely keeping her before the sea.   I spoke out
then, and said, "Let every one here thank the Lord for our
preservation!"   All the voices answered (even the child's),
"We thank the Lord!"   I then said the Lord's Prayer, and all
hands said it after me with a solemn murmuring.   Then I gave
the word "Cheerily, O men, Cheerily!" and I felt that they
were handling the boat again as a boat ought to be handled.

The Surf-boat now burnt another blue-light to show us
where they were, and we made for her, and laid ourselves as
nearly alongside of her as we dared.   I had always kept my
boats with a coil or two of good stout stuff in each of them,
so both boats had a rope at hand.   We made a shift, with
much labour and trouble, to get near enough to one another
to divide the blue-lights (they were no use after that night,
for the sea-water soon got at them), and to get a tow-rope out
between us.   All night long we kept together, sometimes
obliged to cast off the rope, and sometimes getting it out
again, and all of us wearying for the morning—which appeared so long in coming that old Mr. Rarx screamed out,
in spite of his fears of me, "The world is drawing to an end,
and the sun will never rise any more!"

When the day broke, I found that we were all huddled

The Wreck of the Golden Mary

together in a miserable manner.   We were deep in the water; being, as I found on mustering, thirty-one in number, or at least six too many.   In the Surf-boat they were fourteen in number, being at least four too many.   The first thing I did, was to get myself passed to the rudder—which I took from that time—and to get Mrs. Atherfield, her child, and Miss Coleshaw, passed on to sit next me.   As to old Mr. Rarx, I put him in the bow, as far from us as I could.   And I put some of the best men near us in order that if I should drop there might be a skilful hand ready to take the helm.

The sea moderating as the sun came up, though the sky was cloudy and wild, we spoke the other boat, to know what stores they had, and to overhaul what we had.   I had a compass in my pocket, a small telescope, a double-barrelled pistol, a knife, and a fire-box and matches.   Most of my men had knives, and some had a little tobacco : some, a pipe as well.   We had a mug among us, and an iron spoon.   As to provisions, there were in my boat two bags of biscuit, one piece of raw beef, one piece of raw pork, a bag of coffee, roasted but not ground (thrown in, I imagine, by mistake, for something else), two small casks of water, and about half-a-gallon of rum in a keg.   The Surf-boat, having rather more rum than we, and fewer to drink it, gave us, as I estimated, another quart into our keg.   In return, we gave them three double handfuls of coffee, tied up in a piece of a handkerchief ; they reported that they had aboard besides, a bag of biscuit, a piece of beef, a small cask of water, a small box of lemons, and a Dutch cheese.   It took a long time to make these exchanges, and they were not made without risk to both parties ; the sea running quite high enough to make our approaching near to one another very hazardous.   In the bundle with the coffee, I conveyed to John Steadiman (who had a ship's compass with him), a paper written in pencil, and torn from my pocket-book, containing the course I meant to steer, in the hope of making land, or being picked up by some vessel—I say in the hope, though I had little hope of either deliverance.   I then sang out to him, so as all might hear, that if we two boats could live or die together, we would ; but, that if we should be parted by the weather, and join company no more, they should have our prayers and blessings, and we asked for theirs.   We then gave them three cheers, which they returned, and I saw the men's heads droop in both boats as they fell to their oars again.

These arrangements had occupied the general attention advantageously for all, though (as I expressed in the last sentence) they ended in a sorrowful feeling. I now said a few words to my fellow-voyagers on the subject of the small stock of food on which our lives depended if they were preserved from the great deep, and on the rigid necessity of our eking it out in the most frugal manner. One and all replied that whatever allowance I thought best to lay down should be strictly kept to. We made a pair of scales out of a thin strap of iron-plating and some twine, and I got together for weights such of the heaviest buttons among us as I calculated made up some fraction over two ounces. This was the allowance of solid food served out once a-day to each, from that time to the end; with the addition of a coffee-berry, or sometimes half a one, when the weather was very fair, for breakfast. We had nothing else whatever, but half a pint of water each per day, and sometimes, when we were coldest and weakest, a teaspoonful of rum each, served out as a dram. I know how learnedly it can be shown that rum is poison, but I also know that in this case, as in all similar cases I have ever read of—which are numerous—no words can express the comfort and support derived from it. Nor have I the least doubt that it saved the lives of far more than half our number. Having mentioned half a pint of water as our daily allowance, I ought to observe that sometimes we had less, and sometimes we had more; for much rain fell, and we caught it in a canvas stretched for the purpose.

Thus, at that tempestuous time of the year, and in that tempestuous part of the world, we shipwrecked people rose and fell with the waves. It is not my intention to relate (if I can avoid it) such circumstances appertaining to our doleful condition as have been better told in many other narratives of the kind than I can be expected to tell them. I will only note, in so many passing words, that day after day and night after night we received the sea upon our backs to prevent it from swamping the boat; that one party was always kept baling, and that every hat and cap among us soon got worn out, though patched up fifty times, as the only vessels we had for that service; that another party lay down in the bottom of the boat, while a third rowed; and that we were soon all in boils and blisters and rags.

The other boat was a source of such anxious interest to

all of us that I used to wonder whether, if we were saved, the time could ever come when the survivors in this boat of ours could be at all indifferent to the fortunes of the survivors in that. We got out a tow-rope whenever the weather permitted, but that did not often happen, and how we two parties kept within the same horizon, as we did, He, who mercifully permitted it to be so for our consolation, only knows. I never shall forget the looks with which, when the morning light came, we used to gaze about us over the stormy waters, for the other boat. We once parted company for seventy-two hours, and we believed them to have gone down, as they did us. The joy on both sides when we came within view of one another again, had something in a manner Divine in it; each was so forgetful of individual suffering, in tears of delight and sympathy for the people in the other boat.

I have been wanting to get round to the individual or personal part of my subject, as I call it, and the foregoing incident puts me in the right way. The patience and good disposition aboard of us, was wonderful. I was not surprised by it in the women; for all men born of women know what great qualities they will show when men will fail; but, I own I was a little surprised by it in some of the men. Among one-and-thirty people assembled at the best of times, there will usually, I should say, be two or three uncertain tempers. I knew that I had more than one rough temper with me among my own people, for I had chosen those for the Long-boat that I might have them under my eye. But, they softened under their misery, and were as considerate of the ladies, and as compassionate of the child, as the best among us, or among men—they could not have been more so. I heard scarcely any complaining. The party lying down would moan a good deal in their sleep, and I would often notice a man—not always the same man, it is to be understood, but nearly all of them at one time or other—sitting moaning at his oar, or in his place, as he looked mistily over the sea. When it happened to be long before I could catch his eye, he would go on moaning all the time in the dismallest manner; but, when our looks met, he would brighten and leave off. I almost always got the impression that he did not know what sound he had been making, but that he thought he had been humming a tune.

Our sufferings from cold and wet were far greater than our sufferings from hunger. We managed to keep the child warm; but, I doubt if any one else among us ever was warm for five minutes together; and the shivering, and the chattering of teeth, were sad to hear. The child cried a little at first for her lost playfellow, the Golden Mary; but hardly ever whimpered afterwards; and when the state of the weather made it possible, she used now and then to be held up in the arms of some of us, to look over the sea for John Steadiman's boat. I see the golden hair and the innocent face now, between me and the driving clouds, like an angel going to fly away.

It had happened on the second day, towards night, that Mrs. Atherfield, in getting Little Lucy to sleep, sang her a song. She had a soft, melodious voice, and, when she had finished it, our people up and begged for another. She sang them another, and after it had fallen dark ended with the Evening Hymn. From that time, whenever anything could be heard above the sea and wind, and while she had any voice left, nothing would serve the people but that she should sing at sunset. She always did, and always ended with the Evening Hymn. We mostly took up the last line, and shed tears when it was done, but not miserably. We had a prayer night and morning, also, when the weather allowed of it.

Twelve nights and eleven days we had been driving in the boat, when old Mr. Rarx began to be delirious, and to cry out to me to throw the gold overboard or it would sink us, and we should all be lost. For days past the child had been declining, and that was the great cause of his wildness. He had been over and over again shrieking out to me to give her all the remaining meat, to give her all the remaining rum, to save her at any cost, or we should all be ruined. At this time, she lay in her mother's arms at my feet. One of her little hands was almost always creeping about her mother's neck or chin. I had watched the wasting of the little hand, and I knew it was nearly over.

The old man's cries were so discordant with the mother's love and submission, that I called out to him in an angry voice, unless he held his peace on the instant, I would order him to be knocked on the head and thrown overboard. He was mute then, until the child died, very peacefully, an hour afterwards: which was known to all in the boat by the mother's breaking out into lamentations for the first time since the wreck—for, she had great fortitude and constancy, though she was a little gentle woman. Old Mr. Rarx then became quite ungovernable, tearing what rags he had on him, raging in imprecations, and calling to me that if I had thrown the gold overboard (always the gold with him !) I might have saved the child. "And now," says he, in a terrible voice, "we shall founder, and all go to the Devil, for our sins will sink us, when we have no innocent child to bear us up !" We so discovered with amazement, that this old wretch had only cared for the life of the pretty little creature dear to all of us, because of the influence he superstitiously hoped she might have in preserving him ! Altogether it was too much for the smith or armourer, who was sitting next the old man, to bear. He took him by the throat and rolled him under the thwarts, where he lay still enough for hours afterwards.

All that thirteenth night, Miss Coleshaw, lying across my knees as I kept the helm, comforted and supported the poor mother. Her child, covered with a pea-jacket of mine, lay in her lap. It troubled me all night to think that there was no Prayer-Book among us, and that I could remember but very few of the exact words of the burial service. When I stood up at broad day, all knew what was going to be done, and I noticed that my poor fellows made the motion of uncovering their heads, though their heads had been stark bare to the sky and sea for many a weary hour. There was a long heavy swell on, but otherwise it was a fair morning, and there were broad fields of sunlight on the waves in the east. I said no more than this: "I am the Resurrection and the Life, saith the Lord. He raised the daughter of Jairus the ruler, and said she was not dead but slept. He raised the widow's son. He arose Himself, and was seen of many. He loved little children, saying, Suffer them to come unto Me, and rebuke them not, for of such is the kingdom of heaven. In His name, my friends, and committed to His merciful goodness !" With those words I laid my rough face softly on the placid little forehead, and buried the Golden Lucy in the grave of the Golden Mary.

Having had it on my mind to relate the end of this dear little child, I have omitted something from its exact place, which I will supply here. It will come quite as well here as anywhere else.

Foreseeing that if the boat lived through the stormy weather, the time must come, and soon come, when we should have absolutely no morsel to eat, I had one moment-ous point often in my thoughts. Although I had, years before that, fully satisfied myself that the instances in which human beings in the last distress have fed upon each other, are exceedingly few, and have very seldom indeed (if ever) occurred when the people in distress, however dreadful their extremity, have been accustomed to moderate forbearance and restraint; I say, though I had long before quite satisfied my mind on this topic, I felt doubtful whether there might not have been in former cases some harm and danger from keeping it out of sight and pretending not to think of it. I felt doubtful whether some minds, growing weak with fasting and exposure and having such a terrific idea to dwell upon in secret, might not magnify it until it got to have an awful attraction about it.   This was not a new thought of mine, for it had grown out of my reading.   However, it came over me stronger than it had ever done before—as it had reason for doing—in the boat, and on the fourth day I decided that I would bring out into the light that unformed fear which must have been more or less darkly in every brain among us.   Therefore, as a means of beguiling the time and inspiring hope, I gave them the best summary in my power of Bligh's voyage of more than three thousand miles, in an open boat, after the Mutiny of the Bounty, and of the wonderful preservation of that boat's crew.   They listened throughout with great interest, and I concluded by telling them, that, in my opinion, the happiest circumstance in the whole narrative was, that Bligh, who was no delicate man either, had solemnly placed it on record therein that he was sure and certain that under no conceivable circumstances whatever would that emaciated party, who had gone through all the pains of famine, have preyed on one another.   I cannot describe the visible relief which this spread through the boat, and how the tears stood in every eye.   From that time I was as well convinced as Bligh himself that there was no danger, and that this phantom, at any rate, did not haunt us.

Now, it was a part of Bligh's experience that when the people in his boat were most cast down, nothing did them so much good as hearing a story told by one of their number. When I mentioned that, I saw that it struck the general attention as much as it did my own, for I had not thought of it until I came to it in my summary.   This was on the day after Mrs. Atherfield first sang to us.   I proposed that, whenever the weather would permit, we should have a story two hours after dinner (I always issued the allowance I have mentioned at one o'clock, and called it by that name), as well as our song at sunset. The proposal was received with a cheerful satisfaction that warmed my heart within me; and I do not say too much when I say that those two periods in the four-and-twenty hours were expected with positive pleasure, and were really enjoyed by all hands. Spectres as we soon were in our bodily wasting, our imaginations did not perish like the gross flesh upon our bones. Music and Adventure, two of the great gifts of Providence to mankind, could charm us long after that was lost.

The wind was almost always against us after the second day; and for many days together we could not nearly hold our own. We had all varieties of bad weather. We had rain, hail, snow, wind, mist, thunder and lightning. Still the boats lived through the heavy seas, and still we perishing people rose and fell with the great waves.

Sixteen nights and fifteen days, twenty nights and nineteen days, twenty-four nights and twenty-three days. So the time went on. Disheartening as I knew that our progress, or want of progress, must be, I never deceived them as to my calculations of it. In the first place, I felt that we were all too near eternity for deceit; in the second place, I knew that if I failed, or died, the man who followed me must have a knowledge of the true state of things to begin upon. When I told them at noon, what I reckoned we had made or lost, they generally received what I said in a tranquil and resigned manner, and always gratefully towards me. It was not unusual at any time of the day for some one to burst out weeping loudly without any new cause; and, when the burst was over, to calm down a little better than before. I had seen exactly the same thing in a house of mourning.

During the whole of this time, old Mr. Rarx had had his fits of calling out to me to throw the gold (always the gold!) overboard, and of heaping violent reproaches upon me for not having saved the child; but now, the food being all gone, and I having nothing left to serve out but a bit of coffee-berry now and then, he began to be too weak to do this, and consequently fell silent. Mrs. Atherfield and Miss Coleshaw generally lay, each with an arm across one of my knees, and her head upon it. They never complained at all. Up to the time of her child's death, Mrs. Atherfield had bound up her own beautiful hair every day; and I took particular notice that this was always before she sang her song at night, when every one looked at her. But she never did it after the loss of her darling; and it would have been now all tangled with dirt and wet, but that Miss Coleshaw was careful of it long after she was herself, and would sometimes smooth it down with her weak thin hands.

We were past mustering a story now; but one day, at about this period, I reverted to the superstition of old Mr. Rarx, concerning the Golden Lucy, and told them that nothing vanished from the eye of God, though much might pass away from the eyes of men. "We were all of us," says I, "children once; and our baby feet have strolled in green woods ashore; and our baby hands have gathered flowers in gardens, where the birds were singing. The children that we were, are not lost to the great knowledge of our Creator. Those innocent creatures will appear with us before Him, and plead for us. What we were in the best time of our generous youth will arise and go with us too. The purest part of our lives will not desert us at the pass to which all of us here present are gliding. What we were then, will be as much in existence before Him, as what we are now." They were no less comforted by this consideration, than I was myself; and Miss Coleshaw, drawing my ear nearer to her lips, said, "Captain Ravender, I was on my way to marry a disgraced and broken man, whom I dearly loved when he was honourable and good. Your words seem to have come out of my own poor heart." She pressed my hand upon it, smiling.

Twenty-seven nights and twenty-six days. We were in no want of rain-water, but we had nothing else. And yet, even now, I never turned my eyes upon a waking face but it tried to brighten before mine. O, what a thing it is, in a time of danger and in the presence of death, the shining of a face upon a face! I have heard it broached that orders should be given in great new ships by electric telegraph. I admire machinery as much as any man, and am as thankful to it as any man can be for what it does for us. But it will never be a substitute for the face of a man, with his soul in it, encouraging another man to be brave and true. Never try it for that. It will break down like a straw.

I now began to remark certain changes in myself which I did not like. They caused me much disquiet. I often saw the Golden Lucy in the air above the boat. I often saw her I have spoken of before, sitting beside me. I saw the Golden

Mary go down, as she really had gone down, twenty times
in a day. And yet the sea was mostly, to my thinking, not
sea neither, but moving country and extraordinary moun-
tainous regions, the like of which have never been beheld. I felt it time to leave my last words regarding John
Steadiman, in case any lips should last out to repeat them to
any living ears. I said that John had told me (as he had on
deck) that he had sung out "Breakers ahead!" the instant
they were audible, and had tried to wear ship, but she struck
before it could be done. (His cry, I dare say, had made my
dream.) I said that the circumstances were altogether without warning, and out of any course that could have been
guarded against; that the same loss would have happened if
I had been in charge; and that John was not to blame, but
from first to last had done his duty nobly, like the man he
was. I tried to write it down in my pocket-book, but could
make no words, though I knew what the words were that
I wanted to make. When it had come to that, her hands—
though she was dead so long—laid me down gently in the
bottom of the boat, and she and the Golden Lucy swung me
to sleep.

All that follows, was written by John Steadiman, Chief Mate:

On the twenty-sixth day after the foundering of the Golden
Mary at sea, I, John Steadiman, was sitting in my place in
the stern-sheets of the Surf-boat, with just sense enough left
in me to steer—that is to say, with my eyes strained, wideawake, over the bows of the boat, and my brains fast asleep
and dreaming—when I was roused upon a sudden by our
second mate, Mr. William Rames.

"Let me take a spell in your place," says he. "And look
you out for the Long-boat astern. The last time she rose
on the crest of a wave, I thought I made out a signal flying
aboard her."

We shifted our places, clumsily and slowly enough, for we
were both of us weak and dazed with wet, cold, and hunger.
I waited some time, watching the heavy rollers astern, before
the Long-boat rose a-top of one of them at the same time
with us. At last, she was heaved up for a moment well in
view, and there, sure enough, was the signal flying aboard of
her—a strip of rag of some sort, rigged to an oar, and hoisted
in her bows.

"What does it mean?" says Rames to me in a quavering, trembling sort of voice. "Do they signal a sail in sight?"

"Hush, for God's sake!" says I, clapping my hand over his mouth. "Don't let the people hear you. They'll all go mad together if we mislead them about that signal. Wait a bit, till I have another look at it."

I held on by him, for he had set me all of a tremble with his notion of a sail in sight, and watched for the Long-boat again. Up she rose on the top of another roller. I made out the signal clearly, that second time, and saw that it was rigged half-mast high.

"Rames," says I, "it's a signal of distress. Pass the word forward to keep her before the sea, and no more. We must get the Long-boat within hailing distance of us, as soon as possible."

I dropped down into my old place at the tiller without another word—for the thought went through me like a knife that something had happened to Captain Ravender. I should consider myself unworthy to write another line of this statement, if I had not made up my mind to speak the truth, the whole truth, and nothing but the truth—and I must, therefore, confess plainly that now, for the first time, my heart sank within me. This weakness on my part was produced in some degree, as I take it, by the exhausting effects of previous anxiety and grief.

Our provisions—if I may give that name to what we had left—were reduced to the rind of one lemon and about a couple of handsfull of coffee-berries. Besides these great distresses, caused by the death, the danger, and the suffering among my crew and passengers, I had had a little distress of my own to shake me still more, in the death of the child whom I had got to be very fond of on the voyage out—so fond that I was secretly a little jealous of her being taken in the Long-boat instead of mine when the ship foundered. It used to be a great comfort to me, and I think to those with me also, after we had seen the last of the Golden Mary, to see the Golden Lucy, held up by the men in the Long-boat, when the weather allowed it, as the best and brightest sight they had to show. She looked, at the distance we saw her from, almost like a little white bird in the air. To miss her for the first time, when the weather lulled a little again, and we all looked out for our white bird and looked in vain, was a sore disappointment. To see the men's heads bowed down and the captain's hand pointing into the sea when we hailed the Long-boat, a few day's after, gave me as heavy a shock and as sharp a pang of heartache to bear as ever I remember suffering in all my life. I only mention these things to show that if I did give way a little at first, under the dread that our captain was lost to us, it was not without having been a good deal shaken beforehand by more trials of one sort or another than often fall to one man's share.

I had got over the choking in my throat with the help of a drop of water, and had steadied my mind again so as to be prepared against the worst, when I heard the hail (Lord help the poor fellows, how weak it sounded !)—

"Surf-boat ahoy !"

I looked up, and there were our companions in misfortune tossing abreast of us; not so near that we could make out the features of any of them, but near enough, with some exertion for people in our condition, to make their voices heard in the intervals when the wind was weakest.

I answered the hail, and waited a bit, and heard nothing, and then sung out the captain's name. The voice that replied did not sound like his; the words that reached us were:

"Chief-mate wanted on board !"

Every man of my crew knew what that meant as well as I did. As second officer in command, there could be but one reason for wanting me on board the Long-boat. A groan went all round us, and my men looked darkly in each other's faces, and whispered under their breaths:

"The captain is dead !"

I commanded them to be silent, and not to make too sure of bad news, at such a pass as things had now come to with us. Then, hailing the Long-boat, I signified that I was ready to go on board when the weather would let me—stopped a bit to draw a good long breath—and then called out as loud as I could the dreadful question:

"Is the captain dead ?"

The black figures of three or four men in the after-part of the Long-boat all stooped down together as my voice reached them. They were lost to view for about a minute; then appeared again—one man among them was held up on his feet by the rest, and he hailed back the blessed words (a very faint hope went a very long way with people in our desperate situation): "Not yet !"

The relief felt by me, and by all with me, when we knew that our captain, though unfitted for duty, was not lost to us, it is not in words—at least, not in such words as a man like me can command—to express. I did my best to cheer the men by telling them what a good sign it was that we were not as badly off yet as we had feared ; and then communicated what instructions I had to give, to William Rames, who was to be left in command in my place when I took charge of the Long-boat. After that, there was no thing to be done, but to wait for the chance of the wind dropping at sunset, and the sea going down afterwards, so as to enable our weak crews to lay the two boats alongside of each other, without undue risk—or, to put it plainer, without saddling ourselves with the necessity for any extraordinary exertion of strength or skill. Both the one and the other had now been starved out of us for days and days together.

At sunset the wind suddenly dropped, but the sea, which had been running high for so long a time past, took hours after that before it showed any signs of getting to rest. The moon was shining, the sky was wonderfully clear, and it could not have been, according to my calculations, far off midnight, when the long, slow, regular swell of the calming ocean fairly set in, and I took the responsibility of lessening the distance between the Long-boat and ourselves.

It was, I dare say, a delusion of mine ; but I thought I had never seen the moon shine so white and ghastly anywhere, either at sea or on land, as she shone that night while we were approaching our companions in misery. Wh··n there was not much more than a boat's length between us, and the white light streamed cold and clear over all our faces, both crews rested on their oars with one great shudder, and stared over the gunwale of either boat, panic-stricken at the first sight of each other.

"Any lives lost among you ?" I asked, in the midst of that frightful silence.

The men in the Long-boat huddled together like sheep at the sound of my voice.

"None yet, but the child, thanks be to God !" answered one among them.

And at the sound of his voice, all my men shrank together like the men in the Long-boat. I was afraid to let the horror produced by our first meeting at close quarters after the dreadful changes that wet, cold, and famine had produced, last one moment longer than could be helped; so, without giving time for any more questions and answers, I commanded the men to lay the two boats close alongside of each other. When I rose up and committed the tiller to the hands of Rames, all my poor fellows raised their white faces imploringly to mine. "Don't leave us, Sir," they said, "don't leave us." "I leave you," says I, "under the command and the guidance of Mr. William Rames, as good a sailor as I am, and as trusty and kind a man as ever stepped. Do your duty by him, as you have done it by me; and remember to the last, that while there is life there is hope. God bless and help you all!" With those words I collected what strength I had left, and caught at two arms that were held out to me, and so got from the stern-sheets of one boat into the stern-sheets of the other.

"Mind where you step, Sir," whispered one of the men who had helped me into the Long-boat. I looked down as he spoke. Three figures were huddled up below me, with the moonshine falling on them in ragged streaks through the gaps between the men standing or sitting above them. The first face I made out was the face of Miss Coleshaw; her eyes were wide open and fixed on me. She seemed still to keep her senses, and, by the alternate parting and closing of her lips, to be trying to speak, but I could not hear that she uttered a single word. On her shoulder rested the head of Mrs. Atherfield. The mother of our poor little Golden Lucy must, I think, have been dreaming of the child she had lost; for there was a faint smile just ruffling the white stillness of her face, when I first saw it turned upward, with peaceful closed eyes towards the heavens. From her, I looked down a little, and there, with his head on her lap, and with one of her hands resting tenderly on his cheek— there lay the Captain, to whose help and guidance, up to this miserable time, we had never looked in vain,—there, worn out at last in our service, and for our sakes, lay the best and bravest man of all our company. I stole my hand in gently through his clothes and laid it on his heart, and felt a little feeble warmth over it, though my cold dulled touch could not detect even the faintest beating. The two men in the stern-sheets with me, noticing what I was doing —knowing I loved him like a brother—and seeing, I suppose, more distress in my face than I myself was conscious of its showing, lost command over themselves altogether, and burst into a piteous moaning, sobbing lamentation over him. One of the two drew aside a jacket from his feet, and showed me that they were bare, except where a wet, ragged strip of stocking still clung to one of them. When the ship struck the Iceberg, he had run on deck leaving his shoes in his cabin. All through the voyage in the boat his feet had been unprotected; and not a soul had discovered it until he dropped! As long as he could keep his eyes open, the very look of them had cheered the men, and comforted and upheld the women. Not one living creature in the boat, with any sense about him, but had felt the good influence of that brave man in one way or another. Not one but had heard him, over and over again, give the credit to others which was due only to himself; praising this man for patience, and thanking that man for help, when the patience and the help had really and truly, as to the best part of both, come only from him. All this, and much more, I heard pouring confusedly from the men's lips while they crouched down, sobbing and crying over their commander, and wrapping the jacket as warmly and tenderly as they could over his cold feet. It went to my heart to check them; but I knew that if this lamenting spirit spread any further, all chance of keeping alight any last sparks of hope and resolution among the boat's company would be lost for ever. Accordingly I sent them to their places, spoke a few encouraging words to the men forward, promising to serve out, when the morning came, as much as I dared, of any eatable thing left in the lockers; called to Rames, in my old boat, to keep as near us as he safely could; drew the garments and coverings of the two poor suffering women more closely about them; and, with a secret prayer to be directed for the best in bearing the awful responsibility now laid on my shoulders, took my Captain's vacant place at the helm of the Long-boat.

This, as well as I can tell it, is the full and true account of how I came to be placed in charge of the lost passengers and crew of the Golden Mary, on the morning of the twenty-seventh day after the ship struck the Iceberg, and foundered at sea.

THE PERILS OF CERTAIN
ENGLISH PRISONERS

[1857]

CHARACTERS

CAPTAIN CARTON, *a naval officer; afterwards Admiral Sir George Carton.*

HARRY CHARKER, *a comrade of Gill Davis's, devoted to duty.*

GILL DAVIS, *a private in the Royal Marines; narrator of the story.*

SERGEANT DROOCE, *a brave but tyrannical non-commissioned officer.*

MR. FISHER, *one of the residents of Silver-Store Island.*

MRS. FISHER, *his wife.*

CHRISTIAN GEORGE KING, *a treacherous half-caste negro.*

MR. KITTEN, *Vice-Commissioner and Deputy-Consul.*

LIEUTENANT LINDERWOOD, *an officer of the Royal Marines.*

MR. MACEY, *a quick, brave, steady gentleman.*

CAPTAIN MARYON, *commander of the* Christopher Columbus.

MISS MARION MARYON, *sister of the preceding; afterwards Lady Carton.*

TOM PACKER, *a wild, unsteady young fellow in the Marines.*

MR. COMMISSIONER PORDAGE, *a stiff-jointed, high-nosed official.*

MRS. PORDAGE, *his wife.*

ISABELLA TOTT ('Mrs. Belltott'), *a young widow, and maid to Miss Maryon.*

THE PERILS OF CERTAIN
ENGLISH PRISONERS

IN TWO CHAPTERS

CHAPTER I

THE ISLAND OF SILVER-STORE

It was in the year of our Lord one thousand seven hundred
and forty-four, that I, Gill Davis to command, His Mark,
having then the honour to be a private in the Royal Marines,
stood a-leaning over the bulwarks of the armed sloop
Christopher Columbus, in the South American waters off the
Mosquito shore.

My lady remarks to me, before I go any further, that there
is no such christian-name as Gill, and that her confident
opinion is, that the name given to me in the baptism wherein
I was made, &c., was Gilbert. She is certain to be right,
but I never heard of it. I was a foundling child, picked up
somewhere or another, and I always understood my christian-
name to be Gill. It is true that I was called Gills when
employed at Snorridge Bottom betwixt Chatham and Maidstone to frighten birds; but that had nothing to do with
the baptism wherein I was made, &c., and wherein a number
of things were promised for me by somebody, who let me
alone ever afterwards as to performing any of them, and who,
I consider, must have been the Beadle. Such name of Gills
was entirely owing to my cheeks, or gills, which at that time
of my life were of a raspy description.

My lady stops me again, before I go any further, by
laughing exactly in her old way and waving the feather of

her pen at me. That action on her part, calls to my mind as I look at her hand with the rings on it——Well! I won't! To be sure it will come in, in its own place. But it's always strange to me, noticing the quiet hand, and noticing it (as I have done, you know, so many times) a-fondling children and grandchildren asleep, to think that when blood and honour were up—there! I won't! not at present!—Scratch it out.

She won't scratch it out, and quite honourable; because we have made an understanding that everything is to be taken down, and that nothing that is once taken down shall be scratched out. I have the great misfortune not to be able to read and write, and I am speaking my true and faithful account of those Adventures, and my lady is writing it, word for word.

I say, there I was, a-leaning over the bulwarks of the sloop Christopher Columbus in the South American waters off the Mosquito shore: a subject of his Gracious Majesty King George of England, and a private in the Royal Marines.

In those climates, you don't want to do much. I was doing nothing. I was thinking of the shepherd (my father, I wonder?) on the hill-sides by Snorridge Bottom, with a long staff, and with a rough white coat in all weathers all the year round, who used to let me lie in a corner of his hut by night, and who used to let me go about with him and his sheep by day when I could get nothing else to do, and who used to give me so little of his victuals and so much of his staff, that I ran away from him—which was what he wanted all along, I expect—to be knocked about the world in preference to Snorridge Bottom. I had been knocked about the world for nine-and-twenty years in all, when I stood looking along those bright blue South American Waters. Looking after the shepherd, I may say. Watching him in a half-waking dream, with my eyes half-shut, as he, and his flock of sheep, and his two dogs, seemed to move away from the ship's side, far away over the blue water, and go right down into the sky.

"It's rising out of the water, steady," a voice said close to me. I had been thinking on so, that it like woke me with a start, though it was no stranger voice than the voice of Harry Charker, my own comrade.

"What's rising out of the water, steady?" I asked my comrade.

"What?" says he. "The Island."

"O! The Island!" says I, turning my eyes towards it. "True. I forgot the Island."

"Forgot the port you're going to? That's odd, ain't it?"

"It is odd," says I.

"And odd," he said, slowly considering with himself, "ain't even. Is it, Gill?"

He had always a remark just like that to make, and seldom another. As soon as he had brought a thing round to what it was not, he was satisfied. He was one of the best of men, and, in a certain sort of a way, one with the least to say for himself. I qualify it, because, besides being able to read and write like a Quarter-master, he had always one most excellent idea in his mind. That was, Duty. Upon my soul, I don't believe, though I admire learning beyond everything, that he could have got a better idea out of all the books in the world, if he had learnt them every word, and been the cleverest of scholars.

My comrade and I had been quartered in Jamaica, and from there we had been drafted off to the British settlement of Belize, lying away West and North of the Mosquito coast. At Belize there had been great alarm of one cruel gang of pirates (there were always more pirates than enough in those Caribbean Seas), and as they got the better of our English cruisers by running into out-of-the-way creeks and shallows, and taking the land when they were hotly pressed, the governor of Belize had received orders from home to keep a sharp look-out for them along shore. Now, there was an armed sloop came once a-year from Port Royal, Jamaica, to the Island, laden with all manner of necessaries, to eat, and to drink, and to wear, and to use in various ways; and it was aboard of that sloop which had touched at Belize, that I was a-standing, leaning over the bulwarks.

The Island was occupied by a very small English colony. It had been given the name of Silver-Store. The reason of its being so called, was, that the English colony owned and worked a silver mine over on the mainland, in Honduras, and used this Island as a safe and convenient place to store their silver in, until it was annually fetched away by the sloop. It was brought down from the mine to the coast on the backs of mules, attended by friendly Indians and guarded by white men; from thence it was conveyed over to Silver-Store, when the weather was fair, in the canoes of that country; from Silver-Store, it was carried to Jamaica by the armed sloop once a-year, as I have already mentioned ; from Jamaica, it went, of course, all over the world.

How I came to be aboard the armed sloop, is easily told. Four-and-twenty marines under command of a lieutenant— that officer's name was Linderwood—had been told off at Belize, to proceed to Silver-Store, in aid of boats and seamen stationed there for the chase of the Pirates. The Island was considered a good post of observation against the pirates, both by land and sea; neither the pirate ship nor yet her boats had been seen by any of us, but they had been so much heard of, that the reinforcement was sent. Of that party, I was one. It included a corporal and a sergeant. Charker was corporal, and the sergeant's name was Drooce. He was the most tyrannical non-commissioned officer in His Majesty's service.

The night came on, soon after I had had the foregoing words with Charker. All the wonderful bright colours went out of the sea and sky in a few minutes, and all the stars in the Heavens seemed to shine out together, and to look down at themselves in the sea, over one another's shoulders, millions deep. Next morning, we cast anchor off the Island. There was a snug harbour within a little reef; there was a sandy beach ; there were cocoa-nut trees with high straight stems, quite bare, and foliage at the top like plumes of magnificent green feathers ; there were all the objects that are usually seen in those parts, and I am not going to describe them, having something else to tell about.

Great rejoicings, to be sure, were made on our arrival. All the flags in the place were hoisted, all the guns in the place were fired, and all the people in the place came down to look at us. One of those Sambo fellows—they call those natives Sambos, when they are half-negro and half-Indian—had come off outside the reef, to pilot us in, and remained on board after we had let go our anchor. He was called Christian George King, and was fonder of all hands than anybody else was. Now, I confess, for myself, that on that first day, if I had been captain of the Christopher Columbus, instead of private in the Royal Marines, I should have kicked Christian George King—who was no more a Christian than he was a King or a George—over the side, without exactly knowing why, except that it was the right thing to do.

But, I must likewise confess, that I was not in a particularly pleasant humour, when I stood under arms that morning, aboard the Christopher Columbus in the harbour of the Island of Silver-Store. I had had a hard life, and the life of the English on the Island seemed too easy and too gay to please me. "Here you are," I thought to myself, "good scholars and good livers; able to read what you like, able to write what you like, able to eat and drink what you like, and spend what you like, and do what you like; and much *you* care for a poor, ignorant Private in the Royal Marines! Yet it's hard, too, I think, that you should have all the halfpence, and I all the kicks; you all the smooth, and I all the rough; you all the oil, and I all the vinegar." It was as envious a thing to think as might be, let alone its being nonsensical; but, I thought it. I took it so much amiss, that, when a very beautiful young English lady came aboard, I grunted to myself, "Ah! *you* have got a lover, I'll be bound!" As if there was any new offence to me in that, if she had!

She was sister to the captain of our sloop, who had been in a poor way for some time, and who was so ill then that he was obliged to be carried ashore. She was the child of a military officer, and had come out there with her sister, who was married to one of the owners of the silver mine, and who had three children with her. It was easy to see that she was the light and spirit of the Island. After I had got a good look at her, I grunted to myself again, in an even worse state of mind than before, "I'll be damned, if I don't hate him, whoever he is!"

My officer, Lieutenant Linderwood, was as ill as the captain of the sloop, and was carried ashore, too. They were both young men of about my age, who had been delicate in the West India climate. I even took *that* in bad part. I thought I was much fitter for the work than they were, and that if all of us had our deserts, I should be both of them rolled into one. (It may be imagined what sort of an officer of marines I should have made, without the power of reading a written order. And as to any knowledge how to command the sloop— Lord! I should have sunk her in a quarter of an hour!)

However, such were my reflections; and when we men were ashore and dismissed, I strolled about the place along with Charker, making my observations in a similar spirit.

It was a pretty place: in all its arrangements partly South American and partly English, and very agreeable to look at on that account, being like a bit of home that had got chipped off and had floated away to that spot, accommodating itself to circumstances as it drifted along. The huts of the Sambos, to the number of five-and-twenty, perhaps, were down by the beach to the left of the anchorage. On the right was a sort of barrack, with a South-American Flag and the Union Jack, flying from the same staff, where the little English colony could all come together, if they saw occasion. It was a walled square of building, with a sort of pleasure-ground inside, and inside that again a sunken block like a powder magazine, with a little square trench round it, and steps down to the door. Charker and I were looking in at the gate, which was not guarded; and I had said to Charker, in reference to the bit like a powder magazine, "That's where they keep the silver you see;" and Charker had said to me, after thinking it over, "And silver ain't gold. Is it, Gill?" when the beautiful young English lady I had been so bilious about, looked out of a door, or a window— at all events looked out, from under a bright awning. She no sooner saw us two in uniform, than she came out so quickly that she was still putting on her broad Mexican hat of plaited straw when we saluted.

"Would you like to come in," she said, "and see the place? It is rather a curious place."

We thanked the young lady, and said we didn't wish to be troublesome; but, she said it could be no trouble to an English soldier's daughter, to show English soldiers how their countrymen and countrywomen fared, so far away from England; and consequently we saluted again, and went in. Then, as we stood in the shade, she showed us (being as affable as beautiful), how the different families lived in their separate houses, and how there was a general house for stores, and a general reading-room, and a general room for music and dancing, and a room for Church; and how there were other houses on the rising ground called the Signal Hill, where they lived in the hotter weather.

"Your officer has been carried up there," she said, "and my brother, too, for the better air. At present, our few residents are dispersed over both spots: deducting, that is to say, such of our number as are always going to, or coming from, or staying at, the mine."

("*He* is among one of those parties," I thought, "and I wish somebody would knock his head off.")

"Some of our married ladies live here," she said, "during at least half the year, as lonely as widows, with their children."

" Many children here, ma'am ? "

" Seventeen.   There are thirteen married ladies, and there are eight like me."

There were not eight like her—there was not one like her —in the world.   She meant single.

" Which, with about thirty Englishmen of various degrees," said the young lady, " form the little colony now on the Island.   I don't count the sailors, for they don't belong to us.   Nor the soldiers," she gave us a gracious smile when she spoke of the soldiers, " for the same reason,"

" Nor the Sambos, ma'am," said I.

" No."

" Under your favour, and with your leave, ma'am," said I, " are they trustworthy ? "

" Perfectly !   We are all very kind to them, and they are very grateful to us."

" Indeed, ma'am ?   Now—Christian George King—— ? "

" Very much attached to us all.   Would die for us."

She was, as in my uneducated way I have observed very beautiful women almost always to be, so composed, that her composure gave great weight to what she said, and I believed it.

Then, she pointed out to us the building like a powder magazine, and explained to us in what manner the silver was brought from the mine, and was brought over from the mainland, and was stored there.   The Christopher Columbus would have a rich lading, she said, for there had been a great yield that year, a much richer yield than usual, and there was a chest of jewels besides the silver.

When we had looked about us, and were getting sheepish, through fearing we were troublesome, she turned us over to a young woman, English born but West-India bred, who served her as her maid.   This young woman was the widow of a non-commissioned officer in a regiment of the line.   She had got married and widowed at St. Vincent, with only a few months between the two events.   She was a little saucy woman, with a bright pair of eyes, rather a neat little foot and figure, and rather a neat little turned-up nose.   The sort of young woman, I considered at the time, who appeared to invite you to give her a kiss, and who would have slapped your face if you accepted the invitation.

I couldn't make out her name at first ; for, when she gave it in answer to my inquiry, it sounded like Belltott, which

G

didn't sound right. But, when we became better acquainted
—which was while Charker and I were drinking sugar-cane
sangaree, which she made in a most excellent manner—I
found that her Christian name was Isabella, which they
shortened into Bell, and that the name of the deceased non-
commissioned officer was Tott. Being the kind of neat little
woman it was natural to make a toy of—I never saw a woman
so like a toy in my life—she had got the plaything name of
Belltott. In short, she had no other name on the Island.
Even Mr. Commissioner Pordage (and *he* was a grave one!)
formally addressed her as Mrs. Belltott. But, I shall come
to Mr. Commissioner Pordage presently.

The name of the captain of the sloop was Captain Maryon,
and therefore it was no news to hear from Mrs. Belltott, that
his sister, the beautiful unmarried young English lady, was
Miss Maryon. The novelty was, that her Christian name was
Marion too. Marion Maryon. Many a time I have run off
those two names in my thoughts, like a bit of verse. Oh
many, and many, and many a time!

We saw out all the drink that was produced, like good
men and true, and then took our leaves, and went down to
the beach. The weather was beautiful; the wind steady, low,
and gentle; the Island, a picture; the sea, a picture; the
sky, a picture. In that country there are two rainy seasons
in the year. One sets in at about our English Midsummer;
the other, about a fortnight after our English Michaelmas.
It was the beginning of August at that time; the first of
these rainy seasons was well over; and everything was in its
most beautiful growth, and had its loveliest look upon it.

"They enjoy themselves here," I says to Charker, turning
surly again. "This is better than private-soldiering."

We had come down to the beach, to be friendly with the
boat's-crew who were camped and hutted there; and we were
approaching towards their quarters over the sand, when
Christian George King comes up from the landing-place at a
wolf's-trot, crying, "Yup, So-Jeer!"—which was that Sambo
Pilot's barbarous way of saying, Hallo, Soldier! I have
stated myself to be a man of no learning, and, if I entertain
prejudices, I hope allowance may be made. I will now confess
to one. It may be a right one or it may be a wrong one;
but, I never did like Natives, except in the form of oysters.

So, when Christian George King, who was individually
unpleasant to me besides, comes a trotting along the sand,

clucking, "Yup, So-Jeer!" I had a thundering good mind
to let fly at him with my right. I certainly should have
done it, but that it would have exposed me to reprimand.

"Yup, So-Jeer!" says he.   "Bad job."

"What do you mean?" says I.

"Yup, So-Jeer!" says he, "Ship Leakee."

"Ship leaky?" says I.

"Iss," says he, with a nod that looked as if it was jerked
out of him by a most violent hiccup—which is the way with
those savages.

I cast my eyes at Charker, and we both heard the pumps
going aboard the sloop, and saw the signal run up, "Come
on board; hands wanted from the shore." In no time some
of the sloop's liberty-men were already running down to the
water's edge, and the party of seamen, under orders against
the Pirates, were putting off to the Columbus in two boats.

"O Christian George King sar berry sorry!" says that
Sambo vagabond, then. "Christian George King cry, English fashion!" His English fashion of crying was to screw
his black knuckles into his eyes, howl like a dog, and roll himself on his back on the sand. It was trying not to kick him,
but I gave Charker the word, "Double-quick, Harry!" and
we got down to the water's edge, and got on board the
sloop.

By some means or other, she had sprung such a leak, that
no pumping would keep her free; and what between the two
fears that she would go down in the harbour, and that, even
if she did not, all the supplies she had brought for the little
colony would be destroyed by the sea-water as it rose in her,
there was great confusion. In the midst of it, Captain Maryon
was heard hailing from the beach. He had been carried down
in his hammock, and looked very bad; but he insisted on
being stood there on his feet; and I saw him, myself, come
off in the boat, sitting upright in the stern-sheets, as if
nothing was wrong with him.

A quick sort of council was held, and Captain Maryon soon
resolved that we must all fall to work to get the cargo out,
and that when that was done, the guns and heavy matters
must be got out, and that the sloop must be hauled ashore,
and careened, and the leak stopped. We were all mustered
(the Pirate-Chase party volunteering), and told off into parties,
with so many hours of spell and so many hours of relief, and
we all went at it with a will. Christian George King was

entered one of the party in which I worked, at his own request, and he went at it with as good a will as any of the rest. He went at it with so much heartiness, to say the truth, that he rose in my good opinion almost as fast as the water rose in the ship. Which was fast enough, and faster.

Mr. Commissioner Pordage kept in a red-and-black japanned box, like a family lump-sugar box, some document or other, which some Sambo chief or other had got drunk and spilt some ink over (as well as I could understand the matter), and by that means had given up lawful possession of the Island. Through having hold of this box, Mr. Pordage got his title of Commissioner. He was styled Consul too, and spoke of himself as "Government."

He was a stiff-jointed, high-nosed old gentleman, without an ounce of fat on him, of a very angry temper and a very yellow complexion. Mrs. Commissioner Pordage, making allowance for difference of sex, was much the same. Mr. Kitten, a small, youngish, bald, botanical and mineralogical gentleman, also connected with the mine—but everybody there was that, more or less—was sometimes called by Mr. Commissioner Pordage, his Vice-commissioner, and sometimes his Deputy-consul. Or sometimes he spoke of Mr. Kitten, merely as being "under Government."

The beach was beginning to be a lively scene with the preparations for careening the sloop, and, with cargo, and spars, and rigging, and water-casks, dotted about it, and with temporary quarters for the men rising up there out of such sails and odds and ends as could be best set on one side to make them, when Mr. Commissioner Pordage comes down in a high fluster, and asks for Captain Maryon. The Captain, ill as he was, was slung in his hammock betwixt two trees, that he might direct; and he raised his head, and answered for himself.

"Captain Maryon," cries Mr. Commissioner Pordage, "this is not official. This is not regular."

"Sir," says the Captain, "it hath been arranged with the clerk and supercargo, that you should be communicated with, and requested to render any little assistance that may lie in your power. I am quite certain that hath been duly done."

"Captain Maryon," replies Mr. Commissioner Pordage, "there hath been no written correspondence. No documents have passed, no memoranda have been made, no minutes have been made, no entries and counter-entries appear in the official muniments. This is indecent. I call upon you, Sir, to desist, until all is regular, or Government will take this up."

"Sir," says Captain Maryon, chafing a little, as he looked out of his hammock; "between the chances of Government taking this up, and my ship taking herself down, I much prefer to trust myself to the former."

"You do, Sir?" cries Mr. Commissioner Pordage.

"I do, Sir," says Captain Maryon, lying down again.

"Then, Mr. Kitten," says the Commissioner, "send up instantly for my Diplomatic coat."

He was dressed in a linen suit at that moment; but, Mr. Kitten started off himself and brought down the Diplomatic coat, which was a blue cloth one, gold-laced, and with a crown on the button.

"Now, Mr. Kitten," says Pordage, "I instruct you, as Vice-commissioner, and Deputy-consul of this place, to demand of Captain Maryon, of the sloop Christopher Columbus, whether he drives me to the act of putting this coat on?"

"Mr. Pordage," says Captain Maryon, looking out of his hammock again, "as I can hear what you say, I can answer it without troubling the gentleman. I should be sorry that you should be at the pains of putting on too hot a coat on my account; but, otherwise, you may put it on hind-side before, or inside-out, or with your legs in the sleeves, or your head in the skirts, for any objection that I have to offer to your thoroughly pleasing yourself."

"Very good, Captain Maryon," says Pordage, in a tremendous passion. "Very good, Sir. Be the consequences on your own head! Mr. Kitten, as it has come to this, help me on with it."

When he had given that order, he walked off in the coat, and all our names were taken, and I was afterwards told that Mr. Kitten wrote from his dictation more than a bushel of large paper on the subject, which cost more before it was done with, than ever could be calculated, and which only got done with after all, by being lost.

Our work went on merrily, nevertheless, and the Christopher Columbus, hauled up, lay helpless on her side like a great fish out of water. While she was in that state, there was a feast, or a ball, or an entertainment, or more properly all three together, given us in honour of the ship, and the ship's company, and the other visitors. At that assembly, I believe, I saw all the inhabitants then upon the Island, without any exception. I took no particular notice of more than a few, but I found it very agreeable in that little corner of the world to see the children, who were of all ages, and mostly very pretty—as they mostly are. There was one handsome elderly lady, with very dark eyes and grey hair, that I inquired about. I was told that her name was Mrs. Venning; and her married daughter, a fair slight thing, was pointed out to me by the name of Fanny Fisher. Quite a child she looked, with a little copy of herself holding to her dress; and her husband, just come back from the mine, exceeding proud of her. They were a good-looking set of people on the whole, but I didn't like them. I was out of sorts; in conversation with Charker, I found fault with all of them. I said of Mrs. Venning, she was proud; of Mrs. Fisher, she was a delicate little baby-fool. What did I think of this one? Why, he was a fine gentleman. What did I say to that one? Why, she was a fine lady. What could you expect them to be (I asked Charker), nursed in that climate, with the tropical night shining for them, musical instruments playing to them, great trees bending over them, soft lamps lighting them, fire-flies sparkling in among them, bright flowers and birds brought into existence to please their eyes, delicious drinks to be had for the pouring out, delicious fruits to be got for the picking, and every one dancing and murmuring happily in the scented air, with the sea breaking low on the reef for a pleasant chorus.

"Fine gentlemen and fine ladies, Harry?" I says to Charker. "Yes, I think so! Dolls! Dolls! Not the sort of stuff for wear, that comes of poor private-soldiering in the Royal Marines!"

However, I could not gainsay that they were very hospitable people, and that they treated us uncommonly well. Every man of us was at the entertainment, and Mrs. Belltott had more partners than she could dance with: though she danced all night, too. As to Jack (whether of the Christopher Columbus, or of the Pirate pursuit party, it made no difference), he danced with his brother Jack, danced with himself, danced with the moon, the stars, the trees, the prospect, anything. I didn't greatly take to the chief-officer of that party, with his bright eyes, brown face, and easy figure. I didn't much like his way when he first happened to come where we were, with Miss Maryon on his arm. "O, Captain Carton," she says, "here are two friends of mine!" He says, "Indeed? These two Marines?"—meaning Charker and self. "Yes," says she, "I showed these two friends of mine when they first came, all the wonders of Silver-Store." He gave us a laughing look, and says he, "You are in luck, men. I would be disrated and go before the mast to-morrow, to be shown the way upward again by such a guide. You are in luck, men." When we had saluted, and he and the lady had waltzed away, I said, "You are a pretty fellow, too, to talk of luck. You may go to the Devil!"

Mr. Commissioner Pordage and Mrs. Commissioner, showed among the company on that occasion like the King and Queen of a much Greater Britain than Great Britain. Only two other circumstances in that jovial night made much separate impression on me. One was this. A man in our draft of marines, named Tom Packer, a wild unsteady young fellow, but the son of a respectable shipwright in Portsmouth Yard, and a good scholar who had been well brought up, comes to me after a spell of dancing, and takes me aside by the elbow, and says, swearing angrily :

"Gill Davis, I hope I may not be the death of Sergeant Drooce one day!"

Now, I knew Drooce had always borne particularly hard on this man, and I knew this man to be of a very hot temper: so, I said :

"Tut, nonsense! don't talk so to me! If there's a man in the corps who scorns the name of an assassin, that man and Tom Packer are one."

Tom wipes his head, being in a mortal sweat, and says he :

"I hope so, but I can't answer for myself when he lords it over me, as he has just now done, before a woman. I tell you what, Gill! Mark my words! It will go hard with Sergeant Drooce, if ever we are in an engagement together, and he has to look to me to save him. Let him say a prayer then, if he knows one, for it's all over with him, and he is on his deathbed. Mark my words!"

I did mark his words, and very soon afterwards, too, as will shortly be taken down.

The other circumstance that I noticed at that ball, was, the gaiety and attachment of Christian George King. The innocent spirits that Sambo Pilot was in, and the impossibility he found himself under of showing all the little colony, but especially the ladies and children, how fond he was of them, how devoted to them, and how faithful to them for life and death, for present, future, and everlasting, made a great impression on me. If ever a man, Sambo or no Sambo, was trustful and trusted, to what may be called quite an infantine and sweetly beautiful extent, surely, I thought that morning when I did at last lie down to rest, it was that Sambo Pilot, Christian George King.

This may account for my dreaming of him. He stuck in my sleep. cornerwise, and I couldn't get him out. He was always flitting about me, dancing round me, and peeping in over my hammock, though I woke and dozed off again fifty times. At last, when I opened my eyes, there he really was, looking in at the open side of the little dark hut; which was made of leaves, and had Charker's hammock slung in it as well as mine.

"So-Jeer!" says he, in a sort of a low croak. "Yup!"

"Hallo!" says I, starting up. "What? You *are* there, are you?"

"Iss," says he. "Christian George King got news."

"What news has he got?"

"Pirates out!"

I was on my feet in a second. So was Charker. We were both aware that Captain Carton, in command of the boats, constantly watched the mainland for a secret signal, though, of course, it was not known to such as us what the signal was.

Christian George King had vanished before we touched the ground. But, the word was already passing from hut to hut to turn out quietly, and we knew that the nimble barbarian had got hold of the truth, or something near it.

In a space among the trees behind the encampment of us visitors, naval and military, was a snugly-screened spot, where we kept the stores that were in use, and did our cookery. The word was passed to assemble here. It was very quickly given, and was given (so far as we were concerned) by Sergeant Drooce, who was as good in a soldier point of view, as he was bad in a tyrannical one. We were ordered to drop into this space, quietly, behind the trees, one by one. As we assembled here, the seamen assembled too. Within ten minutes, as I should estimate, we were all here, except the usual guard upon the beach. The beach (we could see it through the wood) looked as it always had done in the hottest time of the day. The guard were in the shadow of the sloop's hull, and nothing was moving but the sea, and that moved very faintly. Work had always been knocked off at that hour, until the sun grew less fierce, and the sea-breeze rose; so that its being holiday with us, made no difference, just then, in the look of the place. But I may mention that it was a holiday, and the first we had had since our hard work began. Last night's ball had been given, on the leak's being repaired, and the careening done. The worst of the work was over, and to-morrow we were to begin to get the sloop afloat again.

We marines were now drawn up here under arms. The chase-party were drawn up separate. The men of the Columbus were drawn up separate. The officers stepped out into the midst of the three parties, and spoke so as all might hear. Captain Carton was the officer in command, and he had a spy-glass in his hand. His coxswain stood by him with another spy-glass, and with a slate on which he seemed to have been taking down signals.

"Now, men!" says Captain Carton; "I have to let you know, for your satisfaction: Firstly, that there are ten pirate-boats, strongly manned and armed, lying hidden up a creek yonder on the coast, under the overhanging branches of the dense trees. Secondly, that they will certainly come out this night when the moon rises, on a pillaging and murdering expedition, of which some part of the mainland is the object. Thirdly—don't cheer, men!—that we will give chase, and, if we can get at them, rid the world of them, please God!"

Nobody spoke, that I heard, and nobody moved, that I saw. Yet there was a kind of ring, as if every man answered and approved with the best blood that was inside of him.

"Sir," says Captain Maryon, "I beg to volunteer on this service, with my boats. My people volunteer, to the ship's boys."

"In His Majesty's name and service," the other answers, touching his hat, "I accept your aid with pleasure. Lieutenant Linderwood, how will you divide your men?"

I was ashamed—I give it out to be written down as large and plain as possible—I was heart and soul ashamed of my thoughts of those two sick officers, Captain Maryon and Lieutenant Linderwood, when I saw them, then and there. The spirit in those two gentlemen beat down their illness (and very ill I knew them to be) like Saint George beating down the Dragon. Pain and weakness, want of ease and want of rest, had no more place in their minds than fear itself. Meaning now to express for my lady to write down, exactly what I felt then and there, I felt this: "You two brave fellows that I had been so grudgeful of, I know that if you were dying you would put it off to get up and do your best, and then you would be so modest that in lying down again to die, you would hardly say, 'I did it!'"

It did me good. It really did me good.

But, to go back to where I broke off. Says Captain Carton to Lieutenant Linderwood, "Sir, how will you divide your men? There is not room for all; and a few men should, in any case, be left here."

There was some debate about it. At last, it was resolved to leave eight Marines and four seamen on the Island, besides the sloop's two boys. And because it was considered that the friendly Sambos would only want to be commanded in case of any danger (though none at all was apprehended there), the officers were in favour of leaving the two non-commissioned officers, Drooce and Charker. It was a heavy disappointment to them, just as my being one of the left was a heavy disappointment to me—then, but not soon afterwards. We men drew lots for it, and I drew "Island." So did Tom Packer. So, of course, did four more of our rank and file.

When this was settled, verbal instructions were given to all hands to keep the intended expedition secret, in order that the women and children might not be alarmed, or the expedition put in a difficulty by more volunteers. The assembly was to be on that same spot at sunset. Every man was to keep up an appearance, meanwhile, of occupying himself in his usual way. That is to say, every man excepting four old trusty seamen, who were appointed, with an officer, to see to the arms and ammunition, and to muffle the rullocks of the boats, and to make everything as trim and swift and silent as it could be made.

The Sambo Pilot had been present all the while, in case of his being wanted, and had said to the officer in command, five hundred times over if he had said it once, that Christian George King would stay with the So-Jeers, and take care of the booffer ladies and the booffer childs—booffer being that native's expression for beautiful. He was now asked a few questions concerning the putting off of the boats, and in particular whether there was any way of embarking at the back of the Island: which Captain Carton would have half liked to do, and then have dropped round in its shadow and slanted across to the main. But, "No," says Christian George

King. "No, no, no! Told you so, ten time. No, no, no! All reef, all rock, all swim, all drown!" Striking out as he said it, like a swimmer gone mad, and turning over on his back on dry land, and spluttering himself to death, in a manner that made him quite an exhibition.

The sun went down, after appearing to be a long time about it, and the assembly was called. Every man answered to his name, of course, and was at his post. It was not yet black dark, and the roll was only just gone through, when up comes Mr. Commissioner Pordage with his Diplomatic coat on.

"Captain Carton," says he, "Sir, what is this?"

"This, Mr. Commissioner" (he was very short with him), "is an expedition against the Pirates. It is a secret expedition, so please to keep it a secret."

"Sir," says Commissioner Pordage, "I trust there is going to be no unnecessary cruelty committed?"

"Sir," returns the officer, "I trust not."

"That is not enough, Sir," cries Commissioner Pordage, getting wroth. "Captain Carton, I give you notice. Government requires you to treat the enemy with great delicacy, consideration, clemency, and forbearance."

"Sir," says Captain Carton, "I am an English officer, commanding English Men, and I hope I am not likely to disappoint the Government's just expectations. But, I presume you know that these villains under their black flag have despoiled our countrymen of their property, burnt their homes, barbarously murdered them and their little children, and worse than murdered their wives and daughters?"

"Perhaps I do, Captain Carton," answers Pordage, waving his hand, with dignity; "perhaps I do not. It is not customary, Sir, for Government to commit itself."

"It matters very little, Mr. Pordage, whether or no. Believing that I hold my commission by the allowance of God, and not that I have received it direct from the Devil, I shall certainly use it, with all avoidance of unnecessary suffering and with all merciful swiftness of execution, to exterminate these people from the face of the earth. Let me recommend you to go home, Sir, and to keep out of the night-air."

Never another syllable did that officer say to the Commissioner, but turned away to his men. The Commissioner buttoned his Diplomatic coat to the chin, said, "Mr. Kitten, attend me!" gasped, half choked himself, and took himself off.

It now fell very dark, indeed. I have seldom, if ever, seen it darker, nor yet so dark. The moon was not due until one in the morning, and it was but a little after nine when our men lay down where they were mustered. It was pretended that they were to take a nap, but everybody knew that no nap was to be got under the circumstances. Though all were very quiet, there was a restlessness among the people; much what I have seen among the people on a race-course, when the bell has rung for the saddling for a great race with large stakes on it.

At ten, they put off; only one boat putting off at a time; another following in five minutes; both then lying on their oars until another followed. Ahead of all, paddling his own outlandish little canoe without a sound, went the Sambo pilot, to take them safely outside the reef. No light was shown but once, and that was in the commanding officer's own hand. I lighted the dark lantern for him, and he took it from me when he embarked. They had blue-lights and such like with them, but kept themselves as dark as Murder.

The expedition got away with wonderful quietness, and Christian George King soon came back dancing with joy.

"Yup, So-Jeer," says he to myself in a very objectionable kind of convulsions, "Christian George King sar berry glad. Pirates all be blown a-pieces. Yup! Yup!"

My reply to that cannibal was, "However glad you may be, hold your noise, and don't dance jigs and slap your knees about it, for I can't abear to see you do it."

I was on duty then; we twelve who were left being divided into four watches of three each, three hours' spell. I was relieved at twelve. A little before that time, I had challenged, and Miss Maryon and Mrs. Belltott had come in.

"Good Davis," says Miss Maryon, "what is the matter? Where is my brother?"

I told her what was the matter, and where her brother was.

"O Heaven help him!" says she, clasping her hands and looking up—she was close in front of me, and she looked most lovely to be sure; "he is not sufficiently recovered, not strong enough for such strife!"

"If you had seen him, miss," I told her, "as I saw him when he volunteered, you would have known that his spirit is strong enough for any strife. It will bear his body, miss, to wherever duty calls him. It will always bear him to an honourable life, or a brave death."

"Heaven bless you!" says she, touching my arm. "I know it. Heaven bless you!"

Mrs. Belltott surprised me by trembling and saying nothing. They were still standing looking towards the sea and listening, after the relief had come round. It continuing very dark, I asked to be allowed to take them back. Miss Maryon thanked me, and she put her arm in mine, and I did take them back. I have now got to make a confession that will appear singular. After I had left them, I laid myself down on my face on the beach, and cried for the first time since I had frightened birds as a boy at Snorridge Bottom, to think what a poor, ignorant, low-placed, private soldier I was.

It was only for half a minute or so. A man can't at all times be quite master of himself, and it was only for half a minute or so. Then I up and went to my hut, and turned into my hammock, and fell asleep with wet eyelashes, and a sore, sore heart. Just as I had often done when I was a child, and had been worse used than usual.

I slept (as a child under those circumstances might) very sound, and yet very sore at heart all through my sleep. I was awoke by the words, "He is a determined man." I had sprung out of my hammock, and had seized my firelock, and was standing on the ground, saying the words myself. "He is a determined man." But, the curiosity of my state was, that I seemed to be repeating them after somebody, and to have been wonderfully startled by hearing them.

As soon as I came to myself, I went out of the hut, and away to where the guard was. Charker challenged:

"Who goes there?"

"A friend."

"Not Gill?" says he, as he shouldered his piece.

"Gill," says I.

"Why, what the deuce do you do out of your hammock?" says he.

"Too hot for sleep," says I; "is all right?"

"Right!" says Charker, "yes, yes; all's right enough here; what should be wrong here? It's the boats that we want to know of. Except for fire-flies twinkling about, and the lonesome splashes of great creatures as they drop into the water, there's nothing going on here to ease a man's mind from the boats."

The moon was above the sea, and had risen, I should say,

some half-an-hour. As Charker spoke, with his face towards
the sea, I, looking landward, suddenly laid my right hand
on his breast, and said, "Don't move. Don't turn. Don't
raise your voice! You never saw a Maltese face here?"

"No. What do you mean?" he asks, staring at me.

"Nor yet an English face, with one eye and a patch across
the nose?"

"No. What ails you? What do you mean?"

I had seen both, looking at us round the stem of a cocoa-
nut tree, where the moon struck them. I had seen that
Sambo Pilot, with one hand laid on the stem of the tree,
drawing them back into the heavy shadow. I had seen their
naked cutlasses twinkle and shine, like bits of the moonshine
in the water that had got blown ashore among the trees by
the light wind. I had seen it all, in a moment. And I
saw in a moment (as any man would), that the signalled
move of the pirates on the mainland was a plot and a feint;
that the leak had been made to disable the sloop; that the
boats had been tempted away, to leave the Island unprotected;
that the pirates had landed by some secreted way at the
back; and that Christian George King was a double-dyed
traitor and a most infernal villain.

I considered, still all in one and the same moment, that
Charker was a brave man, but not quick with his head; and
that Sergeant Drooce, with a much better head, was close
by. All I said to Charker was, "I am afraid we are betrayed.
Turn your back full to the moonlight on the sea, and cover
the stem of the cocoa-nut tree which will then be right before
you, at the height of a man's heart. Are you right?"

"I am right," says Charker, turning instantly, and falling
into the position with a nerve of iron; "and right ain't left.
Is it, Gill?"

A few seconds brought me to Sergeant Drooce's hut. He
was fast asleep, and being a heavy sleeper, I had to lay my
hand upon him to rouse him. The instant I touched him
he came rolling out of his hammock, and upon me like a
tiger. And a tiger he was, except that he knew what he
was up to, in his utmost heat, as well as any man.

I had to struggle with him pretty hard to bring him to
his senses, panting all the while (for he gave me a breather),
"Sergeant, I am Gill Davis! Treachery! Pirates on the
Island!"

The last words brought him round, and he took his hands

off. "I have seen two of them within this minute," said I. And so I told him what I had told Harry Charker.

His soldierly, though tyrannical, head was clear in an instant. He didn't waste one word, even of surprise. "Order the guard," says he, "to draw off quietly into the Fort." (They called the enclosure I have before mentioned, the Fort, though it was not much of that.) ˙ "Then get you to the Fort as quick as you can, rouse up every soul there, and fasten the gate. I will bring in all those who are up at the Signal Hill. If we are surrounded before we can join you, you must make a sally and cut us out if you can. The word among our men is, 'Women and children!'"

He burst away, like fire going before the wind over dry reeds. He roused up the seven men who were off duty, and had them bursting away with him, before they knew they were not asleep. I reported orders to Charker, and ran to the Fort, as I have never run at any other time in all my life: no, not even in a dream.

The gate was not fast, and had no good fastening: only a double wooden bar, a poor chain, and a bad lock. Those, I secured as well as they could be secured in a few seconds by one pair of hands, and so ran to that part of the building where Miss Maryon lived. I called to her loudly by her name until she answered. I then called loudly all the names I knew—Mrs. Macey (Miss Maryon's married sister), Mr. Macey, Mrs. Venning, Mr. and Mrs. Fisher, even Mr. and Mrs. Pordage. Then I called out, "All you gentlemen here, get up and defend the place! We are caught in a trap. Pirates have landed. We are attacked!"

At the terrible word "Pirates!"—for, those villains had done such deeds in those seas as never can be told in writing, and can scarcely be so much as thought of—cries and screams rose up from every part of the place. Quickly lights moved about from window to window, and the cries moved about with them, and men, women, and children came flying down into the square. I remarked to myself, even then, what a number of things I seemed to see at once. I noticed Mrs. Macey coming towards me, carrying all her three children together. I noticed Mr. Pordage in the greatest terror, in vain trying to get on his Diplomatic coat; and Mr. Kitten respectfully tying his pocket-handkerchief over Mrs. Pordage's nightcap. I noticed Mrs. Belltott run out screaming, and shrink upon the ground near me, and cover her face in her hands, and lie all of a bundle, shivering. But, what I noticed with the greatest pleasure was, the determined eyes with which those men of the Mine that I had thought fine gentlemen, came round me with what arms they had: to the full as cool and resolute as I could be, for my life—ay, and for my soul, too, into the bargain!

The chief person being Mr. Macey, I told him how the three men of the guard would be at the gate directly, if they were not already there, and how Sergeant Drooce and the other seven were gone to bring in the outlying part of the people of Silver-Store. I next urged him, for the love of all who were dear to him, to trust no Sambo, and, above all, if he could get any good chance at Christian George King, not to lose it, but to put him out of the world.

"I will follow your advice to the letter, Davis," says he; "what next?"

My answer was, "I think, Sir, I would recommend you next, to order down such heavy furniture and lumber as can be moved, and make a barricade within the gate."

"That's good again," says he: "will you see it done?"

"I'll willingly help to do it," says I, "unless or until my superior, Sergeant Drooce, gives me other orders."

He shook me by the hand, and having told off some of his companions to help me, bestirred himself to look to the arms and ammunition. A proper quick, brave, steady, ready gentleman!

One of their three little children was deaf and dumb. Miss Maryon had been from the first with all the children, soothing them, and dressing them (poor little things, they had been brought out of their beds), and making them believe that it was a game of play, so that some of them were now even laughing. I had been working hard with the others at the barricade, and had got up a pretty good breastwork within the gate. Drooce and the seven had come back, bringing in the people from the Signal Hill, and had worked along with us: but, I had not so much as spoken a word to Drooce, nor had Drooce so much as spoken a word to me, for we were both too busy. The breastwork was now finished, and I found Miss Maryon at my side, with a child in her arms. Her dark hair was fastened round her head with a band. She had a quantity of it, and it looked even richer and more precious, put up hastily out of her way, than

I had seen it look when it was carefully arranged. She was very pale, but extraordinarily quiet and still.

"Dear good Davis," said she, "I have been waiting to speak one word to you."

I turned to her directly. If I had received a musket-ball in the heart, and she had stood there, I almost believe I should have turned to her before I dropped.

"This pretty little creature," said she, kissing the child in her arms, who was playing with her hair and trying to pull it down, "cannot hear what we say—can hear nothing. I trust you so much, and have such great confidence in you, that I want you to make me a promise."

"What is it, Miss?"

"That if we are defeated, and you are absolutely sure of my being taken, you will kill me."

"I shall not be alive to do it, Miss. I shall have died in your defence before it comes to that. They must step across my body to lay a hand on you."

"But, if you are alive, you brave soldier." How she looked at me! "And if you cannot save me from the Pirates, living, you will save me, dead. Tell me so."

Well! I told her I would do that at the last, if all else failed. She took my hand—my rough, coarse hand—and put it to her lips. She put it to the child's lips, and the child kissed it. I believe I had the strength of half-a-dozen men in me, from that moment, until the fight was over.

All this time, Mr. Commissioner Pordage had been wanting to make a Proclamation to the Pirates to lay down their arms and go away; and everybody had been hustling him about and tumbling over him, while he was calling for pen and ink to write it with. Mrs. Pordage, too, had some curious ideas about the British respectability of her nightcap (which had as many frills to it, growing in layers one inside another, as if it was a white vegetable of the artichoke sort), and she wouldn't take the nightcap off, and would be angry when it got crushed by the other ladies who were handing things about, and, in short, she gave as much trouble as her husband did. But, as we were now forming for the defence of the place, they were both poked out of the way with no ceremony. The children and ladies were got into the little trench which surrounded the silver-house (we were afraid of leaving them in any of the light buildings, lest they should be set on fire), and we made the best disposition we could.

There was a pretty good store, in point of amount, of tolerable swords and cutlasses. Those were issued. There were, also, perhaps a score or so of spare muskets. Those were brought out. To my astonishment, little Mrs. Fisher that I had taken for a doll and a baby, was not only very active in that service, but volunteered to load the spare arms.

"For, I understand it well," says she, cheerfully, without a shake in her voice.

"I am a soldier's daughter and a sailor's sister, and I understand it too," says Miss Maryon, just in the same way.

Steady and busy behind where I stood, those two beautiful and delicate young women fell to handling the guns, hammering the flints, looking to the locks, and quietly directing others to pass up powder and bullets from hand to hand, as unflinching as the best of tried soldiers.

Sergeant Drooce had brought in word that the Pirates were very strong in numbers—over a hundred was his estimate—and that they were not, even then, all landed ; for, he had seen them in a very good position on the further side of the Signal Hill, evidently waiting for the rest of their men to come up. In the present pause, the first we had had since the alarm, he was telling this over again to Mr. Macey, when Mr. Macey suddenly cried out : "The signal ! Nobody has thought of the signal !"

We knew of no signal, so we could not have thought of it.

"What signal may you mean, Sir ?" says Sergeant Drooce, looking sharp at him.

"There is a pile of wood upon the Signal Hill. If it could be lighted—which never has been done yet—it would be a signal of distress to the mainland."

Charker cries, directly : "Sergeant Drooce, dispatch me on that duty. Give me the two men who were on guard with me to-night, and I'll light the fire, if it can be done."

"And if it can't, Corporal—— " Mr. Macey strikes in.

"Look at these ladies and children, Sir !" says Charker. "I'd sooner *light myself*, than not try any chance to save them."

We gave him a Hurrah !—it burst from us, come of it what might—and he got his two men, and was let out at the gate, and crept away. I had no sooner come back to my place from being one of the party to handle the gate, than Miss Maryon said in a low voice behind me :

"Davis, will you look at this powder ? This is not right."

I turned my head. Christian George King again, and treachery again! Sea-water had been conveyed into the magazine, and every grain of powder was spoiled!

"Stay a moment," said Sergeant Drooce, when I had told him, without causing a movement in a muscle of his face: "look to your pouch, my lad. You Tom Packer, look to your pouch, confound you! Look to your pouches, all you Marines."

The same artful savage had got at them, somehow or another, and the cartridges were all unserviceable. "Hum!" says the Sergeant. "Look to your loading, men. You are right so far?"

Yes; we were right so far.

"Well, my lads, and gentlemen all," says the Sergeant, "this will be a hand-to-hand affair, and so much the better."

He treated himself to a pinch of snuff, and stood up, square-shouldered and broad-chested, in the light of the moon—which was now very bright—as cool as if he was waiting for a play to begin. He stood quiet, and we all stood quiet, for a matter of something like half an hour. I took notice from such whispered talk as there was, how little we that the silver did not belong to, thought about it, and how much the people that it did belong to, thought about it. At the end of the half hour, it was reported from the gate that Charker and the two were falling back on us, pursued by about a dozen.

"Sally! Gate-party, under Gill Davis," says the Sergeant, "and bring 'em in! Like men, now!"

We were not long about it, and we brought them in. "Don't take me," says Charker, holding me round the neck, and stumbling down at my feet when the gate was fast, "don't take me near the ladies or the children, Gill. They had better not see Death, till it can't be helped. They'll see it soon enough."

"Harry!" I answered, holding up his head. "Comrade!"

He was cut to pieces. The signal had been secured by the first pirate party that landed; his hair was all singed off, and his face was blackened with the running pitch from a torch.

He made no complaint of pain, or of anything. "Good-bye, old chap," was all he said, with a smile. "I've got my death. And Death ain't life. Is it, Gill?"

Having helped to lay his poor body on one side, I went back to my post. Sergeant Drooce looked at me, with his eyebrows a little lifted. I nodded. "Close up here men, and gentlemen all!" said the Sergeant. "A place too many, in the line."

The Pirates were so close upon us at this time, that the foremost of them were already before the gate. More and more came up with a great noise, and shouting loudly. When we believed from the sound that they were all there, we gave three English cheers. The poor little children joined, and were so fully convinced of our being at play, that they enjoyed the noise, and were heard clapping their hands in the silence that followed.

Our disposition was this, beginning with the rear. Mrs. Venning, holding her daughter's child in her arms, sat on the steps of the little square trench surrounding the silver-house, encouraging and directing those women and children as she might have done in the happiest and easiest time of her life. Then, there was an armed line, under Mr. Macey, across the width of the enclosure, facing that way and having their backs towards the gate, in order that they might watch the walls and prevent our being taken by surprise. Then there was a space of eight or ten feet deep, in which the spare arms were, and in which Miss Maryon and Mrs. Fisher, their hands and dresses blackened with the spoilt gunpowder, worked on their knees, tying such things as knives, old bayonets, and spear-heads, to the muzzles of the useless muskets. Then, there was a second armed line, under Sergeant Drooce, also across the width of the enclosure, but facing to the gate. Then came the breastwork we had made, with a zig-zag way through it for me and my little party to hold good in retreating, as long as we could, when we were driven from the gate. We all knew that it was impossible to hold the place long, and that our only hope was in the timely discovery of the plot by the boats, and in their coming back.

I and my men were now thrown forward to the gate. From a spy-hole, I could see the whole crowd of Pirates. There were Malays among them, Dutch, Maltese, Greeks, Sambos, Negroes, and Convict Englishmen from the West India Islands; among the last, him with the one eye and the patch across the nose. There were some Portuguese, too, and a few Spaniards. The captain was a Portuguese; a little man with very large earrings under a very broad hat, and a great bright shawl twisted about his shoulders. They were all strongly armed, but like a boarding party, with pikes, swords, cutlasses, and axes. I noticed a good many pistols, but not a gun of any kind among them. This gave me to understand that they had considered that a continued roll of musketry might perhaps have been heard on the mainland; also, that for the reason that fire would be seen from the mainland they would not set the Fort in flames and roast us alive; which was one of their favourite ways of carrying on. I looked about for Christian George King, and if I had seen him I am much mistaken if he would not have received my one round of ball-cartridge in his head. But, no Christian George King was visible.

A sort of a wild Portuguese demon, who seemed either fierce-mad or fierce-drunk—but, they all seemed one or the other—came forward with the black flag, and gave it a wave or two. After that, the Portuguese captain called out in shrill English, "I say you! English fools! Open the gate! Surrender!

As we kept close and quiet, he said something to his men which I didn't understand, and when he had said it, the one-eyed English rascal with the patch (who had stepped out when he began), said it again in English. It was only this. "Boys of the black flag, this is to be quickly done. Take all the prisoners you can. If they don't yield, kill the children to make them. Forward!" Then, they all came on at the gate, and, in another half minute were smashing and splitting it in.

We struck at them through the gaps and shivers, and we dropped many of them, too; but, their very weight would have carried such a gate, if they had been unarmed. I soon found Sergeant Drooce at my side, forming us six remaining marines in line—Tom Packer next to me—and ordering us to fall back three paces, and, as they broke in, to give them our one little volley at short distance. "Then," says he, "receive them behind your breastwork on the bayonet, and at least let every man of you pin one of the cursed cockchafers through the body."

We checked them by our fire, slight as it was, and we checked them at the breastwork. However, they broke over it like swarms of devils—they were, really and truly, more devils than men—and then it was hand to hand, indeed.

We clubbed our muskets and laid about us; even then, those two ladies—always behind me—were steady and ready with the arms. I had a lot of Maltese and Malays upon me, and, but for a broadsword that Miss Maryon's own hand put in mine, should have got my end from them. But, was that all? No. I saw a heap of banded dark hair and a white dress come thrice between me and them, under my own raised right arm, which each time might have destroyed the wearer of the white dress; and each time one of the lot went down, struck dead.

Drooce was armed with a broadsword, too, and did such things with it, that there was a cry, in half-a-dozen languages, of "Kill that sergeant!" as I knew, by the cry being raised in English, and taken up in other tongues. I had received a severe cut across the left arm a few moments before, and should have known nothing of it, except supposing that somebody had struck me a smart blow, if I had not felt weak, and seen myself covered with spouting blood, and, at the same instant of time, seen Miss Maryon tearing her dress and binding it with Mrs. Fisher's help round the wound. They called to Tom Packer, who was scouring by, to stop and guard me for one minute, while I was bound, or I should bleed to death in trying to defend myself. Tom stopped directly, with a good sabre in his hand.

In that same moment—all things seem to happen in that same moment, at such a time—half-a-dozen had rushed howling at Sergeant Drooce. The Sergeant, stepping back against the wall, stopped one howl for ever with such a terrible blow, and waited for the rest to come on, with such a wonderfully unmoved face, that they stopped and looked at him.

"See him now!" cried Tom Packer. "Now, when I could cut him out! Gill! Did I tell you to mark my words?"

I implored Tom Packer in the Lord's name, as well as I could in my faintness, to go to the Sergeant's aid.

"I hate and detest him," says Tom, moodily wavering. "Still, he is a brave man." Then he calls out, "Sergeant Drooce, Sergeant Drooce! Tell me you have driven me too hard, and are sorry for it."

The Sergeant, without turning his eyes from his assailants, which would have been instant death to him, answers:

"No. I won't."

"Sergeant Drooce!" cries Tom, in a kind of an agony. "I have passed my word that I would never save you from Death, if I could, but would leave you to die. Tell me you have driven me too hard and are sorry for it, and that shall go for nothing."

One of the group laid the Sergeant's bald bare head open. The Sergeant laid him dead.

"I tell you," says the Sergeant, breathing a little short, and waiting for the next attack, "no. I won't. If you are not man enough to strike for a fellow-soldier because he wants help, and because of nothing else, I'll go into the other world and look for a better man."

Tom swept upon them, and cut him out. Tom and he fought their way through another knot of them, and sent them flying, and came over to where I was beginning again to feel, with inexpressible joy, that I had got a sword in my hand.

They had hardly come to us, when I heard, above all the other noises, a tremendous cry of women's voices. I also saw Miss Maryon, with quite a new face, suddenly clap her two hands over Mrs. Fisher's eyes. I looked towards the silver-house, and saw Mrs. Venning—standing upright on the top of the steps of the trench, with her gray hair and her dark eyes—hide her daughter's child behind her, among the folds of her dress, strike a pirate with her other hand, and fall, shot by his pistol.

The cry arose again, and there was a terrible and confusing rush of the women into the midst of the struggle. In another moment, something came tumbling down upon me that I thought was the wall. It was a heap of Sambos who had come over the wall; and of four men who clung to my legs like serpents, one who clung to my right leg was Christian George King.

"Yup, So-Jeer," says he, "Christian George King sar berry glad So-Jeer a prisoner. Christian George King been waiting for So-Jeer sech long time. Yup, yup!"

What could I do, with five-and-twenty of them on me, but be tied hand and foot? So, I was tied hand and foot. It was all over now—boats not come back—all lost! When I was fast bound and was put up against the wall, the one-eyed English convict came up with the Portuguese Captain, to have a look at me.

"See!" says he. "Here's the determined man! If you had slept sounder, last night, you'd have slept your soundest last night, my determined man."

The Portuguese Captain laughed in a cool way, and with the flat of his cutlass, hit me crosswise, as if I was the bough of a tree that he played with: first on the face, and then across the chest and the wounded arm. I looked him steady in the face without tumbling while he looked at me, I am happy to say ; but, when they went away, I fell, and lay there.

The sun was up, when I was roused and told to come down to the beach and be embarked. I was full of aches and pains, and could not at first remember ; but, I remembered quite soon enough. The killed were lying about all over the place, and the Pirates were burying their dead, and taking away their wounded on hastily-made litters, to the back of the Island. As for us prisoners, some of their boats had come round to the usual harbour, to carry us off. We looked a wretched few, I thought, when I got down there ; still, it was another sign that we had fought well, and made the enemy suffer.

The Portuguese Captain had all the women already embarked in the boat he himself commanded, which was just putting off when I got down. Miss Maryon sat on one side of him, and gave me a moment's look, as full of quiet courage, and pity, and confidence, as if it had been an hour long. On the other side of him was poor little Mrs. Fisher, weeping for her child and her mother. I was shoved into the same boat with Drooce and Packer, and the remainder of our party of marines : of whom we had lost two privates, besides Charker, my poor, brave comrade. We all made a melancholy passage, under the hot sun over to the mainland. There, we landed in a solitary place, and were mustered on the sea sand. Mr. and Mrs. Macey and their children were amongst us, Mr. and Mrs. Pordage, Mr. Kitten, Mr. Fisher, and Mrs. Belltott. We mustered only fourteen men, fifteen women, and seven children. Those were all that remained of the English who had lain down to sleep last night, unsuspecting and happy, on the Island of Silver-Store.

[The second chapter, which was not written by Dickens, describes the Prisoners (twenty-two women and children) taken into the interior by the Pirate Captain, who makes them the material guarantee for the precious metal and jewels left on the Island ; declaring that, if the latter be wrested by English ships from the pirates in charge, he will murder the captives. From their "Prison in the Woods," however (this being the title of the second chapter), they escape by means of rafts down the river ; and the sequel is told in a third and concluding chapter by Dickens.]

CHAPTER III

THE RAFTS ON THE RIVER

WE contrived to keep afloat all that night, and, the stream running strong with us, to glide a long way down the river. But, we found the night to be a dangerous time for such navigation, on account of the eddies and rapids, and it was therefore settled next day that in future we would bring-to at sunset, and encamp on the shore. As we knew of no boats that the Pirates possessed, up at the Prison in the Woods, we settled always to encamp on the opposite side of the stream, so as to have the breadth of the river between our sleep and them. Our opinion was, that if they were acquainted with any near way by land to the mouth of this river, they would come up it in force, and retake us or kill us, according as they could; but that if that was not the case, and if the river ran by none of their secret stations, we might escape.

When I say we settled this or that, I do not mean that we planned anything with any confidence as to what might happen an hour hence. So much had happened in one night, and such great changes had been violently and suddenly made in the fortunes of many among us, that we had got better used to uncertainty, in a little while, than I dare say most people do in the course of their lives.

The difficulties we soon got into, through the off-settings and point-currents of the stream, made the likelihood of our being drowned, alone—to say nothing of our being retaken— as broad and plain as the sun at noonday to all of us. But, we all worked hard at managing the rafts, under the direction of the seamen (of our own skill, I think we never could have prevented them from oversetting), and we also worked hard at making good the defects in their first hasty construction— which the water soon found out. While we humbly resigned ourselves to going down, if it was the will of Our Father that was in Heaven, we humbly made up our minds, that we would all do the best that was in us.

And so we held on, gliding with the stream. It drove us to this bank, and it drove us to that bank, and it turned us, and whirled us; but yet it carried us on. Sometimes much too slowly; sometimes much too fast, but yet it carried us on.

My little deaf and dumb boy slumbered a good deal now, and that was the case with all the children. They caused very little trouble to any one. They seemed, in my eyes, to get more like one another, not only in quiet manner, but in the face, too. The motion of the raft was usually so much the same, the scene was usually so much the same, the sound of the soft wash and ripple of the water was usually so much the same, that they were made drowsy, as they might have been by the constant playing of one tune. Even on the grown people, who worked hard and felt anxiety, the same things produced something of the same effect. Every day was so like the other, that I soon lost count of the days, myself, and had to ask Miss Maryon, for instance, whether this was the third or fourth? Miss Maryon had a pocket-book and pencil, and she kept the log; that is to say, she entered up a clear little journal of the time, and of the distances our seamen thought we had made, each night.

So, as I say, we kept afloat and glided on. All day long, and every day, the water, and the woods, and sky; all day long, and every day, the constant watching of both sides of the river, and far ahead at every bold turn and sweep it made, for any signs of Pirate-boats, or Pirate-dwellings. So, as I say, we kept afloat and glided on. The days melting themselves together to that degree, that I could hardly believe my ears when I asked "How many, now, Miss?" and she answered "Seven."

To be sure, poor Mr. Pordage had, by about now, got his Diplomatic coat into such a state as never was seen. What with the mud of the river, what with the water of the river, what with the sun, and the dews, and the tearing boughs, and the thickets, it hung about him in discoloured shreds like a mop. The sun had touched him a bit. He had taken to always polishing one particular button, which just held on to his left wrist, and to always calling for stationery. I suppose that man called for pens, ink, and paper, tape, and sealing-wax, upwards of one thousand times in four-and-twenty hours. He had an idea that we should never get out of that river unless we were written out of it in a formal Memorandum;

and the more we laboured at navigating the rafts, the more
he ordered us not to touch them at our peril, and the more he
sat and roared for stationery.

Mrs. Pordage, similarly, persisted in wearing her nightcap.
I doubt if any one but ourselves who had seen the progress
of that article of dress, could by this time have told what it
was meant for. It had got so limp and ragged that she
couldn't see out of her eyes for it. It was so dirty, that
whether it was vegetable matter out of a swamp, or weeds out
of the river, or an old porter's-knot from England, I don't
think any new spectator could have said. Yet, this unfortunate old woman had a notion that it was not only vastly
genteel, but that it was the correct thing as to propriety.
And she really did carry herself over the other ladies who
had no nightcaps, and who were forced to tie up their hair
how they could, in a superior manner that was perfectly
amazing.

I don't know what she looked like, sitting in that blessed
nightcap, on a log of wood, outside the hut or cabin upon our
raft. She would have rather resembled a fortune-teller in
one of the picture-books that used to be in the shop-windows
in my boyhood, except for her stateliness. But, Lord bless
my heart, the dignity with which she sat and moped, with
her head in that bundle of tatters, was like nothing else in
the world! She was not on speaking terms with more than
three of the ladies. Some of them had, what she called,
"taken precedence" of her—in getting into, or out of, that
miserable little shelter!—and others had not called to pay
their respects, or something of that kind. So, there she sat,
in her own state and ceremony, while her husband sat on the
same log of wood, ordering us one and all to let the raft go
to the bottom, and to bring him stationery.

What with this noise on the part of Mr. Commissioner
Pordage, and what with the cries of Sergeant Drooce on the
raft astern (which were sometimes more than Tom Packer
could silence), we often made our slow way down the river,
anything but quietly. Yet, that it was of great importance
that no ears should be able to hear us from the woods on the
banks, could not be doubted. We were looked for, to a
certainty, and we might be retaken at any moment. It
was an anxious time; it was, indeed, indeed, an anxious
time.

On the seventh night of our voyage on the rafts, we made

fast, as usual, on the opposite side of the river to that from which we had started, in as dark a place as we could pick out. Our little encampment was soon made, and supper was eaten, and the children fell asleep. The watch was set, and everything made orderly for the night. Such a starlight night, with such blue in the sky, and such black in the places of heavy shade on the banks of the great stream !

Those two ladies, Miss Maryon and Mrs. Fisher, had always kept near me since the night of the attack. Mr. Fisher, who was untiring in the work of our raft, had said to me :

" My dear little childless wife has grown so attached to you, Davis, and you are such a gentle fellow, as well as such a determined one ; " our party had adopted that last expression from the one-eyed English pirate, and I repeat what Mr. Fisher said, only because he said it ; " that it takes a load off my mind to leave her in your charge."

I said to him : " Your lady is in far better charge than mine, Sir, having Miss Maryon to take care of her ; but, you may rely upon it, that I will guard them both—faithful and true."

Says he : " I do rely upon it, Davis, and I heartily wish all the silver on our old Island was yours."

That seventh starlight night, as I have said, we made our camp, and got our supper, and set our watch, and the children fell asleep. It was solemn and beautiful in those wild and solitary parts, to see them, every night before they lay down, kneeling under the bright sky, saying their little prayers at women's laps. At that time we men all uncovered, and mostly kept at a distance. When the innocent creatures rose up, we murmured "Amen!" all together. For, though we had not heard what they said, we knew it must be good for us.

At that time, too, as was only natural, those poor mothers in our company, whose children had been killed, shed many tears. I thought the sight seemed to console them while it made them cry ; but, whether I was right or wrong in that, they wept very much. On this seventh night, Mrs. Fisher had cried for her lost darling until she cried herself asleep. She was lying on a little couch of leaves and such-like (I made the best little couch I could for them every night), and Miss Maryon had covered her, and sat by her, holding her hand. The stars looked down upon them. As for me, I guarded them.

"Davis!" says Miss Maryon. (I am not going to say what a voice she had. I couldn't if I tried.)

"I am here, Miss."

"The river sounds as if it were swollen to-night."

"We all think, Miss, that we are coming near the sea."

"Do you believe now; we shall escape?"

"I do now, Miss, really believe it." I had always said I did; but, I had in my own mind been doubtful.

"How glad you will be, my good Davis, to see England again!"

I have another confession to make that will appear singular. When she said these words, something rose in my throat; and the stars I looked away at, seemed to break into sparkles that fell down my face and burnt it.

"England is not much to me, Miss, except as a name."

"O, so true an Englishman should not say that!—Are you not well to-night, Davis?" Very kindly, and with a quick change.

"Quite well, Miss."

"Are you sure? Your voice sounds altered in my hearing."

"No, Miss, I am a stronger man than ever. But, England is nothing to me."

Miss Maryon sat silent for so long a while, that I believed she had done speaking to me for one time. However, she had not; for by-and-by she said in a distinct clear tone:

"No, good friend; you must not say that England is nothing to you. It is to be much to you, yet—everything to you. You have to take back to England the good name you have earned here, and the gratitude and attachment and respect you have won here: and you have to make some good English girl very happy and proud, by marrying her; and I shall one day see her, I hope, and make her happier and prouder still, by telling her what noble services her husband's were in South America, and what a noble friend he was to me there."

Though she spoke these kind words in a cheering manner, she spoke them compassionately. I said nothing. It will appear to be another strange confession, that I paced to and fro, within call, all that night, a most unhappy man, reproaching myself all the night long. "You are as ignorant as any man alive; you are as obscure as any man alive; you are as poor as any man alive; you are no better than the mud under your foot.". That was the way in which I went on against myself until the morning.

With the day, came the day's labour. What I should have done without the labour, I don't know. We were afloat again at the usual hour, and were again making our way down the river. It was broader, and clearer of obstructions than it had been, and it seemed to flow faster. This was one of Drooce's quiet days; Mr. Pordage, besides being sulky, had almost lost his voice; and we made good way, and with little noise.

There was always a seaman forward on the raft, keeping a bright look-out. Suddenly, in the full heat of the day, when the children were slumbering, and the very trees and reeds appeared to be slumbering, this man—it was Short— holds up his hand, and cries with great caution: "Avast! Voices ahead!"

We held on against the stream as soon as we could bring her up, and the other raft followed suit. At first, Mr. Macey, Mr. Fisher, and myself, could hear nothing; though both the seamen aboard of us agreed that they could hear voices and oars. After a little pause, however, we united in thinking that we *could* hear the sound of voices, and the dip of oars. But, you can hear a long way in those countries, and there was a bend of the river before us, and nothing was to be seen except such waters and such banks as we were now in the eighth day (and might, for the matter of our feelings, have been in the eightieth), of having seen with anxious eyes.

It was soon decided to put a man ashore, who should creep through the wood, see what was coming, and warn the rafts. The rafts in the meantime to keep the middle of the stream. The man to be put ashore, and not to swim ashore, as the first thing could be more quickly done than the second. The raft conveying him, to get back into midstream, and to hold on along with the other, as well as it could, until signalled by the man. In case of danger, the man to shift for himself until it should be safe to take him on board again. I volunteered to be the man.

We knew that the voices and oars must come up slowly against the stream; and our seamen knew, by the set of the stream, under which bank they would come. I was put ashore accordingly. The raft got off well, and I broke into the wood.

Steaming hot it was, and a tearing place to get through. So much the better for me, since it was something to contend against and do. I cut off the bend of the river, at a great saving of space, came to the water's edge again, and hid myself, and waited. I could now hear the dip of the oars very distinctly; the voices had ceased.

The sound came on in a regular tune, and as I lay hidden, I fancied the tune so played to be, "Chris'en— George—King! Chris'en—George—King! Chris'en—George—King!" over and over again, always the same, with the pauses always at the same places. I had likewise time to make up my mind that if these were the Pirates, I could and would (barring my being shot) swim off to my raft, in spite of my wound, the moment I had given the alarm, and hold my old post by Miss Maryon.

"Chris'en—George—King! Chris'en—George—King! Chris'en—George—King!" coming up, now, very near.

I took a look at the branches about me, to see where a shower of bullets would be most likely to do me least hurt; and I took a look back at the track I had made in forcing my way in; and now I was wholly prepared and fully ready for them.

"Chris'en—George—King! Chris'en—George—King! Chris'en—George—King!" Here they were!

Who were they? The barbarous Pirates, scum of all nations, headed by such men as the hideous little Portuguese monkey, and the one-eyed English convict with the gash across his face, that ought to have gashed his wicked head off? The worst men in the world picked out from the worst, to do the cruellest and most atrocious deeds that ever stained it? The howling, murdering, black-flag waving, mad, and drunken crowds of devils that had overcome us by numbers and by treachery? No. These were English men in English boats—good blue-jackets and red-coats—marines that I knew myself, and sailors that knew our seamen! At the helm of the first boat, Captain Carton, eager and steady. At the helm of the second boat, Captain Maryon, brave and bold. At the helm of the third boat, an old seaman, with determination carved into his watchful face, like the figure-head of a ship. Every man doubly and trebly armed from head to foot. Every man lying-to at his work, with a will that had all his heart and soul in it. Every man looking out for any trace of friend or enemy, and burning

to be the first to do good or avenge evil. Every man with
his face on fire when he saw me, his countryman who had
been taken prisoner, and hailed me with a cheer, as Captain
Carton's boat ran in and took me on board.

I reported, "All escaped, Sir! All well, all safe, all
here!"

God bless me—and God bless them—what a cheer! It
turned me weak, as I was passed on from hand to hand to
the stern of the boat: every hand patting me or grasping
me in some way or other, in the moment of my going by.

"Hold up, my brave fellow," says Captain Carton, clapping
me on the shoulder like a friend, and giving me a flask.
"Put your lips to that, and they'll be red again. Now, boys,
give way!"

The banks flew by us as if the mightiest stream that ever
ran was with us; and so it was, I am sure, meaning the
stream to those men's ardour and spirit. The banks flew by
us, and we came in sight of the rafts—the banks flew by us,
and we came alongside of the rafts—the banks stopped; and
there was a tumult of laughing and crying, and kissing and
shaking of hands, and catching up of children and setting
of them down again, and a wild hurry of thankfulness and
joy that melted every one and softened all hearts.

I had taken notice, in Captain Carton's boat, that there
was a curious and quite new sort of fitting on board. It
was a kind of a little bower made of flowers, and it was set
up behind the captain, and betwixt him and the rudder.
Not only was this arbour, so to call it, neatly made of
flowers, but it was ornamented in a singular way. Some of
the men had taken the ribbons and buckles off their hats,
and hung them among the flowers; others had made festoons
and streamers of their handkerchiefs, and hung them there;
others had intermixed such trifles as bits of glass and shining
fragments of lockets and tobacco-boxes with the flowers; so
that altogether it was a very bright and lively object in the
sunshine. But why there, or what for, I did not understand.

Now, as soon as the first bewilderment was over, Captain
Carton gave the order to land for the present. But this boat
of his, with two hands left in her, immediately put off again
when the men were out of her, and kept off, some yards from
the shore. As she floated there, with the two hands gently
backing water to keep her from going down the stream, this

The Perils of Certain English Prisoners

(p. 205)

pretty little arbour attracted many eyes. None of the boat's crew, however, had anything to say about it, except that it was the captain's fancy.

The captain—with the women and children clustering round him, and the men of all ranks grouped outside them, and all listening—stood telling how the Expedition, deceived by its bad intelligence, had chased the light Pirate boats all that fatal night, and had still followed in their wake next day, and had never suspected until many hours too late that the great Pirate body had drawn off in the darkness when the chase began, and shot over to the Island. He stood telling how the Expedition, supposing the whole array of armed boats to be ahead of it, got tempted into shallows and went aground ; but not without having its revenge upon the two decoy-boats, both of which it had come up with, overhand, and sent to the bottom with all on board. He stood telling how the Expedition, fearing then that the case stood as it did, got afloat again, by great exertion, after the loss of four more tides, and returned to the Island, where they found the sloop scuttled and the treasure gone. He stood telling how my officer, Lieutenant Linderwood, was left upon the Island, with as strong a force as could be got together hurriedly from the mainland, and how the three boats we saw before us were manned and armed and had come away, exploring the coast and inlets, in search of any tidings of us. He stood telling all this, with his face to the river ; and, as he stood telling it, the little arbour of flowers floated in the sunshine before all the faces there.

Leaning on Captain Carton's shoulder, between him and Miss Maryon, was Mrs. Fisher, her head drooping on her arm. She asked him, without raising it, when he had told so much, whether he had found her mother ?

"Be comforted ! She lies," said the Captain gently, "under the cocoa-nut trees on the beach."

"And my child, Captain Carton, did you find my child, too ? Does my darling rest with my mother ? "

"No. Your pretty child sleeps," said the Captain, "under a shade of flowers."

His voice shook ; but there was something in it that struck all the hearers. At that moment there sprung from the arbour in his boat a little creature, clapping her hands and stretching out her arms, and crying, "Dear papa ! Dear mamma ! I am not killed. I am saved. I am coming to

kiss you.   Take me to them, take me to them, good, kind
sailors!"

Nobody who saw that scene has ever forgotten it, I am
sure, or ever will forget it.   The child had kept quite still,
where her brave grandmamma had put her (first whispering
in her ear, "Whatever happens to me, do not stir, my
dear!"), and had remained quiet until the fort was deserted;
she had then crept out of the trench, and gone into her
mother's house; and there, alone on the solitary Island, in
her mother's room, and asleep on her mother's bed, the
Captain had found her.   Nothing could induce her to be
parted from him after he took her up in his arms, and he
had brought her away with him, and the men had made
the bower for her.   To see those men now, was a sight.
The joy of the women was beautiful; the joy of those
women who had lost their own children was quite sacred
and divine; but, the ecstasies of Captain Carton's boat's
crew, when their pet was restored to her parents, were
wonderful for the tenderness they showed in the midst of
roughness.   As the Captain stood with the child in his arms,
and the child's own little arms now clinging round his neck,
now round her father's, now round her mother's, now round
some one who pressed up to kiss her, the boat's crew shook
hands with one another, waved their hats over their heads,
laughed, sang, cried, danced—and all among themselves,
without wanting to interfere with anybody—in a manner
never to be represented.   At last, I saw the coxswain and
another, two very hard-faced men, with grizzled heads, who
had been the heartiest of the hearty all along, close with one
another, get each of them the other's head under his arm,
and pommel away at it with his fist as hard as he could,
in his excess of joy.

When we had well rested and refreshed ourselves—and
very glad we were to have some of the heartening things to
eat and drink that had come up in the boats—we recom-
menced our voyage down the river: rafts, and boats, and all.
I said to myself, it was a very different kind of voyage now,
from what it had been; and I fell into my proper place and
station among my fellow-soldiers.

But, when we halted for the night, I found that Miss
Maryon had spoken to Captain Carton concerning me.   For,
the Captain came straight up to me, and says he, "My brave
fellow, you have been Miss Maryon's body-guard all along,

and you shall remain so. Nobody shall supersede you in the distinction and pleasure of protecting that young lady." I thanked his honour in the fittest words I could find, and that night I was placed on my old post of watching the place where she slept. More than once in the night, I saw Captain Carton come out into the air, and stroll about there, to see that all was well. I have now this other singular confession to make, that I saw him with a heavy heart. Yes; I saw him with a heavy, heavy heart.

In the daytime, I had the like post in Captain Carton's boat. I had a special station of my own, behind Miss Maryon, and no hands but hers ever touched my wound. (It has been healed these many long years; but, no other hands have ever touched it.) Mr. Pordage was kept tolerably quiet now, with pen and ink, and began to pick up his senses a little. Seated in the second boat, he made documents with Mr. Kitten, pretty well all day; and he generally handed in a Protest about something whenever we stopped. The Captain, however, made so very light of these papers, that it grew into a saying among the men, when one of them wanted a match for his pipe, "Hand us over a Protest, Jack!" As to Mrs. Pordage, she still wore the nightcap, and she now had cut all the ladies on account of her not having been formally and separately rescued by Captain Carton before anybody else. The end of Mr. Pordage, to bring to an end all I know about him, was, that he got great compliments at home for his conduct on these trying occasions, and that he died of yellow jaundice, a Governor and a K.C.B.

Sergeant Drooce had fallen from a high fever into a low one. Tom Packer—the only man who could have pulled the Sergeant through it—kept hospital aboard the old raft, and Mrs. Belltott, as brisk as ever again (but the spirit of that little woman, when things tried it, was not equal to appearances), was head-nurse under his directions. Before we got down to the Mosquito coast, the joke had been made by one of our men, that we should see her gazetted Mrs. Tom Packer, *vice* Belltott exchanged.

When we reached the coast, we got native boats as substitutes for the rafts; and we rowed along under the land; and in that beautiful climate, and upon that beautiful water, the blooming days were like enchantment. Ah! They were running away, faster than any sea or river, and there was no tide to bring them back. We were coming very near the settlement where the people of Silver-Store were to be left, and from which we Marines were under orders to return to Belize.

Captain Carton had, in the boat by him, a curious long-barrelled Spanish gun, and he had said to Miss Maryon one day that it was the best of guns, and had turned his head to me, and said :

"Gill Davis, load her fresh with a couple of slugs, against a chance of showing how good she is."

So, I had discharged the gun over the sea, and had loaded her, according to orders, and there it had lain at the Captain's feet, convenient to the Captain's hand.

The last day but one of our journey was an uncommonly hot day. We started very early ; but, there was no cool air on the sea as the day got on, and by noon the heat was really hard to bear, considering that there were women and children to bear it. Now, we happened to open, just at that time, a very pleasant little cove or bay, where there was a deep shade from a great growth of trees. Now, the Captain, therefore, made the signal to the other boats to follow him in and lie by a while.

The men who were off duty went ashore, and lay down, but were ordered, for caution's sake, not to stray, and to keep within view. The others rested on their oars, and dozed. Awnings had been made of one thing and another, in all the boats, and the passengers found it cooler to be under them in the shade, when there was room enough, than to be in the thick woods. So, the passengers were all afloat, and mostly sleeping. I kept my post behind Miss Maryon, and she was on Captain Carton's right in the boat, and Mrs. Fisher sat on her right again. The Captain had Mrs. Fisher's daughter on his knee. He and the two ladies were talking about the Pirates, and were talking softly ; partly, because people do talk softly under such indolent circumstances, and partly because the little girl had gone off asleep.

I think I have before given it out for my Lady to write down, that Captain Carton had a fine bright eye of his own. All at once, he darted me a side look, as much as to say, "Steady—don't take on—I see something !"—and gave the child into her mother's arms. That eye of his was so easy to understand, that I obeyed it by not so much as looking either to the right or to the left out of a corner of my own.

or changing my attitude the least trifle. The Captain went on talking in the same mild and easy way; but began—with his arms resting across his knees, and his head a little hanging forward, as if the heat were rather too much for him—began to play with the Spanish gun.

"They had laid their plans, you see," says the Captain, taking up the Spanish gun across his knees, and looking, lazily, at the inlaying on the stock, "with a great deal of art; and the corrupt or blundering local authorities were so easily deceived;" he ran his left hand idly along the barrel, but I saw, with my breath held, that he covered the action of cocking the gun with his right—"so easily deceived, that they summoned us out to come into the trap. But my intention as to future operations ——" In a flash the Spanish gun was at his bright eye, and he fired.

All started up; innumerable echoes repeated the sound of the discharge; a cloud of bright-coloured birds flew out of the woods screaming; a handful of leaves were scattered in the place where the shot had struck; a crackling of branches was heard; and some lithe but heavy creature sprang into the air, and fell forward, head down, over the muddy bank.

"What is it?" cries Captain Maryon from his boat. All silent then, but the echoes rolling away.

"It is a Traitor and a Spy," said Captain Carton, handing me the gun to load again. "And I think the other name of the animal is Christian George King!"

Shot through the heart. Some of the people ran round to the spot, and drew him out, with the slime and wet trickling down his face; but his face itself would never stir any more to the end of time.

"Leave him hanging to that tree," cried Captain Carton; his boat's crew giving way, and he leaping ashore. "But first into this wood, every man in his place. And boats! Out of gunshot!"

It was a quick change, well meant and well made, though it ended in disappointment. No Pirates were there; no one but the Spy was found. It was supposed that the Pirates, unable to retake us, and expecting a great attack upon them to be the consequence of our escape, had made from the ruins in the Forest, taken to their ship along with the Treasure, and left the Spy to pick up what intelligence he could. In the evening we went away, and he was left hanging to the tree, all alone, with the red sun making a kind of a dead sunset on his black face.

Next day, we gained the settlement on the Mosquito coast for which we were bound. Having stayed there to refresh seven days, and having been much commended, and highly spoken of, and finely entertained, we Marines stood under orders to march from the Town-Gate (it was neither much of a town nor much of a gate), at five in the morning.

My officer had joined us before then. When we turned out at the gate, all the people were there; in the front of them all those who had been our fellow-prisoners, and all the seamen.

"Davis," says Lieutenant Linderwood. "Stand out, my friend!"

I stood out from the ranks, and Miss Maryon and Captain Carton came up to me.

"Dear Davis," says Miss Maryon, while the tears fell fast down her face. "your grateful friends, in most unwillingly taking leave of you, ask the favour that, while you bear away with you their affectionate remembrance, which nothing can ever impair, you will also take this purse of money—far more valuable to you, we all know, for the deep attachment and thankfulness with which it is offered, than for its own contents, though we hope those may prove useful to you, too, in after life."

I got out, in answer, that I thankfully accepted the attachment and affection, but not the money. Captain Carton looked at me very attentively, and stepped back, and moved away. I made him my bow as he stepped back, to thank him for being so delicate.

"No, Miss," said I, "I think it would break my heart to accept of money. But, if you could condescend to give to a man so ignorant and common as myself, any little thing you have worn—such as a bit of ribbon——"

She took a ring from her finger, and put it in my hand. And she rested her hand in mine, while she said these words:

"The brave gentlemen of old—but not one of them was braver, or had a nobler nature than you—took such gifts from ladies, and did all their good actions for the givers' sakes. If you will do yours for mine, I shall think with pride that I continue to have some share in the life of a gallant and generous man."

For the second time in my life she kissed my hand. I made so bold, for the first time, as to kiss hers; and I tied the ring at my breast, and I fell back to my place.

Then, the horse-litter went out at the gate with Sergeant Drooce in it; and the horse-litter went out at the gate with Mrs. Belltott in it; and Lieutenant Linderwood gave the word of command, "Quick march!" and, cheered and cried for, we went out of the gate too, marching along the level plain towards the serene blue sky, as if we were marching straight to Heaven.

When I have added here that the Pirate scheme was blown to shivers, by the Pirate-ship which had the Treasure on board being so vigorously attacked by one of His Majesty's cruisers, among the West-India Keys, and being so swiftly boarded and carried, that nobody suspected anything about the scheme until three-fourths of the Pirates were killed, and the other fourth were in irons, and the Treasure was recovered; I come to the last singular confession I have got to make.

It is this. I well knew what an immense and hopeless distance there was between me and Miss Maryon; I well knew that I was no fitter company for her than I was for the angels; I well knew that she was as high above my reach as the sky over my head; and yet I loved her. What put it in my low heart to be so daring, or whether such a thing ever happened before or since, as that a man so uninstructed and obscure as myself got his unhappy thoughts lifted up to such a height, while knowing very well how presumptuous and impossible to be realised they were, I am unable to say; still, the suffering to me was just as great as if I had been a gentleman. I suffered agony—agony. I suffered hard, and I suffered long. I thought of her last words to me, however, and I never disgraced them. If it had not been for those dear words, I think I should have lost myself in despair and recklessness.

The ring will be found lying on my heart, of course, and will be laid with me wherever I am laid. I am getting on in years now, though I am able and hearty. I was recommended for promotion, and everything was done to reward me that could be done; but my total want of all learning stood in my way, and I found myself so completely out of the road to it, that I could not conquer any learning, though I tried. I was long in the service, and I respected it, and was respected in it, and the service is dear to me at this present hour.

At this present hour, when I give this out to my Lady to be written down, all my old pain has softened away, and I am as happy as a man can be, at this present fine old country-house of Admiral Sir George Carton, Baronet. It was my Lady Carton who herself sought me out, over a great many miles of the wide world, and found me in Hospital wounded, and brought me here. It is my Lady Carton who writes down my words. My Lady was Miss Maryon. And now, that I conclude what I had to tell, I see my Lady's honoured gray hair droop over her face, as she leans a little lower at her desk; and I fervently thank her for being so tender as I see she is, towards the past pain and trouble of her poor, old, faithful, humble soldier.

GOING INTO SOCIETY

[1858]

CHARACTERS

TOBY MAGSMAN, *a showman.*

NORMANDY, *a 'Bonnet' at a gaming-booth.*

MAJOR TPSCHOFFKI ('Chops'), *a dwarf in the collection of Toby Magsman.*

GOING INTO SOCIETY

<hr>

AT one period of its reverses, the House fell into the occupation of a Showman. He was found registered as its occupier, on the parish books of the time when he rented the House, and there was therefore no need of any clue to his name. But, he himself was less easy to be found; for, he had led a wandering life, and settled people had lost sight of him, and people who plumed themselves on being respectable were shy of admitting that they had ever known anything of him. At last, among the marsh lands near the river's level, that lie about Deptford and the neighbouring market-gardens, a Grizzled Personage in velveteen, with a face so cut up by varieties of weather that he looked as if he had been tattooed, was found smoking a pipe at the door of a wooden house on wheels. The wooden house was laid up in ordinary for the winter, near the mouth of a muddy creek; and everything near it, the foggy river, the misty marshes, and the steaming market-gardens, smoked in company with the grizzled man. In the midst of this smoking party, the funnel-chimney of the wooden house on wheels was not remiss, but took its pipe with the rest in a companionable manner.

On being asked if it were he who had once rented the House to Let, Grizzled Velveteen looked surprised, and said yes. Then his name was Magsman? That was it, Toby Magsman—which lawfully christened Robert; but called in the line, from a infant, Toby. There was nothing agin Toby Magsman, he believed? If there was suspicion of such—mention it!

There was no suspicion of such, he might rest assured. But, some inquiries were making about that House, and would he object to say why he left it?

Not at all; why should he? He left it, along of a Dwarf.

Along of a Dwarf?

Mr. Magsman repeated, deliberately and emphatically, Along of a Dwarf.

Might it be compatible with Mr. Magsman's inclination and convenience to enter, as a favour, into a few particulars?

Mr. Magsman entered into the following particulars.

It was a long time ago, to begin with;—afore lotteries and a deal more was done away with. Mr. Magsman was looking about for a good pitch, and he see that house, and he says to himself, "I'll have you, if you're to be had. If money'll get you, I'll have you."

The neighbours cut up rough, and made complaints; but Mr. Magsman don't know what they *would* have had. It was a lovely thing. First of all, there was the canvas, representin the picter of the Giant, in Spanish trunks and a ruff, who was himself half the heighth of the house, and was run up with a line and pulley to a pole on the roof, so that his Ed was coeval with the parapet. Then, there was the canvas, representin the picter of the Albina lady, showing her white air to the Army and Navy in correct uniform. Then, there was the canvas, representin the picter of the Wild Indian a scalpin a member of some foreign nation. Then, there was the canvas, representin the picter of a child of a British Planter, seized by two Boa Constrictors—not that *we* never had no child, nor no Constrictors neither. Similarly, there was the canvas, representin the picter of the Wild Ass of the Prairies—not that *we* never had no wild asses, nor wouldn't have had 'em at a gift. Last, there was the canvas, representin the picter of the Dwarf, and like him too (considerin), with George the Fourth in such a state of astonishment at him as His Majesty couldn't with his utmost politeness and stoutness express. The front of the House was so covered with canvases, that there wasn't a spark of daylight ever visible on that side. "MAGSMAN'S AMUSEMENTS," fifteen foot long by two foot high, ran over the front door and parlour winders. The passage was a Arbour of green baize and gardenstuff. A barrel-organ performed there unceasing. And as to respectability,—if threepence ain't respectable, what is?

But, the Dwarf is the principal article at present, and he was worth the money. He was wrote up as MAJOR TPSCHOFFKI, OF THE IMPERIAL BULGRADERIAN BRIGADE. Nobody couldn't pronounce the name, and it never was intended anybody should. The public always turned it, as a regular rule, into Chopski. In the line he was called Chops; partly on that account, and partly because his real name, if he ever had any real name (which was very dubious), was Stakes.

He was a uncommon small man, he really was. Certainly not so small as he was made out to be, but where *is* your Dwarf as is? He was a most uncommon small man, with a most uncommon large Ed; and what he had inside that Ed, nobody never knowed but himself: even supposin himself to have ever took stock of it, which it would have been a stiff job for even him to do.

The kindest little man as never growed! Spirited, but not proud. When he travelled with the Spotted Baby—though he knowed himself to be a nat'ral Dwarf, and knowed the Baby's spots to be put upon him artificial, he nursed that Baby like a mother. You never heerd him give a ill-name to a Giant. He *did* allow himself to break out into strong language respectin the Fat Lady from Norfolk; but that was an affair of the 'art; and when a man's 'art has been trifled with by a lady, and the preference giv to a Indian, he ain't master of his actions.

He was always in love, of course; every human nat'ral phenomenon is. And he was always in love with a large woman; *I* never knowed the Dwarf as could be got to love a small one. Which helps to keep 'em the Curiosities they are.

One sing'ler idea he had in that Ed of his, which must have meant something, or it wouldn't have been there. It was always his opinion that he was entitled to property. He never would put his name to anything. He had been taught to write, by the young man without arms, who got his living with his toes (quite a writing-master *he* was, and taught scores in the line), but Chops would have starved to death, afore he'd have gained a bit of bread by putting his hand to a paper. This is the more curious to bear in mind, because HE had no property, nor hope of property, except his house and a sarser. When I say his house, I mean the box, painted and got up outside like a reg'lar six-roomer, that he used to creep into, with a diamond ring (or quite as good to look at) on his forefinger, and ring a little bell out of what the Public believed to be the Drawing-room winder. And when I say a sarser, I mean a Chaney sarser in which he made a collection for himself at the end of every Entertainment. His cue for that, he took from me; "Ladies and gentlemen, the little man will now walk three times round the Cairawan, and retire behind the curtain." When he said anything important, in private life, he mostly wound it up with this form of words, and they was generally the last thing he said to me at night afore he went to bed.

He had what I consider a fine mind—a poetic mind. His ideas respectin his property never come upon him so strong as when he sat upon a barrel-organ and had the handle turned. Arter the wibration had run through him a little time, he would screech out, "Toby, I feel my property coming—grind away! I'm counting my guineas by thousands, Toby—grind away! Toby, I shall be a man of fortun! I feel the Mint a jingling in me, Toby, and I'm swelling out into the Bank of England!" Such is the influence of music on a poetic mind. Not that he was partial to any other music but a barrel-organ; on the contrairy, hated it.

He had a kind of a everlasting grudge agin the Public: which is a thing you may notice in many phenomenons that get their living out of it. What riled him most in the nater of his occupation was, that it kep him out of Society. He was continiwally saying, "Toby, my ambition is, to go into Society. The curse of my position towards the Public is, that it keeps me hout of Society. This don't signify to a low beast of a Indian; he an't formed for Society. This don't signify to a Spotted Baby; *he* an't formed for Society.— I am."

Nobody never could make out what Chops done with his money. He had a good salary, down on the drum every Saturday as the day came round, besides having the run of his teeth—and he was a Woodpecker to eat—but all Dwarfs are. The sarser was a little income, bringing him in so many halfpence that he'd carry 'em for a week together, tied up in a pocket-handkercher. And yet he never had money. And it couldn't be the Fat Lady from Norfolk, as was once supposed, because it stands to reason that when you have a animosity towards a Indian, which makes you grind your teeth at him to his face, and which can hardly hold you from Goosing him audible when he's going through his War-Dance—it stands to reason you wouldn't under them circumstances deprive yourself, to support that Indian in the lap of luxury.

Most unexpected, the mystery came out one day at Egham Races. The Public was shy of bein pulled in, and Chops was ringin his little bell out of his drawing-room winder, and was snarling to me over his shoulder as he kneeled down with his legs out at the back-door—for he couldn't be shoved into his house without kneeling down, and the premises wouldn't accommodate his legs—was snarlin, "Here's a precious Public for you ; why the Devil don't they tumble up ?" when a man in the crowd holds up a carrier-pigeon, and cries out, "If there's any person here as has got a ticket, the Lottery's just drawed, and the number as has come up for the great prize is three, seven, forty-two ! Three, seven, forty-two !" I was givin the man to the Furies myself, for calling off the Public's attention—for the Public will turn away, at any time, to look at anything in preference to the thing showed 'em ; and if you doubt it, get 'em together for any indiwidual purpose on the face of the earth, and send only two people in late, and see if the whole company an't far more interested in takin particular notice of them two than of you—I say, I wasn't best pleased with the man foi callin out, and wasn't blessin him in my own mind, when I see Chops's little bell fly out of winder at a old lady, and he gets up and kicks his box over, exposin the whole secret, and he catches hold of the calves of my legs and he says to me, "Carry me into the wan, Toby, and throw a pail of water over me or I'm a dead man, for I've come into my property !"

Twelve thousand odd hundred pound, was Chops's winnins. He had bought a half-ticket for the twenty-five thousand prize, and it had come up. The first use he made of his property, was, to offer to fight the Wild Indian for five hundred pound a side, him with a poisoned darnin-needle and the Indian with a club ; but the Indian being in want of backers to that amount, it went no further.

Arter he had been mad for a week—in a state of mind, in short, in which, if I had let him sit on the organ for only two minutes, I believe he would have bust—but we kep the organ from him—Mr. Chops come round, and behaved liberal and beautiful to all. He then sent for a young man he knowed, as had a wery genteel appearance and was a Bonnet at a gaming-booth (most respectable brought up, father havin been imminent in the livery stable line but unfort'nate in a commercial crisis, through paintin a old gray, ginger-bay, and sellin him with a Pedigree), and Mr. Chops said to this Bonnet, who said his name was Normandy, which it wasn't:

"Normandy, I'm a goin into Society. Will you go with me ?"

Says Normandy : "Do I understand you, Mr. Chops, to hintimate that the 'ole of the expenses of that move will be borne by yourself?"

"Correct," says Mr. Chops.   "And you shall have a princely allowance too."

The Bonnet lifted Mr. Chops upon a chair, to shake hands with him, and replied in poetry, with his eyes seemingly full of tears :

> "My boat is on the shore,
> And my bark is on the sea,
> And I do not ask for more,
> But I'll Go :—along with thee."

They went into Society, in a chay and four grays with silk jackets. They took lodgings in Pall Mall, London, and they blazed away.

In consequence of a note that was brought to Bartlemy Fair in the autumn of next year by a servant, most wonderful got up in milk-white cords and tops, I cleaned myself and went to Pall Mall, one evening appinted. The gentlemen was at their wine arter dinner, and Mr. Chops's eyes was more fixed in that Ed of his than I thought good for him. There was three of 'em (in company, I mean), and I knowed the third well. When last met, he had on a white Roman shirt, and a bishop's mitre covered with leopard-skin, and played the clarionet all wrong, in a band at a Wild Beast Show.

This gent took on not to know me, and Mr. Chops said : "Gentlemen, this is a old friend of former days :" and Normandy looked at me through a eye-glass, and said, "Magsman, glad to see you !"—which I'll take my oath he wasn't. Mr. Chops, to git him convenient to the table, had his chair on a throne (much of the form of George the Fourth's in the canvas), but he hardly appeared to me to be King there in any other pint of view, for his two gentlemen ordered about like Emperors. They was all dressed like May-Day—gorgeous!—and as to Wine, they swam in all sorts.

I made the round of the bottles, first separate (to say I had done it), and then mixed 'em all together (to say I had done it), and then tried two of 'em as half-and-half, and then t'other two. Altogether, I passed a pleasin evenin, but with a tendency to feel muddled, until I considered it good manners to get up and say, "Mr. Chops, the best of friends must part, I thank you for the wariety of foreign drains you have stood so 'ansome, I looks towards you in red wine,

Going into Society
(p. 218)

and I takes my leave." Mr. Chops replied, "If you'll just hitch me out of this over your right arm, Magsman, and carry me downstairs, I'll see you out." I said I couldn't think of such a thing, but he would have it, so I lifted him off his throne. He smelt strong of Maideary, and I couldn't help thinking as I carried him down that it was like carrying a large bottle full of wine, with a rayther ugly stopper, a good deal out of proportion.

When I set him on the door-mat in the hall, he kep me close to him by holding on to my coat-collar, and he whispers:

"I ain't 'appy, Magsman."

"What's on your mind, Mr. Chops?"

"They don't use me well. They ain't grateful to me. They puts me on the mantel-piece when I won't have in more Champagne-wine, and they locks me in the sideboard when I won't give up my property."

"Get rid of 'em, Mr. Chops."

"I can't. We're in Society together and what would Society say?"

"Come out of Society!" says I.

"I can't. You don't know what you're talking about. When you have once gone into Society, you mustn't come out of it."

"Then if you'll excuse the freedom, Mr. Chops," were my remark, shaking my head grave, "I think it's a pity you ever went in."

Mr. Chops shook that deep Ed of his, to a surprisin extent, and slapped it half-a-dozen times with his hand, and with more Wice than I thought were in him. Then, he says, "You're a good fellow, but you don't understand. Good night, go along. Magsman, the little man will now walk three times round the Cairawan, and retire behind the curtain." The last I see of him on that occasion was his tryin, on the extremest werge of insensibility, to climb up the stairs, one by one, with his hands and knees. They'd have been much too steep for him, if he had been sober ; but he wouldn't be helped.

It warn't long after that, that I read in the newspaper of Mr. Chops's being presented at court. It was printed, "It will be recollected"—and I've noticed in my life, that it is sure to be printed that it *will* be recollected, whenever it won't—"that Mr. Chops is the individual of small stature, whose brilliant success in the last State Lottery attracted so much attention." Well, I says to myself, Such is Life ! He has been and done it in earnest at last! He has astonished George the Fourth!

(On account of which, I had that canvas new-painted, him with a bag of money in his hand, a presentin it to George the Fourth, and a lady in Ostrich Feathers fallin in love with him in a bag-wig, sword, and buckles correct.)

I took the House as is the subject of present inquiries— though not the honour of bein acquainted—and I run Magsman's Amusements in it thirteen months—sometimes one thing, sometimes another, sometimes nothin particular, but always all the canvases outside. One night, when we had played the last company out, which was a shy company, through its raining Heavens hard, I was takin a pipe in the one pair back along with the young man with the toes. which I had taken on for a month (though he never drawed —except on paper), and I heard a kickin at the street door. "Halloa!" I says to the young man, "what's up?" He rubs his eyebrows with his toes, and he says, "I can't imagine, Mr. Magsman"—which he never could imagine nothin, and was monotonous company.

The noise not leavin off, I laid down my pipe, and I took up a candle, and I went down and opened the door. I looked out into the street; but nothin could I see, and nothin was I aware of 'until I turned round quick, because some creetur run between my legs into the passage. There was Mr. Chops!

"Magsman," he says, "take me, on the old terms, and you've got me; if it's done, say done!"

I was all of a maze, but I said, "Done, Sir."

"Done to your done, and double done!" says he. "Have you got a bit of supper in the house?"

Bearin in mind them sparklin warieties of foreign drains as we'd guzzled away at in Pall Mall, I was ashamed to offer him cold sassages and gin-and-water; but he took 'em both and took 'em free; havin a chair for his table, and sittin down at it on a stool, like hold times. I, all of a maze all the while.

It was arter he had made a clean sweep of the sassages (beef, and to the best of my calculations two pound and a quarter), that the wisdom as was in that little man began to come out of him like perspiration.

"Magsman," he says, "look upon me! You see afore you, One as has both gone into Society and come out."

"O! You are out of it, Mr. Chops? How did you get out, Sir?"

"SOLD OUT!" says he. You never saw the like of the

wisdom as his Ed expressed, when he made use of them two words.

"My friend Magsman, I'll impart to you a discovery I've made. It's wallable; it's cost twelve thousand five hundred pound; it may do you good in life.—The secret of this matter is, that it ain't so much that a person goes into Society, as that Society goes into a person."

Not exactly keepin up with his meanin, I shook my head, put on a deep look, and said, "You're right there, Mr. Chops."

"Magsman," he says, twitchin me by the leg, "Society has gone into me, to the tune of every penny of my property."

I felt that I went pale, and though nat'rally a bold speaker, I couldn't hardly say, "Where's Normandy?"

"Bolted. With the plate," said Mr. Chops.

"And t'other one?" meaning him as formerly wore the bishop's mitre.

"Bolted. With the jewels," said Mr. Chops.

I sat down and looked at him, and he stood up and looked at me.

"Magsman," he says, and he seemed to myself to get wiser as he got hoarser; "Society, taken in the lump, is all dwarfs. At the court of St. James's, they was all a doing my old business—all a goin three times round the Cairawan, in the hold court-suits and properties. Elsewheres, they was most of 'em ringin their little bells out of make-believes. Everywheres, the sarser was a goin round. Magsman, the sarser is the uniwersal Institution!"

I perceived, you understand, that he was soured by his misfortuns, and I felt for Mr. Chops.

"As to Fat Ladies," says he, giving his head a tremendious one agin the wall, "there's lots of *them* in Society, and worse than the original. *Hers* was a outrage upon Taste—simply a outrage upon Taste—awakenin contempt—carryin its own punishment in the form of a Indian!" Here he giv himself another tremendious one. "But *theirs*, Magsman, *theirs* is mercenary outrages. Lay in Cashmeer shawls, buy bracelets, strew 'em and a lot of 'andsome fans and things about your rooms, let it be known that you give away like water to all as come to admire, and the Fat Ladies that don't exhibit for so much down upon the drum, will come from all the pints of the compass to flock about you, whatever you are. They'll drill holes in your 'art, Magsman, like a Cullender. And when you've no more left to give, they'll laugh at you to your face, and leave you to have your bones picked dry by Wulturs, like the dead Wild Ass of the Prairies that you deserve to be!" Here he giv himself the most tremendious one of all, and dropped.

I thought he was gone. His Ed was so heavy, and he knocked it so hard, and he fell so stoney, and the sassagerial disturbance in him must have been so immense, that I thought he was gone. But, he soon come round with care, and he sat up on the floor, and he said to me, with wisdom comin out of his eyes, if ever it come:

"Magsman! The most material difference between the two states of existence through which your unappy friend has passed;" he reached out his poor little hand, and his tears dropped down on the moustachio which it was a credit to him to have done his best to grow, but it is not in mortals to command success,—"the difference is this. When I was out of Society, I was paid light for being seen. When I went into Society, I paid heavy for being seen. I prefer the former, even if I wasn't forced upon it. Give me out through the trumpet, in the hold way, to-morrow."

Arter that, he slid into the line again as easy as if he had been iled all over. But the organ was kep from him, and no allusions was ever made, when a company was in, to his property. He got wiser every day; his views of Society and the Public was luminous, bewilderin, awful; and his Ed got bigger and bigger as his Wisdom expanded it.

He took well, and pulled 'em in most excellent for nine weeks. At the expiration of that period, when his Ed was a sight, he expressed one evenin, the last Company havin been turned out, and the door shut, a wish to have a little music.

"Mr. Chops," I said (I never dropped the "Mr." with him; the world might do it, but not me); "Mr. Chops, are you sure as you are in a state of mind and body to sit upon the organ?"

His answer was this: "Toby, when next met with on the tramp, I forgive her and the Indian. And I am."

It was with fear and trembling that I began to turn the handle; but he sat like a lamb. It will be my belief to my dying day, that I see his Ed expand as he sat; you may therefore judge how great his thoughts was. He sat out all the changes, and then he come off.

"Toby," he says, with a quiet smile, "the little man will now walk three times round the Cairawan, and retire behind the curtain."

When we called him in the morning, we found him gone into a much better Society than mine or Pall Mall's. I giv Mr. Chops as comfortable a funeral as lay in my power, followed myself as Chief, and had the George the Fourth canvas carried first, in the form of a banner. But, the House was so dismal arterwards, that I giv it up, and took to the Wan again.

"I don't triumph," said Jarber, folding up the second manuscript, and looking hard at Trottle. "I don't triumph over this worthy creature. I merely ask him if he is satisfied now?"

"How can he be anything else?" I said, answering for Trottle, who sat obstinately silent. "This time, Jarber, you have not only read us a delightfully amusing story, but you have also answered the question about the House. Of course it stands empty now. Who would think of taking it after it had been turned into a caravan?" I looked at Trottle, as I said those last words, and Jarber waved his hand indulgently in the same direction.

"Let this excellent person speak," said Jarber. "You were about to say, my good man——?"

"I only wished to ask, Sir," said Trottle doggedly, "if you could kindly oblige me with a date or two in connexion with that last story?"

"A date!" repeated Jarber. "What does the man want with dates?"

"I should be glad to know, with great respect," persisted Trottle, "if the person named Magsman was the last tenant who lived in the House. It's my opinion—if I may be excused for giving it—that he most decidedly was not."

With those words, Trottle made a low bow, and quietly left the room.

There is no denying that Jarber, when we were left together, looked sadly discomposed. He had evidently forgotten to inquire about dates; and, in spite of his magnificent talk about his series of discoveries, it was quite as plain that the two stories he had just read, had really and truly exhausted his present stock. I thought myself bound, in common gratitude, to help him out of his embarrassment by a timely suggestion. So I proposed that he should come to tea again, on the next Monday evening, the thirteenth, and should make such inquiries in the meantime, as might enable him to dispose triumphantly of Trottle's objection.

He gallantly kissed my hand, made a neat little speech of acknowledgment, and took his leave. For the rest of the week I would not encourage Trottle by allowing him to refer to the House at all. I suspected he was making his own inquiries about dates, but I put no questions to him.

On Monday evening, the thirteenth, that dear unfortunate Jarber came, punctual to the appointed time. He looked so terribly harassed, that he was really quite a spectacle of feebleness and fatigue. I saw, at a glance, that the question of dates had gone against him, that Mr. Magsman had not been the last tenant of the House, and that the reason of its emptiness was still to seek.

"What I have gone through," said Jarber, "words are not eloquent enough to tell. O Sophonisba, I have begun another series of discoveries! Accept the last two as stories laid on your shrine; and wait to blame me for leaving your curiosity unappeased, until you have heard Number Three."

Number Three looked like a very short manuscript, and I said as much. Jarber explained to me that we were to have some poetry this time. In the course of his investigations he had stepped into the Circulating Library, to seek for information on the one important subject. All the Library-people knew about the House was, that a female relative of the last tenant, as they believed, had, just after that tenant left, sent a little manuscript poem to them which she described as referring to events that had actually passed in the House; and which she wanted the proprietor of the Library to publish. She had written no address on her letter; and the proprietor had kept the manuscript ready to be given back to her (the publishing of poems not being in his line) when she might call for it. She had never called for it; and the poem had been lent to Jarber, at his express request, to read to me.

Before he began, I rang the bell for Trottle; being determined to have him present at the new reading, as a wholesome check on his obstinacy. To my surprise Peggy answered the bell, and told me that Trottle had stepped out without saying where. I instantly felt the strongest possible conviction that he was at his old tricks: and that his stepping out in the evening, without leave, meant—Philandering.

Controlling myself on my visitor's account, I dismissed Peggy, stifled my indignation, and prepared, as politely as might be, to listen to Jarber.

THE HAUNTED HOUSE

[1859]

THE HAUNTED HOUSE

IN TWO CHAPTERS[1]

THE MORTALS IN THE HOUSE

UNDER none of the accredited ghostly circumstances, and environed by none of the conventional ghostly surroundings, did I first make acquaintance with the house which is the subject of this Christmas piece. I saw it in the daylight, with the sun upon it. There was no wind, no rain, no lightning, no thunder, no awful or unwonted circumstance, of any kind, to heighten its effect. More than that: I had come to it direct from a railway station: it was not more than a mile distant from the railway station; and, as I stood outside the house, looking back upon the way I had come, I could see the goods train running smoothly along the embankment in the valley. I will not say that everything was utterly commonplace, because I doubt if anything can be that, except to utterly commonplace people—and there my vanity steps in; but, I will take it on myself to say that anybody might see the house as I saw it, any fine autumn morning.

The manner of my lighting on it was this.

I was travelling towards London out of the North, intending to stop by the way, to look at the house. My health required a temporary residence in the country; and a friend of mine who knew that, and who had happened to drive past the house, had written to me to suggest it as a likely place.

[1] The original has eight chapters, which will be found in *All the Year Round*, vol. ii., old series; but those not printed here, excepting a page at the close, were not written by Dickens.

I had got into the train at midnight, and had fallen asleep, and had woke up and had sat looking out of window at the brilliant Northern Lights in the sky, and had fallen asleep again, and had woke up again to find the night gone, with the usual discontented conviction on me that I hadn't been to sleep at all;—upon which question, in the first imbecility of that condition, I am ashamed to believe that I would have done wager by battle with the man who sat opposite me. That opposite man had had, through the night—as that opposite man always has—several legs too many, and all of them too long. In addition to this unreasonable conduct (which was only to be expected of him), he had had a pencil and a pocket-book, and had been perpetually listening and taking notes. It had appeared to me that these aggravating notes related to the jolts and bumps of the carriage, and I should have resigned myself to his taking them, under a general supposition that he was in the civil-engineering way of life, if he had not sat staring straight over my head whenever he listened. He was a goggle-eyed gentleman of a perplexed aspect, and his demeanour became unbearable.

It was a cold, dead morning (the sun not being up yet), and when I had out-watched the paling light of the fires of the iron country, and the curtain of heavy smoke that hung at once between me and the stars and between me and the day, I turned to my fellow-traveller and said:

"I *beg* your pardon, Sir, but do you observe anything particular in me?" For, really, he appeared to be taking down, either my travelling-cap or my hair, with a minuteness that was a liberty.

The goggle-eyed gentleman withdrew his eyes from behind me, as if the back of the carriage were a hundred miles off, and said, with a lofty look of compassion for my insignificance:

"In you, Sir?—B."

"B, Sir?" said I, growing warm.

"I have nothing to do with you, Sir," returned the gentleman; "pray let me listen—O."

He enunciated this vowel after a pause, and noted it down.

At first I was alarmed, for an Express lunatic and no communication with the guard, is a serious position. The thought came to my relief that the gentleman might be what is popularly called a Rapper: one of a sect for (some of) whom I have the highest respect, but whom I don't believe in. I was going to ask him the question, when he took the bread out of my mouth.

"You will excuse me," said the gentleman contemptuously, "if I am too much in advance of common humanity to trouble myself at all about it. I have passed the night—as indeed I pass the whole of my time now—in spiritual intercourse."

"O!" said I, something snappishly.

"The conferences of the night began," continued the gentleman, turning several leaves of his note-book, "with this message: 'Evil communications corrupt good manners.'"

"Sound," said I; "but, absolutely new?"

"New from spirits," returned the gentleman.

I could only repeat my rather snappish "O!" and ask if I might be favoured with the last communication.

"'A bird in the hand,'" said the gentleman, reading his last entry with great solemnity, "'is worth two in the Bosh.'"

"Truly I am of the same opinion," said I; "but shouldn't it be Bush?"

"It came to me, Bosh," returned the gentleman.

The gentleman then informed me that the spirit of Socrates had delivered this special revelation in the course of the night. "My friend, I hope you are pretty well. There are two in this railway carriage. How do you do? There are seventeen thousand four hundred and seventy-nine spirits here, but you cannot see them. Pythagoras is here. He is not at liberty to mention it, but hopes you like travelling." Galileo likewise had dropped in, with this scientific intelligence. "I am glad to see you, *amico. Come sta?* Water will freeze when it is cold enough. *Addio!*" In the course of the night, also, the following phenomena had occurred. Bishop Butler had insisted on spelling his name, "Bubler," for which offence against orthography and good manners he had been dismissed as out of temper. John Milton (suspected of wilful mystification) had repudiated the authorship of Paradise Lost, and had introduced, as joint authors of that poem, two Unknown gentlemen, respectively named Grungers and Scadgingtone. And Prince Arthur, nephew of King John of England, had described himself as tolerably comfortable in the seventh circle, where he was learning to paint on velvet, under the direction of Mrs. Trimmer and Mary Queen of Scots.

If this should meet the eye of the gentleman who favoured

me with these disclosures, I trust he will excuse my confessing that the sight of the rising sun, and the contemplation of the magnificent Order of the vast Universe, made me impatient of them. In a word, I was so impatient of them, that I was mightily glad to get out at the next station, and to exchange these clouds and vapours for the free air of Heaven.

By that time it was a beautiful morning. As I walked away among such leaves as had already fallen from the golden, brown, and russet trees ; and as I looked around me on the wonders of Creation, and thought of the steady, unchanging, and harmonious laws by which they are sustained ; the gentleman's spiritual intercourse seemed to me as poor a piece of journey-work as ever this world saw. In which heathen state of mind, I came within view of the house, and stopped to examine it attentively.

It was a solitary house, standing in a sadly neglected garden : a pretty even square of some two acres. It was a house of about the time of George the Second ; as stiff, as cold, as formal, and in as bad taste, as could possibly be desired by the most loyal admirer of the whole quartet of Georges. It was uninhabited, but had, within a year or two, been cheaply repaired to render it habitable ; I say cheaply, because the work had been done in a surface manner, and was already decaying as to the paint and plaster, though the colours were fresh. A lop-sided board drooped over the garden wall, announcing that it was "to let on very reasonable terms, well furnished." It was much too closely and heavily shadowed by trees, and, in particular, there were six tall poplars before the front windows, which were excessively melancholy, and the site of which had been extremely ill chosen.

It was easy to see that it was an avoided house—a house that was shunned by the village, to which my eye was guided by a church spire some half a mile off—a house that nobody would take. And the natural inference was, that it had the reputation of being a haunted house.

No period within the four-and-twenty hours of day and night is so solemn to me, as the early morning. In the summer time, I often rise very early, and repair to my room to do a day's work before breakfast, and I am always on those occasions deeply impressed by the stillness and solitude around me. Besides that there is something awful in the being surrounded by familiar faces asleep—in the knowledge that those who are dearest to us and to whom we are dearest, are profoundly unconscious of us, in an impassive state, anticipative of that mysterious condition to which we are all tending—the stopped life, the broken threads of yesterday, the deserted seat, the closed book, the unfinished but abandoned occupation, all are images of Death. The tranquillity of the hour is the tranquillity of Death. The colour and the chill have the same association. Even a certain air that familiar household objects take upon them when they first emerge from the shadows of the night into the morning, of being newer, and as they used to be long ago, has its counterpart in the subsidence of the worn face of maturity or age, in death, into the old youthful look. Moreover, I once saw the apparition of my father, at this hour. He was alive and well, and nothing ever came of it, but I saw him in the daylight, sitting with his back towards me, on a seat that stood beside my bed. His head was resting on his hand, and whether he was slumbering or grieving, I could not discern. Amazed to see him there, I sat up, moved my position, leaned out of bed, and watched him. As he did not move, I spoke to him more than once. As he did not move then, I became alarmed and laid my hand upon his shoulder, as I thought—and there was no such thing.

For all these reasons, and for others less easily and briefly statable, I find the early morning to be my most ghostly time. Any house would be more or less haunted, to me, in the early morning; and a haunted house could scarcely address me to greater advantage than then.

I walked on into the village, with the desertion of this house upon my mind, and I found the landlord of the little inn, sanding his doorstep. I bespoke breakfast, and broached the subject of the house.

"Is it haunted?" I asked.

The landlord looked at me, shook his head, and answered, "I say nothing."

"Then it *is* haunted?"

"Well!" cried the landlord, in an outburst of frankness that had the appearance of desperation—"I wouldn't sleep in it."

"Why not?"

"If I wanted to have all the bells in a house ring, with nobody to ring 'em; and all the doors in a house bang, with

I

nobody to bang 'em; and all sorts of feet treading about, with no feet there; why, then," said the landlord, "I'd sleep in that house."

"Is anything seen there?"

The landlord looked at me again, and then, with his former appearance of desperation, called down his stable-yard for "Ikey!"

The call produced a high-shouldered young fellow, with a round red face, a short crop of sandy hair, a very broad humorous mouth, a turned-up nose, and a great sleeved waistcoat of purple bars, with mother-of-pearl buttons, that seemed to be growing upon him, and to be in a fair way— if it were not pruned—of covering his head and overrunning his boots.

"This gentleman wants to know," said the landlord, "if anything's seen at the Poplars."

"'Ooded woman with a howl," said Ikey, in a state of great freshness.

"Do you mean a cry?"

"I mean a bird, Sir."

"A hooded woman with an owl. Dear me! Did you ever see her?"

"I seen the howl."

"Never the woman?"

"Not so plain as the howl, but they always keeps together."

"Has anybody ever seen the woman as plainly as the owl?"

"Lord bless you, Sir! Lots."

"Who?"

"Lord bless you, Sir! Lots."

"The general-dealer opposite, for instance, who is opening his shop?"

"Perkins? Bless you, Perkins wouldn't go a-nigh the place. No!" observed the young man, with considerable feeling; "he an't overwise, an't Perkins, but he an't such a fool as *that*."

(Here, the landlord murmured his confidence in Perkins's knowing better.)

"Who is—or who was—the hooded woman with the owl? Do you know?"

"Well!" said Ikey, holding up his cap with one hand while he scratched his head with the other, "they say, in general, that she was murdered, and the howl he 'ooted the while."

This very concise summary of the facts was all I could learn, except that a young man, as hearty and likely a young man as ever I see, had been took with fits and held down in 'em, after seeing the hooded woman. Also, that a personage, dimly described as "a hold chap, a sort of one-eyed tramp, answering to the name of Joby, unless you challenged him as Greenwood, and then he said, 'Why not? and even if so, mind your own business,'" had encountered the hooded woman, a matter of five or six times. But, I was not materially assisted by these witnesses: inasmuch as the first was in California, and the last was, as Ikey said (and he was confirmed by the landlord), Anywheres.

Now, although I regard with a hushed and solemn fear, the mysteries, between which and this state of existence is interposed the barrier of the great trial and change that fall on all the things that live; and although I have not the audacity to pretend that I know anything of them; I can no more reconcile the mere banging of doors, ringing of bells, creaking of boards, and such-like insignificances, with the majestic beauty and pervading analogy of all the Divine rules that I am permitted to understand, than I had been able, a little while before, to yoke the spiritual intercourse of my fellow-traveller to the chariot of the rising sun. Moreover, I had lived in two haunted houses—both abroad. In one of these, an old Italian palace, which bore the reputation of being very badly haunted indeed, and which had recently been twice abandoned on that account, I lived eight months, most tranquilly and pleasantly: notwithstanding that the house had a score of mysterious bedrooms, which were never used, and possessed, in one large room in which I sat reading, times out of number at all hours, and next to which I slept, a haunted chamber of the first pretensions. I gently hinted these considerations to the landlord. And as to this particular house having a bad name, I reasoned with him, Why, how many things had bad names undeservedly, and how easy it was to give bad names, and did he not think that if he and I were persistently to whisper in the village that any weird-looking old drunken tinker of the neighbourhood had sold himself to the Devil, he would come in time to be suspected of that commercial venture! All this wise talk was perfectly ineffective with the landlord, I am bound to confess, and was as dead a failure as ever I made in my life.

To cut this part of the story short, I was piqued about the haunted house, and was already half resolved to take it. So, after breakfast, I got the keys from Perkins's brother-in-law (a whip and harness maker, who keeps the Post Office, and is under submission to a most rigorous wife of the Doubly Seceding Little Emmanuel persuasion), and went up to the house, attended by my landlord and by Ikey.

Within, I found it, as I had expected, transcendently dismal. The slowly changing shadows waved on it from the heavy trees, were doleful in the last degree; the house was ill-placed, ill-built, ill-planned, and ill-fitted. It was damp, it was not free from dry rot, there was a flavour of rats in it, and it was the gloomy victim of that indescribable decay which settles on all the work of man's hands whenever it is not turned to man's account. The kitchens and offices were too large, and too remote from each other. Above stairs and below, waste tracts of passage intervened between patches of fertility represented by rooms; and there was a mouldy old well with a green growth upon it, hiding like a murderous trap, near the bottom of the back-stairs, under the double row of bells. One of these bells was labelled, on a black ground in faded white letters, MASTER B. This, they told me, was the bell that rang the most.

"Who was Master B. ?" I asked. "Is it known what he did while the owl hooted?"

"Rang the bell," said Ikey.

I was rather struck by the prompt dexterity with which this young man pitched his fur cap at the bell, and rang it himself. It was a loud, unpleasant bell, and made a very disagreeable sound. The other bells were inscribed according to the names of the rooms to which their wires were conducted: as "Picture Room," "Double Room," "Clock Room," and the like. Following Master B.'s bell to its source, I found that young gentleman to have had but indifferent third-class accommodation in a triangular cabin under the cock-loft, with a corner fireplace which Master B. must have been exceedingly small if he were ever able to warm himself at, and a corner chimneypiece like a pyramidal staircase to the ceiling for Tom Thumb. The papering of one side of the room had dropped down bodily, with fragments of plaster adhering to it, and almost blocked up the door. It appeared that Master B., in his spiritual condition, always made a point of pulling the paper down. Neither the landlord nor Ikey could suggest why he made such a fool of himself.

Except that the house had an immensely large rambling loft at top, I made no other discoveries. It was moderately well furnished, but sparely. Some of the furniture—say, a third—was as old as the house; the rest was of various periods within the last half-century. I was referred to a corn-chandler in the market-place of the county town to treat for the house. I went that day, and I took it for six months.

It was just the middle of October when I moved in with my maiden sister (I venture to call her eight-and-thirty, she is so very handsome, sensible, and engaging). We took with us, a deaf stable-man, my bloodhound Turk, two women servants, and a young person called an Odd Girl. I have reason to record of the attendant last enumerated, who was one of the Saint Lawrence's Union Female Orphans, that she was a fatal mistake and a disastrous engagement.

The year was dying early, the leaves were falling fast, it was a raw cold day when we took possession, and the gloom of the house was most depressing. The cook (an amiable woman, but of a weak turn of intellect) burst into tears on beholding the kitchen, and requested that her silver watch might be delivered over to her sister (2 Tuppintock's Gardens, Liggs's Walk, Clapham Rise), in the event of anything happening to her from the damp. Streaker, the housemaid, feigned cheerfulness, but was the greater martyr. The Odd Girl, who had never been in the country, alone was pleased, and made arrangements for sowing an acorn in the garden outside the scullery window, and rearing an oak.

We went, before dark, through all the natural—as opposed to supernatural—miseries incidental to our state. Dispiriting reports ascended (like the smoke) from the basement in volumes, and descended from the upper rooms. There was no rolling-pin, there was no salamander (which failed to surprise me, for I don't know what it is), there was nothing in the house, what there was, was broken, the last people must have lived like pigs, what could the meaning of the landlord be? Through these distresses, the Odd Girl was cheerful and exemplary. But within four hours after dark we had got into a supernatural groove, and the Odd Girl had seen " Eyes," and was in hysterics.

My sister and I had agreed to keep the haunting strictly

to ourselves, and my impression was, and still is, that I had not left Ikey, when he helped to unload the cart, alone with the women, or any one of them, for one minute.   Nevertheless, as I say, the Odd Girl had "seen Eyes" (no other explanation could ever be drawn from her), before nine, and by ten o'clock had had as much vinegar applied to her as would pickle a handsome salmon.

I leave a discerning public to judge of my feelings, when, under these untoward circumstances, at about half-past ten o'clock Master B.'s bell began to ring in a most infuriated manner, and Turk howled until the house resounded with his lamentations!

I hope I may never again be in a state of mind so unchristian as the mental frame in which I lived for some weeks, respecting the memory of Master B.   Whether his bell was rung by rats, or mice, or bats, or wind, or what other accidental vibration, or sometimes by one cause, sometimes another, and sometimes by collusion, I don't know; but, certain it is, that it did ring two nights out of three, until I conceived the happy idea of twisting Master B.'s neck—in other words, breaking his bell short off—and silencing that young gentleman, as to my experience and belief, for ever.

But, by that time, the Odd Girl had developed such improving powers of catalepsy, that she had become a shining example of that very inconvenient disorder.   She would stiffen, like a Guy Fawkes endowed with unreason, on the most irrelevant occasions.   I would address the servants in a lucid manner, pointing out to them that I had painted Master B.'s room and balked the paper, and taken Master B.'s bell away and balked the ringing, and if they could suppose that that confounded boy had lived and died, to clothe himself with no better behaviour than would most unquestionably have brought him and the sharpest particles of a birch-broom into close acquaintance in the present imperfect state of existence, could they also suppose a mere poor human being, such as I was, capable by those contemptible means of counteracting and limiting the powers of the disembodied spirits of the dead, or of any spirits?—I say I would become emphatic and cogent, not to say rather complacent, in such an address, when it would all go for nothing by reason of the Odd Girl's suddenly stiffening from the toes upward, and glaring among us like a parochial petrifaction.

Streaker, the housemaid, too, had an attribute of a most discomfiting nature. I am unable to say whether she was of an unusually lymphatic temperament, or what else was the matter with her, but this young woman became a mere Distillery for the production of the largest and most transparent tears I ever met with. Combined with these characteristics, was a peculiar tenacity of hold in those specimens, so that they didn't fall, but hung upon her face and nose. In this condition, and mildly and deplorably shaking her head, her silence would throw me more heavily than the Admirable Crichton could have done in a verbal disputation for a purse of money. Cook, likewise, always covered me with confusion as with a garment, by neatly winding up the session with the protest that the Ouse was wearing her out, and by meekly repeating her last wishes regarding her silver watch.

As to our nightly life, the contagion of suspicion and fear was among us, and there is no such contagion under the sky. Hooded woman? According to the accounts, we were in a perfect Convent of hooded women. Noises? With that contagion downstairs, I myself have sat in the dismal parlour, listening, until I have heard so many and such strange noises, that they would have chilled my blood if I had not warmed it by dashing out to make discoveries. Try this in bed, in the dead of the night; try this at your own comfortable fireside, in the life of the night. You can fill any house with noises, if you will, until you have a noise for every nerve in your nervous system.

I repeat; the contagion of suspicion and fear was among us, and there is no such contagion under the sky. The women (their noses in a chronic state of excoriation from smelling-salts) were always primed and loaded for a swoon, and ready to go off with hair-triggers. The two elder detached the Odd Girl on all expeditions that were considered doubly hazardous, and she always established the reputation of such adventures by coming back cataleptic. If Cook or Streaker went overhead after dark, we knew we should presently hear a bump on the ceiling; and this took place so constantly, that it was as if a fighting man were engaged to go about the house, administering a touch of his art which I believe is called The Auctioneer, to every domestic he met with.

It was in vain to do anything. It was in vain to be

frightened, for the moment in one's own person, by a real owl, and then to show the owl. It was in vain to discover, by striking an accidental discord on the piano, that Turk always howled at particular notes and combinations. It was in vain to be a Rhadamanthus with the bells, and if an unfortunate bell rang without leave, to have it down inexorably and silence it. It was in vain to fire up chimneys, let torches down the well, charge furiously into suspected rooms and recesses. We changed servants, and it was no better. The new set ran away, and a third set came, and it was no better. At last, our comfortable housekeeping got to be so disorganised and wretched, that I one night dejectedly said to my sister: "Patty, I begin to despair of our getting people to go on with us here, and I think we must give this up."

My sister, who is a woman of immense spirit, replied, "No, John, don't give it up. Don't be beaten, John. There is another way."

"And what is that?" said I.

"John," returned my sister, "if we are not to be driven out of this house, and that for no reason whatever, that is apparent to you or me, we must help ourselves and take the house wholly and solely into our own hands."

"But, the servants," said I.

"Have no servants," said my sister, boldly.

Like most people in my grade of life, I had never thought of the possibility of going on without those faithful obstructions. The notion was so new to me when suggested, that I looked very doubtful.

"We know they come here to be frightened and infect one another, and we know they are frightened and do infect one another," said my sister.

"With the exception of Bottles," I observed, in a meditative tone.

(The deaf stable-man. I kept him in my service, and still keep him, as a phenomenon of moroseness not to be matched in England.)

"To be sure, John," assented my sister; "except Bottles. And what does that go to prove? Bottles talks to nobody, and hears nobody unless he is absolutely roared at, and what alarm has Bottles ever given, or taken? None."

This was perfectly true; the individual in question having retired, every night at ten o'clock, to his bed over the coach-house, with no other company than a pitchfork and a pail of water. That the pail of water would have been over me, and the pitchfork through me, if I had put myself without announcement in Bottles's way after that minute, I had deposited in my own mind as a fact worth remembering. Neither had Bottles ever taken the least notice of any of our many uproars. An imperturbable and speechless man, he had sat at his supper, with Streaker present in a swoon, and the Odd Girl marble, and had only put another potato in his cheek, or profited by the general misery to help himself to beefsteak pie.

"And so," continued my sister, "I exempt Bottles. And considering, John, that the house is too large, and perhaps too lonely, to be kept well in hand by Bottles, you, and me, I propose that we cast about among our friends for a certain selected number of the most reliable and willing—form a Society here for three months—wait upon ourselves and one another—live cheerfully and socially—and see what happens."

I was so charmed with my sister, that I embraced her on the spot, and went into her plan with the greatest ardour.

We were then in the third week of November; but, we took our measures so vigorously, and were so well seconded by the friends in whom we confided, that there was still a week of the month unexpired, when our party all came down together merrily, and mustered in the haunted house.

I will mention, in this place, two small changes that I made while my sister and I were yet alone. It occurring to me as not improbable that Turk howled in the house at night, partly because he wanted to get out of it, I stationed him in his kennel outside, but unchained; and I seriously warned the village that any man who came in his way must not expect to leave him without a rip in his own throat. I then casually asked Ikey if he were a judge of a gun? On his saying, "Yes, Sir, I knows a good gun when I sees her," I begged the favour of his stepping up to the house and looking at mine.

"*She's* a true one, Sir," said Ikey, after inspecting a double-barrelled rifle that I bought in New York a few years ago. "No mistake about *her*, Sir,"

"Ikey," said I, "don't mention it; I have seen something in this house."

"No, Sir?" he whispered, greedily opening his eyes. "'Ooded lady, Sir?"

"Don't be frightened," said I. "It was a figure rather like you."

"Lord, Sir?"

"Ikey!" said I, shaking hands with him warmly: I may say affectionately; "if there is any truth in these ghost-stories, the greatest service I can do you, is, to fire at that figure. And I promise you, by Heaven and earth, I will do it with this gun if I see it again!"

The young man thanked me, and took his leave with some little precipitation, after declining a glass of liquor. I imparted my secret to him, because I had never quite forgotten his throwing his cap at the bell; because I had, on another occasion, noticed something very like a fur cap, lying not far from the bell, one night when it had burst out ringing; and because I had remarked that we were at our ghostliest whenever he came up in the evening to comfort the servants. Let me do Ikey no injustice. He was afraid of the house, and believed in its being haunted; and yet he would play false on the haunting side, so surely as he got an opportunity. The Odd Girl's case was exactly similar. She went about the house in a state of real terror, and yet lied monstrously and wilfully, and invented many of the alarms she spread, and made many of the sounds we heard. I had had my eye on the two, and I know it. It is not necessary for me, here, to account for this preposterous state of mind; I content myself with remarking that it is familiarly known to every intelligent man who has had fair medical, legal, or other watchful experience; that it is as well established and as common a state of mind as any with which observers are acquainted; and that it is one of the first elements, above all others, rationally to be suspected in, and strictly looked for, and separated from, any question of this kind.

To return to our party. The first thing we did when we were all assembled, was, to draw lots for bedrooms. That done, and every bedroom, and, indeed, the whole house, having been minutely examined by the whole body, we allotted the various household duties, as if we had been on a gipsy party, or a yachting party, or a hunting party, or were shipwrecked. I then recounted the floating rumours concerning the hooded lady, the owl, and Master B.: with others, still more filmy, which had floated about during our occupation, relative to some ridiculous old ghost of the female gender who went up and down, carrying the ghost of a round table; and also to an impalpable Jackass, whom nobody was ever able to catch. Some of these ideas I really believe our people below had communicated to one another in some diseased way, without conveying them in words. We then gravely called one another to witness, that we were not there to be deceived, or to deceive—which we considered pretty much the same thing—and that, with a serious sense of responsibility, we would be strictly true to one another, and would strictly follow out the truth. The understanding was established, that any one who heard unusual noises in the night, and who wished to trace them, should knock at my door; lastly, that on Twelfth Night, the last night of holy Christmas, all our individual experiences since that then present hour of our coming together in the haunted house, should be brought to light for the good of all; and that we would hold our peace on the subject till then, unless on some remarkable provocation to break silence.

We were, in number and in character, as follows:

First—to get my sister and myself out of the way—there were we two. In the drawing of lots, my sister drew her own room, and I drew Master B.'s. Next, there was our first cousin John Herschel, so called after the great astronomer: than whom I suppose a better man at a telescope does not breathe. With him, was his wife: a charming creature to whom he had been married in the previous spring. I thought it (under the circumstances) rather imprudent to bring her, because there is no knowing what even a false alarm may do at such a time; but I suppose he knew his own business best, and I must say that if she had been *my* wife, I never could have left her endearing and bright face behind. They drew the Clock Room. Alfred Starling, an uncommonly agreeable young fellow of eight-and-twenty for whom I have the greatest liking, was in the Double Room; mine, usually, and designated by that name from having a dressing-room within it, with two large and cumbersome windows, which no wedges *I* was ever able to make, would keep from shaking, in any weather, wind or no wind. Alfred is a young fellow who pretends to be "fast" (another word for loose, as I understand the term), but who is much too good and sensible for that nonsense, and who would have distinguished himself before now, if his father had not unfortunately left him a small independence of two hundred a year, on the strength of which his only occupation in life has been to spend six.

I am in hopes, however, that his Banker may break, or that he may enter into some speculation guaranteed to pay twenty per cent.; for, I am convinced that if he could only be ruined, his fortune is made. Belinda Bates, bosom friend of my sister, and a most intellectual, amiable, and delightful girl, got the Picture Room. She has a fine genius for poetry, combined with real business earnestness, and "goes in "—to use an expression of Alfred's—for Woman's mission, Woman's rights, Woman's wrongs, and everything that is woman's with a capital W, or is not and ought to be, or is and ought not to be. "Most praiseworthy, my dear, and Heaven prosper you!" I whispered to her on the first night of my taking leave of her at the Picture-Room door, "but don't overdo it. And in respect of the great necessity there is, my darling, for more employments being within the reach of Woman than our civilisation has as yet assigned to her, don't fly at the unfortunate men, even those men who are at first sight in your way, as if they were the natural oppressors of your sex; for, trust me, Belinda, they do sometimes spend their wages among wives and daughters, sisters, mothers, aunts, and grandmothers; and the play is, really, not *all* Wolf and Red Riding-Hood, but has other parts in it." However, I digress.

Belinda, as I have mentioned, occupied the Picture Room. We had but three other chambers: the Corner Room, the Cupboard Room, and the Garden Room. My old friend, Jack Governor, "slung his hammock," as he called it, in the Corner Room. I have always regarded Jack as the finest-looking sailor that ever sailed. He is gray now, but as handsome as he was a quarter of a century ago—nay, handsomer. A portly, cheery, well-built figure of a broad-shouldered man, with a frank smile, a brilliant dark eye, and a rich dark eyebrow. I remember those under darker hair, and they look all the better for their silver setting. He has been wherever his Union namesake flies, has Jack, and I have met old shipmates of his, away in the Mediterranean and on the other side of the Atlantic, who have beamed and brightened at the casual mention of his name, and have cried, "You know Jack Governor? Then you know a prince of men!" That he is! And so unmistakably a naval officer, that if you were to meet him coming out of an Esquimaux snow-hut in seal's skin, you would be vaguely persuaded he was in full naval uniform.

Jack once had that bright clear eye of his on my sister; but, it fell out that he married another lady and took her to South America, where she died. This was a dozen years ago or more. He brought down with him to our haunted house a little cask of salt beef; for, he is always convinced that all salt beef not of his own pickling, is mere carrion, and invariably, when he goes to London, packs a piece in his portmanteau. He had also volunteered to bring with him one "Nat Beaver," an old comrade of his, captain of a merchantman. Mr. Beaver, with a thick-set wooden face and figure, and apparently as hard as a block all over, proved to be an intelligent man, with a world of watery experiences in him, and great practical knowledge. At times, there was a curious nervousness about him, apparently the lingering result of some old illness; but, it seldom lasted many minutes. He got the Cupboard Room, and lay there next to Mr. Undery, my friend and solicitor: who came down, in an amateur capacity, "to go through with it," as he said, and who plays whist better than the whole Law List, from the red cover at the beginning to the red cover at the end.

I never was happier in my life, and I believe it was the universal feeling among us. Jack Governor, always a man of wonderful resources, was Chief Cook, and made some of the best dishes I ever ate, including unapproachable curries. My sister was pastrycook and confectioner. Starling and I were Cook's Mate, turn and turn about, and on special occasions the chief cook "pressed" Mr. Beaver. We had a great deal of out-door sport and exercise, but nothing was neglected within, and there was no ill-humour or misunderstanding among us, and our evenings were so delightful that we had at least one good reason for being reluctant to go to bed.

We had a few night alarms in the beginning. On the first night, I was knocked up by Jack with a most wonderful ship's lantern in his hand, like the gills of some monster of the deep, who informed me that he "was going aloft to the main truck," to have the weathercock down. It was a stormy night, and I remonstrated; but Jack called my attention to its making a sound like a cry of despair, and said somebody would be "hailing a ghost" presently, if it wasn't done. So, up to the top of the house, where I could hardly stand for the wind, we went, accompanied by Mr. Beaver; and there Jack, lantern and all, with Mr. Beaver after him, swarmed up to the top of a cupola, some two dozen feet above the chimneys, and stood upon nothing particular, coolly knocking the weathercock off, until they both got into such good spirits with the wind and the height, that I thought they would never come down. Another night, they turned out again, and had a chimney-cowl off. Another night, they cut a sobbing and gulping water-pipe away. Another night, they found out something else. On several occasions, they both, in the coolest manner, simultaneously dropped out of their respective bedroom windows, hand over hand by their counterpanes, to "overhaul" something mysterious in the garden.

The engagement among us was faithfully kept, and nobody revealed anything. All we knew was, if any one's room were haunted, no one looked the worse for it.

THE GHOST IN MASTER B.'S ROOM

WHEN I established myself in the triangular garret which had gained so distinguished a reputation, my thoughts naturally turned to Master B. My speculations about him were uneasy and manifold. Whether his Christian name was Benjamin, Bissextile (from his having been born in Leap Year), Bartholomew, or Bill. Whether the initial letter belonged to his family name, and that was Baxter, Black, Brown, Barker, Buggins, Baker, or Bird. Whether he was a foundling, and had been baptized B. Whether he was a lion-hearted boy, and B. was short for Briton, or for Bull. Whether he could possibly have been kith and kin to an illustrious lady who brightened my own childhood, and had come of the blood of the brilliant Mother Bunch?

With these profitless meditations I tormented myself much. I also carried the mysterious letter into the appearance and pursuits of the deceased; wondering whether he dressed in Blue, wore Boots (he couldn't have been Bald), was a boy of Brains, liked Books, was good at Bowling, had any skill as a Boxer, even in his Buoyant Boyhood Bathed from a Bathing-machine at Bognor, Bangor, Bournemouth, Brighton, or Broadstairs, like a Bounding Billiard Ball?

So, from the first, I was haunted by the letter B.

It was not long before I remarked that I never by any

The Haunted House

hazard had a dream of Master B., or of anything belonging
to him.   But, the instant I awoke from sleep, at whatever
hour of the night, my thoughts took him up, and roamed
away, trying to attach his initial letter to something that
would fit it and keep it quiet.

For six nights, I had been worried thus in Master B.'s room,
when I began to perceive that things were going wrong.

The first appearance that presented itself was early in the
morning when it was but just daylight and no more.   I was
standing shaving at my glass, when I suddenly discovered,
to my consternation and amazement, that I was shaving—not
myself—I am fifty—but a boy.   Apparently Master B.!

I trembled and looked over my shoulder; nothing there.
I looked again in the glass, and distinctly saw the features
and expression of a boy, who was shaving, not to get rid of
a beard, but to get one.   Extremely troubled in my mind,
I took a few turns in the room, and went back to the looking-
glass, resolved to steady my hand and complete the operation
in which I had been disturbed.   Opening my eyes, which I
had shut while recovering my firmness, I now met in the
glass, looking straight at me, the eyes of a young man of four
or five and twenty.   Terrified by this new ghost, I closed my
eyes, and made a strong effort to recover myself.   Opening
them again, I saw, shaving his cheek in the glass, my father,
who has long been dead.   Nay, I even saw my grandfather
too, whom I never did see in my life.

Although naturally much affected by these remarkable
visitations, I determined to keep my secret, until the time
agreed upon for the present general disclosure.   Agitated by
a multitude of curious thoughts, I retired to my room, that
night, prepared to encounter some new experience of a spectral
character.   Nor was my preparation needless, for, waking
from an uneasy sleep at exactly two o'clock in the morning,
what were my feelings to find that I was sharing my bed
with the skeleton of Master B.!

I sprang up, and the skeleton sprang up also.   I then heard
a plaintive voice saying, "Where am I?   What is become
of me?" and, looking hard in that direction, perceived the
ghost of Master B.

The young spectre was dressed in an obsolete fashion : or
rather, was not so much dressed as put into a case of inferior
pepper-and-salt cloth, made horrible by means of shining
buttons.   I observed that these buttons went, in a double

row, over each shoulder of the young ghost, and appeared to descend his back. He wore a frill round his neck. His right hand (which I distinctly noticed to be inky) was laid upon his stomach; connecting this action with some feeble pimples on his countenance, and his general air of nausea, I concluded this ghost to be the ghost of a boy who had habitually taken a great deal too much medicine.

"Where am I?" said the little spectre, in a pathetic voice. "And why was I born in the Calomel days, and why did I have all that Calomel given me?"

I replied, with sincere earnestness, that upon my soul I couldn't tell him.

"Where is my little sister," said the ghost, "and where my angelic little wife, and where is the boy I went to school with?"

I entreated the phantom to be comforted, and above all things to take heart respecting the loss of the boy he went to school with. I represented to him that probably that boy never did, within human experience, come out well, when discovered. I urged that I myself had, in later life, turned up several boys whom I went to school with, and none of them had at all answered. I expressed my humble belief that that boy never did answer. I represented that he was a mythic character, a delusion, and a snare. I recounted how, the last time I found him, I found him at a dinner party behind a wall of white cravat, with an inconclusive opinion on every possible subject, and a power of silent boredom absolutely Titanic. I related how, on the strength of our having been together at "Old Doylance's," he had asked himself to breakfast with me (a social offence of the largest magnitude); how, fanning my weak embers of belief in Doylance's boys, I had let him in; and how, he had proved to be a fearful wanderer about the earth, pursuing the race of Adam with inexplicable notions concerning the currency, and with a proposition that the Bank of England should, on pain of being abolished, instantly strike off and circulate, God knows how many thousand millions of ten-and-sixpenny notes.

The ghost heard me in silence, and with a fixed stare. "Barber!" it apostrophised me when I had finished.

"Barber?" I repeated—for I am not of that profession.

"Condemned," said the ghost, "to shave a constant change of customers—now, me—now, a young man—now, thyself as thou art—now, thy father—now, thy grandfather; condemned,

too, to lie down with a skeleton every night, and to rise with
it every morning——"

(I shuddered on hearing this dismal announcement).

"Barber! Pursue me!"

I had felt, even before the words were uttered, that I was
under a spell to pursue the phantom. I immediately did
so, and was in Master B.'s room no longer.

Most people know what long and fatiguing night journeys
had been forced upon the witches who used to confess, and
who, no doubt, told the exact truth—particularly as they
were always assisted with leading questions, and the Torture
was always ready. I asseverate that, during my occupation
of Master B.'s room, I was taken by the ghost that haunted
it, on expeditions fully as long and wild as any of those.
Assuredly, I was presented to no shabby old man with a
goat's horns and tail (something between Pan and an old
clothesman), holding conventional receptions, as stupid as
those of real life and less decent; but, I came upon other
things which appeared to me to have more meaning.

Confident that I speak the truth and shall be believed, I
declare without hesitation that I followed the ghost, in the
first instance on a broom-stick, and afterwards on a rocking-
horse. The very smell of the animal's paint—especially
when I brought it out, by making him warm—I am ready
to swear to. I followed the ghost, afterwards, in a hackney
coach; an institution with the peculiar smell of which, the
present generation is unacquainted, but to which I am again
ready to swear as a combination of stable, dog with the mange,
and very old bellows. (In this, I appeal to previous generations to confirm or refute me.) I pursued the phantom, on a
headless donkey: at least, upon a donkey who was so interested
in the state of his stomach that his head was always down
there, investigating it; on ponies, expressly born to kick up
behind; on roundabouts and swings, from fairs; in the first
cab—another forgotten institution where the fare regularly
got into bed, and was tucked up with the driver.

Not to trouble you with a detailed account of all my
travels in pursuit of the ghost of Master B., which were
longer and more wonderful than those of Sinbad the Sailor,
I will confine myself to one experience from which you may
judge of many.

I was marvellously changed. I was myself, yet not myself.
I was conscious of something within me, which has been the

same all through my life, and which I have always recognised
under all its phases and varieties as never altering, and yet I
was not the I who had gone to bed in Master B.'s room.
I had the smoothest of faces and the shortest of legs, and
I had taken another creature like myself, also with the
smoothest of faces and the shortest of legs, behind a door,
and was confiding to him a proposition of the most astounding nature.

This proposition was, that we should have a Seraglio.

The other creature assented warmly. He had no notion
of respectability, neither had I. It was the custom of the
East, it was the way of the good Caliph Haroun Alraschid
(let me have the corrupted name again for once, it is so
scented with sweet memories!), the usage was highly laudable,
and most worthy of imitation. "O, yes! Let us," said the
other creature with a jump, "have a Seraglio."

It was not because we entertained the faintest doubts of
the meritorious character of the Oriental establishment we
proposed to import, that we perceived it must be kept a secret
from Miss Griffin. It was because we knew Miss Griffin to be
bereft of human sympathies, and incapable of appreciating the
greatness of the great Haroun. Mystery impenetrably shrouded
from Miss Griffin then, let us entrust it to Miss Bule.

We were ten in Miss Griffin's establishment by Hamp-
stead Ponds; eight ladies and two gentlemen. Miss Bule,
whom I judge to have attained the ripe age of eight or nine,
took the lead in society. I opened the subject to her in the
course of the day, and proposed that she should become the
Favourite.

Miss Bule, after struggling with the diffidence so natural
to, and charming in, her adorable sex, expressed herself as
flattered by the idea, but wished to know how it was proposed to provide for Miss Pipson? Miss Bule—who was
understood to have vowed towards that young lady, a friendship, halves, and no secrets, until death, on the Church Service and Lessons complete in two volumes with case and
lock—Miss Bule said she could not, as the friend of Pipson,
disguise from herself, or me, that Pipson was not one of
the common.

Now, Miss Pipson, having curly light hair and blue eyes
(which was my idea of anything mortal and feminine that
was called Fair), I promptly replied that I regarded Miss
Pipson in the light of a Fair Circassian.

"And what then?" Miss Bule pensively asked.

I replied that she must be inveigled by a Merchant, brought to me veiled, and purchased as a slave.

[The other creature had already fallen into the second male place in the State, and was set apart for Grand Vizier. He afterwards resisted this disposal of events, but had his hair pulled until he yielded.]

"Shall I not be jealous?" Miss Bule inquired, casting down her eyes.

"Zobeide, no," I replied; "you will ever be the favourite Sultana; the first place in my heart, and on my throne, will be ever yours."

Miss Bule, upon that assurance, consented to propound the idea to her seven beautiful companions. It occurring to me, in the course of the same day, that we knew we could trust a grinning and good-natured soul called Tabby, who was the serving drudge of the house, and had no more figure than one of the beds, and upon whose face there was always more or less black-lead, I slipped into Miss Bule's hand after supper, a little note to that effect: dwelling on the black-lead as being in a manner deposited by the finger of Providence, pointing Tabby out for Mesrour, the celebrated chief of the Blacks of the Hareem.

There were difficulties in the formation of the desired institution, as there are in all combinations. The other creature showed himself of a low character, and, when defeated in aspiring to the throne, pretended to have conscientious scruples about prostrating himself before the Caliph; wouldn't call him Commander of the Faithful; spoke of him slightingly and inconsistently as a mere "chap;" said he, the other creature, "wouldn't play"—Play!—and was otherwise coarse and offensive. This meanness of disposition was, however, put down by the general indignation of an united Seraglio, and I became blessed in the smiles of eight of the fairest of the daughters of men.

The smiles could only be bestowed when Miss Griffin was looking another way, and only then in a very wary manner, for there was a legend among the followers of the Prophet that she saw with a little round ornament in the middle of the pattern on the back of her shawl. But every day after dinner, for an hour, we were all together, and then the Favourite and the rest of the Royal Hareem competed who should most beguile the leisure of the Serene Haroun reposing from the cares of State—which were generally, as in most affairs of State, of an arithmetical character, the Commander of the Faithful being a fearful boggler at a sum.

On these occasions, the devoted Mesrour, chief of the Blacks of the Hareem, was always in attendance (Miss Griffin usually ringing for that officer, at the same time, with great vehemence), but never acquitted himself in a manner worthy of his historical reputation. In the first place, his bringing a broom into the Divan of the Caliph, even when Haroun wore on his shoulders the red robe of anger (Miss Pipson's pelisse), though it might be got over for the moment, was never to be quite satisfactorily accounted for. In the second place, his breaking out into grinning exclamations of "Lork you pretties!" was neither Eastern nor respectful. In the third place, when specially instructed to say "Bismillah!" he always said "Hallelujah!" This officer, unlike his class, was too good-humoured altogether, kept his mouth open far too wide, expressed approbation to an incongruous extent, and even once—it was on the occasion of the purchase of the Fair Circassian for five hundred thousand purses of gold, and cheap, too—embraced the Slave, the Favourite, and the Caliph, all round. (Parenthetically let me say God bless Mesrour, and may there have been sons and daughters on that tender bosom, softening many a hard day since!)

Miss Griffin was a model of propriety, and I am at a loss to imagine what the feelings of the virtuous woman would have been, if she had known, when she paraded us down the Hampstead-road two and two, that she was walking with a stately step at the head of Polygamy and Mahomedanism. I believe that a mysterious and terrible joy with which the contemplation of Miss Griffin, in this unconscious state, inspired us, and a grim sense prevalent among us that there was a dreadful power in our knowledge of what Miss Griffin (who knew all things that could be learnt out of book) didn't know, were the mainspring of the preservation of our secret. It was wonderfully kept, but was once upon the verge of self-betrayal. The danger and escape occurred upon a Sunday. We were all ten ranged in a conspicuous part of the gallery at church, with Miss Griffin at our head—as we were every Sunday—advertising the establishment in an unsecular sort of way—when the description of Solomon in his domestic glory happened to be read. The moment that monarch was thus referred to, conscience whispered me, "Thou, too, Haroun!" The officiating minister had a cast in his eye, and it assisted conscience by giving him the appearance of reading personally at me. A crimson blush, attended by a fearful perspiration, suffused my features. The Grand Vizier became more dead than alive, and the whole Seraglio reddened as if the sunset of Bagdad shone direct upon their lovely faces. At this portentous time the awful Griffin rose, and balefully surveyed the children of Islam. My own impression was, that Church and State had entered into a conspiracy with Miss Griffin to expose us, and that we should all be put into white sheets, and exhibited in the centre aisle. But, so Westerly—if I may be allowed the expression as opposite to Eastern associations—was Miss Griffin's sense of rectitude, that she merely suspected Apples, and we were saved.

I have called the Seraglio, united. Upon the question, solely, whether the Commander of the Faithful durst exercise a right of kissing in that sanctuary of the palace, were its peerless inmates divided. Zobeide asserted a counter-right in the Favourite to scratch, and the fair Circassian put her face, for refuge, into a green baize bag, originally designed for books. On the other hand, a young antelope of transcendent beauty from the fruitful plains of Camden-town (whence she had been brought, by traders, in the half-yearly caravan that crossed the intermediate desert after the holidays), held more liberal opinions, but stipulated for limiting the benefit of them to that dog, and son of a dog, the Grand Vizier—who had no rights, and was not in question. At length, the difficulty was compromised by the installation of a very youthful slave as Deputy. She, raised upon a stool, officially received upon her cheeks the salutes intended by the gracious Haroun for other Sultanas, and was privately rewarded from the coffers of the Ladies of the Hareem.

And now it was, at the full height of enjoyment of my bliss, that I became heavily troubled. I began to think of my mother, and what she would say to my taking home at Midsummer eight of the most beautiful of the daughters of men, but all unexpected. I thought of the number of beds we made up at our house, of my father's income, and of the baker, and my despondency redoubled. The Seraglio and malicious Vizier, divining the cause of their Lord's unhappiness, did their utmost to augment it. They professed unbounded fidelity, and declared that they would live and die with him. Reduced to the utmost wretchedness by these protestations of attachment, I lay awake, for hours at a time, ruminating on my frightful lot. In my despair, I think I might have taken an early opportunity of falling on my knees before Miss Griffin, avowing my resemblance to Solomon, and praying to be dealt with according to the outraged laws of my country, if an unthought-of means of escape had not opened before me.

One day, we were out walking, two and two—on which occasion the Vizier had his usual instructions to take note of the boy at the turnpike, and if he profanely gazed (which he always did) at the beauties of the Hareem, to have him bowstrung in the course of the night—and it happened that our hearts were veiled in gloom. An unaccountable action on the part of the antelope had plunged the State into disgrace. That charmer, on the representation that the previous day was her birthday, and that vast treasures had been sent in a hamper for its celebration (both baseless assertions), had secretly but most pressingly invited thirty-five neighbouring princes and princesses to a ball and supper: with a special stipulation that they were "not to be fetched till twelve." This wandering of the antelope's fancy, led to the surprising arrival at Miss Griffin's door, in divers equipages and under various escorts, of a great company in full dress, who were deposited on the top step in a flush of high expectancy, and who were dismissed in tears. At the beginning of the double knocks attendant on these ceremonies, the antelope had retired to a back attic, and bolted herself in ; and at every new arrival, Miss Griffin had gone so much more and more distracted, that at last she had been seen to tear her front. Ultimate capitulation on the part of the offender, had been followed by solitude in the linen-closet, bread and water and a lecture to all, of vindictive length, in which Miss Griffin had used expressions : Firstly, "I believe you all of you knew of it ; " Secondly, "Every one of you is as wicked as another ; " Thirdly, "A pack of little wretches."

Under these circumstances, we were walking drearily along; and I especially, with my Moosulmaun responsibilities heavy on me, was in a very low state of mind ; when a strange man accosted Miss Griffin, and, after walking on at her side for a little while and talking with her, looked at me. Supposing him to be a minion of the law, and that my hour was come, I instantly ran away, with the general purpose of making for Egypt.

The whole Seraglio cried out, when they saw me making off as fast as my legs would carry me (I had an impression that the first turning on the left, and round by the public-house, would be the shortest way to the Pyramids), Miss Griffin screamed after me, the faithless Vizier ran after me, and the boy at the turnpike dodged me into a corner, like a sheep, and cut me off. Nobody scolded me when I was taken and brought back; Miss Griffin only said, with a stunning gentleness, This was very curious! Why had I run away when the gentleman looked at me?

If I had had any breath to answer with, I dare say I should have made no answer; having no breath, I certainly made none. Miss Griffin and the strange man took me between them, and walked me back to the palace in a sort of state; but not at all (as I couldn't help feeling, with astonishment), in culprit state.

When we got there, we went into a room by ourselves, and Miss Griffin called in to her assistance, Mesrour, chief of the dusky guards of the Hareem. Mesrour, on being whispered to, began to shed tears.

"Bless you, my precious!" said that officer, turning to me; "your pa's took bitter bad!"

I asked, with a fluttered heart, "Is he very ill?"

"Lord temper the wind to you, my lamb!" said the good Mesrour, kneeling down, that I might have a comforting shoulder for my head to rest on, "your pa's dead!"

Haroun Alraschid took to flight at the words; the Seraglio vanished; from that moment, I never again saw one of the eight of the fairest of the daughters of men.

I was taken home, and there was Debt at home as well as Death, and we had a sale there. My own little bed was so superciliously looked upon by a Power unknown to me, hazily called "The Trade," that a brass coal-scuttle, a roasting-jack, and a birdcage, were obliged to be put into it to make a Lot of it, and then it went for a song. So I heard mentioned, and I wondered what song, and thought what a dismal song it must have been to sing!

Then, I was sent to a great, cold, bare, school of big boys; where everything to eat and wear was thick and clumpy, without being enough; where everybody, large and small, was cruel; where the boys knew all about the sale, before I got there, and asked me what I had fetched, and who had bought me, and hooted at me, "Going, going, gone!" I never whispered in that wretched place that I had been Haroun, or had had a Seraglio: for, I knew that if I mentioned my reverses, I should be so worried, that I should have to drown myself in the muddy pond near the playground, which looked like the beer.

Ah me, ah me! No other ghost has haunted the boy's room, my friends, since I have occupied it, than the ghost of my own childhood, the ghost of my own innocence, the ghost of my own airy belief. Many a time have I pursued the phantom: never with this man's stride of mine to come up with it, never with these man's hands of mine to touch it, never more to this man's heart of mine to hold it in its purity. And here you see me working out, as cheerfully and thankfully as I may, my doom of shaving in the glass a constant change of customers, and of lying down and rising up with the skeleton allotted to me for my mortal companion.

A MESSAGE FROM THE SEA

[*Written in collaboration with* WILKIE COLLINS]

[1860]

CHARACTERS

LAWRENCE CLISSOLD, *a fraudulent clerk.*

CAPTAIN JORGAN, *a frank, open-hearted American ship-owner.*

MR. TOM PETTIFER, *a ship's steward.*

MRS. RAYBROCK, *a comely elderly woman; draper and village postmistress.*

ALFRED RAYBROCK, *her son; an honest, manly young fisherman.*

HUGH RAYBROCK, *eldest son of Mrs. Raybrock; a ship-wrecked mariner.*

MRS. MARGARET RAYBROCK, *his devoted wife.*

MR. TREGARTHEN, *an agreeable but rather infirm man.*

KITTY TREGARTHEN, *his daughter; Alfred Raybrock's sweetheart.*

A MESSAGE FROM THE SEA

CHAPTER I

THE VILLAGE

AND a mighty sing'lar and pretty place it is, as ever I saw in all the days of my life!" said Captain Jorgan, looking up at it.

Captain Jorgan had to look high to look at it, for the village was built sheer up the face of a steep and lofty cliff. There was no road in it, there was no wheeled vehicle in it, there was not a level yard in it. From the sea-beach to the cliff-top two irregular rows of white houses, placed opposite to one another, and twisting here and there, and there and here, rose, like the sides of a long succession of stages of crooked ladders, and you climbed up the village or climbed down the village by the staves between, some six feet wide or so, and made of sharp irregular stones. The old pack-saddle, long laid aside in most parts of England as one of the appendages of its infancy, flourished here intact. Strings of pack-horses and pack-donkeys toiled slowly up the staves of the ladders, bearing fish, and coal, and such other cargo as was unshipping at the pier from the dancing fleet of village boats, and from two or three little coasting traders. As the beasts of burden ascended laden, or descended light, they got so lost at intervals in the floating clouds of village smoke, that they seemed to dive down some of the village chimneys, and come to the surface again far off, high above others. No two houses in the village were alike, in chimney, size, shape, door, window, gable, roof-tree, anything. The sides of the ladders were musical with water, running clear and bright. The staves were musical with the clattering

feet of the pack-horses and pack-donkeys, and the voices of
the fishermen urging them up, mingled with the voices of
the fishermen's wives and their many children. The pier was
musical with the wash of the sea, the creaking of capstans
and windlasses, and the airy fluttering of little vanes and
sails. The rough, sea-bleached boulders of which the pier
was made, and the whiter boulders of the shore, were brown
with drying nets. The red-brown cliffs, richly wooded to
their extremest verge, had their softened and beautiful forms
reflected in the bluest water, under the clear North Devonshire sky of a November day without a cloud. The village
itself was so steeped in autumnal foliage, from the houses
lying on the pier to the topmost round of the topmost ladder,
that one might have fancied it was out a bird's-nesting, and
was (as indeed it was) a wonderful climber. And mentioning birds, the place was not without some music from them
too ; for the rook was very busy on the higher levels, and the
gull with his flapping wings was fishing in the bay, and the
lusty little robin was hopping among the great stone blocks
and iron rings of the breakwater, fearless in the faith of his
ancestors, and the Children in the Wood.

Thus it came to pass that Captain Jorgan, sitting balancing
himself on the pier-wall, struck his leg with his open hand,
as some men do when they are pleased—and as he always
did when he was pleased—and said,—

"A mighty sing'lar and pretty place it is, as ever I saw in
all the days of my life ! "

Captain Jorgan had not been through the village, but had
come down to the pier by a winding side-road, to have
a preliminary look at it from the level of his own natural
element. He had seen many things and places, and had
stowed them all away in a shrewd intellect and a vigorous
memory. He was an American born, was Captain Jorgan,
—a New-Englander,—but he was a citizen of the world, and
a combination of most of the best qualities of most of its
best countries.

For Captain Jorgan to sit anywhere in his long-skirted
blue coat and blue trousers, without holding converse with
everybody within speaking distance, was a sheer impossibility.
So the captain fell to talking with the fishermen, and to
asking them knowing questions about the fishery, and the
tides, and the currents, and the race of water off that point
yonder, and what you kept in your eye, and got into a line

with what else when you ran into the little harbour ; and other nautical profundities. Among the men who exchanged ideas with the captain was a young fellow, who exactly hit his fancy,—a young fisherman of two or three and twenty, in the rough sea-dress of his craft, with a brown face, dark curling hair, and bright, modest eyes under his Sou'wester hat, and with a frank, but simple and retiring manner, which the captain found uncommonly taking. "I'd bet a thousand dollars," said the captain to himself, "that your father was an honest man ! "

"Might you be married now ? " asked the captain, when he had had some talk with this new acquaintance.

"Not yet."

"Going to be ? " said the captain.

"I hope so."

The captain's keen glance followed the slightest possible turn of the dark eye, and the slightest possible tilt of the Sou'wester hat. The captain then slapped both his legs, and said to himself,—

"Never knew such a good thing in all my life ! There's his sweetheart looking over the wall ! "

There was a very pretty girl looking over the wall, from a little platform of cottage, vine, and fuchsia ; and she certainly did not look as if the presence of this young fisherman in the landscape made it any the less sunny and hopeful for her.

Captain Jorgan, having doubled himself up to laugh with that hearty good-nature which is quite exultant in the innocent happiness of other people, had undoubled himself, and was going to start a new subject, when there appeared coming down the lower ladders of stones, a man whom he hailed as "Tom Pettifer, Ho ! " Tom Pettifer, Ho, responded with alacrity, and in speedy course descended on the pier.

"Afraid of a sun-stroke in England in November, Tom, that you wear your tropical hat, strongly paid outside and paper-lined inside, here ? " said the captain, eyeing it.

"It's as well to be on the safe side, Sir," replied Tom.

"Safe side ! " repeated the captain, laughing. "You'd guard against a sun-stroke, with that old hat, in an Ice Pack. Wa'al ! What have you made out at the Post-office ? "

"It *is* the Post-office, Sir."

"What's the Post-office ? " said the captain.

"The name, Sir. The name keeps the Post-office."

"A coincidence ! " said the captain. "A lucky hit ! Show

me where it is. Good-bye, shipmates, for the present! I shall come and have another look at you, afore I leave, this afternoon."

This was addressed to all there, but especially the young fisherman; so all there acknowledged it, but especially the young fisherman. "*He's* a sailor!" said one to another, as they looked after the captain moving away. That he was; and so outspeaking was the sailor in him, that although his dress had nothing nautical about it, with the single exception of its colour, but was a suit of a shore-going shape and form, too long in the sleeves and too short in the legs, and too unaccommodating everywhere, terminating earthward in a pair of Wellington boots, and surmounted by a tall, stiff hat, which no mortal could have worn at sea in any wind under heaven; nevertheless, a glimpse of his sagacious, weather-beaten face, or his strong, brown hand, would have established the captain's calling. Whereas Mr. Pettifer—a man of a certain plump neatness, with a curly whisker, and elaborately nautical in a jacket, and shoes, and all things correspondent —looked no more like a seaman, beside Captain Jorgan, than he looked like a sea-serpent.

The two climbed high up the village,—which had the most arbitrary turns and twists in it, so that the cobbler's house came dead across the ladder, and to have held a reasonable course, you must have gone through his house, and through him too, as he sat at his work between two little windows, with one eye microscopically on the geological formation of that part of Devonshire, and the other telescopically on the open sea,—the two climbed high up the village, and stopped before a quaint little house, on which was painted, "MRS. RAYBROCK, DRAPER;" and also "POST-OFFICE." Before it, ran a rill of murmuring water, and access to it was gained by a little plank-bridge.

"Here's the name," said Captain Jorgan, "sure enough. You can come in if you like, Tom."

The captain opened the door, and passed into an odd little shop, about six feet high, with a great variety of beams and bumps in the ceiling, and, besides the principal window giving on the ladder of stones, a purblind little window of a single pane of glass, peeping out of an abutting corner at the sun-lighted ocean, and winking at its brightness.

"How do you do, ma'am?" said the captain. "I am very glad to see you. I have come a long way to see you."

"*Have* you, Sir? Then I am sure I am very glad to see *you*, though I don't know you from Adam."

Thus a comely elderly woman, short of stature, plump of form, sparkling and dark of eye, who, perfectly clean and neat herself, stood in the midst of her perfectly clean and neat arrangements, and surveyed Captain Jorgan with smiling curiosity. "Ah! but you are a sailor, Sir," she added, almost immediately, and with a slight movement of her hands, that was not very unlike wringing them; "then you are heartily welcome."

"Thank'ee, ma'am," said the captain, "I don't know what it is, I am sure, that brings out the salt in me, but everybody seems to see it on the crown of my hat and the collar of my coat. Yes, ma'am, I am in that way of life."

"And the other gentleman, too," said Mrs. Raybrock.

"Well now, ma'am," said the captain, glancing shrewdly at the other gentleman, "you are that nigh right, that he goes to sea,—if that makes him a sailor. This is my steward, ma'am, Tom Pettifer; he's been a'most all trades you could name, in the course of his life,—would have bought all your chairs and tables once, if you had wished to sell 'em,—but now he's my steward. My name's Jorgan, and I'm a shipowner, and I sail my own and my partners' ships, and have done so this five-and-twenty year. According to custom I am called Captain Jorgan, but I am no more a captain, bless your heart! than you are."

"Perhaps you'll come into my parlour, Sir, and take a chair?" said Mrs. Raybrock.

"Ex-actly what I was going to propose myself, ma'am. After you."

Thus replying, and enjoining Tom to give an eye to the shop, Captain Jorgan followed Mrs. Raybrock into the little, low back-room,—decorated with divers plants in pots, teatrays, old china teapots, and punch-bowls,—which was at once the private sitting-room of the Raybrock family and the inner cabinet of the post-office of the village of Steepways.

"Now, ma'am," said the captain, "it don't signify a cent to you where I was born, except——" But here the shadow of some one entering fell upon the captain's figure, and he broke off to double himself up, slap both his legs, and ejaculate, "Never knew such a thing in all my life! Here he is again! How are you?"

These words referred to the young fellow who had so taken

Captain Jorgan's fancy down at the pier. To make it all quite complete he came in accompanied by the sweetheart whom the captain had detected looking over the wall. A prettier sweetheart the sun could not have shone upon that shining day. As she stood before the captain, with her rosy lips just parted in surprise, her brown eyes a little wider open than was usual from the same cause, and her breathing a little quickened by the ascent (and possibly by some mysterious hurry and flurry at the parlour door, in which the captain had observed her face to be for a moment totally eclipsed by the Sou'wester hat), she looked so charming, that the captain felt himself under a moral obligation to slap both his legs again. She was very simply dressed, with no other ornament than an autumnal flower in her bosom. She wore neither hat nor bonnet, but merely a scarf or kerchief, folded squarely back over the head, to keep the sun off,—according to a fashion that may be sometimes seen in the more genial parts of England as well as of Italy, and which is probably the first fashion of head-dress that came into the world when grasses and leaves went out.

"In my country," said the captain, rising to give her his chair, and dexterously sliding it close to another chair on which the young fisherman must necessarily establish himself,—"in my country we should call Devonshire beauty first-rate!"

Whenever a frank manner is offensive, it is because it is strained or feigned; for there may be quite as much intolerable affectation in plainness as in mincing nicety. All that the captain said and did was honestly according to his nature; and his nature was open nature and good nature; therefore, when he paid this little compliment, and expressed with a sparkle or two of his knowing eye, "I see how it is, and nothing could be better," he had established a delicate confidence on that subject with the family.

"I was saying to your worthy mother," said the captain to the young man, after again introducing himself by name and occupation,—"I was saying to your mother (and you're very like her) that it didn't signify where I was born, except that I was raised on question-asking ground, where the babies as soon as ever they come into the world, inquire of their mothers, 'Neow, how old may *you* be, and wa'at air you a goin' to name me?'—which is a fact." Here he slapped his leg. "Such being the case, I may be excused for asking you if your name's Alfred?"

"Yes, Sir, my name is Alfred," returned the young man.

"I am not a conjurer," pursued the captain, "and don't think me so, or I shall right soon undeceive you. Likewise don't think, if you please, though I *do* come from that country of the babies, that I am asking questions for question-asking's sake, for I am not. Somebody belonging to you went to sea?"

"My elder brother, Hugh," returned the young man. He said it in an altered and lower voice, and glanced at his mother, who raised her hands hurriedly, and put them together across her black gown, and looked eagerly at the visitor.

"No! For God's sake, don't think that!" said the captain, in a solemn way; "I bring no good tidings of him."

There was a silence, and the mother turned her face to the fire and put her hand between it and her eyes. The young fisherman slightly motioned toward the window, and the captain, looking in that direction, saw a young widow, sitting at a neighbouring window across a little garden, engaged in needlework, with a young child sleeping on her bosom. The silence continued until the captain asked of Alfred,—

"How long is it since it happened?"

"He shipped for his last voyage better than three years ago."

"Ship struck upon some reef or rock, as I take it," said the captain, "and all hands lost?"

"Yes."

"Wa'al!" said the captain, after a shorter silence, "Here I sit who may come to the same end, like enough. He holds the seas in the hollow of His hand. We must all strike somewhere and go down. Our comfort, then, for ourselves and one another is to have done our duty. I'd wager your brother did his!"

"He did!" answered the young fisherman. "If ever man strove faithfully on all occasions to do his duty, my brother did. My brother was not a quick man (anything but that), but he was a faithful, true, and just man. We were the sons of only a small tradesman in this county, Sir; yet our father was as watchful of his good name as if he had been a king."

"A precious sight more so, I hope,—bearing in mind the general run of that class of crittur," said the captain. "But I interrupt."

"My brother considered that our father left the good name to us, to keep clear and true."

"Your brother considered right," said the captain; "and you couldn't take care of a better legacy. But again I interrupt."

"No; for I have nothing more to say. We know that Hugh lived well for the good name, and we feel certain that he died well for the good name. And now it has come into my keeping. And that's all."

"Well spoken!" cried the captain. "Well spoken, young man! Concerning the manner of your brother's death,"—by this time the captain had released the hand he had shaken, and sat with his own broad, brown hands spread out on his knees, and spoke aside,—"concerning the manner of your brother's death, it may be that I have some information to give you; though it may not be, for I am far from sure. Can we have a little talk alone?"

The young man rose; but not before the captain's quick eye had noticed that, on the pretty sweetheart's turning to the window to greet the young widow with a nod and a wave of the hand, the young widow had held up to her the needlework on which she was engaged, with a patient and pleasant smile. So the captain said, being on his legs, —

"What might she be making now?"

"What is Margaret making, Kitty?" asked the young fisherman,—with one of his arms apparently mislaid somewhere.

As Kitty only blushed in reply, the captain doubled himself up as far as he could, standing, and said, with a slap of his leg, —

"In my country we should call it wedding-clothes. Fact! We should, I do assure you."

But it seemed to strike the captain in another light too; for his laugh was not a long one, and he added, in quite a gentle tone,—

"And it's very pretty, my dear, to see her—poor young thing, with her fatherless child upon her bosom—giving up her thoughts to your home and your happiness. It's very pretty, my dear, and it's very good. May your marriage be more prosperous than hers, and be a comfort to her too. May the blessed sun see you all happy together, in possession of the good name, long after I have done ploughing the great salt field that is never sown!"

Kitty answered very earnestly, "O! Thank you, Sir, with all my heart!" And, in her loving little way, kissed her hand to him, and possibly by implication to the young fisherman, too, as the latter held the parlour-door open for the captain to pass out.

CHAPTER II

THE MONEY

"THE stairs are very narrow, Sir," said Alfred Raybrock to Captain Jorgan.

"Like my cabin-stairs," returned the captain, "on many a voyage."

"And they are rather inconvenient for the head."

"If my head can't take care of itself by this time, after all the knocking about the world it has had," replied the captain, as unconcernedly as if he had no connexion with it, "it's not worth looking after."

Thus they came into the young fisherman's bedroom, which was as perfectly neat and clean as the shop and parlour below; though it was but a little place, with a sliding window, and a phrenological ceiling expressive of all the peculiarities of the house-roof. Here the captain sat down on the foot of the bed, and glancing at a dreadful libel on Kitty which ornamented the wall,—the production of some wandering limner, whom the captain secretly admired as having studied portraiture from the figure-heads of ships, —motioned to the young man to take the rush-chair on the other side of the small. round table. That done, the captain put his hand in the deep breast-pocket of his long-skirted blue coat, and took out of it a strong square case-bottle,— not a large bottle, but such as may be seen in any ordinary ship's medicine-chest. Setting this bottle on the table without removing his hand from it, Captain Jorgan then spake as follows:—

"In my last voyage homeward-bound," said the captain, "and that's the voyage off of which I now come straight, I encountered such weather off the Horn as is not very often met with, even there. I have rounded that stormy Cape pretty often, and I believe I first beat about there in the identical storms that blew the Devil's horns and tail off, and led to the horns being worked up into toothpicks for the plantation overseers in my country, who may be seen (if you travel down South, or away West, fur enough) picking their teeth with 'em, while the whips, made of the tail, flog hard. In this last voyage, homeward-bound for Liverpool from South America, I say to you, my young friend, it blew. Whole measures! No half measures, nor making believe to blow; it blew! Now I warn't blown clean out of the water into the sky,—though I expected to be even that,—but I was blown clean out of my course; and when at last it fell calm, it fell dead calm, and a strong current set one way, day and night, night and day, and I drifted—drifted—drifted—out of all the ordinary tracks and courses of ships, and drifted yet, and yet drifted. It behooves a man who takes charge of fellow-critturs' lives, never to rest from making himself master of his calling. I never did rest, and consequently I knew pretty well ('specially looking over the side in the dead calm of that strong current) what dangers to expect, and what precautions to take against 'em. In short, we were driving head on to an island. There was no island in the chart, and, therefore, you may say it was ill-manners in the island to be there; I don't dispute its bad breeding, but there it was. Thanks be to Heaven, I was as ready for the island as the island was ready for me. I made it out myself from the masthead, and I got enough way upon her in good time to keep her off. I ordered a boat to be lowered and manned, and went in that boat myself to explore the island. There was a reef outside it, and, floating in a corner of the smooth water within the reef, was a heap of sea-weed, and entangled in that sea-weed was this bottle."

Here the captain took his hand from the bottle for a moment, that the young fisherman might direct a wondering glance at it; and then replaced his hand and went on:—

"If ever you come—or even if ever you don't come—to a desert place, use you your eyes and your spy-glass well; for the smallest thing you see may prove of use to you, and may have some information or some warning in it. That's the principle on which I came to see this bottle. I picked up the bottle and ran the boat alongside the island, and made fast and went ashore armed, with a part of my boat's crew. We found that every scrap of vegetation on the island (I give it you as my opinion, but scant and scrubby at the best of times) had been consumed by fire. As we were making our way, cautiously and toilsomely, over the pulverised embers, one of my people sank into the earth breast-high. He turned pale, and "Haul me out smart, shipmates," says he, "for my feet are among bones." We soon got him on his legs again, and then we dug up the spot, and we found that the man was right, and that his feet had been among bones. More than that, they were human bones; though whether the remains of one man, or of two or three men, what with calcination and ashes, and what with a poor practical knowledge of anatomy, I can't undertake to say. We examined the whole island and made out nothing else, save and except that, from its opposite side, I sighted a considerable tract of land, which land I was able to identify, and according to the bearings of which (not to trouble you with my log) I took a fresh departure. When I got aboard again I opened the bottle, which was oilskin-covered as you see, and glass-stoppered as you see. Inside of it," pursued the captain, suiting his action to his words, "I found this little crumpled, folded paper, just as you see. Outside of it was written, as you see, these words: '*Whoever finds this, is solemnly entreated by the dead to convey it unread to Alfred Raybrock, Steepways, North Devon, England.*' A sacred charge," said the captain, concluding his narrative, "and, Alfred Raybrock, there it is!"

"This is my poor brother's writing!"

"I suppose so," said Captain Jorgan. "I'll take a look out of this little window while you read it."

"Pray no, Sir! I should be hurt. My brother couldn't know it would fall into such hands as yours."

The captain sat down again on the foot of the bed, and the young man opened the folded paper with a trembling hand, and spread it on the table. The ragged paper, evidently creased and torn both before and after being written on. was much blotted and stained, and the ink had faded and run, and many words were wanting. What the captain and the young fisherman made out together, after much re-reading and much humouring of the folds of the paper, is given on the next page.

The young fisherman had become more and more agitated, as the writing had become clearer to him. He now left it lying before the captain, over whose shoulder he had been reading it, and dropping into his former seat, leaned forward on the table and laid his face in his hands.

"What, man," urged the captain, "don't give in! Be up and doing *like* a man!"

"It is selfish, I know,—but doing what, doing what?' cried the young fisherman, in complete despair, and stamping his sea-boot on the ground.

"Doing what?" returned the captain. "Something! I'd go down to the little breakwater below yonder, and take

a wrench at one of the salt-rusted iron rings there, and either wrench it up by the roots or wrench my teeth out of my head, sooner than I'd do nothing. Nothing!" ejaculated the captain. "Any fool or fainting heart can do *that*, and nothing can come of nothing,—which was pretended to be found out, I believe, by one of them Latin critters," said the captain with the deepest disdain; "as if Adam hadn't found it out, afore ever he so much as named the beasts!"

Yet the captain saw, in spite of his bold words, that there was some greater reason than he yet understood for the young man's distress. And he eyed him with a sympathising curiosity.

"Come, come!" continued the captain. "Speak out. What is it, boy!"

"You have seen how beautiful she is, Sir," said the young man, looking up for the moment, with a flushed face and rumpled hair.

"Did any man ever say she warn't beautiful?" retorted the captain. "If so, go and lick him."

The young man laughed fretfully in spite of himself, and said,

"It's not that, it's not that."

"Wa'al, then, what is it?" said the captain in a more soothing tone.

The young fisherman mournfully composed himself to tell the captain what it was, and began: "We were to have been married next Monday week——"

"Were to have been!" interrupted Captain Jorgan. "And are to be? Hey?"

Young Raybrock shook his head, and traced out with his forefinger the words, "*poor father's five hundred pounds,*" in the written paper.

"Go along," said the captain. "Five hundred pounds? Yes?"

"That sum of money," pursued the young fisherman, entering with the greatest earnestness on his demonstration, while the captain eyed him with equal earnestness, "was all my late father possessed. When he died, he owed no man more than he left means to pay, but he had been able to lay by only five hundred pounds."

"Five hundred pounds," repeated the captain. "Yes?"

"In his lifetime, years before, he had expressly laid the money aside to leave to my mother,—like to settle upon her, if I make myself understood."

"Yes?"

"He had risked it once—my father put down in writing at that time, respecting the money—and was resolved never to risk it again."

"Not a spec'lator," said the captain. "My country wouldn't have suited him. Yes?"

"My mother has never touched the money till now. And

now it was to have been laid out, this very next week, in buying me a handsome share in our neighbouring fishery here, to settle me in life with Kitty."

The captain's face fell, and he passed and repassed his sun-browned right hand over his thin hair, in a discomfited manner.

"Kitty's father has no more than enough to live on, even in the sparing way in which we live about here. He is a kind of bailiff or steward of manor rights here, and they are not much, and it is but a poor little office. He was better off once, and Kitty must never marry to mere drudgery and hard living."

The captain still sat stroking his thin hair, and looking at the young fisherman.

"I am as certain that my father had no knowledge that any one was wronged as to this money, or that any restitution ought to be made, as I am certain that the sun now shines. But, after this solemn warning from my brother's grave in the sea, that the money is Stolen Money," said Young Raybrock, forcing himself to the utterance of the words, "can I doubt it? Can I touch it?"

"About not doubting, I ain't so sure," observed the captain; "but about not touching—no—I don't think you can."

"See then," said Young Raybrock, "why I am so grieved. Think of Kitty. Think what I have got to tell her!"

His heart quite failed him again when he had come round to that, and he once more beat his sea-boot softly on the floor. But not for long; he soon began again, in a quietly resolute tone.

"However! Enough of that! You spoke some brave words to me just now, Captain Jorgan, and they shall not be spoken in vain. I have got to do something. What I have got to do, before all other things, is to trace out the meaning of this paper, for the sake of the Good Name that has no one else to put it right. And still for the sake of the Good Name, and my father's memory, not a word of this writing must be breathed to my mother, or to Kitty, or to any human creature. You agree in this?"

"I don't know what they'll think of us below," said the captain, "but for certain I can't oppose it. Now, as to tracing. How will you do?"

They both, as by consent, bent over the paper again, and again carefully puzzled out the whole of the writing.

"I make out that this would stand, if all the writing was here, 'Inquire among the old men living there, for'—some one. Most like, you'll go to this village named here?" said the captain, musing, with his finger on the name.

"Yes! And Mr. Tregarthen is a Cornishman, and—to be sure!—comes from Lanrean."

"Does he?" said the captain quietly. "As I ain't acquainted with him, who may he be?"

"Mr. Tregarthen is Kitty's father."

"Ay, ay!" cried the captain. "Now you speak! Tregarthen knows this village of Lanrean, then?"

"Beyond all doubt he does. I have often heard him mention it, as being his native place. He knows it well."

"Stop half a moment," said the captain. "We want a name here. You could ask Tregarthen (or if you couldn't I could) what names of old men he remembers in his time in those diggings? Hey?"

"I can go straight to his cottage, and ask him now."

"Take me with you," said the captain, rising in a solid way that had a most comfortable reliability in it, "and just a word more first. I have knocked about harder than you, and have got along further than you. I have had, all my sea-going life long, to keep my wits polished bright with acid and friction, like the brass cases of the ship's instruments. I'll keep you company on this expedition. Now you don't live by talking any more than I do. Clench that hand of yours in this hand of mine, and that's a speech on both sides."

Captain Jorgan took command of the expedition with that hearty shake. He at once refolded the paper exactly as before, replaced it in the bottle, put the stopper in, put the oilskin over the stopper, confided the whole to Young Raybrock's keeping, and led the way downstairs.

But it was harder navigation below-stairs than above. The instant they set foot in the parlour the quick, womanly eye detected that there was something wrong. Kitty exclaimed, frightened, as she ran to her lover's side, "Alfred! What's the matter?" Mrs. Raybrock cried out to the captain, "Gracious! what have you done to my son to change him like this all in a minute?" And the young widow—who was there with her work upon her arm—was at first so agitated that she frightened the little girl she held in her hand, who hid her face in her mother's skirts and screamed. The captain, conscious of being held responsible for this domestic change, contemplated it with quite a guilty expression of countenance, and looked to the young fisherman to come to his rescue.

"Kitty, darling," said Young Raybrock, "Kitty, dearest love, I must go away to Lanrean, and I don't know where else or how much further, this very day. Worse than that —our marriage, Kitty, must be put off, and I don't know for how long."

Kitty stared at him, in doubt and wonder and in anger, and pushed him from her with her hand.

"Put off?" cried Mrs. Raybrock. "The marriage put off? And you going to Lanrean! Why, in the name of the dear Lord?"

"Mother dear, I can't say why; I must not say why. It would be dishonourable and undutiful to say why."

"Dishonourable and undutiful?" returned the dame. "And is there nothing dishonourable or undutiful in the boy's breaking the heart of his own plighted love, and his mother's heart too, for the sake of the dark secrets and counsels of a wicked stranger? Why did you ever come here?" she apostrophised the innocent captain. "Who wanted you? Where did you come from? Why couldn't you rest in your own bad place, wherever it is, instead of disturbing the peace of quiet unoffending folk like us?"

"And what," sobbed the poor little Kitty, "have I ever done to you, you hard and cruel captain, that you should come and serve me so?"

And then they both began to weep most pitifully, while the captain could only look from the one to the other, and lay hold of himself by the coat collar.

"Margaret," said the poor young fisherman, on his knees at Kitty's feet, while Kitty kept both her hands before her tearful face, to shut out the traitor from her view,—but kept her fingers wide asunder and looked at him all the time,— "Margaret, you have suffered so much, so uncomplainingly, and are always so careful and considerate! Do take my part, for poor Hugh's sake!"

The quiet Margaret was not appealed to in vain. "I will, Alfred," she returned, "and I do. I wish this gentleman had never come near us," whereupon the captain laid hold of himself the tighter; "but I take your part for all that. I am sure you have some strong reason and some sufficient reason for what you do, strange as it is, and even for not saying why you do it, strange as that is. And, Kitty darling, you are bound to think so more than any one, for true love believes everything, and bears everything, and trusts everything. And, mother dear, you are bound to think so too, for you know you have been blest with good sons, whose word was always as good as their oath, and who were brought up in as true a sense of honour as any gentleman in this land. And I am sure you have no more call, mother, to doubt your living son than to doubt your dead son; and for the sake of the dear dead, I stand up for the dear living."

"Wa'al now," the captain struck in, with enthusiasm, "this I say, That whether your opinions flatter me or not, you are a young woman of sense, and spirit, and feeling; and I'd sooner have you by my side, in the hour of danger, than a good half of the men I've ever fallen in with—or fallen out with, ayther."

Margaret did not return the captain's compliment, or appear fully to reciprocate his good opinion, but she applied herself to the consolation of Kitty, and of Kitty's mother-in-law that was to have been next Monday week, and soon restored the parlour to a quiet condition.

"Kitty, my darling," said the young fisherman, "I must go to your father to entreat him still to trust me in spite of this wretched change and mystery, and to ask him for some directions concerning Lanrean. Will you come home? Will you come with me, Kitty?"

Kitty answered not a word, but rose sobbing, with the end of her simple head-dress at her eyes. Captain Jorgan followed the lovers out, quite sheepishly, pausing in the shop to give an instruction to Mr. Pettifer.

"Here, Tom!" said the captain, in a low voice. "Here's something in your line. Here's an old lady poorly and low in her spirits. Cheer her up a bit, Tom. Cheer 'em all up."

Mr. Pettifer, with a brisk nod of intelligence, immediately assumed his steward face, and went with his quiet, helpful, steward step into the parlour, where the captain had the great satisfaction of seeing him, through the glass door, take the child in his arms (who offered no objection), and bend over Mrs. Raybrock, administering soft words of consolation.

"Though what he finds to say, unless he's telling her that 't'll soon be over, or that most people is so at first, or that it'll do her good afterward, I cannot imaginate!" was the captain's reflection as he followed the lovers.

He had not far to follow them, since it was but a short
descent down the stony ways to the cottage of Kitty's father.
But short as the distance was, it was long enough to enable
the captain to observe that he was fast becoming the village
Ogre; for there was not a woman standing working at her
door, or a fisherman coming up or going down, who saw
Young Raybrock unhappy and little Kitty in tears, but he
or she instantly darted a suspicious and indignant glance at
the captain, as the foreigner who must somehow be responsible for this unusual spectacle. Consequently, when they
came into Tregarthen's little garden,—which formed the
platform from which the captain had seen Kitty peeping
over the wall,—the captain brought to, and stood off and on
at the gate, while Kitty hurried to hide her tears in her own
room, and Alfred spoke with her father, who was working
in the garden. He was a rather infirm man, but could
scarcely be called old yet, with an agreeable face and a promising air of making the best of things. The conversation
began on his side with great cheerfulness and good humour,
but soon became distrustful, and soon angry. That was the
captain's cue for striking both into the conversation and the
garden.

"Morning, Sir!" said Captain Jorgan. "How do you do?"

"The gentleman I am going away with," said the young
fisherman to Tregarthen.

"O!" returned Kitty's father, surveying the unfortunate
captain with a look of extreme disfavour. "I confess that
I can't say I am glad to see you."

"No," said the captain, "and, to admit the truth, that
seems to be the general opinion in these parts. But don't
be hasty; you may think better of me by-and-by."

"I hope so," observed Tregarthen.

"Wa'al, *I* hope so," observed the captain, quite at his
ease; "more than that, I believe so,—though you don't.
Now, Mr. Tregarthen, you don't want to exchange words of
mistrust with me; and if you did, you couldn't, because I
wouldn't. You and I are old enough to know better than
to judge against experience from surfaces and appearances;
and if you haven't lived to find out the evil and injustice of
such judgments, you are a lucky man."

The other seemed to shrink under this remark, and replied,
"Sir, I *have* lived to feel it deeply."

"Wa'al," said the captain, mollified, "then I've made

a good cast without knowing it. Now, Tregarthen, there stands the lover of your only child, and here stand I who know his secret. I warrant it a righteous secret, and none of his making, though bound to be of his keeping. I want to help him out with it, and tewwards that end we ask you to favour us with the names of two or three old residents in the village of Lanrean. As I am taking out my pocket-book and pencil to put the names down, I may as well observe to you that this, wrote atop of the first page here, is my name and address: 'Silas Jonas Jorgan, Salem, Massachusetts, United States.' If ever you take it in your head to run over any morning, I shall be glad to welcome you. Now, what may be the spelling of these said names?"

"There was an elderly man," said Tregarthen, "named David Polreath. He may be dead."

"Wa'al, said the captain, cheerfully, "if Polreath's dead and buried, and can be made of any service to us, Polreath won't object to our digging of him up. Polreath's down, anyhow."

"There was another named Penrewen. I don't know his Christian name."

"Never mind his Chris'en name," said the captain. "Penrewen, for short."

"There was another named John Tredgear."

"And a pleasant-sounding name, too," said the captain; John Tredgear's booked."

"I can recall no other except old Parvis."

"One of old Parvis's fam'ly I reckon," said the captain, "kept a dry-goods store in New York city, and realised a handsome competency by burning his house to ashes. Same name, anyhow. David Polreath, Unchris'en Penrewen, John Tredgear, and old Arson Parvis."

"I cannot recall any others at the moment."

"Thank'ee," said the captain. "And so, Tregarthen, hoping for your good opinion yet, and likewise for the fair Devonshire Flower's, your daughter's, I give you my hand, Sir, and wish you good-day."

Young Raybrock accompanied him disconsolately; for there was no Kitty at the window when he looked up, no Kitty in the garden when he shut the gate, no Kitty gazing after them along the stony ways when they began to climb back.

"Now I tell you what," said the captain. "Not being at

present calc'lated to promote harmony in your family, I won't come in. You go and get your dinner at home, and I'll get mine at the little hotel. Let our hour of meeting be two o'clock, and you'll find me smoking a cigar in the sun afore the hotel door. Tell Tom Pettifer, my steward, to consider himself on duty, and to look after your people till we come back; you'll find he'll have made himself useful to 'em already, and will be quite acceptable."

All was done as Captain Jorgan directed. Punctually at two o'clock the young fisherman appeared with his knapsack at his back; and punctually at two o'clock the captain jerked away the last feather-end of his cigar.

"Let me carry your baggage, Captain Jorgan; I can easily take it with mine."

"Thank'ee," said the captain. "I'll carry it myself. It's only a comb."

They climbed out of the village, and paused among the trees and fern on the summit of the hill above, to take breath, and to look down at the beautiful sea. Suddenly the captain gave his leg a resounding slap, and cried, "Never knew such a right thing in all my life!"—and ran away.

The cause of this abrupt retirement on the part of the captain was little Kitty among the trees. The captain went out of sight and waited, and kept out of sight and waited, until it occurred to him to beguile the time with another cigar. He lighted it, and smoked it out, and still he was out of sight and waiting. He stole within sight at last, and saw the lovers, with their arms entwined and their bent heads touching, moving slowly among the trees. It was the golden time of the afternoon then, and the captain said to himself, "Golden sun, golden sea, golden sails, golden leaves, golden love, golden youth,—a golden state of things altogether!"

Nevertheless the captain found it necessary to hail his young companion before going out of sight again. In a few moments more he came up and they began their journey.

"That still young woman with the fatherless child," said Captain Jorgan, as they fell into step, "didn't throw her words away; but good honest words are never thrown away. And now that I am conveying you off from that tender little thing that loves, and relies, and hopes, I feel just as if I was the snarling crittur in the picters, with the tight legs, the long nose, and the feather in his cap, the tips of whose moustaches get up nearer to his eyes the wickeder he gets."

The young fisherman knew nothing of Mephistopheles; but he smiled when the captain stopped to double himself up and slap his leg, and they went along in right good-fellowship.[1]

CHAPTER V

THE RESTITUTION

CAPTAIN JORGAN, up and out betimes, had put the whole village of Lanrean under an amicable cross-examination, and was returning to the King Arthur's Arms to breakfast, none the wiser for his trouble, when he beheld the young fisherman advancing to meet him, accompanied by a stranger. A glance at this stranger assured the captain that he could be no other than the Seafaring Man; and the captain was about to hail him as a fellow-craftsman, when the two stood still and silent before the captain, and the captain stood still, silent, and wondering before them.

"Why, what's this?" cried the captain, when at last he broke the silence. "You two are alike. You two are much alike! What's this?"

Not a word was answered on the other side, until after the seafaring brother had got hold of the captain's right hand, and the fisherman brother had got hold of the captain's left hand; and if ever the captain had had his fill of hand-shaking, from his birth to that hour, he had it then. And presently up and spoke the two brothers, one at a time, two at a time, two dozen at a time for the bewilderment into which they plunged the captain, until he gradually had Hugh Raybrock's deliverance made clear to him, and also unravelled the fact that the person referred to in the half-obliterated paper was Tregarthen himself.

[1] NOTE.—The third and fourth chapters of this Christmas number were not by Dickens. After the first and second he did not resume the pen until the chapter entitled the "Restitution," here numbered as the fifth. For the two intervening chapters the reader is referred to the number as republished in the volume of the *Nine Christmas numbers of All the Year Round*.

"Formerly, dear Captain Jorgan," said Alfred, "of Lanrean, you recollect? Kitty and her father came to live at Steepways after Hugh shipped on his last voyage."

"Ay, ay!" cried the captain, fetching a breath. "*Now* you have me in tow. Then your brother here don't know his sister-in-law that is to be so much as by name?"

"Never saw her; never heard of her!"

"Ay, ay, ay!" cried the captain. "Why then we every one go back together—paper, writer, and all—and take Tregarthen into the secret we kept from him?"

"Surely," said Alfred, "we can't help it now. We must go through with our duty."

"Not a doubt," returned the captain. "Give me an arm apiece, and let us set this ship-shape."

So walking up and down in the shrill wind on the wild moor, while the neglected breakfast cooled within, the captain and the brothers settled their course of action.

It was that they should all proceed by the quickest means they could secure to Barnstaple, and there look over the father's books and papers in the lawyer's keeping; as Hugh had proposed to himself to do if ever he reached home. That, enlightened or unenlightened, they should then return to Steepways and go straight to Mr. Tregarthen, and tell him all they knew, and see what came of it, and act accordingly. Lastly, that when they got there they should enter the village with all precautions against Hugh's being recognised by any chance; and that to the captain should be consigned the task of preparing his wife and mother for his restoration to this life.

"For you see," quoth Captain Jorgan, touching the last head, "it requires caution any way, great joys being as dangerous as great griefs, if not more dangerous, as being more uncommon (and therefore less provided against) in this round world of ours. And besides, I should like to free my name with the ladies, and take you home again at your brightest and luckiest; so don't let's throw away a chance of success."

The captain was highly lauded by the brothers for his kind interest and foresight.

"And now stop!" said the captain, coming to a standstill, and looking from one brother to the other, with quite a new rigging of wrinkles about each eye; "you are of opinion," to the elder, "that you are ra'ather slow?"

"I assure you I am very slow," said the honest Hugh.

"Wa'al," replied the captain, "I assure *you* that to the best of my belief I am ra'ather smart. Now a slow man ain't good at quick business, is he?"

That was clear to both.

"You," said the captain, turning to the younger brother, "are a little in love; ain't you?"

"Not a little, Captain Jorgan."

"Much or little, you're sort preoccupied; ain't you?"

It was impossible to be denied.

"And a sort preoccupied man ain't good at quick business, is he?" said the captain.

Equally clear on all sides.

"Now," said the captain, "I ain't in love myself, and I've made many a smart run across the ocean, and I should like to carry on and go ahead with this affair of yours and make a run slick through it. Shall I try? Will you hand it over to me?"

They were both delighted to do so, and thanked him heartily.

"Good," said the captain, taking out his watch. "This is half-past eight A.M., Friday morning. I'll jot that down, and we'll compute how many hours we've been out when we run into your mother's post-office. There! The entry's made, and now we go ahead."

They went ahead so well that before the Barnstaple lawyer's office was open next morning, the captain was sitting whistling on the step of the door, waiting for the clerk to come down the street with his key and open it. But instead of the clerk there came the master, with whom the captain fraternised on the spot to an extent that utterly confounded him.

As he personally knew both Hugh and Alfred, there was no difficulty in obtaining immediate access to such of the father's papers as were in his keeping. These were chiefly old letters and cash accounts; from which the captain, with a shrewdness and dispatch that left the lawyer far behind, established with perfect clearness, by noon. the following particulars:—

That one Lawrence Clissold had borrowed of the deceased, at a time when he was a thriving young tradesman in the town of Barnstaple, the sum of five hundred pounds. That he had borrowed it on the written statement that it was to be laid out in furtherance of a speculation which he expected would raise him to independence ; he being, at the time of writing that letter, no more than a clerk in the house of Dringworth Brothers, America-square, London. That the money was borrowed for a stipulated period ; but that, when the term was out, the aforesaid speculation failed, and Clissold was without means of repayment. That, hereupon, he had written to his creditor, in no very persuasive terms, vaguely requesting further time. That the creditor had refused this concession, declaring that he could not afford delay. That Clissold then paid the debt, accompanying the remittance of the money with an angry letter describing it as having been advanced by a relative to save him from ruin. That, in acknowledging the receipt, Raybrock had cautioned Clissold to seek to borrow money of him no more, as he would never so risk money again.

Before the lawyer the captain said never a word in reference to these discoveries. But when the papers had been put back in their box, and he and his two companions were well out of the office, his right leg suffered for it, and he said,—

"So far this run's begun with a fair wind and a prosperous ; for don't you see that all this agrees with that dutiful trust in his father maintained by the slow member of the Raybrock family ?"

Whether the brothers had seen it before or no, they saw it now. Not that the captain gave them much time to contemplate the state of things at their ease, for he instantly whipped them into a chaise again, and bore them off to Steepways. Although the afternoon was but just beginning to decline when they reached it, and it was broad daylight, still they had no difficulty, by dint of muffling the returned sailor up, and ascending the village rather than descending it, in reaching Tregarthen's cottage unobserved. Kitty was not visible, and they surprised Tregarthen sitting writing in the small bay-window of his little room.

"Sir," said the captain, instantly shaking hands with him, pen and all, "I'm glad to see you, Sir. How do you do, Sir ? I told you you'd think better of me by-and-by, and I congratulate you on going to do it."

Here the captain's eye fell on Tom Pettifer Ho, engaged in preparing some cookery at the fire.

"That critter," said the captain, smiting his leg, "is

a born steward, and never ought to have been in any
other way of life. Stop where you are, Tom, and make
yourself useful. Now, Tregarthen, I'm going to try a
chair."

Accordingly the captain drew one close to him, and went
on:—

"This loving member of the Raybrock family you know,
Sir. This slow member of the same family you don't know,
Sir. Wa'al, these two are brothers,—fact! Hugh's come
to life again, and here he stands. Now see here, my friend!
You don't want to be told that he was cast away, but you
do want to be told (for there's a purpose in it) that he was
cast away with another man. That man by name was
Lawrence Clissold."

At the mention of this name Tregarthen started and
changed colour. "What's the matter?" said the captain.

"He was a fellow-clerk of mine thirty—five-and-thirty—
years ago."

"True," said the captain, immediately catching at the
clew: " Dringworth Brothers, America-square, London City."

The other started again, nodded, and said, "That was the
house."

"Now," pursued the captain, "between those two men
cast away there arose a mystery concerning the round
sum of five hundred pound."

Again Tregarthen started, changing colour. Again the
captain said, "What's the matter?"

As Tregarthen only answered, "Please to go on," the
captain recounted, very tersely and plainly, the nature of
Clissold's wanderings on the barren island, as he had condensed them in his mind from the seafaring man. Tregarthen
became greatly agitated during this recital, and at length
exclaimed,—

"Clissold was the man who ruined me! I have suspected
it for many a long year, and now I know it."

"And how," said the captain, drawing his chair still closer
to Tregarthen, and clapping his hand upon his shoulder,—
" how may you know it?"

"When we were fellow-clerks," replied Tregarthen, "in
that London house, it was one of my duties to enter daily
in a certain book an account of the sums received that day
by the firm, and afterward paid into the bankers'. One
memorable day,—a Wednesday, the black day of my life,—

among the sums I so entered was one of five hundred pounds."

"I begin to make it out," said the captain. "Yes?"

"It was one of Clissold's duties to copy from this entry a memorandum of the sums which the clerk employed to go to the bankers' paid in there. It was my duty to hand the money to Clissold; it was Clissold's to hand it to the clerk, with that memorandum of his writing. On that Wednesday I entered a sum of five hundred pounds received. I handed that sum, as I handed the other sums in the day's entry, to Clissold. I was absolutely certain of it at the time; I have been absolutely certain of it ever since. A sum of five hundred pounds was afterward found by the house to have been that day wanting from the bag, from Clissold's memorandum, and from the entries in my book. Clissold, being questioned, stood upon his perfect clearness in the matter, and emphatically declared that he asked no better than to be tested by 'Tregarthen's book.' My book was examined, and the entry of five hundred pounds was not there."

"How not there," said the captain, "when you made it yourself?"

Tregarthen continued:—

"I was then questioned. Had I made the entry? Certainly I had. The house produced my book, and it was not there. I could not deny my book; I could not deny my writing. I knew there must be forgery by some one; but the writing was wonderfully like mine, and I could impeach no one if the house could not. I was required to pay the money back. I did so; and I left the house, almost broken-hearted, rather than remain there,—even if I could have done so,—with a dark shadow of suspicion always on me. I returned to my native place, Lanrean, and remained there, clerk to a mine, until I was appointed to my little post here."

"I well remember," said the captain, "that I told you that if you had no experience of ill judgments on deceiving appearances, you were a lucky man. You went hurt at that, and I see why. I'm sorry."

"Thus it is," said Tregarthen. "Of my own innocence I have of course been sure; it has been at once my comfort and my trial. Of Clissold I have always had suspicions almost amounting to certainty; but they have never been confirmed until now. For my daughter's sake and for my own I have carried this subject in my own heart, as the only secret of my life, and have long believed that it would die with me."

"Wa'al, my good Sir," said the captain cordially, "the present question is, and will be long, I hope, concerning living, and not dying. Now, here are our two honest friends, the loving Raybrock and the slow. Here they stand, agreed on one point, on which I'd back 'em round the world, and right across it from north to south, and then again from east to west, and through it, from your deepest Cornish mine to China. It is, that they will never use this same so-often-mentioned sum of money, and that restitution of it must be made to you. These two, the loving member and the slow, for the sake of the right and of their father's memory, will have it ready for you to-morrow. Take it, and ease their minds and mine, and end a most unfort'nate transaction."

Tregarthen took the captain by the hand, and gave his hand to each of the young men, but positively and finally answered No. He said, they trusted to his word, and he was glad of it, and at rest in his mind; but there was no proof, and the money must remain as it was. All were very earnest over this; and earnestness in men, when they are right and true, is so impressive, that Mr. Pettifer deserted his cookery and looked on quite moved.

"And so," said the captain, "so we come—as that lawyer-crittur over yonder where we were this morning might—to mere proof; do we? We must have it; must we? How? From this Clissold's wanderings, and from what you say, it ain't hard to make out that there was a neat forgery of your writing committed by the too-smart rowdy that was grease and ashes when I made his acquaintance, and a substitution of a forged leaf in your book for a real and true leaf torn out. Now was that real and true leaf then and there destroyed? No,—for says he, in his drunken way, he slipped it into a crack in his own desk, because you came into the office before there was time to burn it, and could never get back to it arterwards. Wait a bit. Where is that desk now? Do you consider it likely to be in America-square, London City?"

Tregarthen shook his head.

"The house has not, for years, transacted business in that place. I have heard of it, and read of it, as removed, enlarged, every way altered. Things alter so fast in these times."

"You think so," returned the captain, with compassion; "but you should come over and see *me* afore you talk about *that*. Wa'al, now. This desk, this paper,—this paper, this desk," said the captain, ruminating and walking about, and looking, in his uneasy abstraction, into Mr. Pettifer's hat on a table, among other things. "This desk, this paper,—this paper, this desk," the captain continued, musing and roaming about the room, "I'd give—— "

However, he gave nothing, but took up his steward's hat instead, and stood looking into it, as if he had just come into church. After that he roamed again, and again said, "This desk, belonging to this house of Dringworth Brothers, America-square, London City—— "

Mr. Pettifer, still strangely moved, and now more moved than before, cut the captain off as he backed across the room, and bespake him thus:—

"Captain Jorgan, I have been wishful to engage your attention, but I couldn't do it. I am unwilling to interrupt Captain Jorgan, but I must do it. *I* know something about that house."

The captain stood stock-still and looked at him,—with his (Mr. Pettifer's) hat under his arm.

"You're aware," pursued his steward, "that I was once in the broking business, Captain Jorgan?"

"I was aware," said the captain, "that you had failed in that calling, and in half the businesses going, Tom."

"Not quite so, Captain Jorgan; but I failed in the broking business. I was partners with my brother, Sir. There was a sale of old office furniture at Dringworth Brothers' when the house was moved from America-square, and me and my brother made what we call in the trade a Deal there, Sir. And I'll make bold to say, Sir, that the only thing I ever had from my brother, or from any relation,—for my relations have mostly taken property from me instead of giving me any,—was an old desk we bought at that same sale, with a crack in it. My brother wouldn't have given me even that, when we broke partnership, if it had been worth anything."

"Where is that desk now?" said the captain.

"Well, Captain Jorgan," replied the steward, "I couldn't say for certain where it is now; but when I saw it last,—which was last time we were outward bound,—it was at a very nice lady's at Wapping, along with a little chest of mine which was detained for a small matter of a bill owing."

The captain, instead of paying that rapt attention to his steward which was rendered by the other three persons present, went to church again, in respect of the steward's hat. And a most especially agitated and memorable face the captain produced from it, after a short pause.

"Now, Tom," said the captain, "I spoke to you, when we first came here, respecting your constitutional weakness on the subject of sunstroke."

"You did, Sir."

"Will my slow friend," said the captain, "lend me his arm, or I shall sink right back'ards into this blessed steward's cookery? Now, Tom," pursued the captain, when the required assistance was given, "on your oath as a steward, didn't you take that desk to pieces to make a better one of it, and put it together fresh,—or something of the kind?"

"On my oath I did, Sir," replied the steward.

"And by the blessing of Heaven, my friends, one and all," cried the captain, radiant with joy,—"of the Heaven that put it into this Tom Pettifer's head to take so much care of his head against the bright sun,—he lined his hat with the original leaf in Tregarthen's writing,—and here it is!"

With that the captain, to the utter destruction of Mr. Pettifer's favourite hat, produced the book-leaf, very much worn, but still legible, and gave both his legs such tremendous slaps that they were heard far off in the bay, and never accounted for.

"A quarter past five P.M.," said the captain, pulling out his watch, "and that's thirty-three hours and a quarter in all, and a pritty run!"

How they were all overpowered with delight and triumph; how the money was restored, then and there, to Tregarthen; how Tregarthen, then and there, gave it all to his daughter; how the captain undertook to go to Dringworth Brothers and re-establish the reputation of their forgotten old clerk; how Kitty came in, and was nearly torn to pieces, and the marriage was reappointed, needs not to be told. Nor how she and the young fisherman went home to the post-office to prepare the way for the captain's coming, by declaring him to be the mightiest of men, who had made all their fortunes, —and then dutifully withdrew together, in order that he might have the domestic coast entirely to himself. How he availed himself of it is all that remains to tell.

Deeply delighted with his trust, and putting his heart into it, he raised the latch of the post-office parlour where Mrs. Raybrock and the young widow sat, and said,—

"May I come in?"

"Sure you may, Captain Jorgan!" replied the old lady. "And good reason you have to be free of the house, though you have not been too well used in it by some who ought to have known better. I ask your pardon."

"No you don't, ma'am," said the captain, "for I won't let you. Wa'al, to be sure!"

By this time he had taken a chair on the hearth between them.

"Never felt such an evil spirit in the whole course of my life! There! I tell you! I could a'most have cut my own connexion. Like the dealer in my country, away West, who when he had let himself be outdone in a bargain, said to himself, 'Now I tell you what! I'll never speak to you again.' And he never did, but joined a settlement of oysters, and translated the multiplication table into their language,— which is a fact that can be proved. If you doubt it, mention it to any oyster you come across, and see if he'll have the face to contradict it."

He took the child from her mother's lap and set it on his knee.

"Not a bit afraid of me now, you see. Knows I am fond of small people. I have a child, and she's a girl, and I sing to her sometimes."

"What do you sing?" asked Margaret.

"Not a long song, my dear.

"Silas Jorgan
Played the organ.

That's about all. And sometimes I tell her stories,—stories of sailors supposed to be lost, and recovered after all hope was abandoned." Here the captain musingly went back to his song,—

"Silas Jorgan
Played the organ;"

repeating it with his eyes on the fire, as he softly danced the child on his knee. For he felt that Margaret had stopped working.

"Yes," said the captain, still looking at the fire, "I make up stories and tell 'em to that child. Stories of shipwreck on desert islands, and long delay in getting back to civilised lands. It is to stories the like of that. mostly, that

> "Silas Jorgan
> Plays the organ."

There was no light in the room but the light of the fire; for the shades of night were on the village, and the stars had begun to peep out of the sky one by one, as the houses of the village peeped out from among the foliage when the night departed. The captain felt that Margaret's eyes were upon him, and thought it discreetest to keep his own eyes on the fire.

"Yes; I make 'em up," said the captain. "I make up stories of brothers brought together by the good providence of GoD,—of sons brought back to mothers, husbands brought back to wives, fathers raised from the deep, for little children like herself."

Margaret's touch was on his arm, and he could not choose but look round now. Next moment her hand moved imploringly to his breast, and she was on her knees before him,—supporting the mother, who was also kneeling.

"What's the matter?" said the captain. "What's the matter?

> "Silas Jorgan
> Played the——"

Their looks and tears were too much for him, and he could not finish the song, short as it was.

"Mistress Margaret, you have borne ill fortune well. Could you bear good fortune equally well, if it was to come?"

"I hope so. I thankfully and humbly and earnestly hope so!"

"Wa'al, my dear," said the captain, "p'r'aps it has come. He's—don't be frightened—shall I say the word—— "

"Alive?"

"Yes!"

The thanks they fervently addressed to Heaven were again too much for the captain, who openly took out his handkerchief and dried his eyes.

"He's no further off," resumed the captain, "than my country. Indeed, he's no further off than his own native country. To tell you the truth, he's no further off than

Falmouth. Indeed, I doubt if he's quite so fur. Indeed, if you was sure you could bear it nicely, and I was to do no more than whistle for him——"

The captain's trust was discharged. A rush came, and they were all together again.

This was a fine opportunity for Tom Pettifer to appear with a tumbler of cold water, and he presently appeared with it, and administered it to the ladies; at the same time soothing them, and composing their dresses, exactly as if they had been passengers crossing the Channel. The extent to which the captain slapped his legs, when Mr. Pettifer acquitted himself of this act of stewardship, could have been thoroughly appreciated by no one but himself; inasmuch as he must have slapped them black and blue, and they must have smarted tremendously.

He couldn't stay for the wedding, having a few appointments to keep at the irreconcilable distance of about four thousand miles. So next morning all the village cheered him up to the level ground above, and there he shook hands with a complete Census of its population, and invited the whole, without exception, to come and stay several months with him at Salem, Mass., U.S. And there as he stood on the spot where he had seen that little golden picture of love and parting, and from which he could that morning contemplate another golden picture with a vista of golden years in it, little Kitty put her arms around his neck, and kissed him on both his bronzed cheeks, and laid her pretty face upon his storm-beaten breast, in sight of all,—ashamed to have called such a noble captain names. And there the captain waved his hat over his head three final times; and there he was last seen, going away accompanied by Tom Pettifer Ho, and carrying his hands in his pockets. And there, before that ground was softened with the fallen leaves of three more summers, a rosy little boy took his first unsteady run to a fair young mother's breast, and the name of that infant fisherman was Jorgan Raybrock.

TOM TIDDLER'S GROUND

[1861]

CHARACTERS

MISS KITTY KIMMEENS, *a loving, self-helpful, cheerful little child.*

THE LANDLORD of '*The Peal of Bells*'.

MR. MOPES THE HERMIT, *a morbid and misanthropical man, secluding himself for the sake of notoriety.*

MISS PUPFORD, *proprietress of an establishment for young ladies.*

THE TINKER, *a man who obstinately refuses to interest himself in Mr. Mopes.*

THE TRAVELLER, *an intruder on 'Tom Tiddler's Ground'.*

TOM TIDDLER'S GROUND

IN THREE CHAPTERS[1]

CHAPTER I

PICKING UP SOOT AND CINDERS

"And why Tom Tiddler's ground?" asked the Traveller.

"Because he scatters halfpence to Tramps and such-like," returned the Landlord, "and of course they pick 'em up. And this being done on his own land (which it *is* his own land, you observe, and were his family's before him), why it is but regarding the halfpence as gold and silver, and turning the ownership of the property a bit round your finger, and there you have the name of the children's game complete. And it's appropriate too," said the Landlord, with his favourite action of stooping a little, to look across the table out of window at vacancy, under the window-blind which was half drawn down. " Leastwise it has been so considered by many gentlemen which have partook of chops and tea in the present humble parlour."

The Traveller was partaking of chops and tea in the present humble parlour, and the Landlord's shot was fired obliquely at him.

"And you call him a Hermit?" said the Traveller.

"They call him such," returned the Landlord, evading personal responsibility; "he is in general so considered."

"What *is* a Hermit?" asked the Traveller.

"What is it?" repeated the Landlord, drawing his hand across his chin.

[1] The original has seven chapters; but those not printed here were not written by Dickens.

"Yes, what is it?"

The Landlord stooped again, to get a more comprehensive view of vacancy under the window-blind, and—with an asphyxiated appearance on him as one unaccustomed to definition—made no answer.

"I'll tell you what I suppose it to be," said the Traveller. "An abominably dirty thing."

"Mr. Mopes is dirty, it cannot be denied," said the Landlord.

"Intolerably conceited."

"Mr. Mopes is vain of the life he leads, some do say," replied the Landlord, as another concession.

"A slothful, unsavoury, nasty reversal of the laws of human nature," said the Traveller; "and for the sake of God's working world and its wholesomeness, both moral and physical, I would put the thing on the treadmill (if I had my way) wherever I found it; whether on a pillar, or in a hole; whether on Tom Tiddler's ground, or the Pope of Rome's ground, or a Hindoo fakeer's ground, or any other ground."

"I don't know about putting Mr. Mopes on the treadmill," said the Landlord, shaking his head very seriously. "There ain't a doubt but what he has got landed property."

"How far may it be to this said Tom Tiddler's ground?" asked the Traveller.

"Put it at five mile," returned the Landlord.

"Well! When I have done my breakfast," said the Traveller, "I'll go there. I came over here this morning, to find it out and see it."

"Many does," observed the Landlord.

The conversation passed, in the Midsummer weather of no remote year of grace, down among the pleasant dales and trout-streams of a green English county. No matter what county. Enough that you may hunt there, shoot there, fish there, traverse long grass-grown Roman roads there, open ancient barrows there, see many a square mile of richly cultivated land there, and hold Arcadian talk with a bold peasantry, their country's pride, who will tell you (if you want to know) how pastoral housekeeping is done on nine shillings a week.

Mr. Traveller sat at his breakfast in the little sanded parlour of the Peal of Bells village alehouse, with the dew and dust of an early walk upon his shoes—an early walk by road and meadow and coppice, that had sprinkled him bountifully with little blades of grass, and scraps of new hay, and with leaves both young and old, and with other such fragrant tokens of the freshness and wealth of summer. The window through which the landlord had concentrated his gaze upon vacancy was shaded, because the morning sun was hot and bright on the village street. The village street was like most other village streets: wide for its height, silent for its size, and drowsy in the dullest degree. The quietest little dwellings with the largest of window-shutters (to shut up Nothing as carefully as if it were the Mint, or the Bank of England) had called in the Doctor's house so suddenly, that his brass door-plate and three stories stood among them as conspicuous and different as the Doctor himself in his broadcloth, among the smock-frocks of his patients. The village residences seemed to have gone to law with a similar absence of consideration, for a score of weak little lath-and-plaster cabins clung in confusion about the Attorney's red-brick house, which, with glaring doorsteps and a most terrific scraper, seemed to serve all manner of ejectments upon them. They were as various as labourers—high-shouldered, wry-necked, one-eyed, goggle-eyed, squinting, bow-legged, knock-kneed, rheumatic, crazy. Some of the small tradesmen's houses, such as the crockery-shop and the harness-maker's, had a Cyclops window in the middle of the gable, within an inch or two of its apex, suggesting that some forlorn rural Prentice must wriggle himself into that apartment horizontally, when he retired to rest, after the manner of the worm. So bountiful in its abundance was the surrounding country, and so lean and scant the village, that one might have thought the village had sown and planted everything it once possessed, to convert the same into crops. This would account for the bareness of the little shops, the bareness of the few boards and trestles designed for market purposes in a corner of the street, the bareness of the obsolete Inn and Inn Yard, with the ominous inscription "Excise Office" not yet faded out from the gateway, as indicating the very last thing that poverty could get rid of. This would also account for the determined abandonment of the village by one stray dog, fast lessening in the perspective where the white posts and the pond were, and would explain his conduct on the hypothesis that he was going (through the act of suicide) to convert himself into manure, and become a part proprietor in turnips or mangold-wurzel.

Mr. Traveller having finished his breakfast and paid his

moderate score, walked out to the threshold of the Peal of Bells, and, thence directed by the pointing finger of his host, betook himself towards the ruined hermitage of Mr. Mopes the hermit.

For, Mr. Mopes, by suffering everything about him to go to ruin, and by dressing himself in a blanket and skewer, and by steeping himself in soot and grease and other nastiness, had acquired great renown in all that country-side—far greater renown than he could ever have won for himself, if his career had been that of any ordinary Christian, or decent Hottentot. He had even blanketed and skewered and sooted and greased himself into the London papers. And it was curious to find, as Mr. Traveller found by stopping for a new direction at this farm-house or at that cottage as he went along, with how much accuracy the morbid Mopes had counted on the weakness of his neighbours to embellish him. A mist of home-brewed marvel and romance surrounded Mopes, in which (as in all fogs) the real proportions of the real object were extravagantly heightened. He had murdered his beautiful beloved in a fit of jealousy and was doing penance; he had made a vow under the influence of grief; he had made a vow under the influence of a fatal accident; he had made a vow under the influence of religion; he had made a vow under the influence of drink; he had made a vow under the influence of disappointment; he had never made any vow, but "had got led into it" by the possession of a mighty and most awful secret; he was enormously rich, he was stupendously charitable, he was profoundly learned, he saw spectres, he knew and could do all kinds of wonders. Some said he went out every night, and was met by terrified wayfarers stalking along dark roads, others said he never went out, some knew his penance to be nearly expired, others had positive information that his seclusion was not a penance at all, and would never expire but with himself. Even, as to the easy facts of how old he was, or how long he had held verminous occupation of his blanket and skewer, no consistent information was to be got, from those who must know if they would. He was represented as being all the ages between five-and-twenty and sixty, and as having been a hermit seven years, twelve, twenty, thirty,—though twenty, on the whole, appeared the favourite term.

"Well, well!" said Mr. Traveller. "At any rate, let us see what a real live Hermit looks like."

So, Mr. Traveller went on, and on, and on, until he came to Tom Tiddler's ground.

It was a nook in a rustic by-road, which the genius of Mopes had laid waste as completely, as if he had been born an Emperor and a Conqueror. Its centre object was a dwelling-house, sufficiently substantial, all the window-glass of which had been long ago abolished by the surprising genius of Mopes, and all the windows of which were barred across with rough-split logs of trees nailed over them on the outside. A rickyard, hip-high in vegetable rankness and ruin, contained outbuildings, from which the thatch had lightly fluttered away, on all the winds of all the seasons of the year, and from which the planks and beams had heavily dropped and rotted. The frosts and damps of winter, and the heats of summer, had warped what wreck remained, so that not a post or a board retained the position it was meant to hold, but everything was twisted from its purpose, like its owner, and degraded and debased. In this homestead of the sluggard, behind the ruined hedge, and sinking away among the ruined grass and the nettles, were the last perishing fragments of certain ricks: which had gradually mildewed and collapsed, until they looked like mounds of rotten honeycomb, or dirty sponge. Tom Tiddler's ground could even show its ruined water; for, there was a slimy pond into which a tree or two had fallen—one soppy trunk and branches lay across it then —which in its accumulation of stagnant weed, and in its black decomposition, and in all its foulness and filth, was almost comforting, regarded as the only water that could have reflected the shameful place without seeming polluted by that low office.

Mr. Traveller looked all around him on Tom Tiddler's ground, and his glance at last encountered a dusky Tinker lying among the weeds and rank grass, in the shade of the dwelling-house. A rough walking-staff lay on the ground by his side, and his head rested on a small wallet. He met Mr. Traveller's eye without lifting up his head, merely depressing his chin a little (for he was lying on his back) to get a better view of him.

"Good day!" said Mr. Traveller.

"Same to you, if you like it," returned the Tinker.

"Don't *you* like it? It's a very fine day."

"I ain't partickler in weather," returned the Tinker, with a yawn.

Mr. Traveller had walked up to where he lay, and was looking down at him. "This is a curious place," said Mr. Traveller.

"Ay, I suppose so!" returned the Tinker. "Tom Tiddler's ground, they call this."

"Are you well acquainted with it?"

"Never saw it afore to-day," said the Tinker, with another yawn, "and don't care if I never see it again. There was a man here just now, told me what it was called. If you want to see Tom himself, you must go in at that gate." He faintly indicated with his chin a little mean ruin of a wooden gate at the side of the house.

"Have you seen Tom?"

"No, and I ain't partickler to see him. I can see a dirty man anywhere."

"He does not live in the house, then?" said Mr. Traveller, casting his eyes upon the house anew.

"The man said," returned the Tinker, rather irritably,— "him as was here just now,—'this what you're a lying on, mate, is Tom Tiddler's ground. And if you want to see Tom,' he says, 'you must go in at that gate.' The man come out at that gate himself, and he ought to know."

"Certainly," said Mr. Traveller.

"Though, perhaps," exclaimed the Tinker, so struck by the brightness of his own idea, that it had the electric effect upon him of causing him to lift up his head an inch or so, "perhaps he was a liar! He told some rum'uns—him as was here just now did, about this place of Tom's. He says —him as was here just now—'When Tom shut up the house, mate, to go to rack, the beds was left, all made, like as if somebody was a going to sleep in every bed. And if you was to walk through the bedrooms now, you'd see the ragged mouldy bedclothes a heaving and a heaving like seas. And a heaving and a heaving with what?' he says. 'Why, with the rats under 'em.'"

"I wish I had seen that man," Mr. Traveller remarked.

"You'd have been welcome to see him instead of me seeing him," growled the Tinker; "for he was a long-winded one."

Not without a sense of injury in the remembrance, the Tinker gloomily closed his eyes. Mr. Traveller, deeming the Tinker a short-winded one, from whom no further breath of information was to be derived, betook himself to the gate.

Swung upon its rusty hinges, it admitted him into a yard in which there was nothing to be seen but an outhouse attached to the ruined building, with a barred window in it. As there were traces of many recent footsteps under this window, and as it was a low window, and unglazed, Mr. Traveller made bold to peep within the bars. And there to be sure he had a real live Hermit before him, and could judge how the real dead Hermits used to look.

He was lying on a bank of soot and cinders, on the floor, in front of a rusty fireplace. There was nothing else in the dark little kitchen, or scullery, or whatever his den had been originally used as, but a table with a litter of old bottles on it. A rat made a clatter among these bottles, jumped down, and ran over the real live Hermit on his way to his hole, or the man in *his* hole would not have been so easily discernible. Tickled in the face by the rat's tail, the owner of Tom Tiddler's ground opened his eyes, saw Mr. Traveller, started up, and sprang to the window.

"Humph!" thought Mr. Traveller, retiring a pace or two from the bars. "A compound of Newgate, Bedlam, a Debtors' Prison in the worst time, a chimney-sweep, a mudlark, and the Noble Savage! A nice old family, the Hermit family. Hah!"

Mr. Traveller thought this, as he silently confronted the sooty object in the blanket and skewer (in sober truth it wore nothing else), with the matted hair and the staring eyes. Further, Mr. Traveller thought, as the eye surveyed him with a very obvious curiosity in ascertaining the effect they produced, "Vanity, vanity, vanity! Verily, all is vanity!"

"What is your name, Sir, and where do you come from?" asked Mr. Mopes the Hermit—with an air of authority, but in the ordinary human speech of one who has been to school.

Mr. Traveller answered the inquiries.

"Did you come here, Sir, to see *me?*"

"I did. I heard of you, and I came to see you.—I know you like to be seen." Mr. Traveller coolly threw the last words in, as a matter of course, to forestall an affectation of resentment or objection that he saw rising beneath the grease and grime of the face. They had their effect.

"So," said the Hermit, after a momentary silence, unclasping the bars by which he had previously held, and seating himself behind them on the ledge of the window, with his bare legs and feet crouched up, "you know I like to be seen?"

Mr. Traveller looked about him for something to sit on, and, observing a billet of wood in a corner, brought it near the window. Deliberately seating himself upon it, he answered, "Just so."

Each looked at the other, and each appeared to take some pains to get the measure of the other.

"Then you have come to ask me why I lead this life," said the Hermit, frowning in a stormy manner. "I never tell that to any human being. I will not be asked that."

"Certainly you will not be asked that by me," said Mr. Traveller, "for I have not the slightest desire to know."

"You are an uncouth man," said Mr. Mopes the Hermit.

"You are another," said Mr. Traveller.

The Hermit, who was plainly in the habit of overawing his visitors with the novelty of his filth and his blanket and skewer, glared at his present visitor in some discomfiture and surprise: as if he had taken aim at him with a sure gun, and his piece had missed fire.

"Why do you come here at all?" he asked, after a pause.

"Upon my life," said Mr. Traveller, "I was made to ask myself that very question only a few minutes ago—by a Tinker too."

As he glanced towards the gate in saying it, the Hermit glanced in that direction likewise.

"Yes He is lying on his back in the sunlight outside," said Mr. Traveller, as if he had been asked concerning the man, "and he won't come in; for he says—and really very reasonably—'What should I come in for? I can see a dirty man anywhere.'"

"You are an insolent person. Go away from my premises. Go!" said the Hermit, in an imperious and angry tone.

"Come, come!" returned Mr. Traveller, quite undisturbed. "This is a little too much. You are not going to call yourself clean? Look at your legs. And as to these being your premises:—they are in far too disgraceful a condition to claim any privilege of ownership, or anything else."

The Hermit bounced down from his window-ledge, and cast himself on his bed of soot and cinders.

"I am not going," said Mr. Traveller, glancing in after him; "you won't get rid of me in that way. You had better come and talk."

"I won't talk." said the Hermit, flouncing round to get his back towards the window.

"Then I will," said Mr. Traveller. "Why should you take it ill that I have no curiosity to know why you live this highly absurd and highly indecent life? When I contemplate a man in a state of disease, surely there is no moral obligation on me to be anxious to know how he took it."

After a short silence, the Hermit bounced up again, and came back to the barred window.

"What? You are not gone?" he said, affecting to have supposed that he was.

"Nor going," Mr. Traveller replied; "I design to pass this summer day here."

"How dare you come, Sir, upon my premises—— " the Hermit was returning, when his visitor interrupted him.

"Really, you know, you must *not* talk about your premises. I cannot allow such a place as this to be dignified with the name of premises."

"How dare you," said the Hermit, shaking his bars, "come in at my gate, to taunt me with being in a diseased state?"

"Why, Lord bless my soul," returned the other, very composedly, "you have not the face to say that you are in a wholesome state? Do allow me again to call your attention to your legs. Scrape yourself anywhere— with anything —and then tell me you are in a wholesome state. The fact is, Mr. Mopes, that you are not only a Nuisance—— "

"A Nuisance?" repeated the Hermit, fiercely.

"What is a place in this obscene state of dilapidation but a Nuisance? What is a man in your obscene state of dilapidation but a Nuisance? Then, as you very well know, you cannot do without an audience, and your audience is a Nuisance. You attract all the disreputable vagabonds and prowlers within ten miles around, by exhibiting yourself to them in that objectionable blanket, and by throwing copper money among them, and giving them drink out of those very dirty jars and bottles that I see in there (their stomachs need be strong!); and in short," said Mr. Traveller, summing up in a quietly and comfortably settled manner, "you are a Nuisance, and this kennel is a Nuisance, and the audience that you cannot possibly dispense with is a Nuisance, and the Nuisance is not merely a local Nuisance, because it is a general Nuisance to know that there *can be* such a Nuisance left in civilisation so very long after its time."

"Will you go away? I have a gun in here," said the Hermit.

"Pooh!"

"I *have!*"

"Now, I put it to you. Did I say you had not? And as to going away, didn't I say I am not going away? You have made me forget where I was. I now remember that I was remarking on your conduct being a Nuisance. Moreover, it is in the last and lowest degree inconsequent foolishness and weakness."

"Weakness?" echoed the Hermit.

"Weakness," said Mr. Traveller, with his former comfortably settled final air.

"I weak, you fool?" cried the Hermit, "I, who have held to my purpose, and my diet, and my only bed there, all these years?"

"The more the years, the weaker you," returned Mr. Traveller. "Though the years are not so many as folks say, and as you willingly take credit for. The crust upon your face is thick and dark, Mr. Mopes, but I can see enough of you through it, to see that you are still a young man."

"Inconsequent foolishness is lunacy, I suppose?" said the Hermit.

"I suppose it is very like it," answered Mr. Traveller.

"Do I converse like a lunatic?"

"One of us two must have a strong presumption against him of being one, whether or no. Either the clean and decorously clad man, or the dirty and indecorously clad man. I don't say which."

"Why, you self-sufficient bear," said the Hermit, "not a day passes but I am justified in my purpose by the conversations I hold here; not a day passes but I am shown, by everything I hear and see here, how right and strong I am in holding my purpose."

Mr. Traveller, lounging easily on his billet of wood, took out a pocket pipe and began to fill it. "Now, that a man," he said, appealing to the summer sky as he did so, "that a man—even behind bars, in a blanket and skewer—should tell me that he can see, from day to day, any orders or conditions of men, women, or children, who can by any possibility teach him that it is anything but the miserablest drivelling for a human creature to quarrel with his social nature—not to go so far as to say, to renounce his common human decency, for that is an extreme case; or who can teach him that he can in any wise separate himself from his kind and the habits of his kind, without becoming a deteriorated spectacle calculated to give the Devil (and perhaps the monkeys) pleasure,—is something wonderful! I repeat," said Mr. Traveller, beginning to smoke, "the unreasoning hardihood of it is something wonderful—even in a man with the dirt upon him an inch or two thick—behind bars—in a blanket and skewer!"

The Hermit looked at him irresolutely, and retired to his soot and cinders and lay down, and got up again and came to the bars, and again looked at him irresolutely, and finally said with sharpness: "I don't like tobacco."

"I don't like dirt," rejoined Mr. Traveller; "tobacco is an excellent disinfectant. We shall both be the better for my pipe. It is my intention to sit here through this summer day, until that blessed summer sun sinks low in the west, and to show you what a poor creature you are, through the lips of every chance wayfarer who may come in at your gate."

"What do you mean?" inquired the Hermit, with a furious air.

"I mean that yonder is your gate, and there are you, and here am I; I mean that I know it to be a moral impossibility that any person can stray in at that gate from any point of the compass, with any sort of experience, gained at first hand, or derived from another, that can confute me and justify you."

"You are an arrogant and boastful hero," said the Hermit. "You think yourself profoundly wise."

"Bah!" returned Mr. Traveller, quietly smoking. "There is little wisdom in knowing that every man must be up and doing, and that all mankind are made dependent on one another."

"You have companions outside," said the Hermit. "I am not to be imposed upon by your assumed confidence in the people who may enter."

"A depraved distrust," returned the visitor, compassionately raising his eyebrows, "of course belongs to your state. I can't help that."

"Do you mean to tell me you have no confederates?"

"I mean to tell you nothing but what I have told you. What I have told you is, that it is a moral impossibility that any son or daughter of Adam can stand on this ground that I put my foot on, or on any ground that mortal treads, and gainsay the healthy tenure on which we hold our existence."

"Which is," sneered the Hermit, "according to you—— "

"Which is," returned the other, "according to Eternal Providence, that we must arise and wash our faces and do our gregarious work and act and re-act on one another, leaving only the idiot and the palsied to sit blinking in the corner. Come!" apostrophising the gate. "Open Sesame! Show his eyes and grieve his heart! I don't care who comes, for I know what must come of it!"

With that, he faced round a little on his billet of wood towards the gate; and Mr. Mopes, the Hermit, after two or three ridiculous bounces of indecision at his bed and back again, submitted to what he could not help himself against, and coiled himself on his window-ledge, holding to his bars and looking out rather anxiously.

CHAPTER VI

PICKING UP MISS KIMMEENS

THE day was by this time waning, when the gate again opened, and, with the brilliant golden light that streamed from the declining sun and touched the very bars of the sooty creature's den, there passed in a little child; a little girl with beautiful bright hair. She wore a plain straw hat, had a door-key in her hand, and tripped towards Mr. Traveller as if she were pleased to see him and were going to repose some childish confidence in him, when she caught sight of the figure behind the bars, and started back in terror.

"Don't be alarmed, darling!" said Mr. Traveller, taking her by the hand.

"Oh, but I don't like it!" urged the shrinking child; "it's dreadful."

"Well! I don't like it either," said Mr. Traveller.

"Who has put it there?" asked the little girl. "Does it bite?"

"No,—only barks. But can't you make up your mind to see it, my dear?" For she was covering her eyes.

"O no no no!" returned the child. "I cannot bear to look at it!"

Mr. Traveller turned his head towards his friend in there, as much as to ask him how he liked that instance of his success, and then took the child out at the still open gate, and stood talking to her for some half an hour in the mellow sunlight. At length he returned, encouraging her as she held his arm with both her hands; and laying his protecting hand upon her head and smoothing her pretty hair, he addressed his friend behind the bars as follows:

Miss Pupford's establishment for six young ladies of tender years, is an establishment of a compact nature, an establishment in miniature, quite a pocket establishment. Miss Pupford, Miss Pupford's assistant with the Parisian accent, Miss Pupford's cook, and Miss Pupford's housemaid, complete what Miss Pupford calls the educational and domestic staff of her Lilliputian College.

Miss Pupford is one of the most amiable of her sex; it necessarily follows that she possesses a sweet temper, and would own to the possession of a great deal of sentiment if she considered it quite reconcilable with her duty to parents. Deeming it not in the bond, Miss Pupford keeps it as far out of sight as she can—which (God bless her!) is not very far.

Miss Pupford's assistant with the Parisian accent, may be regarded as in some sort an inspired lady, for she never conversed with a Parisian, and was never out of England—except once in the pleasure-boat Lively, in the foreign waters that ebb and flow two miles off Margate at high water. Even under those geographically favourable circumstances for the acquisition of the French language in its utmost politeness and purity, Miss Pupford's assistant did not fully profit by the opportunity; for the pleasure-boat, Lively, so strongly asserted its title to its name on that occasion, that she was reduced to the condition of lying in the bottom of the boat pickling in brine—as if she were being salted down for the use of the Navy—undergoing at the same time great mental alarm, corporeal distress, and clear-starching derangement.

When Miss Pupford and her assistant first foregathered, is not known to men, or pupils. But, it was long ago. A belief would have established itself among pupils that the two once went to school together, were it not for the difficulty and audacity of imagining Miss Pupford born without mittens, and without a front, and without a bit of gold wire among her front teeth, and without little dabs of powder on her neat little face and nose. Indeed, whenever Miss Pupford gives a little lecture on the mythology of the misguided heathens (always carefully excluding Cupid from recognition), and tells how Minerva sprang, perfectly equipped, from the brain of Jupiter, she is half supposed to hint, "So I myself came into the world, completely up in Pinnock, Mangnall, Tables, and the use of the Globes."

Howbeit, Miss Pupford and Miss Pupford's assistant are old old friends. And it is thought by pupils that, after pupils are gone to bed, they even call one another by their christian names in the quiet little parlour. For, once upon a time on a thunderous afternoon, when Miss Pupford fainted away without notice, Miss Pupford's assistant (never heard, before or since, to address her otherwise than as Miss Pupford) ran to her, crying out "My dearest Euphemia!" And Euphemia is Miss Pupford's christian name on the sampler (date picked out) hanging up in the College-hall, where the two peacocks, terrified to death by some German text that is waddling down hill after them out of a cottage, are scuttling away to hide their profiles in two immense bean-stalks growing out of flower-pots.

Also, there is a notion latent among pupils, that Miss Pupford was once in love, and that the beloved object still moves upon this ball. Also, that he is a public character, and a personage of vast consequence. Also, that Miss Pupford's assistant knows all about it. For, sometimes of an afternoon when Miss Pupford has been reading the paper through her little gold eye-glass (it is necessary to read it on the spot, as the boy calls for it, with ill-conditioned punctuality, in an hour), she has become agitated, and has said to her assistant "G!" Then Miss Pupford's assistant has gone to Miss Pupford, and Miss Pupford has pointed out, with her eye-glass, G in the paper, and then Miss Pupford's assistant has read about G, and has shown sympathy. So stimulated has the pupil-mind been in its time to curiosity on the subject of G, that once, under temporary circumstances favourable to the bold sally, one fearless pupil did actually obtain possession of the paper, and range all over it in search of G, who had been discovered therein by Miss Pupford not

ten minutes before. But no G could be identified, except
one capital offender who had been executed in a state of
great hardihood, and it was not to be supposed that Miss
Pupford could ever have loved *him*. Besides, he couldn't be
always being executed. Besides, he got into the paper again,
alive, within a month.

On the whole, it is suspected by the pupil-mind that G is
a short chubby old gentleman, with little black sealing-wax
boots up to his knees, whom a sharply observant pupil, Miss
Linx, when she once went to Tunbridge Wells with Miss
Pupford for the holidays, reported on her return (privately
and confidentially) to have seen come capering up to Miss
Pupford on the Promenade, and to have detected in the act
of squeezing Miss Pupford's hand, and to have heard
pronounce the words, "Cruel Euphemia, ever thine!"—or
something like that. Miss Linx hazarded a guess that he
might be House of Commons, or Money Market, or Court
Circular, or Fashionable Movements; which would account
for his getting into the paper so often. But, it was fatally
objected by the pupil-mind, that none of those notabilities
could possibly be spelt with a G.

There are other occasions, closely watched and perfectly
comprehended by the pupil-mind, when Miss Pupford imparts
with mystery to her assistant that there is special excitement
in the morning paper. These occasions are, when Miss
Pupford finds an old pupil coming out under the head of
Births, or Marriages. Affectionate tears are invariably seen
in Miss Pupford's meek little eyes when this is the case; and
the pupil-mind, perceiving that its order has distinguished
itself—though the fact is never mentioned by Miss Pupford
—becomes elevated, and feels that it likewise is reserved for
greatness.

Miss Pupford's assistant with the Parisian accent has a
little more bone than Miss Pupford, but is of the same trim
orderly diminutive cast, and, from long contemplation, admiration, and imitation of Miss Pupford, has grown like her.
Being entirely devoted to Miss Pupford, and having a pretty
talent for pencil-drawing, she once made a portrait of that
lady : which was so instantly identified and hailed by the
pupils, that it was done on stone at five shillings. Surely
the softest and milkiest stone that ever was quarried, received
that likeness of Miss Pupford ! The lines of her placid little
nose are so undecided in it that strangers to the work of

art are observed to be exceedingly perplexed as to where the
nose goes to, and involuntarily feel their own noses in a
disconcerted manner. Miss Pupford being represented in a
state of dejection at an open window, ruminating over a bowl
of goldfish, the pupil-mind has settled that the bowl was
presented by G, and that he wreathed the bowl with flowers
of soul, and that Miss Pupford is depicted as waiting for
him on a memorable occasion when he was behind his
time.

The approach of the last Midsummer holidays had a
particular interest for the pupil-mind, by reason of its
knowing that Miss Pupford was bidden, on the second day
of those holidays, to the nuptials of a former pupil. As it
was impossible to conceal the fact—so extensive were the
dressmaking preparations—Miss Pupford openly announced
it. But, she held it due to parents to make the announcement with an air of gentle melancholy, as if marriage were
(as indeed it exceptionally has been) rather a calamity.
With an air of softened resignation and pity, therefore, Miss
Pupford went on with her preparations: and meanwhile no
pupil ever went upstairs, or came down, without peeping in
at the door of Miss Pupford's bedroom (when Miss Pupford
wasn't there), and bringing back some surprising intelligence
concerning the bonnet.

The extensive preparations being completed on the day
before the holidays, an unanimous entreaty was preferred to
Miss Pupford by the pupil-mind—finding expression through
Miss Pupford's assistant—that she would deign to appear
in all her splendour. Miss Pupford consenting, presented a
lovely spectacle. And although the oldest pupil was barely
thirteen, every one of the six became in two minutes perfect
in the shape, cut, colour, price, and quality, of every article
Miss Pupford wore.

Thus delightfully ushered in, the holidays began. Five of
the six pupils kissed little Kitty Kimmeens twenty times over
(round total, one hundred times, for she was very popular),
and so went home. Miss Kitty Kimmeens remained behind,
for her relations and friends were all in India, far away.
A self-helpful steady little child is Miss Kitty Kimmeens:
a dimpled child too, and a loving.

So, the great marriage-day came, and Miss Pupford, quite
as much fluttered as any bride could be (G! thought Miss
Kitty Kimmeens), went away, splendid to behold, in the

carriage that was sent for her. But not Miss Pupford only went away ; for Miss Pupford's assistant went away with her, on a dutiful visit to an aged uncle—though surely the venerable gentleman couldn't live in the gallery of the church where the marriage was to be, thought Miss Kitty Kimmeens—and yet Miss Pupford's assistant had let out that she was going there. Where the cook was going, didn't appear, but she generally conveyed to Miss Kimmeens that she was bound, rather against her will, on a pilgrimage to perform some pious office that rendered new ribbons necessary to her best bonnet, and also sandals to her shoes.

"So you see," said the housemaid, when they were all gone, "there's nobody left in the house but you and me, Miss Kimmeens."

"Nobody else," said Miss Kitty Kimmeens, shaking her curls a little sadly. "Nobody ! "

"And you wouldn't like your Bella to go too ; would you, Miss Kimmeens ? " said the housemaid. (She being Bella.)

"N—no," answered little Miss Kimmeens.

"Your poor Bella is forced to stay with you, whether she likes it or not ; ain't she, Miss Kimmeens ? "

" *Don't* you like it ? " inquired Kitty.

"Why, you're such a darling, Miss, that it would be unkind of your Bella to make objections. Yet my brother-in-law has been took unexpected bad by this morning's post. And your poor Bella is much attached to him, letting alone her favourite sister, Miss Kimmeens."

" Is he very ill ? " asked little Kitty.

"Your poor Bella has her fears so, Miss Kimmeens," returned the housemaid, with her apron at her eyes. "It was but his inside, it is true, but it might mount, and the doctor said that if it mounted he wouldn't answer." Here the housemaid was so overcome that Kitty administered the only comfort she had ready : which was a kiss.

"If it hadn't been for disappointing Cook, dear Miss Kimmeens," said the housemaid, "your Bella would have asked her to stay with you. For Cook is sweet company, Miss Kimmeens, much more so than your own poor Bella."

"But you are very nice, Bella."

"Your Bella could wish to be so, Miss Kimmeens," returned the housemaid, "but she knows full well that it do not lay in her power this day."

With which despondent conviction, the housemaid drew

a heavy sigh, and shook her head, and dropped it on one side.

"If it had been anyways right to disappoint Cook," she pursued, in a contemplative and abstracted manner, "it might have been so easy done! I could have got to my brother-in-law's, and had the best part of the day there, and got back, long before our ladies come home at night, and neither the one nor the other of them need never have known it. Not that Miss Pupford would at all object, but that it might put her out, being tender-hearted. Hows'ever, your own poor Bella, Miss Kimmeens," said the housemaid, rousing herself, "is forced to stay with you, and you're a precious love, if not a liberty."

"Bella," said little Kitty, after a short silence.

"Call your own poor Bella, *your* Bella, dear," the housemaid besought her.

"My Bella, then."

"Bless your considerate heart!" said the housemaid.

"If you would not mind leaving me, I should not mind being left. I am not afraid to stay in the house alone. And you need not be uneasy on my account, for I would be very careful to do no harm."

"O! As to harm, you more than sweetest, if not a liberty," exclaimed the housemaid, in a rapture, "your Bella could trust you anywhere, being so steady, and so answerable. The oldest head in this house (me and Cook says), but for its bright hair, is Miss Kimmeens. But no, I will not leave you; for you would think your Bella unkind."

"But if you are my Bella, you *must* go," returned the child.

"Must I?" said the housemaid, rising, on the whole with alacrity. "What must be, must be, Miss Kimmeens. Your own poor Bella acts according, though unwilling. But go or stay, your own poor Bella loves you, Miss Kimmeens."

It was certainly go, and not stay, for within five minutes Miss Kimmeens's own poor Bella—so much improved in point of spirits as to have grown almost sanguine on the subject of her brother-in-law—went her way, in apparel that seemed to have been expressly prepared for some festive occasion. Such are the changes of this fleeting world, and so short-sighted are we poor mortals!

When the house door closed with a bang and a shake, it seemed to Miss Kimmeens to be a very heavy house door, shutting her up in a wilderness of a house. But, Miss Kimmeens being, as before stated, of a self-reliant and methodical character, presently began to parcel out the long summer-day before her.

And first she thought she would go all over the house, to make quite sure that nobody with a great-coat on and a carving-knife in it, had got under one of the beds or into one of the cupboards. Not that she had ever before been troubled by the image of anybody armed with a great-coat and a carving-knife, but that it seemed to have been shaken into existence by the shake and the bang of the great street door, reverberating through the solitary house. So, little Miss Kimmeens looked under the five empty beds of the five departed pupils, and looked under her own bed, and looked under Miss Pupford's bed, and looked under Miss Pupford's assistant's bed. And when she had done this, and was making the tour of the cupboards, the disagreeable thought came into her young head, What a very alarming thing it would be to find somebody with a mask on, like Guy Fawkes, hiding bolt upright in a corner and pretending not to be alive! However, Miss Kimmeens having finished her inspection without making any such uncomfortable discovery, sat down in her tidy little manner to needlework, and began stitching away at a great rate.

The silence all about her soon grew very oppressive, and the more so because of the odd inconsistency that the more silent it was, the more noises there were. The noise of her own needle and thread as she stitched, was infinitely louder in her ears than the stitching of all the six pupils, and of Miss Pupford, and of Miss Pupford's assistant, all stitching away at once on a highly emulative afternoon. Then, the school-room clock conducted itself in a way in which it had never conducted itself before—fell lame, somehow, and yet persisted in running on as hard and as loud as it could: the consequence of which behaviour was, that it staggered among the minutes in a state of the greatest confusion, and knocked them about in all directions without appearing to get on with its regular work. Perhaps this alarmed the stairs: but be that as it might, they began to creak in a most unusual manner, and then the furniture began to crack, and then poor little Miss Kimmeens, not liking the furtive aspect of things in general, began to sing as she stitched. But. it was not her own voice that she heard—it was some-

body else making believe to be Kitty, and singing excessively
flat, without any heart—so as that would never mend matters,
she left off again.

By and by, the stitching became so palpable a failure that
Miss Kitty Kimmeens folded her work neatly, and put it
away in its box, and gave it up. Then the question arose
about reading. But no; the book that was so delightful
when there was somebody she loved for her eyes to fall on
when they rose from the page, had not more heart in it than
her own singing now. The book went to its shelf as the
needlework had gone to its box, and, since something *must*
be done—thought the child, "I'll go put my room to rights."

She shared her room with her dearest little friend among
the other five pupils, and why then should she now conceive
a lurking dread of the little friend's bedstead? But she did.
There was a stealthy air about its innocent white curtains,
and there were even dark hints of a dead girl lying under
the coverlet. The great want of human company, the great
need of a human face, began now to express itself in the
facility with which the furniture put on strange exaggerated
resemblances to human looks. A chair with a menacing
frown was horribly out of temper in a corner; a most vicious
chest of drawers snarled at her from between the windows.
It was no relief to escape from those monsters to the looking-
glass, for the reflection said, "What? Is that you all alone
there? How you stare!" And the background was all a
great void stare as well.

The day dragged on, dragging Kitty with it very slowly
by the hair of her head, until it was time to eat. There
were good provisions in the pantry, but their right flavour
and relish had evaporated with the five pupils, and Miss
Pupford, and Miss Pupford's assistant, and the cook and
housemaid. Where was the use of laying the cloth symmetrically for one small guest, who had gone on ever since the
morning growing smaller and smaller, while the empty house
had gone on swelling larger and larger? The very Grace
came out wrong, for who were "we" who were going to receive
and be thankful? So, Miss Kimmeens was *not* thankful, and
found herself taking her dinner in very slovenly style—
gobbling it up, in short, rather after the manner of the lower
animals, not to particularise the pigs.

But, this was by no means the worst of the change wrought
out in the naturally loving and cheery little creature as the

solitary day wore on. She began to brood and be suspicious.
She discovered that she was full of wrongs and injuries. All
the people she knew, got tainted by her lonely thoughts and
turned bad.

It was all very well for papa, a widower in India, to send
her home to be educated, and to pay a handsome round sum
every year for her to Miss Pupford, and to write charming
letters to his darling little daughter; but what did he care
for her being left by herself, when he was (as no doubt he
always was) enjoying himself in company from morning till
night? Perhaps he only sent her here, after all, to get her
out of the way. It looked like it—looked like it to-day,
that is, for she had never dreamed of such a thing before.

And this old pupil who was being married. It was
insupportably conceited and selfish in the old pupil to be
married. She was very vain, and very glad to show off; but
it was highly probable that she wasn't pretty; and even if
she were pretty (which Miss Kimmeens now totally denied),
she had no business to be married; and, even if marriage
were conceded, she had no business to ask Miss Pupford to
her wedding. As to Miss Pupford, she was too old to go
to any wedding. She ought to know that. She had much
better attend to her business. She had thought she looked
nice in the morning, but she didn't look nice. She was a
stupid old thing. G was another stupid old thing. Miss
Pupford's assistant was another. They were all stupid old
things together.

More than that: it began to be obvious that this was a
plot. They had said to one another, "Never mind Kitty;
you get off, and I'll get off; and we'll leave Kitty to look
after herself. Who cares for *her?*" To be sure they were
right in that question; for who *did* care for her, a poor
little lonely thing against whom they all planned and plotted?
Nobody, nobody! Here Kitty sobbed.

At all other times she was the pet of the whole house,
and loved her five companions in return with a child's
tenderest and most ingenuous attachment; but now, the five
companions put on ugly colours, and appeared for the first
time under a sullen cloud. There they were, all at their
homes that day, being made much of, being taken out, being
spoilt and made disagreeable, and caring nothing for her.
It was like their artful selfishness always to tell her when
they came back, under pretence of confidence and friendship,

all those details about where they had been, and what they
had done and seen, and how often they had said, "O! If
we had only darling little Kitty here!" Here indeed! I
dare say! When they came back after the holidays, they
were used to being received by Kitty, and to saying that
coming to Kitty was like coming to another home. Very
well then, why did they go away? If they meant it, why
did they go away? Let them answer that. But they didn't
mean it, and couldn't answer that, and they didn't tell the
truth, and people who didn't tell the truth were hateful.
When they came back next time, they should be received
in a new manner; they should be avoided and shunned.

And there, the while she sat all alone revolving how ill
she was used, and how much better she was than the people
who were not alone, the wedding breakfast was going on:
no question of it! With a nasty great bride-cake, and with
those ridiculous orange-flowers, and with that conceited
bride, and that hideous bridegroom, and those heartless
bridesmaids, and Miss Pupford stuck up at the table! They
thought they were enjoying themselves, but it would come
home to them one day to have thought so. They would all
be dead in a few years, let them enjoy themselves ever so
much. It was a religious comfort to know that.

It was such a comfort to know it, that little Miss Kitty
Kimmeens suddenly sprang from the chair in which she had
been musing in a corner, and cried out, "O those envious
thoughts are not mine, O this wicked creature isn't me!
Help me, somebody! I go wrong, alone by my weak self!
Help me, anybody!"

"—Miss Kimmeens is not a professed philosopher, Sir,"
said Mr. Traveller, presenting her at the barred window, and
smoothing her shining hair, "but I apprehend there was some
tincture of philosophy in her words, and in the prompt action
with which she followed them. That action was, to emerge
from her unnatural solitude, and look abroad for wholesome
sympathy, to bestow and to receive. Her footsteps strayed
to this gate, bringing her here by chance, as an apposite
contrast to you. The child came out, Sir. If you have the
wisdom to learn from a child (but I doubt it, for that requires
more wisdom than one in your condition would seem to
possess), you cannot do better than imitate the child, and
come out too—from that very demoralising hutch of yours."

CHAPTER VII

PICKING UP THE TINKER

It was now sunset. The Hermit had betaken himself to his bed of cinders half an hour ago, and lying on it in his blanket and skewer with his back to the window, took not the smallest heed of the appeal addressed to him.

All that had been said for the last two hours, had been said to a tinkling accompaniment performed by the Tinker, who had got to work upon some villager's pot or kettle, and was working briskly outside. This music still continuing, seemed to put it into Mr. Traveller's mind to have another word or two with the Tinker. So, holding Miss Kimmeens (with whom he was now on the most friendly terms) by the hand, he went out at the gate to where the Tinker was seated at his work on the patch of grass on the opposite side of the road, with his wallet of tools open before him, and his little fire smoking.

"I am glad to see you employed," said Mr. Traveller.

"I am glad to *be* employed," returned the Tinker, looking up as he put the finishing touches to his job. "But why are you glad?"

"I thought you were a iazy fellow when I saw you this morning."

"I was only disgusted," said the Tinker.

"Do you mean with the fine weather?"

"With the fine weather?" repeated the Tinker, staring.

"You told me you were not particular as to weather, and I thought——"

"Ha, ha! How should such as me get on, if we *was* particular as to weather? We must take it as it comes, and make the best of it. There's something good in all weathers. If it don't happen to be good for my work to-day, it's good for some other man's to-day, and will come round to me to-morrow. We must all live."

"Pray shake hands," said Mr. Traveller.

"Take care, Sir," was the Tinker's caution, as he reached up his hand in surprise; "the black comes off."

"I am glad of it," said Mr. Traveller. "I have been for several hours among other black that does not come off."

"You are speaking of Tom in there?"

"Yes."

"Well now," said the Tinker, blowing the dust off his job: which was finished. "Ain't it enough to disgust a pig, if he could give his mind to it?"

"If he could give his mind to it," returned the other, smiling, "the probability is that he wouldn't be a pig."

"There you clench the nail," returned the Tinker. "Then what's to be said for Tom?"

"Truly, very little."

"Truly nothing you mean, Sir," said the Tinker, as he put away his tools.

"A better answer, and (I freely acknowledge) my meaning. I infer that he was the cause of your disgust?"

"Why, look'ee here, Sir," said the Tinker, rising to his feet, and wiping his face on the corner of his black apron energetically; "I leave you to judge!—I ask you!—Last night I has a job that needs to be done in the night, and I works all night. Well, there's nothing in that. But this morning I comes along this road here, looking for a sunny and soft spot to sleep in, and I sees this desolation and ruination. I've lived myself in desolation and ruination; I knows many a fellow-creetur that's forced to live life long in desolation and ruination; and I sits me down and takes pity on it, as I casts my eyes about. Then comes up the long-winded one as I told you of, from that gate, and spins himself out like a silkworm concerning the Donkey (if my Donkey at home will excuse me) as has made it all—made it of his own choice! And tells me, if you please, of his likewise choosing to go ragged and naked, and grimy—maskerading, mountebanking, in what is the real hard lot of thousands and thousands! Why, then I say it's a unbearable and nonsensical piece of inconsistency, and I'm disgusted. I'm ashamed and disgusted!"

"I wish you would come and look at him," said Mr. Traveller, clapping the Tinker on the shoulder.

"Not I, Sir," he rejoined. "I ain't a going to flatter him up by looking at him!"

"But he is asleep."

"Are you sure he is asleep?" asked the Tinker, with an unwilling air, as he shouldered his wallet.

"Sure."

"Then I'll look at him for a quarter of a minute," said the Tinker, "since you so much wish it; but not a moment longer."

They all three went back across the road; and, through the barred window, by the dying glow of the sunset coming in at the gate—which the child held open for its admission —he could be pretty clearly discerned lying on his bed.

"You see him?" asked Mr. Traveller.

"Yes," returned the Tinker, "and he's worse than I thought him."

Mr. Traveller then whispered in few words what he had done since morning; and asked the Tinker what he thought of that?

"I think," returned the Tinker, as he turned from the window, "that you've wasted a day on him."

"I think so too; though not, I hope, upon myself. Do you happen to be going anywhere near the Peal of Bells?"

"That's my direct way, Sir," said the Tinker.

"I invite you to supper there. And as I learn from this young lady that she goes some three-quarters of a mile in the same direction, we will drop her on the road, and we will spare time to keep her company at her garden gate until her own Bella comes home."

So, Mr. Traveller, and the child, and the Tinker, went along very amicably in the sweet-scented evening; and the moral with which the Tinker dismissed the subject was, that he said in his trade that metal that rotted for want of use, had better be left to rot, and couldn't rot too soon, considering how much true metal rotted from over-use and hard service.

SOMEBODY'S LUGGAGE

[1862]

CHARACTERS

BEBELLE (Gabrielle), *a little orphan girl; the protégée of Corporal Théophile.*

MADAME BOUCLET, *Mr. Langley's landlady.*

CHRISTOPHER, *head waiter at a London hotel.*

MR. LANGLEY ('Mr. the Englishman'), *a lodger at Madame Bouclet's.*

MISS MARTIN, *a young lady who makes out the bills at the bar of a London hotel.*

MONSIEUR MUTUEL, *a friend of Madame Bouclet's.*

MRS. PRATCHETT, *head chambermaid at a London hotel.*

CORPORAL THÉOPHILE, *a brave French soldier.*

SOMEBODY'S LUGGAGE

IN FOUR CHAPTERS

CHAPTER I

HIS LEAVING IT TILL CALLED FOR

THE writer of these humble lines being a Waiter, and having come of a family of Waiters, and owning at the present time five brothers who are all Waiters, and likewise an only sister who is a Waitress, would wish to offer a few words respecting his calling; first having the pleasure of hereby in a friendly manner offering the Dedication of the same unto JOSEPH, much respected Head Waiter at the Slamjam Coffee-house, London, E.C., than which a individual more eminently deserving of the name of man, or a more amenable honour to his own head and heart, whether considered in the light of a Waiter or regarded as a human being, do not exist.

In case confusion should arise in the public mind (which it is open to confusion on many subjects) respecting what is meant or implied by the term Waiter, the present humble lines would wish to offer an explanation. It may not be generally known that the person as goes out to wait is *not* a Waiter. It may not be generally known that the hand as is called in extra, at the Freemasons' Tavern, or the London, or the Albion, or otherwise, is *not* a Waiter. Such hands may be took on for Public Dinners by the bushel (and you may know them by their breathing with difficulty when in attendance, and taking away the bottle ere yet it is half out); but such are *not* Waiters. For you cannot lay down the tailoring, or the shoemaking, or the brokering, or the greengrocering, or the pictorial-periodicalling, or the second-hand wardrobe, or the small fancy businesses,—you cannot lay down those lines of life at your will and pleasure by the half-day or evening, and take up Waitering. You may suppose you can, but you cannot; or you may go so far as to say you do, but you do not. Nor yet can you lay down the gentleman's-service when stimulated by prolonged incompatibility on the part of Cooks (and here it may be remarked that Cooking and Incompatibility will be mostly found united), and take up Waitering. It has been ascertained that what a gentleman will sit meek under, at home, he will not bear out of doors, at the Slamjam or any similar establishment. Then, what is the inference to be drawn respecting true Waitering? You must be bred to it. You must be born to it.

Would you know how born to it, Fair Reader,—if of the adorable female sex? Then learn from the biographical experience of one that is a Waiter in the sixty-first year of his age.

You were conveyed,—ere yet your dawning powers were otherwise developed than to harbour vacancy in your inside,—you were conveyed, by surreptitious means, into a pantry adjoining the Admiral Nelson, Civic and General Dining-Rooms, there to receive by stealth that healthful sustenance which is the pride and boast of the British female constitution. Your mother was married to your father (himself a distant Waiter) in the profoundest secrecy; for a Waitress known to be married would ruin the best of businesses,—it is the same as on the stage. Hence your being smuggled into the pantry, and that—to add to the infliction—by an unwilling grandmother. Under the combined influence of the smells of roast and boiled, and soup, and gas, and malt liquors, you partook of your earliest nourishment; your unwilling grandmother sitting prepared to catch you when your mother was called and dropped you; your grandmother's shawl ever ready to stifle your natural complainings; your innocent mind surrounded by uncongenial cruets, dirty plates, dish-covers, and cold gravy; your mother calling down the pipe for veals and porks, instead of soothing you with nursery rhymes. Under these untoward circumstances you were early weaned. Your unwilling grandmother, ever growing more unwilling as your food assimilated less, then contracted habits of shaking you till your system

curdled, and your food would not assimilate at all.   At
length she was no longer spared, and could have been
thankfully spared much sooner.   When your brothers began
to appear in succession, your mother retired, left off her
smart dressing (she had previously been a smart dresser),
and her dark ringlets (which had previously been flowing),
and haunted your father late of nights, lying in wait for
him, through all weathers, up the shabby court which led
to the back door of the Royal Old Dust-Bin (said to have
been so named by George the Fourth), where your father
was Head.   But the Dust-Bin was going down then, and
your father took but little,—excepting from a liquid point of
view.   Your mother's object in those visits was of a housekeeping character, and you was set on to whistle your father
out.   Sometimes he came out, but generally not.   Come
or not come, however, all that part of his existence which
was unconnected with open Waitering was kept a close
secret, and was acknowledged by your mother to be a close
secret, and you and your mother flitted about the court,
close secrets both of you, and would scarcely have confessed
under torture that you knew your father, or that your father
had any name than Dick (which wasn't his name, though
he was never known by any other), or that he had kith or
kin or chick or child.   Perhaps the attraction of this mystery,
combined with your father's having a damp compartment to
himself, behind a leaky cistern, at the Dust-Bin,—a sort of
a cellar compartment, with a sink in it, and a smell, and
a plate-rack, and a bottle-rack, and three windows that didn't
match each other or anything else, and no daylight,— caused
your young mind to feel convinced that you must grow up
to be a Waiter too; but you did feel convinced of it, and
so did all your brothers, down to your sister.   Every one of
you felt convinced that you was born to the Waitering.   At
this stage of your career, what was your feelings one day
when your father came home to your mother in open broad
daylight,—of itself an act of Madness on the part of a Waiter,
—and took to his bed (leastwise, your mother and family's
bed), with the statement that his eyes were devilled kidneys.
Physicians being in vain, your father expired, after repeating
at intervals for a day and a night, when gleams of reason
and old business fitfully illuminated his being, "Two and
two is five.   And three is sixpence."   Interred in the parochial
department of the neighbouring churchyard, and accompanied

to the grave by as many Waiters of long standing as could spare the morning time from their soiled glasses (namely, one), your bereaved form was attired in a white neckankecher, and you was took on from motives of benevolence at The George and Gridiron, theatrical and supper. Here, supporting nature on what you found in the plates (which was as it happened, and but too often thoughtlessly, immersed in mustard), and on what you found in the glasses (which rarely went beyond driblets and lemon), by night you dropped asleep standing, till you was cuffed awake, and by day was set to polishing every individual article in the coffee-room. Your couch being sawdust; your counterpane being ashes of cigars. Here, frequently hiding a heavy heart under the smart tie of your white neckankecher (or correctly speaking lower down and more to the left), you picked up the rudiments of knowledge from an extra, by the name of Bishops, and by calling plate-washer, and gradually elevating your mind with chalk on the back of the corner-box partition, until such time as you used the inkstand when it was out of hand, attained to manhood, and to be the Waiter that you find yourself.

I could wish here to offer a few respectful words on behalf of the calling so long the calling of myself and family, and the public interest in which is but too often very limited. We are not generally understood. No, we are not. Allowance enough is not made for us. For, say that we ever show a little drooping listlessness of spirits, or what might be termed indifference or apathy. Put it to yourself what would your own state of mind be, if you was one of an enormous family every member of which except you was always greedy, and in a hurry. Put it to yourself that you was regularly replete with animal food at the slack hours of one in the day and again at nine P.M., and that the repleter you was, the more voracious all your fellow-creatures came in. Put it to yourself that it was your business, when your digestion was well on, to take a personal interest and sympathy in a hundred gentlemen fresh and fresh (say, for the sake of argument, only a hundred), whose imaginations was given up to grease and fat and gravy and melted butter, and abandoned to questioning you about cuts of this, and dishes of that,—each of 'em going on as if him and you and the bill of fare was alone in the world. Then look what you are expected to know. You are never out, but they seem to think you regularly attend everywhere. "What's this, Christopher, that I hear about the smashed Excursion Train?" —"How are they doing at the Italian Opera, Christopher?" —"Christopher, what are the real particulars of this business at the Yorkshire Bank?" Similarly a ministry gives me more trouble than it gives the Queen. As to Lord Palmerston, the constant and wearing connexion into which I have been brought with his lordship during the last few years is deserving of a pension. Then look at the Hypocrites we are made, and the lies (white, I hope) that are forced upon us! Why must a sedentary-pursuited Waiter be considered to be a judge of horseflesh, and to have a most tremenjous interest in horse-training and racing? Yet it would be half our little incomes out of our pockets if we didn't take on to have those sporting tastes. It is the same (inconceivable why!) with Farming. Shooting, equally so. I am sure that so regular as the months of August, September, and October come round, I am ashamed of myself in my own private bosom for the way in which I make believe to care whether or not the grouse is strong on the wing (much their wings, or drumsticks either, signifies to me, uncooked!), and whether the partridges is plentiful among the turnips, and whether the pheasants is shy or bold, or anything else you please to mention. Yet you may see me, or any other Waiter of my standing, holding on by the back of the box, and leaning over a gentleman with his purse out and his bill before him, discussing these points in a confidential tone of voice, as if my happiness in life entirely depended on 'em.

I have mentioned our little incomes. Look at the most unreasonable point of all, and the point on which the greatest injustice is done us! Whether it is owing to our always carrying so much change in our right-hand trousers-pocket, and so many halfpence in our coat-tails, or whether it is human nature (which I were loth to believe), what is meant by the everlasting fable that Head Waiters is rich? How did that fable get into circulation? Who first put it about, and what are the facts to establish the unblushing statement? Come forth, thou slanderer, and refer the public to the Waiter's will in Doctors' Commons supporting thy malignant hiss! Yet this is so commonly dwelt upon—especially by the screws who give Waiters the least—that denial is vain ; and we are obliged, for our credit's sake, to carry our heads as if we were going into a business, when of the two we are much more likely to go into a union. There was formerly a screw as frequented the Slamjam ere yet the present writer had quitted that establishment on a question of tea-ing his assistant staff out of his own pocket, which screw carried the taunt to its bitterest height. Never soaring above threepence, and as often as not grovelling on the earth a penny lower, he yet represented the present writer as a large holder of Consols, a lender of money on mortgage, a Capitalist. He has been overheard to dilate to other customers on the allegation that the present writer put out thousands of pounds at interest in Distilleries and Breweries. "Well, Christopher," he would say (having grovelled his lowest on the earth, half a moment before), "looking out for a House to open, eh? Can't find a business to be disposed of on a scale as is up to your resources, humph?" To such a dizzy precipice of falsehood has this misrepresentation taken wing, that the well-known and highly-respected OLD CHARLES, long eminent at the West Country Hotel, and by some considered the Father of the Waitering, found himself under the obligation to fall into it through so many years that his own wife (for he had an unbeknown old lady in that capacity towards himself) believed it! And what was the consequence? When he was borne to his grave on the shoulders of six picked Waiters, with six more for change, six more acting as pall-bearers, all keeping step in a pouring shower without a dry eye visible, and a concourse only inferior to Royalty, his pantry and lodgings was equally ransacked high and low for property, and none was found! How could it be found, when, beyond his last monthly collection of walking-sticks, umbrellas, and pocket-handkerchiefs (which happened to have been not yet disposed of, though he had ever been through life punctual in clearing off his collections by the month), there was no property existing? Such, however, is the force of this universal libel, that the widow of Old Charles, at the present hour an inmate of the Almshouses of the Cork-Cutters' Company, in Blue Anchor-road (identified sitting at the door of one of 'em, in a clean cap and a Windsor arm-chair, only last Monday), expects John's hoarded wealth to be found hourly! Nay, ere yet he had succumbed to the grisly dart, and when his portrait was painted in oils life-size, by subscription of the frequenters of the West Country, to hang over the coffee-room chimneypiece, there were not wanting those who contended that what is termed the accessories of such a portrait ought to be the Bank of England out of window, and a strong-box on the table. And but for better-regulated minds contending for a bottle and screw and the attitude of drawing,—and carrying their point,—it would have been so handed down to posterity.

I am now brought to the title of the present remarks. Having, I hope without offence to any quarter, offered such observations as I felt it my duty to offer, in a free country which has ever dominated the seas, on the general subject, I will now proceed to wait on the particular question.

At a momentous period of my life, when I was off, so far as concerned notice given, with a House that shall be nameless, —for the question on which I took my departing stand was a fixed charge for waiters, and no House as commits itself to that eminently un-English act of more than foolishness and baseness shall be advertised by me,—I repeat, at a momentous crisis, when I was off with a House too mean for mention, and not yet on with that to which I have ever since had the honour of being attached in the capacity of Head[1], I was casting about what to do next. Then it were that proposals were made to me on behalf of my present establishment. Stipulations were necessary on my part, emendations were necessary on my part: in the end, ratifications ensued on both sides, and I entered on a new career.

We are a bed business, and a coffee-room business. We are not a general dining business, nor do we wish it. In consequence, when diners drop in, we know what to give 'em as will keep 'em away another time. We are a Private Room or Family business also ; but coffee-room principal. Me and the Directory and the Writing Materials and cetrer occupy a place to ourselves—a place fended off up a step or two at the end of the coffee-room, in what I call the good old-fashioned style. The good old-fashioned style is, that whatever you want, down to a wafer, you must be olely and solely dependent on the Head Waiter for. You must put yourself a new-born Child into his hands. There is no other way in which a business untinged with Continental Vice can be conducted. (It were bootless to add, that if languages is required to be jabbered and English is not good enough, both families and gentlemen had better go somewhere else.)

[1] Its name and address at length, with other full particulars, all editorially struck out.

When I began to settle down in this right-principled and well-conducted House, I noticed, under the bed in No. 24 B (which it is up a angle off the staircase, and usually put off upon the lowly-minded), a heap of things in a corner. I asked our Head Chambermaid in the course of the day,

"What are them things in 24 B?"

To which she answered with a careless air,

"Somebody's Luggage."

Regarding her with a eye not free from severity, I says,

"Whose Luggage?"

Evading my eye, she replied,

"Lor! How should *I* know!"

—Being, it may be right to mention, a female of some pertness, though acquainted with her business.

A Head Waiter must be either Head or Tail. He must be at one extremity or the other of the social scale. He cannot be at the waist of it, or anywhere else but the extremities. It is for him to decide which of the extremities.

On the eventful occasion under consideration, I give Mrs. Pratchett so distinctly to understand my decision, that I broke her spirit as towards myself, then and there, and for good. Let not inconsistency be suspected on account of my mentioning Mrs. Pratchett as "Mrs.," and having formerly remarked that a waitress must not be married. Readers are respectfully requested to notice that Mrs. Pratchett was not a waitress, but a chambermaid. Now a chambermaid *may* be married; if Head, generally is married,—or says so. It comes to the same thing as expressing what is customary. (N.B. Mr. Pratchett is in Australia, and his address there is "the Bush.")

Having took Mrs. Pratchett down as many pegs as was essential to the future happiness of all parties, I requested her to explain herself.

"For instance," I says, to give her a little encouragement, "who is Somebody?"

"I give you my sacred honour, Mr. Christopher," answers Pratchett, "that I haven't the faintest notion."

But for the manner in which she settled her cap-strings, I should have doubted this; but in respect of positiveness it was hardly to be discriminated from an affidavit.

"Then you never saw him?" I followed her up with.

"Nor yet," said Mrs. Pratchett, shutting her eyes and making as if she had just took a pill of unusual circumference,

—which gave a remarkable force to her denial,—" nor yet any servant in this house. All have been changed, Mr. Christopher, within five year, and Somebody left his Luggage here before then."

Inquiry of Miss Martin yielded (in the language of the Bard of A. 1.) " confirmation strong." So it had really and truly happened. Miss Martin is the young lady at the bar as makes out our bills; and though higher than I could wish considering her station, is perfectly well-behaved.

Farther investigations led to the disclosure that there was a bill against this Luggage to the amount of two sixteen six. The luggage had been lying under the bedstead of 24 B over six year. The bedstead is a four-poster, with a deal of old hanging and valance, and is, as I once said, probably connected with more than 24 Bs.—which I remember my hearers was pleased to laugh at, at the time.

I don't know why,—when DO we know why?—but this Luggage laid heavy on my mind. I fell a wondering about Somebody, and what he had got and been up to. I couldn't satisfy my thoughts why he should leave so much Luggage against so small a bill. For I had the Luggage out within a day or two and turned it over, and the following were the items:—A black portmanteau, a black bag, a desk, a dressing-case, a brown-paper parcel, a hat-box, and an umbrella strapped to a walking-stick. It was all very dusty and fluey. I had our porter up to get under the bed and fetch it out; and though he habitually wallows in dust,—swims in it from morning to night, and wears a close-fitting waistcoat with black calimanco sleeves for the purpose,—it made him sneeze again, and his throat was that hot with it that it was obliged to be cooled with a drink of Allsopp's draft.

The Luggage so got the better of me, that instead of having it put back when it was well dusted and washed with a wet cloth,—previous to which it was so covered with feathers that you might have thought it was turning into poultry, and would by and by begin to Lay,—I say, instead of having it put back, I had it carried into one of my places downstairs. There from time to time I stared at it and stared at it, till it seemed to grow big and grow little, and come forward at me and retreat again, and go through all manner of performances resembling intoxication. When this had lasted weeks,—I may say months, and not be far out,— I one day thought of asking Miss Martin for the particulars

So far from throwing a light upon the subject, this bill appeared to me, if I may so express my doubts, to involve it in a yet more lurid halo. Speculating it over with the Mistress, she informed me that the luggage had been advertised in the Master's time as being to be sold after such and such a day to pay expenses, but no farther steps had been taken. (I may here remark, that the Mistress is a widow in her fourth year. The Master was possessed of one of those unfortunate constitutions in which Spirits turns to Water, and rises in the ill-starred Victim.)

My speculating it over, not then only, but repeatedly, sometimes with the Mistress, sometimes with one, sometimes with another, led up to the Mistress's saying to me,—whether at first in joke or in earnest, or half joke and half earnest, it matters not:

"Christopher, I am going to make you a handsome offer."

(If this should meet her eye—a lovely blue,—may she not take it ill my mentioning that if I had been eight or ten year younger, I would have done as much by her! That is, I would have made her a offer. It is for others than me to denominate it a handsome one.)

"Christopher, I am going to make you a handsome offer."

"Put a name to it, ma'am."

"Look here, Christopher. Run over the articles of Somebody's Luggage. You've got it all by heart, I know."

"A black portmanteau, ma'am, a black bag, a desk, a dressing-case, a brown-paper parcel, a hat-box, and an umbrella strapped to a walking-stick."

"All just as they were left. Nothing opened, nothing tampered with."

"You are right, ma'am. All locked but the brown-paper parcel, and that sealed."

The Mistress was leaning on Miss Martin's desk at the bar-window, and she taps the open book that lays upon the desk,—she has a pretty-made hand to be sure,—and bobs her head over it and laughs.

"Come," says she, "Christopher. Pay me Somebody's bill, and you shall have Somebody's Luggage."

I rather took to the idea from the first moment; but,

"It mayn't be worth the money," I objected, seeming to hold back.

"That's a Lottery," says the Mistress, folding her arms upon the book,—it ain't her hands alone that's pretty made, the observation extends right up her arms. "Won't you venture two pound sixteen shillings and sixpence in the Lottery? Why, there's no blanks!" says the Mistress, laughing and bobbing her head again, "you *must* win. If you lose, you must win! All prizes in this Lottery! Draw a blank, and remember, Gentlemen-Sportsmen, you'll still be entitled to a black portmanteau. a black bag, a desk, a dressing-case, a sheet of brown paper, a hat-box, and an umbrella strapped to a walking-stick!"

To make short of it, Miss Martin come round me, and Mrs. Pratchett come round me, and the Mistress she was completely round me already, and all the women in the house come round me, and if it had been Sixteen two instead of Two sixteen, I should have thought myself well out of it. For what can you do when they do come round you?

So I paid the money—down—and such a laughing as there was among 'em! But I turned the tables on 'em regularly, when I said:

"My family-name is Blue-Beard. I'm going to open Somebody's Luggage all alone in the Secret Chamber, and not a female eye catches sight of the contents!"

Whether I thought proper to have the firmness to keep to this, don't signify, or whether any female eye, and if any, how many, was really present when the opening of the Luggage came off. Somebody's Luggage is the question at present: Nobody's eyes, nor yet noses.

What I still look at most, in connexion with that Luggage, is the extraordinary quantity of writing-paper, and all written on! And not our paper neither,—not the paper charged in the bill, for we know our paper,—so he must have been always at it. And he had crumpled up this writing of his, everywhere, in every part and parcel of his luggage. There was writing in his dressing-case, writing in his boots, writing among his shaving-tackle, writing in his hat-box, writing folded away down among the very whalebones of his umbrella.

His clothes wasn't bad, what there was of 'em. His dressing-case was poor,—not a particle of silver stopper,—bottle apertures with nothing in 'em, like empty little dog-kennels,—and a most searching description of tooth-powder diffusing itself around, as under a deluded mistake that all the chinks in the fittings was divisions in teeth. His clothes

I parted with, well enough, to a second-hand dealer not far from St. Clement's Danes, in the Strand,—him as the officers in the Army mostly dispose of their uniforms to, when hard pressed with debts of honour, if I may judge from their coats and epaulets diversifying the window with their backs towards the public. The same party bought in one lot the portmanteau, the bag, the desk, the dressing-case, the hat-box, the umbrella, strap, and walking-stick. On my remarking that I should have thought those articles not quite in his line, he said : "No more ith a man'th grandmother, Mithter Chrithtopher; but if any man will bring hith grandmother here, and offer her at a fair trifle below what the'll feth with good luck when the'th thcoured and turned— I'll buy her ! "

These transactions brought me home, and, indeed, more than home, for they left a goodish profit on the original investment. And now there remained the writings ; and the writings I particular wish to bring under the candid attention of the reader.

I wish to do so without postponement, for this reason. This is to say, namely, viz. i.e., as follows, thus :—Before I proceed to recount the mental sufferings of which I became the prey in consequence of the writings, and before following up that harrowing tale with a statement of the wonderful and impressive catastrophe, as thrilling in its nature as unlooked for in any other capacity, which crowned the ole and filled the cup of unexpectedness to overflowing, the writings themselves ought to stand forth to view. Therefore it is that they now come next. One word to introduce them, and I lay down my pen (I hope, my unassuming pen) until I take it up to trace the gloomy sequel of a mind with something on it.

He was a smeary writer, and wrote a dreadful bad hand. Utterly regardless of ink, he lavished it on every undeserving object,—on his clothes, his desk, his hat, the handle of his tooth-brush, his umbrella. Ink was found freely on the coffee-room carpet by No. 4 table, and two blots was on his restless couch. A reference to the document I have given entire will show that on the morning of the third of February, eighteen fifty-six, he procured his no less than fifth pen and paper. To whatever deplorable act of ungovernable com-position he immolated those materials obtained from the bar, there is no doubt that the fatal deed was committed in bed, and that it left its evidences but too plainly, long afterwards, upon the pillow-case.

He had put no Heading to any of his writings. Alas! Was he likely to have a Heading without a Head, and where was *his* Head when he took such things into it? In some cases, such as his Boots, he would appear to have hid the writings; thereby involving his style in greater obscurity. But his boots was at least pairs,—and no two of his writings can put in any claim to be so regarded. Here follows (not to give more specimens) what was found in—

CHAPTER II

HIS BOOTS

"Eh! well then, Monsieur Mutuel! What do I know, what can I say? I assure you that he calls himself Monsieur The Englishman."

"Pardon. But I think it is impossible," said Monsieur Mutuel,—a spectacled, snuffy, stooping old gentleman in carpet shoes and a cloth cap with a peaked shade, a loose blue frock-coat reaching to his heels, a large limp white shirt-frill, and cravat to correspond,—that is to say, white was the natural colour of his linen on Sundays, but it toned down with the week.

"It is," repeated Monsieur Mutuel, his amiable old walnut-shell countenance very walnut-shelly indeed as he smiled and blinked in the bright morning sunlight,—"it is, my cherished Madame Bouclet, I think, impossible!"

"Hey!" (with a little vexed cry and a great many tosses of her head.) "But it is not impossible that you are a Pig!" retorted Madame Bouclet, a compact little woman of thirty-five or so. "See then,—look there,—read! 'On the second floor Monsieur L'Anglais.' Is it not so?"

"It is so," said Monsieur Mutuel.

"Good. Continue your morning walk. Get out!" Madame Bouclet dismissed him with a lively snap of her fingers.

The morning walk of Monsieur Mutuel was in the brightest patch that the sun made in the Grande Place of a dull old fortified French town. The manner of his morning walk was with his hands crossed behind him; an umbrella, in figure the express image of himself, always in one hand; a snuff-box in the other. Thus, with the shuffling gait of the Elephant (who really does deal with the very worst trousers-maker employed by the Zoological world, and who appeared to have recommended him to Monsieur Mutuel), the old gentle-man sunned himself daily when sun was to be had—of course, at the same time sunning a red ribbon at his button-hole; for was he not an ancient Frenchman?

Being told by one of the angelic sex to continue his morning walk and get out, Monsieur Mutuel laughed a walnut-shell laugh, pulled off his cap at arm's length with the hand that contained his snuff-box, kept it off for a con-siderable period after he had parted from Madame Bouclet, and continued his morning walk and got out, like a man of gallantry as he was.

The documentary evidence to which Madame Bouclet had referred Monsieur Mutuel was the list of her lodgers, sweetly written forth by her own Nephew and Bookkeeper, who held the pen of an Angel, and posted up at the side of her gate-way, for the information of the Police: "Au second, M. L'Anglais, Propriétaire." On the second floor, Mr. The Englishman, man of property. So it stood; nothing could be plainer.

Madame Bouclet now traced the line with her forefinger, as it were to confirm and settle herself in her parting snap at Monsieur Mutuel, and so placing her right hand on her hip with a defiant air, as if nothing should ever tempt her to unsnap that snap, strolled out into the Place to glance up at the windows of Mr. The Englishman. That worthy happening to be looking out of window at the moment, Madame Bouclet gave him a graceful salutation with her head, looked to the right and looked to the left to account to him for her being there, considered for a moment, like one who accounted to herself for somebody she had expected not being there, and re-entered her own gateway. Madame Bouclet let all her house giving on the Place in furnished flats or floors, and lived up the yard behind in company with Monsieur Bouclet her husband (great at billiards), an inherited brewing business, several fowls, two carts, a nephew, a little dog in a big kennel, a grape-vine, a counting-house, four horses, a married sister (with a share in the brewing business), the husband and two children of the married sister, a parrot, a drum (performed on by the little boy of the married sister), two billeted soldiers, a quantity of pigeons, a fife (played by the nephew in a ravishing manner), several domestics and supernumeraries, a perpetual flavour of coffee and soup, a terrific range of artificial rocks and wooden precipices at least four feet high, a small fountain, and half-a-dozen large sunflowers.

Now the Englishman, in taking his Appartement,—or, as one might say on our side of the Channel, his set of chambers,—had given his name, correct to the letter, LANGLEY. But as he had a British way of not opening his mouth very wide on foreign soil, except at meals, the Brewery had been able to make nothing of it but L'Anglais. So Mr. The Englishman he had become and he remained.

"Never saw such a people!" muttered Mr. The Englishman, as he now looked out of window. "Never did, in my life!"

This was true enough, for he had never before been out of his own country,—a right little island, a tight little island, a bright little island, a show-fight little island, and full of merit of all sorts; but not the whole round world.

"These chaps," said Mr. The Englishman to himself, as his eye rolled over the Place, sprinkled with military here and there, "are no more like soldiers—" Nothing being sufficiently strong for the end of his sentence, he left it unended.

This again (from the point of view of his experience) was strictly correct; for though there was a great agglomeration of soldiers in the town and neighbouring country, you might have held a grand Review and Field-day of them every one, and looked in vain among them all for a soldier choking behind his foolish stock, or a soldier lamed by his ill-fitting shoes, or a soldier deprived of the use of his limbs by straps and buttons, or a soldier elaborately forced to be self-helpless in all the small affairs of life. A swarm of brisk, bright, active, bustling, handy, odd, skirmishing fellows, able to turn cleverly at anything, from a siege to soup, from great guns to needles and thread, from the broadsword exercise to slicing an onion, from making war to making omelets, was all you would have found.

What a swarm! From the Great Place under the eye of Mr. The Englishman, where a few awkward squads from the last conscription were doing the goose-step—some members of those squads still as to their bodies, in the chrysalis peasant-state of Blouse, and only military butterflies as to their regimentally-clothed legs—from the Great Place, away outside the fortifications, and away for miles along the dusty roads, soldiers swarmed. All day long, upon the grass-grown ramparts of the town, practising soldiers trumpeted and bugled; all day long, down in angles of dry trenches, prac-tising soldiers drummed and drummed.   Every forenoon, soldiers burst out of the great barracks into the sandy gymnasium-ground hard by, and flew over the wooden horse, and hung on to flying ropes, and dangled upside-down between parallel bars, and shot themselves off wooden platforms,—splashes, sparks, coruscations, showers of soldiers. At every corner of the town-wall, every guard-house, every gateway, every sentry-box, every drawbridge, every reedy ditch, and rushy dike, soldiers, soldiers, soldiers. And the town being pretty well all wall, guard-house, gateway, sentry-box, drawbridge, reedy ditch, and rushy dike, the town was pretty well all soldiers.

What would the sleepy old town have been without the soldiers, seeing that even with them it had so overslept itself as to have slept its echoes hoarse, its defensive bars and locks and bolts and chains all rusty, and its ditches stagnant! From the days when VAUBAN engineered it to that perplex-ing extent that to look at it was like being knocked on the head with it, the stranger becoming stunned and stertorous under the shock of its incomprehensibility,—from the days when VAUBAN made it the express incorporation of every substantive and adjective in the art of military engineering, and not only twisted you into it and twisted you out of it, to the right, to the left, opposite, under here, over there, in the dark, in the dirt, by the gateway, archway, covered way, dry way, wet way, fosse, portcullis, drawbridge, sluice, squat tower, pierced wall, and heavy battery, but likewise took a fortifying dive under the neighbouring country, and came to the surface three or four miles off, blowing out incomprehen-sible mounds and batteries among the quiet crops of chicory and beet-root,—from those days to these the town had been asleep, and dust and rust and must had settled on its drowsy Arsenals and Magazines, and grass had grown up in its silent streets.

On market-days alone, its Great Place suddenly leaped out

of bed. On market-days, some friendly enchanter struck his staff upon the stones of the Great Place, and instantly arose the liveliest booths and stalls, and sittings and standings, and a pleasant hum of chaffering and huckstering from many hundreds of tongues, and a pleasant, though peculiar, blending of colours,—white caps, blue blouses, and green vegetables,—and at last the Knight destined for the adventure seemed to have come in earnest, and all the Vaubanois sprang up awake. And now, by long, low-lying avenues of trees, jolting in white-hooded donkey-cart, and on donkey-back, and in tumbril and wagon, and cart and cabriolet, and afoot with barrow and burden,—and along the dikes and ditches and canals, in little peak-prowed country boats,—came peasant-men and women in flocks and crowds, bringing articles for sale. And here you had boots and shoes, and sweetmeats and stuffs to wear, and here (in the cool shade of the Town-hall) you had milk and cream and butter and cheese, and here you had fruits and onions and carrots, and all things needful for your soup, and here you had poultry and flowers and protesting pigs, and here new shovels, axes, spades, and bill-hooks for your farming work, and here huge mounds of bread, and here your unground grain in sacks, and here your children's dolls, and here the cake-seller, announcing his wares by beat and roll of drum. And hark! fanfaronade of trumpets, and here into the Great Place, resplendent in an open carriage, with four gorgeously-attired servitors up behind, playing horns, drums, and cymbals, rolled "the Daughter of a Physician" in massive golden chains and earrings, and blue-feathered hat, shaded from the admiring sun by two immense umbrellas of artificial roses, to dispense (from motives of philanthropy) that small and pleasant dose which had cured so many thousands! Toothache, earache, headache, heartache, stomachache, debility, nervousness, fits, fainting, fever, ague, all equally cured by the small and pleasant dose of the great Physician's great daughter! The process was this,—she, the Daughter of a Physician, proprietress of the superb equipage you now admired with its confirmatory blasts of trumpet, drum, and cymbal, told you so: On the first day after taking the small and pleasant dose, you would feel no particular influence beyond a most harmonious sensation of indescribable and irresistible joy; on the second day you would be so astonishingly better that you would think yourself changed into somebody else; on the third day you would be entirely free from your disorder, whatever its nature and however long you had had it, and would seek out the Physician's Daughter to throw yourself at her feet, kiss the hem of her garment, and buy as many more of the small and pleasant doses as by the sale of all your few effects you could obtain; but she would be inaccessible,—gone for herbs to the Pyramids of Egypt,—and you would be (though cured) reduced to despair! Thus would the Physician's Daughter drive her trade (and briskly too), and thus would the buying and selling and mingling of tongues and colours continue, until the changing sunlight, leaving the Physician's Daughter in the shadow of high roofs, admonished her to jolt out westward, with a departing effect of gleam and glitter on the splendid equipage and brazen blast. And now the enchanter struck his staff upon the stones of the Great Place once more, and down went the booths, the sittings and standings, and vanished the merchandise, and with it the barrows, donkeys, donkey-carts, and tumbrils, and all other things on wheels and feet, except the slow scavengers with unwieldy carts and meagre horses clearing up the rubbish, assisted by the sleek town pigeons, better plumped out than on non-market days. While there was yet an hour or two to wane before the autumn sunset, the loiterer outside town-gate and drawbridge, and postern and double-ditch, would see the last white-hooded cart lessening in the avenue of lengthening shadows of trees, or the last country boat, paddled by the last market-woman on her way home, showing black upon the reddening, long, low, narrow dike between him and the mill; and as the paddle-parted scum and weed closed over the boat's track, he might be comfortably sure that its sluggish rest would be troubled no more until next market-day.

As it was not one of the Great Place's days for getting out of bed, when Mr. The Englishman looked down at the young soldiers practising the goose-step there, his mind was left at liberty to take a military turn.

"These fellows are billeted everywhere about," said he; "and to see them lighting the people's fires, boiling the people's pots, minding the people's babies, rocking the people's cradles, washing the people's greens, and making themselves generally useful, in every sort of unmilitary way, is most ridiculous! Never saw such a set of fellows,—never did in my life!"

All perfectly true again. Was there not Private Valentine in that very house, acting as sole housemaid, valet, cook, steward, and nurse, in the family of his captain, Monsieur le Capitaine de la Cour,—cleaning the floors, making the beds, doing the marketing, dressing the captain, dressing the dinners, dressing the salads, and dressing the baby, all with equal readiness? Or, to put him aside, he being in loyal attendance on his Chief, was there not Private Hyppolite, billeted at the Perfumer's two hundred yards off, who, when not on duty, volunteered to keep shop while the fair Perfumeress stepped out to speak to a neighbour or so, and laughingly sold soap with his war-sword girded on him? Was there not Emile, billeted at the Clock-maker's, perpetually turning to of an evening, with his coat off, winding up the stock? Was there not Eugène, billeted at the Tinman's, cultivating, pipe in mouth, a garden four feet square, for the Tinman, in the little court, behind the shop, and extorting the fruits of the earth from the same, on his knees, with the sweat of his brow? Not to multiply examples, was there not Baptiste, billeted on the poor Water-carrier, at that very instant sitting on the pavement in the sunlight, with his martial legs asunder, and one of the Water-carrier's spare pails between them, which (to the delight and glory of the heart of the Water-carrier coming across the Place from the fountain, yoked and burdened) he was painting bright-green outside and bright-red within? Or, to go no farther than the Barber's at the very next door, was there not Corporal Théophile——

"No," said Mr. The Englishman, glancing down at the Barber's, "he is not there at present. There's the child, though."

A mere mite of a girl stood on the steps of the Barber's shop, looking across the Place. A mere baby, one might call her, dressed in the close white linen cap which small French country children wear (like the children in Dutch pictures), and in a frock of homespun blue, that had no shape except where it was tied round her little fat throat. So that, being naturally short and round all over, she looked, behind, as if she had been cut off at her natural waist, and had had her head neatly fitted on it.

"There's the child, though."

To judge from the way in which the dimpled hand was rubbing the eyes, the eyes had been closed in a nap, and were newly opened. But they seemed to be looking so intently across the Place, that the Englishman looked in the same direction.

"O!" said he presently. "I thought as much. The Corporal's there."

The Corporal, a smart figure of a man of thirty, perhaps a thought under the middle size, but very neatly made,—a sunburnt Corporal with a brown peaked beard,—faced about at the moment, addressing voluble words of instruction to the squad in hand. Nothing was amiss or awry about the Corporal. A lithe and nimble Corporal, quite complete, from the sparkling dark eyes under his knowing uniform cap to his sparkling white gaiters. The very image and presentment of a Corporal of his country's army, in the line of his shoulders, the line of his waist, the broadest line of his Bloomer trousers, and their narrowest line at the calf of his leg.

Mr. The Englishman looked on, and the child looked on, and the Corporal looked on (but the last-named at his men), until the drill ended a few minutes afterwards, and the military sprinkling dried up directly, and was gone. Then said Mr. The Englishman to himself, "Look here! By George!" And the Corporal, dancing towards the Barber's with his arms wide open, caught up the child, held her over his head in a flying attitude, caught her down again, kissed her, and made off with her into the Barber's house.

Now Mr. The Englishman had had a quarrel with his erring and disobedient and disowned daughter, and there was a child in that case too. Had not his daughter been a child, and had she not taken angel-flights above his head as this child had flown above the Corporal's?

"He's a "—National Participled—" fool!" said the Englishman, and shut his window.

But the windows of the house of Memory, and the windows of the house of Mercy, are not so easily closed as windows of glass and wood. They fly open unexpectedly; they rattle in the night; they must be nailed up. Mr. The Englishman had tried nailing them, but had not driven the nails quite home. So he passed but a disturbed evening and a worse night.

By nature a good-tempered man? No; very little gentleness, confounding the quality with weakness. Fierce and wrathful when crossed? Very, and stupendously unreasonable. Moody? Exceedingly so. Vindictive? Well; he *had* had scowling thoughts that he would formally curse his daughter, as he had seen it done on the stage. But remembering that the real Heaven is some paces removed from the mock one in the great chandelier of the Theatre, he had given that up.

And he had come abroad to be rid of his repudiated daughter for the rest of his life. And here he was.

At bottom, it was for this reason, more than for any other, that Mr. The Englishman took it extremely ill that Corporal Théophile should be so devoted to little Bebelle, the child at the Barber's shop. In an unlucky moment he had chanced to say to himself, "Why, confound the fellow, he is not her father!" There was a sharp sting in the speech which ran into him suddenly, and put him in a worse mood. So he had National Participled the unconscious Corporal with most hearty emphasis, and had made up his mind to think no more about such a mountebank.

But it came to pass that the Corporal was not to be dismissed. If he had known the most delicate fibres of the Englishman's mind, instead of knowing nothing on earth about him, and if he had been the most obstinate Corporal in the Grand Army of France, instead of being the most obliging, he could not have planted himself with more determined immovability plump in the midst of all the Englishman's thoughts. Not only so, but he seemed to be always in his view. Mr. The Englishman had but to look out of window, to look upon the Corporal with little Bebelle. He had but to go for a walk, and there was the Corporal walking with Bebelle. He had but to come home again, disgusted, and the Corporal and Bebelle were at home before him. If he looked out at his back windows early in the morning, the Corporal was in the Barber's back yard, washing and dressing and brushing Bebelle. If he took refuge at his front windows, the Corporal brought his breakfast out into the Place, and shared it there with Bebelle. Always Corporal and always Bebelle. Never Corporal without Bebelle. Never Bebelle without Corporal.

Mr. The Englishman was not particularly strong in the French language as a means of oral communication, though he read it very well. It is with languages as with people,— when you only know them by sight, you are apt to mistake them ; you must be on speaking terms before you can be said to have established an acquaintance.

Somebody's Luggage

For this reason, Mr. The Englishman had to gird up his loins considerably before he could bring himself to the point of exchanging ideas with Madame Bouclet on the subject of this Corporal and this Bebelle. But Madame Bouclet looking in apologetically one morning to remark, that, O Heaven! she was in a state of desolation because the lamp-maker had not sent home that lamp confided to him to repair, but that truly he was a lamp-maker against whom the whole world shrieked out, Mr. The Englishman seized the occasion.

"Madame, that baby—— "

"Pardon, monsieur. That lamp."

"No, no, that little girl."

"But, pardon!" said Madame Bouclet, angling for a clew, "one cannot light a little girl, or send her to be repaired?"

"The little girl—at the house of the barber."

"Ah-h-h!" cried Madame Bouclet, suddenly catching the idea with her delicate little line and rod. "Little Bebelle? Yes, yes, yes! And her friend the Corporal? Yes, yes, yes, yes! So genteel of him,—is it not?"

"He is not—— ?"

"Not at all; not at all! He is not one of her relations. Not at all!"

"Why, then, he—— "

"Perfectly!" cried Madame Bouclet, "you are right, monsieur. It is so genteel of him. The less relation, the more genteel. As you say."

"Is she—— ?"

"The child of the barber?" Madame Bouclet whisked up her skilful little line and rod again. "Not at all, not at all! She is the child of—in a word, of no one."

"The wife of the barber, then—— ?"

"Indubitably. As you say. The wife of the barber receives a small stipend to take care of her. So much by the month. Eh, then! It is without doubt very little, for we are all poor here."

"You are not poor, madame."

"As to my lodgers," replied Madame Bouclet, with a smiling and a gracious bend of her head, "no. As to all things else, so-so."

"You flattter me, madame."

"Monsieur, it is you who flatter me in living here."

Certain fishy gasps on Mr. The Englishman's part, denoting that he was about to resume his subject under difficulties,

Madame Bouclet observed him closely, and whisked up her delicate line and rod again with triumphant success.

"O no, monsieur, certainly not.   The wife of the barber is not cruel to the poor child, but she is careless.   Her health is delicate, and she sits all day, looking out at window. Consequently, when the Corporal first came, the poor little Bebelle was much neglected."

"It is a curious—— " began Mr. The Englishman.

"Name?   That Bebelle?   Again you are right, monsieur. But it is a playful name for Gabrielle."

"And so the child is a mere fancy of the Corporal's?" said Mr. The Englishman, in a gruffly disparaging tone of voice.

"Eh, well!" returned Madame Bouclet, with a pleading shrug: "one must love something. Human nature is weak."

("Devilish weak," muttered the Englishman, in his own language.)

"And the Corporal," pursued Madame Bouclet, "being billeted at the barber's,—where he will probably remain a long time, for he is attached to the General,—and finding the poor unowned child in need of being loved, and finding himself in need of loving,—why, there you have it all, you see!"

Mr. The Englishman accepted this interpretation of the matter with an indifferent grace, and observed to himself, in an injured manner, when he was again alone: "I shouldn't mind it so much, if these people were not such a"—National Participled—"sentimental people!"

There was a Cemetery outside the town, and it happened ill for the reputation of the Vaubanois, in this sentimental connexion, that he took a walk there that same afternoon. To be sure there were some wonderful things in it (from the Englishman's point of view), and of a certainty in all Britain you would have found nothing like it.   Not to mention the fanciful flourishes of hearts and crosses in wood and iron, that were planted all over the place, making it look very like a Firework-ground, where a most splendid pyro-technic display might be expected after dark, there were so many wreaths upon the graves, embroidered, as it might be, "To my mother," "To my daughter," "To my father," "To my brother," "To my sister," "To my friend," and those many wreaths were in so many stages of elaboration and decay, from the wreath of yesterday, all fresh colour and bright beads, to the wreath of last year, a poor mouldering

wisp of straw! There were so many little gardens and grottoes
made upon graves, in so many tastes, with plants and shells
and plaster figures and porcelain pitchers, and so many odds
and ends! There were so many tributes of remembrance
hanging up, not to be discriminated by the closest inspection
from little round waiters, whereon were depicted in glowing
hues either a lady or a gentleman with a white pocket-handkerchief out of all proportion, leaning, in a state of the most
faultless mourning and most profound affliction, on the most
architectural and gorgeous urn! There were so many surviving wives who had put their names on the tombs of their
deceased husbands, with a blank for the date of their own
departure from this weary world; and there were so many
surviving husbands who had rendered the same homage to
their deceased wives; and out of the number there must have
been so many who had long ago married again! In fine,
there was so much in the place that would have seemed
mere frippery to a stranger, save for the consideration that
the lightest paper flower that lay upon the poorest heap of
earth was never touched by a rude hand, but perished there,
a sacred thing!

"Nothing of the solemnity of Death here," Mr. The
Englishman had been going to say, when this last consideration touched him with a mild appeal, and on the whole he
walked out without saying it. "But these people are," he
insisted, by way of compensation, when he was well outside
the gate, "they are so"—Participled—"sentimental!"

His way back lay by the military gymnasium-ground.
And there he passed the Corporal glibly instructing young
soldiers how to swing themselves over rapid and deep water-
courses on their way to Glory, by means of a rope, and
himself deftly plunging off a platform, and flying a hundred
feet or two, as an encouragement to them to begin. And
there he also passed, perched on a crowning eminence
(probably by the Corporal's careful hands), the small Bebelle,
with her round eyes wide open, surveying the proceeding
like a wondering sort of blue and white bird.

"If that child was to die," this was his reflection as he
turned his back and went his way,—"and it would almost
serve the fellow right for making such a fool of himself,—I
suppose we should have *him* sticking up a wreath and a waiter
in that fantastic burying-ground."

Nevertheless, after another early morning or two of looking

out of window, he strolled down into the Place, when the Corporal and Bebelle were walking there, and touching his hat to the Corporal (an immense achievement), wished him Good-day.

"Good-day, monsieur."

"This is a rather pretty child you have here," said Mr. The Englishman, taking her chin in his hand, and looking down into her astonished blue eyes.

"Monsieur, she is a very pretty child," returned the Corporal, with a stress on his polite correction of the phrase.

"And good?" said the Englishman.

"And very good.   Poor little thing!"

"Hah!" The Englishman stooped down and patted her cheek, not without awkwardness, as if he were going too far in his conciliation.   "And what is this medal round your neck, my little one?"

Bebelle having no other reply on her lips than her chubby right fist, the Corporal offered his services as interpreter.

"Monsieur demands, what is this, Bebelle?"

"It is the Holy Virgin," said Bebelle.

"And who gave it you?" asked the Englishman.

"Théophile."

"And who is Théophile?"

Bebelle broke into a laugh, laughed merrily and heartily, clapped her chubby hands, and beat her little feet on the stone pavement of the Place.

"He doesn't know Théophile! Why, he doesn't know any one! He doesn't know anything!" Then, sensible of a small solecism in her manners, Bebelle twisted her right hand in a leg of the Corporal's Bloomer trousers, and, laying her cheek against the place, kissed it.

"Monsieur Théophile, I believe?" said the Englishman to the Corporal.

"It is I, monsieur."

"Permit me." Mr. The Englishman shook him heartily by the hand and turned away. But he took it mighty ill that old Monsieur Mutuel in his patch of sunlight, upon whom he came as he turned, should pull off his cap to him with a look of pleased approval. And he muttered, in his own tongue, as he returned the salutation, "Well, walnut-shell! And what business is it of *yours?*"

Mr. The Englishman went on for many weeks passing but disturbed evenings and worse nights, and constantly experiencing that those aforesaid windows in the houses of Memory and Mercy rattled after dark, and that he had very imperfectly nailed them up. Likewise, he went on for many weeks daily improving the acquaintance of the Corporal and Bebelle. That is to say, he took Bebelle by the chin, and the Corporal by the hand, and offered Bebelle sous and the Corporal cigars, and even got the length of changing pipes with the Corporal and kissing Bebelle. But he did it all in a shamefaced way, and always took it extremely ill that Monsieur Mutuel in his patch of sunlight should note what he did. Whenever that seemed to be the case, he always growled in his own tongue, "There you are again, walnut-shell! What business is it of *yours?*"

In a word, it had become the occupation of Mr. The Englishman's life to look after the Corporal and little Bebelle, and to resent old Monsieur Mutuel's looking after *him.* An occupation only varied by a fire in the town one windy night, and much passing of water-buckets from hand to hand (in which the Englishman rendered good service), and much beating of drums,—when all of a sudden the Corporal disappeared.

Next, all of a sudden, Bebelle disappeared.

She had been visible a few days later than the Corporal, —sadly deteriorated as to washing and brushing,—but she had not spoken when addressed by Mr. The Englishman, and had looked scared and had run away. And now it would seem that she had run away for good. And there lay the Great Place under the windows, bare and barren.

In his shamefaced and constrained way, Mr. The Englishman asked no question of any one, but watched from his front windows and watched from his back windows, and lingered about the Place, and peeped in at the Barber's shop, and did all this and much more with a whistling and tune-humming pretence of not missing anything, until one afternoon when Monsieur Mutuel's patch of sunlight was in shadow, and when, according to all rule and precedent, he had no right whatever to bring his red ribbon out of doors, behold here he was, advancing with his cap already in his hand twelve paces off!

Mr. The Englishman had got as far into his usual objurgation as, "What bu—si— " when he checked himself.

"Ah, it is sad, it is sad! Hélas, it is unhappy, it is sad!" Thus old Monsieur Mutuel, shaking his grey head.

"What busin—at least, I would say, what do you mean, Monsieur Mutuel?"

"Our Corporal. Hélas, our dear Corporal!"

"What has happened to him?"

"You have not heard?"

"No."

"At the fire. But he was so brave, so ready. Ah, too brave, too ready!"

"May the Devil carry you away!" the Englishman broke in impatiently; "I beg your pardon,—I mean me,—I am not accustomed to speak French,—go on, will you?"

"And a falling beam——"

"Good God!" exclaimed the Englishman. "It was a private soldier who was killed?"

"No. A Corporal, the same Corporal, our dear Corporal. Beloved by all his comrades. The funeral ceremony was touching,—penetrating. Monsieur The Englishman, your eyes fill with tears."

"What bu—si——"

"Monsieur The Englishman, I honour those emotions. I salute you with profound respect. I will not obtrude myself upon your noble heart."

Monsieur Mutuel,—a gentleman in every thread of his cloudy linen, under whose wrinkled hand every grain in the quarter of an ounce of poor snuff in his poor little tin box became a gentleman's property,—Monsieur Mutuel passed on, with his cap in his hand.

"I little thought," said the Englishman, after walking for several minutes, and more than once blowing his nose, "when I was looking round that cemetery—I'll go there!"

Straight he went there, and when he came within the gate he paused, considering whether he should ask at the lodge for some direction to the grave. But he was less than ever in a mood for asking questions, and he thought, "I shall see something on it to know it by."

In search of the Corporal's grave he went softly on, up this walk and down that, peering in, among the crosses and hearts and columns and obelisks and tombstones, for a recently disturbed spot. It troubled him now to think how many dead there were in the cemetery,—he had not thought them a tenth part so numerous before,—and after he had walked and sought for some time, he said to himself, as he struck down a new vista of tombs, "I might suppose that every one was dead but I."

Not every one. A live child was lying on the ground asleep. Truly he had found something on the Corporal's grave to know it by, and the something was Bebelle.

With such a loving will had the dead soldier's comrades worked at his resting-place, that it was already a neat garden. On the green turf of the garden Bebelle lay sleeping, with her cheek touching it. A plain, unpainted little wooden Cross was planted in the turf, and her short arm embraced this little Cross, as it had many a time embraced the Corporal's neck. They had put a tiny flag (the flag of France) at his head, and a laurel garland.

Mr. The Englishman took off his hat, and stood for a while silent. Then, covering his head again, he bent down on one knee, and softly roused the child.

"Bebelle! My little one!"

Opening her eyes, on which the tears were still wet, Bebelle was at first frightened; but seeing who it was, she suffered him to take her in his arms, looking steadfastly at him.

"You must not lie here, my little one. You must come with me."

"No, no. I can't leave Théophile. I want the good dear Théophile."

"We will go and seek him, Bebelle. We will go and look for him in England. We will go and look for him at my daughter's, Bebelle."

"Shall we find him there?"

"We shall find the best part of him there. Come with me, poor forlorn little one. Heaven is my witness," said the Englishman, in a low voice, as, before he rose, he touched the turf above the gentle Corporal's breast, "that I thankfully accept this trust!"

It was a long way for the child to have come unaided. She was soon asleep again, with her embrace transferred to the Englishman's neck. He looked at her worn shoes, and her galled feet, and her tired face, and believed that she had come there every day.

He was leaving the grave with the slumbering Bebelle in his arms, when he stopped, looked wistfully down at it, and looked wistfully at the other graves around. "It is the innocent custom of the people," said Mr. The Englishman, with hesitation. "I think I should like to do it. No one sees."

Careful not to wake Bebelle as he went, he repaired to the lodge where such little tokens of remembrance were sold, and bought two wreaths. One, blue and white and glistening silver, "To my friend;" one of a soberer red and black and yellow, "To my friend." With these he went back to the grave, and so down on one knee again. Touching the child's lips with the brighter wreath, he guided her hand to hang it on the Cross; then hung his own wreath there. After all, the wreaths were not far out of keeping with the little garden. To my friend. To my friend.

Mr. The Englishman took it very ill when he looked round a street corner into the Great Place, carrying Bebelle in his arms, that old Mutuel should be there airing his red ribbon. He took a world of pains to dodge the worthy Mutuel, and devoted a surprising amount of time and trouble to skulking into his own lodging like a man pursued by Justice. Safely arrived there at last, he made Bebelle's toilet with as accurate a remembrance as he could bring to bear upon that work of the way in which he had often seen the poor Corporal make it, and having given her to eat and drink, laid her down on his own bed. Then he slipped out into the Barber's shop, and after a brief interview with the Barber's wife, and a brief recourse to his purse and card-case, came back again with the whole of Bebelle's personal property in such a very little bundle that it was quite lost under his arm.

As it was irreconcilable with his whole course and character that he should carry Bebelle off in state, or receive any compliments or congratulations on that feat, he devoted the next day to getting his two portmanteaus out of the house by artfulness and stealth, and to comporting himself in every particular as if he were going to run away,—except, indeed, that he paid his few debts in the town, and prepared a letter to leave for Madame Bouclet, enclosing a sufficient sum of money in lieu of notice. A railway train would come through at midnight, and by that train he would take away Bebelle to look for Théophile in England and at his forgiven daughter's.

At midnight, on a moonlight night, Mr. The Englishman came creeping forth like a harmless assassin, with Bebelle on his breast instead of a dagger. Quiet the Great Place, and quiet the never-stirring streets; closed the cafés; huddled together motionless their billiard-balls; drowsy the guard or sentinel on duty here and there; lulled for the time, by sleep, even the insatiate appetite of the Office of Town-dues.

Mr. The Englishman left the Place behind, and left the streets behind, and left the civilian-inhabited town behind, and descended down among the military works of Vauban, hemming all in. As the shadow of the first heavy arch and postern fell upon him and was left behind, as the shadow of the second heavy arch and postern fell upon him and was left behind, as his hollow tramp over the first drawbridge was succeeded by a gentler sound, as his hollow tramp over the second drawbridge was succeeded by a gentler sound, as he overcame the stagnant ditches one by one, and passed out where the flowing waters were and where the moonlight, so the dark shades and the hollow sounds and the unwhole-somely locked currents of his soul were vanquished and set free. See to it, Vaubans of your own hearts, who gird them in with triple walls and ditches, and with bolt and chain and bar and lifted bridge,—raze those fortifications, and lay them level with the all-absorbing dust, before the night cometh when no hand can work!

All went prosperously, and he got into an empty carriage in the train, where he could lay Bebelle on the seat over against him, as on a couch, and cover her from head to foot with his mantle. He had just drawn himself up from per-fecting this arrangement, and had just leaned back in his own seat contemplating it with great satisfaction, when he became aware of a curious appearance at the open carriage window,—a ghostly little tin box floating up in the moon-light, and hovering there.

He leaned forward, and put out his head. Down among the rails and wheels and ashes, Monsieur Mutuel, red ribbon and all!

"Excuse me, Monsieur The Englishman," said Monsieur Mutuel, holding up his box at arm's length, the carriage being so high and he so low; "but I shall reverence the little box for ever, if your so generous hand will take a pinch from it at parting."

Mr. The Englishman reached out of the window before complying, and—without asking the old fellow what busi-ness it was of his—shook hands and said, "Adieu! God bless you!"

"And, Mr. The Englishman, God bless *you!*" cried Madame Bouclet, who was also there among the rails and wheels and ashes. "And God will bless you in the happiness of the protected child now with you. And God will bless you in your own child at home. And God will bless you in your own remembrances. And this from me!"

He had barely time to catch a bouquet from her hand, when the train was flying through the night. Round the paper that enfolded it was bravely written (doubtless by the nephew who held the pen of an Angel), "Homage to the friend of the friendless."

"Not bad people, Bebelle!" said Mr. The Englishman, softly drawing the mantle a little from her sleeping face, that he might kiss it, "though they are so——"

Too "sentimental" himself at the moment to be able to get out that word, he added nothing but a sob, and travelled for some miles, through the moonlight, with his hand before his eyes.

CHAPTER III

HIS BROWN-PAPER PARCEL

My works are well known. I am a young man in the Art line. You have seen my works many a time, though it's fifty thousand to one if you have seen me. You say you don't want to see me? You say your interest is in my works, and not in me? Don't be too sure about that. Stop a bit.

Let us have it down in black and white at the first go off, so that there may be no unpleasantness or wrangling afterwards. And this is looked over by a friend of mine, a ticket writer, that is up to literature. I am a young man in the Art line—in the Fine-Art line. You have seen my works over and over again, and you have been curious about me, and you think you have seen me. Now, as a safe rule, you never have seen me, and you never do see me, and you never will see me. I think that's plainly put—and it's what knocks me over.

If there's a blighted public character going, I am the party.

It has been remarked by a certain (or an uncertain) philosopher, that the world knows nothing of its greatest men. He might have put it plainer if he had thrown his eye in my direction. He might have put it, that while the world knows something of them that apparently go in and win, it knows nothing of them that really go in and don't win. There it is again in another form—and that's what knocks me over.

Not that it's only myself that suffers from injustice, but that I am more alive to my own injuries than to any other man's. Being, as I have mentioned, in the Fine-Art line, and not the Philanthropic line, I openly admit it. As to company in injury, I have company enough. Who are you passing every day at your Competitive Excruciations? The fortunate candidates whose heads and livers you have turned upside down for life? Not you. You are really passing the Crammers and Coaches. If your principle is right, why don't you turn out to-morrow morning with the keys of your cities on velvet cushions, your musicians playing, and your flags flying, and read addresses to the Crammers and Coaches on your bended knees, beseeching them to come out and govern you? Then, again, as to your public business of all sorts, your Financial statements and your Budgets; the Public knows much, truly, about the real doers of all that! Your Nobles and Right Honourables are first-rate men? Yes, and so is a goose a first-rate bird. But I'll tell you this about the goose;—you'll find his natural flavour disappointing, without stuffing.

Perhaps I am soured by not being popular? But suppose I AM popular. Suppose my works never fail to attract. Suppose that, whether they are exhibited by natural light or by artificial, they inevitably draw the public. Then no doubt they are preserved in some Collection? No, they are not; they are not preserved in any Collection. Copyright? No, nor yet copyright. Anyhow they must be somewhere? Wrong again, for they are often nowhere.

Says you, "At all events, you are in a moody state of mind, my friend." My answer is, I have described myself as a public character with a blight upon him—which fully accounts for the curdling of the milk in *that* cocoa-nut.

Those that are acquainted with London are aware of a locality on the Surrey side of the river Thames, called the Obelisk, or, more generally, the Obstacle. Those that are not acquainted with London will also be aware of it, now that I have named it. My lodging is not far from that locality. I am a young man of that easy disposition, that I lie abed till it's absolutely necessary to get up and earn something, and then I lie abed again till I have spent it.

It was on an occasion when I had had to turn to with a view to victuals, that I found myself walking along the Waterloo Road, one evening after dark, accompanied by an acquaintance and fellow-lodger in the gas-fitting way of life. He is very good company, having worked at the theatres, and, indeed, he has a theatrical turn himself, and wishes to be brought out in the character of Othello; but whether on account of his regular work always blacking his face and hands more or less, I cannot say.

"Tom," he says, "what a mystery hangs over you!"

"Yes, Mr. Click"—the rest of the house generally give him his name, as being first, front, carpeted all over, his own furniture, and if not mahogany, an out-and-out imitation —"yes, Mr. Click, a mystery does hang over me."

"Makes you low, you see, don't it?" says he, eyeing me sideways.

"Why, yes, Mr. Click, there are circumstances connected with it that have," I yielded to a sigh, "a lowering effect."

"Gives you a touch of the misanthrope too, don't it?" says he. "Well, I'll tell you what. If I was you, I'd shake it off."

"If I was you, I would, Mr. Click; but, if you was me, you wouldn't.

"Ah!" says he, "there's something in that."

When we had walked a little further, he took it up again by touching me on the chest.

"You see, Tom, it seems to me as if, in the words of the poet who wrote the domestic drama of The Stranger, you had a silent sorrow there."

"I have, Mr. Click."

"I hope, Tom," lowering his voice in a friendly way, "it isn't coining, or smashing?"

"No, Mr. Click. Don't be uneasy."

"Nor yet forg——" Mr. Click checked himself, and added, "counterfeiting anything, for instance?"

"No, Mr. Click. I am lawfully in the Art line—Fine-Art line—but I can say no more."

"Ah! Under a species of star? A kind of malignant spell? A sort of a gloomy destiny? A cankerworm pegging away at your vitals in secret, as well as I make it out?" said Mr. Click, eyeing me with some admiration.

I told Mr. Click that was about it, if we came to particulars; and I thought he appeared rather proud of me.

'Our conversation had brought us to a crowd of people, the greater part struggling for a front place from which to see something on the pavement, which proved to be various designs executed in coloured chalks on the pavement stones, lighted by two candles stuck in mud sconces. The subjects consisted of a fine fresh salmon's head and shoulders, supposed to have been recently sent home from the fishmonger's; a moonlight night at sea (in a circle); dead game; scroll-work; the head of a hoary hermit engaged in devout contemplation; the head of a pointer smoking a pipe; and a cherubim, his flesh creased as in infancy, going on a horizontal errand against the wind. All these subjects appeared to me to be exquisitely done.

On his knees on one side of this gallery, a shabby person of modest appearance who shivered dreadfully (though it wasn't at all cold), was engaged in blowing the chalk-dust off the moon, toning the outline of the back of the hermit's head with a bit of leather, and fattening the down-stroke of a letter or two in the writing. I have forgotten to mention that writing formed a part of the composition, and that it also—as it appeared to me—was exquisitely done. It ran as follows, in fine round characters: "An honest man is the noblest work of God. 1 2 3 4 5 6 7 8 9 0. £ s. d. Employment in an office is humbly requested. Honour the Queen. Hunger is a 0 9 8 7 6 5 4 3 2 1 sharp thorn. Chip chop, cherry chop, fol de rol de ri do. Astronomy and mathematics. I do this to support my family."

Murmurs of admiration at the exceeding beauty of this performance went about among the crowd. The artist, having finished his touching (and having spoilt those places), took his seat on the pavement, with his knees crouched up very nigh his chin; and halfpence began to rattle in.

"A pity to see a man of that talent brought so low; ain't it?" said one of the crowd to me.

"What he might have done in the coach-painting, or house-decorating!" said another man, who took up the first speaker because I did not.

"Why, he writes—alone—like the Lord Chancellor!" said another man.

"Better," said another. "I know *his* writing. *He* couldn't support his family this way."

Then, a woman noticed the natural fluffiness of the hermit's hair, and another woman, her friend, mentioned of the salmon's gills that you could almost see him gasp. Then, an elderly country gentleman stepped forward and asked the modest man how he executed his work? And the modest man took some scraps of brown paper with colours in 'em out of his pockets, and showed them. Then a fair-complexioned donkey, with sandy hair and spectacles, asked if the hermit was a portrait? To which the modest man, casting a sorrowful glance upon it, replied that it was, to a certain extent, a recollection of his father. This caused a boy to yelp out, "Is the Pinter a smoking the pipe your mother?" who was immediately shoved out of view by a sympathetic carpenter with his basket of tools at his back.

At every fresh question or remark the crowd leaned forward more eagerly, and dropped the halfpence more freely, and the modest man gathered them up more meekly. At last, another elderly gentleman came to the front, and gave the artist his card, to come to his office to-morrow, and get some copying to do. The card was accompanied by sixpence, and the artist was profoundly grateful, and, before he put the card in his hat, read it several times by the light of his candles to fix the address well in his mind, in case he should lose it. The crowd was deeply interested by this last incident, and a man in the second row with a gruff voice growled to the artist, "You've got a chance in life now, ain't you?" The artist answered (sniffing in a very low-spirited way, however), "I'm thankful to hope so." Upon which there was a general chorus of "*You* are all right," and the halfpence slackened very decidedly.

I felt myself pulled away by the arm, and Mr. Click and I stood alone at the corner of the next crossing.

"Why, Tom," said Mr. Click, "what a horrid expression of face you've got!"

"Have I?" says I.

"Have you?" says Mr. Click. "Why, you looked as if you would have his blood?"

"Whose blood?"

"The artist's."

"The artist's?" I repeated. And I laughed, frantically, wildly, gloomily, incoherently, disagreeably. I am sensible that I did. I know I did.

Mr. Click stared at me in a scared sort of a way, but said

nothing until we had walked a street's length. He then stopped short, and said, with excitement on the part of his forefinger:

"Thomas, I find it necessary to be plain with you. I don't like the envious man. I have identified the cankerworm that's pegging away at *your* vitals, and it's envy, Thomas."

"Is it?" says I.

"Yes, it is," says he. "Thomas, beware of envy. It is the green-eyed monster which never did and never will improve each shining hour, but quite the reverse. I dread the envious man, Thomas. I confess that I am afraid of the envious man, when he is so envious as you are. Whilst you contemplated the works of a gifted rival, and whilst you heard that rival's praises, and especially whilst you met his humble glance as he put that card away, your countenance was so malevolent as to be terrific. Thomas, I have heard of the envy of them that follows the Fine-Art line, but I never believed it could be what yours is. I wish you well, but I take my leave of you. And if you should ever get into trouble through knifeing—or say, garotting—a brother artist, as I believe you will, don't call me to character, Thomas, or I shall be forced to injure your case."

Mr. Click parted from me with those words, and we broke off our acquaintance.

I became enamoured. Her name was Henrietta. Contending with my easy disposition, I frequently got up to go after her. She also dwelt in the neighbourhood of the Obstacle, and I did fondly hope that no other would interpose in the way of our union.

To say that Henrietta was volatile is but to say that she was woman. To say that she was in the bonnet-trimming is feebly to express the taste which reigned predominant in her own.

She consented to walk with me. Let me do her the justice to say that she did so upon trial. "I am not," said Henrietta, "as yet prepared to regard you, Thomas, in any other light than as a friend; but as a friend I am willing to walk with you, on the understanding that softer sentiments may flow."

We walked.

Under the influence of Henrietta's beguilements, I now got out of bed daily. I pursued my calling with an industry before unknown, and it cannot fail to have been observed at that period, by those most familiar with the streets of London, that there was a larger supply. But hold! The time is not yet come!

One evening in October I was walking with Henrietta, enjoying the cool breezes wafted over Vauxhall Bridge. After several slow turns, Henrietta gaped frequently (so inseparable from woman is the love of excitement), and said, "Let's go home by Grosvenor Place, Piccadilly, and Waterloo" —localities, I may state for the information of the stranger and the foreigner, well known in London, and the last a Bridge.

"No. Not by Piccadilly, Henrietta," said I.

"And why not Piccadilly, for goodness' sake?" said Henrietta.

Could I tell her? Could I confess to the gloomy presentiment that overshadowed me? Could I make myself intelligible to her? No.

"I don't like Piccadilly, Henrietta."

"But I do," said she. "It's dark now, and the long rows of lamps in Piccadilly after dark are beautiful. I *will* go to Piccadilly!"

Of course we went. It was a pleasant night, and there were numbers of people in the streets. It was a brisk night, but not too cold, and not damp. Let me darkly observe, it was the best of all nights—FOR THE PURPOSE.

As we passed the garden wall of the Royal Palace, going up Grosvenor Place, Henrietta murmured:

"I wish I was a Queen!"

"Why so, Henrietta?"

"I would make *you* Something," said she, and crossed her two hands on my arm, and turned away her head.

Judging from this that the softer sentiments alluded to above had begun to flow, I adapted my conduct to that belief. Thus happily we passed on into the detested thoroughfare of Piccadilly. On the right of that thoroughfare is a row of trees, the railing of the Green Park, and a fine broad eligible piece of pavement.

"Oh my!" cried Henrietta presently. "There's been an accident!"

I looked to the left, and said, "Where, Henrietta?"

"Not there, stupid!" said she. "Over by the Park railings Where the crowd is. Oh no, it's not an accident, it's something else to look at! What's them lights?"

She referred to two lights twinkling low amongst the legs of the assemblage: two candles on the pavement.

"Oh, do come along!" cried Henrietta, skipping across the road with me. I hung back, but in vain. "Do let's look!"

Again, designs upon the pavement. Centre compartment, Mount Vesuvius going it (in a circle), supported by four oval compartments, severally representing a ship in heavy weather, a shoulder of mutton attended by two cucumbers, a golden harvest with distant cottage of proprietor, and a knife and fork after nature; above the centre compartment a bunch of grapes, and over the whole a rainbow. The whole, as it appeared to me, exquisitely done.

The person in attendance on these works of art was in all respects, shabbiness excepted, unlike the former personage His whole appearance and manner denoted briskness. Though threadbare, he expressed to the crowd that poverty had not subdued his spirit, or tinged with any sense of shame this honest effort to turn his talents to some account. The writing which formed part of his composition was conceived in a similarly cheerful tone. It breathed the following sentiments: "The writer is poor, but not despondent. To a British 1 2 3 4 5 6 7 8 9 0 Public he £ s. d. appeals. Honour to our brave Army! And also 0 9 8 7 6 5 4 3 2 1 to our gallant Navy. BRITONS STRIKE the A B C D E F G writer in common chalks would be grateful for any suitable employment HOME! HURRAH!" The whole of this writing appeared to me to be exquisitely done.

But this man, in one respect like the last, though seemingly hard at it with a great show of brown paper and rubbers, was only really fattening the down-stroke of a letter here and there, or blowing the loose chalk off the rainbow, or toning the outside edge of the shoulder of mutton. Though he did this with the greatest confidence, he did it (as it struck me) in so ignorant a manner, and so spoilt everything he touched, that when he began upon the purple smoke from the chimney of the distant cottage of the proprietor of the golden harvest (which smoke was beautifully soft), I found myself saying aloud, without considering of it:

"Let that alone, will you?"

"Halloa!" said the man next me in the crowd, jerking me roughly from him with his elbow, "why didn't you send a telegram? If we had known you was coming, we'd have provided something better for you. You understand the man's work better than he does himself, don't you? Have you made your will? You're too clever to live long."

"Don't be hard upon the gentleman, Sir," said the person in attendance on the works of art, with a twinkle in his eye as he looked at me; "he may chance to be an artist himself. If so, Sir, he will have a fellow-feeling with me, Sir, when I" —he adapted his action to his words as he went on, and gave a smart slap of his hands between each touch, working himself all the time about and about the composition— "when I lighten the bloom of my grapes—shade off the orange in my rainbow—dot the i of my Britons—throw a yellow light into my cow-cum-*ber*—insinuate another morsel of fat into my shoulder of mutton—dart another zigzag flash of lightning at my ship in distress!"

He seemed to do this so neatly, and was so nimble about it, that the halfpence came flying in.

"Thanks, generous public, thanks!" said the professor. " You will stimulate me to further exertions! My name will be found in the list of British Painters yet. I shall do better than this, with encouragement. I shall indeed."

"You never can do better than that bunch of grapes," said Henrietta. "Oh, Thomas, them grapes!"

"Not better than *that*, lady? I hope for the time when I shall paint anything but your own bright eyes and lips equal to life."

"(Thomas, did you ever?) But it must take a long time, Sir," said Henrietta, blushing, "to paint equal to that."

"I was prenticed to it, Miss," said the young man, smartly touching up the composition—"prenticed to it in the caves of Spain and Portingale, ever so long and two year over."

There was a laugh from the crowd; and a new man who had worked himself in next me, said, "He's a smart chap, too; ain't he?"

"And what a eye!" exclaimed Henrietta softly.

"Ah! He need have a eye," said the man.

"Ah! He just need," was murmured among the crowd.

"He couldn't come that 'ere burning mountain without a eye," said the man. He had got himself accepted as an authority, somehow, and everybody looked at his finger as it pointed out Vesuvius. "To come that effect in a general illumination would require a eye; but to come it with two dips—why, it's enough to blind him!"

That impostor, pretending not to have heard what was

said, now winked to any extent with both eyes at once, as if
the strain upon his sight was too much, and threw back his
long hair—it was very long—as if to cool his fevered brow.
I was watching him doing it, when Henrietta suddenly
whispered, "Oh, Thomas, how horrid you look!" and pulled
me out by the arm.

Remembering Mr. Click's words, I was confused when I
retorted, "What do you mean by horrid?"

"Oh gracious! Why, you looked," said Henrietta, "as if
you would have his blood."

I was going to answer, "So I would, for twopence——from
his nose," when I checked myself and remained silent.

We returned home in silence. Every step of the way, the
softer sentiments that had flowed, ebbed twenty mile an hour.
Adapting my conduct to the ebbing, as I had done to the
flowing, I let my arm drop limp, so as she could scarcely
keep hold of it, and I wished her such a cold good night at
parting, that I keep within the bounds of truth when I
characterise it as a Rasper.

In the course of the next day I received the following
document:

"Henrietta informs Thomas that my eyes are open to you.
I must ever wish you well, but walking and us is separated
by an unfarmable abyss. One so malignant to superiority—
Oh that look at him!—can never never conduct
"HENRIETTA

"P.S.—To the altar."

Yielding to the easiness of my disposition, I went to bed
for a week, after receiving this letter. During the whole of
such time, London was bereft of the usual fruits of my labour.
When I resumed it, I found that Henrietta was married to
the artist of Piccadilly.

Did I say to the artist? What fell words were those,
expressive of what a galling hollowness, of what a bitter
mockery! I—I—I—am the artist. I was the real artist of
Piccadilly, I was the real artist of the Waterloo Road, I am
the only artist of all those pavement-subjects which daily and
nightly arouse your admiration. I do 'em, and I let 'em out.
The man you behold with the papers of chalks and the
rubbers, touching up the down-strokes of the writing and
shading off the salmon, the man you give the credit to, the

man you give the money to, hires—yes! and I live to tell it!
—hires those works of art of me, and brings nothing to 'em
but the candles.

Such is genius in a commercial country. I am not up to the
shivering, I am not up to the liveliness, I am not up to the
wanting-employment-in-an-office move; I am only up to
originating and executing the work. In consequence of which
you never see me; you think you see me when you see somebody else, and that somebody else is a mere Commercial
character. The one seen by self and Mr. Click in the Waterloo
Road can only write a single word, and that I taught him,
and it's MULTIPLICATION—which you may see him execute
upside down, because he can't do it the natural way. The
one seen by self and Henrietta by the Green Park railings
can just smear into existence the two ends of a rainbow,
with his cuff and a rubber—if very hard put upon making a
show—but he could no more come the arch of the rainbow,
to save his life, than he could come the moonlight, fish,
volcano, shipwreck, mutton, hermit, or any of my most
celebrated effects.

To conclude as I began: if there's a blighted public
character going, I am the party. And often as you have
seen, do see, and will see, my Works, it's fifty thousand to
one if you'll ever see me, unless, when the candles are burnt
down and the Commercial character is gone, you should
happen to notice a neglected young man perseveringly rubbing
out the last traces of the pictures, so that nobody can renew
the same. That's me.

CHAPTER IV

HIS WONDERFUL END

IT will have been, ere now, perceived that I sold the foregoing writings. From the fact of their being printed in
these pages, the inference will, ere now, have been drawn by
the reader (may I add, the gentle reader?) that I sold them
to One who never yet—— [1]

Having parted with the writings on most satisfactory

[1] The remainder of this complimentary sentence editorially struck
out.

terms,—for, in opening negotiations with the present Journal, was I not placing myself in the hands of One of whom it may be said, in the words of Another,[1]—I resumed my usual functions. But I too soon discovered that peace of mind had fled from a brow which, up to that time, Time had merely took the hair off, leaving an unruffled expanse within.

It were superfluous to veil it,—the brow to which I allude is my own.

Yes, over that brow uneasiness gathered like the sable wing of the fabled bird, as—as no doubt will be easily identified by all right-minded individuals. If not, I am unable, on the spur of the moment, to enter into particulars of him. The reflection that the writings must now inevitably get into print, and that He might yet live and meet with them, sat like the Hag of Night upon my jaded form. The elasticity of my spirits departed. Fruitless was the Bottle, whether Wine or Medicine. I had recourse to both, and the effect of both upon my system was witheringly lowering.

In this state of depression, into which I subsided when I first began to revolve what could I ever say if He—the unknown—was to appear in the Coffee-room and demand reparation, I one forenoon in this last November received a turn that appeared to be given me by the finger of Fate and Conscience, hand in hand. I was alone in the Coffee-room, and had just poked the fire into a blaze, and was standing with my back to it, trying whether heat would penetrate with soothing influence to the Voice within, when a young man in a cap, of an intelligent countenance, though requiring his hair cut, stood before me.

" Mr. Christopher, the Head Waiter ? "

" The same."

The young man shook his hair out of his vision,—which it impeded,—took a packet from his breast, and handing it over to me, said, with his eye (or did I dream ?) fixed with a lambent meaning on me, "THE PROOFS."

Although I smelt my coat-tails singeing at the fire, I had not the power to withdraw them. The young man put the packet in my faltering grasp, and repeated,—let me do him the justice to add, with civility :

"THE PROOFS. A. Y. R."

With those words he departed.

[1] The remainder of this complimentary sentence editorially struck out.

A. Y. R.? And You Remember. Was that his meaning? At Your Risk. Were the letters short for *that* reminder? Anticipate Your Retribution. Did they stand for *that* warning? Out-dacious Youth Repent? But no; for that, a O was happily wanting, and the vowel here was a A.

I opened the packet, and found that its contents were the foregoing writings printed just as the reader (may I add the discerning reader?) peruses them. In vain was the reassuring whisper,—A. Y. R., All the Year Round,—it could not cancel the Proofs. Too appropriate name. The Proofs of my having sold the Writings.

My wretchedness daily increased. I had not thought of the risk I ran, and the defying publicity I put my head into, until all was done, and all was in print. Give up the money to be off the bargain and prevent the publication, I could not. My family was down in the world, Christmas was coming on, a brother in the hospital and a sister in the rheumatics could not be entirely neglected. And it was not only ins in the family that had told on the resources of one unaided Waitering; outs were not wanting. A brother out of a situation, and another brother out of money to meet an acceptance, and another brother out of his mind, and another brother out at New York (not the same, though it might appear so), had really and truly brought me to a stand till I could turn myself round. I got worse and worse in my meditations, constantly reflecting "The Proofs," and reflecting that when Christmas drew nearer, and the Proofs were published, there could be no safety from hour to hour but that He might confront me in the Coffee-room, and in the face of day and his country demand his rights.

The impressive and unlooked-for catastrophe towards which I dimly pointed the reader (shall I add, the highly intellectual reader?) in my first remarks now rapidly approaches.

It was November still, but the last echoes of the Guy Foxes had long ceased to reverberate. We was slack,— several joints under our average mark, and wine, of course, proportionate. So slack had we become at last, that Beds Nos. 26, 27, 28, and 31, having took their six o'clock dinners, and dozed over their respective pints, had drove away in their respective Hansoms for their respective Night Mail-trains and left us empty.

I had took the evening paper to No. 6 table,—which is warm and most to be preferred,—and, lost in the all-absorb-

ing topics of the day, had dropped into a slumber. I was
recalled to consciousness by the well-known intimation,
"Waiter!" and replying, "Sir!" found a gentleman standing at No. 4 table. The reader (shall I add, the observant
reader?) will please to notice the locality of the gentleman,
—*at No. 4 table.*

He had one of the new-fangled uncollapsible bags in his
hand (which I am against, for I don't see why you shouldn't
collapse, while you are about it, as your fathers collapsed
before you), and he said :

"I want to dine, waiter. I shall sleep here to-night."

"Very good, Sir. What will you take for dinner, Sir?"

"Soup, bit of codfish, oyster sauce, and the joint."

"Thank you, Sir."

I rang the chambermaid's bell; and Mrs. Pratchett
marched in, according to custom, demurely carrying a lighted
flat candle before her, as if she was one of a long public
procession, all the other members of which was invisible.

In the meanwhile the gentleman had gone up to the mantelpiece, right in front of the fire, and had laid his forehead
against the mantelpiece (which it is a low one, and brought
him into the attitude of leap-frog), and had heaved a tremenjous sigh. His hair was long and lightish; and when
he laid his forehead against the mantelpiece, his hair all fell
in a dusty fluff together over his eyes; and when he now
turned round and lifted up his head again, it all fell in
a dusty fluff together over his ears. This give him a wild
appearance, similar to a blasted heath.

"O! The chambermaid. Ah!" He was turning something in his mind. "To be sure. Yes. I won't go upstairs
now, if you will take my bag. It will be enough for the
present to know my number.—Can you give me 24 B?"

(O Conscience, what a Adder art thou!)

Mrs. Pratchett allotted him the room, and took his bag
to it. He then went back before the fire, and fell a biting
his nails.

"Waiter!" biting between the words, "give me," bite,
"pen and paper; and in five minutes," bite, "let me have, if
you please," bite, "a," bite, "Messenger."

Unmindful of his waning soup, he wrote and sent off six
notes before he touched his dinner. Three were City; three
West-End. The City letters were to Cornhill, Ludgate-hill,
and Farringdon-street. The West-End letters were to Great

Marlborough-street, New Burlington-street, and Piccadilly. Everybody was systematically denied at every one of the six places, and there was not a vestige of any answer. Our light porter whispered to me, when he came back with that report, "All Booksellers."

But before then he had cleared off his dinner, and his bottle of wine. He now—mark the concurrence with the document formerly given in full!—knocked a plate of biscuits off the table with his agitated elber (but without breakage), and demanded boiling brandy-and-water.

Now fully convinced that it was Himself, I perspired with the utmost freedom. When he become flushed with the heated stimulant referred to, he again demanded pen and paper, and passed the succeeding two hours in producing a manuscript which he put in the fire when completed. He then went up to bed, attended by Mrs. Pratchett. Mrs. Pratchett (who was aware of my emotions) told me, on coming down, that she had noticed his eye rolling into every corner of the passages and staircase, as if in search of his Luggage, and that, looking back as she shut the door of 24 B, she perceived him with his coat already thrown off immersing himself bodily under the bedstead, like a chimley-sweep before the application of machinery.

The next day—I forbear the horrors of that night—was a very foggy day in our part of London, insomuch that it was necessary to light the Coffee-room gas. We was still alone, and no feverish words of mine can do justice to the fitfulness of his appearance as he sat at No. 4 table, increased by there being something wrong with the meter.

Having again ordered his dinner, he went out, and was out for the best part of two hours. Inquiring on his return whether any of the answers had arrived, and receiving an unqualified negative, his instant call was for Mulligatawny, the Cayenne Pepper, and Orange Brandy.

Feeling that the mortal struggle was now at hand, I also felt that I must be equal to him, and with that view resolved that whatever he took I would take. Behind my partition, but keeping my eye on him over the curtain, I therefore operated on Mulligatawny, Cayenne Pepper, and Orange Brandy. And at a later period of the day, when he again said, "Orange Brandy," I said so too, in a lower tone, to George, my Second Lieutenant (my First was absent on leave), who acts between me and the bar.

Throughout that awful day he walked about the Coffee-room continually. Often he came close up to my partition, and then his eye rolled within, too evidently in search of any signs of his Luggage. Half-past six came, and I laid his cloth. He ordered a bottle of Old Brown. I likewise ordered a bottle of Old Brown. He drank his. I drank mine (as nearly as my duties would permit) glass for glass against his. He topped with coffee and a small glass. I topped with coffee and a small glass. He dozed. I dozed. At last, "Waiter!"—and he ordered his bill. The moment was now at hand when we two must be locked in the deadly grapple.

Swift as the arrow from the bow, I had formed my resolution ; in other words, I had hammered it out between nine and nine. It was, that I would be the first to open up the subject with a full acknowledgment, and would offer any gradual settlement within my power. He paid his bill (doing what was right by attendance) with his eye rolling about him to the last for any tokens of his Luggage. One only time our gaze then met, with the lustrous fixedness (I believe I am correct in imputing that character to it?) of the well-known Basilisk. The decisive moment had arrived.

With a tolerable steady hand, though with humility, I laid The Proofs before him.

"Gracious Heavens!" he cries out, leaping up, and catching hold of his hair. "What's this? Print!"

"Sir," I replied, in a calming voice, and bending forward, "I humbly acknowledge to being the unfortunate cause of it. But I hope, Sir, that when you have heard the circumstances explained, and the innocence of my intentions——"

To my amazement, I was stopped short by his catching me in both his arms, and pressing me to his breast-bone ; where I must confess to my face (and particular, nose) having undergone some temporary vexation from his wearing his coat buttoned high up, and his buttons being uncommon hard.

"Ha, ha, ha!" he cries, releasing me with a wild laugh, and grasping my hand. "What is your name, my Benefactor?"

"My name, Sir" (I was crumpled, and puzzled to make him out), "is Christopher; and I hope, Sir, that, as such, when you've heard my ex——"

"In print!" he exclaims again, dashing the proofs over and over as if he was bathing in them. "In print!! O Christopher! Philanthropist! Nothing can recompense you, —but what sum of money would be acceptable to you?"

I had drawn a step back from him, or I should have suffered from his buttons again.

"Sir, I assure you, I have been already well paid, and——"

"No, no, Christopher! Don't talk like that! What sum of money would be acceptable to you, Christopher? Would you find twenty pounds acceptable, Christopher?"

However great my surprise, I naturally found words to say, "Sir, I am not aware that the man was ever yet born without more than the average amount of water on the brain as would *not* find twenty pounds acceptable. But—extremely obliged to you, Sir, I'm sure;" for he had tumbled it out of his purse and crammed it in my hand in two bank-notes; "but I could wish to know, Sir, if not intruding, how I have merited this liberality?"

"Know then, my Christopher," he says, "that from boyhood's hour I have unremittingly and unavailingly endeavoured to get into print. Know, Christopher, that all the Booksellers alive—and several dead—have refused to put me into print. Know, Christopher, that I have written unprinted Reams. But they shall be read to you, my friend and brother. You sometimes have a holiday?"

Seeing the great danger I was in, I had the presence of mind to answer, "Never!" To make it more final, I added, "Never! Not from the cradle to the grave."

"Well," says he, thinking no more about that, and chuckling at his proofs again. "But I am in print! The first flight of ambition emanating from my father's lowly cot is realised at length! The golden bow,"—he was getting on,—"struck by the magic hand, has emitted a complete and perfect sound! When did this happen, my Christopher?"

"Which happen, Sir?"

"This," he held it out at arm's length to admire it,—"this Per-rint."

When I had given him my detailed account of it, he grasped me by the hand again, and said:

"Dear Christopher, it should be gratifying to you to know that you are an instrument in the hands of Destiny. Because you *are*."

A passing Something of a melancholy cast put it into my head to shake it, and to say, "Perhaps we all are."

"I don't mean that," he answered; "I don't take that wide range; I confine myself to the special case. Observe me well, my Christopher! Hopeless of getting rid, through any effort of my own, of any of the manuscripts among my Luggage,—all of which, send them where I would, were always coming back to me,—it is now some seven years since I left that Luggage here, on the desperate chance, either that the too, too faithful manuscripts would come back to me no more, or that some one less accursed than I might give them to the world.   You follow me, my Christopher?"

"Pretty well, Sir."   I followed him so far as to judge that he had a weak head, and that the Orange, the Boiling, and Old Brown combined was beginning to tell. (The Old Brown, being heady, is best adapted to seasoned cases.)

"Years elapsed, and those compositions slumbered in dust. At length, Destiny, choosing her agent from all mankind, sent You here, Christopher, and lo! the Casket was burst asunder, and the Giant was free!"

He made hay of his hair after he said this, and he stood a-tiptoe.

"But," he reminded himself in a state of excitement, "we must sit up all night, my Christopher.   I must correct these Proofs for the press.   Fill all the inkstands, and bring me several new pens."

He smeared himself and he smeared the Proofs, the night through, to that degree that when Sol gave him warning to depart (in a four-wheeler), few could have said which was them, and which was him, and which was blots.   His last instructions was, that I should instantly run and take his corrections to the office of the present Journal.   I did so. They most likely will not appear in print, for I noticed a message being brought round from Beauford Printing House, while I was a throwing this concluding statement on paper, that the ole resources of that establishment was unable to make out what they meant.   Upon which a certain gentleman in company, as I will not more particularly name,—but of whom it will be sufficient to remark, standing on the broad basis of a wave-girt isle, that whether we regard him in the light of,—[1] laughed, and put the corrections in the fire.

[1] The remainder of this complimentary parenthesis editorially struck out.

NOTE.—Dickens partly contributed to another of the chapters, entitled "His Umbrella;" but for this the reader is referred to the number as republished in a collected volume—the *Nine Christmas numbers of All the Year Round*.

MRS. LIRRIPER'S LODGINGS

[1863]

CHARACTERS

MR. EDSON, *a gentleman from the country, who takes lodgings for himself and wife at Mrs. Lirriper's.*

MRS. PEGGY EDSON, *his wife; a pretty and delicate young lady.*

MAJOR JEMMY JACKMAN, *a parlour-boarder at Mrs. Lirriper's, and her warm friend.*

JANE, *a housemaid in Miss Wozenham's service.*

JEMMY JACKMAN LIRRIPER, *the son of Mrs. Edson.*

MRS. EMMA LIRRIPER ('Gran'); *a good-natured London lodging-house keeper; the narrator of the story.*

CAROLINE MAXEY, *one of Mrs. Lirriper's servant-girls.*

MARY ANNE PERKINSOP, *another of Mrs. Lirriper's servant-girls.*

SOPHY ('Willing Sophy'), *a poor, half-starved creature, but always smiling and cheerful.*

MISS WOZENHAM, *a lodging-house keeper, and a rival to Mrs. Lirriper.*

MRS. LIRRIPER'S LODGINGS

IN TWO CHAPTERS

CHAPTER I

HOW MRS. LIRRIPER CARRIED ON THE BUSINESS

WHOEVER would begin to be worried with letting Lodgings
that wasn't a lone woman with a living to get is a thing
inconceivable to me, my dear; excuse the familiarity, but it
comes natural to me in my own little room, when wishing
to open my mind to those that I can trust, and I should be
truly thankful if they were all mankind, but such is not so,
for have but a Furnished bill in the window and your watch
on the mantelpiece, and farewell to it if you turn your back
for but a second, however gentlemanly the manners; nor is
being of your own sex any safeguard, as I have reason, in the
form of sugar-tongs to know, for that lady (and a fine woman
she was) got me to run for a glass of water, on the plea of
going to be confined, which certainly turned out true, but it
was in the Station-house.

Number Eighty-one Norfolk Street, Strand—situated midway between the City and St. James's, and within five minutes'
walk of the principal places of public amusement—is my
address. I have rented this house many years, as the parish
rate-books will testify; and I could wish my landlord was as
alive to the fact as I am myself; but no, bless you, not a
half a pound of paint to save his life, nor so much, my dear,
as a tile upon the roof, though on your bended knees.

My dear, you never have found Number Eighty-one Norfolk
Street Strand advertised in Bradshaw's *Railway Guide*, and

with the blessing of Heaven you never will or shall so find it. Some there are who do not think it lowering themselves to make their names that cheap, and even going the lengths of a portrait of the house not like it with a blot in every window and a coach and four at the door, but what will suit Wozenham's lower down on the other side of the way will not suit me, Miss Wozenham having her opinions and me having mine, though when it comes to systematic underbidding capable of being proved on oath in a court of justice and taking the form of " If Mrs. Lirriper names eighteen shillings a week, I name fifteen and six," it then comes to a settlement between yourself and your conscience, supposing for the sake of argument your name to be Wozenham, which I am well aware it is not or my opinion of you would be greatly lowered, and as to airy bedrooms and a night-porter in constant attendance the less said the better, the bedrooms being stuffy and the porter stuff.

It is forty years ago since me and my poor Lirriper got married at St. Clement's Danes, where I now have a sitting in a very pleasant pew with genteel company and my own hassock, and being partial to evening service not too crowded. My poor Lirriper was a handsome figure of a man, with a beaming eye and a voice as mellow as a musical instrument made of honey and steel, but he had ever been a free liver being in the commercial travelling line and travelling what he called a limekiln road—"a dry road, Emma my dear," my poor Lirriper says to me, "where I have to lay the dust with one drink or another all day long and half the night, and it wears me Emma"—and this led to his running through a good deal and might have run through the turnpike too when that dreadful horse that never would stand still for a single instant set off, but for its being night and the gate shut, and consequently took his wheel, my poor Lirriper and the gig smashed to atoms and never spoke afterwards. He was a handsome figure of a man, and a man with a jovial heart and a sweet temper; but if they had come up then they never could have given you the mellowness of his voice, and indeed I consider photographs wanting in mellowness as a general rule and making you look like a new-ploughed field.

My poor Lirriper being behindhand with the world and being buried at Hatfield church in Hertfordshire, not that it was his native place but that he had a liking for the

Salisbury Arms where we went upon our wedding-day and passed as happy a fortnight as ever happy was, I went round to the creditors and I says "Gentlemen I am acquainted with the fact that I am not answerable for my late husband's debts but I wish to pay them for I am his lawful wife and his good name is dear to me. I am going into the Lodgings gentlemen as a business and if I prosper every farthing that my late husband owed shall be paid for the sake of the love I bore him, by this right hand." It took a long time to do but it was done, and the silver cream-jug which is between ourselves and the bed and the mattress in my room upstairs (or it would have found legs so sure as ever the Furnished bill was up) being presented by the gentlemen engraved "To Mrs. Lirriper a mark of grateful respect for her honourable conduct" gave me a turn which was too much for my feelings, till Mr. Betley which at that time had the parlours and loved his joke says "Cheer up Mrs. Lirriper, you should feel as if it was only your christening and they were your godfathers and godmothers which did promise for you." And it brought me round, and I don't mind confessing to you my dear that I then put a sandwich and a drop of sherry in a little basket and went down to Hatfield churchyard outside the coach and kissed my hand and laid it with a kind of proud and swelling love on my husband's grave, though bless you it had taken me so long to clear his name that my wedding-ring was worn quite fine and smooth when I laid it on the green waving grass.

I am an old woman now and my good looks are gone but that's me my dear over the plate-warmer and considered like in the times when you used to pay two guineas on ivory and took your chance pretty much how you came out, which made you very careful how you left it about afterwards because people were turned so red and uncomfortable by mostly guessing it was somebody else quite different, and there was once a certain person that had put his money in a hop business that came in one morning to pay his rent and his respects being the second floor that would have taken it down from its hook and put it in his breast-pocket—you understand my dear—for the L, he says of the original—only there was no mellowness in *his* voice and I wouldn't let him, but his opinion of it you may gather from his saying to it "Speak to me Emma!" which was far from a rational observation no doubt but still a tribute to its being a likeness, and I think myself it *was* like me when I was young and wore that sort of stays.

But it was about the Lodgings that I was intending to hold forth and certainly I ought to know something of the business having been in it so long, for it was early in the second year of my married life that I lost my poor Lirriper and I set up at Islington directly afterwards and afterwards came here, being two houses and eight-and-thirty years and some losses and a deal of experience.

Girls are your first trial after fixtures and they try you even worse than what I call the Wandering Christians, though why *they* should roam the earth looking for bills and then coming in and viewing the apartments and stickling about terms and never at all wanting them or dreaming of taking them being already provided, is a mystery I should be thankful to have explained if by any miracle it could be. It's wonderful they live so long and thrive so on it but I suppose the exercise makes it healthy, knocking so much and going from house to house and up and down stairs all day, and then their pretending to be so particular and punctual is a most astonishing thing, looking at their watches and saying " Could you give me the refusal of the rooms till twenty minutes past eleven the day after to-morrow in the forenoon, and supposing it to be considered essential by my friend from the country could there be a small iron bedstead put in the little room upon the stairs ? " Why when I was new to it my dear I used to consider before I promised and to make my mind anxious with calculations and to get quite wearied out with disappointments, but now I says " Certainly by all means " well knowing it's a Wandering Christian and I shall hear no more about it, indeed by this time I know most of the Wandering Christians by sight as well as they know me, it being the habit of each individual revolving round London in that capacity to come back about twice a year, and it's very remarkable that it runs in families and the children grow up to it, but even were it otherwise I should no sooner hear of the friend from the country which is a certain sign than I should nod and say to myself You're a Wandering Christian, though whether they are (as I *have* heard) persons of small property with a taste for regular employment and frequent change of scene I cannot undertake to tell you.

Girls as I was beginning to remark are one of your first

and your lasting troubles, being like your teeth which begin
with convulsions and never cease tormenting you from the
time you cut them till they cut you, and then you don't
want to part with them which seems hard but we must all
succumb or buy artificial, and even where you get a will nine
times out of ten you'll get a dirty face with it and naturally
lodgers do not like good society to be shown in with a smear
of black across the nose or a smudgy eyebrow. Where they
pick the black up is a mystery I cannot solve, as in the case
of the willingest girl that ever came into a house half-starved
poor thing, a girl so willing that I called her Willing Sophy
down upon her knees scrubbing early and late and ever
cheerful but always smiling with a black face. And I says
to Sophy, "Now Sophy my good girl have a regular day for
your stoves and keep the width of the Airy between yourself
and the blacking and do not brush your hair with the
bottoms of the saucepans and do not meddle with the snuffs
of the candles and it stands to reason that it can no longer
be" yet there it was and always on her nose, which turning
up and being broad at the end seemed to boast of it and
caused warning from a steady gentleman and excellent lodger
with breakfast by the week but a little irritable and use of a
sitting-room when required, his words being "Mrs. Lirriper I
have arrived at the point of admitting that the Black is a man
and a brother, but only in a natural form and when it can't
be got off." Well consequently I put poor Sophy on to other
work and forbid her answering the door or answering a bell
on any account but she was so unfortunately willing that
nothing would stop her flying up the kitchen-stairs whenever
a bell was heard to tingle. I put it to her "O Sophy Sophy
for goodness' goodness' sake where does it come from?" To
which that poor unlucky willing mortal bursting out crying
to see me so vexed replied "I took a deal of black into me
ma'am when I was a small child being much neglected and I
think it must be, that it works out," so it continuing to work
out of that poor thing and not having another fault to find
with her I says "Sophy what do you seriously think of my
helping you away to New South Wales where it might not
be noticed?" Nor did I ever repent the money which was
well spent, for she married the ship's cook on the voyage
(himself a Mulotter) and did well and lived happy, and so
far as ever I heard it was *not* noticed in a new state of society
to her dying day.

In what way Miss Wozenham lower down on the other side of the way reconciled it to her feelings as a lady (which she is not) to entice Mary Anne Perkinsop from my service is best known to herself, I do not know and I do not wish to know how opinions are formed at Wozenham's on any point. But Mary Anne Perkinsop although I behaved handsomely to her and she behaved unhandsomely to me was worth her weight in gold as overawing lodgers without driving them away, for lodgers would be far more sparing of their bells with Mary Anne than I ever knew them to be with Maid or Mistress, which is a great triumph especially when accompanied with a cast in the eye and a bag of bones, but it was the steadiness of her way with them through her father's having failed in Pork. It was Mary Anne's looking so respectable in her person and being so strict in her spirits that conquered the tea-and-sugarest gentleman (for he weighed them both in a pair of scales every morning) that I have ever had to deal with and no lamb grew meeker, still it afterwards came round to me that Miss Wozenham happening to pass and seeing Mary Anne take in the milk of a milkman that made free in a rosy-faced way (I think no worse of him) with every girl in the street but was quite frozen up like the statue at Charing-cross by her, saw Mary Anne's value in the lodging business and went as high as one pound per quarter more, consequently Mary Anne with not a word betwixt us says "If *you* will provide yourself Mrs. Lirriper in a month from this day *I* have already done the same," which hurt me and I said so, and she then hurt me more by insinuating that her father having failed in Pork had laid her open to it.

My dear I do assure you it's a harassing thing to know what kind of girls to give the preference to, for if they are lively they get bell'd off their legs and if they are sluggish you suffer from it yourself in complaints and if they are sparkling-eyed they get made love to, and if they are smart in their persons they try on your Lodgers' bonnets and if they are musical I defy you to keep them away from bands and organs, and allowing for any difference you like in their heads their heads will be always out of window just the same. And then what the gentlemen like in girls the ladies don't, which is fruitful hot water for all parties, and then there's temper though such a temper as Caroline Maxey's I hope not often. A good-looking black-eyed girl was Caroline and a comely-made girl to your cost when she did break out and laid about her, as took place first and last through a new-married couple come to see London in the first floor and the lady very high and it *was* supposed not liking the good looks of Caroline having none of her own to spare, but anyhow she did try Caroline though that was no excuse. So one afternoon Caroline comes down into the kitchen flushed and flashing, and she says to me " Mrs. Lirriper that woman in the first has aggravated me past bearing," I says "Caroline keep your temper." Caroline says with a curdling laugh "Keep my temper? You're right Mrs. Lirriper, so I will. Capital D her!" bursts out Caroline (you might have struck me into the centre of the earth with a feather when she said it) "I'll give her a touch of the temper that *I* keep!" Caroline downs with her hair my dear, screeches and rushes upstairs, I following as fast as my trembling legs could bear me, but before I got into the room the dinner-cloth and pink-and-white service all dragged off upon the floor with a crash and the new-married couple on their backs in the firegrate, him with the shovel and tongs and a dish of cucumber across him and a mercy it was summer-time. "Caroline" I says " be calm," but she catches off my cap and tears it in her teeth as she passes me, then pounces on the new-married lady makes her a bundle of ribbons takes her by the two ears and knocks the back of her head upon the carpet Murder screaming all the time Policemen running down the street and Wozenham's windows (judge of my feelings when I came to know it) thrown up and Miss Wozenham calling out from the balcony with crocodile's tears " It's Mrs. Lirriper been overcharging somebody to madness —she'll be murdered—I always thought so—Pleeseman save her!" My dear four of them and Caroline behind the chiffoniere attacking with the poker and when disarmed prize-fighting with her double fists, and down and up and up and down and dreadful! But I couldn't bear to see the poor young creature roughly handled and her hair torn when they got the better of her, and I says "Gentlemen Policemen pray remember that her sex is the sex of your mothers and sisters and your sweethearts, and God bless them and you!" And there she was sitting down on the ground handcuffed, taking breath against the skirting-board and them cool with their coats in strips, and all she says was " Mrs. Lirriper I'm sorry as ever I touched *you*, for you're a kind motherly old

thing," and it made me think that I had often wished
I had been a mother indeed and how would my heart have
felt if I had been the mother of that girl! Well you know
it turned out at the Police-office that she had done it before,
and she had her clothes away and was sent to prison, and
when she was to come out I trotted off to the gate in the
evening with just a morsel of jelly in that little basket of
mine to give her a mite of strength to face the world again,
and there I met with a very decent mother waiting for her
son through bad company and a stubborn one he was with
his half-boots not laced. So out came Caroline and I says
"Caroline come along with me and sit down under the wall
where it's retired and eat a little trifle that I have brought
with me to do you good," and she throws her arms round
my neck and says sobbing "O why were you never a mother
when there are such mothers as there are?" she says, and in
half a minute more she begins to laugh and says "Did
I really tear your cap to shreds?" and when I told her
"You certainly did so Caroline" she laughed again and said
while she patted my face "Then why do you wear such
queer old caps you dear old thing? If you hadn't worn such
queer old caps I don't think I should have done it even
then." Fancy the girl! Nothing could get out of her what
she was going to do except O she would do well enough, and
we parted she being very thankful and kissing my hands,
and I nevermore saw or heard of that girl, except that I shall
always believe that a very genteel cap which was brought
anonymous to me one Saturday night in an oilskin basket
by a most impertinent young sparrow of a monkey whistling
with dirty shoes on the clean steps and playing the harp on
the Airy railings with a hoop-stick came from Caroline.

What you lay yourself open to my dear in the way of
being the object of uncharitable suspicions when you go into
the Lodging business I have not the words to tell you, but
never was I so dishonourable as to have two keys nor would
I willingly think it even of Miss Wozenham lower down on
the other side of the way sincerely hoping that it may not
be, though doubtless at the same time money cannot come
from nowhere and it is not reason to suppose that Bradshaws
put it in for love be it blotty as it may. It *is* a hardship
hurting to the feelings that Lodgers open their minds so wide
to the idea that you are trying to get the better of them
and shut their minds so close to the idea that they are

trying to get the better of you, but as Major Jackman says to me "I know the ways of this circular world Mrs. Lirriper, and that's one of 'em all round it" and many is the little ruffle in my mind that the Major has smoothed, for he is a clever man who has seen much. Dear dear, thirteen years have passed though it seems but yesterday since I was sitting with my glasses on at the open front parlour window one evening in August (the parlours being then vacant) reading yesterday's paper my eyes for print being poor though still I am thankful to say a long sight at a distance, when I hear a gentleman come posting across the road and up the street in a dreadful rage talking to himself in a fury and d'ing and c'ing somebody. "By George!" says he out loud and clutching his walking-stick, "I'll go to Mrs. Lirriper's. Which is Mrs. Lirriper's?" Then looking round and seeing me he flourishes his hat right off his head as if I had been the queen and he says, "Excuse the intrusion madam, but pray madam can you tell me at what number in this street there resides a well-known and much-respected lady by the name of Lirriper?" A little flustered though I must say gratified I took off my glasses and courtesied and said "Sir, Mrs. Lirriper is your humble servant." "Astonishing!" says he. "A million pardons! Madam, may I ask you to have the kindness to direct one of your domestics to open the door to a gentleman in search of apartments, by the name of Jackman?" I had never heard the name but a politer gentleman I never hope to see, for says he "Madam I am shocked at your opening the door yourself to no worthier a fellow than Jemmy Jackman. After you madam. I never precede a lady." Then he comes into the parlours and he sniffs, and he says "Hah! These are parlours! Not musty cupboards" he says "but parlours, and no smell of coal-sacks." Now my dear it having been remarked by some inimical to the whole neighbourhood that it always smells of coal-sacks which might prove a drawback to Lodgers if encouraged, I says to the Major gently though firmly that I think he is referring to Arundel or Surrey or Howard but not Norfolk. "Madam" says he "I refer to Wozenham's lower down over the way—madam you can form no notion what Wozenham's is—madam it is a vast coal-sack, and Miss Wozenham has the principles and manners of a female heaver—madam from the manner in which I have heard her mention you I know she has no appreciation of a lady, and from the

manner in which she has conducted herself towards me I
know she has no appreciation of a gentleman—madam my
name is Jackman—should you require any other reference
than what I have already said, I name the Bank of England
—perhaps you know it!" Such was the beginning of the
Major's occupying the parlours and from that hour to this
the same and a most obliging Lodger and punctual in all
respects except one irregular which I need not particularly
specify, but made up for by his being a protection and at
all times ready to fill in the papers of the Assessed Taxes
and Juries and that, and once collared a young man with the
drawing-room clock under his coat, and once on the parapets
with his own hands and blankets put out the kitchen chimney
and afterwards attending the summons made a most eloquent
speech against the Parish before the magistrates and saved
the engine, and ever quite the gentleman though passionate.
And certainly Miss Wozenham's detaining the trunks and
umbrella was not in a liberal spirit though it may have been
according to her rights in law or an act *I* would myself have
stooped to, the Major being so much the gentleman that
though he is far from tall he seems almost so when he has
his shirt-frill out and his frock-coat on and his hat with the
curly brims, and in what service he was I cannot truly tell
you my dear whether Militia or Foreign, for I never heard
him even name himself as Major but always simple "Jemmy
Jackman" and once soon after he came when I felt it my
duty to let him know that Miss Wozenham had put it
about that he was no Major and I took the liberty of adding
"which you are Sir" his words were "Madam at any rate I
am not a Minor, and sufficient for the day is the evil thereof"
which cannot be denied to be the sacred truth, nor yet his
military ways of having his boots with only the dirt brushed
off taken to him in the front parlour every morning on a
clean plate and varnishing them himself with a little sponge
and a saucer and a whistle in a whisper so sure as ever his
breakfast is ended, and so neat his ways that it never soils
his linen which is scrupulous though more in quality than
quantity, neither that nor his mustachios which to the best of
my belief are done at the same time and which are as black
and shining as his boots, his head of hair being a lovely white.

It was the third year nearly up of the Major's being in
the parlours that early one morning in the month of February
when Parliament was coming on and you may therefore

suppose a number of impostors were about ready to take hold of anything they could get, a gentleman and a lady from the country came in to view the Second, and I well remember that I had been looking out of window and had watched them and the heavy sleet driving down the street together looking for bills. I did not quite take to the face of the gentleman though he was good-looking too but the lady was a very pretty young thing and delicate, and it seemed too rough for her to be out at all though she had only come from the Adelphi Hotel which would not have been much above a quarter of a mile if the weather had been less severe. Now it did so happen my dear that I had been forced to put five shillings weekly additional on the Second in consequence of a loss from running away full dressed as if going out to a dinner-party, which was very artful and had made me rather suspicious taking it along with Parliament, so when the gentleman proposed three months certain and the money in advance and leave then reserved to renew on the same terms for six months more, I says I was not quite certain but that I might have engaged myself to another party but would step downstairs and look into it if they would take a seat. They took a seat and I went down to the handle of the Major's door that I had already began to consult finding it a great blessing, and I knew by his whistling in a whisper that he was varnishing his boots which was generally considered private, however he kindly calls out "If it's you, madam, come in," and I went in and told him.

"Well, madam," says the Major rubbing his nose—as I did fear at the moment with the black sponge but it was only his knuckle, he being always neat and dexterous with his fingers—"well, madam, I suppose you would be glad of the money?"

I was delicate of saying "Yes" too out, for a little extra colour rose into the Major's cheeks and there was irregularity which I will not particularly specify in a quarter which I will not name.

"I am of opinion, madam," says the Major "that when money is ready for you—when it is ready for you, Mrs. Lirriper—you ought to take it. What is there against it, madam, in this case upstairs?"

"I really cannot say there is anything against it, Sir, still I thought I would consult you."

"You said a newly-married couple, I think, madam?" says the Major.

I says "Ye-es. Evidently. And indeed the young lady mentioned to me in a casual way that she had not been married many months."

The Major rubbed his nose again and stirred the varnish round and round in its little saucer with his piece of sponge and took to his whistling in a whisper for a few moments. Then he says "You would call it a Good Let, madam?"

"O certainly a Good Let Sir."

"Say they renew for the additional six months. Would it put you about very much madam if—if the worst was to come to the worst?" said the Major.

"Well I hardly know," I says to the Major. "It depends upon circumstances. Would *you* object Sir for instance?"

"I?" says the Major. "Object? Jemmy Jackman? Mrs. Lirriper close with the proposal."

So I went upstairs and accepted, and they came in next day which was Saturday and the Major was so good as to draw up a Memorandum of an agreement in a beautiful round hand and expressions that sounded to me equally legal and military, and Mr. Edson signed it on the Monday morning and the Major called upon Mr. Edson on the Tuesday and Mr. Edson called upon the Major on the Wednesday and the Second and the parlours were as friendly as could be wished.

The three months paid for had run out and we had got without any fresh overtures as to payment into May my dear, when there came an obligation upon Mr. Edson to go a business expedition right across the Isle of Man, which fell quite unexpected upon that pretty little thing and is not a place that according to my views is particularly in the way to anywhere at any time but that may be a matter of opinion. So short a notice was it that he was to go next day, and dreadfully she cried poor pretty, and I am sure I cried too when I saw her on the cold pavement in the sharp east wind —it being a very backward spring that year—taking a last leave of him with her pretty bright hair blowing this way and that and her arms clinging round his neck and him saying "There there there. Now let me go Peggy." And by that time it was plain that what the Major had been so accommodating as to say he would not object to happening in the house, would happen in it, and I told her as much when he was gone while I comforted her with my arm up the staircase, for I says "You will soon have others to keep up for my pretty and you must think of that."

His letter never came when it ought to have come and what she went through morning after morning when the postman brought none for her the very postman himself compassionated when she ran down to the door, and yet we cannot wonder at its being calculated to blunt the feelings to have all the trouble of other people's letters and none of the pleasure and doing it oftener in the mud and mizzle than not and at a rate of wages more resembling Little Britain than Great. But at last one morning when she was too poorly to come running downstairs he says to me with a pleased look in his face that made me next to love the man in his uniform coat though he was dripping wet "I have taken you first in the street this morning Mrs. Lirriper, for here's the one for Mrs. Edson." I went up to her bedroom with it as fast as ever I could go, and she sat up in bed when she saw it and kissed it and tore it open and then a blank stare came upon her. "It's very short!" she says lifting her large eyes to my face. "O Mrs. Lirriper it's very short!" I says "My dear Mrs. Edson no doubt that's because your husband hadn't time to write more just at that time." "No doubt, no doubt," says she, and puts her two hands on her face and turns round in her bed.

I shut her softly in and I crept downstairs and I tapped at the Major's door, and when the Major having his thin slices of bacon in his own Dutch oven saw me he came out of his chair and put me down on the sofa. "Hush!" says he, "I see something's the matter. Don't speak—take time." I says "O Major I'm afraid there's cruel work upstairs." "Yes yes," says he "I had begun to be afraid of it—take time." And then in opposition to his own words he rages out frightfully, and says "I shall never forgive myself madam, that I, Jemmy Jackman, didn't see it all that morning—didn't go straight upstairs when my boot-sponge was in my hand—didn't force it down his throat—and choke him dead with it on the spot!"

The Major and me agreed when we came to ourselves that just at present we could do no more than take on to suspect nothing and use our best endeavours to keep that poor young creature quiet, and what I ever should have done without the Major when it got about among the organ-men that quiet was our object is unknown, for he made lion and tiger war upon them to that degree that without seeing it I could not have believed it was in any gentleman to have such a power of bursting out with fire-irons walking-sticks water-jugs coals potatoes off his table the very hat off his head, and at the same time so furious in foreign languages that they would stand with their handles half-turned fixed like the Sleeping Ugly—for I cannot say Beauty.

Ever to see the postman come near the house now gave me such a fear that it was a reprieve when he went by, but in about another ten days or a fortnight he says again, "Here's one for Mrs. Edson.—Is she pretty well?" "She is pretty well postman, but not well enough to rise so early as she used" which was so far gospel-truth.

I carried the letter in to the Major at his breakfast and I says tottering "Major I have not the courage to take it up to her."

"It's an ill-looking villain of a letter," says the Major.

"I have not the courage Major" I says again in a tremble "to take it up to her."

After seeming lost in consideration for some moments the Major says, raising his head as if something new and useful had occurred to his mind "Mrs. Lirriper, I shall never forgive myself that I, Jemmy Jackman, didn't go straight upstairs that morning when my boot-sponge was in my hand—and force it down his throat—and choke him dead with it."

"Major" I says a little hasty "you didn't do it which is a blessing, for it would have done no good and I think your sponge was better employed on your own honourable boots."

So we got to be rational, and planned that I should tap at her bedroom door and lay the letter on the mat outside and wait on the upper landing for what might happen, and never was gunpowder cannon-balls or shells or rockets more dreaded than that dreadful letter was by me as I took it to the second floor.

A terrible loud scream sounded through the house the minute after she had opened it, and I found her on the floor lying as if her life was gone. My dear I never looked at the face of the letter which was lying open by her, for there was no occasion.

Everything I needed to bring her round the Major brought up with his own hands, besides running out to the chemist's

for what was not in the house and likewise having the
fiercest of all his many skirmishes with a musical instrument representing a ball-room I do not know in what
particular country and company waltzing in and out at
folding-doors with rolling eyes.   When after a long time
I saw her coming to, I slipped on the landing till I heard
her cry, and then I went in and says cheerily "Mrs. Edson
you're not well my dear and it's not to be wondered at," as
if I had not been in before.   Whether she believed or dis-
believed I cannot say and it would signify nothing if I could,
but I stayed by her for hours and then she God ever blesses
me! and says she will try to rest for her head is bad.

"Major," I whispers, looking in at the parlours, "I beg
and pray of you don't go out."

The Major whispers, "Madam, trust me I will do no such
a thing.   How is she?"

I says "Major the good Lord above us only knows what
burns and rages in her poor mind.   I left her sitting at her
window.   I am going to sit at mine."

It came on afternoon and it came on evening.   Norfolk is
a delightful street to lodge in—provided you don't go lower
down—but of a summer evening when the dust and waste
paper lie in it and stray children play in it and a kind of a
gritty calm and bake settles on it and a peal of church-
bells is practising in the neighbourhood it is a trifle dull,
and never have I seen it since at such a time and never
shall I see it evermore at such a time without seeing the
dull June evening when that forlorn young creature sat at
her open corner window on the Second and me at my open
corner window (the other corner) on the Third.   Something
merciful, something wiser and better far than my own self,
had moved me while it was yet light to sit in my bonnet
and shawl, and as the shadows fell and the tide rose I
could sometimes—when I put out my head and looked at
her window below—see that she leaned out a little looking
down the street.   It was just settling dark when I saw *her*
in the street.

So fearful of losing sight of her that it almost stops my
breath while I tell it, I went downstairs faster than I ever
moved in all my life and only tapped with my hand at the
Major's door in passing it and slipping out.   She was gone
already.   I made the same speed down the street and when
I came to the corner of Howard-street I saw that she had

turned it and was there plain before me going towards the west. O with what a thankful heart I saw her going along!

She was quite unacquainted with London and had very seldom been out for more than an airing in our own street where she knew two or three little children belonging to neighbours and had sometimes stood among them at the street looking at the water. She must be going at hazard I knew, still she kept the bye-streets quite correctly as long as they would serve her, and then turned up into the Strand. But at every corner I could see her head turned one way, and that way was always the river way.

It may have been only the darkness and quiet of the Adelphi that caused her to strike into it but she struck into it much as readily as if she had set out to go there, which perhaps was the case. She went straight down to the Terrace and along it and looked over the iron rail, and I often woke afterwards in my own bed with the horror of seeing her do it. The desertion of the wharf below and the flowing of the high water there seemed to settle her purpose. She looked about as if to make out the way down, and she struck out the right way or the wrong way—I don't know which, for I don't know the place before or since—and I followed her the way she went.

It was noticeable that all this time she never once looked back. But there was now a great change in the manner of her going, and instead of going at a steady quick walk with her arms folded before her,—among the dark dismal arches she went in a wild way with her arms opened wide, as if they were wings and she was flying to her death.

We were on the wharf and she stopped. I stopped. I saw her hands at her bonnet-strings, and I rushed between her and the brink and took her round the waist with both my arms. She might have drowned me, I felt then, but she could never have got quit of me.

Down to that moment my mind had been all in a maze and not half an idea had I had in it what I should say to her, but the instant I touched her it came to me like magic and I had my natural voice and my senses and even almost my breath.

"Mrs. Edson!" I says "My dear! Take care. How ever did you lose your way and stumble on a dangerous place like this? Why you must have come here by the most perplexing streets in all London. No wonder you are lost, I'm sure.

Mrs. Lirriper's Lodgings

And this place too! Why I thought nobody ever got here, except me to order my coals and the Major in the parlours to smoke his cigar!"—for I saw that blessed man close by, pretending to it.

"Hah—Hah—Hum!" coughs the Major.

"And good gracious me" I says, "why here he is!"

"Halloa! who goes there?" says the Major in a military manner.

"Well!" I says, "if this don't beat everything! Don't you know us Major Jackman?"

"Halloa!" says the Major. "Who calls on Jemmy Jackman?" (and more out of breath he was, and did it less like life than I should have expected.)

"Why here's Mrs. Edson Major" I says, "strolling out to cool her poor head which has been very bad, has missed her way and got lost, and Goodness knows where she might have got to but for me coming here to drop an order into my coal merchant's letter-box and you coming here to smoke your cigar!—And you really are not well enough my dear" I says to her "to be half so far from home without me.—And your arm will be very acceptable I am sure Major" I says to him "and I know she may lean upon it as heavy as she likes." And now we had both got her—thanks be Above! —one on each side.

She was all in a cold shiver and she so continued till I laid her on her own bed, and up to the early morning she held me by the hand and moaned and moaned "O wicked, wicked, wicked!" But when at last I made believe to droop my head and be overpowered with a dead sleep, I heard that poor young creature give such touching and such humble thanks for being preserved from taking her own life in her madness that I thought I should have cried my eyes out on the counterpane and I knew she was safe.

Being well enough to do and able to afford it, me and the Major laid our little plans next day while she was asleep worn out, and so I says to her as soon as I could do it nicely: "Mrs. Edson my dear, when Mr. Edson paid me the rent for these farther six months——"

She gave a start and I felt her large eyes look at me, but I went on with it and with my needlework.

"—I can't say that I am quite sure I dated the receipt right. Could you let me look at it?"

She laid her frozen cold hand upon mine and she looked

through me when I was forced to look up from my needlework, but I had taken the precaution of having on my
spectacles.

"I have no receipt" says she.

"Ah! Then he has got it" I says in a careless way.
"It's of no great consequence.   A rec ipt's a receipt."

From that time she always had hold of my hand when I
could spare it which was generally only when I read to her,
for of course she and me had our bits of needlework to plod
at and neither of us was very handy at those little things,
though I am still rather proud of my share in them too
considering.   And though she took to all I read to her, I
used to fancy that next to what was taught upon the Mount
she took most of all to His gentle compassion for us poor
women and to His young life and to how His mother was
proud of Him and treasured His sayings in her heart.   She
had a grateful look in her eyes that never never never will
be out of mine until they are closed in my last sleep, and
when I chanced to look at her without thinking of it I would
always meet that look, and she would often offer me her
trembling lip to kiss, much more like a little affectionate half-
brokenhearted child than ever I can imagine any grown
person.

One time the trembling of this poor lip was so strong and
her tears ran down so fast that I thought she was going to
tell me all her woe, so I takes her two hands in mine and
I says:

"No my dear not now, you had best not try to do it now.
Wait for better times when you have got over this and
are strong, and then you shall tell me whatever you will.
Shall it be agreed?"

With our hands still joined she nodded her head many
times, and she lifted my hands and put them to her lips
and to her bosom.

"Only one word now my dear" I says.   "Is there any
one?"

She looked inquiringly "Any one?"

"That I can go to?"

She shook her head.

"No one that I can bring?"

She shook her head.

"No one is wanted by *me* my dear.   Now that may be considered past and gone."

Not much more than a week afterwards—for this was far on in the time of our being so together—I was bending over at her bedside with my ear down to her lips, by turns listening for her breath and looking for a sign of life in her face. At last it came in a solemn way—not in a flash but like a kind of pale faint light brought very slow to the face.

She said something to me that had no sound in it, but I saw she asked me:

"Is this death?"

And I says:

"Poor dear poor dear, I think it is."

Knowing somehow that she wanted me to move her weak right hand, I took it and laid it on her breast and then folded her other hand upon it, and she prayed a good good prayer and I joined in it poor me though there were no words spoke. Then I brought the baby in its wrappers from where it lay, and I says:

"My dear this is sent to a childless old woman. This is for me to take care of."

The trembling lip was put up towards my face for the last time, and I dearly kissed it.

"Yes my dear," I says. "Please God! Me and the Major."

I don't know how to tell it right, but I saw her soul brighten and leap up, and get free and fly away in the grateful look.

*　　*　　*　　*　　*　　*

So this is the why and wherefore of its coming to pass my dear that we called him Jemmy, being after the Major his own godfather with Lirriper for a surname being after myself, and never was a dear child such a brightening thing in a Lodgings or such a playmate to his grandmother as Jemmy to this house and me, and always good and minding what he was told (upon the whole) and soothing for the temper and making everything pleasanter except when he grew old enough to drop his cap down Wozenham's Airy and they wouldn't hand it up to him, and being worked into a state I put on my best bonnet and gloves and parasol with the child in my hand and I says "Miss Wozenham I little thought ever to have entered *your* house but unless my grandson's cap is instantly restored, the laws of this country regulating the property of the Subject shall at length decide betwixt yourself and me, cost what it may." With a sneer upon her face which did strike me I must say as being expressive of two keys but it may have been a mistake and if there is any doubt let Miss Wozenham have the full benefit of it as is but right, she rang the bell and she says "Jane, is there a street-child's old cap down our Airy?" I says "Miss Wozenham before your housemaid answers that question you must allow me to inform you to your face that my grandson is *not* a street-child and is *not* in the habit of wearing old caps. In fact" I says "Miss Wozenham I am far from sure that my grandson's cap may not be newer than your own" which was perfectly savage in me, her lace being the commonest machine-make washed and torn besides, but I had been put into a state to begin with fomented by impertinence. Miss Wozenham says red in the face "Jane you heard my question, is there any child's cap down our Airy?" "Yes ma'am" says Jane "I think I did see some such rubbish a-lying there." "Then" says Miss Wozenham "let these visitors out, and then throw up that worthless article out of my premises." But here the child who had been staring at Miss Wozenham with all his eyes and more, frowns down his little eyebrows purses up his little mouth puts his chubby legs far apart turns his little dimpled fists round and round slowly over one another like a little coffee-mill, and says to her "Oo impdent to mi Gran, me tut oor hi!" "O!" says Miss Wozenham looking down scornfully at the Mite "this is not a street-child is it not? Really!" I bursts out laughing and I says "Miss Wozenham if this ain't a pretty sight to you I don't envy your feelings and I wish you good-day. Jemmy come along with Gran." And I was still in the best of humours though his cap came flying up into the street as if it had been just turned on out of the water-plug, and I went home laughing all the way, all owing to that dear boy.

The miles and miles that me and the Major have travelled with Jemmy in the dusk between the lights are not to be calculated, Jemmy driving on the coach-box which is the Major's brass-bound writing desk on the table, me inside in the easy-chair and the Major Guard up behind with a brown-paper horn doing it really wonderful. I do assure you my dear that sometimes when I have taken a few winks in my place inside the coach and have come half awake by the flashing light of the fire and have heard that precious pet driving and the Major blowing up behind to have the change of horses ready when we got to the Inn, I have half believed we were on the old North Road that my poor Lirriper knew so well. Then to see that child and the Major both wrapped up getting down to warm their feet and going stamping about and having glasses of ale out of the paper match-boxes on the chimney-piece is to see the Major enjoying it fully as much as the child I am very sure, and it's equal to any play when Coachee opens the coach-door to look in at me inside and say "Wery 'past that 'tage.—'Prightened old lady?"

But what my inexpressible feelings were when we lost that child can only be compared to the Major's which were not a shade better, through his straying out at five years old and eleven o'clock in the forenoon and never heard of by word or sign or deed till half-past nine at night, when the Major had gone to the Editor of the *Times* newspaper to put in an advertisement, which came out next day four-and-twenty hours after he was found, and which I mean always carefully to keep in my lavender drawer as the first printed account of him. The more the day got on, the more I got distracted and the Major too and both of us made worse by the composed ways of the police though very civil and obliging and what I must call their obstinacy in not entertaining the idea that he was stolen. "We mostly find mum" says the sergeant who came round to comfort me, which he didn't at all and he had been one of the private constables in Caroline's time to which he referred in his opening words when he said "Don't give way to uneasiness in your mind mum, it'll all come as right as my nose did when I got the same barked by that young woman in your second floor"—says this sergeant "we mostly find mum as people ain't over-anxious to have what I may call second-hand children. *You'll* get him back mum." "O but my dear good Sir" I says clasping my hands and wringing them and clasping them again "he is such an uncommon child!" "Yes mum" says the sergeant, "we mostly find that too mum. The question is what his clothes were worth." "His clothes" I says "were not worth much Sir for he had only got his playing-dress on, but the dear child!—" "All right mum" says the sergeant. "*You'll* get him back mum. And even if he'd had his best clothes on, it wouldn't come to worse than his being found wrapped up in a cabbage-leaf, a shivering in a lane." His words pierced my heart like daggers and daggers, and me and the Major ran in and out like wild things all day long till the Major returning from his interview with the Editor of the *Times* at night rushes into my little room hysterical and squeezes my hand and wipes his eyes and says " Joy joy—officer in plain clothes came up on the steps as I was letting myself in—compose your feelings— Jemmy's found."   Consequently I fainted away and when I came to, embraced the legs of the officer in plain clothes who seemed to be taking a kind of a quiet inventory in his mind of the property in my little room with brown whiskers, and I says " Blessings on you Sir where is the Darling ? " and he says " In Kennington Station House."   I was dropping at his feet Stone at the image of that Innocence in cells with mur- derers when he adds " He followed the Monkey."   I says deeming it slang language " O Sir explain for a loving grand- mother what Monkey ! "   He says " Him in the spangled cap with the strap under the chin, as won't keep on— him as sweeps the crossings on a round table and don't want to draw his sabre more than he can help."   Then I understood it all and most thankfully thanked him, and me and the Major and him drove over to Kennington and there we found our boy lying quite comfortable before a blazing fire having sweetly played himself to sleep upon a small accordion nothing like so big as a flat-iron which they had been so kind to lend him for the purpose and which it appeared had been stopped upon a very young person.

My dear the system upon which the Major commenced and as I may say perfected Jemmy's learning when he was so small that if the dear was on the other side of the table you had to look under it instead of over it to see him with his mother's own bright hair in beautiful curls, is a thing that ought to be known to the Throne and Lords and Commons and then might obtain some promotion for the Major which he well deserves and would be none the worse for (speaking between friends) L. S. D.-ically.   When the Major first under- took his learning he says to me :

" I'm going madam," he says " to make our child a Calcu- lating Boy."

" Major," I says, " you terrify me and may do the pet a permanent injury you would never forgive yourself."

" Madam," says the Major, " next to my regret that when I had my boot-sponge in my hand, I didn't choke that scoundrel with it—on the spot——"

" There !   For Gracious' sake," I interrupts, " let his con- science find him without sponges."

" —I say next to that regret, madam," says the Major

"would be the regret with which my breast," which he tapped, "would be surcharged if this fine mind was not early cultivated. But mark me madam," says the Major holding up his forefinger "cultivated on a principle that will make it a delight."

"Major" I says "I will be candid with you and tell you openly that if ever I find the dear child fall off in his appetite I shall know it is his calculations and shall put a stop to them at two minutes' notice. Or if I find them mounting to his head" I says, "or striking anyways cold to his stomach or leading to anything approaching flabbiness in his legs, the result will be the same, but Major you are a clever man and have seen much and you love the child and are his own godfather, and if you feel a confidence in trying try."

"Spoken madam" says the Major "like Emma Lirriper. All I have to ask, madam, is that you will leave my godson and myself to make a week or two's preparations for surprising you, and that you will give me leave to have up and down any small articles not actually in use that I may require from the kitchen."

"From the kitchen Major?" I says half feeling as if he had a mind to cook the child.

"From the kitchen" says the Major, and smiles and swells, and at the same time looks taller.

So I passed my word and the Major and the dear boy were shut up together for half an hour at a time through a certain while, and never could I hear anything going on betwixt them but talking and laughing and Jemmy clapping his hands and screaming out numbers, so I says to myself "it has not harmed him yet" nor could I on examining the dear find any signs of it anywhere about him which was likewise a great relief. At last one day Jemmy brings me a card in joke in the Major's neat writing "The Messrs. Jemmy Jackman" for we had given him the Major's other name too "request the honour of Mrs. Lirriper's company at the Jackman Institution in the front parlour this evening at five, military time, to witness a few slight feats of elementary arithmetic." And if you'll believe me there in the front parlour at five punctual to the moment was the Major behind the Pembroke table with both leaves up and a lot of things from the kitchen tidily set out on old newspapers spread atop of it, and there was the Mite stood up on a chair with his rosy cheeks flushing and his eyes sparkling clusters of diamonds.

"Now Gran" says he, " oo tit down and don't oo touch ler poople "—for he saw with every one of those diamonds of his that I was going to give him a squeeze.

"Very well Sir" I says "I am obedient in this good company I am sure." And I sits down in the easy-chair that was put for me, shaking my sides.

But picture my admiration when the Major going on almost as quick as if he was conjuring sets out all the articles he names, and says "Three saucepans, an Italian iron, a hand-bell, a toasting-fork, a nutmeg-grater, four potlids, a spice-box, two egg-cups, and a chopping-board—how many ? " and when that Mite instantly cries " Tifteen, tut down tive and carry ler 'toppin-board " and then claps his hands draws up his legs and dances on his chair.

My dear with the same astonishing ease and correctness him and the Major added up the tables chairs and sofy, the picters fenders and fire-irons their own selves me and the cat and the eyes in Miss Wozenham's head, and whenever the sum was done Young Roses and Diamonds claps his hands and draws up his legs and dances on his chair.

The pride of the Major ! (" *Here's* a mind ma'am ! " he says to me behind his hand.)

Then he says aloud, " We now come to the next elementary rule,—which is called—— "

"Umtraction ! " cries Jemmy.

"Right," says the Major. " We have here a toasting-fork, a potato in its natural state, two potlids, one egg-cup, a wooden spoon, and two skewers, from which it is necessary for commercial purposes to subtract a sprat-gridiron, a small pickle-jar, two lemons, one pepper-castor, a blackbeetle-trap, and a knob of the dresser-drawer—what remains ? "

"Toatin-fork ! " cries Jemmy.

"In numbers how many ? " says the Major.

"One ! " cries Jemmy.

(" *Here's* a boy, ma'am ! " says the Major to me behind his hand.)

Then the Major goes on :

"We now approach the next elementary rule,—which is entitled—— "

"Tickleication " cries Jemmy.

" Correct " says the Major.

But my dear to relate to you in detail the way in which they multiplied fourteen sticks of firewood by two bits of

ginger and a larding-needle, or divided pretty well everything
else there was on the table by the heater of the Italian iron
and a chamber candlestick, and got a lemon over, would make
my head spin round and round and round as it did at the
time.   So I says "if you'll excuse my addressing the chair
Professor Jackman I think the period of the lecture has now
arrived when it becomes necessary that I should take a good
hug of this young scholar." Upon which Jemmy calls out
from his station on the chair, "Gran oo open oor arms and
me'll make a 'pring into 'em." So I opened my arms to him
as I had opened my sorrowful heart when his poor young
mother lay a dying, and he had his jump and we had a good
long hug together and the Major prouder than any peacock
says to me behind his hand, "You need not let him know it
madam" (which I certainly need not for the Major was quite
audible) "but he is a boy!"

In this way Jemmy grew and grew and went to day-school
and continued under the Major too, and in summer we were
as happy as the days were long, and in winter we were as
happy as the days were short and there seemed to rest a
Blessing on the Lodgings for they as good as Let themselves
and would have done it if there had been twice the accommodation, when sore and hard against my will I one day says
to the Major:

"Major you know what I am going to break to you.   Our
boy must go to boarding-school."

It was a sad sight to see the Major's countenance drop, and
I pitied the good soul with all my heart.

"Yes Major" I says, "though he is as popular with the
Lodgers as you are yourself and though he is to you and me
what only you and me know, still it is in the course of things
and Life is made of partings and we must part with our
Pet."

Bold as I spoke, I saw two Majors and half-a-dozen fire-
places, and when the poor Major put one of his neat bright-
varnished boots upon the fender and his elbow on his knee and
his head upon his hand and rocked himself a little to and fro,
I was dreadfully cut up.

"But" says I clearing my throat "you have so well prepared him Major—he has had such a Tutor in you—that he
will have none of the first drudgery to go through.   And he
is so clever besides that he'll soon make his way to the front
rank."

"He is a boy" says the Major—having sniffed—"that has not his like on the face of the earth."

"True as you say Major, and it is not for us merely for our own sakes to do anything to keep him back from being a credit and an ornament wherever he goes and perhaps even rising to be a great man, is it Major? He will have all my little savings when my work is done (being all the world to me) and we must try to make him a wise man and a good man, mustn't we Major?"

"Madam" says the Major rising "Jemmy Jackman is becoming an older file than I was aware of, and you put him to shame. You are thoroughly right madam. You are simply and undeniably right.—And if you'll excuse me, I'll take a walk."

So the Major being gone out and Jemmy being at home, I got the child into my little room here and I stood him by my chair and I took his mother's own curls in my hand and I spoke to him loving and serious. And when I had reminded the darling how that he was now in his tenth year and when I had said to him about his getting on in life pretty much what I had said to the Major I broke to him how that we must have this same parting, and there I was forced to stop for there I saw of a sudden the well-remembered lip with its tremble, and it so brought back that time! But with the spirit that was in him he controlled it soon and he says gravely nodding through his tears, "I understand Gran—I know it *must* be, Gran,—go on Gran, don't be afraid of *me*." And when I had said all that ever I could think of, he turned his bright steady face to mine and he says just a little broken here and there "You shall see Gran that I can be a man and that I can do anything that is grateful and loving to you—and if I don't grow up to be what you would like to have me—I hope it will be—because I shall die." And with that he sat down by me and I went on to tell him of the school of which I had excellent recommendations and where it was and how many scholars and what games they played as I had heard and what length of holidays, to all of which he listened bright and clear. And so it came that at last he says "And now dear Gran let me kneel down here where I have been used to say my prayers and let me fold my face for just a minute in your gown and let me cry, for you have been more than father—more than mother—more than brothers sisters friends—to me!" And so he did cry and I too and we were both much the better for it.

From that time forth he was true to his word and ever blithe and ready, and even when me and the Major took him down into Lincolnshire he was far the gayest of the party though for sure and certain he might easily have been that, but he really was and put life into us only when it came to the last Good-bye, he says with a wistful look, "You wouldn't have me not really sorry would you Gran?" and when I says "No dear, Lord forbid!" he says "I am glad of that!" and ran in out of sight.

But now that the child was gone out of the Lodgings the Major fell into a regularly moping state. It was taken notice of by all the Lodgers that the Major moped. He hadn't even the same air of being rather tall that he used to have, and if he varnished his boots with a single gleam of interest it was as much as he did.

One evening the Major came into my little room to take a cup of tea and a morsel of buttered toast and to read Jemmy's newest letter which had arrived that afternoon (by the very same postman more than middle-aged upon the Beat now), and the letter raising him up a little I says to the Major:

"Major you mustn't get into a moping way."

The Major shook his head. "Jemmy Jackman madam," he says with a deep sigh, "is an older file than I thought him."

"Moping is not the way to grow younger Major."

"My dear madam," says the Major, "is there *any* way of growing younger?"

Feeling that the Major was getting rather the best of that point I made a diversion to another.

"Thirteen years! Thir-teen years! Many Lodgers have come and gone, in the thirteen years that you have lived in the parlours Major."

"Hah!" says the Major warming. "Many madam, many."

"And I should say you have been familiar with them all?"

"As a rule (with its exceptions like all rules) my dear madam" says the Major, "they have honoured me with their acquaintance, and not unfrequently with their confidence."

Watching the Major as he drooped his white head and stroked his black mustachios and moped again, a thought which I think must have been going about looking for an

owner somewhere dropped into my old noddle if you will
excuse the expression.

"The walls of my Lodgings" I says in a casual way—for
my dear it is of no use going straight at a man who mopes—
"might have something to tell if they could tell it."

The Major neither moved nor said anything but I saw he
was attending with his shoulders my dear—attending with his
shoulders to what I said. In fact I saw that his shoulders
were struck by it.

"The dear boy was always fond of story-books" I went on,
like as if I was talking to myself. "I am sure this house—
his own home—might write a story or two for his reading
one day or another."

The Major's shoulders gave a dip and a curve and his
head came up in his shirt-collar. The Major's head came up
in his shirt-collar as I hadn't seen it come up since Jemmy
went to school.

"It is unquestionable that in intervals of cribbage and a
friendly rubber, my dear madam," says the Major, "and also
over what used to be called in my young times—in the salad
days of Jemmy Jackman—the social glass, I have exchanged
many a reminiscence with your Lodgers."

My remark was—I confess I made it with the deepest and
artfullest of intentions—"I wish our dear boy had heard
them!"

"Are you serious madam?" asks the Major starting and
turning full round.

"Why not Major?"

"Madam" says the Major, turning up one of his cuffs,
"they shall be written for him."

"Ah! Now you speak" I says giving my hands a pleased
clap. "Now you are in a way out of moping Major!"

"Between this and my holidays—I mean the dear boy's"
says the Major turning up his other cuff, "a good deal may
be done towards it."

"Major you are a clever man and you have seen much
and not a doubt of it."

"I'll begin," says the Major looking as tall as ever he did,
"to-morrow."

My dear the Major was another man in three days and he
was himself again in a week and he wrote and wrote and
wrote with his pen scratching like rats behind the wainscot,
and whether he had many grounds to go upon or whether he

did at all romance I cannot tell you, but what he has written is in the left-hand glass closet of the little bookcase close behind you.

CHAPTER II

HOW THE PARLOURS ADDED A FEW WORDS

I HAVE the honour of presenting myself by the name of Jackman. I esteem it a proud privilege to go down to posterity through the instrumentality of the most remarkable boy that ever lived,— by the name of JEMMY JACKMAN LIRRIPER, —and of my worthy and most highly respected friend, Mrs. Emma Lirriper, of Eighty-one, Norfolk Street, Strand, in the County of Middlesex, in the United Kingdom of Great Britain and Ireland.

It is not for me to express the rapture with which we received that dear and eminently remarkable boy, on the occurrence of his first Christmas holidays. Suffice it to observe that when he came flying into the house with two splendid prizes (Arithmetic, and Exemplary Conduct), Mrs. Lirriper and myself embraced with emotion, and instantly took him to the Play, where we were all three admirably entertained.

Nor is it to render homage to the virtues of the best of her good and honoured sex—whom, in deference to her unassuming worth, I will only here designate by the initials E. L.—that I add this record to the bundle of papers with which our, in a most distinguished degree, remarkable boy has expressed himself delighted, before reconsigning the same to the left-hand glass closet of Mrs. Lirriper's little bookcase.

Neither is it to obtrude the name of the old original superannuated obscure Jemmy Jackman, once (to his degradation) of Wozenham's, long (to his elevation) of Lirriper's. If I could be consciously guilty of that piece of bad taste, it would indeed be a work of supererogation, now that the name is borne by JEMMY JACKMAN LIRRIPER.

No, I take up my humble pen to register a little record of our strikingly remarkable boy, which my poor capacity regards as presenting a pleasant little picture of the dear boy's mind.   The picture may be interesting to himself when he is a man.

Our first reunited Christmas-day was the most delightful one we have ever passed together. ' Jemmy was never silent for five minutes, except in church-time.   He talked as we sat by the fire, he talked when we were out walking, he talked as we sat by the fire again, he talked incessantly at dinner, though he made a dinner almost as remarkable as himself. It was the spring of happiness in his fresh young heart flowing and flowing, and it fertilised (if I may be allowed so bold a figure) my much-esteemed friend, and J. J. the present writer.

There were only we three.   We dined in my esteemed friend's little room, and our entertainment was perfect.   But everything in the establishment is, in neatness, order, and comfort, always perfect.   After dinner our boy slipped away to his old stool at my esteemed friend's knee, and there, with his hot chestnuts and his glass of brown sherry (really, a most excellent wine!) on a chair for a table, his face outshone the apples in the dish.

We talked of these jottings of mine, which Jemmy had read through and through by that time; and so it came about that my esteemed friend remarked, as she sat smoothing Jemmy's curls:

"And as you belong to the house too, Jemmy,—and so much more than the Lodgers, having been born in it,—why, your story ought to be added to the rest, I think, one of these days."

Jemmy's eyes sparkled at this, and he said, "So I think, Gran."

Then he sat looking at the fire, and then he began to laugh in a sort of confidence with the fire, and then he said, folding his arms across my esteemed friend's lap, and raising his bright face to hers: "Would you like to hear a boy's story, Gran?"

"Of all things," replied my esteemed friend.

"Would you, godfather?"

"Of all things," I too replied.

"Well, then," said Jemmy, "I'll tell you one."

Here our indisputably remarkable boy gave himself a hug, and laughed again, musically, at the idea of his coming out in that new line.   Then he once more took the fire into the same sort of confidence as before, and began:

"Once upon a time, When pigs drank wine, And monkeys chewed tobaccer, 'Twas neither in your time nor mine, But that's no macker——"

"Bless the child!" cried my esteemed friend, "what's amiss with his brain?"

"It's poetry, Gran," returned Jemmy, shouting with laughter. "We always begin stories that way at school."

"Gave me quite a turn, Major," said my esteemed friend, fanning herself with a plate. "Thought he was light-headed!"

"In those remarkable times, Gran and godfather, there was once a boy,—not me, you know."

"No, no," says my respected friend, "not you. Not him, Major, you understand?"

"No, no," says I.

"And he went to school in Rutlandshire——"

"Why not Lincolnshire?" says my respected friend.

"Why not, you dear old Gran? Because *I* go to school in Lincolnshire, don't I?"

"Ah, to be sure!" says my respected friend. "And it's not Jemmy, you understand, Major?"

"No, no," says I.

"Well!" our boy proceeded, hugging himself comfortably, and laughing merrily (again in confidence with the fire), before he again looked up in Mrs. Lirriper's face, "and so he was tremendously in love with his schoolmaster's daughter, and she was the most beautiful creature that ever was seen, and she had brown eyes, and she had brown hair all curling beautifully, and she had a delicious voice, and she was delicious altogether, and her name was Seraphina."

"What's the name of *your* schoolmaster's daughter, Jemmy?" asks my respected friend.

"Polly!" replied Jemmy, pointing his forefinger at her. "There now! Caught you! Ha, ha, ha!"

When he and my respected friend had had a laugh and a hug together, our admittedly remarkable boy resumed with a great relish:

"Well! And so he loved her. And so he thought about her, and dreamed about her, and made her presents of oranges and nuts, and would have made her presents of pearls and diamonds if he could have afforded it out of his pocket-money, but he couldn't. And so her father—O, he WAS a Tartar! Keeping the boys up to the mark, holding examinations once a month, lecturing upon all sorts of subjects at all sorts of times, and knowing everything in the world out of book.   And so this boy——"

"Had he any name?" asks my respected friend.

"No, he hadn't, Gran. Ha, ha! There now! Caught you again!"

After this, they had another laugh and another hug, and then our boy went on.

"Well! And so this boy, he had a friend about as old as himself at the same school, and his name (for He *had* a name, as it happened) was—let me remember—was Bobbo."

"Not Bob," says my respected friend.

"Of course not," says Jemmy.   "What made you think it was, Gran?   Well! And so this friend was the cleverest and bravest and best-looking and most generous of all the friends that ever were, and so he was in love with Seraphina's sister, and so Seraphina's sister was in love with him, and so they all grew up."

"Bless us!" says my respected friend.   "They were very sudden about it."

"So they all grew up," our boy repeated, laughing heartily, "and Bobbo and this boy went away together on horseback to seek their fortunes, and they partly got their horses by favour, and partly in a bargain; that is to say, they had saved up between them seven and fourpence, and the two horses, being Arabs, were worth more, only the man said he would take that, to favour them.   Well! And so they made their fortunes and came prancing back to the school, with their pockets full of gold, enough to last for ever.   And so they rang at the parents' and visitors' bell (not the back gate), and when the bell was answered they proclaimed 'The same as if it was scarlet fever!   Every boy goes home for an indefinite period!'   And then there was great hurrahing, and then they kissed Seraphina and her sister,—each his own love, and not the other's on any account,—and then they ordered the Tartar into instant confinement."

"Poor man!" said my respected friend.

"Into instant confinement, Gran," repeated Jemmy, trying to look severe and roaring with laughter; "and he was to have nothing to eat but the boys' dinners, and was to drink half a cask of their beer every day.   And so then the preparations were made for the two weddings, and there were hampers, and potted things, and sweet things, and nuts, and postage-stamps, and all manner of things.   And so they were so jolly, that they let the Tartar out, and he was jolly too."

"I am glad they let him out," says my respected friend, "because he had only done his duty."

"O, but hadn't he overdone it, though!" cried Jemmy. "Well! And so then this boy mounted his horse, with his bride in his arms, and cantered away, and cantered on and on till he came to a certain place where he had a certain Gran and a certain godfather,—not you two, you know."

"No, no," we both said.

"And there he was received with great rejoicings, and he filled the cupboard and the bookcase with gold, and he showered it out on his Gran and his godfather because they were the two kindest and dearest people that ever lived in this world. And so while they were sitting up to their knees in gold, a knocking was heard at the street door, and who should it be but Bobbo, also on horseback with his bride in his arms, and what had he come to say but that he would take (at double rent) all the Lodgings for ever, that were not wanted by this boy and this Gran and this godfather, and that they would all live together, and all be happy! And so they were, and so it never ended!"

"And was there no quarrelling?" asked my respected friend, as Jemmy sat upon her lap and hugged her.

"No! Nobody ever quarrelled."

"And did the money never melt away?"

"No! Nobody could ever spend it all."

"And did none of them ever grow older?"

"No! Nobody ever grew older after that."

"And did none of them ever die?"

"O, no, no, no, Gran!" exclaimed our dear boy, laying his cheek upon her breast, and drawing her closer to him. "Nobody ever died."

"Ah, Major, Major!" says my respected friend, smiling benignly upon me, "this beats our stories. Let us end with the Boy's story, Major, for the Boy's story is the best that is ever told!"

In submission to which request on the part of the best of women, I have here noted it down as faithfully as my best abilities, coupled with my best intentions, would admit, subscribing it with my name,

J. JACKMAN.

The Parlours.
Mrs. Lirriper's Lodgings.

MRS. LIRRIPER'S LEGACY

[1864]

CHARACTERS

MR. BUFFLE, *a collector of assessed taxes, of disagreeable official manners.*

MRS. BUFFLE, *his wife; a woman who gives herself important airs.*

MISS ROBINA BUFFLE, *their daughter; a thin young lady.*

MR. EDSON, *a former lodger of Mrs. Lirriper's.*

GEORGE, *a weak-headed young man, articled to Mr. Buffle.*

MAJOR JEMMY JACKMAN, *a lodger at Mrs. Lirriper's, and her warm friend.*

DR. JOSHUA LIRRIPER, *Mrs. Lirriper's good-for-nothing brother-in-law.*

MRS. LIRRIPER ('Gran'), *a lodging-house keeper.*

JEMMY JACKMAN LIRRIPER, *the son of Mr. Edson, and adopted by Mrs. Lirriper.*

WINIFRED MADGERS, *a servant-girl at Mrs. Lirriper's, and a 'Plymouth sister'.*

SALLY RAIRYGANOO, *another of Mrs. Lirriper's domestic servants.*

MISS WOZENHAM, *the keeper of a rival lodging-house.*

in my own quiet room in my own Lodging-House Number
Eighty-one Norfolk Street Strand London situated midway
between the city and St. James's—if anything is where it
used to be with these hotels calling themselves Limited but
called unlimited by Major Jackman rising up everywhere
and rising up into flagstaffs where they can't go any higher,
but my mind of those monsters is give me a landlord's or
landlady's wholesome face when I come off a journey and
not a brass plate with an electrified number clicking out of it
which it's not in nature can be glad to see me and to which
I don't want to be hoisted like molasses at the Docks and
left there telegraphing for help with the most ingenious
instruments but quite in vain—being here my dear I have
no call to mention that I am still in the Lodgings as a
business hoping to die in the same and if agreeable to the
clergy partly read over at Saint Clement's Danes and concluded in Hatfield churchyard when lying once again by my
poor Lirriper ashes to ashes and dust to dust.

Neither should I tell you any news my dear in telling you
that the Major is still a fixture in the Parlours quite as
much so as the roof of the house, and that Jemmy is of
boys the best and brightest and has ever had kept from him
the cruel story of his poor pretty young mother Mrs. Edson
being deserted in the second floor and dying in my arms,
fully believing that I am his born Gran and him an orphan,
though what with engineering since he took a taste for it
and him and the Major making Locomotives out of parasols
broken iron pots and cotton-reels and them absolutely a
getting off the line and falling over the table and injuring
the passengers almost equal to the originals it really is
quite wonderful. And when I says to the Major, "Major
can't you by *any* means give us a communication with the
guard?" the Major says quite huffy, "No madam it's not
to be done," and when I says "Why not?" the Major says,
"That is between us who are in the Railway Interest madam
and our friend the Right Honourable Vice-President of the
Board of Trade" and if you'll believe me my dear the Major
wrote to Jemmy at school to consult him on the answer
I should have before I could get even that amount of
unsatisfactoriness out of the man, the reason being that
when we first began with the little model and the working
signals beautiful and perfect (being in general as wrong as
the real) and when I says laughing "What appointment am

I to hold in this undertaking gentlemen?" Jemmy hugs me round the neck and tells me dancing, "You shall be the Public Gran" and consequently they put upon me just as much as ever they like and I sit a growling in my easy-chair.

My dear whether it is that a grown man as clever as the Major cannot give half his heart and mind to anything—even a plaything—but must get into right down earnest with it, whether it is so or whether it is not so I do not undertake to say, but Jemmy is far outdone by the serious and believing ways of the Major in the management of the United Grand Junction Lirriper and Jackman Great Norfolk Parlour Line, "For" says my Jemmy with the sparkling eyes when it was christened, "we must have a whole mouthful of name Gran or our dear old Public" and there the young rogue kissed me, "won't stump up." So, the Public took the shares—ten at ninepence, and immediately when that was spent twelve Preference to one-and-sixpence—and they were all signed by Jemmy and countersigned by the Major, and between ourselves much better worth the money than some shares I have paid for in my time. In the same holidays the line was made and worked and opened and ran excursions and had collisions and burst its boilers and all sorts of accidents and offences all most regular correct and pretty. The sense of responsibility entertained by the Major as a military style of station-master my dear starting the down train behind time and ringing one of those little bells that you buy with the little coal-scuttles off the tray round the man's neck in the street did him honour, but noticing the Major of a night when he is writing out his monthly report to Jemmy at school of the state of the Rolling Stock and the Permanent Way and all the rest of it (the whole kept upon the Major's sideboard and dusted with his own hands every morning before varnishing his boots) I notice him as full of thought and care as full can be and frowning in a fearful manner, but indeed the Major does nothing by halves as witness his great delight in going out surveying with Jemmy when he has Jemmy to go with, carrying a chain and a measuring-tape and driving I don't know what improvements right through Westminster Abbey and fully believed in the streets to be knocking everything upside down by Act of Parliament. As please Heaven will come to pass when Jemmy takes to that as a profession!

Mentioning my poor Lirriper brings into my head his own

youngest brother the Doctor though Doctor of what I am sure it would be hard to say unless Liquor, for neither Physic nor Music nor yet Law does Joshua Lirriper know a morsel of except continually being summoned to the County Court and having orders made upon him which he runs away from, and once was taken in the passage of this very house with an umbrella up and the Major's hat on, giving his name with the door-mat round him as Sir Johnson Jones, K.C.B. in spectacles residing at the Horse Guards. On which occasion he had got into the house not a minute before, through the girl letting him on the mat when he sent in a piece of paper twisted more like one of those spills for lighting candles than a note, offering me the choice between thirty shillings in hand and his brains on the premises marked immediate and waiting for an answer. My dear it gave me such a dreadful turn to think of the brains of my poor dear Lirriper's own flesh and blood flying about the new oilcloth however unworthy to be so assisted, that I went out of my room here to ask him what he would take once for all not to do it for life when I found him in the custody of two gentlemen that I should have judged to be in the feather-bed trade if they had not announced the law, so fluffy were their personal appearance. "Bring your chains, Sir," says Joshua to the littlest of the two in the biggest hat, "rivet on my fetters!" Imagine my feelings when I pictered him clanking up Norfolk-street in irons and Miss Wozenham looking out of window! "Gentlemen," I says all of a tremble and ready to drop "please to bring him into Major Jackman's apartments." So they brought him into the Parlours, and when the Major spies his own curly-brimmed hat on him which Joshua Lirriper had whipped off its Peg in the passage for a military disguise he goes into such a tearing passion that he tips it off his head with his hand and kicks it up to the ceiling with his foot where it grazed long afterwards. "Major" I says "be cool and advise me what to do with Joshua my dead and gone Lirriper's own youngest brother." "Madam" says the Major "my advice is that you board and lodge him in a Powder Mill, with a handsome gratuity to the proprietor when exploded." "Major" I says "as a Christian you cannot mean your words." "Madam" says the Major "by the Lord I do!" and indeed the Major besides being with all his merits a very passionate man for his size had a bad opinion of Joshua on account of former troubles even unattended by liberties taken with his apparel. When Joshua Lirriper hears this conversation betwixt us he turns upon the littlest one with the biggest hat and says "Come Sir! Remove me to my vile dungeon. Where is my mouldy straw?" My dear at the picter of him rising in my mind dressed almost entirely in padlocks like Baron Trenck in Jemmy's book I was so overcome that I burst into tears and I says to the Major, "Major take my keys and settle with these gentlemen or I shall never know a happy minute more," which was done several times both before and since, but still I must remember that Joshua Lirriper has his good feelings and shows them in being always so troubled in his mind when he cannot wear mourning for his brother. Many a long year have I left off my widow's mourning not being wishful to intrude, but the tender point in Joshua that I cannot help a little yielding to is when he writes "One single sovereign would enable me to wear a decent suit of mourning for my much-loved brother. I vowed at the time of his lamented death that I would ever wear sables in memory of him but Alas how short-sighted is man, How keep that vow when penniless!" It says a good deal for the strength of his feelings that he couldn't have been seven year old when my poor Lirriper died and to have kept to it ever since is highly creditable. But we know there's good in all of us,—if we only knew where it was in some of us,—and though it was far from delicate in Joshua to work upon the dear child's feelings when first sent to school and write down into Lincolnshire for his pocket-money by return of post and got it, still he is my poor Lirriper's own youngest brother and mightn't have meant not paying his bill at the Salisbury Arms when his affection took him down to stay a fortnight at Hatfield churchyard and might have meant to keep sober but for bad company. Consequently if the Major *had* played on him with the garden-engine which he got privately into his room without my knowing of it, I think that much as I should have regretted it there would have been words betwixt the Major and me. Therefore my dear though he played on Mr. Buffle by mistake being hot in his head, and though it might have been misrepresented down at Wozenham's into not being ready for Mr. Buffle in other respects he being the Assessed Taxes, still I do not so much regret it as perhaps I ought. And whether Joshua Lirriper will yet do well in life I cannot say, but I did hear of his coming out at a Private Theatre in the character of a Bandit without receiving any offers afterwards from the regular managers.

Mentioning Mr. Buffle gives an instance of there being good in persons where good is not expected, for it cannot be denied that Mr. Buffle's manners when engaged in his business were not agreeable. To collect is one thing, and to look about as if suspicious of the goods being gradually removing in the dead of the night by a back door is another, over-taxing you have no control but suspecting is voluntary. Allowances too must ever be made for a gentleman of the Major's warmth not relishing being spoke to with a pen in the mouth, and while I do not know that it is more irritable to my own feelings to have a low-crowned hat with a broad brim kept on in doors than any other hat still I can appreciate the Major's, besides which without bearing malice or vengeance the Major is a man that scores up arrears as his habit always was with Joshua Lirriper. So at last my dear the Major lay in wait for Mr. Buffle and it worrited me a good deal. Mr. Buffle gives his rap of two sharp knocks one day and the Major bounces to the door. "Collector has called for two quarters' Assessed Taxes" says Mr. Buffle. "They are ready for him" says the Major and brings him in here. But on the way Mr. Buffle looks about him in his usual suspicious manner and the Major fires and asks him "Do you see a Ghost Sir?" "No Sir" says Mr. Buffle. "Because I have before noticed you" says the Major "apparently looking for a spectre very hard beneath the roof of my respected friend. When you find that supernatural agent, be so good as point him out Sir." Mr. Buffle stares at the Major and then nods at me. "Mrs. Lirriper Sir" says the Major going off into a perfect steam and introducing me with his hand. "Pleasure of knowing her" says Mr. Buffle. "A—hum!—Jemmy Jackman Sir!" says the Major introducing himself. "Honour of knowing you by sight" says Mr. Buffle. "Jemmy Jackman Sir" says the Major wagging his head sideways in a sort of obstinate fury "presents to you his esteemed friend that lady Mrs. Emma Lirriper of Eighty-one Norfolk Street Strand London in the County of Middlesex in the United Kingdom of Great Britain and Ireland. Upon which occasion Sir," says the Major, "Jemmy Jackman takes your hat off." Mr. Buffle looks at his hat where the Major drops it on the floor, and he picks it up and puts it on again. "Sir" says the Major very red and looking him full in the face "there are two quarters of the Gallantry Taxes due and the Collector has called." Upon which if you can believe my words my dear the Major drops Mr. Buffle's hat off again. "This——" Mr. Buffle begins very angry with his pen in his mouth, when the Major steaming more and more says "Take your bit out Sir! Or by the whole infernal system of Taxation of this country and every individual figure in the National Debt, I'll get upon your back and ride you like a horse!" which it's my belief he would have done and even actually jerking his neat little legs ready for a spring as it was. "This," says Mr. Buffle without his pen "is an assault and I'll have the law of you." "Sir" replies the Major "if you are a man of honour, your Collector of whatever may be due on the Honourable Assessment by applying to Major Jackman at the Parlours Mrs. Lirriper's Lodgings, may obtain what he wants in full at any moment."

When the Major glared at Mr. Buffle with those meaning words my dear I literally gasped for a teaspoonful of salvo-latile in a wineglass of water, and I says "Pray let it go no farther gentlemen I beg and beseech of you!" But the Major could be got to do nothing else but snort long after Mr. Buffle was gone, and the effect it had upon my whole mass of blood when on the next day of Mr. Buffle's rounds the Major spruced himself up and went humming a tune up and down the street with one eye almost obliterated by his hat there are not expressions in Johnson's dictionary to state. But I safely put the street door on the jar and got behind the Major's blinds with my shawl on and my mind made up the moment I saw danger to rush out screeching till my voice failed me and catch the Major round the neck till my strength went and have all parties bound. I had not been behind the blinds a quarter of an hour when I saw Mr. Buffle approaching with his Collecting-books in his hand. The Major likewise saw him approaching and hummed louder and himself approached. They met before the Airy railings. The Major takes off his hat at arm's length and says "Mr. Buffle I believe?" Mr. Buffle takes off *his* hat at arm's length and says "That is my name Sir." Says the Major "Have you any commands for me, Mr. Buffle?" Says Mr. Buffle "Not any Sir." Then my dear both of 'em bowed very low and haughty and parted, and whenever Mr. Buffle made his rounds in future him and the Major always met and bowed before the Airy railings, putting me

much in mind of Hamlet and the other gentleman in
mourning before killing one another, though I could have
wished the other gentleman had done it fairer and even if
less polite no poison.

Mr. Buffle's family were not liked in this neighbourhood,
for when you are a householder my dear you'll find it does
not come by nature to like the Assessed, and it was considered besides that a one-horse pheayton ought not to have
elevated Mrs. Buffle to that height especially when purloined
from the Taxes which I myself did consider uncharitable. But
they were *not* liked and there was that domestic unhappiness
in the family in consequence of their both being very hard
with Miss Buffle and one another on account of Miss Buffle's
favouring Mr. Buffle's articled young gentleman, that it *was*
whispered that Miss Buffle would go either into a consumption or a convent she being so very thin and off her appetite
and two close-shaved gentlemen with white bands round
their necks peeping round the corner whenever she went out
in waistcoats resembling black pinafores. So things stood
towards Mr. Buffle when one night I was woke by a frightful noise and a smell of burning, and going to my bedroom
window saw the whole street in a glow. Fortunately we
had two sets empty just then and before I could hurry on
some clothes I heard the Major hammering at the attics'
doors and calling out "Dress yourselves!—Fire! Don't be
frightened!—Fire! Collect your presence of mind!—Fire!
All right—Fire!" most tremenjously. As I opened my
bedroom door the Major came tumbling in over himself and
me, and caught me in his arms. "Major" I says breathless "where is it?" "I don't know dearest madam" says
the Major—"Fire! Jemmy Jackman will defend you to the
last drop of his blood—Fire! If the dear boy was at home
what a treat this would be for him—Fire!" and altogether
very collected and bold except that he couldn't say a single
sentence without shaking me to the very centre with roaring
Fire. We ran down to the drawing-room and put our heads
out of window, and the Major calls to an unfeeling young
monkey, scampering by be joyful and ready to split "Where
is it?—Fire!" The monkey answers without stopping "O
here's a lark! Old Buffle's been setting his house alight
to prevent its being found out that he boned the Taxes.
Hurrah! Fire!" And then the sparks came flying up and
the smoke came pouring down and the crackling of flames

and spatting of water and banging of engines and hacking of axes and breaking of glass and knocking at doors and the shouting and crying and hurrying and the heat and altogether gave me a dreadful palpitation. "Don't be frightened dearest madam," says the Major, "—Fire! There's nothing to be alarmed at—Fire! Don't open the street door till I come back—Fire! I'll go and see if I can be of any service—Fire! You're quite composed and comfortable ain't you?—Fire, Fire, Fire!" It was in vain for me to hold the man and tell him he'd be galloped to death by the engines—pumped to death by his over-exertions—wet-feeted to death by the slop and mess—flattened to death when the roofs fell in—his spirit was up and he went scampering off after the young monkey with all the breath he had and none to spare, and me and the girls huddled together at the parlour windows looking at the dreadful flames above the houses over the way, Mr. Buffle's being round the corner. Presently what should we see but some people running down the street straight to our door, and then the Major directing operations in the busiest way, and then some more people and then—carried in a chair similar to Guy Fawkes—Mr. Buffle in a blanket!

My dear the Major has Mr. Buffle brought up our steps and whisked into the parlour and carted out on the sofy, and then he and all the rest of them without so much as a word burst away again full speed, leaving the impression of a vision except for Mr. Buffle awful in his blanket with his eyes a rolling. In a twinkling they all burst back again with Mrs. Buffle in another blanket, which whisked in and carted out on the sofy they all burst off again and all burst back again with Miss Buffle in another blanket, which again whisked in and carted out they all burst off again and all burst back again with Mr. Buffle's articled young gentleman in another blanket—him a holding round the necks of two men carrying him by the legs, similar to the picter of the disgraceful creetur who has lost the fight (but where the chair I do not know) and his hair having the appearance of newly played upon. When all four of a row, the Major rubs his hands and whispers me with what little hoarseness he can get together. "If our dear remarkable boy was only at home what a delightful treat this would be for him!"

My dear we made them some hot tea and toast and some hot brandy-and-water with a little comfortable nutmeg in it, and at first they were scared and low in their spirits but being fully insured got sociable. And the first use Mr. Buffle made of his tongue was to call the Major his Preserver and his best of friends and to say "My for ever dearest Sir let me make you known to Mrs. Buffle" which also addressed him as her Preserver and her best of friends and was fully as cordial as the blanket would admit of. Also Miss Buffle. The articled young gentleman's head was a little light and he sat a moaning "Robina is reduced to cinders, Robina is reduced to cinders!" Which went more to the heart on account of his having got wrapped in his blanket as if he was looking out of a violinceller case, until Mr. Buffle says "Robina speak to him!" Miss Buffle says "Dear George!" and but for the Major's pouring down brandy-and-water on the instant which caused a catching in his throat owing to the nutmeg and a violent fit of coughing it might have proved too much for his strength. When the articled young gentleman got the better of it Mr. Buffle leaned up against Mrs. Buffle being two bundles, a little while in confidence, and then says with tears in his eyes which the Major noticing wiped, "We have not been an united family, let us after this danger become so, take her George." The young gentleman could not put his arm out far to do it, but his spoken expressions were very beautiful though of a wandering class. And I do not know that I ever had a much pleasanter meal than the breakfast we took together after we had all dozed, when Miss Buffle made tea very sweetly in quite the Roman style as depicted formerly at Covent Garden Theatre and when the whole family was most agreeable, as they have ever proved since that night when the Major stood at the foot of the Fire-Escape and claimed them as they came down —the young gentleman head-foremost, which accounts. And though I do not say that we should be less liable to think ill of one another if strictly limited to blankets, still I do say that we might most of us come to a better understanding if we kept one another less at a distance.

Why there's Wozenham's lower down on the other side of the street. I had a feeling of much soreness several years respecting what I must still ever call Miss Wozenham's systematic underbidding and the likeness of the house in Bradshaw having far too many windows and a most umbrageous and outrageous Oak which never yet was seen in Norfolk-street nor yet a carriage and four at Wozenham's

door, which it would have been far more to Bradshaw's credit
to have drawn a cab.   This frame of mind continued bitter
down to the very afternoon in January last when one of my
girls, Sally Rairyganoo which I still suspect of Irish extrac-
tion though family represented Cambridge, else why abscond
with a bricklayer of the Limerick persuasion and be married
in pattens not waiting till his black eye was decently got
round with all the company fourteen in number and one
horse fighting outside on the roof of the vehicle,—I repeat
my dear my ill-regulated state of mind towards Miss Wozenham continued down to the very afternoon of January last
past when Sally Rairyganoo came banging (I can use no
milder expression) into my room with a jump which may be
Cambridge and may not, and said "Hurroo Missis! Miss
Wozenham's sold up!"   My dear when I had it thrown in
my face and conscience that the girl Sally had reason to
think I could be glad of the ruin of a fellow-creeter, I burst
into tears and dropped back in my chair and I says "I am
ashamed of myself!"

Well!   I tried to settle to my tea but I could not do it
what with thinking of Miss Wozenham and her distresses.
It was a wretched night and I went up to a front window and
looked over at Wozenham's and as well as I could make it out
down the street in the fog it was the dismallest of the dismal
and not a light to be seen.   So at last I says to myself "This
will not do," and I puts on my oldest bonnet and shawl not
wishing Miss Wozenham to be reminded of my best at such
a time, and lo and behold you I goes over to Wozenham's and
knocks.   "Miss Wozenham at home?" I says turning my
head when I heard the door go.   And then I saw it was Miss
Wozenham herself who had opened it and sadly worn she was
poor thing and her eyes all swelled and swelled with crying.
"Miss Wozenham" I says "it is several years since there was
a little unpleasantness betwixt us on the subject of my grandson's cap being down your Airy.   I have overlooked it and
I hope you have done the same."   "Yes Mrs. Lirriper" she
says in a surprise "I have."   "Then my dear" I says "I
should be glad to come in and speak a word to you."   Upon
my calling her my dear Miss Wozenham breaks out a crying
most pitiful, and a not unfeeling elderly person that might
have been better shaved in a nightcap with a hat over it offering a polite apology for the mumps having worked themselves
into his constitution, and also for sending home to his wife on

the bellows which was in his hand as a writing-desk, looks out of the back parlour and says "The lady wants a word of comfort" and goes in again. So I was able to say quite natural "Wants a word of comfort does she Sir? Then please the pigs she shall have it!" And Miss Wozenham and me we go into the front room with a wretched light that seemed to have been crying too and was sputtering out, and I says "Now my dear, tell me all," and she rings her hands and says "O Mrs. Lirriper that man is in possession here, and I have not a friend in the world who is able to help me with a shilling."

It doesn't signify a bit what a talkative old body like me said to Miss Wozenham when she said that, and so I'll tell you instead my dear that I'd have given thirty shillings to have taken her over to tea, only I durstn't on account of the Major. Not you see but what I knew I could draw the Major out like thread and wind him round my finger on most subjects and perhaps even on that if I was to set myself to it, but him and me had so often belied Miss Wozenham to one another that I was shamefaced, and I knew she had offended his pride and never mine, and likewise I felt timid that that Rairyganoo girl might make things awkward. So I says "My dear if you could give me a cup of tea to clear my muddle of a head I should better understand your affairs." And we had the tea and the affairs too and after all it was but forty pound, and —— There! she's as industrious and straight a creeter as ever lived and has paid back half of it already, and where's the use of saying more, particularly when it ain't the point? For the point is that when she was a kissing my hands and holding them in hers and kissing them again and blessing blessing blessing, I cheered up at last and I says "Why what a waddling old goose I have been my dear to take you for something so very different!" "Ah but I too" says she "how have *I* mistaken *you!*" "Come for goodness' sake tell me" I says "what you thought of me?" "O" says she "I thought you had no feeling for such a hard hand-to-mouth life as mine, and were rolling in affluence." I says shaking my sides (and very glad to do it for I had been a choking quite long enough) "Only look at my figure my dear and give me your opinion whether if I was in affluence I should be likely to roll in it?" That did it! We got as merry as grigs (whatever *they* are, if you happen to know my dear—*I* don't) and I went home to my blessed home as happy and as thankful as could be. But before I make an end of it, think even of my having misunderstood the Major! Yes! For next forenoon the Major came into my little room with his brushed hat in his hand and he begins " My dearest madam—— " and then put his face in his hat as if he had just come into church. As I sat all in a maze he came out of his hat and began again. " My esteemed and beloved friend—— " and then went into his hat again. " Major," I cries out frightened " has anything happened to our darling boy?" " No, no, no " says the Major "but Miss Wozenham has been here this morning to make her excuses to me, and by the Lord I can't get over what she told me." " Hoity toity,Major," I says " you don't know yet that I was afraid of you last night and didn't think half as well of you as I ought! So come out of church Major and forgive me like a dear old friend and I'll never do so any more." And I leave you to judge my dear whether I ever did or will. And how affecting to think of Miss Wozenham out of her small income and her losses doing so much for her poor old father, and keeping a brother that had had the mis- fortune to soften his brain against the hard mathematics as neat as a new pin in the three back represented to lodgers as a lumber-room and consuming a whole shoulder of mutton whenever provided!

And now my dear I really am a going to tell you about my Legacy if you're inclined to favour me with your attention, and I did fully intend to have come straight to it only one thing does so bring up another. It was the month of June and the day before Midsummer Day when my girl Winifred Madgers—she was what is termed a Plymouth Sister, and the Plymouth Brother that made away with her was quite right, for a tidier young woman for a wife never came into a house and afterwards called with the beautifullest Plymouth Twins —it was the day before Midsummer Day when Winifred Madgers comes and says to me " A gentleman from the Consul's wishes particular to speak to Mrs. Lirriper." If you'll believe me my dear the Consols at the bank where I have a little matter for Jemmy got into my head, and I says " Good gracious I hope he ain't had any dreadful fall!" Says Winifred " He don't look as if he had ma'am." And I says " Show him in."

The gentleman came in dark and with his hair cropped what I should consider too close, and he says very polite " Madame Lirrwiper!" " I says " Yes Sir. Take a chair."

" I come," says he "frrwom the Frrwench Consul's.   So I
saw at once that it wasn't the Bank of England.   "We have
rrweceived," says the gentleman turning his r's very curious
and skilful, "frrwom the Mairrwie at Sens, a communication
which I will have the honour to rrwead.   Madame Lirrwiper
understands Frrwench?"   "O dear no Sir!" says I.   "Madame
Lirriper don't understand anything of the sort."   "It matters
not." says the gentleman, "I will trrwanslate."

With that my dear the gentleman after reading something
about a Department and a Marie (which Lord forgive me I supposed till the Major came home was Mary, and never was I more
puzzled than to think how that young woman came to have
so much to do with it) translated a lot with the most obliging
pains, and it came to this:—That in the town of Sens in
France an unknown Englishman lay a dying.   That he was
speechless and without motion.   That in his lodging there
was a gold watch and a purse containing such and such money
and a trunk containing such and such clothes, but no passport
and no papers, except that on his table was a pack of cards and
that he had written in pencil on the back of the ace of hearts:
"To the authorities.   When I am dead, pray send what is
left, as a last Legacy, to Mrs. Lirriper Eighty-one Norfolk
Street Strand London."   When the gentleman had explained
all this, which seemed to be drawn up much more methodical
than I should have given the French credit for, not at that
time knowing the nation, he put the document into my hand.
And much the wiser I was for that you may be sure, except
that it had the look of being made out upon grocery paper and
was stamped all over with eagles.

"Does Madame Lirrwiper" says the gentleman, "believe
she rrwecognises her unfortunate compatrrwiot?"

You may imagine the flurry it put me into my dear to be
talked to about my compatriots.

I says "Excuse me.   Would you have the kindness Sir to
make your language as simple as you can?"

"This Englishman unhappy, at the point of death.   This
compatrrwiot afflicted," says the gentleman.

"Thank you, Sir," I says "I understand you now.   No Sir
I have not the least idea who this can be."

" Has Madame Lirrwiper no son, no nephew, no godson, no
frrwiend, no acquaintance of any kind in Frrwance?"

"To my certain knowledge" says I "no relation or friend,
and to the best of my belief no acquaintance."

"Pardon me. You take Locataires?" says the gentleman.

My dear fully believing he was offering me something with his obliging foreign manners,—snuff for anything I knew,—I gave a little bend of my head and I says if you'll credit it, "No I thank you. I have not contracted the habit."

The gentleman looks perplexed and says "Lodgers!"

"Oh!" says I laughing. "Bless the man! Why yes to be sure!"

"May it not be a former lodger?" says the gentleman. "Some lodger that you pardoned some rrwent? You have pardoned lodgers some rrwent?"

"Hem! It has happened Sir" says I, "but I assure you I can call to mind no gentleman of that description that this is at all likely to be."

In short my dear, we could make nothing of it, and the gentleman noted down what I said and went away. But he left me the paper of which he had two with him, and when the Major came in I says to the Major as I put it in his hand "Major here's Old Moore's Almanac with the hieroglyphic complete, for your opinion."

It took the Major a little longer to read than I should have thought, judging from the copious flow with which he seemed to be gifted when attacking the organ-men, but at last he got through it, and stood a gazing at me in amazement.

"Major" I says "you're paralysed."

"Madam" says the Major, "Jemmy Jackman is doubled up."

Now it did so happen that the Major had been out to get a little information about railroads and steamboats, as our boy was coming home for his Midsummer holidays next day and we were going to take him somewhere for a treat and a change. So while the Major stood a gazing it came into my head to say to him "Major I wish you'd go and look at some of your books and maps, and see whereabouts this same town of Sens is in France."

The Major he roused himself and he went into the Parlours and he poked about a little, and he came back to me and he says, "Sens my dearest madam is seventy-odd miles south of Paris."

With what I may truly call a desperate effort "Major," I says "we'll go there with our blessed boy."

If ever the Major was beside himself it was at the thoughts of that journey. All day long he was like the wild man of the woods after meeting with an advertisement in the papers telling him something to his advantage, and early next morning hours before Jemmy could possibly come home he was outside in the street ready to call out to him that we was all a going to France. Young Rosycheeks you may believe was as wild as the Major, and they did carry on to that degree that I says "If you two children ain't more orderly I'll pack you both off to bed." And then they fell to cleaning up the Major's telescope to see France with, and went out and bought a leather bag with a snap to hang round Jemmy, and him to carry the money like a little Fortunatus with his purse.

If I hadn't passed my word and raised their hopes, I doubt if I could have gone through with the undertaking but it was too late to go back now. So on the second day after Midsummer Day we went off by the morning mail. And when we came to the sea which I had never seen but once in my life and that when my poor Lirriper was courting me, the freshness of it and the deepness and the airiness and to think that it had been rolling ever since and that it was always a rolling and so few of us minding, made me feel quite serious. But I felt happy too and so did Jemmy and the Major and not much motion on the whole, though me with a swimming in the head and a sinking but able to take notice that the foreign insides appear to be constructed hollower than the English, leading to much more tremenjous noises when bad sailors.

But my dear the blueness and the lightness and the coloured look of everything and the very sentry-boxes striped and the shining rattling drums and the little soldiers with their waists and tidy gaiters, when we got across to the Continent—it made me feel as if I don't know what—as if the atmosphere had been lifted off me. And as to lunch why bless you if I kept a man-cook and two kitchen-maids I couldn't get it done for twice the money, and no injured young woman a glaring at you and grudging you and acknowledging your patronage by wishing that your food might choke you, but so civil and so hot and attentive and every way comfortable except Jemmy pouring wine down his throat by tumblers-full and me expecting to see him drop under the table.

And the way in which Jemmy spoke his French was a real charm. It was often wanted of him, for whenever anybody spoke a syllable to me I says "Non-comprenny, you're very kind, but it's no use—Now Jemmy!" and then

Jemmy he fires away at 'em lovely, the only thing wanting in Jemmy's French being as it appeared to me that he hardly ever understood a word of what they said to him which made it scarcely of the use it might have been though in other respects a perfect Native, and regarding the Major's fluency I should have been of the opinion judging French by English that there might have been a greater choice of words in the language though still I must admit that if I hadn't known him when he asked a military gentleman in a grey cloak what o'clock it was I should have took him for a Frenchman born.

Before going on to look after my Legacy we were to make one regular day in Paris, and I leave you to judge my dear what a day *that* was with Jemmy and the Major and the telescope and me and the prowling young man at the inn door (but very civil too) that went along with us to show the sights. All along the railway to Paris Jemmy and the Major had been frightening me to death by stooping down on the platforms at stations to inspect the engines under-neath their mechanical stomachs, and by creeping in and out I don't know where all, to find improvements for the United Grand Junction Parlour, but when we got out into the brilliant streets on a bright morning they gave up all their London improvements as a bad job and gave their minds to Paris. Says the prowling young man to me "Will I speak Inglis No?" So I says "If you can young man I shall take it as a favour," but after half-an-hour of it when I fully believed the man had gone mad and me too I says "Be so good as fall back on your French Sir," knowing that then I shouldn't have the agonies of trying to understand him, which was a happy release. Not that I lost much more than the rest either, for I generally noticed that when he had described something very long indeed and I says to Jemmy "What does he say Jemmy?" Jemmy says looking with vengeance in his eye "He is so jolly indistinct!" and that when he had described it longer all over again and I says to Jemmy "Well Jemmy what's it all about?" Jemmy says "He says the building was repaired in seventeen hundred and four, Gran."

Wherever that prowling young man formed his prowling habits I cannot be expected to know, but the way in which he went round the corner while we had our breakfasts and was there again when we swallowed the last crumb was most marvellous, and just the same at dinner and at night, prowling equally at the theatre and the inn gateway and the shop doors when we bought a trifle or two and everywhere else but troubled with a tendency to spit. And of Paris I can tell you no more my dear than that it's town and country both in one, and carved stone and long streets of high houses and gardens and fountains and statues and trees and gold, and immensely big soldiers and immensely little soldiers and the pleasantest nurses with the whitest caps a playing at skipping-rope with the bunchiest babies in the flattest caps, and clean table-cloths spread everywhere for dinner and people sitting out of doors smoking and sipping all day long and little plays being acted in the open air for little people and every shop a complete and elegant room, and everybody seeming to play at everything in this world. And as to the sparkling lights my dear after dark, glittering high up and low down and on before and on behind and all round, and the crowd of theatres and the crowd of people and the crowd of all sorts, it's pure enchantment. And pretty well the only thing that grated on me was that whether you pay your fare at the railway or whether you change your money at a money-dealer's or whether you take your ticket at the theatre, the lady or gentleman is caged up (I suppose by government) behind the strongest iron bars having more of a Zoological appearance than a free country.

Well to be sure when I did after all get my precious bones to bed that night, and my Young Rogue came in to kiss me and asks "What do you think of this lovely lovely Paris, Gran?" I says "Jemmy I feel as if it was beautiful fireworks being let off in my head." And very cool and refreshing the pleasant country was next day when we went on to look after my Legacy, and rested me much and did me a deal of good.

So at length and at last my dear we come to Sens, a pretty little town with a great two-towered cathedral and the rooks flying in and out of the loopholes and another tower atop of one of the towers like a sort of a stone pulpit. In which pulpit with the birds skimming below him if you'll believe me, I saw a speck while I was resting at the inn before dinner which they made signs to me was Jemmy and which really was. I had been a fancying as I sat in the balcony of the hotel that an Angel might light there and call down to the people to be good, but I little thought what Jemmy all unknown to himself was a calling down from that high place to some one in the town.

The pleasantest-situated inn my dear! Right under the two towers, with their shadows a changing upon it all day like a kind of a sundial, and country people driving in and out of the courtyard in carts and hooded cabriolets and such like, and a market outside in front of the cathedral, and all so quaint and like a picter. The Major and me agreed that whatever came of my Legacy this was the place to stay in for our holiday, and we also agreed that our dear boy had best not be checked in his joy that night by the sight of the Englishman if he was still alive, but that we would go together and alone. For you are to understand that the Major not feeling himself quite equal in his wind to the height to which Jemmy had climbed, had come back to me and left him with the Guide.

So after dinner when Jemmy had set off to see the river, the Major went down to the Mairie, and presently came back with a military character in a sword and spurs and a cocked hat and a yellow shoulder-belt and long tags about him that he must have found inconvenient. And the Major says "The Englishman still lies in the same state dearest madam. This gentleman will conduct us to his lodging." Upon which the military character pulled off his cocked hat to me, and I took notice that he had shaved his forehead in imitation of Napoleon Bonaparte but not like.

We went out at the courtyard gate and past the great doors of the cathedral and down a narrow High-street where the people were sitting chatting at their shop doors and the children were at play. The military character went in front and he stopped at a pork-shop with a little statue of a pig sitting up, in the window, and a private door that a donkey was looking out of.

When the donkey saw the military character he came slipping out on the pavement to turn round and then clattered along the passage into a back yard. So the coast being clear, the Major and me were conducted up the common stair and into the front room on the second, a bare room with a red tiled floor and the outside lattice blinds pulled close to darken it. As the military character opened the blinds I saw the tower where I had seen Jemmy, darkening as the sun got low, and I turned to the bed by the wall and saw the Englishman.

It was some kind of brain fever he had had, and his hair was all gone, and some wetted folded linen lay upon his head. I looked at him very attentive as he lay there all wasted away with his eyes closed, and I says to the Major:

"I never saw this face before."

The Major looked at him very attentive too, and he says:

"*I* never saw this face before."

When the Major explained our words to the military character, that gentleman shrugged his shoulders and showed the Major the card on which it was written about the Legacy for me. It had been written with a weak and trembling hand in bed, and I knew no more of the writing than of the face. Neither did the Major.

Though lying there alone, the poor creetur was as well taken care of as could be hoped, and would have been quite unconscious of any one's sitting by him then. I got the Major to say that we were not going away at present and that I would come back to-morrow and watch a bit by the bedside. But I got him to add—and I shook my head hard to make it stronger—"We agree that we never saw this face before."

Our boy was greatly surprised when we told him sitting out in the balcony in the starlight, and he ran over some of those stories of former Lodgers, of the Major's putting down, and asked wasn't it possible that it might be this lodger or that lodger. It was not possible, and we went to bed.

In the morning just at breakfast-time the military character came jingling round, and said that the doctor thought from the signs he saw there might be some rally before the end. So I says to the Major and Jemmy, "You two boys go and enjoy yourselves, and I'll take my Prayer Book and go sit by the bed." So I went, and I sat there some hours, reading a prayer for him poor soul now and then, and it was quite on in the day when he moved his hand.

He had been so still, that the moment he moved I knew of it, and I pulled off my spectacles and laid down my book and rose and looked at him. From moving one hand he began to move both, and then his action was the action of a person groping in the dark. Long after his eyes had opened, there was a film over them and he still felt for his way out into light. But by slow degrees his sight cleared and his hands stopped. He saw the ceiling, he saw the wall, he saw me. As his sight cleared, mine cleared too, and when at last we looked in one another's faces, I started back and I cries passionately:

"O you wicked wicked man! Your sin has found you out!"

For I knew him, the moment life looked out of his eyes, to be Mr. Edson, Jemmy's father who had so cruelly deserted Jemmy's young unmarried mother who had died in my arms, poor tender creetur, and left Jemmy to me.

"You cruel wicked man! You bad black traitor!"

With the little strength he had, he made an attempt to turn over on his wretched face to hide it. His arm dropped out of the bed and his head with it, and there he lay before me crushed in body and in mind. Surely the miserablest sight under the summer sun!

"O blessed Heaven," I says a crying, "teach me what to say to this broken mortal! I am a poor sinful creetur, and the Judgment is not mine."

As I lifted my eyes up to the clear bright sky, I saw the high tower where Jemmy had stood above the birds, seeing that very window; and the last look of that poor pretty young mother when her soul brightened and got free, seemed to shine down from it.

"O man, man, man!" I says, and I went on my knees beside the bed; "if your heart is rent asunder and you are truly penitent for what you did, Our Saviour will have mercy on you yet!"

As I leaned my face against the bed, his feeble hand could just move itself enough to touch me. I hope the touch was penitent. It tried to hold my dress and keep hold, but the fingers were too weak to close.

I lifted him back upon the pillows and I says to him:

"Can you hear me?"

He looked yes.

"Do you know me?"

He looked yes, even yet more plainly.

"I am not here alone. The Major is with me. You recollect the Major?"

Yes. That is to say he made out yes, in the same way as before.

"And even the Major and I are not alone. My grandson—his godson—is with us. Do you hear? My grandson."

The fingers made another trial to catch at my sleeve, but could only creep near it and fall.

"Do you know who my grandson is?"

Yes.

"I pitied and loved his lonely mother. When his mother lay a dying I said to her, 'My dear, this baby is sent to a childless old woman.' He has been my pride and joy ever since. I love him as dearly as if he had drunk from my breast. Do you ask to see my grandson before you die?"

Yes.

"Show me, when I leave off speaking, if you correctly understand what I say. He has been kept unacquainted with the story of his birth. He has no knowledge of it. No suspicion of it. If I bring him here to the side of this bed, he will suppose you to be a perfect stranger. It is more than I can do to keep from him the knowledge that there is such wrong and misery in the world; but that it was ever so near him in his innocent cradle I have kept from him, and I do keep from him, and I ever will keep from him, for his mother's sake, and for his own."

He showed me that he distinctly understood, and the tears fell from his eyes.

"Now rest, and you shall see him."

So I got him a little wine and some brandy, and I put things straight about his bed. But I began to be troubled in my mind lest Jemmy and the Major might be too long of coming back. What with this occupation for my thoughts and hands, I didn't hear a foot upon the stairs, and was startled when I saw the Major stopped short in the middle of the room by the eyes of the man upon the bed, and knowing him then, as I had known him a little while ago.

There was anger in the Major's face, and there was horror and repugnance and I don't know what. So I went up to him and I led him to the bedside, and when I clasped my hands and lifted of them up, the Major did the like.

"O Lord" I says "Thou knowest what we two saw together of the sufferings and sorrows of that young creetur now with Thee. If this dying man is truly penitent, we two together humbly pray Thee to have mercy on him!"

The Major says "Amen!" and then after a little stop I whispers him, "Dear old friend fetch our beloved boy." And the Major, so clever as to have got to understand it all without being told a word, went away and brought him.

Never never never shall I forget the fair bright face of our boy when he stood at the foot of the bed, looking at his unknown father. And O so like his dear young mother then!

Mrs. Lirriper

"Jemmy," I says, "I have found out all about this poor gentleman who is so ill, and he did lodge in the old house once. And as he wants to see all belonging to it, now that he is passing away, I sent for you."

"Ah poor man!" says Jemmy stepping forward and touching one of his hands with great gentleness. "My heart melts for him. Poor, poor man!"

The eyes that were so soon to close for ever turned to me, and I was not that strong in the pride of my strength that I could resist them.

"My darling boy, there is a reason in the secret history of this fellow-creetur lying as the best and worst of us must all lie one day, which I think would ease his spirit in his last hour if you would lay your cheek against his forehead and say, 'May God forgive you!'"

"O Gran," says Jemmy with a full heart "I am not worthy!" But he leaned down and did it. Then the faltering fingers made out to catch hold of my sleeve at last, and I believe he was a-trying to kiss me when he died.

*   *   *   *   *   *

There my dear! There you have the story of my Legacy in full, and it's worth ten times the trouble I have spent upon it if you are pleased to like it.

You might suppose that it set us against the little French town of Sens, but no we didn't find that. I found myself that I never looked up at the high tower atop of the other tower, but the days came back again when that fair young creetur with her pretty bright hair trusted in me like a mother, and the recollection made the place so peaceful to me as I can't express. And every soul about the hotel down to the pigeons in the courtyard made friends with Jemmy and the Major, and went lumbering away with them on all sorts of expeditions in all sorts of vehicles drawn by rampagious cart-horses—with heads and without,—mud for paint and ropes for harness,—and every new friend dressed in blue like a butcher, and every new horse standing on his hind legs wanting to devour and consume every other horse, and every man that had a whip to crack crack-crack-crack-crack-cracking it as if it was a schoolboy with his first. As to the Major my dear that man lived the greater part of his time with a little tumbler in one hand and a bottle of small wine in the other, and whenever he saw anybody else with a little tumbler, no matter who it was,—the military character with

the tags, or the inn-servants at their supper in the court-
yard, or townspeople a chatting on a bench, or country
people a starting home after Market,—down rushes the
Major to clink his glass against their glasses and cry,—
Hola! Vive Somebody! or Vive Something! as if he was
beside himself. And though I could not quite approve of
the Major's doing it, still the ways of the world are the
ways of the world varying according to the different parts
of it, and dancing at all in the open Square with a lady that
kept a barber's shop my opinion is that the Major was right
to dance his best and to lead off with a power that I did not
think was in him, though I was a little uneasy at the Barri-
cading sound of the cries that were set up by the other
dancers and the rest of the company, until when I says
"What are they ever calling out Jemmy?" Jemmy says,
"They're calling out Gran, Bravo the Military English!
Bravo the Military English!" which was very gratifying to
my feelings as a Briton and became the name the Major was
known by.

But every evening at a regular time we all three sat out
in the balcony of the hotel at the end of the courtyard, looking up at the golden and rosy light as it changed on the
great towers, and looking at the shadows of the towers as
they changed on all about us ourselves included, and what
do you think we did there? My dear, if Jemmy hadn't
brought some other of those stories of the Major's taking
down from the telling of former lodgers at Eighty-one Norfolk-
street, and if he didn't bring 'em out with this speech:

"Here you are Gran! Here you are godfather! More of
'em! I'll read. And though you wrote 'em for me, godfather, I know you won't disapprove of my making 'em over
to Gran; will you?"

"No, my dear boy," says the Major. "Everything we
have is hers, and we are hers."

"Hers ever affectionately and devotedly J. Jackman, and
J. Jackman Lirriper," cries the Young Rogue giving me a
close hug. "Very well then godfather. Look here. As
Gran is in the Legacy way just now, I shall make these
stories a part of Gran's Legacy. I'll leave 'em to her. What
do you say godfather?"

"Hip hip Hurrah!" says the Major.

"Very well then," cries Jemmy all in a bustle. "Vive
the Military English! Vive the Lady Lirriper! Vive the

Jemmy Jackman Ditto! Vive the Legacy! Now, you look
out, Gran. And you look out, godfather. *I*'ll read! And
I'll tell you what I'll do besides. On the last night of our
holiday here when we are all packed and going away, I'll
top up with something of my own."

"Mind you do Sir" says I.

CHAPTER II

MRS. LIRRIPER RELATES HOW JEMMY TOPPED UP

WELL my dear and so the evening readings of those jottings
of the Major's brought us round at last to the evening when
we were all packed and going away next day, and I do assure
you that by that time though it was deliciously comfortable
to look forward to the dear old house in Norfolk-street again,
I had formed quite a high opinion of the French nation and
had noticed them to be much more homely and domestic in
their families and far more simple and amiable in their lives
than I had ever been led to expect, and it did strike me
between ourselves that in one particular they might be
imitated to advantage by another nation which I will not
mention, and that is in the courage with which they take
their little enjoyments on little means and with little things
and don't let solemn big-wigs stare them out of countenance
or speechify them dull, of which said solemn big-wigs I have
ever had the one opinion that I wish they were all made
comfortable separately in coppers with the lids on and never
let out any more.

"Now young man." I says to Jemmy when we brought
our chairs into the balcony that last evening, "you please to
remember who was to 'top up.'"

"All right Gran" says Jemmy. "I am the illustrious
personage."

But he looked so serious after he had made me that light
answer, that the Major raised his eyebrows at me and I
raised mine at the Major.

"Gran and godfather," says Jemmy, "you can hardly
think how much my mind has run on Mr. Edson's death."

It gave me a little check. "Ah! it was a sad scene my
love" I says, "and sad remembrances come back stronger
than merry. But this" I says after a little silence, to rouse

myself and the Major and Jemmy all together, "is not top-ping up. Tell us your story my dear."

"I will" says Jemmy.

"What is the date Sir?" says I. "Once upon a time when pigs drank wine?"

"No Gran," says Jemmy, still serious; "once upon a time when the French drank wine."

Again I glanced at the Major, and the Major glanced at me.

"In short, Gran and godfather," says Jemmy, looking up, "the date is this time, and I'm going to tell you Mr. Edson's story."

The flutter that it threw me into. The change of colour on the part of the Major!

"That is to say, you understand," our bright-eyed boy says, "I am going to give you my version of it. I shall not ask whether it's right or not, firstly because you said you knew very little about it, Gran, and secondly because what little you did know was a secret."

I folded my hands in my lap and I never took my eyes off Jemmy as he went running on.

"The unfortunate gentleman" Jemmy commences, "who is the subject of our present narrative was the son of Some-body, and was born Somewhere, and chose a profession Somehow. It is not with those parts of his career that we have to deal; but with his early attachment to a young and beautiful lady."

I thought I should have dropped. I durstn't look at the Major; but I knew what his state was, without looking at him.

"The father of our ill-starred hero" says Jemmy, copying as it seemed to me the style of some of his story-books, "was a worldly man who entertained ambitious views for his only son and who firmly set his face against the contemplated alliance with a virtuous but penniless orphan. Indeed he went so far as roundly to assure our hero that unless he weaned his thoughts from the object of his devoted affection, he would disinherit him. At the same time, he proposed as a suitable match the daughter of a neighbouring gentleman of a good estate, who was neither ill-favoured nor unamiable, and whose eligibility in a pecuniary point of view could not be disputed. But young Mr. Edson, true to the first and only love that had inflamed his breast, rejected all considera-tions of self-advancement, and, deprecating his father's anger in a respectful letter, ran away with her."

My dear I had begun to take a turn for the better, but when it come to running away I began to take another turn for the worse.

"The lovers" says Jemmy "fled to London and were united at the altar of Saint Clement's Danes. And it is at this period of their simple but touching story that we find them inmates of the dwelling of a highly-respected and beloved lady of the name of Gran, residing within a hundred miles of Norfolk-street."

I felt that we were almost safe now, I felt that the dear boy had no suspicion of the bitter truth, and I looked at the Major for the first time and drew a long breath. The Major gave me a nod.

"Our hero's father" Jemmy goes on "proving implacable and carrying his threat into unrelenting execution, the struggles of the young couple in London were severe, and would have been far more so, but for their good angel's having conducted them to the abode of Mrs. Gran ; who, divining their poverty (in spite of their endeavours to conceal it from her), by a thousand delicate arts smoothed their rough way, and alleviated the sharpness of their first distress."

Here Jemmy took one of my hands in one of his, and began a marking the turns of his history by making me give a beat from time to time upon his other hand.

"After a while, they left the house of Mrs. Gran, and pursued their fortunes through a variety of successes and failures elsewhere. But in all reverses, whether for good or evil, the words of Mr. Edson to the fair young partner of his life were, 'Unchanging Love and Truth will carry us through all!'"

My hand trembled in the dear boy's, those words so wofully unlike the fact.

"Unchanging Love and Truth" says Jemmy over again, as if he had a proud kind of a noble pleasure in it, "will carry us through all! Those were his words. And so they fought their way, poor but gallant and happy, until Mrs. Edson gave birth to a child."

"A daughter," I says.

"No," says Jemmy, "a son. And the father was so proud of it that he could hardly bear it out of his sight. But a dark cloud overspread the scene. Mrs. Edson sickened, drooped, and died.

"Ah! Sickened, drooped, and died!" I says.

"And so Mr. Edson's only comfort, only hope on earth, and only stimulus to action, was his darling boy. As the child grew older, he grew so like his mother that he was her living picture. It used to make him wonder why his father cried when he kissed him. But unhappily he was like his mother in constitution as well as in face, and he died too before he had grown out of childhood. Then Mr. Edson, who had good abilities, in his forlornness and despair, threw them all to the winds. He became apathetic, reckless, lost. Little by little he sank down, down, down, down, until at last he almost lived (I think) by gaming. And so sickness overtook him in the town of Sens in France, and he lay down to die. But now that he laid him down when all was done, and looked back upon the green Past beyond the time when he had covered it with ashes, he thought gratefully of the good Mrs. Gran long lost sight of, who had been so kind to him and his young wife in the early days of their marriage, and he left the little that he had as a last Legacy to her. And she, being brought to see him, at first no more knew him than she would know from seeing the ruin of a Greek or Roman Temple, what it used to be before it fell; but at length she remembered him. And then he told her, with tears, of his regret for the misspent part of his life, and besought her to think as mildly of it as she could, because it was the poor fallen Angel of his unchanging Love and Constancy after all. And because she had her grandson with her, and he fancied that his own boy, if he had lived, might have grown to be something like him, he asked her to let him touch his forehead with his cheek and say certain parting words."

Jemmy's voice sank low when it got to that and tears filled my eyes, and filled the Major's.

"You little Conjurer" I says, "how did you ever make it all out? Go in and write it every word down, for it's a wonder."

Which Jemmy did, and I have repeated it to you my dear from his writing.

Then the Major took my hand and kissed it, and said, "Dearest madam all has prospered with us."

"Ah Major" I says drying my eyes, "we needn't have been afraid. We might have known it. Treachery don't come natural to beaming youth; but trust and pity, love and constancy,—they do, thank God!"

DOCTOR MARIGOLD

[1865]

CHARACTERS

JOHN DERRICK, *valet to the haunted juryman.*

THE HAUNTED JURYMAN, *the narrator of the trial for murder.*

DOCTOR MARIGOLD, *a 'Cheap Jack': the narrator of the story.*

MRS. MARIGOLD, *his wife.*

LITTLE SOPHY MARIGOLD, *their child.*

WILLUM MARIGOLD, *father of Doctor Marigold.*

MIM, *a showman.*

PICKLESON ('Rinaldo di Velasco'), *an amiable but timid giant.*

SOPHY, *a deaf and dumb girl adopted by Doctor Marigold.*

DOCTOR MARIGOLD

IN THREE CHAPTERS

CHAPTER I

TO BE TAKEN IMMEDIATELY

I AM a Cheap Jack, and my own father's name was Willum Marigold. It was in his lifetime supposed by some that his name was William, but my own father always consistently said, No, it was Willum. On which point I content myself with looking at the argument this way: If a man is not allowed to know his own name in a free country, how much is he allowed to know in a land of slavery? As to looking at the argument through the medium of the Register, Willum Marigold come into the world before Registers come up much,—and went out of it too. They wouldn't have been greatly in his line neither, if they had chanced to come up before him.

I was born on the Queen's highway, but it was the King's at that time. A doctor was fetched to my own mother by my own father, when it took place on a common; and in consequence of his being a very kind gentleman, and accepting no fee but a tea-tray, I was named Doctor, out of gratitude and compliment to him. There you have me. Doctor Marigold.

I am at present a middle-aged man of a broadish build, in cords, leggings, and a sleeved waistcoat the strings of which is always gone behind. Repair them how you will, they go like fiddle-strings. You have been to the theatre, and you have seen one of the wiolin-players screw up his wiolin, after listening to it as if it had been whispering the secret to him that it feared it was out of order, and then you have heard it snap. That's as exactly similar to my waistcoat as a waistcoat and a wiolin can be like one another.

I am partial to a white hat, and I like a shawl round my neck wore loose and easy. Sitting down is my favourite posture. If I have a taste in point of personal jewelry, it is mother-of-pearl buttons. There you have me again, as large as life.

The doctor having accepted a tea-tray, you'll guess that my father was a Cheap Jack before me. You are right. He was. It was a pretty tray. It represented a large lady going along a serpentining up-hill gravel-walk, to attend a little church. Two swans had likewise come astray with the same intentions. When I call her a large lady, I don't mean in point of breadth, for there she fell below my views, but she more than made it up in heighth; her heighth and slimness was—in short THE heighth of both.

I often saw that tray, after I was the innocently smiling cause (or more like screeching one) of the doctor's standing it up on a table against the wall in his consulting-room. Whenever my own father and mother were in that part of the country, I used to put my head (I have heard my own mother say it was flaxen curls at that time, though you wouldn't know an old hearth-broom from it now till you come to the handle, and found it wasn't me) in at the doctor's door, and the doctor was always glad to see me, and said, "Aha, my brother practitioner! Come in, little M.D. How are your inclinations as to sixpence?"

You can't go on for ever, you'll find, nor yet could my father nor yet my mother. If you don't go off as a whole when you are about due, you're liable to go off in part, and two to one your head's the part. Gradually my father went off his, and my mother went off hers. It was in a harmless way, but it put out the family where I boarded them. The old couple, though retired, got to be wholly and solely devoted to the Cheap Jack business, and were always selling the family off. Whenever the cloth was laid for dinner, my father began rattling the plates and dishes, as we do in our line when we put up crockery for a bid, only he had lost the trick of it, and mostly let 'em drop and broke 'em. As the old lady had been used to sit in the cart, and hand the articles out one by one to the old gentleman on the footboard

to sell, just in the same way she handed him every item of
the family's property, and they disposed of it in their own
imaginations from morning to night.   At last the old gentleman, lying bedridden in the same room with the old lady,
cries out in the old patter, fluent, after having been silent for
two days and nights: "Now here, my jolly companions
every one,—which the Nightingale club in a village was
held, At the sign of the Cabbage and Shears, Where the
singers no doubt would have greatly excelled, But for want
of taste, voices, and ears,—now, here, my jolly companions,
every one, is a working model of a used-up old Cheap Jack,
without a tooth in his head, and with a pain in every bone:
so like life that it would be just as good if it wasn't better,
just as bad if it wasn't worse, and just as new if it wasn't
worn out.   Bid for the working model of the old Cheap Jack,
who has drunk more gunpowder-tea with the ladies in his
time than would blow the lid off a washerwoman's copper,
and carry it as many thousands of miles higher than the
moon as naught nix naught, divided by the national debt,
carry nothing to the poor-rates, three under, and two over.
Now, my hearts of oak and men of straw, what do you say
for the lot?   Two shillings, a shilling, tenpence, eightpence,
sixpence, fourpence. Twopence? Who said twopence? The
gentleman in the scarecrow's hat?   I am ashamed of the
gentleman in the scarecrow's hat.   I really am ashamed of
him for his want of public spirit. Now I'll tell you what I'll
do with you.   Come! I'll throw you in a working model of
a old woman that was married to the old Cheap Jack so long
ago that upon my word and honour it took place in Noah's
Ark, before the Unicorn could get in to forbid the banns
by blowing a tune upon his horn.   There now! Come!
What do you say for both?   I'll tell you what I'll do with
you.   I don't bear you malice for being so backward.   Here!
If you make me a bid that'll only reflect a little credit on
your town, I'll throw you in a warming-pan for nothing, and
lend you a toasting-fork for life.   Now come; what do you
say after that splendid offer?   Say two pound, say thirty
shillings, say a pound, say ten shillings, say five, say two and
six?   You don't say even two and six?   You say two and
three?   No.   You shan't have the lot for two and three.   I'd
sooner give it to you, if you was good-looking enough.
Here!   Missis!   Chuck the old man and woman into the
cart, put the horse to, and drive 'em away and bury 'em!"

Such were the last words of Willum Marigold, my own father, and they were carried out, by him and by his wife, my own mother, on one and the same day, as I ought to know, having followed as mourner.

My father had been a lovely one in his time at the Cheap Jack work, as his dying observations went to prove. But I top him. I don't say it because it's myself, but because it has been universally acknowledged by all that has had the means of comparison. I have worked at it. I have measured myself against other public speakers,—Members of Parliament, Platforms, Pulpits, Counsel learned in the law,—and where I have found 'em good, I have took a bit of imagination from 'em, and where I have found 'em bad, I have let 'em alone. Now I'll tell you what. I mean to go down into my grave declaring that of all the callings ill used in Great Britain, the Cheap Jack calling is the worst used. Why ain't we a profession? Why ain't we endowed with privileges? Why are we forced to take out a hawkers's license, when no such thing is expected of the political hawkers? Where's the difference betwixt us? Except that we are Cheap Jacks, and they are Dear Jacks, *I* don't see any difference but what's in our favour.

For look here! Say it's election time. I am on the footboard of my cart in the market-place, on a Saturday night. I put up a general miscellaneous lot. I say: "Now here, my free and independent woters, I'm a going to give you such a chance as you never had in all your born days, nor yet the days preceding. Now I'll show you what I am a going to do with you. Here's a pair of razors that'll shave you closer than the Board of Guardians; here's a flat-iron worth its weight in gold; here's a frying-pan artificially flavoured with essence of beefsteaks to that degree that you've only got for the rest of your lives to fry bread and dripping in it and there you are replete with animal food; here's a genuine chronometer watch in such a solid silver case that you may knock at the door with it when you come home late from a social meeting, and rouse your wife and family, and save up your knocker for the postman; and here's half-a-dozen dinner plates that you may play the cymbals with to charm the baby when it's fractious. Stop! I'll throw you in another article, and I'll give you that, and it's a rolling-pin; and if the baby can only get it well into its mouth when its teeth is coming and rub the gums once with it, they'll come through

double, in a fit of laughter equal to being tickled. Stop
again! I'll throw you in another article, because I don't like
the looks of you, for you haven't the appearance of buyers
unless I lose by you, and because I'd rather lose than not
take money to-night, and that's a looking-glass in which you
may see how ugly you look when you don't bid. What do
you say now? Come! Do you say a pound? Not you, for
you haven't got it. Do you say ten shillings? Not you, for
you owe more to the tallyman. Well then, I'll tell you
what I'll do with you. I'll heap 'em all on the footboard of
the cart,—there they are! razors, flat-iron, frying-pan, chronometer watch, dinner plates, rolling-pin, and looking-glass,—
take 'em all away for four shillings, and I'll give you sixpence
for your trouble!" This is me, the Cheap Jack. But on
the Monday morning, in the same market-place, comes the
Dear Jack on the hustings—*his* cart—and what does *he* say?
"Now my free and independent woters, I am a going to give
you such a chance" (he begins just like me) "as you never
had in all your born days, and that's the chance of sending
Myself to Parliament. Now I'll tell you what I am a going
to do for you. Here's the interests of this magnificent town
promoted above all the rest of the civilised and uncivilised
earth. Here's your railways carried, and your neighbours'
railways jockeyed. Here's all your sons in the Post-office.
Here's Britannia smiling on you. Here's the eyes of Europe
on you. Here's uniwersal prosperity for you, repletion of
animal food, golden cornfields, gladsome homesteads, and
rounds of applause from your own hearts, all in one lot, and
that's myself. Will you take me as I stand? You won't?
Well, then, I'll tell you what I'll do with you. Come now!
I'll throw you in anything you ask for. There! Church-
rates, abolition of church-rates, more malt tax, no malt tax,
uniwersal education to the highest mark, or uniwersal ignorance to the lowest, total abolition of flogging in the army or
a dozen for every private once a month all round. Wrongs
of Men or Rights of Women—only say which it shall be,
take 'em or leave 'em, and I'm of your opinion altogether,
and the lot's your own on your own terms. There! You
won't take it yet! Well, then, I'll tell you what I'll do with
you. Come! You *are* such free and independent woters,
and I *am* so proud of you,—you *are* such a noble and enlightened constituency, and I *am* so ambitious of the honour
and dignity of being your member, which is by far the

highest level to which the wings of the human mind can soar,— that I'll tell you what I'll do with you. I'll throw you in all the public-houses in your magnificent town for nothing. Will that content you? It won't? You won't take the lot yet? Well, then, before I put the horse in and drive away, and make the offer to the next most magnificent town that can be discovered, I'll tell you what I'll do. Take the lot, and I'll drop two thousand pound in the streets of your magnificent town for them to pick up that can. Not enough? Now look here. This is the very furthest that I'm a going to. I'll make it two thousand five hundred. And still you won't? Here, missis! Put the horse—no, stop half a moment, I shouldn't like to turn my back upon you neither for a trifle, I'll make it two thousand seven hundred and fifty pound. There! Take the lot on your own terms, and I'll count out two thousand seven hundred and fifty pound on the footboard of the cart, to be dropped in the streets of your magnificent town for them to pick up that can. What do you say? Come now! You won't do better, and you may do worse. You take it? Hooray! Sold again, and got the seat!"

These Dear Jacks soap the people shameful, but we Cheap Jacks don't. We tell 'em the truth about themselves to their faces, and scorn to court 'em. As to wenturesomeness in the way of puffing up the lots, the Dear Jacks beats us hollow. It is considered in the Cheap Jack calling, that better patter can be made out of a gun than any article we put up from the cart, except a pair of spectacles. I often hold forth about a gun for a quarter of an hour, and feel as if I need never leave off. But when I tell 'em what the gun can do, and what the gun has brought down, I never go half so far as the Dear Jacks do when they make speeches in praise of *their* guns—their great guns that set 'em on to do it. Besides, I'm in business for myself: I ain't sent down into the market-place to order, as they are. Besides, again, my guns don't know what I say in their laudation, and their guns do, and the whole concern of 'em have reason to be sick and ashamed all round. These are some of my arguments for declaring that the Cheap Jack calling is treated ill in Great Britain, and for turning warm when I think of the other Jacks in question setting themselves up to pretend to look down upon it.

I courted my wife from the footboard of the cart. I did

indeed. She was a Suffolk young woman, and it was in Ipswich market-place right opposite the corn-chandler's shop. I had noticed her up at a window last Saturday that was, appreciating highly. I had took to her, and I had said to myself, "If not already disposed of, I'll have that lot." Next Saturday that come, I pitched the cart on the same pitch, and I was in very high feather indeed, keeping 'em laughing the whole of the time, and getting off the goods briskly. At last I took out of my waistcoat-pocket a small lot wrapped in soft paper, and I put it this way (looking up at the window where she was). "Now here, my blooming English maidens, is an article, the last article of the present evening's sale, which I offer to only you, the lovely Suffolk Dumplings biling over with beauty, and I won't take a bid of a thousand pounds for from any man alive. Now what is it? Why, I'll tell you what it is. It's made of fine gold, and it's not broke, though there's a hole in the middle of it, and it's stronger than any fetter that ever was forged, though it's smaller than any finger in my set of ten. Why ten? Because, when my parents made over my property to me, I tell you true, there was twelve sheets, twelve towels, twelve table-cloths, twelve knives, twelve forks, twelve tablespoons, and twelve teaspoons, but my set of fingers was two short of a dozen, and could never since be matched. Now what else is it? Come, I'll tell you. It's a hoop of solid gold, wrapped in a silver curl-paper, that I myself took off the shining locks of the ever-beautiful old lady in Threadneedle-street, London city; I wouldn't tell you so if I hadn't the paper to show, or you mightn't believe it even of me. Now what else is it? It's a man-trap and a handcuff, the parish stocks and a leg-lock, all in gold and all in one. Now what else is it? It's a wedding-ring. Now I'll tell you what I'm a going to do with it. I'm not a going to offer this lot for money; but I mean to give it to the next of you beauties that laughs, and I'll pay her a visit to-morrow morning at exactly half after nine o'clock as the chimes go, and I'll take her out for a walk to put up the banns." *She* laughed, and got the ring handed up to her. When I called in the morning, she says, "O dear! It's never you, and you never mean it?" "It's ever me," says I, "and I am ever yours, and I ever mean it." So we got married, after being put up three times—which, by the bye, is quite in the Cheap Jack way again, and shows once more how the Cheap Jack customs pervade society.

She wasn't a bad wife, but she had a temper. If she could have parted with that one article at a sacrifice, I wouldn't have swopped her away in exchange for any other woman in England. Not that I ever did swop her away, for we lived together till she died, and that was thirteen year. Now, my lords and ladies and gentlefolks all, I'll let you into a secret, though you won't believe it. Thirteen year of temper in a Palace would try the worst of you, but thirteen year of temper in a Cart would try the best of you. You are kept so very close to it in a cart, you see. There's thousands of couples among you getting on like sweet ile upon a whetstone in houses five and six pairs of stairs high, that would go to the Divorce Court in a cart. Whether the jolting makes it worse, I don't undertake to decide; but in a cart it does come home to you, and stick to you. Wiolence in a cart is *so* wiolent, and aggrawation in a cart is *so* aggrawating.

We might have had such a pleasant life! A roomy cart, with the large goods hung outside, and the bed slung underneath it when on the road, an iron pot and a kettle, a fireplace for the cold weather, a chimney for the smoke, a hanging-shelf and a cupboard, a dog and a horse. What more do you want? You draw off upon a bit of turf in a green lane or by the roadside, you hobble your old horse and turn him grazing, you light your fire upon the ashes of the last visitors, you cook your stew, and you wouldn't call the Emperor of France your father. But have a temper in the cart, flinging language and the hardest goods in stock at you, and where are you then? Put a name to your feelings.

My dog knew as well when she was on the turn as I did. Before she broke out, he would give a howl, and bolt. How he knew it, was a mystery to me; but the sure and certain knowledge of it would wake him up out of his soundest sleep, and he would give a howl, and bolt. At such times I wished I was him.

The worst of it was, we had a daughter born to us, and I love children with all my heart. When she was in her furies she beat the child. This got to be so shocking, as the child got to be four or five year old, that I have many a time gone on with my whip over my shoulder, at the old horse's head, sobbing and crying worse than ever little Sophy did. For how could I prevent it? Such a thing is not to be tried with such a temper—in a cart—without coming to a fight. It's in the natural size and formation of a cart to bring it to a fight. And then the poor child got worse terrified than before, as well as worse hurt generally, and her mother made complaints to the next people we lighted on, and the word went round, "Here's a wretch of a Cheap Jack been a beating his wife."

Little Sophy was such a brave child! She grew to be quite devoted to her poor father, though he could do so little to help her. She had a wonderful quantity of shining dark hair, all curling natural about her. It is quite astonishing to me now, that I didn't go tearing mad when I used to see her run from her mother before the cart, and her mother catch her by this hair, and pull her down by it, and beat her.

Such a brave child I said she was! Ah! with reason.

"Don't you mind next time, father dear," she would whisper to me, with her little face still flushed, and her bright eyes still wet; "if I don't cry out, you may know I am not much hurt. And even if I do cry out, it will only be to get mother to let go and leave off." What I have seen the little spirit bear—for me—without crying out!

Yet in other respects her mother took great care of her. Her clothes were always clean and neat, and her mother was never tired of working at 'em. Such is the inconsistency in things. Our being down in the marsh country in unhealthy weather, I consider the cause of Sophy's taking bad low fever; but however she took it, once she got it she turned away from her mother for evermore, and nothing would persuade her to be touched by her mother's hand. She would shiver and say, "No, no, no," when it was offered at, and would hide her face on my shoulder, and hold me tighter round the neck.

The Cheap Jack business had been worse than ever I had known it, what with one thing and what with another (and not least with railroads, which will cut it all to pieces, I expect, at last), and I was run dry of money. For which reason, one night at that period of little Sophy's being so bad, either we must have come to a dead-lock for victuals and drink, or I must have pitched the cart as I did.

I couldn't get the dear child to lie down or leave go of me, and indeed I hadn't the heart to try, so I stepped out on the footboard with her holding round my neck. They all set up a laugh when they see us, and one chuckle-headed Joskin (that I hated for it) made the bidding, "Tuppence for her!"

" Now, you country boobies," says I, feeling as if my heart was a heavy weight at the end of a broken sashline, "I give you notice that I am a going to charm the money out of your pockets, and to give you so much more than your money's worth that you'll only persuade yourselves to draw your Saturday night's wages ever again arterwards by the hopes of meeting me to lay 'em out with, which you never will, and why not? Because I've made my fortune by selling my goods on a large scale for seventy-five per cent. less than I give for 'em, and I am consequently to be elevated to the House of Peers next week, by the title of the Duke of Cheap and Markis Jackaloorul. Now let's know what you want to-night, and you shall have it. But first of all, shall I tell you why I have got this little girl round my neck? You don't want to know? Then you shall. She belongs to the Fairies. She's a fortune-teller. She can tell me all about you in a whisper, and can put me up to whether you're going to buy a lot or leave it. Now do you want a saw? No, she says you don't, because you're too clumsy to use one. Else here's a saw which would be a lifelong blessing to a handy man, at four shillings, at three and six, at three, at two and six, at two, at eighteen-pence. But none of you shall have it at any price, on account of your well-known awkwardness, which would make it manslaughter. The same objection applies to this set of three planes which I won't let you have neither, so don't bid for 'em. Now I am a going to ask her what you do want." (Then I whispered, "Your head burns so, that I am afraid it hurts you bad, my pet," and she answered, without opening her heavy eyes, "Just a little, father.") "O! This little fortune-teller says it's a memorandum-book you want. Then why didn't you mention it? Here it is. Look at it. Two hundred super-fine hot-pressed wire-wove pages—if you don't believe me, count 'em—ready ruled for your expenses, an everlastingly pointed pencil to put 'em down with, a double-bladed pen-knife to scratch 'em out with, a book of printed tables to calculate your income with, and a camp-stool to sit down upon while you give your mind to it! Stop! And an umbrella to keep the moon off when you give your mind to it on a pitch-dark night. Now I won't ask you how much for the lot, but how little? How little are you thinking of? Don't be ashamed to mention it, because my fortune-teller knows already." (Then making believe to whisper, I kissed her, and she kissed me.) "Why, she says you are thinking of as little as three and threepence! I couldn't have believed it, even of you, unless she told me. Three and threepence! And a set of printed tables in the lot that'll calculate your income up to forty thousand a year! With an income of forty thousand a year, you grudge three and sixpence. Well then, I'll tell you my opinion. I so despise the threepence, that I'd sooner take three shillings. There. For three shillings, three shillings, three shillings! Gone. Hand 'em over to the lucky man."

As there had been no bid at all, everybody looked about and grinned at everybody, while I touched little Sophy's face and asked her if she felt faint, or giddy. "Not very, father. It will soon be over." Then turning from the pretty patient eyes, which were opened now, and seeing nothing but grins across my lighted grease-pot, I went on again in my Cheap Jack style. "Where's the butcher?" (My sorrowful eye had just caught sight of a fat young butcher on the outside of the crowd.) "She says the good luck is the butcher's. Where is he?" Everybody handed on the blushing butcher to the front, and there was a roar, and the butcher felt himself obliged to put his hand in his pocket, and take the lot. The party so picked out, in general, does feel obliged to take the lot—good four times out of six. Then we had another lot, the counterpart of that one, and sold it sixpence cheaper, which is always wery much enjoyed. Then we had the spectacles. It ain't a special profitable lot, but I put 'em on, and I see what the Chancellor of the Exchequer is going to take off the taxes, and I see what the sweetheart of the young woman in the shawl is doing at home, and I see what the Bishops has got for dinner, and a deal more that seldom fails to fetch 'em up in their spirits; and the better their spirits, the better their bids. Then we had the ladies' lot,—the teapot, tea-caddy, glass sugar-basin, half-a-dozen spoons, and caudle-cup—and all the time I was making similar excuses to give a look or two and say a word or two to my poor child. It was while the second ladies' lot was holding 'em enchained that I felt her lift herself a little on my shoulder, to look across the dark street. "What troubles you, darling?" "Nothing troubles me, father. I am not at all troubled. But don't I see a pretty churchyard over there?" "Yes, my dear." "Kiss me twice, dear father, and lay me down to rest upon that churchyard grass so soft and green." I staggered back into the cart with her head dropped on my shoulder, and I says to her mother, "Quick. Shut the door! Don't let those laughing people see!" "What's the matter?" she cries. "O woman, woman," I tells her, "you'll never catch my little Sophy by her hair again, for she has flown away from you!"

Maybe those were harder words than I meant 'em; but from that time forth my wife took to brooding, and would sit in the cart or walk beside it, hours at a stretch, with her arms crossed, and her eyes looking on the ground. When her furies took her (which was rather seldomer than before) they took her in a new way, and she banged herself about to that extent that I was forced to hold her. She got none the better for a little drink now and then, and through some years I used to wonder, as I plodded along at the old horse's head, whether there was many carts upon the road that held so much dreariness as mine, for all my being looked up to as the King of the Cheap Jacks. So sad our lives went on till one summer evening, when, as we were coming into Exeter, out of the farther West of England, we saw a woman beating a child in a cruel manner, who screamed, "Don't beat me! O mother, mother, mother!" Then my wife stopped her ears, and ran away like a wild thing, and next day she was found in the river.

Me and my dog were all the company left in the cart now; and the dog learned to give a short bark when they wouldn't bid, and to give another and a nod of his head when I asked him, "Who said half a crown? Are you the gentleman, Sir, that offered half a crown?" He attained to an immense height of popularity, and I shall always believe taught himself entirely out of his own head to growl at any person in the crowd that bid as low as sixpence. But he got to be well on in years, and one night when I was conwulsing York with the spectacles, he took a conwulsion on his own account upon the very footboard by me, and it finished him.

Being naturally of a tender turn, I had dreadful lonely feelings on me arter this. I conquered 'em at selling times, having a reputation to keep (not to mention keeping myself), but they got me down in private, and rolled upon me. That's often the way with us public characters. See us on the footboard, and you'd give pretty well anything you possess to be us. See us off the footboard, and you'd add a trifle to be off your bargain. It was under those circumstances that I come acquainted with a giant. I might have been too high to fall into conversation with him, had it not been for my lonely feelings. For the general rule is, going round the country, to draw the line at dressing up. When a man can't trust his getting a living to his undisguised abilities, you consider him below your sort. And this giant when on view figured as a Roman.

He was a languid young man, which I attribute to the distance betwixt his extremities. He had a little head and less in it, he had weak eyes and weak knees, and altogether you couldn't look at him without feeling that there was greatly too much of him both for his joints and his mind. But he was an amiable though timid young man (his mother let him out, and spent the money), and we come acquainted when he was walking to ease the horse betwixt two fairs. He was called Rinaldo di Velasco, his name being Pickleson.

This giant, otherwise Pickleson, mentioned to me under the seal of confidence that, beyond his being a burden to himself, his life was made a burden to him by the cruelty of his master towards a step-daughter who was deaf and dumb. Her mother was dead, and she had no living soul to take her part, and was used most hard. She travelled with his master's caravan only because there was nowhere to leave her, and this giant, otherwise Pickleson, did go so far as to believe that his master often tried to lose her. He was such a very languid young man, that I don't know how long it didn't take him to get this story out, but it passed through his defective circulation to his top extremity in course of time.

When I heard this account from the giant, otherwise Pickleson, and likewise that the poor girl had beautiful long dark hair, and was often pulled down by it and beaten, I couldn't see the giant through what stood in my eyes. Having wiped 'em, I give him sixpence (for he was kept as short as he was long), and he laid it out in two three-penn'orths of gin-and-water, which so brisked him up, that he sang the Favourite Comic of Shivery Shakey, ain't it cold? —a popular effect which his master had tried every other means to get out of him as a Roman wholly in vain.

His master's name was Mim, a wery hoarse man, and I knew him to speak to. I went to that Fair as a mere civilian, leaving the cart outside the town, and I looked about the back of the Vans while the performing was going on, and at last, sitting dozing against a muddy cart-wheel, I came upon the poor girl who was deaf and dumb. At the first look I might almost have judged that she had escaped from the Wild Beast Show; but at the second I thought better of her, and thought that if she was more cared for and more kindly used she would be like my child. She was just the same age that my own daughter would have been, if her pretty head had not fell down upon my shoulder that unfortunate night.

To cut it short, I spoke confidential to Mim while he was beating the gong outside betwixt two lots of Pickleson's publics, and I put it to him, "She lies heavy on your own hands; what'll you take for her?" Mim was a most ferocious swearer. Suppressing that part of his reply which was much the longest part, his reply was, "A pair of braces." "Now I'll tell you," says I, "what I'm a going to do with you. I'm a going to fetch you half-a-dozen pair of the primest braces in the cart, and then to take her away with me." Says Mim (again ferocious), "I'll believe it when I've got the goods, and no sooner." I made all the haste I could, lest he should think twice of it, and the bargain was completed, which Pickleson he was thereby so relieved in his mind that he come out at his little back door, longways like a serpent, and give us Shivery Shakey in a whisper among the wheels at parting.

It was happy days for both of us when Sophy and me began to travel in the cart. I at once give her the name of Sophy, to put her ever towards me in the attitude of my own daughter. We soon made out to begin to understand one another, through the goodness of the Heavens, when she knowed that I meant true and kind by her. In a very little time she was wonderful fond of me. You have no idea what it is to have anybody wonderful fond of you, unless you have been got down and rolled upon by the lonely feelings that I have mentioned as having once got the better of me.

You'd have laughed—or the rewerse—it's according to your disposition—if you could have seen me trying to teach Sophy. At first I was helped—you'd never guess by what —milestones. I got some large alphabets in a box, all the letters separate on bits of bone, and saying we was going to WINDSOR, I give her those letters in that order, and then at every milestone I showed her those same letters in that same order again, and pointed towards the abode of royalty. Another time I give her CART, and then chalked the same

upon the cart. Another time I give her DOCTOR MARI-
GOLD, and hung a corresponding inscription outside my
waistcoat. People that met us might stare a bit and laugh.
but what did *I* care, if she caught the idea? She caught it
after long patience and trouble, and then we did begin to
get on swimmingly, I believe you! At first she was a little
given to consider me the cart, and the cart the abode of
royalty, but that soon wore off.

We had our signs, too, and they was hundreds in number.
Sometimes she would sit looking at me and considering hard
how to communicate with me about something fresh,—how
to ask me what she wanted explained,—and then she was
(or I thought she was; what does it signify?) so like my
child with those years added to her, that I half-believed it
was herself, trying to tell me where she had been to up in
the skies, and what she had seen since that unhappy night
when she flied away. She had a pretty face, and now that
there was no one to drag at her bright dark hair, and it was
all in order, there was a something touching in her looks that
made the cart most peaceful and most quiet, though not
at all melancholy. [N.B. In the Cheap Jack patter, we
generally sound it lemonjolly, and it gets a laugh.]

The way she learnt to understand any look of mine was
truly surprising. When I sold of a night, she would sit in
the cart unseen by them outside, and would give a eager
look into my eyes when I looked in, and would hand me
straight the precise article or articles I wanted. And then
she would clap her hands, and laugh for joy. And as for me,
seeing her so bright, and remembering what she was when I
first lighted on her, starved and beaten and ragged, leaning
asleep against the muddy cart-wheel, it give me such heart
that I gained a greater heighth of reputation than ever, and
I put Pickleson down (by the name of Mim's Travelling
Giant otherwise Pickleson) for a fypunnote in my will.

This happiness went on in the cart till she was sixteen
year old. By which time I began to feel not satisfied that
I had done my whole duty by her, and to consider that she
ought to have better teaching than I could give her. It drew
a many tears on both sides when I commenced explaining
my views to her; but what's right is right, and you can't
neither by tears nor laughter do away with its character.

So I took her hand in mine, and I went with her one day
to the Deaf and Dumb establishment in London, and when

the gentleman come to speak to us, I says to him: "Now I'll tell you what I'll do with you, Sir. I am nothing but a Cheap Jack, but of late years I have laid by for a rainy day notwithstanding. This is my only daughter (adopted), and you can't produce a deafer nor a dumber. Teach her the most that can be taught her in the shortest separation that can be named,—state the figure for it,—and I am game to put the money down. I won't bate you a single farthing, Sir, but I'll put down the money here and now, and I'll thankfully throw you in a pound to take it. There!" The gentleman smiled, and then, "Well, well," says he, "I must first know what she has learned already. How do you communicate with her?" Then I showed him, and she wrote in printed writing many names of things and so forth; and we held some sprightly conversation, Sophy and me, about a little story in a book which the gentleman showed her, and which she was able to read. "This is most extraordinary," says the gentleman; "is it possible that you have been her only teacher?" "I have been her only teacher, Sir," I says, "besides herself." "Then," says the gentleman, and more acceptable words was never spoken to me, "you're a clever fellow, and a good fellow." This he makes known to Sophy, who kisses his hands, clasps her own, and laughs and cries upon it.

We saw the gentleman four times in all, and when he took down my name and asked how in the world it ever chanced to be Doctor, it come out that he was own nephew by the sister's side, if you'll believe me, to the very Doctor that I was called after. This made our footing still easier, and he says to me:

"Now, Marigold, tell me what more do you want your adopted daughter to know?"

"I want her, Sir, to be cut off from the world as little as can be, considering her deprivations, and therefore to be able to read whatever is wrote with perfect ease and pleasure."

"My good fellow," urges the gentleman, opening his eyes wide, "why *I* can't do that myself!"

I took his joke, and gave him a laugh (knowing by experience how flat you fall without it), and I mended my words accordingly.

"What do you mean to do with her afterwards?" asks the gentleman, with a sort of a doubtful eye. "To take her about the country?"

"In the cart, Sir, but only in the cart. She will live a private life, you understand, in the cart. I should never think of bringing her infirmities before the public. I wouldn't make a show of her for any money."

The gentleman nodded, and seemed to approve.

"Well," says he, "can you part with her for two years?"

"To do her that good,—yes, Sir."

"There's another question," says the gentleman, looking towards her,—"can she part with you for two years?"

I don't know that it was a harder matter of itself (for the other was hard enough to me), but it was harder to get over. However, she was pacified to it at last, and the separation betwixt us was settled. How it cut up both of us when it took place, and when I left her at the door in the dark of an evening, I don't tell. But I know this; remembering that night, I shall never pass that same establishment without a heartache and a swelling in the throat; and I couldn't put you up the best of lots in sight of it with my usual spirit, —no, not even the gun, nor the pair of spectacles,—for five hundred pound reward from the Secretary of State for the Home Department, and throw in the honour of putting my legs under his mahogany arterwards.

Still, the loneliness that followed in the cart was not the old loneliness, because there was a term put to it, however long to look forward to; and because I could think, when I was anyways down, that she belonged to me and I belonged to her. Always planning for her coming back, I bought in a few months' time another cart, and what do you think I planned to do with it? I'll tell you. I planned to fit it up with shelves and books for her reading, and to have a seat in it where I could sit and see her read, and think that I had been her first teacher. Not hurrying over the job, I had the fittings knocked together in contriving ways under my own inspection, and here was her bed in a berth with curtains, and there was her reading-table, and here was her writing-desk, and elsewhere was her books in rows upon rows, picters and no picters, bindings and no bindings, gilt-edged and plain, just as I could pick 'em up for her in lots up and down the country, North and South and West and East, Winds liked best and winds liked least, Here and there and gone astray, Over the hills and far away. And when I had got together pretty well as many books as the cart would neatly hold, a new scheme come into my head, which, as it turned out, kept my time and attention a good deal employed, and helped me over the two years' stile.

Without being of an awaricious temper, I like to be the owner of things. I shouldn't wish, for instance, to go partners with yourself in the Cheap Jack cart. It's not that I mistrust you, but that I'd rather know it was mine. Similarly, very likely you'd rather know it was yours. Well! A kind of a jealousy began to creep into my mind when I reflected that all those books would have been read by other people long before they was read by her. It seemed to take away from her being the owner of 'em like. In this way, the question got into my head: Couldn't I have a book new-made express for her, which she should be the first to read?

It pleased me, that thought did; and as I never was a man to let a thought sleep (you must wake up all the whole family of thoughts you've got and burn their nightcaps, or you won't do in the Cheap Jack line), I set to work at it. Considering that I was in the habit of changing so much about the country, and that I should have to find out a literary character here to make a deal with, and another literary character there to make a deal with, as opportunities presented, I hit on the plan that this same book should be a general miscellaneous lot,—like the razors, flat-iron, chronometer watch, dinner plates, rolling-pin, and looking-glass,— and shouldn't be offered as a single indiwidual article, like the spectacles or the gun. When I had come to that conclusion, I come to another, which shall likewise be yours.

Often had I regretted that she never had heard me on the footboard, and that she never could hear me. It ain't that *I* am vain, but that *you* don't like to put your own light under a bushel. What's the worth of your reputation, if you can't convey the reason for it to the person you most wish to value it? Now I'll put it to you. Is it worth sixpence, fippence, fourpence, threepence, twopence, a penny, a halfpenny, a farthing? No, it ain't. Not worth a farthing. Very well, then. My conclusion was that I would begin her book with some account of myself. So that, through reading a specimen or two of me on the footboard, she might form an idea of my merits there. I was aware that I could'nt do myself justice. A man can't write his eye (at least *I* don't know how to), nor yet can a man write his voice, nor the rate of his talk, nor the quickness of his action, nor his general spicy way. But he can write his turns of speech, when he is a public speaker,—and indeed I have heard that he very often does, before he speaks 'em.

Well! Having formed that resolution, then come the question of a name. How did I hammer that hot iron into shape? This way. The most difficult explanation I had ever had with her was, how I come to be called Doctor, and yet was no Doctor. After all, I felt that I had failed of getting it correctly into her mind, with my utmost pains. But trusting to her improvement in the two years, I thought that I might trust to her understanding it when she should come to read it as put down by my own hand. Then I thought I would try a joke with her and watch how it took, by which of itself I might fully judge of her understanding it. We had first discovered the mistake we had dropped into, through her having asked me to prescribe for her when she had supposed me to be a Doctor in a medical point of view; so thinks I, "Now, if I give this book the name of my Prescriptions, and if she catches the idea that my only Prescriptions are for her amusement and interest,—to make her laugh in a pleasant way, or to make her cry in a pleasant way,—it will be a delightful proof to both of us that we have got over our difficulty." It fell out to absolute perfection. For when she saw the book, as I had it got up,—the printed and pressed book,—lying on her desk in her cart, and saw the title, DOCTOR MARIGOLD'S PRESCRIPTIONS, she looked at me for a moment with astonishment, then fluttered the leaves, then broke out a laughing in the charmingest way, then felt her pulse and shook her head, then turned the pages pretending to read them most attentive, then kissed the book to me, and put it to her bosom with both her hands. I never was better pleased in all my life!

But let me not anticipate. (I take that expression out of a lot of romances I bought for her. I never opened a single one of 'em—and I have opened many—but I found the romancer saying "let me not anticipate." Which being so, I wonder why he did anticipate, or who asked him to it.) Let me not, I say, anticipate. This same book took up all my spare time. It was no play to get the other articles together in the general miscellaneous lot, but when it come to my own article! There! I couldn't have believed the blotting, nor yet the buckling to at it, nor the patience over it. Which again is like the footboard. The public have no idea.

At last it was done, and the two years' time was gone after

all the other time before it, and where it's all gone to, who knows? The new cart was finished,—yellow outside, relieved with wermilion and brass fittings,—the old horse was put in it, a new 'un and a boy being laid on for the Cheap Jack cart, and I cleaned myself up to go and fetch her. Bright cold weather it was, cart chimneys smoking, carts pitched private on a piece of waste ground over at Wandsworth, where you may see 'em from the Sou'western Railway when not upon the road. (Look out of the right-hand window going down.)

"Marigold," says the gentleman, giving his hand hearty, "I am very glad to see you."

"Yet I have my doubts, Sir," says I, "if you can be half as glad to see me as I am to see you."

"The time has appeared so long,—has it, Marigold?"

"I won't say that, Sir, considering its real length; but——"

"What a start, my good fellow!"

Ah! I should think it was! Grown such a woman, so pretty, so intelligent, so expressive! I knew then that she must be really like my child, or I could never have known her, standing quiet by the door.

"You are affected," says the gentleman in a kindly manner.

"I feel, Sir," says I, "that I am but a rough chap in a sleeved waistcoat."

"I feel," says the gentleman, "that it was you who raised her from misery and degradation, and brought her into communication with her kind. But why do we converse alone together, when we can converse so well with her? Address her in your own way."

"I am such a rough chap in a sleeved waistcoat, Sir," says I, "and she is such a graceful woman, and she stands so quiet at the door!"

"Try if she moves at the old sign," says the gentleman.

They had got it up together o' purpose to please me! For when I give her the old sign, she rushed to my feet, and dropped upon her knees, holding up her hands to me with pouring tears of love and joy; and when I took her hands and lifted her, she clasped me round the neck, and lay there; and I don't know what a fool I didn't make of myself, until we all three settled down into talking without sound, as if there was a something soft and pleasant spread over the whole world for us.

[A portion is here omitted from the text, having reference to the sketches contributed by other writers; but the reader will be pleased to have what follows retained in a note:

"Now I'll tell you what I am a-going to do with you. I am a-going to offer you the general miscellaneous lot, her own book, never read by anybody else but me, added to and completed by me after her first reading of it, eight-and-forty printed pages, six-and-ninety columns, Whiting's own work, Beaufort House to wit, thrown off by the steam-ingine, best of paper, beautiful green wrapper, folded like clean linen come home from the clear-starcher's, and so exquisitely stitched that, regarded as a piece of needlework alone, it's better than the sampler of a seamstress undergoing a Competitive examination for Starvation before the Civil Service Commissioners—and I offer the lot for what? For eight pound? Not so much. For six pound? Less. For four pound. Why, I hardly expect you to believe me, but that's the sum. Four pound! The stitching alone cost half as much again. Here's forty-eight original pages, ninety-six original columns, for four pound. You want more for the money? Take it. Three whole pages of advertisements of thrilling interest thrown in for nothing. Read 'em and believe 'em. More? My best of wishes for your merry Christmases and your happy New Years, your long lives and your true prosperities. Worth twenty pound good if they are delivered as I send them. Remember! Here's a final prescription added, "To be taken for life," which will tell you how the cart broke down, and where the journey ended. You think Four Pound too much? And still you think so? Come! I'll tell you what then. Say Four Pence, and keep the secret."]

CHAPTER II

TO BE TAKEN WITH A GRAIN OF SALT

I HAVE always noticed a prevalent want of courage, even among persons of superior intelligence and culture, as to imparting their own psychological experiences when those have been of a strange sort. Almost all men are afraid that what they could relate in such wise would find no parallel or response in a listener's internal life, and might be suspected or laughed at. A truthful traveller, who should have seen some extraordinary creature in the likeness of a sea-serpent, would have no fear of mentioning it; but the same traveller, having had some singular presentiment, impulse, vagary of thought, vision (so called), dream, or other remarkable mental impression, would hesitate considerably before he would own to it. To this reticence I attribute much of the obscurity in which such subjects are involved. We do not habitually communicate our experiences of these subjective things as we do our experiences of objective creation. The consequence is, that the general stock of experience in this regard appears exceptional, and really is so, in respect of being miserably imperfect.

In what I am going to relate, I have no intention of setting up, opposing, or supporting, any theory whatever. I know the history of the Bookseller of Berlin, I have studied the case of the wife of a late Astronomer Royal as related by Sir David Brewster, and I have followed the minutest details of a much more remarkable case of Spectral Illusion occurring within my private circle of friends. It may be necessary to state as to this last, that the sufferer (a lady) was in no degree, however distant, related to me. A mistaken assumption on that head might suggest an explanation of a part of my own case,—but only a part,—which would be wholly without foundation. It cannot be referred to my inheritance of any developed peculiarity, nor had I ever before any at all similar experience, nor have I ever had any at all similar experience since.

It does not signify how many years ago, or how few, a certain murder was committed in England, which attracted great attention. We hear more than enough of murderers as they rise in succession to their atrocious eminence, and I would bury the memory of this particular brute, if I could, as his body was buried, in Newgate Jail. I purposely abstain from giving any direct clew to the criminal's individuality.

When the murder was first discovered, no suspicion fell— or I ought rather to say, for I cannot be too precise in my facts, it was nowhere publicly hinted that any suspicion fell —on the man who was afterwards brought to trial. As no reference was at that time made to him in the newspapers, it is obviously impossible that any description of him can at that time have been given in the newspapers. It is essential that this fact be remembered.

Unfolding at breakfast my morning paper, containing the account of that first discovery, I found it to be deeply interesting, and I read it with close attention. I read it twice, if not three times. The discovery had been made in a bedroom, and, when I laid down the paper, I was aware of a flash—rush—flow—I do not know what to call it,—no word I can find is satisfactorily descriptive,—in which I seemed to see that bedroom passing through my room, like a picture impossibly painted on a running river. Though almost instantaneous in its passing, it was perfectly clear; so clear that I distinctly, and with a sense of relief, observed the absence of the dead body from the bed.

It was in no romantic place that I had this curious sensation, but in chambers in Piccadilly, very near to the corner of St. James's-street. It was entirely new to me. I was in my easy-chair at the moment, and the sensation was accompanied with a peculiar shiver which started the chair from its position. (But it is to be noted that the chair ran easily on castors.) I went to one of the windows (there are two in the room, and the room is on the second floor) to refresh my eyes with the moving objects down in Piccadilly. It was a bright autumn morning, and the street was sparkling and cheerful. The wind was high. As I looked out, it brought down from the Park a quantity of fallen leaves, which a gust took, and whirled into a spiral pillar. As the pillar fell and the leaves dispersed, I saw two men on the opposite side of the way, going from West to East. They were one behind the other. The foremost man often looked back over his shoulder. The second man followed him, at a distance of some thirty paces, with his right hand menacingly raised. First, the singularity and steadiness of this threatening gesture in so public a thoroughfare attracted my attention; and next, the more remarkable circumstance that nobody heeded it. Both men threaded their way among the other passengers with a smoothness hardly consistent even with the action of walking on a pavement; and no single creature, that I could see, gave them place, touched them, or looked after them. In passing before my windows, they both stared up at me. I saw their two faces very distinctly, and I knew that I could recognise them anywhere. Not that I had consciously noticed anything very remarkable in either face, except that the man who went first had an unusually lower-ing appearance, and that the face of the man who followed him was of the colour of impure wax.

I am a bachelor, and my valet and his wife constitute my whole establishment. My occupation is in a certain Branch Bank, and I wish that my duties as head of a Department were as light as they are popularly supposed to be. They kept me in town that autumn, when I stood in need of change. I was not ill, but I was not well. My reader is to make the most that can be reasonably made of my feeling jaded, having a depressing sense upon me of a monotonous life, and being "slightly dyspeptic." I am assured by my renowned doctor that my real state of health at that time justifies no stronger description, and I quote his own from his written answer to my request for it.

As the circumstances of the murder, gradually unravelling, took stronger and stronger possession of the public mind, I kept them away from mine by knowing as little about them as was possible in the midst of the universal excitement. But I knew that a verdict of Wilful Murder had been found against the suspected murderer, and that he had been committed to Newgate for trial. I also knew that his trial had been postponed over one Sessions of the Central Criminal Court, on the ground of general prejudice and want of time for the preparation of the defence. I may further have known, but I believe I did not, when, or about when, the Sessions to which his trial stood postponed would come on.

My sitting-room, bedroom, and dressing-room, are all on one floor. With the last there is no communication but through the bedroom. True, there is a door in it, once com-municating with the staircase; but a part of the fitting of my bath has been—and had then been for some years—fixed across it. At the same period, and as a part of the same arrangement, the door had been nailed up and canvased over.

I was standing in my bedroom late one night, giving some directions to my servant before he went to bed. My face was towards the only available door of communication with the dressing-room, and it was closed. My servant's back was towards that door. While I was speaking to him, I saw it open, and a man look in, who very earnestly and mysteriously beckoned to me. That man was the man who had gone second of the two along Piccadilly, and whose face was the colour of impure wax.

The figure, having beckoned, drew back, and closed the door. With no longer pause than was made by my crossing the bedroom, I opened the dressing-room door, and looked in. I had a lighted candle already in my hand. I felt no inward expectation of seeing the figure in the dressing-room, and I did not see it there.

Conscious that my servant stood amazed, I turned round to him, and said : " Derrick, could you believe that in my cool senses I fancied I saw a—— " As I there laid my hand upon his breast, with a sudden start he trembled violently, and said, " O Lord, yes, Sir ! A dead man beckoning ! "

Now I do not believe that this John Derrick, my trusty and attached servant for more than twenty years, had any impression whatever of having seen any such figure, until I touched him. The change in him was so startling, when I touched him, that I fully believe he derived his impression in some occult manner from me at that instant.

I bade John Derrick bring some brandy, and I gave him a dram, and was glad to take one myself. Of what had preceded that night's phenomenon, I told him not a single word. Reflecting on it, I was absolutely certain that I had never seen that face before, except on the one occasion in Piccadilly. Comparing its expression when beckoning at the door with its expression when it had stared up at me as I stood at my window, I came to the conclusion that on the first occasion it had sought to fasten itself upon my memory, and that on the second occasion it had made sure of being immediately remembered.

I was not very comfortable that night, though I felt a certainty, difficult to explain, that the figure would not return. At daylight I fell into a heavy sleep, from which I was awakened by John Derrick's coming to my bedside with a paper in his hand.

This paper, it appeared, had been the subject of an alter-cation at the door between its bearer and my servant. It was a summons to me to serve upon a Jury at the forth-coming Sessions of the Central Criminal Court at the Old Bailey. I had never before been summoned on such a Jury, as John Derrick well knew. He believed—I am not certain at this hour whether with reason or otherwise—that that class of Jurors were customarily chosen on a lower qualifica-tion than mine, and he had at first refused to accept the summons. The man who served it had taken the matter very coolly. He had said that my attendance or non-attendance was nothing to him; there the summons was; and I should deal with it at my own peril, and not at his.

For a day or two I was undecided whether to respond to this call, or take no notice of it. I was not conscious of the slightest mysterious bias, influence, or attraction, one way or other. Of that I am as strictly sure as of every other statement that I make here. Ultimately I decided, as a break in the monotony of my life, that I would go.

The appointed morning was a raw morning in the month of November. There was a dense brown fog in Piccadilly, and it became positively black and in the last degree oppressive East of Temple Bar. I found the passages and staircases of the Court-House flaringly lighted with gas, and the Court itself similarly illuminated. I *think* that, until I was conducted by officers into the Old Court and saw its crowded state. I did not know that the Murderer was to be tried that day. I *think* that, until I was so helped into the Old Court with considerable difficulty, I did not know into which of the two Courts sitting my summons would take me. But this must not be received as a positive assertion, for I am not completely satisfied in my mind on either point.

I took my seat in the place appropriated to Jurors in waiting, and I looked about the Court as well as I could through the cloud of fog and breath that was heavy in it. I noticed the black vapour hanging like a murky curtain outside the great windows, and I noticed the stifled sound of wheels on the straw or tan that was littered in the street; also, the hum of the people gathered there, which a shrill whistle, or a louder song or hail than the rest, occasionally pierced. Soon afterwards the Judges, two in number, entered, and took their seats. The buzz in the Court was awfully hushed. The direction was given to put the Murderer to the bar. He appeared there. And in that same instant I recognised in him the first of the two men who had gone down Piccadilly.

If my name had been called then, I doubt if I could have answered to it audibly. But it was called about sixth or eighth in the panel, and I was by that time able to say " Here! " Now, observe. As I stepped into the box, the prisoner, who had been looking on attentively, but with no sign of concern, became violently agitated, and beckoned to his attorney. The prisoner's wish to challenge me was so

manifest, that it occasioned a pause, during which the
attorney, with his hand upon the dock, whispered with his
client, and shook his head.   I afterwards had it from that
gentleman, that the prisoner's first affrighted words to him
were, "*At all hazards, challenge that man!*" But that, as he
would give no reason for it, and admitted that he had not
even known my name until he heard it called and I appeared,
it was not done.

Both on the ground already explained, that I wish to
avoid reviving the unwholesome memory of that Murderer,
and also because a detailed account of his long trial is by no
means indispensable to my narrative, I shall confine myself
closely to such incidents in the ten days and nights during
which we, the Jury, were kept together, as directly bear on
my own curious personal experience.   It is in that, and not
in the Murderer, that I seek to interest my reader.   It is to
that, and not to a page of the Newgate Calendar, that I
beg attention.

I was chosen Foreman of the Jury.   On the second morning of the trial, after evidence had been taken for two hours
(I heard the church clocks strike), happening to cast my eyes
over my brother jurymen, I found an inexplicable difficulty
in counting them.   I counted them several times, yet always
with the same difficulty.   In short, I made them one too many.

I touched the brother juryman whose place was next me,
and I whispered to him, "Oblige me by counting us."   He
looked surprised by the request, but turned his head and
counted.   "Why," says he, suddenly, "we are Thirt—; but
no, it's not possible.   No.   We are twelve."

According to my counting that day, we were always right
in detail, but in the gross we were always one too many.
There was no appearance—no figure—to account for it; but
I had now an inward foreshadowing of the figure that was
surely coming.

The Jury were housed at the London Tavern.   We all
slept in one large room on separate tables, and we were constantly in the charge and under the eye of the officer sworn
to hold us in safe-keeping.   I see no reason for suppressing
the real name of that officer.   He was intelligent, highly
polite, and obliging, and (I was glad to hear) much respected
in the City.   He had an agreeable presence, good eyes,
enviable black whiskers, and a fine sonorous voice.   His
name was Mr. Harker.

When we turned into our twelve beds at night, Mr. Harker's bed was drawn across the door. On the night of the second day, not being disposed to lie down, and seeing Mr. Harker sitting on his bed, I went and sat beside him, and offered him a pinch of snuff. As Mr. Harker's hand touched mine in taking it from my box, a peculiar shiver crossed him, and he said, "Who is this?"

Following Mr. Harker's eyes, and looking along the room, I saw again the figure I expected,—the second of the two men who had gone down Piccadilly. I rose, and advanced a few steps; then stopped, and looked round at Mr. Harker. He was quite unconcerned, laughed, and said in a pleasant way, "I thought for a moment we had a thirteenth juryman, without a bed. But I see it is the moonlight."

Making no revelation to Mr. Harker, but inviting him to take a walk with me to the end of the room, I watched what the figure did. It stood for a few moments by the bedside of each of my eleven brother jurymen, close to the pillow. It always went to the right-hand side of the bed, and always passed out crossing the foot of the next bed. It seemed, from the action of the head, merely to look down pensively at each recumbent figure. It took no notice of me, or of my bed, which was that nearest to Mr. Harker's. It seemed to go out where the moonlight came in, through a high window, as by an aërial flight of stairs.

Next morning at breakfast, it appeared that everybody present had dreamed of the murdered man last night, except myself and Mr. Harker.

I now felt as convinced that the second man who had gone down Piccadilly was the murdered man (so to speak), as if it had been borne into my comprehension by his immediate testimony. But even this took place, and in a manner for which I was not at all prepared.

On the fifth day of the trial, when the case for the prosecution was drawing to a close, a miniature of the murdered man, missing from his bedroom upon the discovery of the deed, and afterwards found in a hiding-place where the Murderer had been seen digging, was put in evidence. Having been identified by the witness under examination, it was handed up to the Bench, and thence handed down to be inspected by the Jury. As an officer in a black gown was making his way with it across to me, the figure of the second man who had gone down Piccadilly impetuously started from the crowd, caught the miniature from the officer, and gave it to me with his own hands, at the same time saying, in a low and hollow tone,—before I saw the miniature, which was in a locket,—"*I was younger then, and my face was not then drained of blood.*" It also came between me and the brother juryman to whom I would have given the miniature, and between him and the brother juryman to whom he would have given it, and so passed it on through the whole of our number, and back into my possession. Not one of them, however, detected this.

At table, and generally when we were shut up together in Mr. Harker's custody, we had from the first naturally discussed the day's proceedings a good deal. On that fifth day, the case for the prosecution being closed, and we having that side of the question in a completed shape before us, our discussion was more animated and serious. Among our number was a vestryman,—the densest idiot I have ever seen at large,—who met the plainest evidence with the most preposterous objections, and who was sided with by two flabby parochial parasites; all the three impanelled from a district so delivered over to Fever that they ought to have been upon their own trial for five hundred Murders. When these mischievous blockheads were at their loudest, which was towards midnight, while some of us were already preparing for bed, I again saw the murdered man. He stood grimly behind them, beckoning to me. On my going towards them, and striking into the conversation, he immediately retired. This was the beginning of a separate series of appearances, confined to that long room in which *we* were confined. Whenever a knot of my brother jurymen laid their heads together, I saw the head of the murdered man among theirs. Whenever their comparison of notes was going against him, he would solemnly and irresistibly beckon to me.

It will be borne in mind that down to the production of the miniature, on the fifth day of the trial, I had never seen the Appearance in Court. Three changes occurred now that we entered on the case for the defence. Two of them I will mention together, first. The figure was now in Court continually, and it never there addressed itself to me, but always to the person who was speaking at the time. For instance: the throat of the murdered man had been cut straight across.

In the opening speech for the defence, it was suggested that the deceased might have cut his own throat. At that very moment, the figure, with its throat in the dreadful condition referred to (this it had concealed before), stood at the speaker's elbow, motioning across and across its windpipe, now with the right hand, now with the left, vigorously suggesting to the speaker himself the impossibility of such a wound having been self-inflicted by either hand. For another instance: a witness to character, a woman, deposed to the prisoner's being the most amiable of mankind. The figure at that instant stood on the floor before her, looking her full in the face, and pointing out the prisoner's evil countenance with an extended arm and an outstretched finger.

The third change now to be added impressed me strongly as the most marked and striking of all. I do not theorise upon it; I accurately state it, and there leave it. Although the Appearance was not itself perceived by those whom it addressed, its coming close to such persons was invariably attended by some trepidation or disturbance on their part. It seemed to me as if it were prevented, by laws to which I was not amenable, from fully revealing itself to others, and yet as if it could invisibly, dumbly, and darkly overshadow their minds. When the leading counsel for the defence suggested that hypothesis of suicide, and the figure stood at the learned gentleman's elbow, frightfully sawing at its severed throat, it is undeniable that the counsel faltered in his speech, lost for a few seconds the thread of his ingenious discourse, wiped his forehead with his handkerchief, and turned extremely pale. When the witness to character was confronted by the Appearance, her eyes most certainly did follow the direction of its pointed finger, and rest in great hesitation and trouble upon the prisoner's face. Two additional illustrations will suffice. On the eighth day of the trial, after the pause which was every day made early in the afternoon for a few minutes' rest and refreshment, I came back into court with the rest of the Jury some little time before the return of the Judges. Standing up in the box and looking about me, I thought the figure was not there, until, chancing to raise my eyes to the gallery, I saw it bending forward, and leaning over a very decent woman, as if to assure itself whether the Judges had resumed their seats or not. Immediately afterwards that woman screamed, fainted, and was carried out. So with the venerable, sagacious, and patient Judge who conducted the trial. When the case was over, and he settled himself and his papers to sum up, the murdered man, entering by the Judges' door, advanced to his Lordship's desk, and looked eagerly over his shoulder at the pages of his notes which he was turning. A change came over his Lordship's face; his hand stopped; the peculiar shiver, that I knew so well, passed over him; he faltered, "Excuse me, gentlemen, for a few moments. I am somewhat oppressed by the vitiated air;" and did not recover until he had drunk a glass of water.

Through all the monotony of six of those interminable ten days,—the same Judges and others on the bench, the same Murderer in the dock, the same lawyers at the table, the same tones of question and answer rising to the roof of the Court, the same scratching of the Judge's pen, the same ushers going in and out, the same lights kindled at the same hour when there had been any natural light of day, the same foggy curtain outside the great windows when it was foggy, the same rain pattering and dripping when it was rainy, the same footmarks of turnkeys and prisoner day after day on the same sawdust, the same keys locking and unlocking the same heavy doors,—through all the wearisome monotony which made me feel as if I had been Foreman of the Jury for a vast period of time, and Piccadilly had flourished coevally with Babylon, the murdered man never lost one trace of his distinctness in my eyes, nor was he at any moment less distinct than anybody else. I must not omit, as a matter of fact, that I never once saw the Appearance which I call by the name of the murdered man look at the Murderer. Again and again I wondered, "Why does he not?" But he never did.

Nor did he look at me, after the production of the miniature, until the last closing minutes of the trial arrived. We retired to consider, at seven minutes before ten at night. The idiotic vestryman and his two parochial parasites gave us so much trouble that we twice returned into Court to beg to have certain extracts from the Judge's notes re-read. Nine of us had not the smallest doubt about those passages, neither, I believe, had any one in the Court; the dunder-headed triumvirate, however, having no idea but obstruction, disputed them for that very reason. At length we prevailed, and finally the Jury returned into Court at ten minutes past twelve.

The murdered man at that time stood directly opposite the Jury-box, on the other side of the Court. As I took my place, his eyes rested on me with great attention ; he seemed satisfied, and slowly shook a great grey veil, which he carried on his arm for the first time, over his head and whole form. As I gave in our verdict, " Guilty," the veil collapsed, all was gone, and his place was empty.

The Murderer, being asked by the Judge, according to usage, whether he had anything to say before sentence of Death should be passed upon him, indistinctly muttered something which was described in the leading newspapers of the following day as "a few rambling, incoherent, and half-audible words, in which he was understood to complain that he had not had a fair trial, because the Foreman of the Jury was prepossessed against him." The remarkable declaration that he really made was this : *"My Lord, I knew I was a doomed man, when the Foreman of my Jury came into the box. My Lord, I knew he would never let me off, because, before I was taken, he somehow got to my bedside in the night, woke me, and put a rope round my neck."*

CHAPTER III

TO BE TAKEN FOR LIFE

So every item of my plan was crowned with success. Our reunited life was more than all that we had looked forward to. Content and joy went with us as the wheels of the two carts went round, and the same stopped with us when the two carts stopped. I was as pleased and as proud as a Pug-Dog with his muzzle black-leaded for a evening party, and his tail extra curled by machinery.

But I had left something out of my calculations. Now, what had I left out? To help you to guess I'll say, a figure. Come. Make a guess and guess right. Nought? No. Nine? No. Eight? No. Seven? No. Six? No. Five? No. Four? No. Three? No. Two? No. One? No. Now I'll tell you what I'll do with you. I'll say it's another sort of figure altogether. There. Why then, says you, it's a mortal figure. No, nor yet a mortal figure. By such means you get yourself penned into a corner, and you can't help guessing a *im*mortal figure. That's about it. Why didn't you say so sooner?

Yes. It was a immortal figure that I had altogether left out of my calculations. Neither man's, nor woman's, but a child's. Girl's or boy's? Boy's. "I, says the sparrow, with my bow and arrow." Now you have got it.

We were down at Lancaster, and I had done two nights more than fair average business (though I cannot in honour recommend them as a quick audience) in the open square there, near the end of the street where Mr. Sly's King's Arms and Royal Hotel stands. Mim's travelling giant, otherwise Pickleson, happened at the self-same time to be trying it on in the town. The genteel lay was adopted with him. No hint of a van. Green baize alcove leading up to Pickleson in a Auction Room. Printed poster, " Free list suspended, with the exception of that proud boast of an enlightened country, a free press. Schools admitted by private arrangement. Nothing to raise a blush in the cheek of youth or shock the most fastidious." Mim swearing most horrible and terrific, in a pink calico pay-place, at the slackness of the public. Serious handbill in the shops, importing that it was all but impossible to come to a right understanding of the history of David without seeing Pickleson.

I went to the Auction Room in question, and I found it entirely empty of everything but echoes and mouldiness, with the single exception of Pickleson on a piece of red drugget. This suited my purpose, as I wanted a private and confidential word with him, which was: "Pickleson. Owing much happiness to you, I put you in my will for a fypunnote ; but, to save trouble, here's fourpunten down, which may equally suit your views, and let us so conclude the transaction." Pickleson, who up to that remark had had the dejected appearance of a long Roman rushlight that couldn't anyhow get lighted, brightened up at his top extremity, and made his acknowledgments in a way which (for him) was parliamentary eloquence. He likewise did add, that, having ceased to draw as a Roman, Mim had made proposals for his going in as a converted Indian Giant worked upon by The Dairyman's Daughter. This, Pickleson, having no acquaintance with the tract named after that young woman, and not being willing to couple gag with his serious views, had declined to do, thereby leading to words and the total stoppage of the unfortunate young man's beer. All of which, during the whole of the interview, was confirmed by the ferocious growling of Mim down below in the pay-place, which shook the giant like a leaf.

But what was to the present point in the remarks of the travelling giant, otherwise Pickleson, was this: "Doctor Marigold,"—I give his words without a hope of conveying their feebleness,—"who is the strange young man that hangs about your carts?"—"The strange young *man?*" I gives him back, thinking that he meant her, and his languid circulation had dropped a syllable. "Doctor," he returns, with a pathos calculated to draw a tear from even a manly eye, "I am weak, but not so weak yet as that I don't know my words. I repeat them, Doctor. The strange young man." It then appeared that Pickleson, being forced to stretch his legs (not that they wanted it) only at times when he couldn't be seen for nothing, to wit in the dead of the night and towards daybreak, had twice seen hanging about my carts, in that same town of Lancaster where I had been only two nights, this same unknown young man.

It put me rather out of sorts. What it meant as to particulars I no more foreboded then than you forebode now, but it put me rather out of sorts. Howsoever, I made light of it to Pickleson, and I took leave of Pickleson, advising him to spend his legacy in getting up his stamina, and to continue to stand by his religion. Towards morning I kept a look out for the strange young man, and—what was more— I saw the strange young man. He was well dressed and well looking. He loitered very nigh my carts, watching them like as if he was taking care of them, and soon after daybreak turned and went away. I sent a hail after him, but he never started or looked round, or took the smallest notice.

We left Lancaster within an hour or two, on our way towards Carlisle. Next morning, at daybreak, I looked out again for the strange young man. I did not see him. But next morning I looked out again, and there he was once more. I sent another hail after him, but as before he gave not the slightest sign of being anyways disturbed. This put a thought into my head. Acting on it I watched him in different manners and at different times not necessary to enter into, till I found that this strange young man was deaf and dumb.

The discovery turned me over, because I knew that a part

of that establishment where she had been was allotted to
young men (some of them well off), and I thought to myself, "If she favours him, where am I? and where is all that
I have worked and planned for?" Hoping—I must confess to
the selfishness—that she might *not* favour him, I set myself
to find out. At last I was by accident present at a meeting
between them in the open air, looking on leaning behind a
fir-tree without their knowing of it. It was a moving meeting for all the three parties concerned. I knew every syllable that passed between them as well as they did. I listened
with my eyes, which had come to be as quick and true with
deaf and dumb conversation as my ears with the talk of
people that can speak. He was a-going out to China as
clerk in a merchant's house, which his father had been before
him. He was in circumstances to keep a wife, and he wanted
her to marry him and go along with him. She persisted,
no. He asked if she didn't love him. Yes, she loved him
dearly, dearly; but she could never disappoint her beloved,
good, noble, generous, and I don't-know-what-all father (meaning me, the Cheap Jack in the sleeved waistcoat), and she
would stay with him, Heaven bless him! though it was to
break her heart. Then she cried most bitterly, and that
made up my mind.

While my mind had been in an unsettled state about
her favouring this young man, I had felt that unreasonable
towards Pickleson, that it was well for him he had got his
legacy down. For I often thought, "If it hadn't been for
this same weak-minded giant, I might never have come to
trouble my head and wex my soul about the young man."
But, once that I knew she loved him,—once that I had seen
her weep for him,—it was a different thing. I made it right
in my mind with Pickleson on the spot, and I shook myself
together to do what was right by all.

She had left the young man by that time (for it took a
few minutes to get me thoroughly well shook together), and
the young man was leaning against another of the fir-trees,—
of which there was a cluster,—with his face upon his arm.
I touched him on the back. Looking up and seeing me, he
says, in our deaf-and-dumb talk, "Do not be angry."

"I am not angry, good boy. I am your friend. Come
with me."

I left him at the foot of the steps of the Library Cart, and
I went up alone. She was drying her eyes.

"You have been crying, my dear."

"Yes, father."

"Why?"

"A headache."

"Not a heartache?"

"I said a headache, father."

"Doctor Marigold must prescribe for that headache."

She took up the book of my Prescriptions, and held it up with a forced smile; but seeing me keep still and look earnest, she softly laid it down again, and her eyes were very attentive.

"The Prescription is not there, Sophy."

"Where is it?"

"Here, my dear."

I brought her young husband in, and I put her hand in his, and my only farther words to both of them were these: "Doctor Marigold's last Prescription. To be taken for life." After which I bolted.

When the wedding came off, I mounted a coat (blue, and bright buttons), for the first and last time in all my days, and I give Sophy away with my own hand. There were only us three and the gentleman who had had charge of her for those two years. I give the wedding dinner of four in the Library Cart. Pigeon-pie, a leg of pickled pork, a pair of fowls, and suitable garden stuff. The best of drinks. I give them a speech, and the gentleman give us a speech, and all our jokes told, and the whole went off like a sky-rocket. In the course of the entertainment I explained to Sophy that I should keep the Library Cart as my living-cart when not upon the road, and that I should keep all her books for her just as they stood, till she come back to claim them. So she went to China with her young husband, and it was a parting sorrowful and heavy, and I got the boy I had another service; and so as of old, when my child and wife were gone, I went plodding along alone, with my whip over my shoulder, at the old horse's head.

Sophy wrote me many letters, and I wrote her many letters. About the end of the first year she sent me one in an unsteady hand: "Dearest father, not a week ago I had a darling little daughter, but I am so well that they let me write these words to you. Dearest and best father, I hope my child may not be deaf and dumb, but I do not yet know." When I wrote back, I hinted the question; but as

Sophy never answered that question, I felt it to be a sad one, and I never repeated it. For a long time our letters were regular, but then they got irregular, through Sophy's husband being moved to another station, and through my being always on the move. But we were in one another's thoughts, I was equally sure, letters or no letters.

Five years, odd months, had gone since Sophy went away. I was still the King of the Cheap Jacks, and at a greater height of popularity than ever. I had had a first-rate autumn of it, and on the twenty-third of December, one thousand eight hundred and sixty-four, I found myself at Uxbridge, Middlesex, clean sold out. So I jogged up to London with the old horse, light and easy, to have my Christmas-eve and Christmas-day alone by the fire in the Library Cart, and then to buy a regular new stock of goods all round, to sell 'em again and get the money.

I am a neat hand at cookery, and I'll tell you what I knocked up for my Christmas-eve dinner in the Library Cart. I knocked up a beefsteak-pudding for one, with two kidneys, a dozen oysters, and a couple of mushrooms thrown in. It's a pudding to put a man in good humour with everything, except the two bottom buttons of his waistcoat. Having relished that pudding and cleared away, I turned the lamp low, and sat down by the light of the fire, watching it as it shone upon the backs of Sophy's books.

Sophy's books so brought up Sophy's self, that I saw her touching face quite plainly, before I dropped off dozing by the fire. This may be a reason why Sophy, with her deaf-and-dumb child in her arms, seemed to stand silent by me all through my nap. I was on the road, off the road, in all sorts of places, North and South and West and East, Winds liked best and winds liked least, Here and there and gone astray, Over the hills and far away, and still she stood silent by me, with her silent child in her arms. Even when I woke with a start, she seemed to vanish, as if she had stood by me in that very place only a single instant before.

I had started at a real sound, and the sound was on the steps of the cart. It was the light hurried tread of a child, coming clambering up. That tread of a child had once been so familiar to me, that for half a moment I believed I was a-going to see a little ghost.

But the touch of a real child was laid upon the outer handle of the door, and the handle turned, and the door opened a little way, and a real child peeped in. A bright little comely girl with large dark eyes.

Looking full at me, the tiny creature took off her mite of a straw hat, and a quantity of dark curls fell all about her face. Then she opened her lips, and said in a pretty voice,

" Grandfather ! "

" Ah, my God ! " I cries out. "She can speak ! "

" Yes, dear grandfather. And I am to ask you whether there was ever any one that I remind you of ? "

In a moment Sophy was round my neck, as well as the child, and her husband was a-wringing my hand with his face hid, and we all had to shake ourselves together before we could get over it. And when we did begin to get over it, and I saw the pretty child a-talking, pleased and quick and eager and busy, to her mother, in the signs that I had first taught her mother, the happy and yet pitying tears fell rolling down my face.

MUGBY JUNCTION

[1866]

CHARACTERS

BEATRICE, *a careworn woman, the wife of Tresham.*

EZEKIEL, *a boy in the refreshment-room at Mugby Junction.*

MR. JACKSON ('Barbox Brothers'), *a former clerk in the firm of Barbox Brothers, later its sole surviving representative.*

LAMPS, *a railway servant employed at Mugby Junction.*

PHŒBE, *his crippled daughter.*

MISS PIFF, *an attendant in the refreshment-room.*

POLLY, *daughter of Beatrice and Tresham.*

THE SIGNALMAN, *a cool, clear-headed man, but haunted by an apparition; the subject of a Ghost-story by Mr. Jackson.*

MR. SNIFF, *an 'odd man' employed in the refreshment-room.*

MRS. SNIFF, *his wife; chief assistant of the refreshment-room manageress.*

TRESHAM, *a former friend of Mr. Jackson's.*

MISS WHIFF, *an attendant in the refreshment-room.*

MUGBY JUNCTION

IN FOUR CHAPTERS

CHAPTER I

BARBOX BROTHERS

I

"GUARD! What place is this?"

"Mugby Junction, Sir."

"A windy place!"

"Yes, it mostly is, Sir."

"And looks comfortless indeed!"

"Yes, it generally does, Sir."

"Is it a rainy night still?"

"Pours, Sir."

"Open the door. I'll get out."

"You'll have, Sir," said the guard, glistening with drops of wet, and looking at the tearful face of his watch by the light of his lantern as the traveller descended, "three minutes here."

"More, I think.—For I am not going on."

"Thought you had a through ticket, Sir?"

"So I have, but I shall sacrifice the rest of it. I want my luggage."

"Please to come to the van and point it out, Sir. Be good enough to look very sharp, Sir. Not a moment to spare."

The guard hurried to the luggage van, and the traveller

hurried after him.   The guard got into it, and the traveller looked into it.

"Those two large black portmanteaus in the corner where your light shines.   Those are mine."

"Name upon 'em, Sir?"

"Barbox Brothers."

"Stand clear, Sir, if you please.   One.   Two.   Right!" Lamp waved.   Signal lights ahead already changing.   Shriek from engine.   Train gone.

"Mugby Junction!" said the traveller, pulling up the woollen muffler round his throat with both hands.   "At past three o'clock of a tempestuous morning!   So!"

He spoke to himself.   There was no one else to speak to. Perhaps, though there had been any one else to speak to, he would have preferred to speak to himself.   Speaking to himself he spoke to a man within five years of fifty either way, who had turned grey too soon, like a neglected fire; a man of pondering habit, brooding carriage of the head, and suppressed internal voice; a man with many indications on him of having been much alone.

He stood unnoticed on the dreary platform, except by the rain and by the wind.   Those two vigilant assailants made a rush at him.   "Very well," said he, yielding.   "It signifies nothing to me to what quarter I turn my face."

Thus, at Mugby Junction, at past three o'clock of a tempestuous morning, the traveller went where the weather drove him.

Not but what he could make a stand when he was so minded, for, coming to the end of the roofed shelter (it is of considerable extent at Mugby Junction), and looking out upon the dark night, with a yet darker spirit-wing of storm beating its wild way through it, he faced about, and held his own as ruggedly in the difficult direction as he had held it in the easier one.   Thus, with a steady step, the traveller went up and down, up and down, up and down, seeking nothing and finding it.

A place replete with shadowy shapes, this Mugby Junction in the black hours of the four-and-twenty.   Mysterious goods trains, covered with palls and gliding on like vast weird funerals, conveying themselves guiltily away from the presence of the few lighted lamps, as if their freight had come to a secret and unlawful end.   Half-miles of coal pursuing in a Detective manner, following when they lead, stopping when they stop, backing when they back. Red-hot embers showering out upon the ground, down this dark avenue, and down the other, as if torturing fires were being raked clear; concurrently, shrieks and groans and grinds invading the ear, as if the tortured were at the height of their suffering. Iron-barred cages full of cattle jangling by midway, the drooping beasts with horns entangled, eyes frozen with terror, and mouths too : at least they have long icicles (or what seem so) hanging from their lips. Unknown languages in the air, conspiring in red, green, and white characters. An earthquake, accompanied with thunder and lightning, going up express to London. Now, all quiet, all rusty, wind and rain in possession, lamps extinguished, Mugby Junction dead and indistinct, with its robe drawn over its head, like Cæsar.

Now, too, as the belated traveller plodded up and down, a shadowy train went by him in the gloom which was no other than the train of a life. From whatsoever intangible deep cutting or dark tunnel it emerged, here it came, unsummoned and unannounced, stealing upon him, and passing away into obscurity. Here mournfully went by a child who had never had a childhood or known a parent, inseparable from a youth with a bitter sense of his nameless-ness, coupled to a man the enforced business of whose best years had been distasteful and oppressive, linked to an un-grateful friend, dragging after him a woman once beloved. Attendant, with many a clank and wrench, were lumbering cares, dark meditations, huge dim disappointments, monoto-nous years, a long jarring line of the discords of a solitary and unhappy existence.

" —Yours, Sir ? "

The traveller recalled his eyes from the waste into which they had been staring, and fell back a step or so under the abruptness, and perhaps the chance appropriateness, of the question.

" Oh ! My thoughts were not here for the moment. Yes. Yes. Those two portmanteaus are mine. Are you a Porter ? "

" On Porter's wages, Sir. But I am Lamps."

The traveller looked a little confused.

" Who did you say you are ? "

" Lamps, Sir," showing an oily cloth in his hand, as further explanation.

" Surely, surely. Is there any hotel or tavern here ? "

"Not exactly here, Sir. There is a Refreshment Room here, but——" Lamps, with a mighty serious look, gave his head a warning roll that plainly added—"but it's a blessed circumstance for you that it's not open."

"You couldn't recommend it, I see, if it was available?"

"Ask your pardon, Sir. If it was——?"

"Open?"

"It ain't my place, as a paid servant of the company, to give my opinion on any of the company's toepics,"—he pronounced it more like toothpicks,—"beyond lamp-ile and cottons," returned Lamps in a confidential tone; "but, speaking as a man, I wouldn't recommend my father (if he was to come to life again) to go and try how he'd be treated at the Refreshment Room. Not speaking as a man, no, I would *not.*"

The traveller nodded conviction. "I suppose I can put up in the town? There is a town here?" For the traveller (though a stay-at-home compared with most travellers) had been, like many others, carried on the steam winds and the iron tides through that Junction before, without having ever, as one might say, gone ashore there.

"Oh yes, there's a town, Sir! Anyways, there's town enough to put up in. But," following the glance of the other at his luggage, "this is a very dead time of the night with us, Sir. The deadest time. I might a'most call it our deadest and buriedest time."

"No porters about?"

"Well, Sir, you see," returned Lamps, confidential again, "they in general goes off with the gas. That's how it is. And they seem to have overlooked you, through your walking to the furder end of the platform. But, in about twelve minutes or so, she may be up."

"Who may be up?"

"The three forty-two, Sir. She goes off in a sidin' till the Up X passes, and then she"—here an air of hopeful vagueness pervaded Lamps—"does all as lays in her power."

"I doubt if I comprehend the arrangement."

"I doubt if anybody do, Sir. She's a Parliamentary, Sir. And, you see, a Parliamentary, or a Skirmishun——"

"Do you mean an Excursion?"

"That's it, Sir.—A Parliamentary or a Skirmishun, she mostly *doos* go off into a sidin'. But, when she *can* get a chance, she's whistled out of it, and she's whistled up into

doin' all as,"—Lamps again wore the air of a highly
sanguine man who hoped for the best,—"all as lays in her
power."

He then explained that porters on duty, being required
to be in attendance on the Parliamentary matron in question,
would doubtless turn up with the gas. In the meantime, if
the gentleman would not very much object to the smell of
lamp-oil, and would accept the warmth of his little room——
The gentleman, being by this time very cold, instantly closed
with the proposal.

A greasy little cabin it was, suggestive, to the sense of
smell, of a cabin in a Whaler. But there was a bright fire
burning in its rusty grate, and on the floor there stood
a wooden stand of newly trimmed and lighted lamps, ready
for carriage service. They made a bright show, and their
light, and the warmth, accounted for the popularity of the
room, as borne witness to by many impressions of velveteen
trousers on a form by the fire, and many rounded smears
and smudges of stooping velveteen shoulders on the adjacent
wall. Various untidy shelves accommodated a quantity of
lamps and oil-cans, and also a fragrant collection of what
looked like the pocket-handkerchiefs of the whole lamp
family.

As Barbox Brothers (so to call the traveller on the warranty
of his luggage) took his seat upon the form, and warmed
his now ungloved hands at the fire, he glanced aside at
a little deal desk, much blotched with ink, which his elbow
touched. Upon it were some scraps of coarse paper, and
a superannuated steel pen in very reduced and gritty circumstances.

From glancing at the scraps of paper, he turned involuntarily to his host, and said, with some roughness:

"Why, you are never a poet, man?"

Lamps had certainly not the conventional appearance of
one, as he stood modestly rubbing his squab nose with
a handkerchief so exceedingly oily, that he might have been
in the act of mistaking himself for one of his charges. He
was a spare man of about the Barbox Brothers' time of life,
with his features whimsically drawn upward as if they were
attracted by the roots of his hair. He had a peculiarly
shining transparent complexion, probably occasioned by
constant oleaginous application; and his attractive hair,
being cut short, and being grizzled, and standing straight

up on end as if it in its turn were attracted by some invisible magnet above it, the top of his head was not very unlike a lamp-wick.

"But, to be sure, it's no business of mine," said Barbox Brothers. "That was an impertinent observation on my part. Be what you like."

"Some people, Sir," remarked Lamps in a tone of apology, "are sometimes what they don't like."

"Nobody knows that better than I do," sighed the other. "I have been what I don't like, all my life."

"When I first took, Sir," resumed Lamps, "to composing little Comic-Songs-like——"

Barbox Brothers eyed him with great disfavour.

"—To composing little Comic-Songs-like—and what was more hard—to singing 'em afterwards," said Lamps, "it went against the grain at that time, it did indeed."

Something that was not all oil here shining in Lamps's eye, Barbox Brothers withdrew his own a little disconcerted, looked at the fire, and put a foot on the top bar. "Why did you do it, then?" he asked after a short pause; abruptly enough, but in a softer tone. "If you didn't want to do it, why did you do it? Where did you sing them? Public-house?"

To which Mr. Lamps returned the curious reply: "Bed-side."

At this moment, while the traveller looked at him for elucidation, Mugby Junction started suddenly, trembled violently, and opened its gas eyes. "She's got up!" Lamps announced, excited. "What lays in her power is sometimes more, and sometimes less; but it's laid in her power to get up to-night, by George!"

The legend "Barbox Brothers," in large white letters on two black surfaces, was very soon afterwards trundling on a truck through a silent street, and, when the owner of the legend had shivered on the pavement half an hour, what time the porter's knocks at the Inn Door knocked up the whole town first, and the Inn last, he groped his way into the close air of a shut-up house, and so groped between the sheets of a shut-up bed that seemed to have been expressly refrigerated for him when last made.

II

"You remember me, Young Jackson?"

"What do I remember if not you? You are my first remembrance. It was you who told me that was my name. It was you who told me that on every twentieth of December my life had a penitential anniversary in it called a birthday. I suppose the last communication was truer than the first!"

"What am I like, Young Jackson?"

"You are like a blight all through the year to me. You hard-lined, thin-lipped, repressive, changeless woman with a wax mask on. You are like the Devil to me; most of all when you teach me religious things, for you make me abhor them."

"You remember me, Mr. Young Jackson?" In another voice from another quarter.

"Most gratefully, Sir. You were the ray of hope and prospering ambition in my life. When I attended your course, I believed that I should come to be a great healer, and I felt almost happy—even though I was still the one boarder in the house with that horrible mask, and ate and drank in silence and constraint with the mask before me, every day. As I had done every, every, every day, through my school-time and from my earliest recollection."

"What am I like, Mr. Young Jackson?"

"You are like a Superior Being to me. You are like Nature beginning to reveal herself to me. I hear you again, as one of the hushed crowd of young men kindling under the power of your presence and knowledge, and you bring into my eyes the only exultant tears that ever stood in them."

"You remember Me, Mr. Young Jackson?" In a grating voice from quite another quarter.

"Too well. You made your ghostly appearance in my life one day, and announced that its course was to be suddenly and wholly changed. You showed me which was my wearisome seat in the Galley of Barbox Brothers. (When *they* were, if they ever were, is unknown to me; there was nothing of them but the name when I bent to the oar.) You told me what I was to do, and what to be paid; you told me afterwards, at intervals of years, when I was to sign for the Firm, when I became a partner, when I became the Firm. I know no more of it, or of myself."

"What am I like, Mr. Young Jackson?"

"You are like my father, I sometimes think. You are hard enough and cold enough so to have brought up an acknowledged son. I see your scanty figure, your close brown suit, and your tight brown wig; but you, too, wear a wax mask to your death. You never by a chance remove it—it never by a chance falls off—and I know no more of you."

Throughout this dialogue, the traveller spoke to himself at his window in the morning, as he had spoken to himself at the Junction overnight. And as he had then looked in the darkness, a man who had turned grey too soon, like a neglected fire: so he now looked in the sunlight, an ashier grey, like a fire which the brightness of the sun put out.

The firm of Barbox Brothers had been some offshoot or irregular branch of the Public Notary and bill-broking tree. It had gained for itself a griping reputation before the days of Young Jackson, and the reputation had stuck to it and to him. As he had imperceptibly come into possession of the dim den up in the corner of a court off Lombard Street, on whose grimy windows the inscription Barbox Brothers had for many long years daily interposed itself between him and the sky, so he had insensibly found himself a personage held in chronic distrust, whom it was essential to screw tight to every transaction in which he engaged, whose word was never to be taken without his attested bond, whom all dealers with openly set up guards and wards against. This character had come upon him through no act of his own. It was as if the original Barbox had stretched himself down upon the office floor, and had thither caused to be conveyed Young Jackson in his sleep, and had there effected a metempsychosis and exchange of persons with him. The discovery—aided in its turn by the deceit of the only woman he had ever loved, and the deceit of the only friend he had ever made; who eloped from him to be married together—the discovery, so followed up, completed what his earliest rearing had begun. He shrank, abashed, within the form of Barbox, and lifted up his head and heart no more.

But he did at last effect one great release in his condition. He broke the oar he had plied so long, and he scuttled and sank the galley. He prevented the gradual retirement of an old conventional business from him, by taking the initiative and retiring from it. With enough to live on (though, after all, with not too much), he obliterated the firm of Barbox Brothers from the pages of the Post-Office Directory and the face of the earth, leaving nothing of it but its name on two portmanteaus.

"For one must have some name in going about, for people to pick up," he explained to Mugby High Street, through the Inn window, "and that name at least was real once. Whereas, Young Jackson!—Not to mention its being a sadly satirical misnomer for Old Jackson."

He took up his hat and walked out, just in time to see, passing along on the opposite side of the way, a velveteen man, carrying his day's dinner in a small bundle that might have been larger without suspicion of gluttony, and pelting away towards the Junction at a great pace.

"There's Lamps!" said Barbox Brothers. "And by-the-bye——"

Ridiculous, surely, that a man so serious, so self-contained, and not yet three days emancipated from a routine of drudgery, should stand rubbing his chin in the street, in a brown study about Comic Songs.

"Bedside?" said Barbox Brothers testily. "Sings them at the bedside? Why at the bedside, unless he goes to bed drunk? Does, I shouldn't wonder. But it's no business of mine. Let me see. Mugby Junction, Mugby Junction. Where shall I go next? As it came into my head last night when I woke from an uneasy sleep in the carriage and found myself here, I can go anywhere from here. Where shall I go? I'll go and look at the Junction by daylight. There's no hurry, and I may like the look of one Line better than another."

But there were so many Lines. Gazing down upon them from a bridge at the Junction, it was as if the concentrating Companies formed a great Industrial Exhibition of the works of extraordinary ground spiders that spun iron. And then so many of the Lines went such wonderful ways, so crossing and curving among one another, that the eye lost them. And then some of them appeared to start with the fixed intention of going five hundred miles, and all of a sudden gave it up at an insignificant barrier, or turned off into a workshop. And then others, like intoxicated men, went a little way very straight, and surprisingly slued round and came back again. And then others were so chock-full of trucks of coal, others were so blocked with trucks of casks, others were so gorged with trucks of ballast, others were so set apart for wheeled objects like immense iron cotton-reels : while others were so bright and clear, and others were so delivered over to rust and ashes and idle wheelbarrows out of work, with their legs in the air (looking much like their masters on strike), that there was no beginning, middle, or end to the bewilderment.

Barbox Brothers stood puzzled on the bridge, passing his right hand across the lines on his forehead, which multiplied while he looked down, as if the railway Lines were getting themselves photographed on that sensitive plate. Then was heard a distant ringing of bells and blowing of whistles. Then, puppet-looking heads of men popped out of boxes in perspective, and popped in again. Then, prodigious wooden razors, set up on end, began shaving the atmosphere. Then, several locomotive engines in several directions began to scream and be agitated. Then, along one avenue a train came in. Then, along another two trains appeared that didn't come in, but stopped without. Then, bits of trains broke off. Then, a struggling horse became involved with them. Then, the locomotives shared the bits of trains, and ran away with the whole.

"I have not made my next move much clearer by this. No hurry. No need to make up my mind to-day, or to-morrow, nor yet the day after. I'll take a walk."

It fell out somehow (perhaps he meant it should) that the walk tended to the platform at which he had alighted, and to Lamps's room. But Lamps was not in his room. A pair of velveteen shoulders were adapting themselves to one of the impressions on the wall by Lamps's fireplace, but otherwise the room was void. In passing back to get out of the station again, he learnt the cause of this vacancy, by catching sight of Lamps on the opposite line of railway, skipping along the top of a train, from carriage to carriage, and catching lighted namesakes thrown up to him by a coadjutor.

"He is busy. He has not much time for composing or singing Comic Songs this morning, I take it."

The direction he pursued now was into the country, keeping very near to the side of one great Line of railway, and within easy view of others. "I have half a mind," he said, glancing around, "to settle the question from this point, by saying, 'I'll take this set of rails, or that, or t'other, and stick to it.' They separate themselves from the confusion, out here, and go their ways."

Ascending a gentle hill of some extent, he came to a few cottages. There, looking about him as a very reserved man might who had never looked about him in his life before, he saw some six or eight young children come merrily trooping and whooping from one of the cottages, and disperse. But not until they had all turned at the little garden-gate, and kissed their hands to a face at the upper window: a low window enough, although the upper, for the cottage had but a story of one room above the ground.

Now, that the children should do this was nothing; but that they should do this to a face lying on the sill of the open window, turned towards them in a horizontal position, and apparently only a face, was something noticeable. He looked up at the window again. Could only see a very fragile, though a very bright face, lying on one cheek on the window-sill. The delicate smiling face of a girl or woman. Framed in long bright brown hair, round which was tied a light blue band or fillet, passing under the chin.

He walked on, turned back, passed the window again, shyly glanced up again. No change. He struck off by a winding branch-road at the top of the hill—which he must otherwise have descended—kept the cottages in view, worked his way round at a distance so as to come out once more into the main road, and be obliged to pass the cottages again. The face still lay on the window-sill, but not so much inclined towards him. And now there were a pair of delicate hands too. They had the action of performing on some musical instrument, and yet it produced no sound that reached his ears.

"Mugby Junction must be the maddest place in England," said Barbox Brothers, pursuing his way down the hill. "The first thing I find here is a Railway Porter who composes comic songs to sing at his bedside. The second thing I find here is a face, and a pair of hands playing a musical instrument that *don't* play!"

The day was a fine bright day in the early beginning of November, the air was clear and inspiriting, and the landscape was rich in beautiful colours. The prevailing colours in the court off Lombard Street, London city, had been few and sombre. Sometimes, when the weather elsewhere was very bright indeed, the dwellers in those tents enjoyed a pepper-

and-salt-coloured day or two, but their atmosphere's usual wear was slate or snuff-coloured.

He relished his walk so well that he repeated it next day. He was a little earlier at the cottage than on the day before, and he could hear the children upstairs singing to a regular measure, and clapping out the time with their hands.

"Still, there is no sound of any musical instrument," he said, listening at the corner, "and yet I saw the performing hands again as I came by. What are the children singing? Why, good Lord, they can never be singing the multiplication table?"

They were, though, and with infinite enjoyment. The mysterious face had a voice attached to it, which occasionally led or set the children right. Its musical cheerfulness was delightful. The measure at length stopped, and was succeeded by a murmuring of young voices, and then by a short song which he made out to be about the current month of the year, and about what work it yielded to the labourers in the fields and farmyards. Then there was a stir of little feet, and the children came trooping and whooping out, as on the previous day. And again, as on the previous day, they all turned at the garden-gate, and kissed their hands—evidently to the face on the window-sill, though Barbox Brothers from his retired post of disadvantage at the corner could not see it.

But, as the children dispersed, he cut off one small straggler —a brown-faced boy with flaxen hair—and said to him:

"Come here, little one. Tell me, whose house is that?"

The child, with one swarthy arm held up across his eyes, half in shyness, and half ready for defence said from behind the inside of his elbow:

"Phœbe's."

"And who," said Barbox Brothers, quite as much embarrassed by his part in the dialogue as the child could possibly be by his, "is Phœbe?"

To which the child made answer: "Why, Phœbe, of course."

The small but sharp observer had eyed his questioner closely, and had taken his moral measure. He lowered his guard, and rather assumed a tone with him: as having discovered him to be an unaccustomed person in the art of polite conversation.

"Phœbe," said the child, "can't be anybobby else but Phœbe. Can she?"

"No, I suppose not."

"Well," returned the child, "then why did you ask me?"

Deeming it prudent to shift his ground, Barbox Brothers took up a new position.

"What do you do there? Up there in that room where the open window is. What do you do there?"

"Cool," said the child.

"Eh?"

"Co-o-ol," the child repeated in a louder voice, lengthening out the word with a fixed look and great emphasis, as much as to say: "What's the use of your having grown up, if you're such a donkey as not to understand me?"

"Ah! School, school," said Barbox Brothers. "Yes, yes, yes. And Phœbe teaches you?"

The child nodded.

"Good boy."

"Tound it out, have you?" said the child.

"Yes, I have found it out. What would you do with twopence, if I gave it you?"

"Pend it."

The knock-down promptitude of this reply leaving him not a leg to stand upon, Barbox Brothers produced the twopence with great lameness, and withdrew in a state of humiliation.

But, seeing the face on the window-sill as he passed the cottage, he acknowledged its presence there with a gesture, which was not a nod, not a bow, not a removal of his hat from his head, but was a diffident compromise between or struggle with all three. The eyes in the face seemed amused, or cheered, or both, and the lips modestly said: "Good day to you, Sir."

"I find I must stick for a time to Mugby Junction," said Barbox Brothers with much gravity, after once more stopping on his return road to look at the Lines where they went their several ways so quietly. "I can't make up my mind yet which iron road to take. In fact, I must get a little accustomed to the Junction before I can decide."

So, he announced at the Inn that he was "going to stay on for the present," and improved his acquaintance with the Junction that night, and again next morning, and again next night and morning: going down to the station, mingling with the people there, looking about him down all the avenues of railway, and beginning to take an interest in the incomings and outgoings of the trains. At first, he often put his head into Lamps's little room, but he never found Lamps there.

A pair or two of velveteen shoulders he usually found there, stooping over the fire, sometimes in connexion with a clasped knife and a piece of bread and meat; but the answer to his inquiry, " Where's Lamps?" was, either that he was " t'other side the line," or, that it was his off-time, or (in the latter case) his own personal introduction to another Lamps who was not his lamps. However, he was not so desperately set upon seeing Lamps now, but he bore the disappointment. Nor did he so wholly devote himself to his severe application to the study of Mugby Junction as to neglect exercise. On the contrary, he took a walk every day, and always the same walk. But the weather turned cold and wet again, and the window was never open.

III

At length, after a lapse of some days, there came another streak of fine bright hardy autumn weather. It was a Saturday. The window was open, and the children were gone. Not surprising, this, for he had patiently watched and waited at the corner until they *were* gone.

"Good day," he said to the face; absolutely getting his hat clear off his head this time.

"Good day to you, Sir."

"I am glad you have a fine sky again to look at."

"Thank you, Sir. It is kind of you."

"You are an invalid, I fear?"

"No, Sir. I have very good health."

"But are you not always lying down?"

"Oh yes, I am always lying down, because I cannot sit up! But I am not an invalid."

The laughing eyes seemed highly to enjoy his great mistake.

"Would you mind taking the trouble to come in, Sir? There is a beautiful view from this window. And you would see that I am not at all ill—being so good as to care."

It was said to help him, as he stood irresolute, but evidently desiring to enter, with his diffident hand on the latch of the garden-gate. It did help him, and he went in.

The room upstairs was a very clean white room with a low roof. Its only inmate lay on a couch that brought her face to a level with the window. The couch was white too; and her simple dress or wrapper being light blue, like the band around her hair, she had an ethereal look, and a fanciful appearance of lying among clouds. He felt that she instinctively perceived him to be by habit a downcast taciturn man; it was another help to him to have established that understanding so easily, and got it over.

There was an awkward constraint upon him, nevertheless, as he touched her hand, and took a chair at the side of her couch.

"I see now," he began, not at all fluently, "how you occupy your hand. Only seeing you from the path outside, I thought you were playing upon something."

She was engaged in very nimbly and dexterously making lace. A lace-pillow lay upon her breast; and the quick movements and changes of her hands upon it, as she worked, had given them the action he had misinterpreted.

"That is curious," she answered with a bright smile. "For I often fancy, myself, that I play tunes while I am at work."

"Have you any musical knowledge?"

She shook her head.

"I think I could pick out tunes, if I had any instrument, which could be made as handy to me as my lace-pillow. But I dare say I deceive myself. At all events, I shall never know."

"You have a musical voice. Excuse me; I have heard you sing."

"With the children?" she answered, slightly colouring. "Oh yes. I sing with the dear children, if it can be called singing."

Barbox Brothers glanced at the two small forms in the room, and hazarded the speculation that she was fond of children, and that she was learned in new systems of teaching them?

"Very fond of them," she said, shaking her head again; "but I know nothing of teaching, beyond the interest I have in it, and the pleasure it gives me when they learn. Perhaps your overhearing my little scholars sing some of their lessons has led you so far astray as to think me a grand teacher? Ah! I thought so! No, I have only read and been told about that system. It seemed so pretty and pleasant, and to treat them so like the merry Robins they are, that I took up with it in my little way. You don't need to be told what a very little way mine is, Sir," she added with a glance at the small forms and round the room.

All this time her hands were busy at her lace-pillow. As they still continued so, and as there was a kind of substitute for conversation in the click and play of its pegs, Barbox Brothers took the opportunity of observing her. He guessed her to be thirty. The charm of her transparent face and large bright brown eyes was, not that they were passively resigned, but that they were actively and thoroughly cheerful. Even her busy hands, which of their own thinness alone might have besought compassion, plied their task with a gay courage that made mere compassion an unjustifiable assumption of superiority, and an impertinence.

He saw her eyes in the act of rising towards his, and he directed his towards the prospect, saying: "Beautiful, indeed!"

"Most beautiful, Sir. I have sometimes had a fancy that I would like to sit up, for once, only to try how it looks to an erect head. But what a foolish fancy that would be to encourage! It cannot look more lovely to any one than it does to me."

Her eyes were turned to it, as she spoke, with most delighted admiration and enjoyment. There was not a trace in it of any sense of deprivation.

"And those threads of railway, with their puffs of smoke and steam changing places so fast, make it so lively for me," she went on. "I think of the number of people who *can* go where they wish, on their business, or their pleasure; I remember that the puffs make signs to me that they are actually going while I look; and that enlivens the prospect with abundance of company, if I want company. There is the great Junction, too. I don't see it under the foot of the hill, but I can very often hear it, and I always know it is there. It seems to join me, in a way, to I don't know how many places and things that *I* shall never see."

With an abashed kind of idea that it might have already joined himself to something he had never seen, he said constrainedly: "Just so."

"And so you see, Sir," pursued Phœbe, "I am not the invalid you thought me, and I am very well off indeed."

"You have a happy disposition," said Barbox Brothers: perhaps with a slight excusatory touch for his own disposition.

"Ah! But you should know my father," she replied. "His is the happy disposition!—Don't mind, Sir!" For his reserve took the alarm at a step upon the stairs, and he distrusted that he would be set down for a troublesome intruder. "This is my father coming."

The door opened, and the father paused there.

"Why, Lamps!" exclaimed Barbox Brothers, starting from his chair. "How do you DO, Lamps?"

To which Lamps responded: "The gentleman for Nowhere! How do you DO, Sir?"

And they shook hands, to the greatest admiration and surprise of Lamps's daughter.

"I have looked you up half-a-dozen times since that night," said Barbox Brothers, "but have never found you."

"So I've heerd on, Sir, so I've heerd on," returned Lamps. "It's your being noticed so often down at the Junction, without taking any train, that has begun to get you the name among us of the gentleman for Nowhere. No offence in my having called you by it when took by surprise, I hope, Sir?"

"None at all. It's as good a name for me as any other you could call me by. But may I ask you a question in the corner here?"

Lamps suffered himself to be led aside from his daughter's couch by one of the buttons of his velveteen jacket.

"Is this the bedside where you sing your songs?"

Lamps nodded.

The gentleman for Nowhere clapped him on the shoulder, and they faced about again.

"Upon my word, my dear," said Lamps then to his daughter, looking from her to her visitor, "it is such an amaze to me, to find you brought acquainted with this gentleman, that I must (if this gentleman will excuse me) take a rounder."

Mr. Lamps demonstrated in action what this meant, by pulling out his oily handkerchief rolled up in the form of a ball, and giving himself an elaborate smear, from behind the right ear, up the cheek, across the forehead, and down the other cheek to behind his left ear. After this operation he shone exceedingly.

"It's according to my custom when particular warmed up by any agitation, Sir," he offered by way of apology. "And really, I am throwed into that state of amaze by finding you brought acquainted with Phœbe, that I—that I think I will, if you'll excuse me, take another rounder." Which he did, seeming to be greatly restored by it.

They were now both standing by the side of her couch,

and she was working at her lace-pillow. "Your daughter tells me," said Barbox Brothers, still in a half-reluctant shamefaced way, "that she never sits up."

"No, Sir, nor never has done. You see, her mother (who died when she was a year and two months old) was subject to very bad fits, and as she had never mentioned to me that she *was* subject to fits, they couldn't be guarded against. Consequently, she dropped the baby when took, and this happened."

"It was very wrong of her," said Barbox Brothers with a knitted brow, "to marry you, making a secret of her infirmity."

"Well, Sir!" pleaded Lamps in behalf of the long-deceased. "You see. Phœbe and me, we have talked that over too. And Lord bless us! Such a number on us has our infirmities, what with fits, and what with misfits, of one sort and another, that if we confessed to 'em all before we got married, most of us might never get married."

"Might not that be for the better?"

"Not in this case, Sir," said Phœbe, giving her hand to her father.

"No, not in this case, Sir," said her father, patting it between his own.

"You correct me," returned Barbox Brothers with a blush; "and I must look so like a Brute, that at all events it would be superfluous in me to confess to *that* infirmity. I wish you would tell me a little more about yourselves. I hardly know how to ask it of you, for I am conscious that I have a bad stiff manner, a dull discouraging way with me, but I wish you would."

"With all our hearts, Sir," returned Lamps gaily for both. "And first of all, that you may know my name——"

"Stay!" interposed the visitor with a slight flush. "What signifies your name? Lamps is name enough for me. I like it. It is bright and expressive. What do I want more?"

"Why, to be sure, Sir," returned Lamps. "I have in general no other name down at the Junction; but I thought, on account of your being here as a first-class single, in a private character, that you might——"

The visitor waved the thought away with his hand, and Lamps acknowledged the mark of confidence by taking another rounder.

"You are hard-worked, I take for granted?" said Barbox

Brothers, when the subject of the rounder came out of it much dirtier than he went into it.

Lamps was beginning, "Not particular so"—when his daughter took him up.

"Oh yes, Sir, he is very hard-worked. Fourteen, fifteen, eighteen hours a day. Sometimes twenty-four hours at a time."

"And you," said Barbox Brothers, "what with your school, Phœbe, and what with your lace-making——"

"But my school is a pleasure to me," she interrupted, opening her brown eyes wider, as if surprised to find him so obtuse. "I began it when I was but a child, because it brought me and other children into company, don't you see? *That* was not work. I carry it on still, because it keeps children about me. *That* is not work. I do it as love, not as work. Then my lace-pillow;" her busy hands had stopped, as if her argument required all her cheerful earnestness, but now went on again at the name; "it goes with my thoughts when I think, and it goes with my tunes when I hum any, and *that's* not work. Why, you yourself thought it was music, you know, Sir. And so it is to me."

"Everything is!" cried Lamps radiantly. "Everything is music to her, Sir."

"My father is, at any rate," said Phœbe, exultingly pointing her thin forefinger at him. "There is more music in my father than there is in a brass band."

"I say! My dear! It's very fillyillially done, you know; but you are flattering your father," he protested, sparkling.

"No, I am not, Sir, I assure you. No, I am not. If you could hear my father sing, you would know I am not. But you never will hear him sing, because he never sings to any one but me. However tired he is, he always sings to me when he comes home. When I lay here long ago, quite a poor little broken doll, he used to sing to me. More than that, he used to make songs, bringing in whatever little jokes we had between us. More than that, he often does so to this day. Oh! I'll tell of you, father, as the gentleman has asked about you. He is a poet, Sir."

"I shouldn't wish the gentleman, my dear," observed Lamps, for the moment turning grave, "to carry away that opinion of your father, because it might look as if I was given to asking the stars in a molloncolly manner what they was up to. Which I wouldn't at once waste the time, and take the liberty, my dear."

"My father," resumed Phœbe, amending her text, " is always on the bright side, and the good side. You told me, just now, I had a happy disposition. How can I help it?"

"Well; but, my dear," returned Lamps argumentatively, "how can *I* help it? Put it to yourself, Sir. Look at her. Always as you see her now. Always working—and after all, Sir, for but a very few shillings a week—always contented, always lively, always interested in others, of all sorts. I said, this moment, she was always as you see her now. So she is, with a difference that comes to much the same. For, when it is my Sunday off and the morning bells have done ringing, I hear the prayers and thanks read in the touchingest way, and I have the hymns sung to me—so soft, Sir, that you couldn't hear 'em out of this room—in notes that seem to me, I am sure, to come from Heaven and go back to it."

It might have been merely through the association of these words with their sacredly quiet time, or it might have been through the larger association of the words with the Redeemer's presence beside the bedridden; but here her dexterous fingers came to a stop on the lace-pillow, and clasped themselves around his neck as he bent down. There was great natural sensibility in both father and daughter, the visitor could easily see; but each made it, for the other's sake, retiring, not demonstrative; and perfect cheerfulness, intuitive or acquired, was either the first or second nature of both. In a very few moments Lamps was taking another rounder with his comical features beaming, while Phœbe's laughing eyes (just a glistening speck or so upon their lashes) were again directed by turns to him, and to her work, and to Barbox Brothers.

"When my father, Sir," she said brightly, "tells you about my being interested in other people, even though they know nothing about me—which, by-the-bye, I told you myself— you ought to know how that comes about. That's my father's doing."

"No, it isn't!" he protested.

"Don't you believe him, Sir; yes, it is. He tells me of everything he sees down at his work. You would be surprised what a quantity he gets together for me every day. He looks into the carriages, and tells me how the ladies are dressed—so that I know all the fashions! He looks into the carriages, and tells me what pairs of lovers he sees, and what new-married couples on their wedding trip—so that I know all about that! He collects chance newspapers and books—

so that I have plenty to read! He tells me about the sick people who are travelling to try to get better—so that I know all about them! In short, as I began by saying, he tells me everything he sees and makes out down at his work, and you can't think what a quantity he does see and make out."

"As to collecting newspapers and books, my dear," said Lamps, "it's clear I can have no merit in that, because they're not my perquisites. You see, Sir, it's this way: A Guard, he'll say to me, 'Hallo, here you are, Lamps. I've saved this paper for your daughter. How is she a-going on?' A Head Porter, he'll say to me, 'Here! Catch hold, Lamps. Here's a couple of wollumes for your daughter. Is she pretty much where she were?' And that's what makes it double welcome, you see. If she had a thousand pound in a box, they wouldn't trouble themselves about her; but being what she is—that is, you understand," Lamps added, somewhat hurriedly, "not having a thousand pound in a box—they take thought for her. And as concerning the young pairs. married and unmarried, it's only natural I should bring home what little I can about *them*, seeing that there's not a Couple of either sort in the neighbourhood that don't come of their own accord to confide in Phœbe."

She raised her eyes triumphantly to Barbox Brothers as she said:

"Indeed, Sir, that is true. If I could have got up and gone to church, I don't know how often I should have been a bridesmaid. But, if I could have done that, some girls in love might have been jealous of me, and, as it is, no girl is jealous of me. And my pillow would not have been half as ready to put the piece of cake under, as I always find it," she added, turning her face on it with a light sigh, and a smile at her father.

The arrival of a little girl, the biggest of the scholars, now led to an understanding on the part of Barbox Brothers, that she was the domestic of the cottage, and had come to take active measures in it, attended by a pail that might have extinguished her, and a broom three times her height. He therefore rose to take his leave, and took it; saying that, if Phœbe had no objection, he would come again.

He had muttered that he would come "in the course of his walks." The course of his walks must have been highly favourable to his return, for he returned after an interval of a single day.

"You thought you would never see me any more, I suppose?" he said to Phœbe as he touched her hand, and sat down by her couch.

"Why should I think so?" was her surprised rejoinder.

"I took it for granted you would mistrust me."

"For granted, Sir? Have you been so much mistrusted?"

"I think I am justified in answering yes. But I may have mistrusted, too, on my part. No matter just now. We were speaking of the Junction last time. I have passed hours there since the day before yesterday."

"Are you now the gentleman for Somewhere?" she asked with a smile.

"Certainly for Somewhere; but I don't yet know Where. You would never guess what I am travelling from. Shall I tell you? I am travelling from my birthday."

Her hands stopped in her work, and she looked at him with incredulous astonishment.

"Yes," said Barbox Brothers, not quite easy in his chair, "from my birthday. I am, to myself, an unintelligible book with the earlier chapters all torn out, and thrown away. My childhood had no grace of childhood, my youth had no charm of youth, and what can be expected from such a lost beginning?" His eyes meeting hers as they were addressed intently to him, something seemed to stir within his breast, whispering: "Was this bed a place for the graces of childhood and the charms of youth to take to kindly? Oh, shame, shame!"

"It is a disease with me," said Barbox Brothers, checking himself, and making as though he had a difficulty in swallowing something, "to go wrong about that. I don't know how I came to speak of that. I hope it is because of an old misplaced confidence in one of your sex involving an old bitter treachery. I don't know. I am all wrong together."

Her hands quietly and slowly resumed their work. Glancing at her, he saw that her eyes were thoughtfully following them.

"I am travelling from my birthday," he resumed, "because it has always been a dreary day to me. My first free birthday coming round some five or six weeks hence, I am travelling to put its predecessors far behind me, and to try to crush the day—or, at all events, put it out of my sight—by heaping new objects on it.

As he paused, she looked at him ; but only shook her head as being quite at a loss.

"This is unintelligible to your happy disposition," he pursued, abiding by his former phrase as if there were some lingering virtue of self-defence in it. "I knew it would be, and am glad it is. However, on this travel of mine (in which I mean to pass the rest of my days, having abandoned all thought of a fixed home), I stopped, as you have heard from your father, at the Junction here. The extent of its ramifications quite confused me as to whither I should go, *from* here. I have not yet settled, being still perplexed among so many roads. What do you think I mean to do? How many of the branching roads can you see from your window?"

Looking out, full of interest, she answered, "Seven."

"Seven," said Barbox Brothers, watching her with a grave smile. "Well! I propose to myself at once to reduce the gross number to those very seven, and gradually to fine them down to one—the most promising for me—and to take that."

"But how will you know, Sir, which *is* the most promising?" she asked, with her brightened eyes roving over the view.

"Ah!" said Barbox Brothers with another grave smile, and considerably improving in his ease of speech. "To be sure. In this way. Where your father can pick up so much every day for a good purpose, I may once and again pick up a little for an indifferent purpose. The gentleman for Nowhere must become still better known at the Junction. He shall continue to explore it, until he attaches something that he has seen, heard, or found out, at the head of each of the seven roads, to the road itself. And so his choice of a road shall be determined by his choice among his discoveries."

Her hands still busy, she again glanced at the prospect, as if it comprehended something that had not been in it before, and laughed as if it yielded her new pleasure.

"But I must not forget," said Barbox Brothers, "(having got so far) to ask a favour. I want your help in this expedient of mine. I want to bring you what I pick up at the heads of the seven roads that you lie here looking out at, and to compare notes with you about it. May I? They say two heads are better than one. I should say myself that probably depends upon the heads concerned. But I am quite sure, though we are so newly acquainted, that your head and your father's have found out better things, Phœbe, than ever mine of itself discovered."

She gave him her sympathetic right hand, in perfect rapture with his proposal, and eagerly and gratefully thanked him.

"That's well!" said Barbox Brothers. "Again I must not forget (having got so far) to ask a favour. Will you shut your eyes?"

Laughing playfully at the strange nature of the request, she did so.

"Keep them shut," said Barbox Brothers, going softly to the door, and coming back. "You are on your honour, mind, not to open your eyes until I tell you that you may?"

"Yes! On my honour."

"Good. May I take your lace-pillow from you for a minute?"

Still laughing and wondering, she removed her hands from it, and he put it aside.

"Tell me. Did you see the puffs of smoke and steam made by the morning fast-train yesterday on road number seven from here?"

"Behind the elm-trees and the spire?"

"That's the road," said Barbox Brothers, directing his eyes towards it.

"Yes. I watched them melt away."

"Anything unusual in what they expressed?"

"No!" she answered merrily.

"Not complimentary to me, for I was in that train. I went—don't open your eyes—to fetch you this, from the great ingenious town. It is not half so large as your lace-pillow, and lies easily and lightly in its place. These little keys are like the keys of a miniature piano, and you supply the air required with your left hand. May you pick out delightful music from it, my dear! For the present—you can open your eyes now—good-bye!"

In his embarrassed way, he closed the door upon himself, and only saw, in doing so, that she ecstatically took the present to her bosom and caressed it. The glimpse gladdened his heart, and yet saddened it; for so might she, if her youth had flourished in its natural course, have taken to her breast that day the slumbering music of her own child's voice.

CHAPTER II

BARBOX BROTHERS AND CO.

WITH good-will and earnest purpose, the gentleman for
Nowhere began, on the very next day, his researches at the
heads of the seven roads.   The results of his researches, as
he and Phœbe afterwards set them down in fair writing,
hold their due places in this veracious chronicle.   But they
occupied a much longer time in the getting together than
they ever will in the perusal.   And this is probably the case
with most reading matter, except when it is of that highly
beneficial kind (for Posterity) which is "thrown off in a few
moments of leisure" by the superior poetic geniuses who
scorn to take prose pains.

It must be admitted, however, that Barbox by no means
hurried himself.   His heart being in his work of good-
nature, he revelled in it.   There was the joy, too (it was a
true joy to him), of sometimes sitting by, listening to Phœbe
as she picked out more and more discourse from her musical
instrument, and as her natural taste and ear refined daily
upon her first discoveries.   Besides being a pleasure, this
was an occupation, and in the course of weeks it consumed
hours.   It resulted that his dreaded birthday was close upon
him before he had troubled himself any more about it.

The matter was made more pressing by the unforeseen
circumstance that the councils held (at which Mr. Lamps,
beaming most brilliantly, on a few rare occasions assisted)
respecting the road to be selected were, after all, in nowise
assisted by his investigations.   For, he had connected this
interest with this road, or that interest with the other, but
could deduce no reason from it for giving any road the preference.   Consequently, when the last council was holden,
that part of the business stood, in the end, exactly where it
had stood in the beginning.

"But, Sir," remarked Phœbe, "we have only six roads after
all.   Is the seventh road dumb?"

"The seventh road? Oh!" said Barbox Brothers, rubbing his chin. "That is the road I took, you know, when I went to get your little present. That is *its* story, Phœbe."

"Would you mind taking that road again, Sir?" she asked with hesitation.

"Not in the least; it is a great high-road after all."

"I should like you to take it," returned Phœbe with a persuasive smile, "for the love of that little present which must ever be so dear to me. I should like you to take it, because that road can never be again like any other road to me. I should like you to take it, in remembrance of your having done me so much good: of your having made me so much happier! If you leave me by the road you travelled when you went to do me this great kindness," sounding a faint chord as she spoke, "I shall feel, lying here watching at my window, as if it must conduct you to a prosperous end, and bring you back some day."

"It shall be done, my dear; it shall be done."

So at last the gentleman for Nowhere took a ticket for Somewhere, and his destination was the great ingenious town.

He had loitered so long about the Junction that it was the eighteenth of December when he left it. "High time," he reflected, as he seated himself in the train, "that I started in earnest! Only one clear day remains between me and the day I am running away from. I'll push onward for the hill-country to-morrow. I'll go to Wales."

It was with some pains that he placed before himself the undeniable advantages to be gained in the way of novel occupation for his senses from misty mountains, swollen streams, rain, cold, a wild seashore, and rugged roads. And yet he scarcely made them out as distinctly as he could have wished. Whether the poor girl, in spite of her new resource, her music, would have any feeling of loneliness upon her now—just at first—that she had not had before; whether she saw those very puffs of steam and smoke that he saw, as he sat in the train thinking of her; whether her face would have any pensive shadow on it as they died out of the distant view from her window; whether, in telling him he had done her so much good, she had not unconsciously corrected his old moody bemoaning of his station in life, by setting him thinking that a man might be a great healer, if he would, and yet not be a great doctor; these and other similar meditations got between him and his Welsh picture. There was within him, too, that

dull sense of vacuity which follows separation from an object
of interest, and cessation of a pleasant pursuit; and this sense,
being quite new to him, made him restless.   Further, in
losing Mugby Junction, he had found himself again ; and he
was not the more enamoured of himself for having lately
passed his time in better company.

But surely here, not far ahead, must be the great ingenious
town.   This crashing and clashing that the train was undergoing, and this coupling on to it of a multitude of new echoes,
could mean nothing less than approach to the great station.
It did mean nothing less.   After some stormy flashes of town
lightning, in the way of swift revelations of red brick blocks
of houses, high red brick chimney-shafts, vistas of red brick
railway-arches, tongues of fire, blocks of smoke, valleys of
canal, and hills of coal, there came the thundering in at the
journey's end.

Having seen his portmanteaus safely housed in the hotel he
chose, and having appointed his dinner hour, Barbox Brothers
went out for a walk in the busy streets.   And now it began
to be suspected by him that Mugby Junction was a Junction
of many branches, invisible as well as visible, and had joined
him to an endless number of by-ways.   For, whereas he
would, but a little while ago, have walked these streets
blindly brooding, he now had eyes and thoughts for a new
external world.   How the many toiling people lived, and
loved, and died ; how wonderful it was to consider the various
trainings of eye and hand, the nice distinctions of sight and
touch, that separated them into classes of workers, and even
into classes of workers at subdivisions of one complete whole
which combined their many intelligences and forces, though
of itself but some cheap object of use or ornament in common
life ; how good it was to know that such assembling in a
multitude on their part, and such contribution of their several
dexterities towards a civilising end, did not deteriorate them
as it was the fashion of the supercilious Mayflies of humanity
to pretend, but engendered among them a self-respect, and
yet a modest desire to be much wiser than they were (the
first evinced in their well-balanced bearing and manner of
speech when he stopped to ask a question ; the second, in the
announcements of their popular studies and amusements on
the public walls) ; these considerations, and a host of such,
made his walk a memorable one.   "I too am but a little part
of a great whole," he began to think ; "and to be serviceable

to myself and others, or to be happy, I must cast my interest into, and draw it out of, the common stock."

Although he had arrived at his journey's end for the day by noon, he had since insensibly walked about the town so far and so long that the lamp-lighters were now at their work in the streets, and the shops were sparkling up brilliantly. Thus reminded to turn towards his quarters, he was in the act of doing so, when a very little hand crept into his, and a very little voice said:

"Oh! if you please, I am lost!"

He looked down, and saw a very little fair-haired girl.

"Yes," she said, confirming her words with a serious nod. "I am indeed. I am lost!"

Greatly perplexed, he stopped, looked about him for help, descried none, and said, bending low:

"Where do you live, my child?"

"I don't know where I live," she returned. "I am lost."

"What is your name?"

"Polly."

"What is your other name?"

The reply was prompt, but unintelligible.

Imitating the sound as he caught it, he hazarded the guess, "Trivits."

"Oh no!" said the child, shaking her head. "Nothing like that."

"Say it again, little one."

An unpromising business. For this time it had quite a different sound.

He made the venture, "Paddens?"

"Oh no!" said the child. "Nothing like that."

"Once more. Let us try it again, dear."

A most hopeless business. This time it swelled into four syllables. "It can't be Tappitarver?" said Barbox Brothers, rubbing his head with his hat in discomfiture.

"No! It ain't," the child quietly assented.

On her trying this unfortunate name once more, with extraordinary efforts at distinctness, it swelled into eight syllables at least.

"Ah! I think," said Barbox Brothers with a desperate air of resignation, "that we had better give it up."

"But I am lost," said the child, nestling her little hand more closely in his, "and you'll take care of me, won't you?"

If ever a man were disconcerted by division between com-

passion on the one hand, and the very imbecility of irresolution on the other, here the man was. "Lost!" he repeated,
looking down at the child. "I am sure *I* am. What is to
be done?"

"Where do *you* live?" asked the child, looking up at him
wistfully.

"Over there," he answered, pointing vaguely in the direction of his hotel.

"Hadn't we better go there?" said the child.

"Really," he replied, "I don't know but what we had."

So they set off, hand-in-hand. He, through comparison of
himself against his little companion, with a clumsy feeling on
him as if he had just developed into a foolish giant. She,
clearly elevated in her own tiny opinion by having got him
so neatly out of his embarrassment.

"We are going to have dinner when we get there, I
suppose?" said Polly.

"Well," he rejoined, "I—— Yes, I suppose we are."

"Do you like your dinner?" asked the child.

"Why, on the whole," said Barbox Brothers, "yes, I think
I do."

"I do mine," said Polly. "Have you any brothers and
sisters?"

"No. Have you?"

"Mine are dead."

"Oh!" said Barbox Brothers. With that absurd sense of
unwieldiness of mind and body weighing him down, he would
have not known how to pursue the conversation beyond this
curt rejoinder, but that the child was always ready for him.

"What," she asked, turning her soft hand coaxingly in
his, "are you going to do to amuse me after dinner?"

"Upon my soul, Polly," exclaimed Barbox Brothers, very
much at a loss, "I have not the slightest idea!"

"Then I tell you what," said Polly. "Have you got any
cards at your house?"

"Plenty," said Barbox Brothers in a boastful vein.

"Very well. Then I'll build houses, and you shall look at
me. You mustn't blow, you know."

"Oh no," said Barbox Brothers. "No, no, no. No blowing. Blowing's not fair."

He flattered himself that he had said this pretty well for
an idiotic monster; but the child, instantly perceiving the
awkwardness of his attempt to adapt himself to her level,

utterly destroyed his hopeful opinion of himself by saying compassionately : "What a funny man you are!"

Feeling, after this melancholy failure, as if he every minute grew bigger and heavier in person, and weaker in mind, Barbox gave himself up for a bad job. No giant ever submitted more meekly to be led in triumph by all-conquering Jack than he to be bound in slavery to Polly.

"Do you know any stories?" she asked him.

He was reduced to the humiliating confession: "No."

"What a dunce you must be, mustn't you?" said Polly.

He was reduced to the humiliating confession : "Yes."

"Would you like me to teach you a story? But you must remember it, you know, and be able to tell it right to somebody else afterwards."

He professed that it would afford him the highest mental gratification to be taught a story, and that he would humbly endeavour to retain it in his mind. Whereupon Polly, giving her hand a new little turn in his, expressive of settling down for enjoyment, commenced a long romance, of which every relishing clause began with the words: "So this," or, "And so this." As, "So this boy;" or, "So this fairy;" or, "And so this pie was four yards round, and two yards and a quarter deep." The interest of the romance was derived from the intervention of this fairy to punish this boy for having a greedy appetite. To achieve which purpose, this fairy made this pie, and this boy ate and ate and ate, and his cheeks swelled and swelled and swelled. There were many tributary circumstances, but the forcible interest culminated in the total consumption of this pie, and the bursting of this boy. Truly he was a fine sight, Barbox Brothers, with serious attentive face, and ear bent down, much jostled on the pavements of the busy town, but afraid of losing a single incident of the epic, lest he should be examined in it by-and-by, and found deficient.

Thus they arrived at the hotel. And there he had to say at the bar, and said awkwardly enough: "I have found a little girl!"

The whole establishment turned out to look at the little girl. Nobody knew her; nobody could make out her name, as she set it forth—except one chambermaid, who said it was Constantinople—which it wasn't.

"I will dine with my young friend in a private room," said Barbox Brothers to the hotel authorities, "and perhaps you will be so good as to let the police know that the pretty baby is here. I suppose she is sure to be inquired for soon, if she has not been already. Come along, Polly."

Perfectly at ease and peace, Polly came along, but, finding the stairs rather stiff work, was carried up by Barbox Brothers. The dinner was a most transcendent success, and the Barbox sheepishness, under Polly's directions how to mince her meat for her, and how to diffuse gravy over the plate with a liberal and equal hand, was another fine sight.

"And now," said Polly, "while we are at dinner, you be good, and tell me that story I taught you."

With the tremors of a Civil Service examination upon him, and very uncertain indeed, not only as to the epoch at which the pie appeared in history, but also as to the measurements of that indispensable fact, Barbox Brothers made a shaky beginning, but under encouragement did very fairly. There was a want of breadth observable in his rendering of the cheeks, as well as the appetite, of the boy ; and there was a certain tameness in his fairy, referable to an under-current of desire to account for her. Still, as the first lumbering performance of a good-humoured monster, it passed muster.

"I told you to be good," said Polly, "and you are good, ain't you ? "

"I hope so," replied Barbox Brothers.

Such was his deference that Polly, elevated on a platform of sofa cushions in a chair at his right hand, encouraged him with a pat or two on the face from the greasy bowl of her spoon, and even with a gracious kiss. In getting on her feet upon her chair, however, to give him this last reward, she toppled forward among the dishes, and caused him to exclaim, as he effected her rescue: "Gracious Angels! Whew! I thought we were in the fire, Polly ! "

"What a coward you are, ain't you ? " said Polly when replaced.

"Yes, I am rather nervous," he replied. "Whew! Don't, Polly ! Don't flourish your spoon, or you'll go over sideways. Don't tilt up your legs when you laugh, Polly, or you'll go over backwards. Whew! Polly, Polly, Polly," said Barbox Brothers, nearly succumbing to despair, "we are environed with dangers ! "

Indeed, he could descry no security from the pitfalls that were yawning for Polly, but in proposing to her, after dinner, to sit upon a low stool. "I will, if you will," said Polly.

So, as peace of mind should go before all, he begged the waiter to wheel aside the table, bring a pack of cards, a couple of footstools, and a screen, and close in Polly and himself before the fire, as it were in a snug room within the room. Then, finest sight of all, was Barbox Brothers on his footstool, with a pint decanter on the rug, contemplating Polly as she built successfully, and growing blue in the face with holding his breath, lest he should blow the house down.

"How you stare, don't you?" said Polly in a houseless pause.

Detected in the ignoble fact, he felt obliged to admit, apologetically: "I am afraid I was looking rather hard at you, Polly."

"Why do you stare?" asked Polly.

"I cannot," he murmured to himself, "recall why.—I don't know, Polly."

"You must be a simpleton to do things and not know why, mustn't you?" said Polly.

In spite of which reproof, he looked at the child again intently, as she bent her head over her card structure, her rich curls shading her face. "It is impossible," he thought, "that I can ever have seen this pretty baby before. Can I have dreamed of her? In some sorrowful dream?"

He could make nothing of it. So he went into the building trade as a journeyman under Polly, and they built three stories high, four stories high; even five.

"I say! Who do you think is coming?" asked Polly, rubbing her eyes after tea.

He guessed: "The waiter?"

"No," said Polly, "the dustman. I am getting sleepy."

A new embarrassment for Barbox Brothers!

"I don't think I am going to be fetched to-night," said Polly. "What do you think?"

He thought not, either. After another quarter of an hour, the dustman not merely impending, but actually arriving, recourse was had to the Constantinopolitan chambermaid: who cheerily undertook that the child should sleep in a comfortable and wholesome room, which she herself would share.

"And I know you will be careful, won't you," said Barbox Brothers, as a new fear dawned upon him, "that she don't fall out of bed?"

Polly found this so highly entertaining that she was under

the necessity of clutching him round the neck with both arms as he sat on his footstool picking up the cards, and rocking him to and fro, with her dimpled chin on his shoulder.

"Oh, what a coward you are, ain't you?" said Polly. "Do *you* fall out of bed?"

"N—not generally, Polly."

"No more do I."

With that, Polly gave him a reassuring hug or two to keep him going, and then giving that confiding mite of a hand of hers to be swallowed up in the hand of the Constantinopolitan chambermaid, trotted off, chattering, without a vestige of anxiety.

He looked after her, had the screen removed and the table and chairs replaced, and still looked after her. He paced the room for half an hour. "A most engaging little creature, but it's not that. A most winning little voice, but it's not that. That has much to do with it, but there is something more. How can it be that I seem to know this child? What was it she imperfectly recalled to me when I felt her touch in the street, and, looking down at her, saw her looking up at me?"

"Mr. Jackson!"

With a start he turned towards the sound of the subdued voice, and saw his answer standing at the door.

"Oh, Mr. Jackson, do not be severe with me! Speak a word of encouragement to me, I beseech you."

"You are Polly's mother."

"Yes."

Yes. Polly herself might come to this, one day. As you see what the rose was in its faded leaves; as you see what the summer growth of the woods was in their wintry branches; so Polly might be traced, one day, in a careworn woman like this, with her hair turned grey. Before him were the ashes of a dead fire that had once burned bright. This was the woman he had loved. This was the woman he had lost. Such had been the constancy of his imagination to her, so had Time spared her under its withholding, that now, seeing how roughly the inexorable hand had struck her, his soul was filled with pity and amazement.

He led her to a chair, and stood leaning on a corner of the chimneypiece, with his head resting on his hand, and his face half averted.

"Did you see me in the street, and show me to your child?" he asked.

"Yes."

"Is the little creature, then, a party to deceit?"

"I hope there is no deceit. I said to her, 'We have lost our way, and I must try to find mine by myself. Go to that gentleman, and tell him you are lost. You shall be fetched by-and-by.' Perhaps you have not thought how very young she is?"

"She is very self-reliant."

"Perhaps because she is so young."

He asked, after a short pause, "Why did you do this?"

"Oh, Mr. Jackson, do you ask me? In the hope that you might see something in my innocent child to soften your heart towards me. Not only towards me, but towards my husband."

He suddenly turned about, and walked to the opposite end of the room. He came back again with a slower step, and resumed his former attitude, saying:

"I thought you had emigrated to America?"

"We did. But life went ill with us there, and we came back."

"Do you live in this town?"

"Yes. I am a daily teacher of music here. My husband is a bookkeeper."

"Are you—forgive my asking—poor?"

"We earn enough for our wants. That is not our distress. My husband is very, very ill of a lingering disorder. He will never recover——"

"You check yourself. If it is for want of the encouraging word you spoke of, take it from me. I cannot forget the old time, Beatrice."

"God bless you!" she replied with a burst of tears, and gave him her trembling hand.

"Compose yourself. I cannot be composed if you are not, for to see you weep distresses me beyond expression. Speak freely to me. Trust me."

She shaded her face with her veil, and after a little while spoke calmly. Her voice had the ring of Polly's.

"It is not that my husband's mind is at all impaired by his bodily suffering, for I assure you that is not the case. But in his weakness, and in his knowledge that he is incurably ill, he cannot overcome the ascendancy of one idea. It preys upon him, embitters every moment of his painful life, and will shorten it."

She stopping, he said again: "Speak freely to me. Trust me."

"We have had five children before this darling, and they all lie in their little graves. He believes that they have withered away under a curse, and that it will blight this child like the rest."

"Under what curse?"

"Both I and he have it on our conscience that we tried you very heavily, and I do not know but that, if I were as ill as he, I might suffer in my mind as he does. This is the constant burden:—'I believe, Beatrice, I was the only friend that Mr. Jackson ever cared to make, though I was so much his junior. The more influence he acquired in the business, the higher he advanced me, and I was alone in his private confidence. I came between him and you, and I took you from him. We were both secret, and the blow fell when he was wholly unprepared. The anguish it caused a man so compressed must have been terrible; the wrath it awakened inappeasable. So, a curse came to be invoked on our poor pretty little flowers, and they fall.'"

"And you, Beatrice," he asked, when she had ceased to speak, and there had been a silence afterwards, "how say you?"

"Until within these few weeks I was afraid of you, and I believed that you would never, never forgive."

"Until within these few weeks," he repeated. "Have you changed your opinion of me within these few weeks?"

"Yes."

"For what reason?"

"I was getting some pieces of music in a shop in this town, when, to my terror, you came in. As I veiled my face and stood in the dark end of the shop, I heard you explain that you wanted a musical instrument for a bedridden girl. Your voice and manner were so softened, you showed such interest in its selection, you took it away yourself with so much tenderness of care and pleasure, that I knew you were a man with a most gentle heart. Oh, Mr. Jackson, Mr. Jackson, if you could have felt the refreshing rain of tears that followed for me!"

Was Phœbe playing at that moment on her distant couch? He seemed to hear her.

"I inquired in the shop where you lived, but could get no information. As I had heard you say that you were going back by the next train (but you did not say where), I resolved to visit the station at about that time of day, as often as I could, between my lessons, on the chance of seeing you again. I have been there very often, but saw you no more until to-day. You were meditating as you walked the street, but the calm expression of your face emboldened me to send my child to you. And when I saw you bend your head to speak tenderly to her, I prayed to GOD to forgive me for having ever brought a sorrow on it. I now pray to you to forgive me, and to forgive my husband. I was very young, he was young too, and, in the ignorant hardihood of such a time of life, we don't know what we do to those who have undergone more discipline. You generous man! You good man! So to raise me up and make nothing of my crime against you!"—for he would not see her on her knees, and soothed her as a kind father might have soothed an erring daughter—"thank you, bless you, thank you!"

When he next spoke, it was after having drawn aside the window curtain and looked out awhile. Then he only said:

"Is Polly asleep?"

"Yes. As I came in, I met her going away upstairs, and put her to bed myself."

"Leave her with me for to-morrow, Beatrice, and write me your address on this leaf of my pocket-book. In the evening I will bring her home to you—and to her father."

*   *   *   *   *   *

"Hallo!" cried Polly, putting her saucy sunny face in at the door next morning when breakfast was ready: "I thought I was fetched last night?"

"So you were, Polly, but I asked leave to keep you here for the day, and to take you home in the evening."

"Upon my word!" said Polly. "You are very cool, ain't you?"

However, Polly seemed to think it a good idea, and added:

"I suppose I must give you a kiss, though you *are* cool."

The kiss given and taken, they sat down to breakfast in a highly conversational tone.

"Of course, you are going to amuse me?" said Polly.

"Oh, of course!" said Barbox Brothers.

In the pleasurable height of her anticipations, Polly found

it indispensable to put down her piece of toast, cross one of her little fat knees over the other, and bring her little fat right hand down into her left hand with a business-like slap. After this gathering of herself together, Polly, by that time a mere heap of dimples, asked in a wheedling manner:

"What are we going to do, you dear old thing?"

"Why, I was thinking," said Barbox Brothers, "—but are you fond of horses, Polly?"

"Ponies, I am," said Polly, "especially when their tails are long. But horses—n—no—too big, you know."

"Well," pursued Barbox Brothers, in a spirit of grave mysterious confidence adapted to the importance of the consultation, "I did see yesterday, Polly, on the walls, pictures of two long-tailed ponies, speckled all over——"

"No, no, NO!" cried Polly, in an ecstatic desire to linger on the charming details. "Not speckled all over!"

"Speckled all over. Which ponies jump through hoops——"

"No, no, NO!" cried Polly as before. "They never jump through hoops!"

"Yes, they do. Oh, I assure you they do! And eat pie in pinafores——"

"Ponies eating pie in pinafores!" said Polly. "What a story-teller you are, ain't you?"

"Upon my honour. —And fire off guns."

(Polly hardly seemed to see the force of the ponies resorting to fire-arms.)

"And I was thinking," pursued the exemplary Barbox, "that if you and I were to go to the Circus where these ponies are, it would do our constitutions good."

"Does that mean amuse us?" inquired Polly. "What long words you do use, don't you?"

Apologetic for having wandered out of his depth, he replied:

"That means amuse us. That is exactly what it means. There are many other wonders besides the ponies, and we shall see them all. Ladies and gentlemen in spangled dresses, and elephants and lions and tigers."

Polly became observant of the teapot, with a curled-up nose indicating some uneasiness of mind.

"They never get out, of course," she remarked as a mere truism.

"The elephants and lions and tigers? Oh, dear no!"

"Oh, dear no!" said Polly. "And of course nobody's afraid of the ponies shooting anybody."

"Not the least in the world."

"No, no, not the least in the world," said Polly.

"I was also thinking," proceeded Barbox, "that if we were to look in at the toy-shop, to choose a doll——"

"Not dressed!" cried Polly with a clap of her hands. "No, no, no, not dressed!"

"Full-dressed. Together with a house, and all things necessary for house-keeping——"

Polly gave a little scream, and seemed in danger of falling into a swoon of bliss.

"What a darling you are!" she languidly exclaimed, leaning back in her chair. "Come and be hugged, or I must come and hug you."

This resplendent programme was carried into execution with the utmost rigour of the law. It being essential to make the purchase of the doll its first feature—or that lady would have lost the ponies—the toy-shop expedition took precedence. Polly in the magic warehouse, with a doll as large as herself under each arm, and a neat assortment of some twenty more on view upon the counter, did indeed present a spectacle of indecision not quite compatible with unalloyed happiness, but the light cloud passed. The lovely specimen oftenest chosen, oftenest rejected, and finally abided by, was of Circassian descent, possessing as much boldness of beauty as was reconcilable with extreme feebleness of mouth, and combining a sky-blue silk pelisse with rose-coloured satin trousers, and a black velvet hat: which this fair stranger to our northern shores would seem to have founded on the portraits of the late Duchess of Kent. The name this distinguished foreigner brought with her from beneath the glowing skies of a sunny clime was (on Polly's authority) Miss Melluka, and the costly nature of her outfit as a housekeeper, from the Barbox coffers, may be inferred from the two facts that her silver tea-spoons were as large as her kitchen poker, and that the proportions of her watch exceeded those of her frying-pan. Miss Melluka was graciously pleased to express her entire approbation of the Circus, and so was Polly; for the ponies *were* speckled, and brought down nobody when they fired, and the savagery of the wild beasts appeared to be mere smoke—which article, in fact, they did produce in large quantities from their insides. The Barbox absorption in the general subject throughout the realisation of these delights was again a sight to see, nor was it less worthy to behold at dinner, when he drank to Miss Melluka, tied stiff in a chair opposite to Polly (the fair Circassian possessing an unbendable spine), and even induced the waiter to assist in carrying out with due decorum the prevailing glorious idea. To wind up, there came the agreeable fever of getting Miss Melluka and all her wardrobe and rich possessions into a fly with Polly, to be taken home. But, by that time, Polly had become unable to look upon such accumulated joys with waking eyes, and had withdrawn her consciousness into the wonderful Paradise of a child's sleep. "Sleep, Polly, sleep," said Barbox Brothers, as her head dropped on his shoulder ; "you shall not fall out of this bed easily, at any rate ! "

What rustling piece of paper he took from his pocket, and carefully folded into the bosom of Polly's frock, shall not be mentioned. He said nothing about it, and nothing shall be said about it. They drove to a modest suburb of the great ingenious town, and stopped at the fore-court of a small house. "Do not wake the child," said Barbox Brothers softly to the driver ; "I will carry her in as she is."

Greeting the light at the opened door which was held by Polly's mother, Polly's bearer passed on with mother and child into a ground-floor room. There, stretched on a sofa, lay a sick man, sorely wasted, who covered his eyes with his emaciated hands.

"Tresham," said Barbox in a kindly voice, "I have brought you back your Polly, fast asleep. Give me your hand, and tell me you are better."

The sick man reached forth his right hand, and bowed his head over the hand into which it was taken, and kissed it. "Thank you, thank you ! I may say that I am well and happy."

"That's brave,"said Barbox. "Tresham, I have a fancy—— Can you make room for me beside you here ? "

He sat down on the sofa as he said the words, cherishing the plump peachy cheek that lay uppermost on his shoulder.

" I have a fancy, Tresham (I am getting quite an old fellow now, you know, and old fellows may take fancies into their heads sometimes), to give up Polly, having found her, to no one but you. Will you take her from me ? "

As the father held out his arms for the child, each of the two men looked steadily at the other.

"She is very dear to you, Tresham?"

"Unutterably dear."

"God bless her! It is not much, Polly," he continued, turning his eyes upon her peaceful face as he apostrophized her, "it is not much, Polly, for a blind and sinful man to invoke a blessing on something so far better than himself as a little child is; but it would be much—much upon his cruel head, and much upon his guilty soul—if he could be so wicked as to invoke a curse. He had better have a millstone round his neck, and be cast into the deepest sea. Live and thrive, my pretty baby!" Here he kissed her. "Live and prosper, and become in time the mother of other little children, like the Angels who behold The Father's face!"

He kissed her again, gave her up gently to both her parents, and went out.

But he went not to Wales. No, he never went to Wales. He went straightway for another stroll about the town, and he looked in upon the people at their work, and at their play, here, there, everywhere, and where not. For he was Barbox Brothers and Co. now, and had taken thousands of partners into the solitary firm.

He had at length got back to his hotel room, and was standing before his fire refreshing himself with a glass of hot drink which he had stood upon the chimneypiece, when he heard the town clocks striking, and, referring to his watch, found the evening to have so slipped away, that they were striking twelve. As he put up his watch again, his eyes met those of his reflection in the chimney-glass.

"Why, it's your birthday already," he said, smiling. "You are looking very well. I wish you many happy returns of the day."

He had never before bestowed that wish upon himself. "By Jupiter!" he discovered, "it alters the whole case of running away from one's birthday! It's a thing to explain to Phœbe. Besides, here is quite a long story to tell her, that has sprung out of the road with no story. I'll go back, instead of going on. I'll go back by my friend Lamps's Up X presently."

He went back to Mugby Junction, and, in point of fact, he established himself at Mugby Junction. It was the convenient place to live in, for brightening Phœbe's life. It was the convenient place to live in, for having her taught music by Beatrice. It was the convenient place to live in, for occasionally borrowing Polly. It was the convenient place to live in, for being joined at will to all sorts of agreeable places and persons. So, he became settled there, and, his house standing in an elevated situation, it is note-worthy of him in conclusion, as Polly herself might (not irreverently) have put it :

> "There was an Old Barbox who lived on a hill,
> And if he ain't gone, he lives there still."

HERE FOLLOWS THE SUBSTANCE OF WHAT WAS SEEN, HEARD, OR OTHERWISE PICKED UP, BY THE GENTLEMAN FOR NOWHERE, IN HIS CAREFUL STUDY OF THE JUNCTION.

CHAPTER III

MAIN LINE: THE BOY AT MUGBY

I AM the boy at Mugby. That's about what *I* am.

You don't know what I mean? What a pity! But I think you do. I think you must. Look here. I am the boy at what is called The Refreshment Room at Mugby Junction, and what's proudest boast is, that it never yet refreshed a mortal being.

Up in a corner of the Down Refreshment Room at Mugby Junction, in the height of twenty-seven cross draughts (I've often counted 'em while they brush the First-Class hair twenty-seven ways), behind the bottles, among the glasses, bounded on the nor'west by the beer, stood pretty far to the right of a metallic object that's at times the tea-urn and at times the soup-tureen, according to the nature of the last twang imparted to its contents which are the same ground-work, fended off from the traveller by a barrier of stale sponge-cakes erected atop of the counter, and lastly exposed sideways to the glare of Our Missis's eye—you ask a Boy so sitiwated, next time you stop in a hurry at Mugby, for anything to drink ; you take particular notice that he'll try to seem not to hear you, that he'll appear in a absent manner to survey the Line through a transparent medium composed of your head and body, and that he won't serve you as long as you can possibly bear it. That's me.

What a lark it is! We are the Model Establishment,

we are, at Mugby. Other Refreshment Rooms send their imperfect young ladies up to be finished off by Our Missis. For some of the young ladies, when they're new to the business, come into it mild! Ah! Our Missis, she soon takes that out of 'em. Why, I originally come into the business meek myself. But Our Missis, she soon took that out of *me*.

What a delightful lark it is! I look upon us Refreshmenters as ockipying the only proudly independent footing on the Line. There's Papers, for instance,—my honourable friend, if he will allow me to call him so,—him as belongs to Smith's bookstall. Why, he no more dares to be up to our Refreshmenting games than he dares to jump atop of a locomotive with her steam at full pressure, and cut away upon her alone, driving himself, at limited-mail speed. Papers, he'd get his head punched at every compartment, first, second, and third, the whole length of a train, if he was to ventur to imitate my demeanour. It's the same with the porters, the same with the guards, the same with the ticket clerks, the same the whole way up to the secretary, traffic-manager, or very chairman. There ain't a one among 'em on the nobly independent footing we are. Did you ever catch one of *them*, when you wanted anything of him, making a system of surveying the Line through a transparent medium composed of your head and body? I should hope not.

You should see our Bandolining Room at Mugby Junction. It's led to by the door behind the counter, which you'll notice usually stands ajar, and it's the room where Our Missis and our young ladies Bandolines their hair. You should see 'em at it, betwixt trains, Bandolining away, as if they was anointing themselves for the combat. When you're telegraphed, you should see their noses all a-going up with scorn, as if it was a part of the working of the same Cooke and Wheatstone electrical machinery. You should hear Our Missis give the word, "Here comes the Beast to be Fed!" and then you should see 'em indignantly skipping across the Line, from the Up to the Down, or Wicer Warsaw, and begin to pitch the stale pastry into the plates, and chuck the sawdust sangwiches under the glass covers, and get out the—ha, ha, ha!—the sherry,—O my eye, my eye!—for your Refreshment.

It's only in the Isle of the Brave and Land of the Free (by which, of course, I mean to say Britannia) that Refresh-

menting is so effective, so 'olesome, so constitutional a check
upon the public. There was a Foreigner, which having
politely, with his hat off, beseeched our young ladies and
Our Missis for "a leetel gloss hoff prarndee," and having had
the Line surveyed through him by all and no other acknowledgment, was a-proceeding at last to help himself, as seems
to be the custom in his own country, when Our Missis, with
her hair almost a-coming un-Bandolined with rage, and her
eyes omitting sparks, flew at him, cotched the decanter out
of his hand, and said, "Put it down! I won't allow that!"
The foreigner turned pale, stepped back with his arms
stretched out in front of him, his hands clasped, and his
shoulders riz, and exclaimed: "Ah! Is it possible, this!
That these disdaineous females and this ferocious old woman
are placed here by the administration, not only to empoison
the voyagers, but to affront them! Great Heaven! How
arrives it? The English people. Or is he then a slave?
Or idiot?" Another time, a merry, wideawake American
gent had tried the sawdust and spit it out, and had tried
the Sherry and spit that out, and had tried in vain to sustain
exhausted natur upon Butter-Scotch, and had been rather
extra Bandolined and Line-surveyed through, when, as the
bell was ringing and he paid Our Missis, he says, very loud
and good-tempered: "I tell Yew what 'tis, ma'arm. I la'af.
Theer! I la'af. I Dew. I oughter ha' seen most things,
for I hail from the Onlimited side of the Atlantic Ocean,
and I haive travelled right slick over the Limited, head on
through Jeerusalemm and the East, and likeways France and
Italy, Europe Old World, and am now upon the track to
the Chief Europian Village; but such an Institution as Yew,
and Yewer young ladies, and Yewer fixin's solid and liquid,
afore the glorious Tarnal I never did see yet! And if I
hain't found the eighth wonder of monarchical Creation, in
finding Yew, and Yewer young ladies, and Yewer fixin's
solid and liquid, all as aforesaid, established in a country
where the people air not absolute Loo-naticks, I am Extra
Double Darned with a Nip and Frizzle to the innermostest
grit! Wheerfur—Theer!—I la'af! I Dew, ma'arm. I la'af!"
And so he went, stamping and shaking his sides, along the
platform all the way to his own compartment.

I think it was her standing up agin the Foreigner as giv'
Our Missis the idea of going over to France, and droring
a comparison betwixt Refreshmenting as followed among the

frog-eaters, and Refreshmenting as triumphant in the Isle of the Brave and Land of the Free (by which, of course, I mean to say agin, Britannia). Our young ladies, Miss Whiff, Miss Piff, and Mrs. Sniff, was unanimous opposed to her going; for, as they says to Our Missis one and all, it is well beknown to the hends of the herth as no other nation except Britain has a idea of anythink, but above all of business. Why then should you tire yourself to prove what is already proved? Our Missis, however (being a teazer at all pints) stood out grim obstinate, and got a return pass by South-eastern Tidal, to go right through, if such should be her dispositions, to Marseilles.

Sniff is husband to Mrs. Sniff, and is a regular insignificant cove. He looks arter the sawdust department in a back room, and is sometimes, when we are very hard put to it, let behind the counter with a corkscrew; but never when it can be helped, his demeanour towards the public being disgusting servile. How Mrs. Sniff ever come so far to lower herself as to marry him, I don't know; but I suppose *he* does, and I should think he wished he didn't, for he leads a awful life. Mrs. Sniff couldn't be much harder with him if he was public. Similarly, Miss Whiff and Miss Piff, taking the tone of Mrs. Sniff, they shoulder Sniff about when he *is* let in with a corkscrew, and they whisk things out of his hands when in his servility he is a-going to let the public have 'em, and they snap him up when in the crawling baseness of his spirit he is a-going to answer a public question, and they drore more tears into his eyes than ever the mustard does which he all day long lays on to the sawdust. (But it ain't strong.) Once, when Sniff had the repulsiveness to reach across to get the milk-pot to hand over for a baby, I see Our Missis in her rage catch him by both his shoulders, and spin him out into the Bandolining Room.

But Mrs. Sniff,—how different! She's the one! She's the one as you'll notice to be always looking another way from you, when you look at her. She's the one with the small waist buckled in tight in front, and with the lace cuffs at her wrists, which she puts on the edge of the counter before her, and stands a-smoothing while the public foams. This smoothing the cuffs and looking another way while the public foams is the last accomplishment taught to the young ladies as come to Mugby to be finished by Our Missis; and it's always taught by Mrs. Sniff.

The Boy at Mugby

When Our Missis went away upon her journey, Mrs. Sniff was left in charge. She did hold the public in check most beautiful! In all my time, I never see half so many cups of tea given without milk to people as wanted it with, nor half so many cups of tea with milk given to people as wanted it without. When foaming ensued, Mrs. Sniff would say: "Then you'd better settle it among yourselves, and change with one another." It was a most highly delicious lark. I enjoyed the Refreshmenting business more than ever, and was so glad I had took to it when young.

Our Missis returned. It got circulated among the young ladies, and it as it might be penetrated to me through the crevices of the Bandolining Room, that she had Orrors to reveal, if revelations so contemptible could be dignified with the name. Agitation become awakened. Excitement was up in the stirrups. Expectation stood a-tiptoe. At length it was put forth that on our slacked evening in the week, and at our slackest time of that evening betwixt trains, Our Missis would give her views of foreign Refreshmenting, in the Bandolining Room.

It was arranged tasteful for the purpose. The Bandolining table and glass was hid in a corner, a armchair was elevated on a packing-case for Our Missis's ockypation, a table and a tumbler of water (no sherry in it, thankee) was placed beside it. Two of the pupils, the season being autumn, and hollyhocks and dahlias being in, ornamented the wall with three devices in those flowers. On one might be read, "MAY ALBION NEVER LEARN;" on another, "KEEP THE PUBLIC DOWN;" on another, "OUR REFRESHMENTING CHARTER." The whole had a beautiful appearance, with which the beauty of the sentiments corresponded.

On Our Missis's brow was wrote Severity, as she ascended the fatal platform. (Not that that was anythink new.) Miss Whiff and Miss Piff sat at her feet. Three chairs from the Waiting Room might have been perceived by a average eye, in front of her, on which the pupils was accommodated. Behind them a very close observer might have discerned a Boy. Myself.

"Where," said Our Missis, glancing gloomily around, "is Sniff?"

"I thought it better," answered Mrs. Sniff, "that he should not be let to come in. He is such an Ass."

"No doubt," assented Our Missis. "But for that reason is it not desirable to improve his mind?"

"Oh, nothing will ever improve *him*," said Mrs. Sniff.

"However," pursued Our Missis, "call him in, Ezekiel."

I called him in. The appearance of the low-minded cove was hailed with disapprobation from all sides, on account of his having brought his corkscrew with him. He pleaded "the force of habit."

"The force!" said Mrs. Sniff. "Don't let us have you talking about force, for Gracious' sake. There! Do stand still where you are, with your back against the wall."

He is a smiling piece of vacancy, and he smiled in the mean way in which he will even smile at the public if he gets a chance (language can say no meaner of him), and he stood upright near the door with the back of his head agin the wall, as if he was a-waiting for somebody to come and measure his heighth for the Army.

"I should not enter, ladies," says Our Missis, "on the revolting disclosures I am about to make, if it was not in the hope that they will cause you to be yet more implacable in the exercise of the power you wield in a constitutional country, and yet more devoted to the constitutional motto which I see before me,"—it was behind her, but the words sounded better so,—"'May Albion never learn!'"

Here the pupils as had made the motto admired it, and cried, "Hear! Hear! Hear!" Sniff, showing an inclination to join in chorus, got himself frowned down by every brow.

"The baseness of the French," pursued Our Missis, "as displayed in the fawning nature of their Refreshmenting, equals, if not surpasses, anythink as was ever heard of the baseness of the celebrated Bonaparte."

Miss Whiff, Miss Piff, and me, we drored a heavy breath, equal to saying, "We thought as much!" Miss Whiff and Miss Piff seeming to object to my droring mine along with theirs, I drored another to aggravate 'em.

"Shall I be believed," says Our Missis, with flashing eyes, "when I tell you that no sooner had I set my foot upon that treacherous shore——"

Here Sniff, either bursting out mad, or thinking aloud, says, in a low voice: "Feet. Plural, you know."

The cowering that come upon him when he was spurned by all eyes, added to his being beneath contempt, was sufficient punishment for a cove so grovelling. In the midst of a silence rendered more impressive by the turned-

up female noses with which it was pervaded, Our Missis
went on :

"Shall I be believed when I tell you, that no sooner had
I landed," this word with a killing look at Sniff, "on that
treacherous shore, than I was ushered into a Refreshment
Room where there were—I do not exaggerate—actually
eatable things to eat?"

A groan burst from the ladies. I not only did myself the
honour of jining, but also of lengthening it out.

"Where there were," Our Missis added, "not only eatable
things to eat, but also drinkable things to drink?"

A murmur, swelling almost into a scream, ariz. Miss Piff,
trembling with indignation, called out, "Name!"

"I *will* name," said Our Missis. "There was roast fowls,
hot and cold ; there was smoking roast veal surrounded with
browned potatoes ; there was hot soup with (again I ask
shall I be credited?) nothing bitter in it, and no flour to
choke off the consumer ; there was a variety of cold dishes
set off with jelly ; there was salad ; there was—mark me !
fresh pastry, and that of a light construction ; there was
a luscious show of fruit ; there was bottles and decanters
of sound small wine, of every size, and adapted to every
pocket ; the same odious statement will apply to brandy ;
and these were set out upon the counter so that all could
help themselves."

Our Missis's lips so quivered, that Mrs. Sniff, though
scarcely less convulsed than she were, got up and held the
tumbler to them.

"This," proceeds Our Missis, "was my first unconstitutional
experience. Well would it have been if it had been my last
and worst. But no. As I proceeded farther into that
enslaved and ignorant land, its aspect became more hideous.
I need not explain to this assembly the ingredients and
formation of the British Refreshment sangwich?"

Universal laughter,—except from Sniff, who, as sangwich-
cutter, shook his head in a state of the utmost dejection as
he stood with it agin the wall.

"Well!" said Our Missis, with dilated nostrils. "Take
a fresh, crisp, long, crusty penny loaf made of the whitest
and best flour. Cut it longwise through the middle. Insert
a fair and nicely fitting slice of ham. Tie a smart piece of
ribbon round the middle of the whole to bind it together.
Add at one end a neat wrapper of clean white paper by

which to hold it.   And the universal French Refreshment
sangwich busts on your disgusted vision."

A cry of "Shame!" from all—except Sniff, which rubbed
his stomach with a soothing hand.

"I need not," said Our Missis, "explain to this assembly
the usual formation and fitting of the British Refreshment
Room?"

No, no, and laughter.   Sniff agin shaking his head in low
spirits agin the wall.

"Well," said Our Missis, "what would you say to a general
decoration of everythink, to hangings (sometimes elegant),
to easy velvet furniture, to abundance of little tables, to
abundance of little seats, to brisk bright waiters, to great
convenience, to a pervading cleanliness and tastefulness
positively addressing the public, and making the Beast
thinking itself worth the pains?"

Contemptuous fury on the part of all the ladies.   Mrs.
Sniff looking as if she wanted somebody to hold her, and
everybody else looking as if they'd rayther not.

"Three times," said Our Missis, working herself into
a truly terrimenjious state,—"three times did I see these
shameful things, only between the coast and Paris, and not
counting either: at Hazebroucke, at Arras, at Amiens.   But
worse remains.   Tell me, what would you call a person who
should propose in England that there should be kept, say at
our own model Mugby Junction, pretty baskets, each holding
an assorted cold lunch and dessert for one, each at a certain
fixed price, and each within a passenger's power to take
away, to empty in the carriage at perfect leisure, and to
return at another station fifty or a hundred miles farther
on?"

There was disagreement what such a person should be
called.   Whether revolutionist, atheist, Bright (*I* said him),
or Un-English.   Miss Piff screeched her shrill opinion last,
in the words: "A malignant maniac!"

"I adopt," says Our Missis, "the brand set upon such
a person by the righteous indignation of my friend Miss Piff.
A malignant maniac.   Know, then, that that malignant
maniac has sprung from the congenial soil of France, and
that his malignant madness was in unchecked action on this
same part of my journey."

I noticed that Sniff was a-rubbing his hands, and that
Mrs. Sniff had got her eye upon him.   But I did not take

more particular notice, owing to the excited state in which the young ladies was, and to feeling myself called upon to keep it up with a howl.

"On my experience south of Paris," said Our Missis, in a deep tone, "I will not expatiate. Too loathsome were the task! But fancy this. Fancy a guard coming round, with the train at full speed, to inquire how many for dinner. Fancy his telegraphing forward the number of dinners. Fancy every one expected, and the table elegantly laid for the complete party. Fancy a charming dinner, in a charming room, and the head-cook, concerned for the honour of every dish, superintending in his clean white jacket and cap. Fancy the Beast travelling six hundred miles on end, very fast, and with great punctuality, yet being taught to expect all this to be done for it!"

A spirited chorus of "The Beast!"

I noticed that Sniff was agin a-rubbing his stomach with a soothing hand, and that he had drored up one leg. But agin I didn't take particular notice, looking on myself as called upon to stimulate public feeling. It being a lark besides.

"Putting everything together," said Our Missis, "French Refreshmenting comes to this, and oh, it comes to a nice total! First: eatable things to eat, and drinkable things to drink."

A groan from the young ladies, kep' up by me.

"Second: convenience, and even elegance."

Another groan from the young ladies, kep' up by me.

"Third: moderate charges."

This time a groan from me, kep' up by the young ladies.

"Fourth:—and here," says Our Missis, "I claim your angriest sympathy,—attention, common civility, nay, even politeness!"

Me and the young ladies regularly raging mad all together.

"And I cannot in conclusion," says Our Missis, with her spitefullest sneer, "give you a completer pictur of that despicable nation (after what I have related), than assuring you that they wouldn't bear our constitutional ways and noble independence at Mugby Junction, for a single month, and that they would turn us to the right-about and put another system in our places, as soon as look at us; perhaps sooner, for I do not believe they have the good taste to care to look at us twice."

The swelling tumult was arrested in its rise. Sniff, bore away by his servile disposition, had drored up his leg with a higher and a higher relish, and was now discovered to be waving his corkscrew over his head. It was at this moment that Mrs. Sniff, who had kep' her eye upon him like the fabled obelisk, descended on her victim. Our Missis followed them both out, and cries was heard in the sawdust department.

You come into the Down Refreshment Room, at the Junction, making believe you don't know me, and I'll pint you out with my right thumb over my shoulder which is Our Missis, and which is Miss Whiff, and which is Miss Piff, and which is Mrs. Sniff. But you won't get a chance to see Sniff. because he disappeared that night. Whether he perished, tore to pieces, I cannot say; but his corkscrew alone remains, to bear witness to the servility of his disposition.

CHAPTER IV

NO. 1 BRANCH LINE: THE SIGNAL-MAN

" HALLOA! Below there!"

When he heard a voice thus calling to him, he was standing at the door of his box, with a flag in his hand, furled round its short pole. One would have thought, considering the nature of the ground, that he could not have doubted from what quarter the voice came; but instead of looking up to where I stood on the top of the steep cutting nearly over his head, he turned himself about, and looked down the Line. There was something remarkable in his manner of doing so, though I could not have said for my life what. But I know it was remarkable enough to attract my notice, even though his figure was foreshortened and shadowed, down in the deep trench, and mine was high above him, so steeped in the glow of an angry sunset, that I had shaded my eyes with my hand before I saw him at all.

"Halloa! Below!"

From looking down the Line, he turned himself about again, and, raising his eyes, saw my figure high above him.

"Is there any path by which I can come down and speak to you?"

He looked up at me without replying, and I looked down at him without pressing him too soon with a repetition of my idle question. Just then there came a vague vibration in the earth and air, quickly changing into a violent pulsation, and an oncoming rush that caused me to start back, as though it had force to draw me down. When such vapour as rose to my height from this rapid train had passed me, and was skimming away over the landscape, I looked down again, and saw him refurling the flag he had shown while the train went by.

I repeated my inquiry. After a pause, during which he seemed to regard me with fixed attention, he motioned with his rolled-up flag towards a point on my level, some two or three hundred yards distant. I called down to him, "All right!" and made for that point. There, by dint of looking closely about me, I found a rough zigzag descending path notched out, which I followed.

The cutting was extremely deep, and unusually precipitate. It was made through a clammy stone, that became oozier and wetter as I went down. For these reasons, I found the way long enough to give me time to recall a singular air of reluctance or compulsion with which he had pointed out the path.

When I came down low enough upon the zigzag descent to see him again, I saw that he was standing between the rails on the way by which the train had lately passed, in an attitude as if he were waiting for me to appear. He had his left hand at his chin, and that left elbow rested on his right hand, crossed over his breast. His attitude was one of such expectation and watchfulness that I stopped a moment, wondering at it.

I resumed my downward way, and stepping out upon the level of the railroad, and drawing nearer to him, saw that he was a dark sallow man, with a dark beard and rather heavy eyebrows. His post was in as solitary and dismal a place as ever I saw. On either side, a dripping-wet wall of jagged stone, excluding all view but a strip of sky; the perspective one way only a crooked prolongation of this great dungeon; the shorter perspective in the other direction terminating in a gloomy red light, and the gloomier entrance to a black tunnel, in whose massive architecture there was a barbarous, depressing, and forbidding air. So little sunlight ever found its way to this spot, that it had an earthy, deadly smell; and so much cold wind rushed through it, that it struck chill to me, as if I had left the natural world.

Before he stirred, I was near enough to him to have touched him. Not even then removing his eyes from mine, he stepped back one step, and lifted his hand.

This was a lonesome post to occupy (I said), and it had riveted my attention when I looked down from up yonder. A visitor was a rarity, I should suppose; not an unwelcome rarity, I hoped? In me, he merely saw a man who had been shut up within narrow limits all his life, and who, being at last set free, had a newly-awakened interest in these great works. To such purpose I spoke to him; but I am far from sure of the terms I used; for, besides that I am not happy in opening any conversation, there was something in the man that daunted me.

He directed a most curious look towards the red light near the tunnel's mouth, and looked all about it, as if something were missing from it, and then looked at me.

That light was part of his charge? Was it not?

He answered in a low voice,—"Don't you know it is?"

The monstrous thought came into my mind, as I perused the fixed eyes and the saturnine face, that this was a spirit, not a man. I have speculated since, whether there may have been infection in his mind.

In my turn, I stepped back. But in making the action, I detected in his eyes some latent fear of me. This put the monstrous thought to flight.

"You look at me," I said, forcing a smile, "as if you had a dread of me."

"I was doubtful," he returned, "whether I had seen you before."

"Where?"

He pointed to the red light he had looked at.

"There?" I said.

Intently watchful of me, he replied (but without sound), "Yes."

"My good fellow, what should I do there? However, be that as it may, I never was there, you may swear."

"I think I may," he rejoined. "Yes; I am sure I may."

His manner cleared, like my own. He replied to my remarks with readiness, and in well-chosen words. Had he much to do there? Yes; that was to say, he had enough responsibility to bear; but exactness and watchfulness were what was required of him, and of actual work—manual labour—he had next to none. To change that signal, to trim those lights, and to turn this iron handle now and then, was all he had to do under that head. Regarding those many long and lonely hours of which I seemed to make so much, he could only say that the routine of his life had shaped itself into that form, and he had grown used to it. He had taught himself a language down here,—if only to know it by sight, and to have formed his own crude ideas of its pronunciation, could be called learning it. He had also worked at fractions and decimals, and tried a little algebra; but he was, and had been as a boy, a poor hand at figures. Was it necessary for him when on duty always to remain in that channel of damp air, and could he never rise into the sunshine from between those high stone walls? Why, that depended upon times and circumstances. Under some conditions there would be less upon the Line than under others, and the same held good as to certain hours of the day and night. In bright weather, he did choose occasions for getting a little above these lower shadows; but, being at all times liable to be called by his electric bell, and at such times listening for it with redoubled anxiety, the relief was less than I would suppose.

He took me into his box, where there was a fire, a desk for an official book in which he had to make certain entries, a telegraphic instrument with its dial, face, and needles, and the little bell of which he had spoken. On my trusting that he would excuse the remark that he had been well educated, and (I hoped I might say without offence), perhaps educated above that station, he observed that instances of slight incongruity in such wise would rarely be found wanting among large bodies of men; that he had heard it was so in workhouses, in the police force, even in that last desperate resource, the army; and that he knew it was so, more or less, in any great railway staff. He had been, when young (if I could believe it, sitting in that hut,—he scarcely could), a student of natural philosophy, and had attended lectures; but he had run wild, misused his opportunities, gone down, and never risen again. He had no complaint to offer about that. He had made his bed, and he lay upon it. It was far too late to make another.

All that I have here condensed he said in a quiet manner,

with his grave dark regards divided between me and the fire. He threw in the word, "Sir," from time to time, and especially when he referred to his youth,—as though to request me to understand that he claimed to be nothing but what I found him. He was several times interrupted by the little bell, and had to read off messages, and send replies. Once he had to stand without the door, and display a flag as a train passed, and make some verbal communication to the driver. In the discharge of his duties, I observed him to be remarkably exact and vigilant, breaking off his discourse at a syllable, and remaining silent until what he had to do was done.

In a word, I should have set this man down as one of the safest of men to be employed in that capacity, but for the circumstance that while he was speaking to me he twice broke off with a fallen colour, turned his face towards the little bell when it did NOT ring, opened the door of the hut (which was kept shut to exclude the unhealthy damp), and looked out towards the red light near the mouth of the tunnel. On both of those occasions, he came back to the fire with the inexplicable air upon him which I had remarked, without being able to define, when we were so far asunder.

Said I, when I rose to leave him, "You almost make me think that I have met with a contented man."

(I am afraid I must acknowledge that I said it to lead him on.)

"I believe I used to be so," he rejoined, in the low voice in which he had first spoken; "but I am troubled, Sir, I am troubled."

He would have recalled the words if he could. He had said them, however, and I took them up quickly.

"With what? What is your trouble?"

"It is very difficult to impart, Sir. It is very, very difficult to speak of. If ever you make me another visit, I will try to tell you."

"But I expressly intend to make you another visit. Say, when shall it be?"

"I go off early in the morning, and I shall be on again at ten to-morrow night, Sir."

"I will come at eleven."

He thanked me, and went out at the door with me. "I'll show my white light, Sir," he said, in his peculiar low voice, "till you have found the way up. When you have found it, don't call out! And when you are at the top, don't call out!"

His manner seemed to make the place strike colder to me, but I said no more than, "Very well."

"And when you come down to-morrow night, don't call out! Let me ask you a parting question. What made you cry, 'Halloa! Below there!' to-night?"

"Heaven knows," said I. "I cried something to that effect——"

"Not to that effect, Sir. Those were the very words. I know them well."

"Admit those were the very words. I said them, no doubt, because I saw you below."

"For no other reason?"

"What other reason could I possibly have?"

"You had no feeling that they were conveyed to you in any supernatural way?"

"No."

He wished me good night, and held up his light. I walked by the side of the down Line of rails (with a very disagreeable sensation of a train coming behind me) until I found the path. It was easier to mount than to descend, and I got back to my inn without any adventure.

Punctual to my appointment, I placed my foot on the first notch of the zigzag next night, as the distant clocks were striking eleven. He was waiting for me at the bottom, with his white light on. "I have not called out," I said, when we came close together; "may I speak now?" "By all means, Sir." "Good night, then, and here's my hand." "Good night, Sir, and here's mine." With that we walked side by side to his box, entered it, closed the door, and sat down by the fire.

"I have made up my mind, Sir," he began, bending forward as soon as we were seated, and speaking in a tone but a little above a whisper, "that you shall not have to ask me twice what troubles me. I took you for some one else yesterday evening. That troubles me."

"That mistake?"

"No. That some one else."

"Who is it?"

"I don't know."

"Like me?"

"I don't know. I never saw the face. The left arm is across the face, and the right arm is waved,—violently waved. This way."

I followed his action with my eyes, and it was the action of an arm gesticulating, with the utmost passion and vehemence, "For God's sake, clear the way!"

"One moonlight night," said the man, "I was sitting here, when I heard a voice cry, 'Halloa! Below there!' I started up, looked from that door, and saw this Some one else standing by the red light near the tunnel, waving as I just now showed you. The voice seemed hoarse with shouting, and it cried, 'Look out! Look out!' And then again, 'Halloa! Below there! Look out!' I caught up my lamp, turned it on red, and ran towards the figure, calling, 'What's wrong? What has happened? Where?' It stood just outside the blackness of the tunnel. I advanced so close upon it that I wondered at its keeping the sleeve across its eyes. I ran right up at it, and had my hand stretched out to pull the sleeve away, when it was gone."

"Into the tunnel?" said I.

"No. I ran on into the tunnel, five hundred yards. I stopped, and held my lamp above my head, and saw the figures of the measured distance, and saw the wet stains stealing down the walls and trickling through the arch. I ran out again faster than I had run in (for I had a mortal abhorrence of the place upon me), and I looked all round the red light with my own red light, and I went up the iron ladder to the gallery atop of it, and I came down again, and ran back here. I telegraphed both ways. 'An alarm has been given. Is anything wrong?' The answer came back, both ways, 'All well.'"

Resisting the slow touch of a frozen finger tracing out my spine, I showed him how that this figure must be a deception of his sense of sight; and how that figures, originating in disease of the delicate nerves that minister to the functions of the eye, were known to have often troubled patients, some of whom had become conscious of the nature of their affliction, and had even proved it by experiments upon themselves. "As to an imaginary cry," said I, "do but listen for a moment to the wind in this unnatural valley while we speak so low, and to the wild harp it makes of the telegraph wires."

That was all very well, he returned, after we had sat listening for a while, and he ought to know something of the wind and the wires,—he who so often passed long winter nights there, alone and watching. But he would beg to remark that he had not finished.

I asked his pardon, and he slowly added these words, touching my arm,—

"Within six hours after the Appearance, the memorable accident on this Line happened, and within ten hours the dead and wounded were brought along through the tunnel over the spot where the figure had stood."

A disagreeable shudder crept over me, but I did my best against it. It was not to be denied, I rejoined, that this was a remarkable coincidence, calculated deeply to impress his mind. But it was unquestionable that remarkable coincidences did continually occur, and they must be taken into account in dealing with such a subject. Though to be sure I must admit, I added (for I thought I saw that he was going to bring the objection to bear upon me), men of common sense did not allow much for coincidences in making the ordinary calculations of life.

He again begged to remark that he had not finished.

I again begged his pardon for being betrayed into interruptions.

"This," he said, again laying his hand upon my arm, and glancing over his shoulder with hollow eyes, "was just a year ago. Six or seven months passed, and I had recovered from the surprise and shock, when one morning, as the day was breaking, I, standing at the door, looked towards the red light, and saw the spectre again." He stopped, with a fixed look at me.

"Did it cry out?"

"No. It was silent."

"Did it wave its arm?"

"No. It leaned against the shaft of the light, with both hands before the face. Like this."

Once more I followed his action with my eyes. It was an action of mourning. I have seen such an attitude in stone figures on tombs.

"Did you go up to it?"

"I came in and sat down, partly to collect my thoughts, partly because it had turned me faint. When I went to the door again, daylight was above me, and the ghost was gone."

"But nothing followed? Nothing came of this?"

He touched me on the arm with his forefinger twice or thrice, giving a ghastly nod each time:—

"That very day, as a train came out of the tunnel, I noticed, at a carriage window on my side, what looked like a confusion of hands and heads, and something waved. I saw it just in time to signal the driver, Stop! He shut off, and put his brake on, but the train drifted past here a hundred and fifty yards or more. I ran after it, and, as I went along, heard terrible screams and cries. A beautiful young lady had died instantaneously in one of the compartments, and was brought in here, and laid down on this floor between us."

Involuntarily I pushed my chair back, as I looked from the boards at which he pointed to himself.

"True, Sir. True. Precisely as it happened, so I tell it you."

I could think of nothing to say, to any purpose, and my mouth was very dry. The wind and the wires took up the story with a long lamenting wail.

He resumed. "Now, Sir, mark this, and judge how my mind is troubled. The spectre came back a week ago. Ever since, it has been there, now and again, by fits and starts."

"At the light?"

"At the Danger-light."

"What does it seem to do?"

He repeated, if possible with increased passion and vehemence, that former gesticulation of, "For God's sake, clear the way!"

Then he went on. "I have no peace or rest for it. It calls to me, for many minutes together, in an agonised manner, 'Below there! Look out! Look out!' It stands waving to me. It rings my little bell——"

I caught at that. "Did it ring your bell yesterday evening when I was here, and you went to the door?"

"Twice."

"Why, see," said I, "how your imagination misleads you. My eyes were on the bell, and my ears were open to the bell, and if I am a living man, it did NOT ring at those times. No, nor at any other time, except when it was rung in the natural course of physical things by the station communicating with you."

He shook his head. "I have never made a mistake as to that yet, Sir. I have never confused the spectre's ring with the man's. The ghost's ring is a strange vibration in the bell that it derives from nothing else, and I have not asserted that the bell stirs to the eye. I don't wonder that you failed to hear it. But I heard it."

The Signal-Man

"And did the spectre seem to be there, when you looked out?"

"It WAS there."

"Both times?"

He repeated firmly: "Both times."

"Will you come to the door with me, and look for it now?"

He bit his under lip as though he were somewhat unwilling, but arose. I opened the door, and stood on the step, while he stood in the doorway. There was the Danger-light. There was the dismal mouth of the tunnel. There were the high, wet stone walls of the cutting. There were the stars above them.

"Do you see it?" I asked him, taking particular note of his face. His eyes were prominent and strained, but not very much more so, perhaps, than my own had been when I had directed them earnestly towards the same spot.

"No," he answered. "It is not there."

"Agreed," said I.

We went in again, shut the door, and resumed our seats. I was thinking how best to improve this advantage, if it might be called one, when he took up the conversation in such a matter-of-course way, so assuming that there could be no serious question of fact between us, that I felt myself placed in the weakest of positions.

"By this time you will fully understand, Sir," he said, "that what troubles me so dreadfully is the question, What does the spectre mean?"

I was not sure, I told him, that I did fully understand.

"What is its warning against?" he said, ruminating, with his eyes on the fire, and only by times turning them on me. "What is the danger? Where is the danger? There is danger overhanging somewhere on the Line. Some dreadful calamity will happen. It is not to be doubted this third time, after what has gone before. But surely this is a cruel haunting of *me*. What can *I* do?"

He pulled out his handkerchief, and wiped the drops from his heated forehead.

"If I telegraph Danger, on either side of me, or on both, I can give no reason for it," he went on, wiping the palms of his hands. "I should get into trouble, and do no good. They would think I was mad. This is the way it would work,—Message: 'Danger! Take care!' Answer: 'What

Danger? Where?' Message: 'Don't know. But, for God's sake, take care!' They would displace me. What else could they do?"

His pain of mind was most pitiable to see. It was the mental torture of a conscientious man, oppressed beyond endurance by an unintelligible responsibility involving life.

"When it first stood under the Danger-light," he went on, putting his dark hair back from his head, and drawing his hands outward across and across his temples in an extremity of feverish distress, "why not tell me where that accident was to happen,—if it must happen? Why not tell me how it could be averted,—if it could have been averted? When on its second coming it hid its face, why not tell me, instead, 'She is going to die. Let them keep her at home'? If it came, on those two occasions, only to show me that its warnings were true, and so to prepare me for the third, why not warn me plainly now? And I, Lord help me! A mere poor signal-man on this solitary station! Why not go to somebody with credit to be believed, and power to act?"

When I saw him in this state, I saw that for the poor man's sake, as well as for the public safety, what I had to do for the time was to compose his mind. Therefore, setting aside all question of reality or unreality between us, I represented to him that whoever thoroughly discharged his duty must do well, and that at least it was his comfort that he understood his duty, though he did not understand these confounding Appearances. In this effort I succeeded far better than in the attempt to reason him out of his conviction. He became calm; the occupations incidental to his post as the night advanced began to make larger demands on his attention: and I left him at two in the morning. I had offered to stay through the night, but he would not hear of it.

That I more than once looked back at the red light as I ascended the pathway, that I did not like the red light, and that I should have slept but poorly if my bed had been under it, I see no reason to conceal. Nor did I like the two sequences of the accident and the dead girl. I see no reason to conceal that either.

But what ran most in my thoughts was the consideration how ought I to act, having become the recipient of this disclosure? I had proved the man to be intelligent, vigilant, painstaking, and exact; but how long might he remain so, in his state of mind? Though in a subordinate position, still he held a most important trust, and would I (for instance) like to stake my own life on the chances of his continuing to execute it with precision?

Unable to overcome a feeling that there would be something treacherous in my communicating what he had told me to his superiors in the Company, without first being plain with himself and proposing a middle course to him, I ultimately resolved to offer to accompany him (otherwise keeping his secret for the present) to the wisest medical practitioner we could hear of in those parts, and to take his opinion. A change in his time of duty would come round next night, he had apprised me, and he would be off an hour or two after sunrise, and on again soon after sunset. I had appointed to return accordingly.

Next evening was a lovely evening, and I walked out early to enjoy it. The sun was not yet quite down when I traversed the field-path near the top of the deep cutting. I would extend my walk for an hour, I said to myself, half an hour on and half an hour back, and it would then be time to go to my signal-man's box.

Before pursuing my stroll, I stepped to the brink, and mechanically looked down, from the point from which I had first seen him. I cannot describe the thrill that seized upon me, when, close at the mouth of the tunnel, I saw the appearance of a man, with his left sleeve across his eyes, passionately waving his right arm.

The nameless horror that oppressed me passed in a moment, for in a moment I saw that this appearance of a man was a man indeed, and that there was a little group of other men, standing at a short distance, to whom he seemed to be rehearsing the gesture he made. The Danger-light was not yet lighted. Against its shaft, a little low hut, entirely new to me, had been made of some wooden supports and tarpaulin. It looked no bigger than a bed.

With an irresistible sense that something was wrong,—with a flashing self-reproachful fear that fatal mischief had come of my leaving the man there, and causing no one to be sent to overlook or correct what he did,—I descended the notched path with all the speed I could make.

"What is the matter?" I asked the men.

"Signal-man killed this morning, Sir."

"Not the man belonging to that box?"

"Yes, Sir."

"Not the man I know?"

"You will recognise him, Sir, if you knew him," said the man who spoke for the others, solemnly uncovering his own head, and raising an end of the tarpaulin, "for his face is quite composed."

"O, how did this happen, how did this happen?" I asked, turning from one to another as the hut closed in again.

"He was cut down by an engine, Sir. No man in England knew his work better. But somehow he was not clear of the outer rail. It was just at broad day. He had struck the light, and had the lamp in his hand. As the engine came out of the tunnel, his back was towards her, and she cut him down. That man drove her, and was showing how it happened. Show the gentleman, Tom."

The man, who wore a rough dark dress, stepped back to his former place at the mouth of the tunnel.

"Coming round the curve in the tunnel, Sir," he said, "I saw him at the end, like as if I saw him down a perspective-glass. There was no time to check speed, and I knew him to be very careful. As he didn't seem to take heed of the whistle, I shut it off when we were running down upon him, and called to him as loud as I could call."

"What did you say?"

"I said, 'Below there! Look out! Look out! For God's sake, clear the way!'"

I started.

"Ah! it was a dreadful time, Sir. I never left off calling to him. I put this arm before my eyes not to see, and I waved this arm to the last; but it was no use."

Without prolonging the narrative to dwell on any one of its curious circumstances more than on any other, I may, in closing it, point out the coincidence that the warning of the Engine-Driver included, not only the words which the unfortunate Signal-man had repeated to me as haunting him, but also the words which I myself—not he—had attached, and that only in my own mind, to the gesticulation he had imitated.

NO THOROUGHFARE

[1867]

[This was written by Wilkie Collins conjointly with Dickens; the only portions furnished exclusively by Dickens being the 'Overture' and the 'Third Act'; Collins contributing to acts first and fourth, and writing the whole of the second.]

CHARACTERS

MR. BINTREY, *legal adviser to Mr. Walter Wilding.*

MADAME DOR, *an elderly companion of Marguerite's.*

MRS. SARAH GOLDSTRAW ('Sally'), *housekeeper to Mr. Wilding.*

MR. JARVIS, *a clerk.*

JOEY LADLE, *head cellarman to Wilding & Co.*

M. JULES OBENREIZER, *London agent for a Swiss firm.*

MISS MARGUERITE OBENREIZER, *his niece.*

MR. GEORGE VENDALE, *a partner in the firm of Wilding & Co.*

MAÎTRE VOIGT, *a handsome old man, chief notary of Neuchâtel.*

MR. WALTER WILDING, *a wine-merchant.*

NO THOROUGHFARE

THE OVERTURE

DAY of the month and year, November the thirtieth, one thousand eight hundred and thirty-five. London Time by the great clock of Saint Paul's, ten at night. All the lesser London churches strain their metallic throats. Some, flippantly begin before the heavy bell of the great cathedral; some, tardily begin three, four, half-a-dozen, strokes behind it; all are in sufficiently near accord, to leave a resonance in the air, as if the winged father who devours his children, had made a sounding sweep with his gigantic scythe in flying over the city.

What is this clock lower than most of the rest, and nearer to the ear, that lags so far behind to-night as to strike into the vibration alone? This is the clock of the Hospital for Foundling Children. Time was, when the Foundlings were received without question in a cradle at the gate. Time is, when inquiries are made respecting them, and they are taken as by favour from the mothers who relinquish all natural knowledge of them and claim to them for evermore.

The moon is at the full, and the night is fair with light clouds. The day has been otherwise than fair, for slush and mud, thickened with the droppings of heavy fog, lie black in the streets. The veiled lady who flutters up and down near the postern-gate of the Hospital for Foundling Children has need to be well shod to-night.

She flutters to and fro, avoiding the stand of hackney-coaches, and often pausing in the shadow of the western end of the great quadrangle wall, with her face turned towards the gate. As above her there is the purity of the moonlit sky, and below her there are the defilements of the pavement, so may she, haply, be divided in her mind between two vistas of reflection or experience. As her footprints crossing and recrossing one another have made a labyrinth in the mire, so may her track in life have involved itself in an intricate and unravellable tangle.

The postern-gate of the Hospital for Foundling Children opens, and a young woman comes out. The lady stands aside, observes closely, sees that the gate is quietly closed again from within, and follows the young woman.

Two or three streets have been traversed in silence before she, following close behind the object of her attention, stretches out her hand and touches her. Then the young woman stops and looks round, startled.

"You touched me last night, and, when I turned my head, you would not speak. Why do you follow me like a silent ghost?"

"It was not," returned the lady, in a low voice, "that I would not speak, but that I could not when I tried."

"What do you want of me? I have never done you any harm?"

"Never."

"Do I know you?"

"No."

"Then what can you want of me?"

"Here are two guineas in this paper. Take my poor little present, and I will tell you."

Into the young woman's face, which is honest and comely, comes a flush as she replies: "There is neither grown person nor child in all the large establishment that I belong to, who hasn't a good word for Sally. I am Sally. Could I be so well thought of, if I was to be bought?"

"I do not mean to buy you; I mean only to reward you very slightly."

Sally firmly, but not ungently, closes and puts back the offering hand. "If there is anything I can do for you, ma'am, that I will not do for its own sake, you are much mistaken in me if you think that I will do it for money. What is it you want?"

"You are one of the nurses or attendants at the Hospital; I saw you leave to-night and last night."

"Yes, I am. I am Sally."

"There is a pleasant patience in your face which makes me believe that very young children would take readily to you."

"God bless 'em! So they do."

The lady lifts her veil, and shows a face no older than the nurse's. A face far more refined and capable than hers, but wild and worn with sorrow.

"I am the miserable mother of a baby lately received under your care. I have a prayer to make to you."

Instinctively respecting the confidence which has drawn aside the veil, Sally—whose ways are all ways of simplicity and spontaneity—replaces it, and begins to cry.

"You will listen to my prayer?" the lady urges. "You will not be deaf to the agonised entreaty of such a broken suppliant as I am?"

"O dear, dear, dear!" cries Sally. "What shall I say, or can I say! Don't talk of prayers. Prayers are to be put up to the Good Father of All, and not to nurses and such. And there! I am only to hold my place for half a year longer, till another young woman can be trained up to it. I am going to be married. I shouldn't have been out last night, and I shouldn't have been out to-night, but that my Dick (he is the young man I am going to be married to) lies ill, and I help his mother and sister to watch him. Don't take on so, don't take on so!"

"O good Sally, dear Sally," moans the lady, catching at her dress entreatingly. "As you are hopeful, and I am hopeless; as a fair way in life is before you, which can never, never, be before me; as you can aspire to become a respected wife, and as you can aspire to become a proud mother, as you are a living loving woman, and must die; for GOD's sake hear my distracted petition!"

"Deary, deary. deary ME!" cries Sally, her desperation culminating in the pronoun, "what am I ever to do? And there! See how you turn my own words back upon me. I tell you I am going to be married, on purpose to make it clearer to you that I am going to leave, and therefore couldn't help you if I would, Poor Thing, and you make it seem to my own self as if I was cruel in going to be married and *not* helping you. It ain't kind. Now, is it kind, Poor Thing?"

"Sally! Hear me, my dear. My entreaty is for no help in the future. It applies to what is past. It is only to be told in two words."

"There! This is worse and worse," cries Sally, "supposing that I understand what two words you mean."

"You do understand. What are the names they have
given my poor baby? I ask no more than that. I have
read of the customs of the place. He has been christened in
the chapel, and registered by some surname in the book. He
was received last Monday evening. What have they called
him?"

Down upon her knees in the foul mud of the by-way into
which they have strayed—an empty street without a thoroughfare giving on the dark gardens of the Hospital—the lady
would drop in her passionate entreaty, but that Sally prevents
her.

"Don't! Don't! You make me feel as if I was setting
myself up to be good. Let me look in your pretty face
again. Put your two hands in mine. Now, promise. You
will never ask me anything more than the two words?"

"Never! Never!"

"You will never put them to a bad use, if I say them?"

"Never! Never!"

"Walter Wilding."

The lady lays her face upon the nurse's breast, draws her
close in her embrace with both arms, murmurs a blessing and
the words, "Kiss him for me!" and is gone.

Day of the month and year, the first Sunday in October,
one thousand eight hundred and forty-seven. London Time
by the great clock of Saint Paul's, half-past one in the afternoon. The clock of the Hospital for Foundling Children is
well up with the Cathedral to-day. Service in the chapel is
over, and the Foundling children are at dinner.

There are numerous lookers-on at the dinner, as the custom
is. There are two or three governors, whole families from
the congregation, smaller groups of both sexes, individual
stragglers of various degrees. The bright autumnal sun
strikes freshly into the wards; and the heavy-framed windows
through which it shines, and the panelled walls on which it
strikes, are such windows and such walls as pervade Hogarth's
pictures. The girls' refectory (including that of the younger
children) is the principal attraction. Neat attendants silently
glide about the orderly and silent tables; the lookers-on
move or stop as the fancy takes them; comments in whispers
on face such a number from such a window are not unfre-
quent; many of the faces are of a character to fix attention.
Some of the visitors from the outside public are accustomed

visitors. They have established a speaking acquaintance with the occupants of particular seats at the tables, and halt at those points to bend down and say a word or two. It is no disparagement to their kindness that those points are generally points where personal attractions are. The monotony of the long spacious rooms and the double lines of faces is agreeably relieved by these incidents, although so slight.

A veiled lady, who has no companion, goes among the company. It would seem that curiosity and opportunity have never brought her there before. She has the air of being a little troubled by the sight, and, as she goes the length of the tables, it is with a hesitating step and an uneasy manner. At length she comes to the refectory of the boys. They are so much less popular than the girls that it is bare of visitors when she looks in at the doorway.

But just within the doorway, chances to stand, inspecting, an elderly female attendant: some order of matron or house-keeper. To whom the lady addresses natural questions: As, how many boys? At what age are they usually put out in life? Do they often take a fancy to the sea? So, lower and lower in tone until the lady puts the question: "Which is Walter Wilding?"

Attendant's head shaken. Against the rules.

"You know which is Walter Wilding?"

So keenly does the attendant feel the closeness with which the lady's eyes examine her face, that she keeps her own eyes fast upon the floor, lest by wandering in the right direction they should betray her.

"I know which is Walter Wilding, but it is not my place, ma'am, to tell names to visitors."

"But you can show me without telling me."

The lady's hand moves quietly to the attendant's hand. Pause and silence.

"I am going to pass round the tables," says the lady's interlocutor, without seeming to address her. "Follow me with your eyes. The boy that I stop at and speak to, will not matter to you. But the boy that I touch, will be Walter Wilding. Say nothing more to me, and move a little away."

Quickly acting on the hint, the lady passes on into the room, and looks about her. After a few moments, the attendant, in a staid official way, walks down outside the line of tables commencing on her left hand. She goes the whole length of the line, turns, and comes back on the inside. Very slightly glancing in the lady's direction, she stops, bends forward, and speaks. The boy whom she addresses, lifts his head and replies. Good humouredly and easily, as she listens to what he says, she lays her hand upon the shoulder of the next boy on his right. That the action may be well noted, she keeps her hand on the shoulder while speaking in return, and pats it twice or thrice before moving away. She completes her tour of the tables, touching no one else, and passes out by a door at the opposite end of the long room.

Dinner is done, and the lady, too, walks down outside the line of tables commencing on her left hand, goes the whole length of the line, turns, and comes back on the inside. Other people have strolled in, fortunately for her, and stand sprinkled about. She lifts her veil, and, stopping at the touched boy, asks how old he is?

"I am twelve, ma'am," he answers, with his bright eyes fixed on hers.

"Are you well and happy?"

"Yes, ma'am."

"May you take these sweetmeats from my hand?"

"If you please to give them to me."

In stooping low for the purpose, the lady touches the boy's face with her forehead and with her hair. Then, lowering her veil again, she passes on, and passes out without looking back.

ACT I

THE CURTAIN RISES

In a court-yard in the City of London, which was No Thoroughfare either for vehicles or foot-passengers; a court-yard diverging from a steep, a slippery, and a winding street connecting Tower-street with the Middlesex shore of the Thames; stood the place of business of Wilding and Co., Wine Merchants. Probably as a jocose acknowledgment of the obstructive character of this main approach, the point nearest to its base at which one could take the river (if so inodorously minded) bore the appellation Break-Neck-Stairs. The court-yard itself had likewise been descriptively entitled in old time, Cripple Corner.

Years before the year one thousand eight hundred and sixty-one, people had left off taking boat at Break-Neck-Stairs, and watermen had ceased to ply there. The slimy little causeway had dropped into the river by a slow process of suicide, and two or three stumps of piles and a rusty iron mooring-ring were all that remained of the departed Break-Neck glories. Sometimes, indeed, a laden coal barge would bump itself into the place, and certain laborious heavers, seemingly mud-engendered, would arise, deliver the cargo in the neighbourhood, shove off. and vanish ; but at most times the only commerce of Break-Neck-Stairs arose out of the conveyance of casks and bottles, both full and empty, both to and from the cellars of Wilding and Co., Wine Merchants. Even that commerce was but occasional, and through three-fourths of its rising tides the dirty indecorous drab of a river would come solitarily oozing and lapping at the rusty ring, as if it had heard of the Doge and the Adriatic, and wanted to be married to the great conserver of its filthiness, the Right Honourable the Lord Mayor.

Some two hundred and fifty yards on the right, up the opposite hill (approaching it from the low ground of Break-Neck-Stairs) was Cripple Corner. There was a pump in Cripple Corner, there was a tree in Cripple Corner. All Cripple Corner belonged to Wilding and Co., Wine Merchants. Their cellars burrowed under it, their mansion towered over it. It really had been a mansion in the days when merchants inhabited the City, and had a ceremonious shelter to the doorway without visible support, like the sounding-board over an old pulpit. It had also a number of long narrow strips of window, so disposed in its grave brick front as to render it symmetrically ugly. It had also, on its roof, a cupola with a bell in it.

"When a man at five-and-twenty can put his hat on, and can say 'this hat covers the owner of this property and of the business which is transacted on this property,' I consider, Mr. Bintrey, that, without being boastful, he may be allowed to be deeply thankful. I don't know how it may appear to you, but so it appears to me."

Thus Mr. Walter Wilding to his man of law, in his own counting-house ; taking his hat down from its peg to suit the action to the word, and hanging it up again when he had done so, not to overstep the modesty of nature.

An innocent, open-speaking, unused-looking man, Mr.

Walter Wilding, with a remarkably pink and white complexion, and a figure much too bulky for so young a man, though of a good stature. With crispy curling brown hair, and amiable bright blue eyes. An extremely communicative man: a man with whom loquacity was the irrestrainable outpouring of contentment and gratitude. Mr. Bintrey, on the other hand, a cautious man, with twinkling beads of eyes in a large overhanging bald head, who inwardly but intensely enjoyed the comicality of openness of speech, or hand, or heart.

"Yes," said Mr. Bintrey. "Yes. Ha, ha!"

A decanter, two wine-glasses, and a plate of biscuits, stood on the desk.

"You like this forty-five-year-old port wine?" said Mr. Wilding.

"Like it?" repeated Mr. Bintrey. "Rather, Sir!"

"It's from the best corner of our best forty-five-year-old bin," said Mr. Wilding.

"Thank you, Sir," said Mr. Bintrey. "It's most excellent."

He laughed again, as he held up his glass and ogled it, at the highly ludicrous idea of giving away such wine.

"And now," said Wilding, with a childish enjoyment in the discussion of affairs, "I think we have got everything straight, Mr. Bintrey."

"Everything straight," said Bintrey.

"A partner secured——"

"Partner secured," said Bintrey.

"A housekeeper advertised for——"

"Housekeeper advertised for," said Bintrey, "'apply personally at Cripple Corner, Great Tower-street, from ten to twelve'—to-morrow, by-the-bye."

"My late dear mother's affairs wound up——"

"Wound up," said Bintrey.

"And all charges paid."

"And all charges paid," said Bintrey, with a chuckle: probably occasioned by the droll circumstance that they had been paid without a haggle.

"The mention of my late dear mother," Mr. Wilding continued, his eyes filling with tears and his pocket-handkerchief drying them, "unmans me still, Mr. Bintrey. You know how I loved her; you (her lawyer) know how she loved me. The utmost love of mother and child was cherished between us, and we never experienced one moment's division or unhappiness from the time when she took me under her care. Thirteen years in all! Thirteen years under my late dear mother's care, Mr. Bintrey, and eight of them her confidentially acknowledged son! You know the story, Mr. Bintrey, who but you, Sir!" Mr. Wilding sobbed and dried his eyes, without attempt at concealment, during these remarks.

Mr. Bintrey enjoyed his comical port, and said, after rolling it in his mouth: "I know the story."

"My late dear mother, Mr. Bintrey," pursued the wine-merchant, "had been deeply deceived, and had cruelly suffered. But on that subject my late dear mother's lips were for ever sealed. By whom deceived, or under what circumstances, Heaven only knows. My late dear mother never betrayed her betrayer."

"She had made up her mind," said Mr. Bintrey, again turning his wine on his palate, "and she could hold her peace." An amused twinkle in his eyes pretty plainly added—"A devilish deal better than *you* ever will!"

"'Honour,'" said Mr. Wilding, sobbing as he quoted from the Commandments, "'thy father and thy mother, that thy days may be long in the land.' When I was in the Foundling, Mr. Bintrey, I was at such a loss how to do it, that I apprehended my days would be short in the land. But I afterwards came to honour my mother deeply, profoundly. And I honour and revere her memory. For seven happy years, Mr. Bintrey," pursued Wilding, still with the same innocent catching in his breath, and the same unabashed tears, "did my excellent mother article me to my predecessors in this business, Pebbleson Nephew. Her affectionate forethought likewise apprenticed me to the Vintners' Company, and made me in time a free Vintner, and—and—everything else that the best of mothers could desire. When I came of age, she bestowed her inherited share in this business upon me; it was her money that afterwards bought out Pebbleson Nephew, and painted in Wilding and Co.; it was she who left me everything she possessed, but the mourning ring you wear. And yet, Mr. Bintrey," with a fresh burst of honest affection, "she is no more. It is little over half a year since she came into the Corner to read on that door-post with her own eyes, WILDING AND CO., WINE MERCHANTS. And yet she is no more!"

"Sad. But the common lot, Mr. Wilding," observed Bintrey. "At some time or other we must all be no more."

He placed the forty-five-year-old port wine in the universal condition, with a relishing sigh.

"So now, Mr. Bintrey," pursued Wilding, putting away his pocket-handkerchief, and smoothing his eyelids with his fingers, "now that I can no longer show my love and honour for the dear parent to whom my heart was mysteriously turned by Nature when she first spoke to me, a strange lady, I sitting at our Sunday dinner-table in the Foundling, I can at least show that I am not ashamed of having been a Foundling, and that I, who never knew a father of my own, wish to be a father to all in my employment. Therefore," continued Wilding, becoming enthusiastic in his loquacity, "therefore, I want a thoroughly good housekeeper to undertake this dwelling-house of Wilding and Co., Wine Merchants, Cripple Corner, so that I may restore in it some of the old relations betwixt employer and employed! So that I may live in it on the spot where my money is made! So that I may daily sit at the head of the table at which the people in my employment eat together, and may eat of the same roast and boiled, and drink of the same beer! So that the people in my employment may lodge under the same roof with me! So that we may one and all—— I beg your pardon, Mr. Bintrey, but that old singing in my head has suddenly come on, and I shall feel obliged if you will lead me to the pump."

Alarmed by the excessive pinkness of his client, Mr. Bintrey lost not a moment in leading him forth into the court-yard. It was easily done; for the counting-house in which they talked together opened on to it, at one side of the dwelling-house. There the attorney pumped with a will, obedient to a sign from the client, and the client laved his head and face with both hands, and took a hearty drink. After these remedies, he declared himself much better.

"Don't let your good feelings excite you," said Bintrey, as they returned to the counting-house, and Mr. Wilding dried himself on a jack-towel behind an inner door.

"No, no. I won't," he returned, looking out of the towel. "I won't. I have not been confused, have I?"

"Not at all. Perfectly clear."

"Where did I leave off, Mr. Bintrey?"

"Well, you left off—but I wouldn't excite myself, if I was you, by taking it up again just yet."

"I'll take care. I'll take care. The singing in my head, came on at where, Mr. Bintrey?"

"At roast, and boiled, and beer," answered the lawyer, prompting—"lodging under the same roof—and one and all——"

"Ah! And one and all singing in the head together——"

"Do you know, I really *would not* let my good feelings excite me, if I was you," hinted the lawyer again, anxiously. "Try some more pump."

"No occasion, no occasion. All right, Mr. Bintrey. And one and all forming a kind of family! You see, Mr. Bintrey, I was not used in my childhood to that sort of individual existence which most individuals have led, more or less, in their childhood. After that time I became absorbed in my late dear mother. Having lost her, I find that I am more fit for being one of a body than one by myself. To be that, and at the same time to do my duty to those dependent on me, and attach them to me, has a patriarchal and pleasant air about it. I don't know how it may appear to you, Mr. Bintrey, but so it appears to me."

"It is not I who am all-important in the case, but you," returned Bintrey. "Consequently, how it may appear to me is of very small importance."

"It appears to *me*," said Mr. Wilding, in a glow, "hopeful, useful, delightful!"

"Do you know," hinted the lawyer again, "I really would not ex——"

"I am not going to. Then there's Handel."

"There's who?" asked Bintrey.

"Handel, Mozart, Haydn, Kent, Purcell, Doctor Arne, Greene, Mendelssohn. I know the choruses to those anthems by heart. Foundling Chapel Collection. Why shouldn't we learn them together?"

"Who learn them together?" asked the lawyer, rather shortly.

"Employer and employed."

"Ay, ay," returned Bintrey, mollified; as if he had half expected the answer to be, Lawyer and client. "That's another thing."

"Not another thing, Mr. Bintrey! The same thing. A part of the bond among us. We will form a Choir in some quiet church near the Corner here, and, having sung together of a Sunday with a relish, we will come home and take an early dinner together with a relish. The object that I have at heart now is, to get this system well in action without delay, so that my new partner may find it founded when he enters on his partnership."

"All good be with it!" exclaimed Bintrey, rising. "May it prosper! Is Joey Ladle to take a share in Handel, Mozart, Haydn, Kent, Purcell, Doctor Arne, Greene, and Mendelssohn?"

"I hope so."

"I wish them all well out of it," returned Bintrey, with much heartiness. "Good-bye, Sir."

They shook hands and parted. Then (first knocking with his knuckles for leave) entered to Mr. Wilding from a door of communication between his private counting-house and that in which his clerks sat, the Head Cellarman of the cellars of Wilding and Co., Wine Merchants, and erst Head Cellarman of the cellars of Pebbleson Nephew. The Joey Ladle in question. A slow and ponderous man, of the dray-man order of human architecture, dressed in a corrugated suit and bibbed apron, apparently a composite of door-mat and rhinoceros-hide.

"Respecting this same boarding and lodging, Young Master Wilding," said he.

"Yes, Joey?"

"Speaking for myself, Young Master Wilding—and I never did speak and I never do speak for no one else—*I* don't want no boarding nor yet no lodging. But if you wish to board me and to lodge me, take me. I can peck as well as most men. Where I peck ain't so high a object with me as What I peck. Nor even so high a object with me as How Much I peck. Is all to live in the house, Young Master Wilding? The two other cellarmen, the three porters, the two 'prentices, and the odd men?"

"Yes. I hope we shall all be an united family, Joey."

"Ah!" said Joey. "I hope they may be."

"They? Rather say we, Joey."

Joey Ladle shook his head. Don't look to me to make we on it, Young Master Wilding, not at my time of life and under the circumstarnces which has formed my disposition. I have said to Pebbleson Nephew many a time, when they have said to me, 'Put a livelier face upon it, Joey'—I have said to them, 'Gentlemen, it is all wery well for you that has been accustomed to take your wine into your systems by the conwivial channel of your throttles, to put a lively face upon it; but,' I says, 'I have been accustomed to take *my* wine in at the pores of the skin, and, took that way, it acts different. It acts depressing. It's one thing, gentlemen,' I says to Pebbleson Nephew, 'to charge your glasses in a dining-room with a Hip Hurrah and a Jolly Companions Every One, and it's another thing to be charged yourself, through the pores, in a low dark cellar and a mouldy atmosphere. It makes all the difference betwixt bubbles and wapours,' I tells Pebbleson Nephew. And so it do. I've been a cellarman my life through, with my mind fully given to the business. What's the consequence? I'm as muddled a man as lives—you won't find a muddleder man than me—nor yet you won't find my equal in molloncolly. Sing of Filling the bumper fair, Every drop you sprinkle, O'er the brow of care, Smooths away a wrinkle? Yes. P'r'aps so. But try filling yourself through the pores, underground, when you don't want to it !"

"I am sorry to hear this, Joey. I had even thought that you might join a singing-class in the house."

"Me, Sir? No, no, Young Master Wilding, you won't catch Joey Ladle muddling the Armory. A pecking-machine, Sir, is all that I am capable of proving myself, out of my cellars ; but that you're welcome to, if you think it's worth your while to keep such a thing on your premises."

"I do, Joey."

"Say no more, Sir. The Business's word is my law. And you're a going to take Young Master George Vendale partner into the old Business ? "

"I am, Joey."

"More changes, you see ! But don't change the name of the Firm again. Don't do it, Young Master Wilding. It was bad luck enough to make it Yourself and Co. Better by far have left it Pebbleson Nephew that good luck always stuck to, You should never change luck when it's good, Sir."

"At all events, I have no intention of changing the name of the House again, Joey."

"Glad to hear it, and wish you good-day, Young Master Wilding. But you had better by half," muttered Joey Ladle inaudibly, as he closed the door and shook his head, "have let the name alone from the first. You had better by half have followed the luck instead of crossing it,"

ENTER THE HOUSEKEEPER

The wine-merchant sat in his dining-room next morning, to receive the personal applicants for the vacant post in his establishment. It was an old-fashioned wainscoted room; the panels ornamented with festoons of flowers carved in wood; with an oaken floor, a well-worn Turkey carpet, and dark mahogany furniture, all of which had seen service and polish under Pebbleson Nephew. The great sideboard had assisted at many business-dinners given by Pebbleson Nephew to their connexion, on the principle of throwing sprats overboard to catch whales; and Pebbleson Nephew's comprehensive three-sided plate-warmer, made to fit the whole front of the large fireplace, kept watch beneath it over a sarcophagus-shaped cellaret that had in its time held many a dozen of Pebbleson Nephew's wine. But the little rubicund old bachelor with a pigtail, whose portrait was over the sideboard (and who could easily be identified as decidedly Pebbleson and decidedly not Nephew), had retired into another sarcophagus, and the plate-warmer had grown as cold as he. So, the golden and black griffins that supported the candelabra, with black balls in their mouths at the end of gilded chains, looked as if in their old age they had lost all heart for playing at ball, and were dolefully exhibiting their chains in the Missionary line of inquiry whether they had not earned emancipation by this time, and were not griffins and brothers.

Such a Columbus of a morning was the summer morning, that it discovered Cripple Corner. The light and warmth pierced in at the open windows, and irradiated the picture of a lady hanging over the chimneypiece, the only other decoration of the walls.

"My mother at five-and-twenty," said Mr. Wilding to himself, as his eyes enthusiastically followed the light to the portrait's face, "I hang up here, in order that visitors may admire my mother in the bloom of her youth and beauty. My mother at fifty I hang in the seclusion of my own chamber, as a remembrance sacred to me. O! It's you, Jarvis!"

These latter words he addressed to a clerk who had tapped at the door, and now looked in.

"Yes, Sir. I merely wished to mention that it's gone ten, Sir, and that there are several females in the Counting-house."

"Dear me!" said the wine-merchant, deepening in the pink of his complexion and whitening in the white, "are there several? So many as several? I had better begin before there are more. I'll see them one by one, Jarvis, in the order of their arrival."

Hastily entrenching himself in his easy-chair at the table behind a great inkstand, having first placed a chair on the other side of the table opposite his own seat, Mr. Wilding entered on his task with considerable trepidation.

He ran the gauntlet that must be run on any such occasion. There were the usual species of profoundly unsympathetic women, and the usual species of much too sympathetic women. There were buccaneering widows who came to seize him, and who griped umbrellas under their arms, as if each umbrella were he, and each griper had got him. There were towering maiden ladies who had seen better days, and who came armed with clerical testimonials to their theology, as if he were Saint Peter with his keys. There were gentle maiden ladies who came to marry him. There were professional housekeepers, like non-commissioned officers, who put him through his domestic exercise, instead of submitting themselves to catechism. There were languid invalids, to whom salary was not so much an object as the comforts of a private hospital. There were sensitive creatures who burst into tears on being addressed, and had to be restored with glasses of cold water. There were some respondents who came two together, a highly promising one and a wholly unpromising one : of whom the promising one answered all questions charmingly, until it would at last appear that she was not a candidate at all, but only the friend of the unpromising one, who had glowered in absolute silence and apparent injury.

At last, when the good wine-merchant's simple heart was failing him, there entered an applicant quite different from all the rest. A woman, perhaps fifty, but looking younger. with a face remarkable for placid cheerfulness, and a manner no less remarkable for its quiet expression of equability of temper. Nothing in her dress could have been changed to her advantage. Nothing in the noiseless self-possession of her manner could have been changed to her advantage. Nothing could have been in better unison with both, than her voice when she answered the question: "What name shall I have the pleasure of noting down?" with the words,

"My name is Sarah Goldstraw. Mrs. Goldstraw. My husband has been dead many years, and we had no family."

Half-a-dozen questions had scarcely extracted as much to the purpose from any one else. The voice dwelt so agreeably on Mr. Wilding's ear as he made his note, that he was rather long about it. When he looked up again, Mrs. Goldstraw's glance had naturally gone round the room, and now returned to him from the chimneypiece. Its expression was one of frank readiness to be questioned, and to answer straight.

"You will excuse my asking you a few questions?" said the modest wine-merchant.

"O, surely, Sir. Or I should have no business here."

"Have you filled the station of housekeeper before?"

"Only once. I have lived with the same widow lady for twelve years. Ever since I lost my husband. She was an invalid, and is lately dead; which is the occasion of my now wearing black."

"I do not doubt that she has left you the best credentials?" said Mr. Wilding.

"I hope I may say, the very best. I thought it would save trouble, Sir, if I wrote down the name and address of her representatives, and brought it with me." Laying a card on the table.

"You singularly remind me, Mrs. Goldstraw," said Wilding, taking the card beside him, "of a manner and tone of voice that I was once acquainted with. Not of an individual—I feel sure of that, though I cannot recall what it is I have in my mind—but of a general bearing. I ought to add, it was a kind and pleasant one."

She smiled, as she rejoined: "At least, I am very glad of that, Sir."

"Yes," said the wine-merchant, thoughtfully repeating his last phrase, with a momentary glance at his future house-keeper, "it was a kind and pleasant one. But that is the most I can make of it. Memory is sometimes like a half-forgotten dream. I don't know how it may appear to you, Mrs. Goldstraw, but so it appears to me."

Probably it appeared to Mrs. Goldstraw in a similar light, for she quietly assented to the proposition. Mr. Wilding then offered to put himself at once in communication with the gentleman named upon the card: a firm of proctors in

Doctors' Commons. To this, Mrs. Goldstraw thankfully assented. Doctors' Commons not being far off, Mr. Wilding suggested the feasibility of Mrs. Goldstraw's looking in again, say in three hours' time. Mrs. Goldstraw readily undertook to do so. In fine, the result of Mr. Wilding's inquiries being eminently satisfactory, Mrs. Goldstraw was that afternoon engaged (on her own perfectly fair terms) to come to-morrow and set up her rest as housekeeper in Cripple Corner.

THE HOUSEKEEPER SPEAKS

On the next day Mrs. Goldstraw arrived, to enter on her domestic duties.

Having settled herself in her own room, without troubling the servants, and without wasting time, the new housekeeper announced herself as waiting to be favoured with any instructions which her master might wish to give her. The wine-merchant received Mrs. Goldstraw in the dining-room, in which he had seen her on the previous day; and, the usual preliminary civilities having passed on either side, the two sat down to take counsel together on the affairs of the house.

"About the meals, Sir?" said Mrs. Goldstraw. "Have I a large, or a small, number to provide for?"

"If I can carry out a certain old-fashioned plan of mine," replied Mr. Wilding, "you will have a large number to provide for. I am a lonely single man, Mrs. Goldstraw; and I hope to live with all the persons in my employment as if they were members of my family. Until that time comes, you will only have me, and the new partner whom I expect immediately, to provide for. What my partner's habits may be, I cannot yet say. But I may describe myself as a man of regular hours, with an invariable appetite that you may depend upon to an ounce."

"About breakfast, Sir?" asked Mrs. Goldstraw. "Is there anything particular—— ?"

She hesitated, and left the sentence unfinished. Her eyes turned slowly away from her master, and looked towards the chimneypiece. If she had been a less excellent and experienced housekeeper, Mr. Wilding might have fancied that her attention was beginning to wander at the very outset of the interview.

"Eight o'clock is my breakfast-hour," he resumed. "It is

one of my virtues to be never tired of broiled bacon, and it is one of my vices to be habitually suspicious of the freshness of eggs." Mrs. Goldstraw looked back at him, still a little divided between her master's chimneypiece and her master. "I take tea," Mr. Wilding went on; "and I am perhaps rather nervous and fidgety about drinking it, within a certain time after it is made. If my tea stands too long——"

He hesitated, on his side, and left the sentence unfinished. If he had not been engaged in discussing a subject of such paramount interest to himself as his breakfast, Mrs. Goldstraw might have fancied that his attention was beginning to wander at the very outset of the interview.

"If your tea stands too long, Sir——?" said the housekeeper, politely taking up her master's lost thread.

"If my tea stands too long," repeated the wine-merchant mechanically, his mind getting farther and farther away from his breakfast, and his eyes fixing themselves more and more inquiringly on his housekeeper's face. "If my tea—— Dear, dear me, Mrs. Goldstraw! what *is* the manner and tone of voice that you remind me of? It strikes me even more strongly to-day, than it did when I saw you yesterday. What can it be?"

"What can it be?" repeated Mrs. Goldstraw.

She said the words, evidently thinking while she spoke them of something else. The wine-merchant, still looking at her inquiringly, observed that her eyes wandered towards the chimneypiece once more. They fixed on the portrait of his mother, which hung there, and looked at it with that slight contraction of the brow which accompanies a scarcely conscious effort of memory. Mr. Wilding remarked:

"My late dear mother, when she was five-and-twenty."

Mrs. Goldstraw thanked him with a movement of the head for being at the pains to explain the picture, and said, with a cleared brow, that it was the portrait of a very beautiful lady.

Mr. Wilding, falling back into his former perplexity, tried once more to recover that lost recollection, associated so closely, and yet so undiscoverably, with his new housekeeper's voice and manner.

"Excuse my asking you a question which has nothing to do with me or my breakfast," he said. "May I inquire if you have ever occupied any other situation than the situation of housekeeper?"

"O yes, Sir. I began life as one of the nurses at the Foundling."

"Why, that's it!" cried the wine-merchant, pushing back his chair. "By heaven! Their manner is the manner you remind me of!"

In an astonished look at him, Mrs. Goldstraw changed colour, checked herself, turned her eyes upon the ground, and sat still and silent.

"What is the matter?" said Mr. Wilding.

"Do I understand that you were in the Foundling, Sir?"

"Certainly. I am not ashamed to own it."

"Under the name you now bear?"

"Under the name of Walter Wilding."

"And the lady—— ?" Mrs. Goldstraw stopped short with a look at the portrait which was now unmistakably a look of alarm.

"You mean my mother," interrupted Mr. Wilding.

"Your—mother," repeated the housekeeper, a little constrainedly, "removed you from the Foundling? At what age, Sir?"

"At between eleven and twelve years old. It's quite a romantic adventure, Mrs. Goldstraw."

He told her the story of the lady having spoken to him, while he sat at dinner with the other boys in the Foundling, and of all that had followed in his innocently communicative way. "My poor mother could never have discovered me," he added, "if she had not met with one of the matrons who pitied her. The matron consented to touch the boy whose name was 'Walter Wilding' as she went round the dinner-tables—and so my mother discovered me again, after having parted from me as an infant at the Foundling doors."

At those words Mrs. Goldstraw's hand, resting on the table, dropped helplessly into her lap. She sat, looking at her new master, with a face that had turned deadly pale, and with eyes that expressed an unutterable dismay.

"What does this mean?" asked the wine-merchant. "Stop!" he cried. "Is there something else in the past time which I ought to associate with you? I remember my mother telling me of another person at the Foundling, to whose kindness she owed a debt of gratitude. When she first parted with me, as an infant, one of the nurses informed her of the name that had been given to me in the institution. You were that nurse?"

"God forgive me, Sir—I was that nurse!"

"God forgive you?"

"We had better get back, Sir (if I may make so bold as to say so), to my duties in the house," said Mrs. Goldstraw. "Your breakfast-hour is eight. Do you lunch, or dine, in the middle of the day?"

The excessive pinkness which Mr. Bintrey had noticed in his client's face began to appear there once more. Mr. Wilding put his hand to his head, and mastered some momentary confusion in that quarter, before he spoke again.

"Mrs. Goldstraw," he said, "you are concealing something from me!"

The housekeeper obstinately repeated, "Please to favour me, Sir, by saying whether you lunch, or dine, in the middle of the day?"

"I don't know what I do in the middle of the day. I can't enter into my household affairs, Mrs. Goldstraw, till I know why you regret an act of kindness to my mother, which she always spoke of gratefully to the end of her life. You are not doing me a service by your silence. You are agitating me, you are alarming me, you are bringing on the singing in my head."

His hand went up to his head again, and the pink in his face deepened by a shade or two.

"It's hard, Sir, on just entering your service," said the housekeeper, "to say what may cost me the loss of your good-will. Please to remember, end how it may, that I only speak because you have insisted on my speaking, and because I see that I am alarming you by my silence. When I told the poor lady, whose portrait you have got there, the name by which her infant was christened in the Foundling, I allowed myself to forget my duty, and dreadful consequences, I am afraid, have followed from it. I'll tell you the truth, as plainly as I can. A few months from the time when I had informed the lady of her baby's name, there came to our institution in the country another lady (a stranger), whose object was to adopt one of our children. She brought the needful permission with her, and after looking at a great many of the children, without being able to make up her mind, she took a sudden fancy to one of the babies—a boy —under my care. Try, pray try, to compose yourself, Sir! It's no use disguising it any longer. The child the stranger took away was the child of that lady whose portrait hangs there!"

Mr. Wilding started to his feet. "Impossible!" he cried out, vehemently. "What are you talking about? What absurd story are you telling me now? There's her portrait! Haven't I told you so already? The portrait of my mother!"

"When that unhappy lady removed you from the Foundling, in after years," said Mrs. Goldstraw, gently, "she was the victim, and you were the victim, Sir, of a dreadful mistake."

He dropped back into his chair. "The room goes round with me," he said. "My head! my head!" The housekeeper rose in alarm, and opened the windows. Before she could get to the door to call for help, a sudden burst of tears relieved the oppression which had at first almost appeared to threaten his life. He signed entreatingly to Mrs. Goldstraw not to leave him. She waited until the paroxysm of weeping had worn itself out. He raised his head as he recovered himself, and looked at her with the angry unreasoning suspicion of a weak man.

"Mistake?" he said, wildly repeating her last word. "How do I know you are not mistaken yourself?"

"There is no hope that I am mistaken, Sir. I will tell you why, when you are better fit to hear it."

"Now! now!"

The tone in which he spoke warned Mrs. Goldstraw that it would be cruel kindness to let him comfort himself a moment longer with the vain hope that she might be wrong. A few words more would end it, and those few words she determined to speak.

"I have told you," she said, "that the child of the lady whose portrait hangs there, was adopted in its infancy, and taken away by a stranger. I am as certain of what I say as that I am now sitting here, obliged to distress you, Sir, sorely against my will. Please to carry your mind on, now, to about three months after that time. I was then at the Foundling, in London, waiting to take some children to our Institution in the country. There was a question that day about naming an infant—a boy—who had just been received. We generally named them out of the Directory. On this occasion, one of the gentlemen who managed the Hospital happened to be looking over the Register. He noticed that the name of the baby who had been adopted ('Walter Wilding') was scratched out—for the reason, of course, that the child had been removed for good from our care. 'Here's a name to let,' he said. 'Give it to the new foundling who has been received to-day.' The name was given, and the child was christened. You, Sir, were that child."

The wine-merchant's head dropped on his breast. "I was that child!" he said to himself, trying helplessly to fix the idea in his mind. "I was that child!"

"Not very long after you had been received into the Institution, Sir," pursued Mrs. Goldstraw, "I left my situation there, to be married. If you will remember that, and if you can give your mind to it, you will see for yourself how the mistake happened. Between eleven and twelve years passed before the lady, whom you have believed to be your mother, returned to the Foundling, to find her son, and to remove him to her own home. The lady only knew that her infant had been called 'Walter Wilding.' The matron who took pity on her, could but point out the only 'Walter Wilding' known in the Institution. I, who might have set the matter right, was far away from the Foundling and all that belonged to it. There was nothing—there was really nothing that could prevent this terrible mistake from taking place. I feel for you—I do indeed, Sir! You must think—and with reason—that it was in an evil hour that I came here (innocently enough, I'm sure), to apply for your housekeeper's place. I feel as if I was to blame—I feel as if I ought to have had more self-command. If I had only been able to keep my face from showing you what that portrait and what your own words put into my mind, you need never, to your dying day, have known what you know now."

Mr. Wilding looked up suddenly. The inbred honesty of the man rose in protest against the housekeeper's last words. His mind seemed to steady itself, for the moment, under the shock that had fallen on it.

"Do you mean to say that you would have concealed this from me if you could?" he exclaimed.

"I hope I should always tell the truth, Sir, if I was asked," said Mrs. Goldstraw. "And I know it is better for *me* that I should not have a secret of this sort weighing on my mind. But is it better for *you*? What use can it serve now——?"

"What use? Why, good Lord! if your story is true—— "

"Should I have told it, Sir, as I am now situated, if it had not been true?"

"I beg your pardon," said the wine-merchant. "You

must make allowance for me. This dreadful discovery is something I can't realise even yet. We loved each other so dearly—I felt so fondly that I was her son. She died, Mrs. Goldstraw, in my arms—she died blessing me as only a mother *could* have blessed me. And now, after all these years, to be told she was *not* my mother! O me, O me! I don t know what I am saying!" he cried, as the impulse of self-control under which he had spoken a moment since, flickered, and died out. "It was not this dreadful grief—it was something else that I had it in my mind to speak of. Yes, yes. You surprised me—you wounded me just now. You talked as if you would have hidden this from me, if you could. Don't talk in that way again. It would have been a crime to have hidden it. You mean well, I know. I don't want to distress you—you are a kind-hearted woman. But you don't remember what my position is. She left me all that I possess, in the firm persuasion that I was her son. I am not her son. I have taken the place, I have innocently got the inheritance of another man. He must be found! How do I know he is not at this moment in misery, without bread to eat? He must be found! My only hope of bearing up against the shock that has fallen on me, is the hope of doing something which *she* would have approved. You must know more, Mrs. Goldstraw, than you have told me yet. Who was the stranger who adopted the child? You must have heard the lady's name?"

"I never heard it, Sir. I have never seen her, or heard of her, since."

"Did she say nothing when she took the child away? Search your memory. She must have said something."

"Only one thing, Sir, that I can remember. It was a miserably bad season, that year; and many of the children were suffering from it. When she took the baby away, the lady said to me, laughing, 'Don't be alarmed about his health. He will be brought up in a better climate than this —I am going to take him to Switzerland.'"

"To Switzerland? What part of Switzerland?"

"She didn't say, Sir."

"Only that faint clue!" said Mr. Wilding. "And a quarter of a century has passed since the child was taken away! What am I to do?"

"I hope you won't take offence at my freedom, Sir," said Mrs. Goldstraw; "but why should you distress yourself

about what is to be done? He may not be alive now, for
anything you know. And, if he is alive, it's not likely he
can be in any distress. The lady who adopted him was a bred-
and-born lady—it was easy to see that. And she must have
satisfied them at the Foundling that she could provide for the
child, or they would never have let her take him away. If
I was in your place, Sir—please to excuse my saying so—
I should comfort myself with remembering that I had loved
that poor lady whose portrait you have got there—truly
loved her as my mother, and that she had truly loved me as
her son. All she gave to you, she gave for the sake of that
love. It never altered while she lived; and it won't alter,
I'm sure, as long as *you* live. How can you have a better
right, Sir, to keep what you have got than that?"

Mr. Wilding's immovable honesty saw the fallacy in his
housekeeper's point of view at a glance.

"You don't understand me," he said. "It's *because* I loved
her that I feel it a duty—a sacred duty—to do justice to
her son. If he is a living man, I must find him: for my
own sake, as well as for his. I shall break down under this
dreadful trial, unless I employ myself—actively, instantly
employ myself—in doing what my conscience tells me ought
to be done. I must speak to my lawyer; I must set my
lawyer at work before I sleep to-night." He approached a
tube in the wall of the room, and called down through it to
the office below. "Leave me for a little, Mrs. Goldstraw,"
he resumed; "I shall be more composed, I shall be better
able to speak to you later in the day. We shall get on well
—I hope we shall get on well together—in spite of what has
happened. It isn't your fault; I know it isn't your fault.
There! there! shake hands; and—and do the best you can
in the house—I can't talk about it now."

The door opened as Mrs. Goldstraw advanced towards it;
and Mr. Jarvis appeared.

"Send for Mr. Bintrey," said the wine-merchant. "Say
I want to see him directly."

The clerk unconsciously suspended the execution of the
order, by announcing "Mr. Vendale," and showing in the new
partner in the firm of Wilding and Co.

"Pray excuse me for one moment, George Vendale," said
Wilding. "I have a word to say to Jarvis. Send for Mr.
Bintrey," he repeated—"send at once."

Mr. Jarvis laid a letter on the table before he left the room.

"From our correspondents at Neuchâtel, I think, Sir. The letter has got the Swiss postmark."

NEW CHARACTERS ON THE SCENE

The words, "The Swiss Postmark," following so soon upon the housekeeper's reference to Switzerland, wrought Mr. Wilding's agitation to such a remarkable height, that his new partner could not decently make a pretence of letting it pass unnoticed.

"Wilding," he asked hurriedly, and yet stopping short and glancing around as if for some visible cause of his state of mind: "what is the matter?"

"My good George Vendale," returned the wine-merchant, giving his hand with an appealing look, rather as if he wanted help to get over some obstacle, than as if he gave it in welcome or salutation: "my good George Vendale, so much is the matter, that I shall never be myself again. It is impossible that I can ever be myself again. For, in fact, I am not myself."

The new partner, a brown-cheeked handsome fellow, of about his own age, with a quick determined eye and an impulsive manner, retorted with natural astonishment: "Not yourself?"

"Not what I supposed myself to be," said Wilding.

"What, in the name of wonder, *did* you suppose yourself to be that you are not?" was the rejoinder, delivered with a cheerful frankness, inviting confidence from a more reticent man. "I may ask without impertinence, now that we are partners."

"There again!" cried Wilding, leaning back in his chair, with a lost look at the other. "Partners! I had no right to come into this business. It was never meant for me. My mother never meant it should be mine. I mean, his mother meant it should be his—if I mean anything—or if I am anybody."

"Come, come," urged his partner, after a moment's pause, and taking possession of him with that calm confidence which inspires a strong nature when it honestly desires to aid a weak one. "Whatever has gone wrong, has gone wrong through no fault of your's, I am very sure. I was not in this counting-house with you, under the old *régime*, for three years, to doubt you, Wilding. We were not younger men than we are, together, for that. Let me begin our partnership by being a serviceable partner, and setting right whatever is wrong. Has that letter anything to do with it?"

"Hah!" said Wilding, with his hand to his temple. "There again! My head! I was forgetting the coincidence. The Swiss postmark."

"At a second glance I see that the letter is unopened, so it is not very likely to have much to do with the matter," said Vendale, with comforting composure. "Is it for you, or for us?"

"For us," said Wilding.

"Suppose I open it and read it aloud, to get it out of our way?"

"Thank you, thank you."

"The letter is only from our champagne-making friends, the house at Neuchâtel. 'Dear Sir. We are in receipt of yours of the 28th ult., informing us that you have taken your Mr. Vendale into partnership, whereon we beg you to receive the assurance of our felicitations. Permit us to embrace the occasion of specially commending to you M. Jules Obenreizer.' Impossible!"

Wilding looked up in quick apprehension, and cried, "Eh?"

"Impossible sort of name," returned his partner, slightly—"Obenreizer. '—Of specially commending to you M. Jules Obenreizer, of Soho-square, London (north side), henceforth fully accredited as our agent, and who has already had the honour of making the acquaintance of your Mr. Vendale, in his (said M. Obenreizer's) native country, Switzerland.' To be sure! pooh pooh, what have I been thinking of! I remember now; 'when travelling with his niece.'"

"With his —— ?" Vendale had so slurred the last word, that Wilding had not heard it.

"When travelling with his Niece. Obenreizer's Niece," said Vendale, in a somewhat superfluously lucid manner. "Niece of Obenreizer. (I met them in my first Swiss tour, travelled a little with them, and lost them for two years; met them again, my Swiss tour before last, and have lost them ever since.) Obenreizer. Niece of Obenreizer. To be sure! Possible sort of name, after all! 'M. Obenreizer is in possession of our absolute confidence, and we do not doubt you will esteem his merits.' Duly signed by the House, 'Defresnier et Cⁱᵉ.' Very well. I undertake to see M. Obenreizer presently, and clear him out of the way. That clears the Swiss postmark out of the way. So now, my dear Wilding, tell me what I can clear out of *your* way, and I'll find a way to clear it."

More than ready and grateful to be thus taken charge of, the honest wine-merchant wrung his partner's hand, and, beginning his tale by pathetically declaring himself an Impostor, told it.

"It was on this matter, no doubt, that you were sending for Bintrey when I came in?" said his partner, after reflecting.

"It was."

"He has experience and a shrewd head; I shall be anxious to know his opinion. It is bold and hazardous in me to give you mine before I know his, but I am not good at holding back. Plainly, then, I do not see these circumstances as you see them. I do not see your position as you see it. As to your being an Impostor, my dear Wilding, that is simply absurd, because no man can be that without being a consenting party to an imposition. Clearly you never were so. As to your enrichment by the lady who believed you to be her son, and whom you were forced to believe, on her showing, to be your mother, consider whether that did not arise out of the personal relations between you. You gradually became much attached to her; she gradually became much attached to you. It was on you, personally you, as I see the case, that she conferred these worldly advantages; it was from her, personally her, that you took them."

"She supposed me," objected Wilding, shaking his head, "to have a natural claim upon her, which I had not."

"I must admit that," replied his partner, "to be true. But if she had made the discovery that you have made, six months before she died, do you think it would have cancelled the years you were together, and the tenderness that each of you had conceived for the other, each on increasing knowledge of the other?"

"What I think," said Wilding, simply but stoutly holding to the bare fact, "can no more change the truth than it can bring down the sky. The truth is that I stand possessed of what was meant for another man."

"He may be dead," said Vendale.

"He may be alive," said Wilding. "And if he is alive, have I not—innocently, I grant you innocently—robbed him of enough? Have I not robbed him of all the happy time that I enjoyed in his stead? Have I not robbed him of the exquisite delight that filled my soul when that dear lady," stretching his hand towards the picture, "told me she was my mother? Have I not robbed him of all the care she lavished on me? Have I not even robbed him of all the devotion and duty that I so proudly gave to her? Therefore it is that I ask myself, George Vendale, and I ask you, where is he? What has become of him?"

"Who can tell?"

"I must try to find out who can tell. I must institute inquiries. I must never desist from prosecuting inquiries. I will live upon the interest of my share—I ought to say his share—in this business, and will lay up the rest for him. When I find him, I may perhaps throw myself upon his generosity; but I will yield up all to him. I will, I swear. As I loved and honoured her," said Wilding, reverently kissing his hand towards the picture, and then covering his eyes with it. "As I loved and honoured her, and have a world of reasons to be grateful to her!" And so broke down again.

His partner rose from the chair he had occupied, and stood beside him with a hand softly laid upon his shoulder. "Walter, I knew you before to-day to be an upright man, with a pure conscience and a fine heart. It is very fortunate for me that I have the privilege to travel on in life so near to so trustworthy a man. I am thankful for it. Use me as your right hand, and rely upon me to the death. Don't think the worse of me if I protest to you that my uppermost feeling at present is a confused, you may call it an unreasonable, one. I feel far more pity for the lady and for you, because you did not stand in your supposed relations, than I can feel for the unknown man (if he ever became a man), because he was unconsciously displaced. You have done well in sending for Mr. Bintrey. What I think will be a part of his advice, I know is the whole of mine. Do not move a step in this serious matter precipitately. The secret must be kept among us with great strictness, for to part with it lightly would be to invite fraudulent claims, to encourage a host of knaves, to let loose a flood of perjury and plotting. I have no more to say now, Walter, than to remind you that you sold me a share in your business, expressly to save yourself from more work than your present health is fit for, and that I bought it expressly to do work, and mean to do it."

With these words, and a parting grip of his partner's

shoulder that gave them the best emphasis they could have had, George Vendale betook himself presently to the counting-house, and presently afterwards to the address of M. Jules Obenreizer.

As he turned into Soho-square, and directed his steps towards its north side, a deepened colour shot across his sun-browned face, which Wilding, if he had been a better observer, or had been less occupied with his own trouble, might have noticed when his partner read aloud a certain passage in their Swiss correspondent's letter, which he had not read so distinctly as the rest.

A curious colony of mountaineers has long been enclosed within that small flat London district of Soho. Swiss watch-makers, Swiss silver-chasers, Swiss jewellers, Swiss importers of Swiss musical boxes and Swiss toys of various kinds, draw close together there. Swiss professors of music, painting, and languages; Swiss artificers in steady work; Swiss cou-riers, and other Swiss servants chronically out of place; in-dustrious Swiss laundresses and clear-starchers; mysteriously existing Swiss of both sexes; Swiss creditable and Swiss dis-creditable; Swiss to be trusted by all means, and Swiss to be trusted by no means; these divers Swiss particles are at-tracted to a centre in the district of Soho. Shabby Swiss eating-houses, coffee-houses, and lodging-houses, Swiss drinks and dishes, Swiss service for Sundays, and Swiss schools for week-days, are all to be found there. Even the native-born English taverns drive a sort of broken-English trade; an-nouncing in their windows Swiss whets and drams, and sheltering in their bars Swiss skirmishes of love and ani-mosity on most nights in the year.

When the new partner in Wilding and Co. rang the bell of a door bearing the blunt inscription OBENREIZER on a brass plate—the inner door of a substantial house, whose ground story was devoted to the sale of Swiss clocks—he passed at once into domestic Switzerland. A white-tiled stove for winter-time filled the fireplace of the room into which he was shown, the room's bare floor was laid together in a neat pattern of several ordinary woods, the room had a prevalent air of surface bareness and much scrubbing; and the little square of flowery carpet by the sofa, and the velvet chimney-board with its capacious clock and vases of artificial flowers, contended with that tone, as if, in bringing out the whole effect, a Parisian had adapted a dairy to domestic purposes.

Mimic water was dropping off a mill-wheel under the clock. The visitor had not stood before it, following it with his eyes, a minute, when M. Obenreizer, at his elbow, startled him by saying, in very good English, very slightly clipped: "How do you do? So glad!"

"I beg your pardon. I didn't hear you come in."

"Not at all! Sit, please."

Releasing his visitor's two arms, which he had lightly pinioned at the elbows by way of embrace, M. Obenreizer also sat, remarking, with a smile: "You are well? So glad!" and touching his elbows again.

"I don't know," said Vendale, after exchange of salutations, "whether you may yet have heard of me from your House at Neuchâtel?"

"Ah, yes!"

"In connexion with Wilding and Co.?"

"Ah, surely!"

"Is it not odd that I should come to you, in London here, as one of the Firm of Wilding and Co., to pay the Firm's respects?"

"Not at all! What did I always observe when we were on the mountains? We call them vast; but the world is so little. So little is the world, that one cannot keep away from persons. There are so few persons in the world, that they continually cross and re-cross. So very little is the world, that one cannot get rid of a person. Not," touching his elbows again, with an ingratiatory smile, "that one would desire to get rid of you."

"I hope not, M. Obenreizer."

"Please call me, in your country, Mr. I call myself so, for I love your country. If I *could* be English! But I am born. And you? Though descended from so fine a family, you have had the condescension to come into trade? Stop though. Wines? Is it trade in England or profession? Not fine art?"

"Mr. Obenreizer," returned Vendale, somewhat out of countenance, "I was but a silly young fellow, just of age, when I first had the pleasure of travelling with you, and when you and I and Mademoiselle your niece—who is well?"

"Thank you. Who is well."

"—Shared some slight glacier dangers together. If, with a boy's vanity, I rather vaunted my family, I hope I did so as a kind of introduction of myself.   It was very weak, and in very bad taste; but perhaps you know our English proverb, 'Live and Learn.'"

"You make too much of it," returned the Swiss.   "And what the devil!   After all, yours *was* a fine family."

George Vendale's laugh betrayed a little vexation as he rejoined: "Well! I was strongly attached to my parents, and when we first travelled together, Mr. Obenreizer, I was in the first flush of coming into what my father and mother left me.   So I hope it may have been, after all, more youthful openness of speech and heart than boastfulness."

"All openness of speech and heart!   No boastfulness!" cried Obenreizer.   "You tax yourself too heavily.   You tax yourself, my faith! as if you was your Government taxing you!   Besides, it commenced with me.   I remember, that evening in the boat upon the lake, floating among the reflections of the mountains and valleys, the crags and pine woods, which were my earliest remembrance, I drew a word-picture of my sordid childhood.   Of our poor hut, by the waterfall which my mother showed to travellers; of the cowshed where I slept with the cow; of my idiot half-brother always sitting at the door, or limping down the Pass to beg; of my half-sister always spinning, and resting her enormous goître on a great stone; of my being a famished naked little wretch of two or three years, when they were men and women with hard hands to beat me, I, the only child of my father's second marriage—if it even was a marriage.   What more natural than for you to compare notes with me, and say, 'We are as one by age; at that same time I sat upon my mother's lap in my father's carriage, rolling through the rich English streets, all luxury surrounding me, all squalid poverty kept far from me.   Such is *my* earliest remembrance as opposed to yours!'"

Mr. Obenreizer was a black-haired young man of a dark complexion, through whose swarthy skin no red glow ever shone.   When colour would have come into another cheek, a hardly discernible beat would come into his, as if the machinery for bringing up the ardent blood were there, but the machinery were dry.   He was robustly made, well proportioned, and had handsome features.   Many would have perceived that some surface change in him would have set them more at their ease with him, without being able to define what change.   If his lips could have been made much thicker, and his neck much thinner, they would have found their want supplied.

But the great Obenreizer peculiarity was, that a certain nameless film would come over his eyes—apparently by the action of his own will—which would impenetrably veil, not only from those tellers of tales, but from his face at large, every expression save one of attention. It by no means followed that his attention should be wholly given to the person with whom he spoke, or even wholly bestowed on present sounds and objects. Rather, it was a comprehensive watchfulness of everything he had in his own mind, and everything that he knew to be, or suspected to be, in the minds of other men.

At this stage of the conversation, Mr. Obenreizer's film came over him.

"The object of my present visit," said Vendale, " is, I need hardly say, to assure you of the friendliness of Wilding and Co., and of the goodness of your credit with us, and of our desire to be of service to you. We hope shortly to offer you our hospitality. Things are not quite in train with us yet, for my partner, Mr. Wilding, is reorganising the domestic part of our establishment, and is interrupted by some private affairs. You don't know Mr. Wilding, I believe?"

Mr. Obenreizer did not.

"You must come together soon. He will be glad to have made your acquaintance, and I think I may predict that you will be glad to have made his. You have not been long established in London, I suppose, Mr. Obenreizer?"

"It is only now that I have undertaken this agency."

"Mademoiselle your niece—is—not married?"

"Not married."

George Vendale glanced about him, as if for any tokens of her.

"She has been in London?"

"She *is* in London."

"When, and where, might I have the honour of recalling myself to her remembrance?"

Mr. Obenreizer, discarding his film and touching his visitor's elbows as before, said lightly : "Come upstairs."

Fluttered enough by the suddenness with which the interview he had sought was coming upon him after all, George Vendale followed upstairs. In a room over the chamber he had just quitted—a room also Swiss-appointed—

a young lady sat near one of three windows, working at an embroidery-frame ; and an older lady sat with her face turned close to another white-tiled stove (though it was summer, and the stove was not lighted), cleaning gloves. The young lady wore an unusual quantity of fair bright hair, very prettily braided about a rather rounder white forehead than the average English type, and so her face might have been a shade—or say a light—rounder than the average English face, and her figure slightly rounder than the figure of the average English girl at nineteen. A remarkable indication of freedom and grace of limb, in her quiet attitude, and a wonderful purity and freshness of colour in her dimpled face and bright grey eyes, seemed fraught with mountain air. Switzerland too, though the general fashion of her dress was English, peeped out of the fanciful bodice she wore, and lurked in the curious clocked red stocking, and in its little silver-buckled shoe. As to the elder lady, sitting with her feet apart upon the lower brass ledge of the stove, supporting a lapful of gloves while she cleaned one stretched on her left hand, she was a true Swiss impersonation of another kind ; from the breadth of her cushion-like back, and the ponderosity of her respectable legs (if the word be admissible), to the black velvet band tied tightly round her throat for the repression of a rising tendency to goître ; or, higher still, to her great copper-coloured gold earrings ; or, higher still, to her head-dress of black gauze stretched on wire.

"Miss Marguerite," said Obenreizer to the young lady, "do you recollect this gentleman ? "

"I think," she answered, rising from her seat, surprised and a little confused : "it is Mr. Vendale ? "

"I think it is," said Obenreizer, dryly. "Permit me, Mr. Vendale. Madame Dor."

The elder lady by the stove, with the glove stretched on her left hand, like a glover's sign, half got up, half looked over her broad shoulder, and wholly plumped down again and rubbed away.

"Madame Dor," said Obenreizer, smiling, "is so kind as to keep me free from stain or tear. Madame Dor humours my weakness for being always neat, and devotes her time to removing every one of my specks and spots."

Madame Dor, with the stretched glove in the air, and her eyes closely scrutinizing its palm, discovered a tough spot in Mr. Obenreizer at that instant, and rubbed hard at him.

George Vendale took his seat by the embroidery-frame (having first taken the fair right hand that his entrance had checked), and glanced at the gold cross that dipped into the bodice, with something of the devotion of a pilgrim who had reached his shrine at last. Obenreizer stood in the middle of the room with his thumbs in his waistcoat-pockets, and became filmy.

"He was saying downstairs, Miss Obenreizer," observed Vendale, "that the world is so small a place, that people cannot escape one another. I have found it much too large for me since I saw you last."

"Have you travelled so far, then?" she inquired.

"Not so far, for I have only gone back to Switzerland each year; but I could have wished—and indeed I have wished very often—that the little world did not afford such opportunities for long escapes as it does. If it had been less, I might have found my fellow-travellers sooner, you know."

The pretty Marguerite coloured, and very slightly glanced in the direction of Madame Dor.

"You find us at length, Mr. Vendale. Perhaps you may lose us again."

"I trust not. The curious coincidence that has enabled me to find you, encourages me to hope not."

"What is that coincidence, Sir, if you please?" A dainty little native touch in this turn of speech, and in its tone, made it perfectly captivating, thought George Vendale, when again he noticed an instantaneous glance towards Madame Dor. A caution seemed to be conveyed in it, rapid flash though it was; so he quietly took heed of Madame Dor from that time forth.

"It is that I happen to have become a partner in a House of business in London, to which Mr. Obenreizer happens this very day to be expressly recommended: and that, too, by another house of business in Switzerland, in which (as it turns out) we both have a commercial interest. He has not told you?"

"Ah!" cried Mr. Obenreizer, striking in, filmless. "No. I had not told Miss Marguerite. The world is so small and so monotonous that a surprise is worth having in such a little jog-trot place. It is as he tells you, Miss Marguerite. He, of so fine a family, and so proudly bred, has condescended to trade. To trade! Like us poor peasants who have risen from ditches!"

A cloud crept over the fair brow, and she cast down her eyes.

"Why, it is good for trade!" pursued Obenreizer, enthusiastically. "It ennobles trade! It is the misfortune of trade, it is its vulgarity, that any low people—for example, we poor peasants—may take to it and climb by it. See you, my dear Vendale!" He spoke with great energy. "The father of Miss Marguerite, my eldest half-brother, more than two times your age or mine, if living now, wandered without shoes, almost without rags, from that wretched Pass—wandered—wandered—got to be fed with the mules and dogs at an Inn in the main valley far away—got to be Boy there—got to be Ostler—got to be Waiter—got to be Cook —got to be Landlord. As Landlord, he took me (could he take the idiot beggar his brother, or the spinning monstrosity his sister?) to put as pupil to the famous watchmaker, his neighbour and friend. His wife dies when Miss Marguerite is born. What is his will, and what are his words to me, when *he* dies, she being between girl and woman? 'All for Marguerite, except so much by the year for you. You are young, but I make her your ward, for you were of the obscurest and the poorest peasantry, and so was I, and so was her mother; we were abject peasants all, and you will remember it.' The thing is equally true of most of my countrymen, now in trade in this your London quarter of Soho. Peasants once; low-born drudging Swiss Peasants. Then how good and great for trade:" here, from having been warm, he became playfully jubilant, and touched the young wine-merchant's elbows again with his light embrace: "to be exalted by gentlemen."

"I do not think so," said Marguerite, with a flushed cheek, and a look away from the visitor, that was almost defiant. "I think it is as much exalted by us peasants."

"Fie, fie, Miss Marguerite," said Obenreizer. "You speak in proud England."

"I speak in proud earnest," she answered, quietly resuming her work, "and I am not English, but a Swiss peasant's daughter."

There was a dismissal of the subject in her words, which Vendale could not contend against. He only said in an earnest manner, "I most heartily agree with you, Miss Obenreizer, and I have already said so, as Mr. Obenreizer will bear witness," which he by no means did, "in this house."

Now, Vendale's eyes were quick eyes, and sharply watch-

ing Madame Dor by times, noted something in the broad
back view of that lady. There was considerable pantomimic
expression in her glove-cleaning. It had been very softly
done when he spoke with Marguerite, or it had altogether
stopped, like the action of a listener. When Obenreizer's
peasant-speech came to an end, she rubbed most vigorously,
as if applauding it. And once or twice, as the glove (which
she always held before her a little above her face) turned in
the air, or as this finger went down, or that went up, he
even fancied that it made some telegraphic communication to
Obenreizer: whose back was certainly never turned upon it,
though he did not seem at all to heed it.

Vendale observed too, that in Marguerite's dismissal of the
subject twice forced upon him to his misrepresentation, there
was an indignant treatment of her guardian which she tried
to check: as though she would have flamed out against him,
but for the influence of fear. He also observed—though this
was not much—that he never advanced within the distance of
her at which he first placed himself: as though there were
limits fixed between them. Neither had he ever spoken of
her without the prefix "Miss," though whenever he uttered
it, it was with the faintest trace of an air of mockery. And
now it occurred to Vendale for the first time that something
curious in the man, which he had never before been able to
define, was definable as a certain subtle essence of mockery
that eluded touch or analysis. He felt convinced that
Marguerite was in some sort a prisoner as to her free-will—
though she held her own against those two combined, by the
force of her character, which was nevertheless inadequate to
her release. To feel convinced of this, was not to feel less
disposed to love her than he had always been. In a word,
he was desperately in love with her, and thoroughly determined
to pursue the opportunity which had opened at last.

For the present, he merely touched upon the pleasure that
Wilding and Co. would soon have in entreating Miss
Obenreizer to honour their establishment with her presence
—a curious old place, though a bachelor house withal—and
so did not protract his visit beyond such a visit's ordinary
length. Going downstairs, conducted by his host, he found
the Obenreizer counting-house at the back of the entrance-
hall, and several shabby men in outlandish garments hanging about, whom Obenreizer put aside that he might pass,
with a few words in *patois.*

"Countrymen," he explained, as he attended Vendale to the door. "Poor compatriots. Grateful and attached, like dogs! Good-bye. To meet again. So glad!"

Two more light touches on his elbows dismissed him into the street.

Sweet Marguerite at her frame, and Madame Dor's broad back at her telegraph, floated before him to Cripple Corner. On his arrival there, Wilding was closeted with Bintrey. The cellar doors happening to be open, Vendale lighted a candle in a cleft stick, and went down for a cellarous stroll. Graceful Marguerite floated before him faithfully, but Madame Dor's broad back remained outside.

The vaults were very spacious, and very old. There had been a stone crypt down there, when bygones were not bygones; some said, part of a monkish refectory; some said, of a chapel; some said, of a Pagan temple. It was all one now. Let who would make what he liked of a crumbled pillar and a broken arch or so. Old Time had made what *he* liked of it, and was quite indifferent to contradiction.

The close air, the musty smell, and the thunderous rumbling in the streets above, as being out of the routine of ordinary life, went well enough with the picture of pretty Marguerite holding her own against those two. So Vendale went on until, at a turning in the vaults, he saw a light like the light he carried.

"O! You are here, are you, Joey?"

"Oughtn't it rather to go, 'O! *You're* here, are you, Master George?' For it's my business to be here. But it ain't yourn."

"Don't grumble, Joey."

"O! *I* don't grumble," returned the Cellarman. "If anything grumbles, it's what I've took in through the pores; it ain't me. Have a care as something in *you* don't begin a grumbling, Master George. Stop here long enough for the wapours to work, and they'll be at it."

His present occupation consisted of poking his head into the bins, making measurements and mental calculations, and entering them in a rhinoceros-hide-looking note-book, like a piece of himself.

"They'll be at it," he resumed, laying the wooden rod that he measured with across two casks, entering his last calculation, and straightening his back, "trust 'em! And so you've regularly come into the business, Master George?"

"Regularly. I hope you don't object, Joey?"

"*I* don't, bless you. But Wapours objects that you're too young. You're both on you too young."

"We shall get over that objection day by day, Joey."

"Ay, Master George; but I shall day by day get over the objection that I'm too old, and so I shan't be capable of seeing much improvement in you."

The retort so tickled Joey Ladle that he grunted forth a laugh and delivered it again, grunting forth another laugh after the second edition of "improvement in you."

"But what's no laughing matter, Master George," he resumed, straightening his back once more, "is, that young Master Wilding has gone and changed the luck. Mark my words. He has changed the luck, and he'll find it out. *I* ain't been down here all my life for nothing! *I* know by what I notices down here, when it's a-going to rain, when it's a-going to hold up, when it's a-going to blow, when it's a-going to be calm. *I* know, by what I notices down here, when the luck's changed, quite as well."

"Has this growth on the roof anything to do with your divination?" asked Vendale, holding his light towards a gloomy ragged growth of dark fungus, pendent from the arches with a very disagreeable and repellent effect. "We are famous for this growth in this vault, aren't we?"

"We are, Master George," replied Joey Ladle, moving a step or two away, "and if you'll be advised by me, you'll let it alone."

Taking up the rod just now laid across the two casks, and faintly moving the languid fungus with it, Vendale asked, "Ay, indeed? Why so?"

"Why, not so much because it rises from the casks of wine, and may leave you to judge what sort of stuff a Cellarman takes into himself when he walks in the same all the days of his life, nor yet so much because at a stage of its growth it's maggots, and you'll fetch 'em down upon you," returned Joey Ladle, still keeping away, "as for another reason, Master George."

"What other reason?"

"(I wouldn't keep on touchin' it, if I was you, Sir.) I'll tell you if you'll come out of the place. First, take a look at its colour, Master George."

"I am doing so."

"Done, Sir. Now, come out of the place."

He moved away with his light. and Vendale followed with his. When Vendale came up with him, and they were going back together, Vendale, eyeing him as they walked through the arches, said : "Well, Joey? The colour."

"Is it like clotted blood, Master George?"

"Like enough, perhaps."

"More than enough, I think," muttered Joey Ladle, shaking his head solemnly.

"Well, say it is like ; say it is exactly like. What then ?"

"Master George, they do say——"

"Who ?"

"How should I know who ?" rejoined the Cellarman, apparently much exasperated by the unreasonable nature of the question. "Them! Them as says pretty well everything, you know. How should I know who They are, if you don't ?"

"True. Go on."

"They do say that the man that gets by any accident a piece of that dark growth right upon his breast, will, for sure and certain, die by murder."

As Vendale laughingly stopped to meet the Cellarman's eyes, which he had fastened on his light while dreamily saying those words, he suddenly became conscious of being struck upon his own breast by a heavy hand. Instantly following with his eyes the action of the hand that struck him—which was his companion's—he saw that it had beaten off his breast a web or clot of the fungus even then floating to the ground.

For a moment he turned upon the Cellarman almost as scared a look as the Cellarman turned upon him. But in another moment they had reached the daylight at the foot of the cellar-steps, and before he cheerfully sprang up them. he blew out his candle and the superstition together.

EXIT WILDING

On the morning of the next day, Wilding went out alone after leaving a message with his clerk. "If Mr. Vendale should ask for me," he said, "or if Mr. Bintrey should call, tell them I am gone to the Foundling." All that his partner had said to him, all that his lawyer, following on the same side, could urge, had left him persisting unshaken in his own point of view. To find the lost man, whose place he had usurped, was now the paramount interest of his life, and to inquire at the Foundling was plainly to take the first step in the direction of discovery. To the Foundling, accordingly, the wine-merchant now went.

The once familiar aspect of the building was altered to him, as the look of the portrait over the chimneypiece was altered to him. His one dearest association with the place which had sheltered his childhood had been broken away from it for ever. A strange reluctance possessed him, when he stated his business at the door. His heart ached as he sat alone in the waiting-room while the Treasurer of the Institution was being sent for to see him. When the interview began, it was only by a painful effort that he could compose himself sufficiently to mention the nature of his errand.

The Treasurer listened with a face which promised all needful attention, and promised nothing more.

"We are obliged to be cautious," he said, when it came to his turn to speak, "about all inquiries which are made by strangers."

"You can hardly consider me a stranger," answered Wilding, simply. "I was one of your poor lost children here, in the bygone time."

The Treasurer politely rejoined that this circumstance inspired him with a special interest in his visitor. But he pressed, nevertheless, for that visitor's motive in making his inquiry. Without further preface, Wilding told him his motive, suppressing nothing. The Treasurer rose, and led the way into the room in which the registers of the institution were kept. "All the information which our books can give is heartily at your service," he said. "After the time that has elapsed I am afraid it is the only information we have to offer you."

The books were consulted, and the entry was found expressed as follows:—

"3d March, 1836. Adopted, and removed from the Foundling Hospital, a male infant, named Walter Wilding. Name and condition of the person adopting the child— Mrs. Jane Ann Miller, widow. Address—Lime-Tree Lodge, Groombridge Wells. References—the Reverend John Harker, Groombridge Wells; and Messrs. Giles, Jeremie, and Giles, bankers, Lombard-street."

"Is that all?" asked the wine-merchant. "Had you no after-communication with Mrs. Miller?"

"None—or some reference to it must have appeared in this book."

"May I take a copy of the entry?"

"Certainly! You are a little agitated. Let me make a copy for you."

"My only chance, I suppose," said Wilding, looking sadly at the copy, "is to inquire at Mrs. Miller's residence, and to try if her references can help me?"

"That is the only chance I see at present," answered the Treasurer. "I heartily wish I could have been of some further assistance to you."

With those farewell words to comfort him, Wilding set forth on the journey of investigation which began from the Foundling doors. The first stage to make for, was plainly the house of business of the bankers in Lombard-street. Two of the partners in the firm were inaccessible to chance-visitors when he asked for them. The third, after raising certain inevitable difficulties, consented to let a clerk examine the Ledger marked with the initial letter "M." The account of Mrs. Miller, widow, of Groombridge Wells, was found. Two long lines, in faded ink, were drawn across it; and at the bottom of the page there appeared this note: "Account closed, September 30th, 1837."

So the first stage of the journey was reached—and so it ended in No Thoroughfare! After sending a note to Cripple Corner to inform his partner that his absence might be prolonged for some hours, Wilding took his place in the train, and started for the second stage on the journey— Mrs. Miller's residence at Groombridge Wells.

Mothers and children travelled with him; mothers and children met each other at the station; mothers and children were in the shops when he entered them to inquire for Lime-Tree Lodge. Everywhere, the nearest and dearest of human relations showed itself happily in the happy light of day. Everywhere, he was reminded of the treasured delusion from which he had been awakened so cruelly—of the lost memory which had passed from him like a reflection from a glass.

Inquiring here, inquiring there, he could hear of no such place as Lime-Tree Lodge. Passing a house-agent's office, he went in wearily, and put the question for the last time. The house-agent pointed across the street to a dreary mansion of many windows, which might have been a manufactory, but which was an hotel. "That's where Lime-Tree Lodge stood, Sir," said the man, "ten years ago."

The second stage reached, and No Thoroughfare again!

But one chance was left. The clerical reference, Mr. Harker, still remained to be found. Customers coming in at the moment to occupy the house-agent's attention, Wilding went down the street, and entering a bookseller's shop, asked if he could be informed of the Reverend John Harker's present address.

The bookseller looked unaffectedly shocked and astonished, and made no answer.

Wilding repeated his question.

The bookseller took up from his counter a prim little volume in a binding of sober grey. He handed it to his visitor, open at the title-page. Wilding read:

"The martyrdom of the Reverend John Harker in New Zealand. Related by a former member of his flock."

Wilding put the book down on the counter. "I beg your pardon," he said, thinking a little, perhaps, of his own present martyrdom while he spoke. The silent bookseller acknowledged the apology by a bow. Wilding went out.

Third and last stage, and No Thoroughfare for the third and last time.

There was nothing more to be done; there was absolutely no choice but to go back to London, defeated at all points. From time to time on the return journey, the wine-merchant looked at his copy of the entry in the Foundling Register. There is one among the many forms of despair—perhaps the most pitiable of all—which persists in disguising itself as Hope. Wilding checked himself in the act of throwing the useless morsel of paper out of the carriage window. "It may lead to something yet," he thought. "While I live, I won't part with it. When I die, my executors shall find it sealed up with my will."

Now, the mention of his will set the good wine-merchant on a new track of thought, without diverting his mind from its engrossing subject. He must make his will immediately.

The application of the phrase No Thoroughfare to the case had originated with Mr. Bintrey. In their first long conference following the discovery, that sagacious personage had a hundred times repeated, with an obstructive shake of the head, "No Thoroughfare, Sir, No Thoroughfare. My belief is that there is no way out of this at this time of day, and my advice is, make yourself comfortable where you are."

In the course of the protracted consultation, a magnum of

the forty-five-year-old port wine had been produced for the
wetting of Mr. Bintrey's legal whistle; but the more clearly
he saw his way through the wine, the more emphatically he
did not see his way through the case; repeating as often as
he set his glass down empty. "Mr. Wilding, No Thoroughfare.
Rest and be thankful."

It is certain that the honest wine-merchant's anxiety to
make a will originated in profound conscientiousness; though
it is possible (and quite consistent with his rectitude) that he
may unconsciously have derived some feeling of relief from
the prospect of delegating his own difficulty to two other
men who were to come after him.   Be that as it may, he
pursued his new track of thought with great ardour, and lost
no time in begging George Vendale and Mr. Bintrey to
meet him in Cripple Corner and share his confidence.

"Being all three assembled with closed doors," said Mr.
Bintrey, addressing the new partner on the occasion, "I wish
to observe, before our friend (and my client) entrusts us with
his further views, that I have endorsed what I understand
from him to have been your advice, Mr. Vendale, and what
would be the advice of every sensible man.   I have told him
that he positively must keep his secret.   I have spoken with
Mrs. Goldstraw, both in his presence and in his absence;
and if anybody is to be trusted (which is a very large IF),
I think she is to be trusted to that extent.   I have pointed
out to our friend (and my client), that to set on foot random
inquiries would not only be to raise the Devil, in the likeness
of all the swindlers in the kingdom, but would also be to
waste the estate.   Now, you see, Mr. Vendale, our friend
(and my client) does not desire to waste the estate, but, on
the contrary, desires to husband it for what he considers—
but I can't say I do—the rightful owner, if such rightful
owner should ever be found.   I am very much mistaken if
he ever will be, but never mind that.   Mr Wilding and I are,
at least, agreed that the estate is not to be wasted.   Now, I
have yielded to Mr. Wilding's desire to keep an advertisement
at intervals flowing through the newspapers, cautiously
inviting any person who may know anything about that
adopted infant, taken from the Foundling Hospital, to come
to my office; and I have pledged myself that such advertisement shall regularly appear.   I have gathered from our
friend (and my client) that I meet you here to-day to take
his instructions, not to give him advice.   I am prepared to

receive his instructions, and to respect his wishes; but you will please observe that this does not imply my approval of either as a matter of professional opinion."

Thus Mr. Bintrey; talking quite as much *at* Wilding as *to* Vendale. And yet, in spite of his care for his client, he was so amused by his client's Quixotic conduct, as to eye him from time to time with twinkling eyes, in the light of a highly comical curiosity.

"Nothing," observed Wilding, "can be clearer. I only wish my head were as clear as yours, Mr. Bintrey."

"If you feel that singing in it coming on," hinted the lawyer, with an alarmed glance, "put it off.—I mean the interview."

"Not at all, I thank you," said Wilding. "What was I going to——"

"Don't excite yourself, Mr. Wilding," urged the lawyer.

"No; I *wasn't* going to," said the wine-merchant. "Mr. Bintrey and George Vendale, would you have any hesitation or objection to become my joint trustees and executors, or can you at once consent?"

"*I* consent," replied George Vendale, readily.

"*I* consent," said Bintrey, not so readily.

"Thank you both. Mr. Bintrey, my instructions for my last will and testament are short and plain. Perhaps you will now have the goodness to take them down. I leave the whole of my real and personal estate, without any exception or reservation whatsoever, to you two, my joint trustees and executors, in trust to pay over the whole to the true Walter Wilding, if he shall be found and identified within two years after the day of my death. Failing that, in trust to you two to pay over the whole as a benefaction and legacy to the Foundling Hospital."

"Those are all your instructions, are they, Mr. Wilding?" demanded Bintrey, after a blank silence, during which nobody had looked at anybody.

"The whole."

"And as to those instructions, you have absolutely made up your mind, Mr. Wilding?"

"Absolutely, decidedly, finally."

"It only remains," said the lawyer, with one shrug of his shoulders, "to get them into technical and binding form, and to execute and attest. Now, does that press? Is there any hurry about it? You are not going to die yet, Sir."

"Mr. Bintrey," answered Wilding, gravely, "when I am going to die is within other knowledge than yours or mine. I shall be glad to have this matter off my mind, if you please."

"We are lawyer and client again," rejoined Bintrey, who, for the nonce, had become almost sympathetic. "If this day week—here, at the same hour—will suit Mr. Vendale and yourself, I will enter in my Diary that I attend you accordingly."

The appointment was made, and in due sequence kept. The will was formally signed, sealed, delivered, and witnessed, and was carried off by Mr. Bintrey for safe storage among the papers of his clients, ranged in their respective iron boxes, with their respective owners' names outside, on iron tiers in his consulting-room, as if that legal sanctuary were a condensed Family Vault of Clients.

With more heart than he had lately had for former subjects of interest, Wilding then set about completing his patriarchal establishment, being much assisted not only by Mrs. Goldstraw but by Vendale too : who, perhaps, had in his mind the giving of an Obenreizer dinner as soon as possible. Anyhow, the establishment being reported in sound working order, the Obenreizers, Guardian and Ward, were asked to dinner, and Madame Dor was included in the invitation. If Vendale had been over head and ears in love before—a phrase not to be taken as implying the faintest doubt about it—this dinner plunged him down in love ten thousand fathoms deep. Yet, for the life of him, he could not get one word alone with charming Marguerite. So surely as a blessed moment seemed to come, Obenreizer, in his filmy state, would stand at Vendale's elbow, or the broad back of Madame Dor would appear before his eyes. That speechless matron was never seen in a front view, from the moment of her arrival to that of her departure—except at dinner. And from the instant of her retirement to the drawing-room, after a hearty participation in that meal, she turned her face to the wall again.

Yet, through four or five delightful though distracting hours, Marguerite was to be seen, Marguerite was to be heard, Marguerite was to be occasionally touched. When they made the round of the old dark cellars, Vendale led her by the hand ; when she sang to him in the lighted room at night, Vendale, standing by her, held her relinquished gloves, and would have bartered against them every drop of the forty-five-year-old, though it had been forty-five times forty-five years old, and its nett price forty-five times forty-five pounds per dozen. And still, when she was gone, and a great gap of an extinguisher was clapped on Cripple Corner, he tormented himself by wondering, Did she think that he admired her! Did she think that he adored her! Did she suspect that she had won him, heart and soul! Did she care to think at all about it! And so, Did she and Didn't she, up and down the gamut, and above the line and below the line, dear, dear! Poor restless heart of humanity! To think that the men who were mummies thousands of years ago, did the same. and ever found the secret how to be quiet after it!

"What do you think, George," Wilding asked him next day. "of Mr. Obenreizer? (I won't ask you what you think of Miss Obenreizer.)"

"I don't know," said Vendale, "and I never did know, what to think of him."

"He is well informed and clever," said Wilding.

"Certainly clever."

"A good musician." (He had played very well, and sung very well, overnight.)

"Unquestionably a good musician."

"And talks well."

"Yes," said George Vendale, ruminating, "and talks well. Do you know, Wilding, it oddly occurs to me, as I think about him. that he doesn't keep silence well!"

"How do you mean? He is not obtrusively talkative."

"No, and I don't mean that. But when he is silent, you can hardly help vaguely, though perhaps most unjustly, mistrusting him. Take people whom you know and like. Take any one you know and like."

"Soon done, my good fellow," said Wilding. "I take you."

"I didn't bargain for that, or foresee it, returned Vendale, laughing. "However, take me. Reflect for a moment. Is your approving knowledge of my interesting face mainly founded (however various the momentary expressions it may include) on my face when I am silent?"

"I think it is," said Wilding.

"I think so too. Now, you see, when Obenreizer speaks— in other words, when he is allowed to explain himself away —he comes out right enough; but when he has not the opportunity of explaining himself away, he comes out rather wrong. Therefore it is, that I say he does not keep silence well. And passing hastily in review such faces as I know, and don't trust, I am inclined to think, now I give my mind to it, that none of them keep silence well."

This proposition in Physiognomy being new to Wilding, he was at first slow to admit it, until asking himself the question whether Mrs. Goldstraw kept silence well, and remembering that her face in repose decidedly invited trustfulness, he was as glad as men usually are to believe what they desire to believe.

But, as he was very slow to regain his spirits or his health, his partner, as another means of setting him up—and perhaps also with contingent Obenreizer views—reminded him of those musical schemes of his in connexion with his family, and how a singing-class was to be formed in the house, and a Choir in a neighbouring church. The class was established speedily, and, two or three of the people having already some musical knowledge, and singing tolerably, the Choir soon followed. The latter was led, and chiefly taught, by Wilding himself: who had hopes of converting his dependants into so many Foundlings, in respect of their capacity to sing sacred choruses.

Now, the Obenreizers being skilled musicians, it was easily brought to pass that they should be asked to join these musical unions. Guardian and Ward consenting, or Guardian consenting for both, it was necessarily brought to pass that Vendale's life became a life of absolute thraldom and enchantment. For, in the mouldy Christopher-Wren church on Sundays, with its dearly beloved brethren assembled and met together, five-and-twenty strong, was not that Her voice that shot like light into the darkest places, thrilling the walls and pillars as though they were pieces of his heart! What time, too, Madame Dor in a corner of the high pew, turning her back upon everybody and everything, could not fail to be Ritualistically right at some moment of the service; like the man whom the doctors recommended to get drunk once a month, and who, that he might not overlook it, got drunk every day.

But, even those seraphic Sundays were surpassed by the Wednesday concerts established for the patriarchal family. At those concerts she would sit down to the piano and sing them, in her own tongue, songs of her own land, songs calling from the mountain-tops to Vendale, "Rise above the grovelling level country; come far away from the crowd; pursue me as I mount higher; higher, higher, melting into the azure distance; rise to my supremest height of all, and love me here!" Then would the pretty bodice, the clocked stocking, and the silver-buckled shoe be, like the broad forehead and the bright eyes, fraught with the spring of a very chamois. until the strain was over.

Not even over Vendale himself did these songs of hers cast a more potent spell than over Joey Ladle in his different way. Steadily refusing to muddle the harmony by taking any share in it, and evincing the supremest contempt for scales and such-like rudiments of music—which, indeed, seldom captivate mere listeners—Joey did at first give up the whole business for a bad job, and the whole of the performers for a set of howling Dervishes. But, descrying traces of un-muddled harmony in a part-song one day, he gave his two under cellarmen faint hopes of getting on towards something in course of time. An anthem of Handel's led to further encouragement from him: though he objected that that great musician must have been down in some of them foreign cellars pretty much, for to go and say the same thing so many times over; which, took it in how you might, he considered a certain sign of your having took it in somehow. On a third occasion, the public appearance of Mr. Jarvis with a flute, and of an odd man with a violin, and the per-formance of a duet by the two, did so astonish him that, solely of his own impulse and motion, he became inspired with the words, "Ann Koar!" repeatedly pronouncing them as if calling in a familiar manner for some lady who had distinguished herself in the orchestra. But this was his final testimony to the merits of his mates, for, the instru-mental duet being performed at the first Wednesday concert, and being presently followed by the voice of Marguerite Obenreizer, he sat with his mouth wide open, entranced, until she had finished; when, rising in his place with much solemnity, and prefacing what he was about to say with a bow that specially included Mr. Wilding in it, he delivered himself of the gratifying sentiment: "Arter that, ye may all on ye get to bed!" And ever afterwards declined to render homage in any other words to the musical powers of the family.

Thus began a separate personal acquaintance between

Marguerite Obenreizer and Joey Ladle. She laughed so
heartily at his compliment, and yet was so abashed by it,
that Joey made bold to say to her, after the concert was
over, he hoped he wasn't so muddled in his head as to have
took a liberty? She made him a gracious reply, and Joey
ducked in return.

"You'll change the luck time about, Miss," said Joey,
ducking again. "It's such as you in the place that can
bring round the luck of the place."

"Can I? Round the luck?" she answered, in her pretty
English, and with a pretty wonder. "I fear I do not understand. I am so stupid."

"Young Master Wilding, Miss," Joey explained confidentially, though not much to her enlightenment, "changed
the luck, afore he took in young Master George. So I say,
and so they'll find. Lord! Only come into the place and
sing over the luck a few times, Miss, and it won't be able to
help itself!"

With this, and with a whole brood of ducks, Joey backed
out of the presence. But Joey being a privileged person,
and even an involuntary conquest being pleasant to youth
and beauty, Marguerite merrily looked out for him next
time.

"Where is my Mr. Joey, please?" she asked Vendale.

So Joey was produced and shaken hands with, and that
became an Institution.

Another Institution arose in this wise. Joey was a little
hard of hearing. He himself said it was "Wapours," and
perhaps it might have been; but whatever the cause of the
effect, there the effect was, upon him. On this first occasion
he had been seen to sidle along the wall, with his left hand
to his left ear, until he had sidled himself into a seat pretty
near the singer, in which place and position he had remained,
until addressing to his friends the amateurs the compliment
before mentioned. It was observed on the following Wednesday that Joey's action as a Pecking Machine was impaired
at dinner, and it was rumoured about the table that this was
explainable by his high-strung expectations of Miss Obenreizer's singing, and his fears of not getting a place where he
could hear every note and syllable. The rumour reaching
Wilding's ears, he in his good nature called Joey to the front
at night before Marguerite began. Thus the Institution
came into being that on succeeding nights, Marguerite,

running her hands over the keys before singing, always said to Vendale, "Where is my Mr. Joey, please?" and that Vendale always brought him forth, and stationed him near by. That he should then, when all eyes were upon him, express in his face the utmost contempt for the exertions of his friends and confidence in Marguerite alone, whom he would stand contemplating, not unlike the rhinoceros out of the spelling-book, tamed and on his hind legs, was a part of the Institution. Also that when he remained after the singing in his most ecstatic state, some bold spirit from the back should say, "What do you think of it, Joey?" and he should be goaded to reply, as having that instant conceived the retort, "Arter that, ye may all on ye get to bed!" These were other parts of the Institution.

But, the simple pleasures and small jests of Cripple Corner were not destined to have a long life. Underlying them from the first was a serious matter, which every member of the patriarchal family knew of, but which, by tacit agreement, all forbore to speak of. Mr. Wilding's health was in a bad way.

He might have overcome the shock he had sustained in the one great affection of his life, or he might have overcome his consciousness of being in the enjoyment of another man's property; but the two together were too much for him. A man haunted by twin ghosts, he became deeply depressed. The inseparable spectres sat at the board with him, ate from his platter, drank from his cup, and stood by his bedside at night. When he recalled his supposed mother's love, he felt as though he had stolen it. When he rallied a little under the respect and attachment of his dependants, he felt as though he were even fraudulent in making them happy, for that should have been the unknown man's duty and gratification.

Gradually, under the pressure of his brooding mind, his body stooped, his step lost its elasticity, his eyes were seldom lifted from the ground. He knew he could not help the deplorable mistake that had been made, but he knew he could not mend it; for the days and weeks went by and no one claimed his name or his possessions. And now there began to creep over him a cloudy consciousness of often-recurring confusion in his head. He would unaccountably lose, sometimes whole hours, sometimes a whole day and night. Once, his remembrance stopped as he sat at the head of the dinner-table, and was blank until daybreak. Another time, it stopped as he was beating time to their singing, and went on again when he and his partner were walking in the courtyard by the light of the moon, half the night later. He asked Vendale (always full of consideration, work, and help) how this was? Vendale only replied, "You have not been quite well; that's all." He looked for explanation into the faces of his people. But they would put it off with, "Glad to see you looking so much better, Sir;" or "Hope you're doing nicely now, Sir;" in which was no information at all.

At length, when the partnership was but five months old, Walter Wilding took to his bed, and his housekeeper became his nurse.

"Lying here, perhaps you will not mind my calling you Sally, Mrs. Goldstraw?" said the poor wine-merchant.

"It sounds more natural to me, Sir, than any other name, and I like it better."

"Thank you, Sally. I think, Sally, I must of late have been subject to fits. Is that so, Sally? Don't mind telling me now."

"It has happened, Sir."

"Ah! That is the explanation!" he quietly remarked. "Mr. Obenreizer, Sally, talks of the world being so small that it is not strange how often the same people come together, and come together at various places, and in various stages of life. But it does seem strange, Sally, that I should, as I may say, come round to the Foundling to die."

He extended his hand to her, and she gently took it.

"You are not going to die, dear Mr. Wilding."

"So Mr. Bintrey said, but I think he was wrong. The old child-feeling is coming back upon me, Sally. The old hush and rest, as I used to fall asleep."

"After an interval he said, in a placid voice, "Please kiss me, Nurse," and, it was evident, believed himself to be lying in the old Dormitory.

As she had been used to bend over the fatherless and motherless children, Sally bent over the fatherless and motherless man, and put her lips to his forehead, murmuring:

"God bless you!"

"God bless you!" he replied, in the same tone.

After another interval, he opened his eyes in his own character, and said: "Don't move me, Sally, because of what I am going to say; I lie quite easily. I think my time is come. I don't know how it may appear to you, Sally, but——"

Insensibility fell upon him for a few minutes; he emerged from it once more.

"—I don't know how it may appear to you, Sally, but so it appears to me."

When he had thus conscientiously finished his favourite sentence, his time came, and he died.

ACT II

VENDALE MAKES LOVE

THE summer and the autumn had passed. Christmas and the New Year were at hand.

As executors honestly bent on performing their duty towards the dead, Vendale and Bintrey had held more than one anxious consultation on the subject of Wilding's will. The lawyer had declared, from the first, that it was simply impossible to take any useful action in the matter at all. The only obvious inquiries to make, in relation to the lost man, had been made already by Wilding himself; with this result, that time and death together had not left a trace of him discoverable. To advertise for the claimant to the property, it would be necessary to mention particulars—a course of proceeding which would invite half the impostors in England to present themselves in the character of the true Walter Wilding. "If we find a chance of tracing the lost man, we will take it. If we don't, let us meet for another consultation on the first anniversary of Wilding's death." So Bintrey advised. And so, with the most earnest desire to fulfil his dead friend's wishes, Vendale was fain to let the matter rest for the present.

Turning from his interest in the past to his interest in the future, Vendale still found himself confronting a doubtful prospect. Months on months had passed since his first visit to Soho-square—and through all that time, the one language in which he had told Marguerite that he loved her was the language of the eyes, assisted, at convenient opportunities, by the language of the hand.

What was the obstacle in his way? The one immovable obstacle which had been in his way from the first. No matter how fairly the opportunities looked, Vendale's efforts to speak with Marguerite alone ended invariably in one and the same result. Under the most accidental circumstances, in the most innocent manner possible, Obenreizer was always in the way.

With the last days of the old year came an unexpected chance of spending an evening with Marguerite, which Vendale resolved should be a chance of speaking privately to her as well. A cordial note from Obenreizer invited him, on New Year's Day, to a little family dinner in Soho-square. "We shall be only four," the note said. "We shall be only two," Vendale determined, "before the evening is out!"

New Year's Day, among the English, is associated with the giving and receiving of dinners, and with nothing more. New Year's Day, among the foreigners, is the grand opportunity of the year for the giving and receiving of presents. It is occasionally possible to acclimatise a foreign custom. In this instance Vendale felt no hesitation about making the attempt. His one difficulty was to decide what his New Year's gift to Marguerite should be. The defensive pride of the peasant's daughter—morbidly sensitive to the inequality between her social position and his—would be secretly roused against him if he ventured on a rich offering. A gift, which a poor man's purse might purchase, was the one gift that could be trusted to find its way to her heart, for the giver's sake. Stoutly resisting temptation, in the form of diamonds and rubies, Vendale bought a brooch of the filigree-work of Genoa—the simplest and most unpretending ornament that he could find in the jeweller's shop.

He slipped his gift into Marguerite's hand as she held it out to welcome him on the day of the dinner.

"This is your first New Year's Day in England," he said. "Will you let me help to make it like a New Year's Day at home?"

She thanked him, a little constrainedly, as she looked at the jeweller's box, uncertain what it might contain. Opening the box, and discovering the studiously simple form under which Vendale's little keepsake offered itself to her, she penetrated his motive on the spot. Her face turned on him brightly, with a look which said, "I own you have pleased and flattered me." Never had she been so charming, in Vendale's eyes, as she was at that moment. Her winter dress—a petticoat of dark silk, with a bodice of black velvet rising to her neck, and enclosing it softly in a little circle of swansdown—heightened, by all the force of contrast, the dazzling fairness of her hair and her complexion. It was only when she turned aside from him to the glass, and, taking out the brooch that she wore, put his New Year's gift in its place, that Vendale's attention wandered far enough away from her to discover the presence of other persons in the room. He now became conscious that the hands of Obenreizer were affectionately in possession of his elbows. He now heard the voice of Obenreizer thanking him for his attention to Marguerite, with the faintest possible ring of mockery in its tone. ("Such a simple present, dear Sir! and showing such nice tact!") He now discovered, for the first time, that there was one other guest, and but one, besides himself, whom Obenreizer presented as a compatriot and friend. The friend's face was mouldy, and the friend's figure was fat. His age was suggestive of the autumnal period of human life. In the course of the evening he developed two extraordinary capacities. One was a capacity for silence; the other was a capacity for emptying bottles.

Madame Dor was not in the room. Neither was there any visible place reserved for her when they sat down to table. Obenreizer explained that it was "the good Dor's simple habit to dine always in the middle of the day. She would make her excuses later in the evening." Vendale wondered whether the good Dor had, on this occasion, varied her domestic employment from cleaning Obenreizer's gloves to cooking Obenreizer's dinner. This at least was certain—the dishes served were, one and all, as achievements in cookery, high above the reach of the rude elementary art of England. The dinner was unobtrusively perfect. As for the wine, the eyes of the speechless friend rolled over it, as in solemn ecstasy. Sometimes he said "Good!" when a bottle came in full; and sometimes he said "Ah!" when a bottle went out empty—and there his contributions to the gaiety of the evening ended.

Silence is occasionally infectious. Oppressed by private anxieties of their own, Marguerite and Vendale appeared to feel the influence of the speechless friend. The whole responsibility of keeping the talk going rested on Obenreizer's shoulders, and manfully did Obenreizer sustain it. He opened his heart in the character of an enlightened foreigner, and sang the praises of England. When other topics ran dry, he returned to this inexhaustible source, and always set the stream running again as copiously as ever. Obenreizer would have given an arm, an eye, or a leg to have been born an Englishman. Out of England there was no such institution as a home, no such thing as a fireside, no such object as a beautiful woman. His dear Miss Marguerite would excuse him. if he accounted for *her* attractions on the theory that English blood must have mixed at some former time with their obscure and unknown ancestry. Survey this English nation, and behold a tall, clean, plump, and solid people! Look at their cities! What magnificence in their public buildings! What admirable order and propriety in their streets! Admire their laws, combining the eternal principle of justice with the other eternal principle of pounds, shillings, and pence; and applying the product to all civil injuries, from an injury to a man's honour, to an injury to a man's nose! You have ruined my daughter—pounds, shillings, and pence! You have knocked me down with a blow in my face—pounds, shillings, and pence! Where was the material prosperity of such a country as *that* to stop? Obenreizer, projecting himself into the future, failed to see the end of it. Obenreizer's enthusiasm entreated permission to exhale itself, English fashion, in a toast. Here is our modest little dinner over, here is our frugal dessert on the table, and here is the admirer of England conforming to national customs, and making a speech! A toast to your white cliffs of Albion, Mr. Vendale! to your national virtues, your charming climate, and your fascinating women! to your Hearths, to your Homes, to your Habeas Corpus, and to all your other institutions! In one word—to England! Heep-heep-heep! hooray!

Obenreizer's voice had barely chanted the last note of the English cheer, the speechless friend had barely drained the last drop out of his glass, when the festive proceedings were interrupted by a modest tap at the door. A woman-servant came in, and approached her master with a little note in her hand. Obenreizer opened the note with a frown; and, after reading it with an expression of genuine annoyance, passed it on to his compatriot and friend. Vendale's spirits rose as he watched these proceedings. Had he found an ally in the annoying little note? Was the long-looked-for chance actually coming at last?

"I am afraid there is no help for it?" said Obenreizer, addressing his fellow-countryman. "I am afraid we must go."

The speechless friend handed back the letter, shrugged his heavy shoulders, and poured himself out a last glass of wine. His fat fingers lingered fondly round the neck of the bottle. They pressed it with a little amatory squeeze at parting. His globular eyes looked dimly, as through an intervening haze, at Vendale and Marguerite. His heavy articulation laboured, and brought forth a whole sentence at a birth. "I think," he said, "I should have liked a little more wine." His breath failed him after that effort; he gasped, and walked to the door.

Obenreizer addressed himself to Vendale with an appearance of the deepest distress.

"I am so shocked, so confused, so distressed," he began. "A misfortune has happened to one of my compatriots. He is alone, he is ignorant of your language—I and my good friend, here, have no choice but to go and help him. What can I say in my excuse? How can I describe my affliction at depriving myself in this way of the honour of your company?"

He paused, evidently expecting to see Vendale take up his hat and retire. Discerning his opportunity at last, Vendale determined to do nothing of the kind. He met Obenreizer dexterously, with Obenreizer's own weapons.

"Pray don't distress yourself," he said. "I'll wait here with the greatest pleasure till you come back."

Marguerite blushed deeply, and turned away to her embroidery-frame in a corner by the window. The film showed itself in Obenreizer's eyes, and the smile came something sourly to Obenreizer's lips. To have told Vendale that there was no reasonable prospect of his coming back in good time, would have been to risk offending a man whose favourable opinion was of solid commercial importance to him. Accepting his defeat with the best possible grace, he declared himself to be equally honoured and delighted by Vendale's proposal. "So frank, so friendly, so English!" He bustled about, apparently looking for something he wanted, disappeared for a moment through the folding-doors communicating with the next room, came back with his hat and coat, and protesting that he would return at the earliest possible moment, embraced Vendale's elbows, and vanished from the scene in company with the speechless friend.

Vendale turned to the corner by the window, in which Marguerite had placed herself with her work. There, as if she had dropped from the ceiling, or come up through the floor—there, in the old attitude, with her face to the stove—sat an Obstacle that had not been foreseen, in the person of Madame Dor! She half got up, half looked over her broad shoulder at Vendale, and plumped down again. Was she at work? Yes. Cleaning Obenreizer's gloves, as before? No; darning Obenreizer's stockings.

The case was now desperate. Two serious considerations presented themselves to Vendale. Was it possible to put Madame Dor into the stove? The stove wouldn't hold her. Was it possible to treat Madame Dor, not as a living woman, but as an article of furniture? Could the mind be brought to contemplate this respectable matron purely in the light of a chest of drawers, with a black gauze head-dress accidentally left on the top of it? Yes, the mind could be brought to do that. With a comparatively trifling effort, Vendale's mind did it. As he took his place on the old-fashioned window-seat, close by Marguerite and her embroidery, a slight movement appeared in the chest of drawers, but no remark issued from it. Let it be remembered that solid furniture is not easy to move, and that it has this advantage in consequence—there is no fear of upsetting it.

Unusually silent and unusually constrained—with the bright colour fast fading from her face, with a feverish energy possessing her fingers—the pretty Marguerite bent over her embroidery, and worked as if her life depended on it. Hardly less agitated himself, Vendale felt the importance of leading her very gently to the avowal which he was eager to make—to the other sweeter avowal still, which he was longing to hear. A woman's love is never to be taken by storm; it yields insensibly to a system of gradual approach. It ventures by the roundabout way, and listens to the low voice. Vendale led her memory back to their past meetings when they were travelling together in Switzerland. They revived the impressions, they recalled the events, of the happy bygone time. Little by little, Marguerite's constraint vanished. She smiled, she was interested, she looked at Vendale, she grew idle with her needle, she made false stitches in her work. Their voices sank lower and lower; their faces bent nearer and nearer to each other as they spoke. And Madame Dor? Madame Dor behaved like an angel. She never looked round;

she never said a word; she went on with Obenreizer's stockings. Pulling each stocking up tight over her left arm, and holding that arm aloft from time to time, to catch the light on her work, there were moments—delicate and indescribable moments—when Madame Dor appeared to be sitting upside down, and contemplating one of her own respectable legs, elevated in the air. As the minutes wore on, these elevations followed each other at longer and longer intervals. Now and again, the black gauze head-dress nodded, dropped forward, recovered itself. A little heap of stockings slid softly from Madame Dor's lap, and remained unnoticed on the floor. A prodigious ball of worsted followed the stockings, and rolled lazily under the table. The black gauze head-dress nodded, dropped forward, recovered itself, nodded again, dropped forward again, and recovered itself no more. A composite sound, partly as of the purring of an immense cat, partly as of the planing of a soft board, rose over the hushed voices of the lovers, and hummed at regular intervals through the room. Nature and Madame Dor had combined together in Vendale's interests. The best of women was asleep.

Marguerite rose to stop—not the snoring—let us say, the audible repose of Madame Dor. Vendale laid his hand on her arm, and pressed her back gently into her chair.

"Don't disturb her," he whispered. "I have been waiting to tell you a secret. Let me tell it now."

Marguerite resumed her seat. She tried to resume her needle. It was useless; her eyes failed her; her hand failed her; she could find nothing.

"We have been talking," said Vendale, "of the happy time when we first met, and first travelled together. I have a confession to make. I have been concealing something. When we spoke of my first visit to Switzerland, I told you of all the impressions I had brought back with me to England —except one. Can you guess what that one is?"

Her eyes looked steadfastly at the embroidery, and her face turned a little away from him. Signs of disturbance began to appear in her neat velvet bodice, round the region of the brooch. She made no reply. Vendale pressed the question without mercy.

"Can you guess what the one Swiss impression is, which I have not told you yet?"

Her face turned back towards him, and a faint smile trembled on her lips.

"An impression of the mountains, perhaps?" she said slyly.

"No; a much more precious impression than that."

"Of the lakes?"

"No. The lakes have not grown dearer and dearer in remembrance to me every day. The lakes are not associated with my happiness in the present, and my hopes in the future. Marguerite! all that makes life worth having hangs, for me, on a word from your lips. Marguerite! I love you!"

Her head drooped as he took her hand. He drew her to him, and looked at her. The tears escaped from her downcast eyes, and fell slowly over her cheeks.

"O, Mr. Vendale," she said sadly, "it would have been kinder to have kept your secret. Have you forgotten the distance between us? It can never, never be!"

"There can be but one distance between us, Marguerite— a distance of your making. My love, my darling, there is no higher rank in goodness, there is no higher rank in beauty, than yours! Come! whisper the one little word which tells me you will be my wife!"

She sighed bitterly. "Think of your family," she murmured; "and think of mine!"

Vendale drew her a little nearer to him.

"If you dwell on such an obstacle as that," he said, "I shall think but one thought—I shall think I have offended you."

She started, and looked up. "O, no!" she exclaimed innocently. The instant the words passed her lips, she saw the construction that might be placed on them. Her confession had escaped her in spite of herself. A lovely flush of colour overspread her face. She made a momentary effort to disengage herself from her lover's embrace. She looked up at him entreatingly. She tried to speak. The words died on her lips in the kiss that Vendale pressed on them. "Let me go, Mr. Vendale!" she said faintly.

"Call me George."

She laid her head on his bosom. All her heart went out to him at last. "George!" she whispered.

"Say you love me!"

Her arms twined themselves gently round his neck. Her lips, timidly touching his cheek, murmured the delicious words—"I love you!"

In the moment of silence that followed, the sound of the

opening and closing of the house-door came clear to them through the wintry stillness of the street.

Marguerite started to her feet.

"Let me go!" she said. "He has come back!"

She hurried from the room, and touched Madame Dor's shoulder in passing. Madame Dor woke up with a loud snort, looked first over one shoulder and then over the other, peered down into her lap, and discovered neither stockings, worsted, nor darning-needle in it. At the same moment, footsteps became audible ascending the stairs. "Mon Dieu!" said Madame Dor, addressing herself to the stove, and trembling violently. Vendale picked up the stockings and the ball, and huddled them all back in a heap over her shoulder. "Mon Dieu!" said Madame Dor, for the second time, as the avalanche of worsted poured into her capacious lap.

The door opened, and Obenreizer came in. His first glance round the room showed him that Marguerite was absent.

"What!" he exclaimed, "my niece is away? My niece is not here to entertain you in my absence? This is unpardonable. I shall bring her back instantly."

Vendale stopped him.

"I beg you will not disturb Miss Obenreizer," he said. "You have returned, I see, without your friend?"

"My friend remains, and consoles our afflicted compatriot. A heart-rending scene, Mr. Vendale! The household gods at the pawnbroker's—the family immersed in tears. We all embraced in silence. My admirable friend alone possessed his composure. He sent out, on the spot, for a bottle of wine."

"Can I say a word to you in private, Mr. Obenreizer?"

"Assuredly." He turned to Madame Dor. "My good creature, you are sinking for want of repose. Mr. Vendale will excuse you."

Madame Dor rose, and set forth sideways on her journey from the stove to bed. She dropped a stocking. Vendale picked it up for her, and opened one of the folding-doors. She advanced a step, and dropped three more stockings. Vendale, stooping to recover them as before, Obenreizer interfered with profuse apologies, and with a warning look at Madame Dor. Madame Dor acknowledged the look by dropping the whole of the stockings in a heap, and then shuffling away panic-stricken from the scene of disaster.

Obenreizer swept up the complete collection fiercely in both hands. "Go!" he cried, giving his prodigious handful a preparatory swing in the air. Madame Dor said, "Mon Dieu," and vanished into the next room, pursued by a shower of stockings.

"What must you think, Mr. Vendale," said Obenreizer, closing the door, "of this deplorable intrusion of domestic details? For myself, I blush at it. We are beginning the New Year as badly as possible; everything has gone wrong to-night. Be seated, pray—and say, what may I offer you? Shall we pay our best respects to another of your noble English institutions? It is my study to be, what you call, jolly. I propose a grog."

Vendale declined the grog with all needful respect for that noble institution.

"I wish to speak to you on a subject in which I am deeply interested," he said. "You must have observed, Mr. Obenreizer, that I have, from the first, felt no ordinary admiration for your charming niece?"

"You are very good. In my niece's name, I thank you."

"Perhaps you may have noticed, latterly, that my admiration for Miss Obenreizer has grown into a tenderer and deeper feeling—?"

"Shall we say friendship, Mr. Vendale?"

"Say love—and we shall be nearer to the truth."

Obenreizer started out of his chair. The faintly discernible beat, which was his nearest approach to a change of colour, showed itself suddenly in his cheeks.

"You are Miss Obenreizer's guardian," pursued Vendale. "I ask you to confer upon me the greatest of all favours—I ask you to give me her hand in marriage."

Obenreizer dropped back into his chair. "Mr. Vendale," he said, "you petrify me."

"I will wait," rejoined Vendale, "until you have recovered yourself."

"One word before I recover myself. You have said nothing about this to my niece?"

"I have opened my whole heart to your niece. And I have reason to hope——"

"What!" interposed Obenreizer. "You have made a proposal to my niece, without first asking for my authority to pay your addresses to her?" He struck his hand on the table, and lost his hold over himself for the first time in

Vendale's experience of him. "Sir!" he exclaimed, indignantly, "what sort of conduct is this? As a man of honour, speaking to a man of honour, how can you justify it?"

"I can only justify it as one of our English institutions," said Vendale quietly. "You admire our English institutions. I can't honestly tell you, Mr. Obenreizer, that I regret what I have done. I can only assure you that I have not acted in the matter with any intentional disrespect towards yourself. This said, may I ask you to tell me plainly what objection you see to favouring my suit?"

"I see this immense objection," answered Obenreizer, "that my niece and you are not on a social equality together. My niece is the daughter of a poor peasant; and you are the son of a gentleman. You do us an honour," he added, lowering hims·lf again gradually to his customary polite level, "which deserves, and has, our most grateful acknowledgments. But the inequality is too glaring; the sacrifice is too great. You English are a proud people, Mr. Vendale. I have observed enough of this country to see that such a marriage as you propose would be a scandal here. Not a hand would be held out to your peasant-wife; and all your best friends would desert you."

"One moment," said Vendale, interposing on his side. "I may claim, without any great arrogance, to know more of my country people in general, and of my own friends in particular, than you do. In the estimation of everybody whose opinion is worth having, my wife herself would be the one sufficient justification of my marriage. If I did not feel certain—observe, I say certain—that I am off·ring her a position which she can accept without so much as the shadow of a humiliation—I would never (cost me what it might) have asked her to be my wife. Is there any other obstacle that you see? Have you any personal objection to me?"

Obenreizer spread out both his hands in courteous protest. "Personal objection!" he exclaimed. "Dear Sir, the bare question is painful to me."

"We are both men of business," pursued Vendale, "and you naturally expect me to satisfy you that I have the means of supporting a wife. I can explain my pecuniary position in two words. I inherit from my parents a fortune of twenty thousand pounds. In half of that sum I have only a life-interest, to which, if I die, leaving a widow, my widow succeeds. If I die, leaving children, the money itself is divided

among them, as they come of age. The other half of my
fortune is at my own disposal, and is invested in the wine-
business. I see my way to greatly improving that business.
As it stands at present, I cannot state my return from my
capital embarked at more than twelve hundred a year. Add
the yearly value of my life-interest—and the total reaches a
present annual income of fifteen hundred pounds. I have the
fairest prospect of soon making it more. In the meantime,
do you object to me on pecuniary grounds ? "

Driven back to his last entrenchment, Obenreizer rose,
and took a turn backwards and forwards in the room. For
the moment, he was plainly at a loss what to say or do next.

" Before I answer that last question," he said, after a little
close consideration with himself, " I beg leave to revert for
a moment to Miss Marguerite. You said something just now
which seemed to imply that she returns the sentiment with
which you are pleased to regard her ? "

" I have the inestimable happiness," said Vendale, " of
knowing that she loves me."

Obenreizer stood silent for a moment, with the film over
his eyes, and the faintly perceptible beat becoming visible
again in his cheeks.

" If you will excuse me for a few minutes," he said, with
ceremonious politeness, " I should like to have the opportunity of speaking to my niece." With those words, he
bowed, and quitted the room.

Left by himself, Vendale's thoughts (as a necessary result
of the interview, thus far) turned instinctively to the consideration of Obenreizer's motives. He had put obstacles in
the way of the courtship ; he was now putting obstacles in
the way of the marriage—a marriage offering advantages
which even his ingenuity could not dispute. On the face of
it, his conduct was incomprehensible. What did it mean ?

Seeking, under the surface, for the answer to that question
—and remembering that Obenreizer was a man of about his
own age ; also, that Marguerite was, strictly speaking, his
half-niece only—Vendale asked himself, with a lover's ready
jealousy, whether he had a rival to fear, as well as a guardian
to conciliate. The thought just crossed his mind, and no
more. The sense of Marguerite's kiss still lingering on his
cheek reminded him gently that even the jealousy of a
moment was now a treason to *her*.

On reflection, it seemed most likely that a personal motive

of another kind might suggest the true explanation of Oben-reizer's conduct. Marguerite's grace and beauty were precious ornaments in that little household. They gave it a special social attraction and a special social importance. They armed Obenreizer with a certain influence in reserve, which he could always depend upon to make his house attractive, and which he might always bring more or less to bear on the forwarding of his own private ends. Was he the sort of man to resign such advantages as were here implied, without obtaining the fullest possible compensation for the loss? A connexion by marriage with Vendale offered him solid advantages, beyond all doubt. But there were hundreds of men in London with far greater power and far wider influence than Vendale possessed. Was it possible that this man's ambition secretly looked higher than the highest prospects that could be offered to him by the alliance now proposed for his niece? As the question passed through Vendale's mind, the man himself reappeared—to answer it, or not to answer it, as the event might prove.

A marked change was visible in Obenreizer when he resumed his place. His manner was less assured, and there were plain traces about his mouth of recent agitation which had not been successfully composed. Had he said something, referring either to Vendale or to himself, which had raised Marguerite's spirit, and which had placed him, for the first time, face to face with a resolute assertion of his niece's will? It might or might not be. This only was certain—he looked like a man who had met with a repulse.

"I have spoken to my niece," he began. "I find, Mr. Vendale, that even your influence has not entirely blinded her to the social objections to your proposal."

"May I ask," returned Vendale, "if that is the only result of your interview with Miss Obenreizer?"

A momentary flash leapt out through the Obenreizer film.

"You are master of the situation," he answered, in a tone of sardonic submission. "If you insist on my admitting it, I do admit it in those words. My niece's will and mine used to be one, Mr. Vendale. You have come between us, and her will is now yours. In my country, we know when we are beaten, and we submit with our best grace. I submit, with my best grace, on certain conditions. Let us revert to the statement of your pecuniary position. I have an objection to you, my dear Sir—a most amazing, a most

audacious objection, from a man in my position to a man in
yours."

"What is it?"

"You have honoured me by making a proposal for my
niece's hand.   For the present (with best thanks and respects),
I beg to decline it."

"Why?"

"Because you are not rich enough."

The objection, as the speaker had foreseen, took Vendale
completely by surprise.   For the moment he was speechless.

"Your income is fifteen hundred a year," pursued Obenreizer.   "In my miserable country I should fall on my
knees before your income, and say, 'What a princely fortune!'   In wealthy England, I sit as I am, and say, 'A
modest independence, dear Sir; nothing more.   Enough,
perhaps, for a wife in your own rank of life, who has no
social prejudices to conquer.   Not more than half enough
for a wife who is a meanly born foreigner, and who has all
your social prejudices against her.'   Sir! if my niece is ever
to marry you, she will have what you call uphill work of it
in taking her place at starting.   Yes, yes; this is not your
view, but it remains, immovably remains, my view for all
that.   For my niece's sake, I claim that this uphill work
shall be made as smooth as possible.   Whatever material
advantages she can have to help her, ought, in common
justice, to be hers.   Now, tell me, Mr. Vendale, on your
fifteen hundred a year can your wife have a house in a fashionable quarter, a footman to open her door, a butler to wait at
her table, and a carriage and horses to drive about in?   I
see the answer in your face—your face says, No.   Very good.
Tell me one more thing, and I have done.   Take the mass
of your educated, accomplished, and lovely country-women,
is it, or is it not, the fact that a lady who has a house in a
fashionable quarter, a footman to open her door, a butler to
wait at her table, and a carriage and horses to drive about
in, is a lady who has gained four steps, in female estimation,
at starting?   Yes? or No?"

"Come to the point," said Vendale.   "You view this
question as a question of terms.   What are your terms?"

"The lowest terms, dear Sir, on which you can provide
your wife with those four steps at starting.   Double your
present income—the most rigid economy cannot do it in
England on less.   You said just now that you expected

greatly to increase the value of your business. To work— and increase it! I am a good devil after all! On the day when you satisfy me, by plain proofs, that your income has risen to three thousand a year, ask me for my niece's hand, and it is yours."

"May I inquire if you have mentioned this arrangement to Miss Obenreizer?"

"Certainly. She has a last little morsel of regard still left for me, Mr. Vendale, which is not yours yet; and she accepts my terms. In other words, she submits to be guided by her guardian's regard for her welfare, and by her guardian's superior knowledge of the world." He threw himself back in his chair, in firm reliance on his position, and in full possession of his excellent temper.

Any open assertion of his own interests, in the situation in which Vendale was now placed, seemed to be (for the present at least) hopeless. He found himself literally left with no ground to stand on. Whether Obenreizer's objections were the genuine product of Obenreizer's own view of the case, or whether he was simply delaying the marriage in the hope of ultimately breaking it off altogether—in either of these events, any present resistance on Vendale's part would be equally useless. There was no help for it but to yield, making the best terms that he could on his own side.

"I protest against the conditions you impose on me," he began.

"Naturally," said Obenreizer; "I dare say I should protest, myself, in your place."

"Say, however," pursued Vendale, "that I accept your terms. In that case, I must be permitted to make two stipulations on my part. In the first place, I shall expect to be allowed to see your niece."

"Aha! to see my niece? and to make her in as great a hurry to be married as you are yourself? Suppose I say, No? you would see her perhaps without my permission?"

"Decidedly!"

"How delightfully frank! How exquisitely English! You shall see her, Mr. Vendale, on certain days, which we will appoint together. What next?"

"Your objection to my income," proceeded Vendale, "has taken me completely by surprise. I wish to be assured against any repetition of that surprise. Your present views of my qualification for marriage require me to have an income of three thousand a year. Can I be certain, in the future, as your experience of England enlarges, that your estimate will rise no higher?"

"In plain English," said Obenreizer, "you doubt my word?"

"Do you purpose to take *my* word for it when I inform you that I have doubled my income?" asked Vendale. "If my memory does not deceive me, you stipulated, a minute since, for plain proofs?"

"Well played, Mr. Vendale! You combine the foreign quickness with the English solidity. Accept my best congratulations. Accept, also, my written guarantee."

He rose; seated himself at a writing-desk at a side-table, wrote a few lines, and presented them to Vendale with a low bow. The engagement was perfectly explicit, and was signed and dated with scrupulous care.

"Are you satisfied with your guarantee?"

"I am satisfied."

"Charmed to hear it, I am sure. We have had our little skirmish—we have really been wonderfully clever on both sides. For the present our affairs are settled. I bear no malice. You bear no malice. Come, Mr. Vendale, a good English shake hands."

Vendale gave his hand, a little bewildered by Obenreizer's sudden transitions from one humour to another.

"When may I expect to see Miss Obenreizer again?" he asked, as he rose to go.

"Honour me with a visit to-morrow," said Obenreizer; "and we will settle it then. Do have a grog before you go! No? Well! well! we will reserve the grog till you have your three thousand a year, and are ready to be married. Aha! When will that be?"

"I made an estimate, some months since, of the capacities of my business," said Vendale. "If that estimate is correct, I shall double my present income——"

"And be married!" added Obenreizer.

"And be married," repeated Vendale, "within a year from this time. Good Night."

VENDALE MAKES MISCHIEF

When Vendale entered his office the next morning, the dull commercial routine at Cripple Corner met him with a new face. Marguerite had an interest in it now! The whole machinery which Wilding's death had set in motion, to realise the value of the business—the balancing of ledgers, the estimating of debts, the taking of stock, and the rest of it—was now transformed into machinery which indicated the chances for and against a speedy marriage. After looking over results, as presented by his accountant, and checking additions and subtractions, as rendered by the clerks, Vendale turned his attention to the stock-taking department next, and sent a message to the cellars, desiring to see the report.

The Cellarman's appearance, the moment he put his head in at the door of his master's private room, suggested that something very extraordinary must have happened that morning. There was an approach to alacrity in Joey Ladle's movements! There was something which actually simulated cheerfulness in Joey Ladle's face!

"What's the matter?" asked Vendale. "Anything wrong?"

"I should wish to mention one thing," answered Joey. "Young Mr. Vendale, I have never set myself up for a prophet."

"Who ever said you did?"

"No prophet, as far as I've heard tell of that profession," proceeded Joey, "ever lived principally underground. No prophet, whatever else he might take in at the pores, ever took in wine from morning to night, for a number of years together. When I said to Young Master Wilding, respecting his changing the name of the firm, that one of these days he might find he'd changed the luck of the firm—did I put myself forward as a prophet? No, I didn't. Has what I said to him come true? Yes, it has. In the time of Pebbleson Nephew, Young Mr. Vendale, no such thing was ever known as a mistake made in a consignment delivered at these doors. There's a mistake been made now. Please to remark that it happened before Miss Margaret came here. For which reason it don't go against what I've said respecting Miss Margaret singing round the luck. Read that, Sir," concluded Joey, pointing attention to a special passage in the report, with a forefinger which appeared to be in process of taking in through the pores nothing more remarkable than dirt. "It's foreign to my nature to crow over the house I serve, but I feel it a kind of a solemn duty to ask you to read that."

Vendale read as follows:—"Note, respecting the Swiss

champagne. An irregularity has been discovered in the last consignment received from the firm of Defresnier and Co." Vendale stopped, and referred to a memorandum-book by his side. "That was in Mr. Wilding's time," he said. "The vintage was a particularly good one, and he took the whole of it. The Swiss champagne has done very well, hasn't it?"

"I don't say it's done badly," answered the Cellarman. "It may have got sick in our customers' bins, or it may have bust in our customers' hands. But I don't say it's done badly with *us*."

Vendale resumed the reading of the note : "We find the number of the cases to be quite correct by the books. But six of them, which present a slight difference from the rest in the brand, have been opened, and have been found to contain a red wine instead of champagne. The similarity in the brands, we suppose, caused a mistake to be made in sending the consignment from Neuchâtel. The error has not been found to extend beyond six cases."

"Is that all!" exclaimed Vendale, tossing the note away from him.

Joey Ladle's eye followed the flying morsel of paper drearily.

"I'm glad to see you take it easy, Sir," he said. "Whatever happens, it will be always a comfort to you to remember that you took it easy at first. Sometimes one mistake leads to another. A man drops a bit of orange-peel on the pavement by mistake, and another man treads on it by mistake, and there's a job at the hospital, and a party crippled for life. I'm glad you take it easy, Sir. In Pebbleson Nephew's time we shouldn't have taken it easy till we had seen the end of it. Without desiring to crow over the house, Young Mr. Vendale, I wish you well through it. No offence, Sir," said the Cellarman, opening the door to go out, and looking in again ominously before he shut it. "I'm muddled and molloncolly, I grant you. But I'm an old servant of Pebbleson Nephew, and I wish you well through them six cases of red wine."

Left by himself, Vendale laughed, and took up his pen. "I may as well send a line to Defresnier and Company," he thought, "before I forget it." He wrote at once in these terms:

"DEAR SIRS. We are taking stock, and a trifling mistake has been discovered in the last consignment of champagne sent by your house to ours. Six of the cases contain red wine—which we hereby return to you. The matter can easily be set right, either by your sending us six cases of the champagne, if they can be produced, or, if not, by your crediting us with the value of six cases on the amount last paid (five hundred pounds) by our firm to yours. Your faithful servants,

"WILDING AND CO."

This letter dispatched to the post, the subject dropped at once out of Vendale's mind. He had other and far more interesting matters to think of. Later in the day he paid the visit to Obenreizer which had been agreed on between them. Certain evenings in the week were set apart which he was privileged to spend with Marguerite—always, however, in the presence of a third person. On this stipulation Obenreizer politely but positively insisted. The one concession he made was to give Vendale his choice of who the third person should be. Confiding in past experience, his choice fell unhesitatingly upon the excellent woman who mended Obenreizer's stockings. On hearing of the responsibility entrusted to her, Madame Dor's intellectual nature burst suddenly into a new stage of development. She waited till Obenreizer's eye was off her—and then she looked at Vendale, and dimly winked.

The time passed—the happy evenings with Marguerite came and went. It was the tenth morning since Vendale had written to the Swiss firm, when the answer appeared on his desk, with the other letters of the day:

"DEAR SIRS. We beg to offer our excuses for the little mistake which has happened. At the same time, we regret to add that the statement of our error, with which you have favoured us, has led to a very unexpected discovery. The affair is a most serious one for you and for us. The particulars are as follows:

"Having no more champagne of the vintage last sent to you, we made arrangements to credit your firm with the value of the six cases, as suggested by yourself. On taking this step, certain forms observed in our mode of doing business necessitated a reference to our bankers' book, as well as to our ledger. The result is a moral certainty that no such remittance as you mention can have reached our house, and a literal certainty that no such remittance has been paid to our account at the bank.

"It is needless, at this stage of the proceedings, to trouble you with details. The money has unquestionably been stolen in the course of its transit from you to us. Certain peculiarities which we observe, relating to the manner in which the fraud has been perpetrated, lead us to conclude that the thief may have calculated on being able to pay the missing sum to our bankers, before an inevitable discovery followed the annual striking of our balance. This would not have happened, in the usual course, for another three months. During that period, but for your letter, we might have remained perfectly unconscious of the robbery that has been committed.

"We mention this last circumstance, as it may help to show you that we have to do, in this case, with no ordinary thief. Thus far we have not even a suspicion of who that thief is. But we believe you will assist us in making some advance towards discovery, by examining the receipt (forged. of course) which has no doubt purported to come to you from our house. Be pleased to look and see whether it is a receipt entirely in manuscript, or whether it is a numbered and printed form which merely requires the filling in of the amount. The settlement of this apparently trivial question is, we assure you, a matter of vital importance. Anxiously awaiting your reply, we remain, with high esteem and consideration,

"DEFRESNIER & CIE."

Vendale had the letter on his desk, and waited a moment to steady his mind under the shock that had fallen on it. At the time of all others when it was most important to him to increase the value of his business, that business was threatened with a loss of five hundred pounds. He thought of Marguerite, as he took the key from his pocket and opened the iron chamber in the wall in which the books and papers of the firm were kept.

He was still in the chamber, searching for the forged receipt, when he was startled by a voice speaking close behind him.

"A thousand pardons," said the voice; "I am afraid I disturb you."

He turned, and found himself face to face with Marguerite's guardian.

"I have called," pursued Obenreizer, "to know if I can be of any use. Business of my own takes me away for some days to Manchester and Liverpool. Can I combine any business of yours with it? I am entirely at your disposal, in the character of commercial traveller for the firm of Wilding and Co."

"Excuse me for one moment," said Vendale; "I will speak to you directly." He turned round again, and continued his search among the papers. "You come at a time when friendly offers are more than usually precious to me," he resumed. "I have had very bad news this morning from Neuchâtel."

"Bad news!" exclaimed Obenreizer. "From Defresnier and Company?"

"Yes. A remittance we sent to them has been stolen. I am threatened with a loss of five hundred pounds. What's that?"

Turning sharply, and looking into the room for the second time, Vendale discovered his envelope-case overthrown on the floor, and Obenreizer on his knees picking up the contents.

"All my awkwardness," said Obenreizer. "This dreadful news of yours startled me; I stepped back——" He became too deeply interested in collecting the scattered envelopes to finish the sentence.

"Don't trouble yourself," said Vendale. "The clerk will pick the things up."

"This dreadful news!" repeated Obenreizer, persisting in collecting the envelopes. "This dreadful news!"

"If you will read the letter," said Vendale, "you will find I have exaggerated nothing. There it is, open on my desk."

He resumed his search, and in a moment more discovered the forged receipt. It was on the numbered and printed form, described by the Swiss firm. Vendale made a memorandum of the number and the date. Having replaced the receipt and locked up the iron chamber, he had leisure to notice Obenreizer, reading the letter in the recess of a window at the far end of the room.

"Come to the fire," said Vendale. "You look perished with the cold out there. I will ring for some more coals."

Obenreizer rose, and came slowly back to the desk. "Marguerite will be as sorry to hear of this as I am," he said, kindly. "What do you mean to do?"

"I am in the hands of Defresnier and Company," answered Vendale. "In my total ignorance of the circumstances, I can only do what they recommend. The receipt which I have just found, turns out to be the numbered and printed form. They seem to attach some special importance to its discovery. You have had experience, when you were in the Swiss house, of their way of doing business. Can you guess what object they have in view?"

Obenreizer offered a suggestion.

"Suppose I examine the receipt?" he said.

"Are you ill?" asked Vendale, startled by the change in his face, which now showed itself plainly for the first time. "Pray go to the fire. You seem to be shivering—I hope you are not going to be ill?"

"Not I!" said Obenreizer. "Perhaps I have caught cold. Your English climate might have spared an admirer of your English institutions. Let me look at the receipt."

Vendale opened the iron chamber. Obenreizer took a chair, and drew it close to the fire. He held both hands over the flames. "Let me look at the receipt," he repeated, eagerly, as Vendale reappeared with the paper in his hand. At the same moment a porter entered the room with a fresh supply of coals. Vendale told him to make a good fire. The man obeyed the order with a disastrous alacrity. As he stepped forward and raised the scuttle, his foot caught in a fold of the rug, and he discharged his entire cargo of coals into the grate. The result was an instant smothering of the flame, and the production of a stream of yellow smoke, without a visible morsel of fire to account for it.

"Imbecile!" whispered Obenreizer to himself, with a look at the man which the man remembered for many a long day afterwards.

"Will you come into the clerks' room?" asked Vendale, "They have a stove there."

"No, no. No matter."

Vendale handed him the receipt. Obenreizer's interest in examining it appeared to have been quenched as suddenly and as effectually as the fire itself. He just glanced over the document, and said, "No; I don't understand it! I am sorry to be of no use."

"I will write to Neuchâtel by to-night's post," said Vendale, putting away the receipt for the second time. "We must wait, and see what comes of it."

"By to-night's post," repeated Obenreizer. "Let me see. You will get the answer in eight or nine days' time. I shall be back before that. If I can be of any service, as commercial traveller, perhaps you will let me know between this and then. You will send me written instructions? My best thanks. I shall be most anxious for your answer from Neuchâtel. Who knows? It may be a mistake, my dear friend, after all. Courage! courage! courage!" He had entered the room with no appearance of being pressed for time. He now snatched up his hat, and took his leave with the air of a man who had not another moment to lose.

Left by himself, Vendale took a turn thoughtfully in the room.

His previous impression of Obenreizer was shaken by what he had heard and seen at the interview which had just taken place. He was disposed, for the first time, to doubt whether, in this case, he had not been a little hasty and hard in his judgment on another man. Obenreizer's surprise and regret, on hearing the news from Neuchâtel, bore the plainest marks of being honestly felt—not politely assumed for the occasion. With troubles of his own to encounter, suffering, to all appearance, from the first insidious attack of a serious illness, he had looked and spoken like a man who really deplored the disaster that had fallen on his friend. Hitherto Vendale had tried vainly to alter his first opinion of Marguerite's guardian, for Marguerite's sake. All the generous instincts in his nature now combined together and shook the evidence which had seemed unanswerable up to this time. "Who knows?" he thought. "I may have read that man's face wrongly, after all."

The time passed—the happy evenings with Marguerite came and went. It was again the tenth morning since Vendale had written to the Swiss firm; and again the answer appeared on his desk with the other letters of the day:

"DEAR SIR. My senior partner, M. Defresnier, has been called away, by urgent business, to Milan. In his absence (and with his full concurrence and authority), I now write to you again on the subject of the missing five hundred pounds.

"Your discovery that the forged receipt is executed upon one of our numbered and printed forms has caused inexpressible surprise and distress to my partner and to myself. At the time when your remittance was stolen, but three keys were in existence opening the strong-box in which our receipt-forms are invariably kept. My partner had one key; I had the other. The third was in the possession of a gentleman who, at that period, occupied a position of trust in our house. We should as soon have thought of suspecting one of ourselves as of suspecting this person. Suspicion now points at him, nevertheless. I cannot prevail on myself to inform you who the person is, so long as there is the shadow of a chance that he may come innocently out of the inquiry which must now be instituted. Forgive my silence; the motive of it is good.

"The form our investigation must now take is simple enough. The handwriting on your receipt must be compared, by competent persons whom we have at our disposal, with certain specimens of handwriting in our possession. I cannot send you the specimens for business reasons, which, when you hear them, you are sure to approve. I must beg you to send me the receipt to Neuchâtel—and, in making this request, I must accompany it by a word of necessary warning.

"If the person, at whom suspicion now points, really proves to be the person who has committed this forgery and theft, I have reason to fear that circumstances may have already put him on his guard. The only evidence against him is the evidence in your hands, and he will move heaven and earth to obtain and destroy it. I strongly urge you not to trust the receipt to the post. Send it to me, without loss of time, by a private hand, and choose nobody for your messenger but a person long established in your own employment, accustomed to travelling, capable of speaking French; a man of courage, a man of honesty, and, above all things, a man who can be trusted to let no stranger scrape acquaintance with him on the route. Tell no one—absolutely no one—but your messenger of the turn this matter has now taken. The safe transit of the receipt may depend on your interpreting *literally* the advice which I give you at the end of this letter.

"I have only to add that every possible saving of time is now of the last importance. More than one of our receipt-forms is missing—and it is impossible to say what new frauds may not be committed, if we fail to lay our hands on the thief.

"Your faithful servant,   "ROLLAND,
"(Signing for Defresnier and Cie.)"

Who was the suspected man? In Vendale's position, it seemed useless to inquire.

Who was to be sent to Neuchâtel with the receipt? Men of courage and men of honesty were to be had at Cripple Corner for the asking. But where was the man who was accustomed to foreign travelling, who could speak the French language, and who could be really relied on to let no stranger scrape acquaintance with him on his route? There was but one man at hand who combined all those requisites in his own person, and that man was Vendale himself.

It was a sacrifice to leave his business; it was a greater sacrifice to leave Marguerite. But a matter of five hundred pounds was involved in the pending inquiry; and a literal interpretation of M. Rolland's advice was insisted on in terms which there was no trifling with. The more Vendale thought of it, the more plainly the necessity faced him, and said, "Go!"

As he locked up the letter with the receipt, the association of ideas reminded him of Obenreizer. A guess at the identity of the suspected man looked more possible now. Obenreizer might know.

The thought had barely passed through his mind, when the door opened, and Obenreizer entered the room.

"They told me at Soho-square you were expected back last night," said Vendale, greeting him. "Have you done well in the country? Are you better?"

A thousand thanks. Obenreizer had done admirably well; Obenreizer was infinitely better. And now, what news? Any letter from Neuchâtel?

"A very strange letter," answered Vendale. "The matter has taken a new turn, and the letter insists—without excepting anybody—on my keeping our next proceedings a profound secret."

"Without excepting anybody?" repeated Obenreizer. As he said the words, he walked away again, thoughtfully, to the window at the other end of the room, looked out for a moment, and suddenly came back to Vendale. "Surely they must have forgotten," he resumed, "or they would have excepted *me*?"

"It is Monsieur Rolland who writes," said Vendale. "And, as you say, he must certainly have forgotten. That view of the matter quite escaped me. I was just wishing I had you to consult, when you came into the room. And here I am tied by a formal prohibition, which cannot possibly have been intended to include you. How very annoying!"

Obenreizer's filmy eyes fixed on Vendale attentively.

"Perhaps it is more than annoying!" he said. "I came this morning not only to hear the news, but to offer myself as messenger, negotiator—what you will. Would you believe it? I have letters which oblige me to go to Switzerland immediately. Messages, documents, anything—I could have taken them all to Defresnier and Rolland for you."

"You are the very man I wanted," returned Vendale. "I had decided, most unwillingly, on going to Neuchâtel myself, not five minutes since, because I could find no one here capable of taking my place. Let me look at the letter again."

He opened the strong room to get at the letter. Obenreizer, after first glancing round him to make sure that they were alone, followed a step or two and waited, measuring Vendale with his eye. Vendale was the tallest man, and unmistakably the strongest man also of the two. Obenreizer turned away, and warmed himself at the fire.

Meanwhile, Vendale read the last paragraph in the letter for the third time. There was the plain warning—there was the closing sentence, which insisted on a literal interpretation of it. The hand, which was leading Vendale in the dark, led him on that condition only. A large sum was at stake: a terrible suspicion remained to be verified. If he acted on his own responsibility, and if anything happened to defeat the object in view, who would be blamed? As a man of business, Vendale had but one course to follow. He locked the letter up again.

"It is most annoying," he said to Obenreizer—"it is a piece of forgetfulness on Monsieur Rolland's part which puts me to serious inconvenience, and places me in an absurdly false position towards you. What am I to do? I am acting in a very serious matter, and acting entirely in the dark. I have no choice but to be guided, not by the spirit, but by the letter of my instructions. You understand me, I am sure? You know, if I had not been fettered in this way, how gladly I should have accepted your services?"

"Say no more!" returned Obenreizer. "In your place I should have done the same. My good friend, I take no offence. I thank you for your compliment. We shall be travelling companions, at any rate," added Obenreizer. "You go, as I go, at once?"

"At once. I must speak to Marguerite first, of course!"

"Surely! surely! Speak to her this evening. Come, and pick me up on the way to the station. We go together by the mail train to-night?"

"By the mail train to-night."

It was later than Vendale had anticipated when he drove up to the house in Soho-square. Business difficulties, occasioned by his sudden departure, had presented themselves by dozens. A cruelly large share of the time which he had hoped to devote to Marguerite had been claimed by duties at his office which it was impossible to neglect.

To his surprise and delight, she was alone in the drawing-room when he entered it.

"We have only a few minutes, George," she said. "But Madame Dor has been good to me—and we can have those few minutes alone." She threw her arms round his neck, and whispered eagerly, "Have you done anything to offend Mr. Obenreizer?"

"I!" exclaimed Vendale, in amazement.

"Hush!" she said, "I want to whisper it. You know the little photograph I have got of you. This afternoon it happened to be on the chimneypiece. He took it up and looked at it—and I saw his face in the glass. I know you have offended him! He is merciless; he is revengeful; he is as secret as the grave. Don't go with him, George—don't go with him!"

"My own love," returned Vendale, "you are letting your fancy frighten you! Obenreizer and I were never better friends than we are at this moment."

Before a word more could be said, the sudden movement of some ponderous body shook the floor of the next room. The shock was followed by the appearance of Madame Dor. "Obenreizer!" exclaimed this excellent person in a whisper, and plumped down instantly in her regular place by the stove.

Obenreizer came in with a courier's bag strapped over his shoulder.

"Are you ready?" he asked, addressing Vendale. "Can I take anything for you? You have no travelling-bag. I have got one. Here is the compartment for papers, open at your service."

"Thank you," said Vendale. "I have only one paper of

importance with me; and that paper I am bound to take
charge of myself. Here it is," he added, touching the
breast-pocket of his coat, "and here it must remain till we
get to Neuchâtel."

As he said those words, Marguerite's hand caught his, and
pressed it significantly. She was looking towards Obenreizer.
Before Vendale could look, in his turn, Obenreizer had wheeled
round, and was taking leave of Madame Dor.

"Adieu, my charming niece!" he said, turning to Marguerite next. "En route, my friend, for Neuchâtel!" He
tapped Vendale lightly over the breast-pocket of his coat,
and led the way to the door.

Vendale's last look was for Marguerite. Marguerite's last
words to him were, "Don't go!"

ACT III

IN THE VALLEY

It was about the middle of the month of February when
Vendale and Obenreizer set forth on their expedition. The
winter being a hard one, the time was bad for travellers.
So bad was it that these two travellers, coming to Strasbourg,
found its great inns almost empty. And even the few
people they did encounter in that city, who had started from
England or from Paris on business journeys towards the
interior of Switzerland, were turning back.

Many of the railroads in Switzerland that tourists pass
easily enough now, were almost or quite impracticable then.
Some were not begun; more were not completed. On such
as were open, there were still large gaps of old road where
communication in the winter season was often stopped; on
others, there were weak points where the new work was not
safe, either under conditions of severe frost, or of rapid thaw.
The running of trains on this last class was not to be counted
on in the worst time of the year, was contingent upon
weather, or was wholly abandoned through the months considered the most dangerous.

At Strasbourg there were more travellers' stories afloat,
respecting the difficulties of the way further on, than there
were travellers to relate them. Many of these tales were as

wild as usual; but the more modestly marvellous did derive some colour from the circumstance that people were indisputably turning back. However, as the road to Basle was open, Vendale's resolution to push on was in no wise disturbed. Obenreizer's resolution was necessarily Vendale's, seeing that he stood at bay thus desperately: He must be ruined, or must destroy the evidence that Vendale carried about him, even if he destroyed Vendale with it.

The state of mind of each of these two fellow-travellers towards the other was this. Obenreizer, encircled by impending ruin through Vendale's quickness of action, and seeing the circle narrowed every hour by Vendale's energy, hated him with the animosity of a fierce cunning lower animal. He had always had instinctive movements in his breast against him; perhaps, because of that old sore of gentleman and peasant; perhaps, because of the openness of his nature; perhaps, because of his better looks; perhaps, because of his success with Marguerite; perhaps, on all those grounds, the two last not the least. And now he saw in him, besides, the hunter who was tracking him down. Vendale, on the other hand, always contending generously against his first vague mistrust, now felt bound to contend against it more than ever: reminding himself, "He is Marguerite's guardian. We are on perfectly friendly terms; he is my companion of his own proposal, and can have no interested motive in sharing this undesirable journey." To which pleas in behalf of Obenreizer, chance added one consideration more, when they came to Basle after a journey of more than twice the average duration.

They had had a late dinner, and were alone in an inn room there, overhanging the Rhine: at that place rapid and deep, swollen and loud. Vendale lounged upon a couch, and Obenreizer walked to and fro: now, stopping at the window, looking at the crooked reflection of the town lights in the dark water (and peradventure thinking, "If I could fling him into it!"); now, resuming his walk with his eyes upon the floor.

"Where shall I rob him, if I can? Where shall I murder him, if I must?" So, as he paced the room, ran the river, ran the river, ran the river.

The burden seemed to him, at last, to be growing so plain, that he stopped; thinking it as well to suggest another burden to his companion.

"The Rhine sounds to-night," he said with a smile, "like

the old waterfall at home. That waterfall which my mother showed to travellers (I told you of it once). The sound of it changed with the weather, as does the sound of all falling waters and flowing waters. When I was pupil of the watch-maker, I remembered it as sometimes saying to me for whole days, 'Who are you, my little wretch? Who are you, my little wretch?' I remembered it as saying, other times, when its sound was hollow, and storm was coming up the Pass: 'Boom, boom, boom. Beat him, beat him, beat him.' Like my mother enraged—if she was my mother."

"If she was?" said Vendale, gradually changing his atti-tude to a sitting one. "If she was? Why do you say 'if'?"

"What do I know?" replied the other negligently, throw-ing up his hands and letting them fall as they would. "What would you have? I am so obscurely born, that how can I say? I was very young, and all the rest of the family were men and women, and my so-called parents were old. Anything is possible of a case like that."

"Did you ever doubt——?"

"I told you once, I doubt the marriage of those two," he replied, throwing up his hands again, as if he were throwing the unprofitable subject away. "But here I am in Creation. *I* come of no fine family. What does it matter?"

"At least you are Swiss," said Vendale, after following him with his eyes to and fro.

"How do I know?" he retorted abruptly, and stopping to look back over his shoulder. "I say to you, at least you are English. How do you know?"

"By what I have been told from infancy."

"Ah! I know of myself that way."

"And," added Vendale, pursuing the thought that he could not drive back, "by my earliest recollections."

"I also. I know of myself that way—if that way satisfies."

"Does it not satisfy you?"

"It must. There is nothing like 'it must' in this little world. It must. Two short words those, but stronger than long proof or reasoning."

"You and poor Wilding were born in the same year. You were nearly of an age," said Vendale, again thoughtfully looking after him as he resumed his pacing up and down.

"Yes. Very nearly."

Could Obenreizer be the missing man? In the unknown associations of things, was there a subtler meaning than he himself thought, in that theory so often on his lips about the smallness of the world? Had the Swiss letter presenting him followed so close on Mrs. Goldstraw's revelation concerning the infant who had been taken away to Switzerland, because he was that infant grown a man? In a world where so many depths lie unsounded, it might be. The chances, or the laws—call them either—that had wrought out the revival of Vendale's own acquaintance with Obenreizer, and had ripened it into intimacy, and had brought them here together this present winter night, were hardly less curious; while read by such a light, they were seen to cohere towards the furtherance of a continuous and an intelligible purpose.

Vendale's awakened thoughts ran high while his eyes musingly followed Obenreizer pacing up and down the room, the river ever running to the tune: "Where shall I rob him, if I can? Where shall I murder him, if I must?" The secret of his dead friend was in no hazard from Vendale's lips; but just as his friend had died of its weight, so did he in his lighter succession feel the burden of the trust, and the obligation to follow any clue, however obscure. He rapidly asked himself, would he like this man to be the real Wilding? No. Argue down his mistrust as he might, he was unwilling to put such a substitute in the place of his late guileless, outspoken, childlike partner. He rapidly asked himself, would he like this man to be rich? No. He had more power than enough over Marguerite as it was, and wealth might invest him with more. Would he like this man to be Marguerite's Guardian, and yet proved to stand in no degree of relationship towards her, however disconnected and distant? No. But these were not considerations to come between him and fidelity to the dead. Let him see to it that they passed him with no other notice than the knowledge that they *had* passed him, and left him bent on the discharge of a solemn duty. And he did see to it, so soon that he followed his companion with ungrudging eyes, while he still paced the room; that companion, whom he supposed to be moodily reflecting on his own birth, and not on another man's—least of all what man's—violent Death.

The road in advance from Basle to Neuchâtel was better than had been represented. The latest weather had done it good. Drivers, both of horses and mules, had come in that evening after dark, and had reported nothing more difficult to be overcome than trials of patience, harness, wheels, axles, and whipcord. A bargain was soon struck for a carriage and horses, to take them on in the morning, and to start before daylight.

"Do you lock your door at night when travelling?" asked Obenreizer, standing warming his hands by the wood fire in Vendale's chamber, before going to his own.

"Not I. I sleep too soundly."

"You are so sound a sleeper?" he retorted, with an admiring look. "What a blessing!"

"Anything but a blessing to the rest of the house," rejoined Vendale, "if I had to be knocked up in the morning from the outside of my bedroom door."

"I, too," said Obenreizer, "leave open my room. But let me advise you, as a Swiss who knows: always, when you travel in my country, put your papers—and, of course, your money—under your pillow. Always the same place."

"You are not complimentary to your countrymen," laughed Vendale.

"My countrymen," said Obenreizer, with that light touch of his friend's elbows by way of Good Night and benediction, "I suppose are like the majority of men. And the majority of men will take what they can get. Adieu! At four in the morning."

"Adieu! At four."

Left to himself, Vendale raked the logs together, sprinkled over them the white wood-ashes lying on the hearth, and sat down to compose his thoughts. But they still ran high on their latest theme, and the running of the river tended to agitate rather than to quiet them. As he sat thinking, what little disposition he had had to sleep departed. He felt it hopeless to lie down yet, and sat dressed by the fire. Marguerite, Wilding, Obenreizer, the business he was then upon, and a thousand hopes and doubts that had nothing to do with it, occupied his mind at once. Everything seemed to have power over him but slumber. The departed disposition to sleep kept far away.

He had sat for a long time thinking, on the hearth, when his candle burned down and its light went out. It was of little moment; there was light enough in the fire. He changed his attitude, and, leaning his arm on the chair-back, and his chin upon that hand, sat thinking still.

But he sat between the fire and the bed, and, as the fire flickered in the play of air from the fast-flowing river, his enlarged shadow fluttered on the white wall by the bedside. His attitude gave it an air, half of mourning and half of bending over the bed imploring. His eyes were observant of it, when he became troubled by the disagreeable fancy that it was like Wilding's shadow, and not his own.

A slight change of place would cause it to disappear. He made the change, and the apparition of his disturbed fancy vanished. He now sat in the shade of a little nook beside the fire, and the door of the room was before him.

It had a long cumbrous iron latch. He saw the latch slowly and softly rise. The door opened a very little, and came to again, as though only the air had moved it. But he saw that the latch was out of the hasp.

The door opened again very slowly, until it opened wide enough to admit some one. It afterwards remained still for a while, as though cautiously held open on the other side. The figure of a man then entered, with its face turned towards the bed, and stood quiet just within the door, until it said, in a low half-whisper, at the same time taking one step forward: "Vendale!"

"What now?" he answered, springing from his seat; "who is it?"

It was Obenreizer, and he uttered a cry of surprise as Vendale came upon him from that unexpected direction. "Not in bed?" he said, catching him by both shoulders with an instinctive tendency to a struggle. "Then something *is* wrong!"

"What do you mean?" said Vendale, releasing himself.

"First tell me; you are not ill?"

"Ill? No."

"I have had a bad dream about you. How is it that I see you up and dressed?"

"My good fellow, I may as well ask you how it is that I see *you* up and undressed?"

"I have told you why. I have had a bad dream about you. I tried to rest after it, but it was impossible. I could not make up my mind to stay where I was without knowing you were safe; and yet I could not make up my mind to come in here. I have been minutes hesitating at the door. It is so easy to laugh at a dream that you have not dreamed. Where is your candle?"

"Burnt out."

"I have a whole one in my room. Shall I fetch it?"

"Do so."

His room was very near, and he was absent for but a few seconds. Coming back with the candle in his hand, he kneeled down on the hearth and lighted it. As he blew with his breath a charred billet into flame for the purpose, Vendale, looking down at him, saw that his lips were white and not easy of control.

"Yes!" said Obenreizer, setting the lighted candle on the table, "it was a bad dream. Only look at me!"

His feet were bare; his red-flannel shirt was thrown back at the throat, and its sleeves were rolled above the elbows; his only other garment, a pair of under pantaloons or drawers, reaching to the ankles, fitted him close and tight. A certain lithe and savage appearance was on his figure, and his eyes were very bright.

"If there had been a wrestle with a robber, as I dreamed," said Obenreizer, "you see, I was stripped for it."

"And armed too," said Vendale, glancing at his girdle.

"A traveller's dagger, that I always carry on the road," he answered carelessly, half drawing it from its sheath with his left hand, and putting it back again. "Do you carry no such thing?"

"Nothing of the kind."

"No pistols?" said Obenreizer, glancing at the table, and from it to the untouched pillow.

"Nothing of the sort."

"You Englishmen are so confident! You wish to sleep?"

"I have wished to sleep this long time, but I can't do it."

"I neither, after the bad dream. My fire has gone the way of your candle. May I come and sit by yours? Two o'clock! It will so soon be four, that it is not worth the trouble to go to bed again."

"I shall not take the trouble to go to bed at all, now," said Vendale; "sit here and keep me company, and welcome."

Going back to his room to arrange his dress, Obenreizer soon returned in a loose cloak and slippers, and they sat down on opposite sides of the hearth. In the interval Vendale had replenished the fire from the wood-basket in his room, and Obenreizer had put upon the table a flask and cup from his.

"Common cabaret brandy, I am afraid," he said, pouring out; "bought upon the road, and not like yours from Cripple Corner. But yours is exhausted; so much the worse. A cold night, a cold time of night, a cold country, and a cold house. This may be better than nothing; try it."

Vendale took the cup, and did so.

"How do you find it?"

"It has a coarse after-flavour," said Vendale, giving back the cup with a slight shudder, "and I don't like it."

"You are right," said Obenreizer, tasting, and smacking his lips; "it *has* a coarse after-flavour, and *I* don't like it. Booh! It burns, though!" He had flung what remained in the cup upon the fire.

Each of them leaned an elbow on the table, reclined his head upon his hand, and sat looking at the flaring logs. Obenreizer remained watchful and still; but Vendale, after certain nervous twitches and starts, in one of which he rose to his feet and looked wildly about him, fell into the strangest confusion of dreams. He carried his papers in a leather case or pocket-book, in an inner breast-pocket of his buttoned travelling-coat; and whatever he dreamed of, in the lethargy that got possession of him, something importunate in these papers called him out of that dream, though he could not wake from it. He was belated on the steppes of Russia (some shadowy person gave that name to the place) with Marguerite; and yet the sensation of a hand at his breast, softly feeling the outline of the pocket-book as he lay asleep before the fire, was present to him. He was ship-wrecked in an open boat at sea, and having lost his clothes, had no other covering than an old sail; and yet a creeping hand, tracing outside all the other pockets of the dress he actually wore, for papers, and finding none answer its touch, warned him to rouse himself. He was in the ancient vault at Cripple Corner, to which was transferred the very bed substantial and present in that very room at Basle; and Wilding (not dead, as he had supposed, and yet he did not wonder much) shook him, and whispered, "Look at that man! Don't you see he has risen, and is turning the pillow? Why should he turn the pillow, if not to seek those papers that are in your breast? Awake!" And yet he slept, and wandered off into other dreams.

Watchful and still, with his elbow on the table, and his head upon that hand, his companion at length said: "Vendale! We are called. Past Four!" Then, opening his eyes, he saw, turned sideways on him, the filmy face of Obenreizer.

"You have been in a heavy sleep," he said.   "The fatigue of constant travelling and the cold!"

"I am broad awake now," cried Vendale, springing up, but with an unsteady footing.   "Haven't you slept at all?"

"I may have dozed, but I seem to have been patiently looking at the fire.   Whether or no, we must wash, and breakfast, and turn out.   Past four, Vendale; past four!"

It was said in a tone to rouse him, for already he was half asleep again.   In his preparation for the day, too, and at his breakfast, he was often virtually asleep while in mechanical action.   It was not until the cold dark day was closing in, that he had any distincter impressions of the ride than jingling bells, bitter weather, slipping horses, frowning hillsides, bleak woods, and a stoppage at some wayside house of entertainment, where they had passed through a cowhouse to reach the travellers' room above.   He had been conscious of little more, except of Obenreizer sitting thoughtful at his side all day, and eyeing him much.

But when he shook off his stupor, Obenreizer was not at his side.   The carriage was stopping to bait at another wayside house; and a line of long narrow carts, laden with casks of wine, and drawn by horses with a quantity of blue collar and head-gear, were baiting too.   These came from the direction in which the travellers were going, and Obenreizer (not thoughtful now, but cheerful and alert) was talking with the foremost driver.   As Vendale stretched his limbs, circulated his blood, and cleared off the lees of his lethargy, with a sharp run to and fro in the bracing air, the line of carts moved on: the drivers all saluting Obenreizer as they passed him.

"Who are those?" asked Vendale.

"They are our carriers—Defresnier and Company's," replied Obenreizer.   "Those are our casks of wine."   He was singing to himself, and lighting a cigar.

"I have been drearily dull company to-day," said Vendale. "I don't know what has been the matter with me."

"You had no sleep last night; and a kind of brain-congestion frequently comes, at first, of such cold," said Obenreizer.   "I have seen it often.   After all, we shall have our journey for nothing, it seems."

"How for nothing?"

"The House is at Milan.   You know, we are a Wine House at Neuchâtel, and a Silk House at Milan?   Well,

Silk happening to press of a sudden, more than Wine,
Defresnier was summoned to Milan. Rolland, the other
partner, has been taken ill since his departure, and the
doctors will allow him to see no one. A letter awaits you
at Neuchâtel to tell you so. I have it from our chief carrier
whom you saw me talking with. He was surprised to see me,
and said he had that word for you if he met you. What do
you do? Go back?"

"Go on," said Vendale.

"On?"

"On? Yes. Across the Alps, and down to Milan."

Obenreizer stopped in his smoking to look at Vendale, and
then smoked heavily, looked up the road, looked down the
road, looked down at the stones in the road at his feet.

"I have a very serious matter in charge," said Vendale;
"more of these missing forms may be turned to as bad
account, or worse; I am urged to lose no time in helping
the House to take the thief; and nothing shall turn me
back."

"No?" cried Obenreizer, taking out his cigar to smile,
and giving his hand to his fellow-traveller. "Then nothing
shall turn *me* back. Ho, driver! Dispatch. Quick there!
Let us push on!"

They travelled through the night. There had been snow,
and there was a partial thaw, and they mostly travelled at a
foot-pace, and always with many stoppages to breathe the
splashed and floundering horses. After an hour's broad daylight, they drew rein at the inn-door at Neuchâtel, having
been some eight-and-twenty-hours in conquering some eighty
English miles.

When they had hurriedly refreshed and changed, they
went together to the house of business of Defresnier and
Company. There they found the letter which the wine-
carrier had described, enclosing the tests and comparisons
of handwriting essential to the discovery of the Forger.
Vendale's determination to press forward, without resting,
being already taken, the only question to delay them was by
what Pass could they cross the Alps? Respecting the state
of the two Passes of the St. Gotthard and the Simplon, the
guides and mule-drivers differed greatly; and both Passes
were still far enough off, to prevent the travellers from
having the benefit of any recent experience of either.
Besides which, they well knew that a fall of snow might

altogether change the described conditions in a single hour, even if they were correctly stated. But, on the whole, the Simplon appearing to be the hopefuller route, Vendale decided to take it. Obenreizer bore little or no part in the discussion, and scarcely spoke.

To Geneva, to Lausanne, along the level margin of the lake to Vevay, so into the winding valley between the spurs of the mountains, and into the valley of the Rhone. The sound of the carriage-wheels, as they rattled on, through the day, through the night, became as the wheels of a great clock, recording the hours. No change of weather varied the journey, after it had hardened into a sullen frost. In a sombre-yellow sky, they saw the Alpine ranges; and they saw enough of snow on nearer and much lower hill-tops and hill-sides, to sully, by contrast, the purity of lake, torrent, and waterfall, and make the villages look discoloured and dirty. But no snow fell, nor was there any snow-drift on the road. The stalking along the valley of more or less of white mist, changing on their hair and dress into icicles, was the only variety between them and the gloomy sky. And still by day, and still by night, the wheels. And still they rolled, in the hearing of one of them, to the burden, altered from the burden of the Rhine; "The time is gone for robbing him alive, and I must murder him."

They came, at length, to the poor little town of Brieg, at the foot of the Simplon. They came there after dark, but yet could see how dwarfed men's works and men became with the immense mountains towering over them. Here they must lie for the night; and here was warmth of fire, and lamp, and dinner, and wine, and after-conference resounding, with guides and drivers. No human creature had come across the Pass for four days. The snow above the snow-line was too soft for wheeled carriage, and not hard enough for sledge. There was snow in the sky. There had been snow in the sky for days past, and the marvel was that it had not fallen, and the certainty was that it must fall. No vehicle could cross. The journey might be tried on mules, or it might be tried on foot; but the best guides must be paid danger-price in either case, and that, too, whether they succeeded in taking the two travellers across, or turned for safety and brought them back.

In this discussion, Obenreizer bore no part whatever. He

sat silently smoking by the fire until the room was cleared
and Vendale referred to him.

"Bah! I am weary of these poor devils and their trade,"
he said, in reply. "Always the same story. It is the story
of their trade to-day, as it was the story of their trade when
I was a ragged boy. What do you and I want? We want
a knapsack each, and a mountain-staff each. We want no
guide; we should guide him; he would not guide us. We
leave our portmanteaus here, and we cross together. We
have been on the mountains together before now, and I am
mountain-born, and I know this Pass—Pass!—rather High
Road!—by heart. We will leave these poor devils, in pity,
to trade with others; but they must not delay us to make
a pretence of earning money. Which is all they mean."

Vendale, glad to be quit of the dispute, and to cut the
knot: active, adventurous, bent on getting forward, and
therefore very susceptible to the last hint: readily assented.
Within two hours, they had purchased what they wanted for
the expedition, had packed their knapsacks, and lay down to
sleep.

At break of day, they found half the town collected in
the narrow street to see them depart. The people talked
together in groups; the guides and drivers whispered apart,
and looked up at the sky; no one wished them a good
journey.

As they began the ascent, a gleam of sun shone from the
otherwise unaltered sky, and for a moment turned the tin
spires of the town to silver.

"A good omen!" said Vendale (though it died out while
he spoke). "Perhaps our example will open the Pass on this
side."

"No; we shall not be followed," returned Obenreizer,
looking up at the sky and back at the valley. "We shall
be alone up yonder."

ON THE MOUNTAIN

The road was fair enough for stout walkers, and the air
grew lighter and easier to breathe as the two ascended. But
the settled gloom remained as it had remained for days back.
Nature seemed to have come to a pause. The sense of
hearing, no less than the sense of sight, was troubled by
having to wait so long for the change, whatever it might be,

that impended. The silence was as palpable and heavy as the lowering clouds—or rather cloud, for there seemed to be but one in all the sky, and that one covering the whole of it.

Although the light was thus dismally shrouded, the prospect was not obscured. Down in the valley of the Rhone behind them, the stream could be traced through all its many windings, oppressively sombre and solemn in its one leaden hue, a colourless waste. Far and high above them, glaciers and suspended avalanches overhung the spots where they must pass, by and by; deep and dark below them on their right, were awful precipice and roaring torrent; tremendous mountains arose in every vista. The gigantic landscape, uncheered by a touch of changing light or a solitary ray of sun, was yet terribly distinct in its ferocity. The hearts of two lonely men might shrink a little, if they had to win their way for miles and hours among a legion of silent and motionless men—mere men like themselves—all looking at them with fixed and frowning front. But how much more, when the legion is of Nature's mightiest works, and the frown may turn to fury in an instant!

As they ascended, the road became gradually more rugged and difficult. But the spirits of Vendale rose as they mounted higher, leaving so much more of the road behind them conquered. Obenreizer spoke little, and held on with a determined purpose. Both, in respect of agility and endurance, were well qualified for the expedition. Whatever the born mountaineer read in the weather-tokens that was illegible to the other, he kept to himself.

"Shall we get across to-day?" asked Vendale.

"No," replied the other. "You see how much deeper the snow lies here than it lay half a league lower. The higher we mount the deeper the snow will lie. Walking is half wading even now. And the days are so short! If we get as high as the fifth Refuge, and lie to-night at the Hospice, we shall do well."

"Is there no danger of the weather rising in the night," asked Vendale, anxiously, "and snowing us up?"

"There is danger enough about us," said Obenreizer, with a cautious glance onward and upward, "to render silence our best policy. You have heard of the Bridge of the Ganther?"

"I have crossed it once."

"In the summer?"

"Yes; in the travelling season."

"Yes; but it is another thing at this season;" with a sneer, as though he were out of temper. "This is not a time of year, or a state of things, on an Alpine Pass, that you gentlemen holiday-travellers know much about."

"You are my Guide," said Vendale, good-humouredly. "I trust to you."

"I am your Guide," said Obenreizer, "and I will guide you to your journey's end. There is the Bridge before us."

They had made a turn into a desolate and dismal ravine, where the snow lay deep below them, deep above them, deep on every side. While speaking, Obenreizer stood pointing at the Bridge, and observing Vendale's face, with a very singular expression on his own.

"If I, as Guide, had sent you over there, in advance, and encouraged you to give a shout or two, you might have brought down upon yourself tons and tons and tons of snow, that would not only have struck you dead, but buried you deep, at a blow."

"No doubt," said Vendale.

"No doubt. But that is not what I have to do, as Guide. So pass silently. Or, going as we go, our indiscretion might else crush and bury *me*. Let us get on!"

There was a great accumulation of snow on the Bridge; and such enormous accumulations of snow overhung them from projecting masses of rock, that they might have been making their way through a stormy sky of white clouds. Using his staff skilfully, sounding as he went, and looking upward, with bent shoulders, as it were to resist the mere idea of a fall from above, Obenreizer softly led. Vendale closely followed. They were yet in the midst of their dangerous way, when there came a mighty rush, followed by a sound as of thunder. Obenreizer clapped his hand on Vendale's mouth and pointed to the track behind them. Its aspect had been wholly changed in a moment. An avalanche had swept over it, and plunged into the torrent at the bottom of the gulf below.

Their appearance at the solitary Inn not far beyond this terrible Bridge, elicited many expressions of astonishment from the people shut up in the house. "We stay but to rest," said Obenreizer, shaking the snow from his dress at the fire. "This gentleman has very pressing occasion to get across; tell them, Vendale."

"Assuredly, I have very pressing occasion. I must cross."

"You hear, all of you. My friend has very pressing occasion to get across, and we want no advice and no help. I am as good a guide, my fellow-countrymen, as any of you. Now, give us to eat and drink."

In exactly the same way, and in nearly the same words, when it was coming on dark and they had struggled through the greatly increased difficulties of the road, and had at last reached their destination for the night, Obenreizer said to the astonished people of the Hospice, gathering about them at the fire, while they were yet in the act of getting their wet shoes off, and shaking the snow from their clothes:

"It is well to understand one another, friends all. This gentleman——"

"—Has," said Vendale, readily taking him up with a smile, "very pressing occasion to get across. Must cross."

"You hear?—has very pressing occasion to get across, must cross. We want no advice and no help. I am mountain-born, and act as Guide. Do not worry us by talking about it, but let us have supper, and wine, and bed."

All through the intense cold of the night, the same awful stillness. Again at sunrise, no sunny tinge to gild or redden the snow. The same interminable waste of deathly white; the same immovable air; the same monotonous gloom in the sky.

"Travellers!" a friendly voice called to them from the door, after they were afoot, knapsack on back and staff in hand, as yesterday; "recollect! There are five places of shelter, near together, on the dangerous road before you; and there is the wooden cross, and there is the next Hospice. Do not stray from the track. If the *Tourmente* comes on, take shelter instantly!"

"The trade of these poor devils!" said Obenreizer to his friend, with a contemptuous backward wave of his hand towards the voice. "How they stick to their trade! You Englishmen say we Swiss are mercenary. Truly, it does look like it."

They had divided between the two knapsacks such refreshments as they had been able to obtain that morning, and as they deemed it prudent to take. Obenreizer carried the wine as his share of the burden; Vendale, the bread and meat and cheese, and the flask of brandy.

They had for some time laboured upward and onward through the snow—which was now above their knees in the track, and of unknown depth elsewhere—and they were still labouring upward and onward through the most frightful part of that tremendous desolation, when snow began to fall. At first, but a few flakes descended slowly and steadily. After a little while the fall grew much denser, and suddenly it began without apparent cause to whirl itself into spiral shapes.   Instantly ensuing upon this last change, an icy blast came roaring at them, and every sound and force imprisoned until now was let loose.

One of the dismal galleries through which the road is carried at that perilous point, a cave eked out by arches of great strength, was near at hand.   They struggled into it, and the storm raged wildly.   The noise of the wind, the noise of the water, the thundering down of displaced masses of rock and snow, the awful voices with which not only that gorge but every gorge in the whole monstrous range seemed to be suddenly endowed, the darkness as of night, the violent revolving of the snow which beat and broke it into spray and blinded them, the madness of everything around insatiate for destruction, the rapid substitution of furious violence for unnatural calm, and hosts of appalling sounds for silence : these were things, on the edge of a deep abyss, to chill the blood, though the fierce wind, made actually solid by ice and snow, had failed to chill it.

Obenreizer, walking to and fro in the gallery without ceasing, signed to Vendale to help him unbuckle his knapsack.   They could see each other, but could not have heard each other speak.   Vendale complying, Obenreizer produced his bottle of wine, and poured some out, motioning Vendale to take that for warmth's sake, and not brandy.   Vendale again complying, Obenreizer seemed to drink after him, and the two walked backwards and forwards side by side ; both well knowing that to rest or sleep would be to die.

The snow came driving heavily into the gallery by the upper end at which they would pass out of it, if they ever passed out ; for greater dangers lay on the road behind them than before.   The snow soon began to choke the arch.   An hour more, and it lay so high as to block out half the returning daylight.   But it froze hard now, as it fell, and could be clambered through or over.   The violence of the mountain storm was gradually yielding to a steady snowfall.

The wind still raged at intervals, but not incessantly ; and when it paused, the snow fell in heavy flakes.

They might have been two hours in their frightful prison, when Obenreizer, now crunching into the mound, now creeping over it with his head bowed down and his body touching the top of the arch, made his way out. Vendale followed close upon him, but followed without clear motive or calculation. For the lethargy of Basle was creeping over him again, and mastering his senses.

How far he had followed out of the gallery, or with what obstacles he had since contended, he knew not. He became roused to the knowledge that Obenreizer had set upon him, and that they were struggling desperately in the snow. He became roused to the remembrance of what his assailant carried in a girdle. He felt for it, drew it, struck at him, struggled again, struck at him again, cast him off, and stood face to face with him.

"I promised to guide you to your journey's end," said Obenreizer, "and I have kept my promise. The journey of your life ends here. Nothing can prolong it. You are sleeping as you stand."

"You are a villain. What have you done to me ?"

"You are a fool. I have drugged you. You are doubly a fool, for I drugged you once before upon the journey, to try you. You are trebly a fool, for I am the thief and forger, and in a few moments I shall take those proofs against the thief and forger from your insensible body."

The entrapped man tried to throw off the lethargy, but its fatal hold upon him was so sure that, even while he heard those words, he stupidly wondered which of them had been wounded, and whose blood it was that he saw sprinkled on the snow.

"What have I done to you," he asked, heavily and thickly, "that you should be—so base—a murderer ? "

"Done to me ? You would have destroyed me, but that you have come to your journey's end. Your cursed activity interposed between me, and the time I had counted on in which I might have replaced the money. Done to me ? You have come in my way—not once, not twice, but again and again and again. Did I try to shake you off in the beginning, or no ? You were not to be shaken off. Therefore you die here."

Vendale tried to think coherently, tried to speak coherently, tried to pick up the iron-shod staff he had let fall ; failing to touch it, tried to stagger on without its aid. All in vain, all in vain ! He stumbled, and fell heavily forward on the brink of the deep chasm.

Stupefied, dozing, unable to stand upon his feet, a veil before his eyes, his sense of hearing deadened, he made such a vigorous rally that, supporting himself on his hands, he saw his enemy standing calmly over him, and heard him speak.

"You call me murderer," said Obenreizer, with a grim laugh. "The name matters very little. But at least I have set my life against yours, for I am surrounded by dangers, and may never make my way out of this place. The *Tourmente* is rising again. The snow is on the whirl. I must have the papers now. Every moment has my life in it."

"Stop !" cried Vendale, in a terrible voice, staggering up with a last flash of fire breaking out of him, and clutching the thievish hands at his breast, in both of his. "Stop ! Stand away from me ! God bless my Marguerite ! Happily she will never know how I died. Stand off from me, and let me look at your murderous face. Let it remind me—of something—left to say."

The sight of him fighting so hard for his senses, and the doubt whether he might not for the instant be possessed by the strength of a dozen men, kept his opponent still. Wildly glaring at him, Vendale faltered out the broken words :

"It shall not be—the trust—of the dead—betrayed by me —reputed parents—misinherited fortune—see to it !"

As his head dropped on his breast, and he stumbled on the brink of the chasm as before, the thievish hands went once more, quick and busy, to his breast. He made a convulsive attempt to cry "No !" desperately rolled himself over into the gulf ; and sank away from his enemy's touch, like a phantom in a dreadful dream.

The mountain storm raged again, and passed again. The awful mountain-voices died away, the moon rose, and the soft and silent snow fell.

Two men and two large dogs came out at the door of the Hospice. The men looked carefully around them, and up at the sky. The dogs rolled in the snow, and took it into their mouths, and cast it up with their paws.

One of the men said to the other : "We may venture now.

No Thoroughfare

We may find them in one of the five Refuges." Each fastened on his back a basket; each took in his hand a strong spiked pole; each girded under his arms a looped end of a stout rope, so that they were tied together.

Suddenly the dogs desisted from their gambols in the snow, stood looking down the ascent, put their noses up, put their noses down, became greatly excited, and broke into a deep loud bay together.

The two men looked in the faces of the two dogs. The two dogs looked, with at least equal intelligence, in the faces of the two men.

"Au secours, then! Help! To the rescue!" cried the two men. The two dogs, with a glad, deep, generous bark, bounded away.

"Two more mad ones!" said the men, stricken motionless, and looking away in the moonlight. "Is it possible in such weather! And one of them a woman!"

Each of the dogs had the corner of a woman's dress in its mouth, and drew her along. She fondled their heads as she came up, and she came up through the snow with an accustomed tread. Not so the large man with her, who was spent and winded.

"Dear guides, dear friends of travellers! I am of your country. We seek two gentlemen crossing the Pass, who should have reached the Hospice this evening."

"They have reached it, Ma'amselle."

"Thank Heaven! O thank Heaven!"

"But, unhappily, they have gone on again. We are setting forth to seek them even now. We had to wait until the *Tourmente* passed. It has been fearful up here."

"Dear guides, dear friends of travellers! Let me go with you. Let me go with you for the love of GOD! One of those gentlemen is to be my husband. I love him, O, so dearly. O so dearly! You see I am not faint, you see I am not tired. I am born a peasant girl. I will show you that I know well how to fasten myself to your ropes. I will do it with my own hands. I will swear to be brave and good. But let me go with you, let me go with you! If any mischance should have befallen him, my love would find him, when nothing else could. On my knees, dear friends of travellers! By the love your dear mothers had for your fathers!"

The good rough fellows were moved. "After all," they murmured to one another, "she speaks but the truth. She knows the ways of the mountains. See how marvellously she has come here. But as to Monsieur there, Ma'amselle?"

"Dear Mr. Joey," said Marguerite, addressing him in his own tongue, "you will remain at the house, and wait for me; will you not?"

"If I know'd which o' you two recommended it," growled Joey Ladle, eyeing the two men with great indignation, "I'd fight you for sixpence, and give you half-a-crown towards your expenses. No, Miss. I'll stick by you as long as there's any sticking left in me, and I'll die for you when I can't do better."

The state of the moon rendering it highly important that no time should be lost, and the dogs showing signs of great uneasiness, the two men quickly took their resolution. The rope that yoked them together was exchanged for a longer one; the party were secured, Marguerite second, and the Cellarman last; and they set out for the Refuges. The actual distance of those places was nothing; the whole five, and the next Hospice to boot, being within two miles; but the ghastly way was whitened out and sheeted over.

They made no miss in reaching the Gallery where the two had taken shelter. The second storm of wind and snow had so wildly swept over it since, that their tracks were gone. But the dogs went to and fro with their noses down, and were confident. The party stopping, however, at the further arch, where the second storm had been especially furious, and where the drift was deep, the dogs became troubled, and went about and about, in quest of a lost purpose.

The great abyss being known to lie on the right, they wandered too much to the left, and had to regain the way with infinite labour through a deep field of snow. The leader of the line had stopped it, and was taking note of the landmarks, when one of the dogs fell to tearing up the snow a little before them. Advancing and stooping to look at it, thinking that some one might be overwhelmed there, they saw that it was stained, and that the stain was red.

The other dog was now seen to look over the brink of the gulf, with his fore legs straightened out, lest he should fall into it, and to tremble in every limb. Then the dog who had found the stained snow joined him, and then they ran to and fro, distressed and whining. Finally, they both stopped on the brink together, and setting up their heads, howled dolefully.

"There is some one lying below," said Marguerite.

"I think so," said the foremost man. "Stand well inward, the two last, and let us look over."

The last man kindled two torches from his basket, and handed them forward. The leader taking one, and Marguerite the other, they looked down; now shading the torches, now moving them to the right or left, now raising them, now depressing them, as moonlight far below contended with black shadows. A piercing cry from Marguerite broke a long silence.

"My God! On a projecting point, where a wall of ice stretches forward over the torrent, I see a human form!"

"Where, Ma'amselle, where?"

"See, there! On the shelf of ice below the dogs!"

The leader, with a sickened aspect, drew inward, and they were all silent. But they were not all inactive, for Marguerite, with swift and skilful fingers, had detached both herself and him from the rope in a few seconds.

"Show me the baskets. These two are the only ropes?"

"The only ropes here, Ma'amselle; but at the Hospice——"

"If he is alive—I know it is my lover—he will be dead before you can return. Dear Guides! Blessed friends of travellers! Look at me. Watch my hands. If they falter or go wrong, make me your prisoner by force. If they are steady and go right, help me to save him!"

She girded herself with a cord under the breast and arms, she formed it into a kind of jacket, she drew it into knots, she laid its end side by side with the end of the other cord, she twisted and twined the two together, she knotted them together, she set her foot upon the knots, she strained them, she held them for the two men to strain at.

"She is inspired," they said to one another.

"By the Almighty's mercy!" she exclaimed. "You both know that I am by far the lightest here. Give me the brandy and the wine, and lower me down to him. Then go for assistance and a stronger rope. You see that when it is lowered to me—look at this about me now—I can make it fast and safe to his body. Alive or dead, I will bring him up, or die with him. I love him passionately. Can I say more?"

They turned to her companion, but he was lying senseless on the snow.

"Lower me down to him," she said, taking two little kegs

they had brought, and hanging them about her, "or I will dash myself to pieces! I am a peasant, and I know no giddiness or fear; and this is nothing to me, and I passionately love him. Lower me down!"

"Ma'amselle, Ma'amselle, he must be dying or dead."

"Dying or dead, my husband's head shall lie upon my breast, or I will dash myself to pieces."

They yielded, overborne. With such precautions as their skill and the circumstances admitted, they let her slip from the summit, guiding herself down the precipitous icy wall with her hand, and they lowered down, and lowered down, and lowered down, until the cry came up: "Enough!"

"Is it really he, and is he dead?" they called down, looking over.

The cry came up: "He is insensible; but his heart beats. It beats against mine."

"How does he lie?"

The cry came up: "Upon a ledge of ice. It has thawed beneath him, and it will thaw beneath me. Hasten. If we die, I am content."

One of the two men hurried off with the dogs at such topmost speed as he could make; the other set up the lighted torches in the snow, and applied himself to recovering the Englishman. Much snow-chafing and some brandy got him on his legs, but delirious and quite unconscious where he was.

The watch remained upon the brink, and his cry went down continually: "Courage! They will soon be here. How goes it?" And the cry came up: "His heart still beats against mine. I warm him in my arms. I have cast off the rope, for the ice melts under us, and the rope would separate me from him; but I am not afraid."

The moon went down behind the mountain tops, and all the abyss lay in darkness. The cry went down: "How goes it?" The cry came up: "We are sinking lower, but his heart still beats against mine."

At length the eager barking of the dogs, and a flare of light upon the snow, proclaimed that help was coming on. Twenty or thirty men, lamps, torches, litters, ropes, blankets, wood to kindle a great fire, restoratives and stimulants, came in fast. The dogs ran from one man to another, and from this thing to that, and ran to the edge of the abyss, dumbly entreating Speed, speed, speed!

The cry went down: "Thanks to God, all is ready. How goes it?"

The cry came up: "We are sinking still, and we are deadly cold. His heart no longer beats against mine. Let no one come down, to add to our weight. Lower the rope only."

The fire was kindled high, a great glare of torches lighted the sides of the precipice, lamps were lowered, a strong rope was lowered. She could be seen passing it round him, and making it secure.

The cry came up into a deathly silence: "Raise! Softly!" They could see her diminished figure shrink, as he was swung into the air.

They gave no shout when some of them laid him on a litter, and others lowered another strong rope. The cry again came up into a deathly silence: "Raise! Softly!" But when they caught her at the brink, then they shouted, then they wept, then they gave thanks to Heaven, then they kissed her feet, then they kissed her dress, then the dogs caressed her, licked her icy hands, and with their honest faces warmed her frozen bosom!

She broke from them all, and sank over him on his litter, with both her loving hands upon the heart that stood still.

ACT IV

THE CLOCK-LOCK

THE pleasant scene was Neuchâtel; the pleasant month was April; the pleasant place was a notary's office; the pleasant person in it was the notary: a rosy, hearty, handsome old man, chief notary of Neuchâtel, known far and wide in the canton as Maître Voigt. Professionally and personally, the notary was a popular citizen. His innumerable kindnesses and his innumerable oddities had for years made him one of the recognised public characters of the pleasant Swiss town. His long brown frock-coat and his black skull-cap, were among the institutions of the place: and he carried a snuff-box which, in point of size, was popularly believed to be without a parallel in Europe.

There was another person in the notary's office, not so pleasant as the notary. This was Obenreizer.

An oddly pastoral kind of office it was, and one that would never have answered in England. It stood in a neat back yard, fenced off from a pretty flower-garden. Goats browsed in the doorway, and a cow was within half-a-dozen feet of keeping company with the clerk. Maître Voigt's room was a bright and varnished little room, with panelled walls, like a toy-chamber. According to the seasons of the year, roses, sunflowers, hollyhocks, peeped in at the windows. Maître Voigt's bees hummed through the office all the summer, in at this window and out at that, taking it frequently in their day's work, as if honey were to be made from Maître Voigt's sweet disposition. A large musical box on the chimney-piece often trilled away at the Overture to Fra Diavolo, or a Selection from William Tell, with a chirruping liveliness that had to be stopped by force on the entrance of a client, and irrepressibly broke out again the moment his back was turned.

"Courage, courage, my good fellow!" said Maître Voigt, patting Obenreizer on the knee, in a fatherly and comforting way. "You will begin a new life to-morrow morning in my office here."

Obenreizer—dressed in mourning, and subdued in manner —lifted his hand, with a white handkerchief in it, to the region of his heart. "The gratitude is here," he said. "But the words to express it are not here."

"Ta-ta-ta! Don't talk to me about gratitude!" said Maître Voigt. "I hate to see a man oppressed. I see you oppressed, and I hold out my hand to you by instinct. Besides, I am not too old yet, to remember my young days. Your father sent me my first client. (It was on a question of half an acre of vineyard that seldom bore any grapes.) Do I owe nothing to your father's son? I owe him a debt of friendly obligation, and I pay it to you. That's rather neatly expressed, I think," added Maître Voigt, in high good humour with himself. "Permit me to reward my own merit with a pinch of snuff!"

Obenreizer dropped his eyes to the ground, as though he were not even worthy to see the notary take snuff.

"Do me one last favour, Sir," he said, when he raised his eyes. "Do not act on impulse. Thus far, you have only a general knowledge of my position. Hear the case for and against me, in its details, before you take me into your office. Let my claim on your benevolence be recognised by your sound reason as well as by your excellent heart. In *that* case, I may hold up my head against the bitterest of my enemies, and build myself a new reputation on the ruins of the character I have lost."

"As you will," said Maître Voigt. "You speak well, my son. You will be a fine lawyer one of these days."

"The details are not many," pursued Obenreizer. "My troubles begin with the accidental death of my late travelling companion, my lost dear friend Mr. Vendale."

"Mr. Vendale," repeated the notary. "Just so. I have heard and read of the name, several times within these two months. The name of the unfortunate English gentleman who was killed on the Simplon. When you got that scar upon your cheek and neck."

"—From my own knife," said Obenreizer, touching what must have been an ugly gash at the time of its infliction.

"From your own knife," assented the notary, "and in trying to save him. Good, good, good. That was very good. Vendale. Yes. I have several times, lately, thought it droll that I should once have had a client of that name."

"But the world, Sir," returned Obenreizer, "is *so* small!" Nevertheless he made a mental note that the notary had once had a client of that name.

"As I was saying, Sir, the death of that dear travelling comrade begins my troubles. What follows? I save myself. I go down to Milan. I am received with coldness by Defresnier and Company. Shortly afterwards, I am discharged by Defresnier and Company. Why? They give no reason why. I ask, do they assail my honour? No answer. I ask, what is the imputation against me? No answer. I ask, where are their proofs against me? No answer. I ask, what am I to think? The reply is, 'M. Obenreizer is free to think what he will. What M. Obenreizer thinks, is of no importance to Defresnier and Company.' And that is all."

"Perfectly. That is all," assented the notary, taking a large pinch of snuff.

"But is that enough, Sir?"

"That is not enough," said Maître Voigt. "The House of Defresnier are my fellow-townsmen—much respected, much esteemed—but the House of Defresnier must not silently destroy a man's character. You can rebut assertion. But how can you rebut silence?"

"Your sense of justice, my dear patron," answered

Obenreizer, "states in a word the cruelty of the case. Does it stop there? No. For, what follows upon that?"

"True, my poor boy," said the notary, with a comforting nod or two; "your ward rebels upon that."

"Rebels is too soft a word," retorted Obenreizer. "My ward revolts from me with horror. My ward defies me. My ward withdraws herself from my authority, and takes shelter (Madame Dor with her) in the house of that English lawyer, Mr. Bintrey, who replies to your summons to her to submit herself to my authority, that she will not do so."

"—And who afterwards writes," said the notary, moving his large snuff-box to look among the papers underneath it for the letter, "that he is coming to confer with me."

"Indeed?" replied Obenreizer, rather checked. "Well, Sir. Have I no legal rights?"

"Assuredly, my poor boy," returned the notary. "All but felons have their legal rights."

"And who calls me felon?" said Obenreizer, fiercely.

"No one. Be calm under your wrongs. If the House of Defresnier would call you felon, indeed, we should know how to deal with them."

While saying these words, he had handed Bintrey's very short letter to Obenreizer, who now read it and gave it back.

"In saying," observed Obenreizer, with recovered composure, "that he is coming to confer with you, this English lawyer means that he is coming to deny my authority over my ward."

"You think so?"

"I am sure of it. I know him. He is obstinate and contentious. You will tell me, my dear Sir, whether my authority is unassailable, until my ward is of age?"

"Absolutely unassailable."

"I will enforce it. I will make her submit herself to it. For," said Obenreizer, changing his angry tone to one of grateful submission, "I owe it to you, Sir; to you, who have so confidingly taken an injured man under your protection, and into your employment."

"Make your mind easy," said Maître Voigt. "No more of this now, and no thanks! Be here to-morrow morning, before the other clerk comes—between seven and eight. You will find me in this room; and I will myself initiate you in your work. Go away! go away! I have letters to write. I won't hear a word more."

Dismissed with this generous abruptness, and satisfied with

the favourable impression he had left on the old man's mind. Obenreizer was at leisure to revert to the mental note he had made that Maître Voigt once had a client whose name was Vendale.

"I ought to know England well enough by this time;" so his meditations ran, as he sat on a bench in the yard; "and it is not a name I ever encountered there, except "—he looked involuntarily over his shoulder—" as *his* name. Is the world so small that I cannot get away from him, even now when he is dead? He confessed at the last that he had betrayed the trust of the dead, and misinherited a fortune. And I was to see to it. And I was to stand off, that my face might remind him of it. Why *my* face, unless it concerned *me?* I am sure of his words, for they have been in my ears ever since. Can there be anything bearing on them, in the keeping of this old idiot? Anything to repair my fortunes, and blacken his memory? He dwelt upon my earliest remembrances, that night at Basle. Why, unless he had a purpose in it?"

Maître Voigt's two largest he-goats were butting at him to butt him out of the place, as if for that disrespectful mention of their master. So he got up and left the place. But he walked alone for a long time on the border of the lake, with his head drooped in deep thought.

Between seven and eight next morning, he presented himself again at the office. He found the notary ready for him, at work on some papers which had come in on the previous evening. In a few clear words, Maître Voigt explained the routine of the office, and the duties Obenreizer would be expected to perform. It still wanted five minutes to eight, when the preliminary instructions were declared to be complete.

"I will show you over the house and the offices," said Maître Voigt, "but I must put away these papers first. They come from the municipal authorities, and they must be taken special care of."

Obenreizer saw his chance, here, of finding out the repository in which his employer's private papers were kept.

"Can't I save you the trouble, Sir?" he asked. "Can't I put those documents away under your directions?"

Maître Voigt laughed softly to himself; closed the portfolio in which the papers had been sent to him; handed it to Obenreizer.

"Suppose you try," he said. "All my papers of importance are kept yonder."

He pointed to a heavy oaken door, thickly studded with nails, at the lower end of the room. Approaching the door, with the portfolio, Obenreizer discovered, to his astonishment, that there were no means whatever of opening it from the outside. There was no handle, no bolt, no key, and (climax of passive obstruction!) no keyhole.

"There is a second door to this room?" said Obenreizer, appealing to the notary.

"No," said Maître Voigt. "Guess again."

"There is a window?"

"Nothing of the sort. The window has been bricked up. The only way in, is the way by that door. Do you give it up?" cried Maître Voigt, in high triumph. "Listen, my good fellow, and tell me if you hear nothing inside?"

Obenreizer listened for a moment, and started back from the door.

"I know!" he exclaimed. "I heard of this when I was apprenticed here at the watchmaker's. Perrin Brothers have finished their famous clock-lock at last—and you have got it?"

"Bravo!" said Maître Voigt. "The clock-lock it is! There, my son! There you have one more of what the good people of this town call, 'Daddy Voigt's follies.' With all my heart! Let those laugh who win. No thief can steal *my* keys. No burglar can pick *my* lock. No power on earth, short of a battering-ram or a barrel of gunpowder, can move that door, till my little sentinel inside—my worthy friend who goes 'Tick, Tick,' as I tell him—says 'Open!' The big door obeys the little Tick, Tick, and the little Tick, Tick, obeys *me*. That!" cried Daddy Voigt, snapping his fingers, "for all the thieves in Christendom!"

"May I see it in action?" asked Obenreizer. "Pardon my curiosity, dear Sir! You know that I was once a tolerable worker in the clock trade."

"Certainly you shall see it in action," said Maître Voigt. "What is the time now? One minute to eight. Watch, and in one minute you will see the door open of itself."

In one minute, smoothly and slowly and silently, as if invisible hands had set it free, the heavy door opened inward, and disclosed a dark chamber beyond. On three sides, shelves filled the walls, from floor to ceiling. Arranged on the shelves, were rows upon rows of boxes made in the pretty inlaid wood-work of Switzerland, and bearing inscribed on their fronts (for the most part in fanciful coloured letters) the names of the notary's clients.

Maître Voigt lighted a taper, and led the way into the room. "You shall see the clock," he said proudly. "I possess the greatest curiosity in Europe. It is only a privileged few whose eyes can look at it. I give the privilege to your good father's son—you shall be one of the favoured few who enter the room with me. See! here it is, on the right-hand wall at the side of the door."

"An ordinary clock," exclaimed Obenreizer. "No! Not an ordinary clock. It has only one hand."

"Aha!" said Maître Voigt. "Not an ordinary clock, my friend. No, no. That one hand goes round the dial. As I put it, so it regulates the hour at which the door shall open. See! the hand points to eight. At eight the door opened, as you saw for yourself."

"Does it open more than once in the four-and-twenty hours?" asked Obenreizer.

"More than once?" repeated the notary, with great scorn. "You don't know, my good friend, Tick-Tick! He will open the door as often as I ask him. All he wants is his directions, and he gets them here. Look below the dial. Here is a half-circle of steel let into the wall, and here is a hand (called the regulator) that travels round it, just as *my* hand chooses. Notice, if you please, that there are figures to guide me on the half-circle of steel. Figure I. means: Open once in the four-and-twenty hours. Figure II. means: Open twice; and so on to the end. I set the regulator every morning, after I have read my letters, and when I know what my day's work is to be. Would you like to see me set it now? What is to-day? Wednesday. Good! This is the day of our rifle-club; there is little business to do; I grant a half-holiday. No work here to-day, after three o'clock. Let us first put away this port-folio of municipal papers. There! No need to trouble Tick-Tick to open the door until eight to-morrow. Good! I leave the dial-hand at eight; I put back the regulator to I.; I close the door; and closed the door remains, past all opening by anybody, till to-morrow morning at eight."

Obenreizer's quickness instantly saw the means by which he might make the clock-lock betray its master's confidence, and place its master's papers at his disposal.

"Stop, Sir!" he cried, at the moment when the notary was closing the door. "Don't I see something moving among the boxes—on the floor there?"

(Maître Voigt turned his back for a moment to look. In that moment, Obenreizer's ready hand put the regulator on, from the figure "I." to the figure "II." Unless the notary looked again at the half-circle of steel, the door would open at eight that evening, as well as at eight next morning, and nobody but Obenreizer would know it.)

"There is nothing!" said Maître Voigt. "Your troubles have shaken your nerves, my son. Some shadow thrown by my taper; or some poor little beetle, who lives among the old lawyer's secrets, running away from the light. Hark! I hear your fellow-clerk in the office. To work! to work! and build to-day the first step that leads to your new fortunes!"

He good-humouredly pushed Obenreizer out before him; extinguished the taper, with a last fond glance at his clock which passed harmlessly over the regulator beneath; and closed the oaken door.

At three, the office was shut up. The notary and everybody in the notary's employment, with one exception, went to see the rifle-shooting. Obenreizer had pleaded that he was not in spirits for a public festival. Nobody knew what had become of him. It was believed that he had slipped away for a solitary walk.

The house and offices had been closed but a few minutes, when the door of a shining wardrobe in the notary's shining room opened, and Obenreizer stepped out. He walked to a window, unclosed the shutters, satisfied himself that he could escape unseen by way of the garden, turned back into the room, and took his place in the notary's easy chair. He was locked up in the house, and there were five hours to wait before eight o'clock came.

He wore his way through the five hours: sometimes reading the books and newspapers that lay on the table: sometimes thinking: sometimes walking to and fro. Sunset came on. He closed the window-shutters before he kindled a light. The candle lighted, and the time drawing nearer and nearer, he sat, watch in hand, with his eyes on the oaken door.

At eight, smoothly and softly and silently the door opened.

One after another, he read the names on the outer rows of boxes. No such name as Vendale! He removed the outer row, and looked at the row behind. These were older boxes, and shabbier boxes. The four first that he examined, were inscribed with French and German names. The fifth bore a name which was almost illegible. He brought it out into the room, and examined it closely. There, covered thickly with time-stains and dust, was the name : "Vendale."

The key hung to the box by a string. He unlocked the box, took out four loose papers that were in it, spread them open on the table, and began to read them. He had not so occupied a minute, when his face fell from its expression of eagerness and avidity, to one of haggard astonishment and disappointment. But, after a little consideration, he copied the papers. He then replaced the papers, replaced the box, closed the door, extinguished the candle, and stole away.

As his murderous and thievish footfall passed out of the garden, the steps of the notary and some one accompanying him stopped at the front door of the house. The lamps were lighted in the little street, and the notary had his door-key in his hand.

"Pray do not pass my house, Mr. Bintrey," he said. "Do me the honour to come in. It is one of our town half-holidays —our Tir—but my people will be back directly. It is droll that you should ask your way to the Hotel of me. Let us eat and drink before you go there."

"Thank you ; not to-night," said Bintrey. "Shall I come to you at ten to-morrow ?"

"I shall be enchanted, Sir, to take so early an opportunity of redressing the wrongs of my injured client," returned the good notary.

"Yes," retorted Bintrey ; "your injured client is all very well—but—a word in your ear."

He whispered to the notary and walked off. When the notary's housekeeper came home, she found him standing at his door motionless, with the key still in his hand, and the door unopened.

OBENREIZER'S VICTORY

The scene shifts again—to the foot of the Simplon, on the Swiss side.

In one of the dreary rooms of the dreary little inn at Briog, Mr. Bintrey and Maître Voigt sat together at a professional council of two. Mr. Bintrey was searching in his dispatch-box. Maître Voigt was looking towards a closed door, painted brown to imitate mahogany, and communicating with an inner room.

"Isn't it time he was here?" asked the notary, shifting his position, and glancing at a second door at the other end of the room, painted yellow to imitate deal.

"He *is* here," answered Bintrey, after listening for a moment.

The yellow door was opened by a waiter, and Obenreizer walked in.

After greeting Maître Voigt with a cordiality which appeared to cause the notary no little embarrassment, Obenreizer bowed with grave and distant politeness to Bintrey. "For what reason have I been brought from Neuchâtel to the foot of the mountain?" he inquired, taking the seat which the English lawyer had indicated to him.

"You shall be quite satisfied on that head before our interview is over," returned Bintrey. "For the present, permit me to suggest proceeding at once to business. There has been a correspondence, Mr. Obenreizer, between you and your niece. I am here to represent your niece."

"In other words, you, a lawyer, are here to represent an infraction of the law."

"Admirably put!" said Bintrey. "If all the people I have to deal with were only like you, what an easy profession mine would be! I am here to represent an infraction of the law— that is your point of view. I am here to make a compromise between you and your niece—that is my point of view."

"There must be two parties to a compromise," rejoined Obenreizer. "I decline, in this case, to be one of them. The law gives me authority to control my niece's actions, until she comes of age. She is not yet of age; and I claim my authority."

At this point Maître Voigt attempted to speak. Bintrey silenced him with a compassionate indulgence of tone and manner, as if he was silencing a favourite child.

"No, my worthy friend, not a word. Don't excite yourself unnecessarily; leave it to me." He turned, and addressed himself again to Obenreizer. "I can think of nothing comparable to you, Mr. Obenreizer, but granite—and even that wears out in course of time. In the interests of peace and quietness—for the sake of your own dignity—relax a little. If you will only delegate your authority to another person whom I know of, that person may be trusted never to lose sight of your niece, night or day!"

"You are wasting your time and mine," returned Oben-reizer. "If my niece is not rendered up to my authority within one week from this day, I invoke the law. If you resist the law, I take her by force."

He rose to his feet as he said the last word. Maître Voigt looked round again towards the brown door which led into the inner room.

"Have some pity on the poor girl," pleaded Bintrey. "Remember how lately she lost her lover by a dreadful death! Will nothing move you?"

"Nothing."

Bintrey, in his turn, rose to his feet, and looked at Maître Voigt. Maître Voigt's hand, resting on the table, began to tremble. Maître Voigt's eyes remained fixed, as if by irresistible fascination, on the brown door. Obenreizer, suspiciously observing him, looked that way too.

"There is somebody listening in there!" he exclaimed, with a sharp backward glance at Bintrey.

"There are two people listening," answered Bintrey.

"Who are they?"

"You shall see."

With that answer, he raised his voice and spoke the next words—the two common words which are on everybody's lips, at every hour of the day: "Come in!"

The brown door opened. Supported on Marguerite's arm —his sunburnt colour gone, his right arm bandaged and slung over his breast—Vendale stood before the murderer, a man risen from the dead.

In the moment of silence that followed, the singing of a caged bird in the courtyard outside was the one sound stirring in the room. Maître Voigt touched Bintrey, and pointed to Obenreizer. "Look at him!" said the notary, in a whisper.

The shock had paralysed every movement in the villain's body, but the movement of the blood. His face was like the face of a corpse. The one vestige of colour left in it was a livid purple streak which marked the course of the scar where his victim had wounded him on the cheek and neck. Speechless, breathless, motionless alike in eye and limb, it seemed as if, at the sight of Vendale, the death to which he had doomed Vendale had struck him where he stood.

"Somebody ought to speak to him," said Maître Voigt. "Shall I?"

Even at that moment Bintrey persisted in silencing the notary, and in keeping the lead in the proceedings to himself. Checking Maître Voigt by a gesture, he dismissed Marguerite and Vendale in these words:—"The object of your appearance here is answered," he said. "If you will withdraw for the present, it may help Mr. Obenreizer to recover himself."

It did help him. As the two passed through the door and closed it behind them, he drew a deep breath of relief. He looked round him for the chair from which he had risen, and dropped into it.

"Give him time!" pleaded Maître Voigt.

"No," said Bintrey. "I don't know what use he may make of it if I do." He turned once more to Obenreizer, and went on. "I owe it to myself," he said—"I don't admit, mind, that I owe it to *you*—to account for my appearance in these proceedings, and to state what has been done under my advice, and on my sole responsibility. Can you listen to me?"

"I can listen to you."

"Recall the time when you started for Switzerland with Mr. Vendale," Bintrey began. "You had not left England four-and-twenty hours before your niece committed an act of imprudence which not even your penetration could foresee. She followed her promised husband on his journey, without asking anybody's advice or permission, and without any better companion to protect her than a Cellarman in Mr. Vendale's employment."

"Why did she follow me on the journey? and how came the Cellarman to be the person who accompanied her?"

"She followed you on the journey," answered Bintrey, "because she suspected there had been some serious collision between you and Mr. Vendale, which had been kept secret from her; and because she rightly believed you to be capable of serving your interests, or of satisfying your enmity, at the price of a crime. As for the Cellarman, he was one, among the other people in Mr. Vendale's establishment, to whom she had applied (the moment your back was turned) to know if anything had happened between their master and you. The Cellarman alone had something to tell her. A senseless superstition, and a common accident which had happened to his master, in his master's cellar, had connected Mr. Vendale in this man's mind with the idea of danger by murder. Your niece surprised him into a confession, which aggravated ten-fold the terrors that possessed her. Aroused to a sense of the mischief he had done, the man, of his own accord, made the one atonement in his power. 'If my master is in danger, Miss,' he said, 'it's my duty to follow him, too; and it's more than my duty to take care of *you.*' The two set forth together—and, for once, a superstition has had its use. It decided your niece on taking the journey; and it led the way to saving a man's life. Do you understand me, so far?"

"I understand you, so far."

"My first knowledge of the crime that you had committed," pursued Bintrey, "came to me in the form of a letter from your niece. All you need know is that her love and her courage recovered the body of your victim, and aided the after-efforts which brought him back to life. While he lay helpless at Brieg, under her care, she wrote to me to come out to him. Before starting, I informed Madame Dor that I knew Miss Obenreizer to be safe, and knew where she was. Madame Dor informed me, in return, that a letter had come for your niece, which she knew to be in your handwriting. I took possession of it, and arranged for the forwarding of any other letters which might follow. Arrived at Brieg, I found Mr. Vendale out of danger, and at once devoted myself to hastening the day of reckoning with you. Defresnier and Company turned you off on suspicion ; acting on information privately supplied by me. Having stripped you of your false character, the next thing to do was to strip you of your authority over your niece. To reach this end, I not only had no scruple in digging the pitfall under your feet in the dark—I felt a certain professional pleasure in fighting you with your own weapons. By my advice the truth has been carefully concealed from you up to this day. By my advice the trap into which you have walked was set for you (you know why, now, as well as I do) in this place. There was but one certain way of shaking the devilish self-control which has hitherto made you a formidable man. That way has been tried, and (look at me as you may) that way has succeeded. The last thing that remains to be done," concluded Bintrey, producing two little slips of manuscript from his dispatch-box, "is to set your niece free. You have attempted murder, and you have committed forgery and theft. We have the evidence ready against you in both cases. If you are convicted as a felon, you know as well as I do what becomes of your authority over your niece. Personally, I should have preferred taking that way out of it. But considerations are pressed on me which I am not able to resist, and this interview must end, as I have told you already, in a compromise. Sign those lines, resigning all authority over Miss Obenreizer, and pledging yourself never to be seen in England or in Switzerland again ; and I will sign an indemnity which secures you against further proceedings on our part."

Obenreizer took the pen, in silence, and signed his niece's release. On receiving the indemnity in return, he rose, but made no movement to leave the room. He stood looking at Maître Voigt with a strange smile gathering at his lips, and a strange light flashing in his filmy eyes.

"What are you waiting for ? " asked Bintrey.

Obenreizer pointed to the brown door. "Call them back," he answered. "I have something to say in their presence before I go."

"Say it in my presence," retorted Bintrey. "I decline to call them back."

Obenreizer turned to Maître Voigt. "Do you remember telling me that you once had an English client named Vendale ? " he asked.

"Well," answered the notary. "And what of that ? "

"Maître Voigt, your clock-lock has betrayed you."

"What do you mean ? "

"I have read the letters and certificates in your client's box. I have taken copies of them. I have got the copies here. Is there, or is there not, a reason for calling them back ? "

For a moment the notary looked to and fro, between Obenreizer and Bintrey, in helpless astonishment. Recovering himself, he drew his brother-lawyer aside, and hurriedly spoke a few words close at his ear. The face of Bintrey—after first faithfully reflecting the astonishment on the face of Maître Voigt —suddenly altered its expression. He sprang, with the activity of a young man, to the door of the inner room, entered it, remained inside for a minute, and returned followed by Marguerite and Vendale. "Now, Mr. Obenreizer," said Bintrey, "the last move in the game is yours. Play it."

"Before I resign my position as that young lady's guardian," said Obenreizer, "I have a secret to reveal in which she is interested. In making my disclosure, I am not claiming her attention for a narrative which she, or any other person present, is expected to take on trust. I am possessed of written proofs, copies of originals, the authenticity of which Maître Voigt himself can attest. Bear that in mind, and permit me to refer you, at starting, to a date long past—the month of February, in the year one thousand eight hundred and thirty-six."

"Mark the date, Mr. Vendale," said Bintrey.

"My first proof," said Obenreizer, taking a paper from his pocket-book. "Copy of a letter, written by an English lady (married) to her sister, a widow. The name of the person writing the letter I shall keep suppressed until I have done. The name of the person to whom the letter is written I am willing to reveal. It is addressed to "Mrs. Jane Anne Miller, of Groombridge-wells, England.'"

Vendale started, and opened his lips to speak. Bintrey instantly stopped him, as he had stopped Maître Voigt. "No," said the pertinacious lawyer. "Leave it to me."

Obenreizer went on :

"It is needless to trouble you with the first half of the letter," he said. "I can give the substance of it in two words. The writer's position at the time is this. She has been long living in Switzerland with her husband—obliged to live there for the sake of her husband's health. They are about to move to a new residence on the Lake of Neuchâtel in a week, and they will be ready to receive Mrs. Miller as visitor in a fortnight from that time. This said, the writer next enters into an important domestic detail. She has been childless for years—she and her husband have now no hope of children ; they are lonely ; they want an interest in life ; they have decided on adopting a child. Here the important part of the letter begins ; and here, therefore, I read it to you word for word."

He folded back the first page of the letter and read as follows:

"* * * Will you help us, my dear sister, to realise our new project ? As English people, we wish to adopt an English child. This may be done, I believe. at the Foundling: my husband's lawyers in London will tell you how. I leave the choice to you, with only these conditions attached to it—that the child is to be an infant under a year old, and is to be a boy. Will you pardon the trouble I am giving you, for my sake ; and will you bring our adopted child to us, with your own children, when you come to Neuchâtel?

"I must add a word as to my husband's wishes in this matter. He is resolved to spare the child whom we make our own any future mortification and loss of self-respect which might be caused by a discovery of his true origin. He will bear my husband's name, and he will be brought up in the belief that he is really our son. His inheritance of what we have to leave will be secured to him—not only according to the laws of England in such cases, but according to the laws of Switzerland also; for we have lived so long in this country, that there is a doubt whether we may not be considered as 'domiciled' in Switzerland. The one precaution left to take is to prevent any after-discovery at the Foundling. Now, our name is a very uncommon one; and if we appear on the Register of the Institution as the persons adopting the child, there is just a chance that something might result from it. Your name, my dear, is the name of thousands of other people; and if *you* will consent to appear on the Register, there need be no fear of any discoveries in that quarter. We are moving, by the doctor's orders, to a part of Switzerland in which our circumstances are quite unknown; and you, as I understand, are about to engage a new nurse for the journey when you come to see us. Under these circumstances, the child may appear as my child, brought back to me under my sister's care. The only servant we take with us from our old home is my own maid, who can be safely trusted. As for the lawyers in England and in Switzerland, it is their profession to keep secrets—and we may feel quite easy in that direction. So there you have our harmless little conspiracy! Write by return of post, my love, and tell me you will join it." * * *

"Do you still conceal the name of the writer of that letter?" asked Vendale.

"I keep the name of the writer till the last," answered Obenreizer, "and I proceed to my second proof—a mere slip of paper this time, as you see. Memorandum given to the Swiss lawyer, who drew the documents referred to in the letter I have just read, expressed as follows:—'Adopted from the Foundling Hospital of England, 3rd March, 1836, a male infant, called, in the Institution, Walter Wilding. Person appearing on the register, as adopting the child, Mrs. Jane

Anne Miller, widow, acting in this matter for her married sister, domiciled in Switzerland.' Patience!" resumed Oben-reizer, as Vendale, breaking loose from Bintrey, started to his feet. "I shall not keep the name concealed much longer. Two more little slips of paper, and I have done. Third proof! Certificate of Doctor Ganz, still living in practice at Neuchâtel, dated July, 1838. The doctor certifies (you shall read it for yourselves directly), first, that he attended the adopted child in its infant maladies; second, that, three months before the date of the certificate, the gentleman adopting the child as his son died; third, that *on* the date of the certificate, his widow and her maid, taking the adopted child with them, left Neuchâtel on their return to England. One more link now added to this, and my chain of evidence is complete. The maid remained with her mistress till her mistress's death, only a few years since. The maid can swear to the identity of the adopted infant, from his childhood to his youth—from his youth to his manhood, as he is now. There is her address in England—and there, Mr. Vendale, is the fourth, and final proof!"

"Why do you address yourself to *me?*" said Vendale, as Obenreizer threw the written address on the table.

Obenreizer turned on him, in a sudden frenzy of triumph.

"*Because you are the man!* If my niece marries you, she marries a bastard, brought up by public charity. If my niece marries you, she marries an impostor, without name or lineage, disguised in the character of a gentleman of rank and family."

"Bravo!" cried Bintrey. "Admirably put, Mr. Obenreizer! It only wants one word more to complete it. She marries—thanks entirely to your exertions—a man who inherits a handsome fortune, and a man whose origin will make him prouder than ever of his peasant-wife. George Vendale, as brother-executors, let us congratulate each other! Our dear dead friend's last wish on earth is accomplished. We have found the lost Walter Wilding. As Mr. Obenreizer said just now—you are the man!"

The words passed by Vendale unheeded. For the moment he was conscious of but one sensation; he heard but one voice. Marguerite's hand was clasping his. Marguerite's voice was whispering to him: "I never loved you, George, as I love you now!"

THE CURTAIN FALLS

May-day. There is merry-making in Cripple Corner, the chimneys smoke, the patriarchal dining-hall is hung with garlands, and Mrs. Goldstraw, the respected housekeeper, is very busy. For, on this bright morning the young master of Cripple Corner is married to its young mistress, far away: to wit, in the little town of Brieg, in Switzerland, lying at the foot of the Simplon Pass where she saved his life.

The bells ring gaily in the little town of Brieg, and flags are stretched across the street, and rifle shots are heard, and sounding music from brass instruments. Streamer-decorated casks of wine have been rolled out under a gay awning in the public way before the Inn, and there will be free feasting and revelry. What with bells and banners, draperies hanging from windows, explosion of gunpowder, and reverberation of brass music, the little town of Brieg is all in a flutter, like the hearts of its simple people.

It was a stormy night last night, and the mountains are covered with snow. But the sun is bright to-day, the sweet air is fresh, the tin spires of the little town of Brieg are burnished silver, and the Alps are ranges of far-off white cloud in a deep blue sky.

The primitive people of the little town of Brieg have built a greenwood arch across the street, under which the newly married pair shall pass in triumph from the church. It is inscribed, on that side, " HONOUR AND LOVE TO MARGUERITE VENDALE!" for the people are proud of her to enthusiasm. This greeting of the bride under her new name is affectionately meant as a surprise, and therefore the arrangement has been made that she, unconscious why, shall be taken to the church by a tortuous back way. A scheme not difficult to carry into execution in the crooked little town of Brieg.

So, all things are in readiness, and they are to go and come on foot. Assembled in the Inn's best chamber, festively adorned, are the bride and bridegroom, the Neuchâtel notary, the London lawyer, Madame Dor, and a certain large mysterious Englishman, popularly known as Monsieur Zhoé-Ladelle. And behold Madame Dor, arrayed in a spotless pair of gloves of her own, with no hand in the air, but both hands clasped round the neck of the bride ; to embrace whom Madame Dor has turned her broad back on the company, consistent to the last.

"Forgive me, my beautiful," pleads Madame Dor, "for that I ever was his she-cat!"

"She-cat, Madame Dor?"

"Engaged to sit watching my so-charming mouse," are the explanatory words of Madame Dor, delivered with a penitential sob.

"Why, you were our best friend! George, dearest, tell Madame Dor. Was she not our best friend?"

"Undoubtedly, darling. What should we have done without her?"

"You are both so generous," cries Madame Dor, accepting consolation, and immediately relapsing. "But I commenced as a she-cat."

"Ah! But like the cat in the fairy-story, good Madame Dor," says Vendale, saluting her cheek, "you were a true woman. And, being a true woman, the sympathy of your heart was with true love."

"I don't wish to deprive Madame Dor of her share in the embraces that are going on," Mr. Bintrey puts in, watch in hand, "and I don't presume to offer any objection to your having got yourselves mixed together, in the corner there, like the three Graces. I merely remark that I think it's time we were moving. What are *your* sentiments on that subject, Mr. Ladle?"

"Clear, Sir," replies Joey, with a gracious grin. "I'm clearer altogether, Sir, for having lived so many weeks upon the surface. I never was half so long upon the surface afore, and it's done me a power of good. At Cripple Corner, I was too much below it. Atop of the Simpleton, I was a deal too high above it. I've found the medium here, Sir. And if ever I take it in convivial, in all the rest of my days, I mean to do it this day, to the toast of 'Bless 'em both.'"

"I, too!" says Bintrey. "And now, Monsieur Voigt, let you and me be two men of Marseilles, and allons, marchons, arm-in-arm!"

They go down to the door, where others are waiting for them, and they go quietly to the church, and the happy marriage takes place. While the ceremony is yet in progress, the notary is called out. When it is finished, he has returned, is standing behind Vendale, and touches him on the shoulder.

"Go to the side door, one moment, Monsieur Vendale. Alone. Leave Madame to me."

At the side door of the church, are the same two men from the Hospice. They are snow-stained and travel-worn. They wish him joy, and then each lays his broad hand upon Vendale's breast, and one says in a low voice, while the other steadfastly regards him: .

"It is here, Monsieur. Your litter. The very same."

"My litter is here? Why?"

"Hush! For the sake of Madame. Your companion of that day——"

"What of him?"

The man looks at his comrade, and his comrade takes him up. Each keeps his hand laid earnestly on Vendale's breast.

"He had been living at the first Refuge, Monsieur, for some days. The weather was now good, now bad."

"Yes?"

"He arrived at our Hospice the day before yesterday, and, having refreshed himself with sleep on the floor before the fire, wrapped in his cloak, was resolute to go on, before dark, to the next Hospice. He had a great fear of that part of the way, and thought it would be worse to-morrow."

"Yes?"

"He went on alone. He had passed the gallery when an avalanche—like that which fell behind you near the Bridge of the Ganther——"

"Killed him?"

"We dug him out, suffocated and broken all to pieces! But, Monsieur, as to Madame. We have brought him here on the litter, to be buried. We must ascend the street outside. Madame must not see. It would be an accursed thing to bring the litter through the arch across the street, until Madame has passed through. As you descend, we who accompany the litter will set it down on the stones of the street the second to the right, and will stand before it. But do not let Madame turn her head towards the street the second to the right. There is no time to lose. Madame will be alarmed by your absence. Adieu!"

Vendale returns to his bride, and draws her hand through his unmaimed arm. A pretty procession awaits them at the main door of the church. They take their station in it, and descend the street amidst the ringing of the bells, the firing of the guns, the waving of the flags, the playing of the music, the shouts, the smiles, and tears, of the excited town. Heads are uncovered as she passes, hands are kissed to her, all the people bless her. "Heaven's benediction on the dear girl! See where she goes in her youth and beauty; she who so nobly saved his life!"

Near the corner of the street the second to the right, he speaks to her, and calls her attention to the windows on the opposite side. The corner well passed, he says: "Do not look round, my darling, for a reason that I have," and turns his head. Then, looking back along the street, he sees the litter and its bearers passing up alone under the arch, as he and she and their marriage train go down towards the shining valley.

THE LAZY TOUR OF TWO IDLE APPRENTICES

[Written in collaboration with WILKIE COLLINS*]*

CHARACTERS

ELLEN, *a fair, flaxen-haired, large-eyed girl; the victim in the story of the Bride's Chamber.*

MR. FRANCIS GOODCHILD, *a laboriously idle fellow.*

MR. ARTHUR HOLLIDAY, *a reckless, rattle-pated, open-hearted young gentleman.*

MR. THOMAS IDLE, *a passive, consistent, born-and-bred idler.*

THE INNKEEPER, *a fine specimen of a north-countryman.*

THE LANDLORD of '*The Two Robins Inn*'.

MR. LORN, *Dr. Speddie's assistant.*

THE ONE OLD MAN, *a cadaverous old man of measured speech, who narrates the story of the Bride's Chamber.*

DR. SPEDDIE, *a tall, thin, large-boned country doctor.*

THE LAZY TOUR OF TWO IDLE APPRENTICES

CHAPTER I

IN the autumn month of September, eighteen hundred and
fifty-seven, wherein these presents bear date, two idle apprentices, exhausted by the long, hot summer, and the long, hot
work it had brought with it, ran away from their employer.
They were bound to a highly meritorious lady (named
Literature), of fair credit and repute, though, it must be
acknowledged, not quite so highly esteemed in the City as
she might be. This is the more remarkable, as there is
nothing against the respectable lady in that quarter, but
quite the contrary; her family having rendered eminent
service to many famous citizens of London. It may be
sufficient to name Sir William Walworth, Lord Mayor under
King Richard II., at the time of Wat Tyler's insurrection,
and Sir Richard Whittington : which latter distinguished
man and magistrate was doubtless indebted to the lady's
family for the gift of his celebrated cat. There is also strong
reason to suppose that they rang the Highgate bells for him
with their own hands.

The misguided young men who thus shirked their duty to
the mistress from whom they had received many favours,
were actuated by the low idea of making a perfectly idle trip,
in any direction. They had no intention of going anywhere
in particular; they wanted to see nothing, they wanted to
know nothing, they wanted to learn nothing, they wanted to

do nothing. They wanted only to be idle. They took to themselves (after HOGARTH), the names of Mr. Thomas Idle and Mr. Francis Goodchild; but there was not a moral pin to choose between them, and they were both idle in the last degree.

Between Francis and Thomas, however, there was this difference of character: Goodchild was laboriously idle, and would take upon himself any amount of pains and labour to assure himself that he was idle; in short, had no better idea of idleness than that it was useless industry. Thomas Idle, on the other hand, was an idler of the unmixed Irish or Neapolitan type; a passive idler, a born-and-bred idler, a consistent idler, who practised what he would have preached if he had not been too idle to preach; a one entire and perfect chrysolite of idleness.

The two idle apprentices found themselves, within a few hours of their escape, walking down into the North of England, that is to say, Thomas was lying in a meadow, looking at the railway trains as they passed over a distant viaduct—which was *his* idea of walking down into the North; while Francis was walking a mile due South against time—which was *his* idea of walking down into the North. In the meantime the day waned, and the milestones remained unconquered.

" Tom," said Goodchild, " the sun is getting low. Up, and let us go forward !"

" Nay," quoth Thomas Idle, "I have not done with Annie Laurie yet." And he proceeded with that idle but popular ballad, to the effect that for the bonnie young person of that name he would "lay him doon and dee"—equivalent, in prose, to lay him down and die.

" What an ass that fellow was !" cried Goodchild, with the bitter emphasis of contempt.

" Which fellow ?" asked Thomas Idle.

" The fellow in your song. Lay him doon and dee ! Finely he'd show off before the girl by doing *that*. A sniveller ! Why couldn't he get up, and punch somebody's head !"

" Whose ?" asked Thomas Idle.

" Anybody's. Everybody's would be better than nobody's ! If I fell into that state of mind about a girl, do you think I'd lay me doon and dee? No, Sir." proceeded Goodchild, with a disparaging assumption of the Scottish accent, "I'd get me oop and peetch into somebody. Wouldn't you?"

"I wouldn't have anything to do with her," yawned Thomas Idle. "Why should I take the trouble?"

"It's no trouble, Tom, to fall in love," said Goodchild, shaking his head.

"It's trouble enough to fall out of it, once you're in it," retorted Tom. "So I keep out of it altogether. It would be better for you, if you did the same."

Mr. Goodchild, who is always in love with somebody, and not unfrequently with several objects at once, made no reply. He heaved a sigh of the kind which is termed by the lower orders "a bellowser," and then, heaving Mr. Idle on his feet (who was not half so heavy as the sigh), urged him northward.

These two had sent their personal baggage on by train: only retaining each a knapsack. Idle now applied himself to constantly regretting the train, to tracking it through the intricacies of Bradshaw's Guide, and finding out where it is now—and where now—and where now—and to asking what was the use of walking, when you could ride at such a pace as that. Was it to see the country? If that was the object, look at it out of the carriage windows. There was a great deal more of it to be seen there than here. Besides, who wanted to see the country? Nobody. And again, whoever did walk? Nobody. Fellows set off to walk, but they never did it. They came back and said they did, but they didn't. Then why should he walk? He wouldn't walk. He swore it by this milestone!

It was the fifth from London, so far had they penetrated into the North. Submitting to the powerful chain of argument, Goodchild proposed a return to the Metropolis, and a falling back upon Euston Square Terminus. Thomas assented with alacrity, and so they walked down into the North by the next morning's express, and carried their knapsacks in the luggage-van.

It was like all other expresses, as every express is and must be. It bore through the harvest country a smell like a large washing-day, and a sharp issue of steam as from a huge brazen tea-urn. The greatest power in nature and art combined, it yet glided over dangerous heights in the sight of people looking up from fields and roads, as smoothly and unreally as a light miniature plaything. Now, the engine shrieked in hysterics of such intensity, that it seemed desirable that the men who had her in charge should hold her feet, slap her hands, and bring her to; now, burrowed into tunnels with a stubborn and undemonstrative energy so confusing that the train seemed to be flying back into leagues of darkness. Here, were station after station, swallowed up by the express without stopping; here, stations where it fired itself in like a volley of cannon-balls, swooped away four country-people with nosegays, and three men of business with portmanteaus, and fired itself off again, bang, bang, bang! At long intervals were uncomfortable refreshment-rooms, made more uncomfortable by the scorn of Beauty towards Beast, the public (but to whom she never relented, as Beauty did in the story, towards the other Beast), and where sensitive stomachs were fed, with a contemptuous sharpness occasioning indigestion. Here, again, were stations with nothing going but a bell, and wonderful wooden razors set aloft on great posts, shaving the air. In these fields, the horses, sheep, and cattle were well used to the thundering meteor, and didn't mind; in those, they were all set scampering together, and a herd of pigs scoured after them. The pastoral country darkened, became coaly, became smoky, became infernal, got better, got worse, improved again, grew rugged, turned romantic; was a wood, a stream, a chain of hills, a gorge, a moor, a cathedral town, a fortified place, a waste. Now, miserable black dwellings, a black canal, and sick black towers of chimneys; now, a trim garden, where the flowers were bright and fair; now, a wilderness of hideous altars all ablaze; now, the water meadows with their fairy rings; now, the mangy patch of unlet building ground outside the stagnant town, with the larger ring where the Circus was last week. The temperature changed, the dialect changed, the people changed, faces got sharper, manner got shorter, eyes got shrewder and harder; yet all so quickly, that the spruce guard in the London uniform and silver lace, had not yet rumpled his shirt-collar, delivered half the dispatches in his shiny little pouch, or read his newspaper.

Carlisle! Idle and Goodchild had got to Carlisle. It looked congenially and delightfully idle. Something in the way of public amusement had happened last month, and something else was going to happen before Christmas; and, in the meantime there was a lecture on India for those who liked it—which Idle and Goodchild did not. Likewise, by those who liked them, there were impressions to be bought of all the vapid prints, going and gone, and of nearly all the

vapid books. For those who wanted to put anything in missionary boxes, here were the boxes. For those who wanted
the Reverend Mr. Podgers (artist's proofs, thirty shillings),
here was Mr. Podgers to any amount. Not less gracious and
abundant, Mr. Codgers also of the vineyard, but opposed to
Mr. Podgers, brotherly tooth and nail. Here, were guide-
books to the neighbouring antiquities, and eke the Lake
country, in several dry and husky sorts; here, many physically
and morally impossible heads of both sexes, for young ladies
to copy, in the exercise of the art of drawing; here, further,
a large impression of Mr. SPURGEON, solid as to the flesh, not
to say even something gross. The working young men of
Carlisle were drawn up, with their hands in their pockets,
across the pavements, four and six abreast, and appeared
(much to the satisfaction of Mr. Idle) to have nothing else to
do. The working and growing young women of Carlisle,
from the age of twelve upwards, promenaded the streets in
the cool of the evening, and rallied the said young men.
Sometimes the young men rallied the young women, as in
the case of a group gathered round an accordion-player, from
among whom a young man advanced behind a young woman
for whom he appeared to have a tenderness, and hinted to
her that he was there and playful, by giving her (he wore
clogs) a kick.

On market morning, Carlisle woke up amazingly, and became (to the two Idle Apprentices) disagreeably and reproachfully busy. There were its cattle market, its sheep market,
and its pig market down by the river, with raw-boned and
shock-headed Rob Roys hiding their Lowland dresses beneath heavy plaids, prowling in and out among the animals,
and flavouring the air with fumes of whiskey. There was
its corn market down the main street, with hum of chaffering over open sacks. There was its general market in
the street too, with heather brooms on which the purple
flower still flourished, and heather baskets primitive and
fresh to behold. With women trying on clogs and caps at
open stalls, and "Bible stalls" adjoining. With "Doctor
Mantle's Dispensary for the cure of all Human Maladies and
no charge for advice," and with Doctor Mantle's "Laboratory
of Medical, Chemical, and Botanical Science"—both healing
institutions established on one pair of trestles, one board, and
one sun-blind. With the renowned phrenologist from
London, begging to be favoured (at sixpence each) with the

company of clients of both sexes, to whom, on examination of their heads, he would make revelations "enabling him or her to know themselves." Through all these bargains and blessings, the recruiting-sergeant watchfully elbowed his way, a thread of War in the peaceful skein. Likewise on the walls were printed hints that the Oxford Blues might not be indisposed to hear of a few fine active young men ; and that whereas the standard of that distinguished corps is full six feet, " growing lads of five feet eleven " need not absolutely despair of being accepted.

Scenting the morning air more pleasantly than the buried majesty of Denmark did, Messrs. Idle and Goodchild rode away from Carlisle at eight o'clock one forenoon, bound for the village of Hesket, Newmarket, some fourteen miles distant. Goodchild (who had already begun to doubt whether he was idle: as his way always is when he has nothing to do) had read of a certain black old Cumberland hill or mountain, called Carrock, or Carrock Fell ; and had arrived at the conclusion that it would be the culminating triumph of Idleness to ascend the same. Thomas Idle, dwelling on the pains inseparable from that achievement, had expressed the strongest doubts of the expediency, and even of the sanity, of the enterprise ; but Goodchild had carried his point, and they rode away.

Up hill and down hill, and twisting to the right, and twisting to the left, and with old Skiddaw (who has vaunted himself a great deal more than his merits deserve ; but that is rather the way of the Lake country), dodging the apprentices in a picturesque and pleasant manner. Good, weatherproof, warm, pleasant houses, well white-limed, scantily dotting the road. Clean children coming out to look, carrying other clean children as big as themselves. Harvest still lying out and much rained upon ; here and there, harvest still unreaped. Well-cultivated gardens attached to the cottages, with plenty of produce forced out of their hard soil. Lonely nooks, and wild ; but people can be born, and married, and buried in such nooks, and can live and love, and be loved, there as elsewhere, thank God ! (Mr. Goodchild's remark.) By-and-by, the village. Black, coarse-stoned, rough-windowed houses ; some with outer staircases, like Swiss houses ; a sinuous and stony gutter winding up hill and round the corner, by way of street. All the children running out directly. Women pausing in washing, to peep from doorways and very little windows. Such were the observations of Messrs. Idle and Goodchild, as their conveyance stopped at the village shoemaker's. Old Carrock gloomed down upon it all in a very ill-tempered state ; and rain was beginning.

The village shoemaker declined to have anything to do with Carrock. No visitors went up Carrock. No visitors came there at all. Aa' the world ganged awa' yon. The driver appealed to the Innkeeper. The Innkeeper had two men working in the fields, and one of them should be called in, to go up Carrock as guide. Messrs. Idle and Goodchild, highly approving, entered the Innkeeper's house, to drink whiskey and eat oatcake.

The Innkeeper was not idle enough—was not idle at all, which was a great fault in him—but was a fine specimen of a north-countryman, or any kind of man. He had a ruddy cheek, a bright eye, a well-knit frame, an immense hand, a cheery outspeaking voice, and a straight, bright, broad look. He had a drawing-room, too, upstairs, which was worth a visit to the Cumberland Fells. (This was Mr. Francis Goodchild's opinion, in which Mr. Thomas Idle did not concur.)

The ceiling of this drawing-room was so crossed and recrossed by beams of unequal lengths, radiating from a centre, in a corner, that it looked like a broken star-fish. The room was comfortably and solidly furnished with good mahogany and horsehair. It had a snug fireside, and a couple of well-curtained windows, looking out upon the wild country behind the house. What it most developed was, an unexpected taste for little ornaments and nick-nacks, of which it contained a most surprising number. They were not very various, consisting in great part of waxen babies with their limbs more or less mutilated, appealing on one leg to the parental affections from under little cupping glasses ; but, Uncle Tom was there, in crockery, receiving theological instructions from Miss Eva, who grew out of his side like a wen, in an exceedingly rough state of profile propagandism. Engravings of Mr. Hunt's country boy, before and after his pie, were on the wall, divided by a highly-coloured nautical piece, the subject of which had all her colours (and more) flying, and was making great way through a sea of a regular pattern, like a lady's collar. A benevolent, elderly gentleman of the last century, with a powdered head, kept guard, in oil and varnish, over a most perplexing piece of furniture

on a table; in appearance between a driving seat and an
angular knife-box, but, when opened, a musical instrument
of tinkling wires, exactly like David's harp packed for travelling.   Everything became a nick-nack in this curious room.
The copper tea-kettle, burnished up to the highest point of
glory, took his station on a stand of his own at the greatest
possible distance from the fireplace, and said: " By your
leave, not a kittle, but a bijou."   The Staffordshire-ware
butter-dish with the cover on, got upon a little round occasional table in a window, with a worked top, and announced
itself to the two chairs accidentally placed there, as an aid
to polite conversation, a graceful trifle in china to be chatted
over by callers, as they airily trifled away the visiting
moments of a butterfly existence, in that rugged old village
on the Cumberland Fells.   The very footstool could not keep
the floor, but got upon a sofa, and therefrom proclaimed
itself, in high relief of white and liver-coloured wool, a
favourite spaniel coiled up for repose.   Though, truly, in
spite of its bright glass eyes, the spaniel was the least successful assumption in the collection: being perfectly flat, and
dismally suggestive of a recent mistake in sitting down on
the part of some corpulent member of the family.

    There were books, too, in this room; books on the table,
books on the chimneypiece, books in an open press in the
corner.   Fielding was there, and Smollett was there, and
Steele and Addison were there, in dispersed volumes; and
there were tales of those who go down to the sea in ships,
for windy nights; and there was really a choice of good
books for rainy days or fine.   It was so very pleasant to see
these things in such a lonesome by-place—so very agreeable
to find these evidences of a taste, however homely, that went
beyond the beautiful cleanliness and trimness of the house—so
fanciful to imagine what a wonder the room must be to the
little children born in the gloomy village—what grand impressions of it those of them who became wanderers over
the earth would carry away; and how, at distant ends of the
world, some old voyagers would die, cherishing the belief that
the finest apartment known to men was once in the Hesket-
Newmarket Inn, in rare old Cumberland—it was such a charmingly lazy pursuit to entertain these rambling thoughts over
the choice oatcake and the genial whiskey, that Mr. Idle and
Mr. Goodchild never asked themselves how it came to pass
that the men in the fields were never heard of more, how

the stalwart landlord replaced them without explanation, how his dog-cart came to be waiting at the door, and how everything was arranged without the least arrangement for climbing to old Carrock's shoulders, and standing on his head.

Without a word of inquiry, therefore, the Two Idle Apprentices drifted out resignedly into a fine, soft, close, drowsy, penetrating rain; got into the landlord's light dog-cart, and rattled off through the village for the foot of Carrock. The journey at the outset was not remarkable. The Cumberland road went up and down like all other roads; the Cumberland curs burst out from backs of cottages and barked like other curs, and the Cumberland peasantry stared after the dog-cart amazedly, as long as it was in sight, like the rest of their race. The approach to the foot of the mountain resembled the approaches to the feet of most other mountains all over the world. The cultivation gradually ceased, the trees grew gradually rare, the road became gradually rougher, and the sides of the mountain looked gradually more and more lofty, and more and more difficult to get up. The dog-cart was left at a lonely farm-house. The landlord borrowed a large umbrella, and, assuming in an instant the character of the most cheerful and adventurous of guides, led the way to the ascent. Mr. Goodchild looked eagerly at the top of the mountain, and, feeling apparently that he was now going to be very lazy indeed, shone all over wonderfully to the eye, under the influence of the contentment within and the moisture without. Only in the bosom of Mr. Thomas Idle did Despondency now hold her gloomy state. He kept it a secret; but he would have given a very handsome sum, when the ascent began, to have been back again at the inn. The sides of Carrock looked fearfully steep, and the top of Carrock was hidden in mist. The rain was falling faster and faster. The knees of Mr. Idle—always weak on walking excursions—shivered and shook with fear and damp. The wet was already penetrating through the young man's outer coat to a brand-new shooting-jacket, for which he had reluctantly paid the large sum of two guineas on leaving town; he had no stimulating refreshment about him but a small packet of clammy gingerbread nuts; he had nobody to give him an arm, nobody to push him gently behind, nobody to pull him up tenderly in front, nobody to speak to who really felt the difficulties of the ascent, the dampness of the rain, the denseness of the mist, and the unutterable folly of

climbing, undriven, up any steep place in the world, when
there is level ground within reach to walk on instead. Was
it for this that Thomas had left London? London, where
there are nice short walks in level public gardens, with benches
of repose set up at convenient distances for weary travellers
—London, where rugg d stone is humanely pounded into little
lumps for the road, and intelligently shaped into smooth slabs
for the pavement! No! it was not for the laborious ascent
of the crags of Carrock that Idle had left his native city,
and travelled to Cumberland. Never did he feel more
disastrously convinced that he had committed a very grave
error in judgment than when he found himself standing in
the rain at the bottom of a steep mountain, and knew that
the responsibility rested on his weak shoulders of actually
getting to the top of it.

The honest landlord went first, the beaming Goodchild
followed, the mournful Idle brought up the rear. From time
to time, the two foremost members of the expedition changed
places in the order of march; but the rearguard never altered
his position. Up the mountain or down the mountain, in
the water or out of it. over the rocks, through the bogs,
skirting the heather, Mr. Thomas Idle was always the last,
and was always the man who had to be looked after and
waited for. At first the ascent was delusively easy. the sides
of the mountain sloped gradually. and the material of which
they were composed was a soft spongy turf, very tender and
pleasant to walk upon. After a hundred yards or so. however, the verdant scene and the easy slope disappeared, and
the rocks began. Not noble, massive rocks, standing upright,
keeping a c rtain regularity in their positions, and possessing,
now and then, flat tops to sit upon, but little irritating, comfortless rocks, littered about anyhow by Nature; treacherous,
disheartening rocks of all sorts of small shapes and small
sizes, bruisers of tender toes and trippers-up of wavering feet.
When these impediments were passed, heather and slough
followed. Here the steepness of the ascent was slightly
mitigated; and here the exploring party of three turned
roun l to look at the view below them. The scene of the
moorland and the fields was like a feeble water-colour drawing
half sponged out. The mist was darkening, the rain was
thickening, the trees were dotted about like spots of faint
shadow, the division-lines which mapped out the fields were
all getting blurred together, and the lonely farm-house where

the dog-cart had been left, loomed spectral in the grey light like the last human dwelling at the end of the habitable world. Was this a sight worth climbing to see? Surely—surely not!

Up again—for the top of Carrock is not reached yet. The landlord, just as good-tempered and obliging as he was at the bottom of the mountain. Mr. Goodchild brighter in the eyes and rosier in the face than ever; full of cheerful remarks ano apt quotations; and walking with a springiness of step wonderful to behold. Mr. Idle, farther and farther in the rear, with the water squeaking in the toes of his boots, with his two-guinea shooting-jacket clinging damply to his aching sides, with his overcoat so full of rain, and standing out so pyramidically stiff, in consequence, from his shoulders downwards, that he felt as if he was walking in a gigantic extinguisher—the despairing spirit within him representing but too aptly the candle that had just been put out. Up and up and up again, till a ridge is reached and the outer edge of the mist on the summit of Carrock is darkly and drizzingly near. Is this the top? No, nothing like the top. It is an aggravating peculiarity of all mountains, that, although they have only one top when they are seen (as they ought always to be seen) from below, they turn out to have a perfect eruption of false tops whenever the traveller is sufficiently ill-advised to go out of his way for the purpose of ascending them. Carrock is but a trumpery little mountain of fifteen hundred feet, and it presumes to have false tops, and even precipices, as if it were Mont Blanc. No matter; Goodchild enjoys it, and will go on; and Idle, who is afraid of being left behind by himself, must follow. On entering the edge of the mist, the landlord stops, and says he hopes that it will not get any thicker. It is twenty years since he last ascended Carrock, and it is barely possible, if the mist increases, that the party may be lost on the mountain. Goodchild hears this dreadful intimation, and is not in the least impressed by it. He marches for the top that is never to be found, as if he was the Wandering Jew, bound to go on for ever, in defiance of everything. The landlord faithfully accompanies him. The two, to the dim eye of Idle, far below, look in the exaggerative mist, like a pair of friendly giants, mounting the steps of some invisible castle together. Up and up, and then down a little, and then up, and then along a strip of level ground, and then up again. The wind, a wind unknown in the happy valley, blows keen and strong; the rain-mist gets impenetrable; a dreary little cairn of stones appears. The landlord adds one to the heap, first walking all round the cairn as if he were about to perform an incantation, then dropping the stone on to the top of the heap with the gesture of a magician adding an ingredient to a cauldron in full bubble. Goodchild sits down by the cairn as if it was his study-table at home; Idle, drenched and panting, stands up with his back to the wind, ascertains distinctly that this is the top at last, looks round with all the little curiosity that is left in him, and gets, in return, a magnificent view of —Nothing!

The effect of this sublime spectacle on the minds of the exploring party is a little injured by the nature of the direct conclusion to which the sight of it points—the said conclusion being that the mountain mist has actually gathered round them, as the landlord feared it would. It now becomes imperatively necessary to settle the exact situation of the farm-house in the valley at which the dog-cart has been left, before the travellers attempt to descend. While the landlord is endeavouring to make this discovery in his own way, Mr. Goodchild plunges his hand under his wet coat, draws out a little red morocco-case, opens it, and displays to the view of his companions a neat pocket-compass. The north is found, the point at which the farm-house is situated is settled, and the descent begins. After a little downward walking, Idle (behind as usual) sees his fellow-travellers turn aside sharply—tries to follow them—loses them in the mist—is shouted after, waited for, recovered—and then finds that a halt has been ordered, partly on his account, partly for the purpose of again consulting the compass.

The point in debate is settled as before between Goodchild and the landlord, and the expedition moves on, not down the mountain, but marching straight forward round the slope of it. The difficulty of following this new route is acutely felt by Thomas Idle. He finds the hardship of walking at all greatly increased by the fatigue of moving his feet straight forward along the side of a slope, when their natural tendency, at every step, is to turn off at a right angle, and go straight down the declivity. Let the reader imagine himself to be walking along the roof of a barn, instead of up or down it, and he will have an exact idea of the pedestrian difficulty in which the travellers had now involved themselves. In ten minutes more Idle was lost in the distance again, was shouted for, waited for, recovered as before; found Goodchild repeating his observation of the compass, and remonstrated warmly against the sideway route that his companions persisted in following. It appeared to the uninstructed mind of Thomas that when three men want to get to the bottom of a mountain, their business is to walk down it; and he put this view of the case, not only with emphasis, but even with some irritability. He was answered from the scientific eminence of the compass on which his companions were mounted, that there was a frightful chasm somewhere near the foot of Carrock, called The Black Arches, into which the travellers were sure to march in the mist, if they risked continuing the descent from the place where they had now halted. Idle received this answer with the silent respect which was due to the commanders of the expedition, and followed along the roof of the barn, or rather the side of the mountain, reflecting upon the assurance which he received on starting again, that the object of the party was only to gain " a certain point," and, this haven attained, to continue the descent afterwards until the foot of Carrock was reached. Though quite unexceptionable as an abstract form of expression, the phrase " a certain point " has the disadvantage of sounding rather vaguely when it is pronounced on unknown ground, under a canopy of mist much thicker than a London fog. Nevertheless, after the compass, this phrase was all the clue the party had to hold by, and Idle clung to the extreme end of it as hopefully as he could.

More sideway walking, thicker and thicker mist, all sorts of points reached except the " certain point;" third loss of Idle, third shouts for him, third recovery of him, third consultation of compass. Mr. Goodchild draws it tenderly from his pocket, and prepares to adjust it on a stone. Something falls on the turf—it is the glass. Something else drops immediately after—it is the needle. The compass is broken, and the exploring party is lost!

It is the practice of the English portion of the human race to receive all great disasters in dead silence. Mr. Goodchild restored the useless compass to his pocket without saying a word, Mr. Idle looked at the landlord, and the landlord looked at Mr. Idle. There was nothing for it now but to go on blindfold, and trust to the chapter of chances. Accordingly, the lost travellers moved forward, still walking round the slope of the mountain, still desperately resolved to avoid the Black Arches, and to succeed in reaching the "certain point."

A quarter of an hour brought them to the brink of a ravine, at the bottom of which there flowed a muddy little stream. Here another halt was called, and another consultation took place. The landlord, still clinging pertinaciously to the idea of reaching the "point," voted for crossing the ravine, and going on round the slope of the mountain. Mr. Goodchild, to the great relief of his fellow-traveller, took another view of the case, and backed Mr. Idle's proposal to descend Carrock at once, at any hazard—the rather as the running stream was a sure guide to follow from the mountain to the valley. Accordingly, the party descended to the rugged and stony banks of the stream; and here again Thomas lost ground sadly, and fell far behind his travelling companions. Not much more than six weeks had elapsed since he had sprained one of his ankles, and he began to feel this same ankle getting rather weak when he found himself among the stones that were strewn about the running water. Goodchild and the landlord were getting farther and farther ahead of him. He saw them cross the stream and disappear round a projection on its banks. He heard them shout the moment after as a signal that they had halted and were waiting for him. Answering the shout, he mended his pace, crossed the stream where they had crossed it, and was within one step of the opposite bank, when his foot slipped on a wet stone, his weak ankle gave a twist outwards, a hot, rending, tearing pain ran through it at the same moment, and down fell the idlest of the Two Idle Apprentices, crippled in an instant.

The situation was now, in plain terms, one of absolute danger. There lay Mr. Idle writhing with pain, there was the mist as thick as ever, there was the landlord as completely lost as the strangers whom he was conducting, and there was the compass broken in Goodchild's pocket. To leave the wretched Thomas on unknown ground was plainly impossible; and to get him to walk with a badly sprained ankle seemed equally out of the question. However, Goodchild (brought back by his cry for help) bandaged the ankle with a pocket-handkerchief, and assisted by the landlord, raised the crippled Apprentice to his legs, offered him a shoulder to lean on, and exhorted him for the sake of the whole party to try if he could walk. Thomas, assisted by the shoulder on one side, and a stick on the other, did try, with what pain and difficulty those only can imagine who have sprained an ankle and have had to tread on it after-wards.   At a pace adapted to the feeble hobbling of a newly-lamed man, the lost party moved on, perfectly ignorant whether they were on the right side of the mountain or the wrong, and equally uncertain how long Idle would be able to contend with the pain in his ankle, before he gave in altogether and fell down again, unable to stir another step.

Slowly and more slowly, as the clog of crippled Thomas weighed heavily and more heavily on the march of the expe-dition, the lost travellers followed the windings of the stream, till they came to a faintly-marked cart-track, branching off nearly at right angles, to the left.   After a little consultation it was resolved to follow this dim vestige of a road in the hope that it might lead to some farm or cottage, at which Idle could be left in safety.   It was now getting on towards the afternoon, and it was fast becoming more than doubtful whether the party, delayed in their progress as they now were, might not be overtaken by the darkness before the right route was found, and be condemned to pass the night on the mountain, without bit or drop to comfort them, in their wet clothes.

The cart-track grew fainter and fainter, until it was washed out altogether by another little stream, dark, turbulent, and rapid.   The landlord suggested, judging by the colour of the water, that it must be flowing from one of the lead mines in the neighbourhood of Carrock ; and the travellers accordingly kept by the stream for a little while, in the hope of possibly wandering towards help in that way.   After walking forward about two hundred yards, they came upon a mine indeed, but a mine, exhausted and abandoned ; a dismal, ruinous place, with nothing but the wreck of its works and buildings left to speak for it.   Here, there were a few sheep feeding. The landlord looked at them earnestly, thought he recognised the marks on them—then thought he did not—finally gave up the sheep in despair—and walked on just as ignorant of the whereabouts of the party as ever.

The march in the dark, literally as well as metaphorically in the dark, had now been continued for three-quarters of an hour from the time when the crippled Apprentice had met with his accident.   Mr. Idle, with all the will to conquer the pain in his ankle, and to hobble on, found the power rapidly failing him, and felt that another ten minutes at most would find him at the end of his last physical resources. He had just made up his mind on this point, and was about to communicate the dismal result of his reflections to his companions, when the mist suddenly brightened, and begun to lift straight ahead. In another minute, the landlord, who was in advance, proclaimed that he saw a tree. Before long, other trees appeared—then a cottage—then a house beyond the cottage, and a familiar line of road rising behind it. Last of all, Carrock itself loomed darkly into view, far away to the right hand. The party had not only got down the mountain without knowing how, but had wandered away from it in the mist, without knowing why—away, far down on the very moor by which they had approached the base of Carrock that morning.

The happy lifting of the mist, and the still happier discovery that the travellers had groped their way, though by a very roundabout direction, to within a mile or so of the part of the valley in which the farm-house was situated, restored Mr. Idle's sinking spirits and reanimated his failing strength. While the landlord ran off to get the dog-cart, Thomas was assisted by Goodchild to the cottage which had been the first building seen when the darkness brightened, and was propped up against the garden wall, like an artist's lay figure waiting to be forwarded, until the dog-cart should arrive from the farm-house below. In due time—and a very long time it seemed to Mr. Idle—the rattle of wheels was heard, and the crippled Apprentice was lifted into the seat. As the dog-cart was driven back to the inn, the landlord related an anecdote which he had just heard at the farm-house, of an unhappy man who had been lost, like his two guests and himself, on Carrock; who had passed the night there alone; who had been found the next morning, "scared and starved;" and who never went out afterwards, except on his way to the grave. Mr. Idle heard this sad story, and derived at least one useful impression from it. Bad as the pain in his ankle was, he contrived to bear it patiently, for he felt grateful that a worse accident had not befallen him in the wilds of Carrock.

CHAPTER II

THE dog-cart, with Mr. Thomas Idle and his ankle on the
hanging seat behind, Mr. Francis Goodchild and the Innkeeper in front, and the rain in spouts and splashes everywhere, made the best of its way back to the little inn; the
broken moor country looking like miles upon miles of Pre-
Adamite sop, or the ruins of some enormous jorum of
antediluvian toast-and-water.   The trees dripped; the eaves
of the scattered cottages dripped; the barren stone walls
dividing the land, dripped; the yelping dogs dripped; carts
and waggons under ill-roofed penthouses, dripped; melancholy cocks and hens perching on their shafts, or seeking
shelter underneath them, dripped; Mr. Goodchild dripped;
Francis Idle dripped; the Innkeeper dripped; the mare
dripped; the vast curtains of mist and cloud passed before
the shadowy forms of the hills, streamed water as they were
drawn across the landscape.   Down such steep pitches that
the mare seemed to be trotting on her head, and up such
steep pitches that she seemed to have a supplementary leg in
her tail, the dog-cart jolted and tilted back to the village.
It was too wet for the women to look out, it was too wet
even for the children to look out; all the doors and windows
were closed, and the only sign of life or motion was in the
rain-punctured puddles.

Whiskey and oil to Thomas Idle's ankle, and whiskey
without oil to Francis Goodchild's stomach, produced an
agreeable change in the systems of both; soothing Mr. Idle's
pain, which was sharp before, and sweetening Mr. Goodchild's temper, which was sweet before.   Portmanteaus being
then opened and clothes changed, Mr. Goodchild, through
having no change of outer garments but broadcloth and
velvet, suddenly became a magnificent portent in the Innkeeper's house, a shining frontispiece to the fashions for the
month, and a frightful anomaly in the Cumberland village.

Greatly ashamed of his splendid appearance, the conscious
Goodchild quenched it as much as possible, in the shadow of

Thomas Idle's ankle, and in a corner of the little covered carriage that started with them for Wigton—a most desirable carriage for any country, except for its having a flat roof and no sides; which caused the plumps of rain accumulating on the roof to play vigorous games of bagatelle into the interior all the way, and to score immensely. It was comfortable to see how the people coming back in open carts from Wigton market made no more of the rain than if it were sunshine; how the Wigton policeman taking a country walk of half-a-dozen miles (apparently for pleasure), in resplendent uniform, accepted saturation as his normal state; how clerks and schoolmasters in black, loitered along the road without umbrellas, getting varnished at every step; how the Cumberland girls, coming out to look after the Cumberland cows, shook the rain from their eyelashes and laughed it away; and how the rain continued to fall upon all, as it only does fall in hill countries.

Wigton market was over, and its bare booths were smoking with rain all down the street. Mr. Thomas Idle, melodramatically carried to the inn's first floor, and laid upon three chairs (he should have had the sofa, if there had been one), Mr. Goodchild went to the window to take an observation of Wigton, and report what he saw to his disabled companion.

"Brother Francis, brother Francis," cried Thomas Idle. "What do you see from the turret?"

"I see," said Brother Francis, "what I hope and believe to be one of the most dismal places ever seen by eyes. I see the houses with their roofs of dull black, their stained fronts, and their dark-rimmed windows, looking as if they were all in mourning. As every little puff of wind comes down the street, I see a perfect train of rain let off along the wooden stalls in the market-place and exploded against me. I see a very big gas lamp in the centre which I know, by a secret instinct, will not be lighted to-night. I see a pump, with a trivet underneath its spout whereon to stand the vessels that are brought to be filled with water. I see a man come to pump, and he pumps very hard, but no water follows, and he strolls empty away."

"Brother Francis, brother Francis," cried Thomas Idle, "what more do you see from the turret, besides the man and the pump, and the trivet and the houses all in mourning and the rain?"

"I see," said Brother Francis, "one, two, three, four, five, linen-drapers' shops in front of me. I see a linen-draper's shop next door to the right—and there are five more linen-drapers' shops down the corner to the left. Eleven homicidal linen-drapers' shops within a short stone's throw, each with its hands at the throats of all the rest! Over the small first-floor of one of these linen-drapers' shops appears the wonderful inscription, BANK."

"Brother Francis, brother Francis," cried Thomas Idle. "what more do you see from the turret, besides the eleven homicidal linen-drapers' shops, and the wonderful inscription, 'Bank,' on the small first-floor, and the man and the pump and the trivet and the houses all in mourning and the rain?"

"I see," said Brother Francis, "the depository for Christian Knowledge, and through the dark vapour I think I again make out Mr. Spurgeon looming heavily. Her Majesty the Queen, God bless her, printed in colours, I am sure I see. I see the *Illustrated London News* of several years ago, and I see a sweetmeat shop—which the proprietor calls a 'Salt Warehouse'—with one small female child in a cotton bonnet looking in on tip-toe, oblivious of rain. And I see a watchmaker's with only three great pale watches of a dull metal hanging in his window, each in a separate pane."

"Brother Francis, brother Francis," cried Thomas Idle, "what more do you see of Wigton, besides these objects, and the man and the pump and the trivet and the houses all in mourning and the rain?"

"I see nothing more," said Brother Francis, "and there is nothing more to see, except the curlpaper bill of the theatre, which was opened and shut last week (the manager's family played all the parts), and the short, square, chinky omnibus that goes to the railway, and leads too rattling a life over the stones to hold together long. O yes! Now, I see two men with their hands in their pockets and their backs towards me."

"Brother Francis, brother Francis," cried Thomas Idle, "what do you make out from the turret, of the expression of the two men with their hands in their pockets and their backs towards you?"

"They are mysterious men," said Brother Francis, "with inscrutable backs. They keep their backs towards me with persistency. If one turns an inch in any direction, the other turns an inch in the same direction. and no more. They turn very stiffly, on a very little pivot, in the middle of the market-place. Their appearance is partly of a mining, partly of a ploughing, partly of a stable, character. They are looking at nothing—very hard. Their backs are slouched, and their legs are curved with much standing about. Their pockets are loose and dog's-eared, on account of their hands being always in them. They stand to be rained upon, without any movement of impatience or dissatisfaction, and they keep so close together that an elbow of each jostles an elbow of the other, but they never speak. They spit at times, but speak not. I see it growing darker and darker, and still I see them, sole visible population of the place, standing to be rained upon with their backs towards me, and looking at nothing very hard."

"Brother Francis, brother Francis," cried Thomas Idle, "before you draw down the blind of the turret and come in to have your head scorched by the hot gas, see if you can, and impart to me, something of the expression of those two amazing men."

"The murky shadows," said Francis Goodchild, "are gathering fast ; and the wings of evening, and the wings of coal, are folding over Wigton. Still, they look at nothing very hard, with their backs towards me. Ah! Now, they turn, and I see—— "

"Brother Francis, brother Francis," cried Thomas Idle, "tell me quickly what you see of the two men of Wigton !"

"I see," said Francis Goodchild, "that they have no expression at all. And now the town goes to sleep, undazzled by the large unlighted lamp in the market-place ; and let no man wake it."

At the close of the next day's journey, Mr. Thomas Idle's ankle became much swollen and inflamed. There are reasons which will presently explain themselves for not publicly indicating the exact direction in which that journey lay, or the place in which it ended. It was a long day's shaking of Thomas Idle over the rough roads, and a long day's getting out and going on before the horses, and fagging up hills, and scouring down hills, on the part of Mr. Goodchild, who in the fatigues of such labours congratulated himself on attaining a high point of idleness. It was at a little town, still in Cumberland, that they halted for the night—a very little town, with the purple and brown moor close upon its one street ; a curious little ancient market-cross set up in the midst of it; and the town itself looking much as if it were a collection of great stones piled on end by the Druids long ago, which a few recluse people had since hollowed out for habitations.

"Is there a doctor here?" asked Mr. Goodchild, on his knee, of the motherly landlady of the little Inn: stopping in his examination of Mr. Idle's ankle, with the aid of a candle.

"Ey, my word!" said the landlady, glancing doubtfully at the ankle for herself; "there's Doctor Speddie."

"Is he a good Doctor?"

"Ey!" said the landlady, "I ca' him so. A' cooms efther nae doctor that I ken. Mair nor which, a's just THE doctor heer."

"Do you think he is at home?"

Her reply was, "Gang awa', Jock, and bring him."

Jock, a white-headed boy, who, under pretence of stirring up some bay salt in a basin of water for the laving of this unfortunate ankle, had greatly enjoyed himself for the last ten minutes in splashing the carpet, set off promptly. A very few minutes had elapsed when he showed the Doctor in, by tumbling against the door before him and bursting it open with his head.

"Gently, Jock, gently," said the Doctor as he advanced with a quiet step. "Gentlemen, a good evening. I am sorry that my presence is required here. A slight accident, I hope? A slip and a fall? Yes, yes, yes. Carrock, indeed? Hah! Does that pain you, Sir? No doubt, it does. It is the great connecting ligament here, you see, that has been badly strained. Time and rest, Sir! They are often the recipe in greater cases," with a slight sigh, "and often the recipe in small. I can send a lotion to relieve you, but we must leave the cure to time and rest."

This he said, holding Idle's foot on his knee between his two hands, as he sat over against him. He had touched it tenderly and skilfully in explanation of what he said, and, when his careful examination was completed, softly returned it to its former horizontal position on a chair.

He spoke with a little irresolution whenever he began, but afterwards fluently. He was a tall, thin, large-boned, old gentleman, with an appearance at first sight of being hard-featured; but, at a second glance, the mild expression of his face and some particular touches of sweetness and patience about his mouth, corrected this impression and assigned his long professional rides, by day and night, in the bleak hill-weather, as the true cause of that appearance. He stooped very little, though past seventy and very grey. His dress was more like that of a clergyman than a country doctor, being a plain black suit, and a plain white neck-kerchief tied behind like a band. His black was the worse for wear, and there were darns in his coat, and his linen was a little frayed at the hems and edges. He might have been poor—it was likely enough in that out-of-the-way spot—or he might have been a little self-forgetful and eccentric. Any one could have seen directly, that he had neither wife nor child at home. He had a scholarly air with him, and that kind of considerate humanity towards others which claimed a gentle consideration for himself. Mr. Goodchild made this study of him while he was examining the limb, and as he laid it down. Mr. Goodchild wishes to add that he considers it a very good likeness.

It came out in the course of a little conversation, that Doctor Speddie was acquainted with some friends of Thomas Idle's, and had, when a young man, passed some years in Thomas Idle's birthplace on the other side of England. Certain idle labours, the fruit of Mr. Goodchild's apprenticeship, also happened to be well known to him. The lazy travellers were thus placed on a more intimate footing with the Doctor than the casual circumstances of the meeting would of themselves have established ; and when Doctor Speddie rose to go home, remarking that he would send his assistant with the lotion, Francis Goodchild said that was unnecessary, for, by the Doctor's leave, he would accompany him, and bring it back. (Having done nothing to fatigue himself for a full quarter of an hour, Francis began to fear that he was not in a state of idleness.)

Doctor Speddie politely assented to the proposition of Francis Goodchild, "as it would give him the pleasure of enjoying a few more minutes of Mr. Goodchild's society than he could otherwise have hoped for," and they went out together into the village street. The rain had nearly ceased, the clouds had broken before a cool wind from the north-east, and stars were shining from the peaceful heights beyond them.

Doctor Speddie's house was the last house in the place. Beyond it, lay the moor, all dark and lonesome. The wind moaned in a low, dull, shivering manner round the little garden, like a houseless creature that knew the winter was coming. It was exceedingly wild and solitary. "Roses," said the Doctor, when Goodchild touched some wet leaves overhanging the stone porch ; "but they get cut to pieces."

The Doctor opened the door with a key he carried, and led the way into a low but pretty ample hall with rooms on either side. The door of one of these stood open, and the Doctor entered it, with a word of welcome to his guest. It, too, was a low room, half surgery and half parlour, with shelves of books and bottles against the walls, which were of a very dark hue. There was a fire in the grate, the night being damp and chill. Leaning against the chimneypiece looking down into it, stood the Doctor's Assistant.

A man of a most remarkable appearance. Much older than Mr. Goodchild had expected, for he was at least two-and-fifty ; but, that was nothing. What was startling in him was his remarkable paleness. His large black eyes, his sunken cheeks, his long and heavy iron-grey hair, his wasted hands, and even the attenuation of his figure, were at first forgotten in his extraordinary pallor. There was no vestige of colour in the man. When he turned his face, Francis Goodchild started as if a stone figure had looked round at him.

"Mr. Lorn," said the Doctor. "Mr. Goodchild."

The Assistant, in a distraught way—as if he had forgotten something—as if he had forgotten everything, even to his own name and himself—acknowledged the visitor's presence, and stepped further back into the shadow of the wall behind him. But, he was so pale that his face stood out in relief against the dark wall, and really could not be hidden so.

"Mr. Goodchild's friend has met with an accident, Lorn," said Doctor Speddie. "We want the lotion for a bad sprain."

A pause.

"My dear fellow, you are more than usually absent to-night. The lotion for a bad sprain."

"Ah! yes! Directly."

He was evidently relieved to turn away, and to take his white face and his wild eyes to a table in a recess among the bottles. But, though he stood there, compounding the lotion with his back towards them, Goodchild could not, for many moments, withdraw his gaze from the man. When he at length did so, he found the Doctor observing him, with some trouble in his face. "He is absent," explained the Doctor, in a low voice. "Always absent. Very absent."

"Is he ill?"

"No, not ill."

"Unhappy?"

"I have my suspicions that he was," assented the Doctor, "once."

Francis Goodchild could not but observe that the Doctor accompanied these words with a benignant and protecting glance at their subject, in which there was much of the expression with which an attached father might have looked at a heavily afflicted son. Yet, that they were not father and son must have been plain to most eyes. The Assistant, on the other hand, turning presently to ask the Doctor some question, looked at him with a wan smile as if he were his whole reliance and sustainment in life.

It was in vain for the Doctor in his easy-chair, to try to lead the mind of Mr. Goodchild in the opposite easy-chair, away from what was before him. Let Mr. Goodchild do what he would to follow the Doctor, his eyes and thoughts reverted to the Assistant. The Doctor soon perceived it, and, after falling silent, and musing in a little perplexity, said:

"Lorn!"

"My dear Doctor."

"Would you go to the Inn, and apply that lotion? You will show the best way of applying it, far better than Mr. Goodchild can."

"With pleasure."

The Assistant took his hat, and passed like a shadow to the door.

"Lorn!" said the Doctor, calling after him.

He returned.

"Mr. Goodchild will keep me company till you come home. Don't hurry. Excuse my calling you back."

"It is not," said the Assistant, with his former smile, "the first time you have called me back, dear Doctor." With those words he went away.

"Mr. Goodchild," said Doctor Speddie, in a low voice, and with his former troubled expression of face, "I have seen that your attention has been concentrated on my friend."

"He fascinates me. I must apologise to you, but he has quite bewildered and mastered me."

"I find that a lonely existence and a long secret," said the Doctor, drawing his chair a little nearer to Mr. Goodchild's, "become in the course of time very heavy. I will tell you something. You may make what use you will of it, under fictitious names. I know I may trust you. I am the more inclined to confidence to-night, through having been unexpectedly led back, by the current of our conversation at the Inn, to scenes in my early life. Will you please to draw a little nearer?"

Mr. Goodchild drew a little nearer, and the Doctor went on thus: speaking, for the most part, in so cautious a voice, that the wind, though it was far from high, occasionally got the better of him.

When this present nineteenth century was younger by a good many years than it is now, a certain friend of mine, named Arthur Holliday, happened to arrive in the town of Doncaster, exactly in the middle of a race-week, or, in other words, in the middle of the month of September. He was one of those reckless, rattle-pated, open-hearted, and open-mouthed young gentlemen, who possess the gift of familiarity in its highest perfection, and who scramble carelessly along the journey of life making friends, as the phrase is, wherever they go. His father was a rich manufacturer, and had bought landed property enough in one of the midland counties to make all the born squires in his neighbourhood thoroughly envious of him. Arthur was his only son, possessor in prospect of the great estate and the great business after his father's death; well supplied with money, and not too rigidly looked after, during his father's lifetime. Report, or scandal, whichever you please, said that the old gentleman had been rather wild in his youthful days, and that, unlike most parents, he was not disposed to be violently indignant when he found that his son took after him. This may be true or not. I myself only knew the elder Mr. Holliday when he was getting on in years; and then he was as quiet and as respectable a gentleman as ever I met with.

Well, one September, as I told you, young Arthur comes to Doncaster, having decided all of a sudden, in his hare-brained way, that he would go to the races. He did not reach the town till towards the close of the evening, and he went at once to see about his dinner and bed at the principal hotel. Dinner they were ready enough to give him; but as for a bed, they laughed when he mentioned it. In the race-week at Doncaster, it is no uncommon thing for

visitors who have not bespoken apartments, to pass the night
in their carriages at the inn doors. As for the lower sort of
strangers, I myself have often seen them, at that full time,
sleeping out on the doorsteps for want of a covered place to
creep under. Rich as he was, Arthur's chance of getting
a night's lodging (seeing that he had not written beforehand
to secure one) was more than doubtful. He tried the second
hotel, and the third hotel, and two of the inferior inns after
that; and was met everywhere by the same form of answer.
No accommodation for the night of any sort was left. All
the bright golden sovereigns in his pocket would not buy
him a bed at Doncaster in the race-week.

To a young fellow of Arthur's temperament, the novelty of
being turned away into the street, like a penniless vagabond,
at every house where he asked for a lodging, presented itself
in the light of a new and highly amusing piece of experience.
He went on, with his carpet-bag in his hand, applying for a
bed at every place of entertainment for travellers that he
could find in Doncaster, until he wandered into the outskirts
of the town. By this time, the last glimmer of twilight had
faded out, the moon was rising dimly in a mist, the wind
was getting cold, the clouds were gathering heavily, and
there was every prospect that it was soon going to rain.

The look of the night had rather a lowering effect on
young Holliday's good spirits. He began to contemplate the
houseless situation in which he was placed, from the serious
rather than the humorous point of view; and he looked
about him, for another public-house to inquire at, with something very like downright anxiety in his mind on the subject
of a lodging for the night. The suburban part of the town
towards which he had now strayed was hardly lighted at all,
and he could see nothing of the houses as he passed them,
except that they got progressively smaller and dirtier, the
farther he went. Down the winding road before him shone
the dull gleam of an oil lamp, the one faint, lonely light that
struggled ineffectually with the foggy darkness all round
him. He resolved to go on as far as this lamp, and then,
if it showed him nothing in the shape of an Inn, to return
to the central part of the town and to try if he could not
at least secure a chair to sit down on, through the night, at
one of the principal Hotels.

As he got near the lamp, he heard voices; and, walking
close under it, found that it lighted the entrance to a narrow

court, on the wall of which was painted a long hand in faded flesh-colour, pointing with a lean forefinger, to this inscription:—

THE TWO ROBINS

Arthur turned into the court without hesitation, to see what The Two Robins could do for him. Four or five men were standing together round the door of the house which was at the bottom of the court, facing the entrance from the street. The men were all listening to one other man, better dressed than the rest, who was telling his audience something, in a low voice, in which they were apparently very much interested.

On entering the passage, Arthur was passed by a stranger with a knapsack in his hand, who was evidently leaving the house.

"No," said the traveller with the knapsack, turning round and addressing himself cheerfully to a fat, sly-looking, bald-headed man, with a dirty white apron on, who had followed him down the passage. "No, Mr. Landlord, I am not easily scared by trifles; but, I don't mind confessing that I can't quite stand *that*."

It occurred to young Holliday, the moment he heard these words, that the stranger had been asked an exorbitant price for a bed at The Two Robins; and that he was unable or unwilling to pay it. The moment his back was turned, Arthur, comfortably conscious of his own well-filled pockets, addressed himself in a great hurry, for fear any other benighted traveller should slip in and forestall him, to the sly-looking landlord with the dirty apron and the bald head.

"If you have got a bed to let," he said, "and if that gentleman who has just gone out won't pay your price for it, I will."

The sly landlord looked hard at Arthur.

"Will you, Sir?" he asked, in a meditative, doubtful way.

"Name your price," said young Holliday, thinking that the landlord's hesitation sprang from some boorish distrust of him. Name your price, and I'll give you the money at once if you like?"

"Are you game for five shillings?" inquired the landlord, rubbing his stubbly double chin, and looking up thoughtfully at the ceiling above him.

Arthur nearly laughed in the man's face; but thinking it

prudent to control himself, offered the five shillings as seriously as he could. The sly landlord held out his hand, then suddenly drew it back again.

"You're acting all fair and above-board by me," he said : "and, before I take your money, I'll do the same by you. Look here, this is how it stands. You can have a bed all to yourself for five shillings ; but you can't have more than a half-share of the room it stands in. Do you see what I mean, young gentleman ? "

"Of course I do," returned Arthur, a little irritably. "You mean that it is a double-bedded room, and that one of the beds is occupied ? "

The landlord nodded his head, and rubbed his double chin harder than ever. Arthur hesitated, and mechanically moved back a step or two towards the door. The idea of sleeping in the same room with a total stranger, did not present an attractive prospect to him. He felt more than half inclined to drop his five shillings into his pocket, and to go out into the street once more.

"Is it yes, or no?" asked the landlord. "Settle it as quick as you can, because there's lots of people wanting a bed at Doncaster to-night, besides you."

Arthur looked towards the court, and heard the rain falling heavily in the street outside. He thought he would ask a question or two before he rashly decided on leaving the shelter of The Two Robins.

"What sort of a man is it who has got the other bed ? " he inquired. "Is he a gentleman ? I mean, is he a quiet, well-behaved person ? "

"The quietest man I ever came across," said the landlord, rubbing his fat hands stealthily one over the other. "As sober as a judge, and as regular as clock-work in his habits. It hasn't struck nine, not ten minutes ago, and he's in his bed already. I don't know whether that comes up to your notion of a quiet man: it goes a long way ahead of mine, I can tell you."

"Is he asleep, do you think ? " asked Arthur.

"I know he's asleep," returned the landlord. "And what's more, he's gone off so fast, that I'll warrant you don't wake him. This way, Sir," said the landlord, speaking over young Holliday's shoulder, as if he was addressing some new guest who was approaching the house.

"Here you are," said Arthur, determined to be beforehand

with the stranger, whoever he might be. "I'll take the bed."
And he handed the five shillings to the landlord, who nodded, dropped the money carelessly into his waistcoat-pocket,
and lighted the candle.

"Come up and see the room," said the host of The Two
Robins, leading the way to the staircase quite briskly, considering how fat he was.

They mounted to the second-floor of the house. The landlord half opened a door, fronting the landing, then stopped,
and turned round to Arthur.

"It's a fair bargain, mind, on my side as well as on yours,'
he said. "You give me five shillings, I give you in return
a clean, comfortable bed ; and I warrant, beforehand, that
you won't be interfered with, or annoyed in any way, by the
man who sleeps in the same room as you." Saying those
words, he looked hard, for a moment, in young Holliday's
face, and then led the way into the room.

It was larger and cleaner than Arthur had expected it
would be. The two beds stood parallel with each other—a
space of about six feet intervening between them. They
were both of the same medium size, and both had the same
plain white curtains, made to draw, if necessary, all round
them. The occupied bed was the bed nearest the window.
The curtains were all drawn round this, except the half curtain at the bottom, on the side of the bed farthest from the
window. Arthur saw the feet of the sleeping man raising
the scanty clothes into a sharp little eminence, as if he was
lying flat on his back. He took the candle, and advanced
softly to draw the curtain—stopped half-way, and listened
for a moment—then turned to the landlord.

"He's a very quiet sleeper," said Arthur.

"Yes," said the landlord, "very quiet."

Young Holliday advanced with the candle, and looked in
at the man cautiously.

"How pale he is!" said Arthur.

"Yes," returned the landlord, "pale enough, isn't he ?"

Arthur looked closer at the man. The bedclothes were
drawn up to his chin, and they lay perfectly still over the
region of his chest. Surprised and vaguely startled, as he
noticed this, Arthur stooped down closer over the stranger ;
looked at his ashy, parted lips ; listened breathlessly for an
instant ; looked again at the strangely still face, and the
motionless lips and chest ; and turned round suddenly on

the landlord, with his own cheeks as pale for the moment as the hollow cheeks of the man on the bed.

"Come here," he whispered, under his breath. "Come here, for God's sake! The man's not asleep—he is dead!"

"You have found that out sooner than I thought you would," said the landlord, composedly. "Yes, he's dead, sure enough. He died at five o'clock to-day."

"How did he die? Who is he?" asked Arthur, staggered, for a moment, by the audacious coolness of the answer.

"As to who is he," rejoined the landlord, "I know no more about him than you do. There are his books and letters and things, all sealed up in that brown-paper parcel, for the Coroner's inquest to open to-morrow or next day. He's been here a week, paying his way fairly enough, and stopping in-doors, for the most part, as if he was ailing. My girl brought him up his tea at five to-day; and as he was pouring of it out, he fell down in a faint, or a fit, or a compound of both, for anything I know. We could not bring him to—and I said he was dead. And the doctor couldn't bring him to—and the doctor said he was dead. And there he is. And the Coroner's inquest's coming as soon as it can. And that's as much as I know about it."

Arthur held the candle close to the man's lips. The flame still burnt straight up, as steadily as before. There was a moment of silence; and the rain pattered drearily through it against the panes of the window.

"If you haven't got nothing more to say to me," continued the landlord, "I suppose I may go. You don't expect your five shillings back, do you? There's the bed I promised you, clean and comfortable. There's the man I warranted not to disturb you, quiet in this world for ever. If you're frightened to stop alone with him, that's not my look out. I've kept my part of the bargain, and I mean to keep the money. I'm not Yorkshire, myself, young gentleman; but I've lived long enough in these parts to have my wits sharpened; and I shouldn't wonder if you found out the way to brighten up yours, next time you come amongst us." With these words, the landlord turned towards the door, and laughed to himself softly, in high satisfaction at his own sharpness.

Startled and shocked as he was, Arthur had by this time sufficiently recovered himself to feel indignant at the trick that had been played on him, and at the insolent manner in which the landlord exulted in it.

"Don't laugh," he said sharply, "till you are quite sure you have got the laugh against me. You shan't have the five shillings for nothing, my man. I'll keep the bed."

"Will you?" said the landlord. "Then I wish you a good night's rest." With that brief farewell, he went out, and shut the door after him.

A good night's rest! The words had hardly been spoken, the door had hardly been closed, before Arthur half-repented the hasty words that had just escaped him. Though not naturally over-sensitive, and not wanting in courage of the moral as well as the physical sort, the presence of the dead man had an instantaneously chilling effect on his mind when he found himself alone in the room—alone, and bound by his own rash words to stay there till the next morning. An older man would have thought nothing of those words, and would have acted, without reference to them, as his calmer sense suggested. But Arthur was too young to treat the ridicule, even of his inferiors, with contempt—too young not to fear the momentary humiliation of falsifying his own foolish boast, more than he feared the trial of watching out the long night in the same chamber with the dead.

"It is but a few hours," he thought to himself, "and I can get away the first thing in the morning."

He was looking towards the occupied bed as that idea passed through his mind, and the sharp angular eminence made in the clothes by the dead man's upturned feet again caught his eye. He advanced and drew the curtains, purposely abstaining, as he did so, from looking at the face of the corpse, lest he might unnerve himself at the outset by fastening some ghastly impression of it on his mind. He drew the curtain very gently, and sighed involuntarily as he closed it. "Poor fellow," he said, almost as sadly as if he had known the man. "Ah, poor fellow!"

He went next to the window. The night was black, and he could see nothing from it. The rain still pattered heavily against the glass. He inferred, from hearing it, that the window was at the back of the house; remembering that the front was sheltered from the weather by the court and the buildings over it.

While he was still standing at the window—for even the dreary rain was a relief, because of the sound it made; a relief, also, because it moved, and had some faint suggestion, in consequence, of life and companionship in it—while he was standing at the window, and looking vacantly into the black darkness outside, he heard a distant church-clock strike ten. Only ten ! How was he to pass the time till the house was astir the next morning ?

Under any other circumstances, he would have gone down to the public-house parlour, would have called for his grog, and would have laughed and talked with the company assembled as familiarly as if he had known them all his life. But the very thought of whiling away the time in this manner was distasteful to him. The new situation in which he was placed seemed to have altered him to himself already. Thus far, his life had been the common, trifling, prosaic, surface-life of a prosperous young man, with no troubles to conquer, and no trials to face. He had lost no relation whom he loved, no friend whom he treasured. Till this night, what share he had of the immortal inheritance that is divided amongst us all, had laid dormant within him. Till this night, Death and he had not once met, even in thought.

He took a few turns up and down the room—then stopped. The noise made by his boots on the poorly carpeted floor, jarred on his ear. He hesitated a little, and ended by taking the boots off, and walking backwards and forwards noiselessly. All desire to sleep or to rest had left him. The bare thought of lying down on the unoccupied bed instantly drew the picture on his mind of a dreadful mimicry of the position of the dead man. Who was he ? What was the story of his past life ? Poor he must have been, or he would not have stopped at such a place as The Two Robins Inn—and weakened, probably, by long illness, or he could hardly have died in the manner in which the landlord had described. Poor, ill, lonely,—dead in a strange place ; dead, with nobody but a stranger to pity him. A sad story : truly, on the mere face of it, a very sad story.

While these thoughts were passing through his mind, he had stopped insensibly at the window, close to which stood the foot of the bed with the closed curtains. At first he looked at it absently ; then he became conscious that his eyes were fixed on it ; and then, a perverse desire took possession of him to do the very thing which he had resolved not to do, up to this time— to look at the dead man.

He stretched out his hand towards the curtains; but checked himself in the very act of undrawing them, turned his back sharply on the bed, and walked towards the chimneypiece, to see what things were placed on it, and to try if he could keep the dead man out of his mind in that way.

There was a pewter inkstand on the chimneypiece, with some mildewed remains of ink in the bottle. There were two coarse china ornaments of the commonest kind ; and there was a square of embossed card, dirty and fly-blown, with a collection of wretched riddles printed on it, in all sorts of zig-zag directions, and in variously coloured inks. He took the card, and went away, to read it, to the table on which the candle was placed ; sitting down, with his back resolutely turned to the curtained bed.

He read the first riddle, the second, the third, all in one corner of the card—then turned it round impatiently to look at another. Before he could begin reading the riddles printed here, the sound of the church-clock stopped him. Eleven. He had got through an hour of the time, in the room with the dead man.

Once more he looked at the card. It was not easy to make out the letters printed on it, in consequence of the dimness of the light which the landlord had left him—a common tallow candle, furnished with a pair of heavy old-fashioned steel snuffers. Up to this time, his mind had been too much occupied to think of the light. He had left the wick of the candle unsnuffed, till it had risen higher than the flame, and had burnt into an odd pent-house shape at the top, from which morsels of the charred cotton fell off, from time to time, in little flakes. He took up the snuffers now, and trimmed the wick. The light brightened directly, and the room became less dismal.

Again he turned to the riddles ; reading them doggedly and resolutely, now in one corner of the card, now in another. All his efforts, however, could not fix his attention on them. He pursued his occupation mechanically, deriving no sort of impression from what he was reading. It was as if a shadow from the curtained bed had got between his mind and the gaily printed letters—a shadow that nothing could dispel. At last, he gave up the struggle, and threw the card from him impatiently, and took to walking softly up and down the room again.

The dead man, the dead man, the *hidden* dead man on the bed ! There was the one persistent idea still haunting him. Hidden ? Was it only the body being there, or was it the body being there, concealed, that was preying on his mind ?

He stopped at the window, with that doubt in him; once more listening to the pattering rain, once more looking out into the black darkness.

Still the dead man! The darkness forced his mind back upon itself, and set his memory at work, reviving, with a painfully-vivid distinctness the momentary impression it had received from the first sight of the corpse. Before long the face seemed to be hovering out in the middle of the darkness, confronting him through the window, with the paleness whiter, with the dreadful dull line of light between the imperfectly-closed eyelids broader than he had seen it—with the parted lips slowly dropping farther and farther away from each other —with the features growing larger and moving closer, till they seemed to fill the window and to silence the rain, and to shut out the night.

The sound of a voice, shouting below-stairs, woke him suddenly from the dream of his own distempered fancy. He recognised it as the voice of the landlord. "Shut up at twelve, Ben," he heard it say. "I'm off to bed."

He wiped away the damp that had gathered on his forehead, reasoned with himself for a little while, and resolved to shake his mind free of the ghastly counterfeit which still clung to it, by forcing himself to confront, if it was only for a moment, the solemn reality. Without allowing himself an instant to hesitate, he parted the curtains at the foot of the bed, and looked through.

There was a sad, peaceful, white face, with the awful mystery of stillness on it, laid back upon the pillow. No stir, no change there! He only looked at it for a moment before he closed the curtains again—but that moment steadied him, calmed him, restored him—mind and body—to himself.

He returned to his old occupation of walking up and down the room; persevering in it, this time, till the clock struck again. Twelve.

As the sound of the clock-bell died away, it was succeeded by the confused noise, downstairs, of the drinkers in the tap-room leaving the house. The next sound, after an interval of silence, was caused by the barring of the door, and the closing of the shutters, at the back of the Inn. Then the silence followed again, and was disturbed no more.

He was alone now—absolutely, utterly, alone with the dead man, till the next morning.

The wick of the candle wanted trimming again. He took up the snuffers—but paused suddenly on the very point of using them, and looked attentively at the candle—then back, over his shoulder, at the curtained bed—then again at the candle. It had been lighted. for the first time, to show him the way upstairs, and three parts of it, at least, were already consumed. In another hour it would be burnt out. In another hour—unless he called at once to the man who had shut up the Inn, for a fresh candle— he would be left in the dark.

Strongly as his mind had been affected since he had entered his room, his unreasonable dread of encountering ridicule, and of exposing his courage to suspicion, had not altogether lost its influence over him, even yet. He lingered irresolutely by the table, waiting till he could prevail on himself to open the door, and call, from the landing, to the man who had shut up the Inn. In his present hesitating frame of mind, it was a kind of relief to gain a few moments only by engaging in the trifling occupation of snuffing the candle. His hand trembled a little, and the snuffers were heavy and awkward to use. When he closed them on the wick, he closed them a hair's breadth too low. In an instant the candle was out, and the room was plunged in pitch darkness.

The one impression which the absence of light immediately produced on his mind, was distrust of the curtained bed— distrust which shaped itself into no distinct idea, but which was powerful enough, in its very vagueness, to bind him down to his chair, to make his heart beat fast, and to set him listening intently. No sound stirred in the room but the familiar sound of the rain against the window, louder and sharper now than he had heard it yet.

Still the vague distrust, the inexpressible' dread possessed him, and kept him to his chair. He had put his carpet-bag on the table, when he first entered the room ; and he now took the key from his pocket, reached out his hand softly, opened the bag, and groped in it for his travelling writing-case, in which he knew that there was a small store of matches. When he had got one of the matches, he waited before he struck it on the coarse wooden table, and listened intently again, without knowing why. Still there was no sound in the room but the steady, ceaseless, rattling sound of the rain.

He lighted the candle again, without another moment of

delay; and, on the instant of its burning up, the first object in the room that his eyes sought for was the curtained bed.

Just before the light had been put out, he had looked in that direction, and had seen no change, no disarrangement of any sort, in the folds of the closely-drawn curtains.

When he looked at the bed, now, he saw, hanging over the side of it, a long white hand.

It lay perfectly motionless, midway on the side of the bed, where the curtain at the head and the curtain at the foot met. Nothing more was visible. The clinging curtains hid everything but the long white hand.

He stood looking at it unable to stir, unable to call out; feeling nothing, knowing nothing, every faculty he possessed gathered up and lost in the one seeing faculty. How long that first panic held him he never could tell afterwards. It might have been only for a moment; it might have been for many minutes together. How he got to the bed—whether he ran to it headlong, or whether he approached it slowly—how he wrought himself up to unclose the curtains and look in, he never has remembered, and never will remember to his dying day. It is enough that he did go to the bed, and that he did look inside the curtains.

The man had moved. One of his arms was outside the clothes; his face was turned a little on the pillow; his eyelids were wide open. Changed as to position, and as to one of the features, the face was, otherwise, fearfully and wonderfully unaltered. The dead paleness and the dead quiet were on it still.

One glance showed Arthur this—one glance, before he flew breathlessly to the door, and alarmed the house.

The man whom the landlord called "Ben," was the first to appear on the stairs. In three words, Arthur told him what had happened, and sent him for the nearest doctor.

I, who tell you this story, was then staying with a medical friend of mine, in practice at Doncaster, taking care of his patients for him, during his absence in London; and I, for the time being, was the nearest doctor. They had sent for me from the Inn, when the stranger was taken ill in the afternoon; but I was not at home, and medical assistance was sought for elsewhere. When the man from The Two Robins rang the night-bell, I was just thinking of going to bed. Naturally enough, I did not believe a word of his story about "a dead man who had come to life again." However, I put on my hat, armed myself with one or two bottles of restorative medicine, and ran to the Inn, expecting to find nothing more remarkable, when I got there, than a patient in a fit.

My surprise at finding that the man had spoken the litเral truth was almost, if not quite, equalled by my astonishment at finding myself face to face with Arthur Holliday as soon as I entered the bedroom. It was no time then for giving or seeking explanations. We just shook hands amazedly; and then I ordered everybody but Arthur out of the room, and hurried to the man on the bed.

The kitchen fire had not been long out. There was plenty of hot water in the boiler, and plenty of flannel to be had. With these, with my medicines, and with such help as Arthur could render under my direction, I dragged the man, literally, out of the jaws of death. In less than an hour from the time when I had been called in, he was alive and talking in the bed on which he had been laid out to wait for the Coroner's inquest.

You will naturally ask me, what had been the matter with him; and I might treat you, in reply, to a long theory, plentifully sprinkled with, what the children call, hard words. I prefer telling you that, in this case, cause and effect could not be satisfactorily joined together by any theory whatever. There are mysteries in life, and the condition of it, which human science has not fathomed yet; and I candidly confess to you, that, in bringing that man back to existence, I was, morally speaking, groping hap-hazard in the dark. I know (from the testimony of the doctor who attended him in the afternoon) that the vital machinery, so far as its action is appreciable by our senses, had, in this case, unquestionably stopped; and I am equally certain (seeing that I recovered him) that the vital principle was not extinct. When I add, that he had suffered from a long and complicated illness, and that his whole nervous system was utterly deranged, I have told you all I really know of the physical condition of my dead-alive patient at The Two Robins Inn.

When he " came to," as the phrase goes, he was a startling object to look at, with his colourless face, his sunken cheeks, his wild black eyes, and his long black hair. The first question he asked me about himself, when he could speak, made me suspect that I had been called in to a man in my own profession. I mentioned to him my surmise; and he told me that I was right.

He said he had come last from Paris, where he had been attached to a hospital. That he had lately returned to England, on his way to Edinburgh, to continue his studies; that he had been taken ill on the journey; and that he had stopped to rest and recover himself at Doncaster. He did not add a word about his name, or who he was: and, of course, I did not question him on the subject. All I inquired, when he ceased speaking, was what branch of the profession he intended to follow.

"Any branch," he said, bitterly, "which will put bread into the mouth of a poor man."

At this, Arthur, who had been hitherto watching him in silent curiosity, burst out impetuously in his usual good-humoured way:—

"My dear fellow!" (everybody was "my dear fellow" with Arthur) "now you have come to life again, don't begin by being downhearted about your prospects. I'll answer for it, I can help you to some capital thing in the medical line—or, if I can't, I know my father can."

The medical student looked at him steadily.

"Thank you," he said, coldly. Then added, "May I ask who your father is?"

"He's well enough known all about this part of the country," replied Arthur. "He is a great manufacturer, and his name is Holliday."

My hand was on the man's wrist during this brief conversation. The instant the name of Holliday was pronounced I felt the pulse under my fingers flutter, stop, go on suddenly with a bound, and beat afterwards, for a minute or two, at the fever rate.

"How did you come here?" asked the stranger, quickly, excitably, passionately almost.

Arthur related briefly what had happened from the time of his first taking the bed at the inn.

"I am indebted to Mr. Holliday's son then for the help that has saved my life," said the medical student, speaking to himself, with a singular sarcasm in his voice. "Come here!"

He held out, as he spoke, his long, white, bony, right hand.

"With all my heart," said Arthur, taking the hand cordially. "I may confess it now," he continued, laughing. "Upon my honour, you almost frightened me out of my wits."

The stranger did not seem to listen. His wild black eyes

were fixed with a look of eager interest on Arthur's face, and his long bony fingers kept tight hold of Arthur's hand. Young Holliday, on his side, returned the gaze, amazed and puzzled by the medical student's odd language and manners. The two faces were close together; I looked at them; and, to my amazement, I was suddenly impressed by the sense of a likeness between them—not in features, or complexion, but solely in expression. It must have been a strong likeness, or I should certainly not have found it out, for I am naturally slow at detecting resemblances between faces.

"You have saved my life," said the strange man, still looking hard in Arthur's face, still holding tightly by his hand. "If you had been my own brother, you could not have done more for me than that."

He laid a singularly strong emphasis on those three words "my own brother," and a change passed over his face as he pronounced them,—a change that no language of mine is competent to describe.

"I hope I have not done being of service to you yet," said Arthur. "I'll speak to my father, as soon as I get home."

"You seem to be fond and proud of your father," said the medical student. "I suppose, in return, he is fond and proud of you?"

"Of course, he is!" answered Arthur, laughing. "Is there anything wonderful in that? Isn't *your* father fond——"

The stranger suddenly dropped young Holliday's hand, and turned his face away.

"I beg your pardon," said Arthur. "I hope I have not unintentionally pained you. I hope you have not lost your father."

"I can't well lose what I have never had," retorted the medical student, with a harsh, mocking laugh.

"What you have never had!"

The strange man suddenly caught Arthur's hand again, suddenly looked once more hard in his face.

"Yes," he said, with a repetition of the bitter laugh. "You have brought a poor devil back into the world, who has no business there. Do I astonish you? Well! I have a fancy of my own for telling you what men in my situation generally keep a secret. I have no name and no father. The merciful law of Society tells me I am Nobody's Son! Ask your father if he will be my father too, and help me on in life with the family name."

Arthur looked at me, more puzzled than ever. I signed to him to say nothing, and then laid my fingers again on the man's wrist. No! In spite of the extraordinary speech that he had just made, he was not, as I had been disposed to suspect, beginning to get light-headed. His pulse, by this time, had fallen back to a quiet, slow beat, and his skin was moist and cool. Not a symptom of fever or agitation about him.

Finding that neither of us answered him, he turned to me, and began talking of the extraordinary nature of his case, and asking my advice about the future course of medical treatment to which he ought to subject himself. I said the matter required careful thinking over, and suggested that I should submit certain prescriptions to him the next morning. He told me to write them at once, as he would, most likely, be leaving Doncaster, in the morning, before I was up. It was quite useless to represent to him the folly and danger of such a proceeding as this. He heard me politely and patiently, but held to his resolution, without offering any reasons or any explanations, and repeated to me, that if I wished to give him a chance of seeing my prescription, I must write it at once. Hearing this, Arthur volunteered the loan of a travelling writing-case, which, he said, he had with him ; and, bringing it to the bed, shook the note-paper out of the pocket of the case forthwith in his usual careless way. With the paper, there fell out on the counterpane of the bed a small packet of sticking-plaster, and a little water-colour drawing of a landscape.

The medical student took up the drawing and looked at it. His eye fell on some initials neatly written, in cypher, in one corner. He started and trembled ; his pale face grew whiter than ever ; his wild black eyes turned on Arthur, and looked through and through him.

"A pretty drawing," he said in a remarkably quiet tone of voice.

"Ah! and done by such a pretty girl," said Arthur. "Oh, such a pretty girl! I wish it was not a landscape—I wish it was a portrait of her!"

"You admire her very much?"

Arthur, half in jest, half in earnest, kissed his hand for answer.

"Love at first sight!" he said, putting the drawing away again. "But the course of it doesn't run smooth. It's the old story. She's monopolised as usual. Trammelled by a rash engagement to some poor man who is never likely to get money enough to marry her. It was lucky I heard of it in time, or I should certainly have risked a declaration when she gave me that drawing. Here, doctor! Here is pen, ink, and paper all ready for you."

"When she gave you that drawing? Gave it. Gave it." He repeated the words slowly to himself, and suddenly closed his eyes. A momentary distortion passed across his face, and I saw one of his hands clutch up the bedclothes and squeeze them hard. I thought he was going to be ill again, and begged that there might be no more talking. He opened his eyes when I spoke, fixed them once more searchingly on Arthur, and said, slowly and distinctly, "You like her, and she likes you. The poor man may die out of your way. Who can tell that she may not give you herself as well as her drawing, after all?"

Before young Holliday could answer, he turned to me, and said in a whisper, "Now for the prescription." From that time, though he spoke to Arthur again, he never looked at him more.

When I had written the prescription, he examined it, approved of it, and then astonished us both by abruptly wishing us good night. I offered to sit up with him, and he shook his head. Arthur offered to sit up with him, and he said, shortly, with his face turned away, "No." I insisted on having somebody left to watch him. He gave way when he found I was determined, and said he would accept the services of the waiter at the Inn.

"Thank you, both," he said, as we rose to go. "I have one last favour to ask—not of you, doctor, for I leave you to exercise your professional discretion—but of Mr. Holliday." His eyes, while he spoke, still rested steadily on me, and never once turned towards Arthur. "I beg that Mr. Holliday will not mention to any one—least of all to his father—the events that have occurred, and the words that have passed, in this room. I entreat him to bury me in his memory, as, but for him, I might have been buried in my grave. I cannot give my reasons for making this strange request. I can only implore him to grant it."

His voice faltered for the first time, and he hid his face on the pillow. Arthur, completely bewildered, gave the required pledge. I took young Holliday away with me, immediately afterwards, to the house of my friend ; determining to go back to the Inn, and to see the medical student again before he had left in the morning.

I returned to the Inn at eight o'clock, purposely abstaining from waking Arthur, who was sleeping off the past night's excitement on one of my friend's sofas. A suspicion had occurred to me as soon as I was alone in my bedroom, which made me resolve that Holliday and the stranger whose life he had saved should not meet again, if I could prevent it. I have already alluded to c rtain reports, or scandals, which I knew of, relating to the early life of Arthur's father. While I was thinking, in my bed, of what had passed at the Inn—of the change in the student's pulse when he heard the name of Holliday ; of the resemblance of expression that I had discovered between his face and Arthur's ; of the emphasis he had laid on those three words, "my own brother ; " and of his incomprehensible acknowledgment of his own illegitimacy—while I was thinking of these things, the reports I have mentioned suddenly flew into my mind, and linked themselves fast to the chain of my previous reflections. Something within me whispered, "It is best that those two young men should not meet again." I felt it before I slept ; I felt it when I woke ; and I went, as I told you, alone to the Inn the next morning.

I had missed my only opportunity of seeing my nameless patient again. He had been gone nearly an hour when I inquired for him.

I have now told you everything that I know for certain, in relation to the man whom I brought back to life in the double-bedded room of the Inn at Doncaster. What I have next to add is matter for inference and surmise, and is not, strictly speaking, matter of fact.

I have to tell you, first, that the medical student turned out to be strangely and unaccountably right in assuming it as more than probable that Arthur Holliday would marry the young lady who had given him the water-colour drawing of the landscape. That marriage took place a little more than a year after the events occurred which I have just been relating. The young couple came to live in the neighbourhood in which I was then established in practice. I was present at the wedding, and was rather surprised to find that Arthur was singularly reserved with me, both before and

after his marriage, on the subject of the young lady's prior
engagement. He only referred to it once, when we were
alone, merely telling me, on that occasion, that his wife had
done all that honour and duty required of her in the matter,
and that the engagement had been broken off with the full
approval of her parents. I never heard more from him than
this. For three years he and his wife lived together happily.
At the expiration of that time, the symptoms of a serious
illness first declared themselves in Mrs. Arthur Holliday.
It turned out to be a long, lingering, hopeless malady. I
attended her throughout. We had been great friends when
she was well, and we became more attached to each other
than ever when she was ill. I had many long and interesting conversations with her in the intervals when she suffered
least. The result of one of these conversations I may briefly
relate, leaving you to draw any inferences from it that you
please.

The interview to which I refer, occurred shortly before her
death. I called one evening, as usual, and found her alone,
with a look in her eyes which told me that she had been
crying. She only informed me at first, that she had been
depressed in spirits; but, by little and little, she became more
communicative, and confessed to me that she had been
looking over some old letters, which had been addressed to
her, before she had seen Arthur, by a man to whom she had
been engaged to be married. I asked her how the engagement
came to be broken off. She replied that it had not been
broken off, but that it had died out in a very mysterious way.
The person to whom she was engaged—her first love, she
called him—was very poor, and there was no immediate
prospect of their being married. He followed my profession,
and went abroad to study. They had corresponded regularly,
until the time when, as she believed, he had returned to
England. From that period she heard no more of him.
He was of a fretful, sensitive temperament; and she feared
that she might have inadvertently done or said something
that offended him. However that might be, he had never
written to her again; and, after waiting a year, she had
married Arthur. I asked when the first estrangement had
begun, and found that the time at which she ceased to hear
anything of her first lover exactly corresponded with the time
at which I had been called in to my mysterious patient at
The Two Robins Inn.

A fortnight after that conversation, she died. In course of time, Arthur married again. Of late years, he has lived principally in London, and I have seen little or nothing of him.

I have many years to pass over before I can approach to anything like a conclusion of this fragmentary narrative. And even when that later period is reached, the little that I have to say will not occupy your attention for more than a few minutes. Between six and seven years ago, the gentleman to whom I introduced you in this room, came to me, with good professional recommendations, to fill the position of my assistant. We met, not like strangers, but like friends—the only difference between us being, that I was very much surprised to see him, and that he did not appear to be at all surprised to see me. If he was my son or my brother, I believe he could not be fonder of me than he is; but he has never volunteered any confidences since he has been here, on the subject of his past life. I saw something that was familiar to me in his face when we first met; and yet it was also something that suggested the idea of change. I had a notion once that my patient at the Inn might be a natural son of Mr. Holliday's; I had another idea that he might also have been the man who was engaged to Arthur's first wife; and I have a third idea, still clinging to me, that Mr. Lorn is the only man in England who could really enlighten me, if he chose, on both those doubtful points. His hair is not black, now, and his eyes are dimmer than the piercing eyes that I remember, but, for all that, he is very like the nameless medical student of my young days—very like him. And, sometimes, when I come home late at night, and find him asleep, and wake him, he looks, in coming to, wonderfully like the stranger at Doncaster, as he raised himself in the bed on that memorable night!

The Doctor paused. Mr. Goodchild, who had been following every word that fell from his lips up to this time, leaned forward eagerly to ask a question. Before he could say a word, the latch of the door was raised, without any warning sound of footsteps in the passage outside. A long, white, bony hand appeared through the opening, gently pushing the door, which was prevented from working freely on its hinges by a fold in the carpet under it.

"That hand! Look at that hand, Doctor!" said Mr. Goodchild, touching him.

At the same moment, the Doctor looked at Mr. Goodchild, and whispered to him, significantly:

"Hush! he has come back."

CHAPTER III

THE Cumberland Doctor's mention of Doncaster Races, inspired Mr. Francis Goodchild with the idea of going down to Doncaster to see the races. Doncaster being a good way off, and quite out of the way of the Idle Apprentices (if anything could be out of their way, who had no way), it necessarily followed that Francis perceived Doncaster in the race-week to be, of all possible idlenesses, the particular idleness that would completely satisfy him.

Thomas, with an enforced idleness grafted on the natural and voluntary power of his disposition, was not of this mind; objecting that a man compelled to lie on his back on a floor, a sofa, a table, a line of chairs, or anything he could get to lie upon, was not in racing condition, and that he desired nothing better than to lie where he was, enjoying himself in looking at the flies on the ceiling. But, Francis Goodchild, who had been walking round his companion in a circuit of twelve miles for two days, and had begun to doubt whether it was reserved for him ever to be idle in his life, not only overpowered this objection, but even converted Thomas Idle to a scheme he formed (another idle inspiration), of conveying the said Thomas to the sea-coast, and putting his injured leg under a stream of salt-water.

Plunging into this happy conception headforemost, Mr. Goodchild immediately referred to the county-map, and ardently discovered that the most delicious piece of sea-coast to be found within the limits of England, Ireland, Scotland, Wales, the Isle of Man, and the Channel Islands, all summed up together, was Allonby on the coast of Cumberland. There was the coast of Scotland opposite to Allonby, said Mr. Goodchild with enthusiasm; there was a fine Scottish mountain on that Scottish coast; there were Scottish lights to be seen shining across the glorious Channel, and at Allonby itself there was every idle luxury (no doubt) that a watering-place could offer to the heart of idle man. Moreover, said Mr. Goodchild, with his finger on the map, this exquisite retreat was approached by a coach-road, from a railway-station called Aspatria—a name, in a manner, suggestive of the departed glories of Greece, associated with one of the most engaging and most famous of Greek women. On this point, Mr. Goodchild continued at intervals to breathe a vein of classic fancy and eloquence exceedingly irksome to Mr. Idle, until it appeared that the honest English pronunciation of that Cumberland country shortened Aspatria into "Spatter." After this supplementary discovery, Mr. Goodchild said no more about it.

By way of Spatter, the crippled Idle was carried, hoisted, pushed, poked, and packed, into and out of carriages, into and out of beds, into and out of tavern resting-places, until he was brought at length within sniff of the sea. And now, behold the apprentices gallantly riding into Allonby in a one-horse fly, bent upon staying in that peaceful marine valley until the turbulent Doncaster time shall come round upon the wheel, in its turn among what are in sporting registers called the "Fixtures" for the month.

"Do you see Allonby!" asked Thomas Idle.

"I don't see it yet," said Francis, looking out of window.

"It must be there," said Thomas Idle.

"I don't see it," returned Francis.

"It must be there," repeated Thomas Idle, fretfully.

"Lord bless me!" exclaimed Francis, drawing in his head, "I suppose this is it!"

"A watering-place," retorted Thomas Idle, with the pardonable sharpness of an invalid, "can't be five gentlemen in straw hats, on a form on one side of a door, and four ladies in hats and falls, on a form on another side of a door, and three geese in a dirty little brook before them, and a boy's legs hanging over a bridge (with a boy's body I suppose on the other side of the parapet), and a donkey running away. What are you talking about?"

"Allonby, gentlemen," said the most comfortable of landladies, as she opened one door of the carriage; "Allonby, gentlemen," said the most attentive of landlords, as he opened the other.

Thomas Idle yielded his arm to the ready Goodchild, and descended from the vehicle. Thomas, now just able to grope his way along, in a doubled-up condition, with the aid of two thick sticks, was no bad embodiment of Commodore Trunnion, or of one of those many gallant Admirals of the stage, who have all ample fortunes, gout, thick sticks, tempers, wards, and nephews. With this distinguished naval appearance upon him, Thomas made a crab-like progress up a clean little bulk-headed staircase, into a clean little bulk-headed room, where he slowly deposited himself on a sofa, with a stick on either hand of him, looking exceedingly grim.

"Francis," said Thomas Idle, "what do you think of this place?"

"I think," returned Mr. Goodchild, in a glowing way, "it is everything we expected."

"Hah!" said Thomas Idle.

"There is the sea," cried Mr. Goodchild, pointing out of window; "and here," pointing to the lunch on the table, "are shrimps. Let us——" here Mr. Goodchild looked out of window, as if in search of something, and looked in again, —"let us eat 'em."

The shrimps eaten and the dinner ordered, Mr. Goodchild went out to survey the watering-place. As Chorus of the Drama, without whom Thomas could make nothing of the scenery, he by-and-by returned, to have the following report screwed out of him.

In brief, it was the most delightful place ever seen.

"But," Thomas Idle asked, "where is it?"

"It's what you may call generally up and down the beach, here and there," said Mr. Goodchild, with a twist of his hand.

"Proceed," said Thomas Idle.

It was, Mr. Goodchild went on to say, in cross-examination, what you might call a primitive place. Large? No, it was not large. Who ever expected it would be large? Shape? What a question to ask! No shape. What sort of a street? Why, no street. Shops? Yes, of course (quite indignant). How many? Who ever went into a place to count the shops? Ever so many. Six? Perhaps. A library? Why, of course (indignant again). Good collection of books? Most likely—couldn't say—had seen nothing in it but a pair of scales. Any reading-room? Of course, there was a reading-room. Where? Where! why, over there. Where was over there? Why, *there!* Let Mr. Idle carry his eye to that bit of waste ground above high-water mark, where the rank grass and loose stones were most in a litter; and he would see a sort of a long ruinous brick loft, next door to a ruinous brick outhouse, which loft had a ladder outside, to get up by. That was the reading-room, and if Mr. Idle didn't like the idea of a weaver's shuttle throbbing under a reading-room, that was his look out. *He* was not to dictate, Mr. Goodchild supposed (indignant again), to the company.

" By-the-by," Thomas Idle observed ; " the company ?"

Well! (Mr. Goodchild went on to report) very nice company. Where were they ? Why, there they were. Mr. Idle could see the tops of their hats, he supposed. What? Those nine straw hats again, five gentlemen's and four ladies' ? Yes, to be sure. Mr. Goodchild hoped the company were not to be expected to wear helmets, to please Mr. Idle.

Beginning to recover his temper at about this point, Mr. Goodchild voluntarily reported that if you wanted to be primitive, you could be primitive here, and that if you wanted to be idle, you could be idle here. In the course of some days, he added, that there were three fishing-boats, but no rigging, and that there were plenty of fishermen who never fished. That they got their living entirely by looking at the ocean. What nourishment they looked out of it to support their strength, he couldn't say ; but, he supposed it was some sort of Iodine. The place was full of their children, who were always upside down on the public buildings (two small bridges over the brook), and always hurting themselves or one another, so that their wailings made more continual noise in the air than could have been got in a busy place. The houses people lodged in, were nowhere in particular, and were in capital accordance with the beach ; being all more or less cracked and damaged as its shells were, and all empty —as its shells were. Among them, was an edifice of destitute appearance, with a number of wall-eyed windows in it, looking desperately out to Scotland as if for help, which said it was a Bazaar (and it ought to know), and where you might buy anything you wanted—supposing what you wanted, was a little camp-stool or a child's wheelbarrow. The brook crawled or stopped between the houses and the sea, and the donkey was always running away, and when he got into the brook he was pelted out with stones, which never hit him, and which always hit some of the children who were upside down on the public buildings, and made their lamentations louder. This donkey was the public excitement of Allonby, and was probably supported at the public expense.

The foregoing descriptions, delivered in separate items, on separate days of adventurous discovery, Mr. Goodchild severally wound up, by looking out of window, looking in again, and saying, "But there is the sea, and here are the shrimps—let us eat 'em."

There were fine sunsets at Allonby when the low flat beach, with its pools of water and its dry patches, changed into long bars of silver and gold in various states of burnishing, and there were fine views—on fine days—of the Scottish coast. But, when it rained at Allonby, Allonby thrown back upon its ragged self, became a kind of place which the donkey seemed to have found out, and to have his highly sagacious reasons for wishing to bolt from. Thomas Idle observed, too, that Mr. Goodchild, with a noble show of disinterestedness, became every day more ready to walk to Maryport and back, for letters; and suspicions began to harbour in the mind of Thomas, that his friend deceived him, and that Maryport was a preferable place.

Therefore, Thomas said to Francis on a day when they had looked at the sea and eaten the shrimps, "My mind misgives me, Goodchild, that you go to Maryport, like the boy in the story-book, to ask *it* to be idle with you."

"Judge, then," returned Francis, adopting the style of the story-book, "with what success. I go to a region which is a bit of water-side Bristol, with a slice of Wapping, a seasoning of Wolverhampton, and a garnish of Portsmouth, and I say, 'Will *you* come and be idle with me?' And it answers, 'No; for I am a great deal too vaporous, and a great deal too rusty, and a great deal too muddy, and a great deal too dirty altogether; and I have ships to load, and pitch and tar to boil, and iron to hammer, and steam to get up, and smoke to make, and stone to quarry, and fifty other disagreeable things to do, and I can't be idle with you.' Then I go into jagged up-hill and down-hill streets, where I am in the pastrycook's shop at one moment, and next moment in savage fastnesses of moor and morass, beyond the confines of civilisation, and I say to those murky and black-dusty streets, 'Will *you* come and be idle with me?' To which they reply, 'No, we can't, indeed, for we haven't the spirits, and we are startled by the echo of your feet on the sharp pavement, and we have so many goods in our shop-windows which nobody wants, and we have so much to do for a limited public which never comes to us to be done for, that we are altogether out of sorts and can't enjoy ourselves with any one.' So I go to the Post-office, and knock at the shutter, and I say to the Post-master, 'Will *you* come and be idle with me?' To which he rejoins, 'No, I really can't, for I live, as you may see, in such a very little Post-office, and pass my life behind such a very little shutter, that my hand, when I put it out, is as the hand of a giant crammed through the window of a dwarf's house at a fair, and I am a mere Post-office anchorite in a cell much too small for him, and I can't get out, and I can't get in, and I have no space to be idle in, even if I would.' So, the boy," said Mr. Goodchild, concluding the tale, "comes back with the letters after all, and lives happy never afterwards."

But it may, not unreasonably, be asked—while Francis Goodchild was wandering hither and thither, storing his mind with perpetual observation of men and things, and sincerely believing himself to be the laziest creature in existence all the time—how did Thomas Idle, crippled and confined to the house, contrive to get through the hours of the day?

Prone on the sofa, Thomas made no attempt to get through the hours, but passively allowed the hours to get through *him*. Where other men in his situation would have read books and improved their minds, Thomas slept and rested his body. Where other men would have pondered anxiously over their future prospects, Thomas dreamed lazily of his past life. The one solitary thing he did, which most other people would have done in his place, was to resolve on making certain alterations and improvements in his mode of existence, as soon as the effects of the misfortune that had overtaken him had all passed away. Remembering that the current of his life had hitherto oozed along in one smooth stream of laziness, occasionally troubled on the surface by a slight passing ripple of industry, his present ideas on the subject of self-reform, inclined him—not as the reader may be disposed to imagine, to project schemes for a new existence of enterprise and exertion—but, on the contrary, to resolve that he would never, if he could possibly help it, be active or industrious again, throughout the whole of his future career.

It is due to Mr. Idle to relate that his mind sauntered towards this peculiar conclusion on distinct and logically-producible grounds. After reviewing, quite at his ease, and with many needful intervals of repose, the generally-placid spectacle of his past existence, he arrived at the discovery that all the great disasters which had tried his patience and equanimity in early life, had been caused by his having allowed himself to be deluded into imitating some pernicious example of activity and industry that had been set him by others. The trials to which he here alludes were three in number, and may be thus reckoned up: First, the disaster of being an unpopular and a thrashed boy at school; secondly, the disaster of falling seriously ill; thirdly, the disaster of becoming acquainted with a great bore.

The first disaster occurred after Thomas had been an idle and a popular boy at school, for some happy years. One Christmas-time, he was stimulated by the evil example of a companion, whom he had always trusted and liked, to be untrue to himself, and to try for a prize at the ensuing half-yearly examination. He did try, and he got a prize— how, he did not distinctly know at the moment, and cannot remember now. No sooner, however, had the book—Moral Hints to the Young on the Value of Time—been placed in his hands, than the first troubles of his life began. The idle boys deserted him, as a traitor to their cause. The industrious boys avoided him, as a dangerous interloper; one of their number, who had always won the prize on previous occasions, expressing just resentment at the invasion of his privileges by calling Thomas into the playground, and then and there administering to him the first sound and genuine thrashing that he had ever received in his life. Unpopular from that moment, as a beaten boy, who belonged to no side and was rejected by all parties, young Idle soon lost caste with his masters, as he had previously lost caste with his schoolfellows. He had forfeited the comfortable reputation of being the one lazy member of the youthful community whom it was quite hopeless to punish. Never again did he hear the headmaster say reproachfully to an industrious boy who had committed a fault, "I might have expected this in Thomas Idle, but it is inexcusable, Sir, in you, who know better." Never more, after winning that fatal prize, did he escape the retributive imposition, or the avenging birch. From that time, the masters made him work, and the boys would not let him play. From that time his social position steadily declined, and his life at school became a perpetual burden to him.

So, again, with the second disaster. While Thomas was lazy, he was a model of health. His first attempt at active exertion and his first suffering from severe illness are connected together by the intimate relations of cause and effect. Shortly after leaving school, he accompanied a party of friends to a cricket-field, in his natural and appropriate character of spectator only. On the ground it was discovered that the players fell short of the required number, and facile Thomas was persuaded to assist in making up the complement. At a certain appointed time, he was roused from peaceful slumber in a dry ditch, and placed before three wickets with a bat in his hand. Opposite to him, behind three more wickets, stood one of his bosom friends, filling the situation (as he was informed) of bowler. No words can describe Mr. Idle's horror and amazement, when he saw this young man—on ordinary occasions, the meekest and mildest of human beings—suddenly contract his eyebrows, compress his lips, assume the aspect of an infuriated savage, run back a few steps, then run forward, and, without the slightest previous provocation, hurl a detestably hard ball with all his might straight at Thomas's legs. Stimulated to preternatural activity of body and sharpness of eye by the instinct of self-preservation, Mr. Idle contrived, by jumping deftly aside at the right moment, and by using his bat (ridiculously narrow as it was for the purpose) as a shield, to preserve his life and limbs from the dastardly attack that had been made on both, to leave the full force of the deadly missile to strike his wicket instead of his leg; and to end the innings, so far as his side was concerned, by being immediately bowled out. Grateful for his escape, he was about to return to the dry ditch, when he was peremptorily stopped, and told that the other side was "going in," and that he was expected to "field." His conception of the whole art and mystery of "fielding," may be summed up in the three words of serious advice which he privately administered to himself on that trying occasion—avoid the ball. Fortified by this sound and salutary principle, he took his own course, impervious alike to ridicule and abuse. Whenever the ball came near him, he thought of his shins, and got out of the way immediately. "Catch it!" "Stop it!" "Pitch it up!" were cries that passed by him like the idle wind that he regarded not. He ducked under it, he jumped over it, he whisked himself away from it on either side. Never once, through the whole innings did he and the ball come together on anything approaching to intimate terms. The unnatural activity of body which was necessarily called forth for the accomplishment of this result threw Thomas Idle, for the first time in his life, into a perspiration. The perspiration, in consequence of his want of practice in the management of that particular result of bodily activity, was suddenly checked; the inevitable chill succeeded; and that, in its turn, was followed by a fever. For the first time since his birth, Mr. Idle found himself confined to his bed for many weeks together, wasted and worn by a long illness, of which his own disastrous muscular exertion had been the sole first cause.

The third occasion on which Thomas found reason to re-proach himself bitterly for the mistake of having attempted to be industrious, was connected with his choice of a calling in life. Having no interest in the Church, he appropriately selected the next best profession for a lazy man in England —the Bar. Although the Benchers of the Inns of Court have lately abandoned their good old principles, and oblige their students to make some show of studying, in Mr. Idle's time no such innovation as this existed. Young men who aspired to the honourable title of barrister were, very properly, not asked to learn anything of the law, but were merely required to eat a certain number of dinners at the table of their Hall, and to pay a certain sum of money; and were called to the Bar as soon as they could prove that they had sufficiently complied with these extremely sensible regula-tions. Never did Thomas move more harmoniously in concert with his elders and betters than when he was qualifying him-self for admission among the barristers of his native country. Never did he feel more deeply what real laziness was in all the serene majesty of its nature, than on the memorable day when he was called to the Bar, after having carefully abstained from opening his law-books during his period of probation, except to fall asleep over them. How he could ever again have become industrious, even for the shortest period, after that great reward conferred upon his idleness, quite passes his comprehension. The kind Benchers did everything they could to show him the folly of exerting himself. They wrote out his probationary exercise for him, and never expected him even to take the trouble of reading it through when it was written. They invited him, with

seven other choice spirits as lazy as himself, to come and be
called to the Bar, while they were sitting over their wine
and fruit after dinner. They put his oaths of allegiance,
and his dreadful official denunciations of the Pope and the
Pretender, so gently into his mouth, that he hardly knew
how the words got there. They wheeled all their chairs
softly round from the table, and sat surveying the young
barristers with their backs to their bottles, rather than stand
up, or adjourn to hear the exercises read. And when Mr.
Idle and the seven unlabouring neophytes, ranged in order,
as a class, with their backs considerately placed against a
screen, had begun, in rotation, to read the exercises which
they had not written, even then, each Bencher, true to the
great lazy principle of the whole proceeding, stopped each
neophyte before he had stammered through his first line,
and bowed to him, and told him politely that he was a
barrister from that moment. This was all the ceremony. It
was followed by a social supper, and by the presentation, in
accordance with ancient custom, of a pound of sweetmeats
and a bottle of Madeira, offered in the way of needful refreshment, by each grateful neophyte to each beneficent Bencher.
It may seem inconceivable that Thomas should ever have
forgotten the great do-nothing principle instilled by such a
ceremony as this; but it is, nevertheless, true, that certain
designing students of industrious habits found him out, took
advantage of his easy humour, persuaded him that it was
discreditable to be a barrister and to know nothing whatever
about the law, and lured him, by the force of their own evil
example, into a conveyancer's chambers, to make up for lost
time, and to qualify himself for practice at the Bar. After
a fortnight of self-delusion, the curtain fell from his eyes;
he resumed his natural character, and shut up his books.
But the retribution which had hitherto always followed his
little casual errors of industry followed them still. He could
get away from the conveyancer's chambers, but he could not
get away from one of the pupils, who had taken a fancy to
him,—a tall, serious, raw-boned, hard-working, disputatious
pupil, with ideas of his own about reforming the Law of
Real Property, who has been the scourge of Mr. Idle's existence ever since the fatal day when he fell into the mistake
of attempting to study the law. Before that time his friends
were all sociable idlers like himself. Since that time the
burden of bearing with a hard-working young man has

become part of his lot in life.   Go where he will now, he can never feel certain that the raw-boned pupil is not affectionately waiting for him round a corner, to tell him a little more about the Law of Real Property.   Suffer as he may under the infliction, he can never complain, for he must always remember, with unavailing regret, that he has his own thoughtless industry to thank for first exposing him to the great social calamity of knowing a bore.

These events of his past life, with the significant results that they brought about, pass drowsily through Thomas Idle's memory, while he lies alone on the sofa at Allonby and elsewhere, dreaming away the time which his fellow-apprentice gets through so actively out of doors.   Remembering the lesson of laziness which his past disasters teach, and bearing in mind also the fact that he is crippled in one leg because he exerted himself to go up a mountain, when he ought to have known that his proper course of conduct was to stop at the bottom of it, he holds now, and will for the future firmly continue to hold, by his new resolution never to be industrious again, on any pretence whatever, for the rest of his life.   The physical results of his accident have been related in a previous chapter.   The moral results now stand on record ; and, with the enumeration of these, that part of the present narrative which is occupied by the Episode of The Sprained Ankle may now perhaps be considered, in all its aspects, as finished and complete.

" How do you propose that we get through this present afternoon and evening?" demanded Thomas Idle, after two or three hours of the foregoing reflections at Allonby.

Mr. Goodchild faltered, looked out of window, looked in again, and said, as he had so often said before, " There is the sea, and here are the shrimps ;—let us eat 'em ! "

But, the wise donkey was at that moment in the act of bolting: not with the irresolution of his previous efforts which had been wanting in sustained force of character, but with real vigour of purpose: shaking the dust off his mane and hind-feet at Allonby, and tearing away from it, as if he had nobly made up his mind that he never would be taken alive.   At sight of this inspiring spectacle, which was visible from his sofa, Thomas Idle stretched his neck and dwelt upon it rapturously.

" Francis Goodchild," he then said, turning to his companion with a solemn air, " this is a delightful little Inn, excellently kept by the most comfortable of landladies and the most attentive of landlords, but——the donkey's right !"

The words, "There is the sea, and here are the——" again trembled on the lips of Goodchild, unaccompanied however by any sound.

"Let us instantly pack the portmanteaus," said Thomas Idle, "pay the bill, and order a fly out, with instructions to the driver to follow the donkey !"

Mr. Goodchild, who had only wanted encouragement to disclose the real state of his feelings, and who had been pining beneath his weary secret, now burst into tears, and confessed that he thought another day in the place would be the death of him.

So, the two idle apprentices followed the donkey until the night was far advanced. Whether he was recaptured by the town-council, or is bolting at this hour through the United Kingdom, they know not. They hope he may be still bolting; if so, their best wishes are with him.

It entered Mr. Idle's head, on the borders of Cumberland, that there could be no idler place to stay at, except by snatches of a few minutes each, than a railway station. "An intermediate station on a line—a junction—anything of that sort," Thomas suggested. Mr. Goodchild approved of the idea as eccentric, and they journeyed on and on, until they came to such a station where there was an Inn.

"Here," said Thomas, "we may be luxuriously lazy; other people will travel for us, as it were, and we shall laugh at their folly."

It was a Junction-Station, where the wooden razors before-mentioned shaved the air very often, and where the sharp electric-telegraph bell was in a very restless condition. All manner of cross-lines of rails came zig-zagging into it, like a Congress of iron vipers; and, a little way out of it, a pointsman in an elevated signal-box was constantly going through the motions of drawing immense quantities of beer at a public-house bar. In one direction, confused perspectives of embankments and arches were to be seen from the platform; in the other, the rails soon disentangled themselves into two tracks, and shot away under a bridge, and curved round a corner. Sidings were there, in which empty luggage-vans and cattle-boxes often butted against each other as if they couldn't agree; and warehouses were there, in which great quantities of goods seemed to have taken the veil (of the consistency of tarpaulin), and to have retired from the world without any hope of getting back to it. Refreshment-rooms were there; one, for the hungry and thirsty Iron Locomotives where their coke and water were ready, and of good quality, for they were dangerous to play tricks with; the other, for the hungry and thirsty human Locomotives, who might take what they could get, and whose chief consolation was provided in the form of three terrific urns or vases of white metal, containing nothing, each forming a breastwork for a defiant and apparently much-injured woman.

Established at this Station, Mr. Thomas Idle and Mr. Francis Goodchild resolved to enjoy it. But, its contrasts were very violent, and there was also an infection in it.

First, as to its contrasts. There were only two, but they were Lethargy and Madness. The Station was either totally unconscious, or wildly raving. By day, in its unconscious state, it looked as if no life could come to it,—as if it were all rust, dust, and ashes—as if the last train for ever, had gone without issuing any Return-Tickets—as if the last Engine had uttered its last shriek and burst. One awkward shave of the air from the wooden razor, and everything changed. Tight office-doors flew open, panels yielded, books, newspapers, travelling-caps and wrappers broke out of brick walls, money chinked, conveyances oppressed by nightmares of luggage came careering into the yard, porters started up from secret places, ditto the much-injured women, the shining bell, who lived in a little tray on stilts by himself, flew into a man's hand and clamoured violently. The pointsman aloft in the signal-box made the motions of drawing, with some difficulty, hogsheads of beer. Down Train! More beer! Up Train! More beer. Cross Junction Train! More beer! Cattle Train! More beer. Goods Train! Simmering, whistling, trembling, rumbling, thundering. Trains on the whole confusion of intersecting rails, crossing one another, bumping one another, hissing one another, backing to go forward, tearing into distance to come close. People frantic. Exiles seeking restoration to their native carriages, and banished to remoter climes. More beer and more bell. Then, in a minute, the Station relapsed into stupor as the stoker of the Cattle Train, the last to depart, went gliding out of it, wiping the long nose of his oil-can with a dirty pocket-handkerchief.

By night, in its unconscious state, the Station was not so much as visible. Something in the air, like an enterprising chemist's established in business on one of the boughs of Jack's beanstalk, was all that could be discerned of it under the stars. In a moment it would break out, a constellation of gas. In another moment, twenty rival chemists, on twenty rival beanstalks, came into existence. Then, the Furies would be seen, waving their lurid torches up and down the confused perspectives of embankments and arches—would be heard, too, wailing and shrieking. Then, the Station would be full of palpitating trains, as in the day : with the heightening difference that they were not so clearly seen as in the day, whereas the Station walls, starting forward under the gas, like a hippopotamus's eyes, dazzled the human locomotives with the sauce-bottle, the cheap music, the bedstead, the distorted range of buildings where the patent safes are made, the gentleman in the rain with the registered umbrella, the lady returning from the ball with the registered respirator, and all their other embellishments. And now, the human locomotives, creased as to their countenances and purblind as to their eyes, would swarm forth in a heap, addressing themselves to the mysterious urns and the much-injured women ; while the iron locomotives, dripping fire and water, shed their steam about plentifully, making the dull oxen in their cages, with heads depressed, and foam hanging from their mouths as their red looks glanced fearfully at the surrounding terrors, seem as though they had been drinking at half-frozen waters and were hung with icicles. Through the same steam would be caught glimpses of their fellow-travellers, the sheep, getting their white kid faces together, away from the bars, and stuffing the interstices with trembling wool. Also, down among the wheels, of the man with the sledge-hammer, ringing the axles of the fast night-train ; against whom the oxen have a misgiving that he is the man with the pole-axe who is to come by-and-by, and so the nearest of them try to get back, and get a purchase for a thrust at him through the bars. Suddenly, the bell would ring, the steam would stop with one hiss and a yell, the chemists on the beanstalks would be busy, the avenging Furies would bestir themselves, the fast night-train would melt from eye and ear, the other trains going their ways more slowly would be heard faintly rattling in the distance like old-fashioned watches running down, the sauce-bottle and cheap music retired from view, even the bedstead went to bed, and there was no such visible thing as the Station to vex the cool wind in its blowing, or perhaps the autumn lightning, as it found out the iron rails.

The infection of the Station was this:—When it was in its raving state, the Apprentices found it impossible to be there, without labouring under the delusion that they were in a hurry. To Mr. Goodchild, whose ideas of idleness were so imperfect, this was no unpleasant hallucination, and accordingly that gentleman went through great exertions in yielding to it, and running up and down the platform, jostling everybody, under the impression that he had a highly important mission somewhere, and had not a moment to lose. But, to Thomas Idle, this contagion was so very unacceptable an incident of the situation, that he struck on the fourth day, and requested to be moved.

"This place fills me with a dreadful sensation," said Thomas, "of having something to do. Remove me, Francis."

"Where would you like to go next?" was the question of the ever-engaging Goodchild.

"I have heard there is a good old Inn at Lancaster, established in a fine old house: an Inn where they give you Bride-cake every day after dinner," said Thomas Idle. "Let us eat Bride-cake without the trouble of being married, or of knowing anybody in that ridiculous dilemma."

Mr. Goodchild, with a lover's sigh, assented. They departed from the Station in a violent hurry (for which, it is unnecessary to observe, there was not the least occasion), and were delivered at the fine old house at Lancaster, on the same night.

It is Mr. Goodchild's opinion, that if a visitor on his arrival at Lancaster could be accommodated with a pole which would push the opposite side of the street some yards farther off, it would be better for all parties. Protesting against being required to live in a trench, and obliged to speculate all day upon what the people can possibly be doing within a mysterious opposite window, which is a shop-window to look at, but not a shop-window in respect of its offering nothing for sale and declining to give any account whatever of itself, Mr. Goodchild concedes Lancaster to be a pleasant place. A place dropped in the midst of a charming landscape, a place with a fine ancient fragment of castle, a place of lovely walks, a place possessing staid old houses richly fitted with old Honduras mahogany, which has grown so dark with time that it seems to have got something of a retrospective mirror-quality into itself, and to show the visitor, in the depth of its grain, through all its polish, the hue of the wretched slaves who groaned long ago under old Lancaster merchants. And Mr. Goodchild adds that the stones of Lancaster do sometimes whisper, even yet, of rich men passed away—upon whose great prosperity some of these old doorways frowned sullen in the brightest weather—that their slave-gain turned to curses, as the Arabian Wizard's money turned to leaves, and that no good ever came of it, even unto the third and fourth generations, until it was wasted and gone.

It was a gallant sight to behold, the Sunday procession of the Lancaster elders to Church—all in black, and looking fearfully like a funeral without the Body—under the escort of Three Beadles.

"Think," said Francis, as he stood at the Inn window, admiring, "of being taken to the sacred edifice by three Beadles! I have, in my early time, been taken out of it by one Beadle; but, to be taken into it by three, O Thomas, is a distinction I shall never enjoy!"

CHAPTER IV

When Mr. Goodchild had looked out of the Lancaster Inn window for two hours on end, with great perseverance, he began to entertain a misgiving that he was growing industrious. He therefore set himself next, to explore the country from the tops of all the steep hills in the neighbourhood.

He came back at dinner-time, red and glowing, to tell Thomas Idle what he had seen. Thomas, on his back reading, listened with great composure, and asked him whether he really had gone up those hills, and bothered himself with those views, and walked all those miles?

"Because I want to know," added Thomas, "what you would say of it, if you were obliged to do it?"

"It would be different, then," said Francis. "It would be work, then; now, it's play."

"Play!" replied Thomas Idle, utterly repudiating the reply. "Play! Here is a man goes systematically tearing himself to pieces, and putting himself through an incessant course of training, as if he were always under articles to fight a match for the champion's belt, and he calls it Play! Play!"

exclaimed Thomas Idle, scornfully contemplating his one boot in the air. "You *can't* play. You don't know what it is. You make work of everything."

The bright Goodchild amiably smiled.

"So you do," said Thomas. "I mean it. To me you are an absolutely terrible fellow. You do nothing like another man. Where another fellow would fall into a footbath of action or emotion, you fall into a mine. Where any other fellow would be a painted butterfly, you are a fiery dragon. Where another man would stake a sixpence, you stake your existence. If you were to go up in a balloon, you would make for Heaven; and if you were to dive into the depths of the earth, nothing short of the other place would content you. What a fellow you are, Francis!"

The cheerful Goodchild laughed.

"It's all very well to laugh, but I wonder you don't feel it to be serious," said Idle. "A man who can do nothing by halves appears to me to be a fearful man."

"Tom, Tom," returned Goodchild, "if I can do nothing by halves, and be nothing by halves, it's pretty clear that you must take me as a whole, and make the best of me."

With this philosophical rejoinder, the airy Goodchild clapped Mr. Idle on the shoulder in a final manner, and they sat down to dinner.

"By-the-by," said Goodchild, "I have been over a lunatic asylum too, since I have been out."

"He has been," exclaimed Thomas Idle, casting up his eyes, "over a lunatic asylum! Not content with being as great an Ass as Captain Barclay in the pedestrian way, he makes a Lunacy Commissioner of himself—for nothing!"

"An immense place," said Goodchild, "admirable offices, very good arrangements, very good attendants; altogether a remarkable place."

"And what did you see there?" asked Mr. Idle, adapting Hamlet's advice to the occasion, and assuming the virtue of interest, though he had it not.

"The usual thing," said Francis Goodchild, with a sigh. "Long groves of blighted men-and-women-trees, interminable avenues of hopeless faces; numbers, without the slightest power of really combining for any earthly purpose; a society of human creatures who have nothing in common but that they have all lost the power of being humanly social with one another."

"Take a glass of wine with me," said Thomas Idle, "and let *us* be social."

"In one gallery, Tom," pursued Francis Goodchild, "which looked to me about the length of the Long Walk at Windsor, more or less —— "

"Probably less," observed Thomas Idle.

"In one gallery, which was otherwise clear of patients (for they were all out), there was a poor little dark-chinned, meagre man, with a perplexed brow and a pensive face, stooping low over the matting on the floor, and picking out with his thumb and forefinger the course of its fibres. The afternoon sun was slanting in at the large end-window, and there were cross patches of light and shade all down the vista, made by the unseen windows and the open doors of the little sleeping-cells on either side. In about the centre of the perspective, under an arch, regardless of the pleasant weather, regardless of the solitude, regardless of approaching footsteps, was the poor little dark-chinned, meagre man, poring over the matting. 'What are you doing there?' said my conductor, when we came to him. He looked up, and pointed to the matting. 'I wouldn't do that, I think,' said my conductor, kindly; 'if I were you, I would go and read, or I would lie down if I felt tired; but I wouldn't do that.' The patient considered a moment, and vacantly answered, 'No, Sir, I won't; I'll—I'll go and read,' and so he lamely shuffled away into one of the little rooms. I turned my head before we had gone many paces. He had already come out again, and was again poring over the matting, and tracking out its fibres with his thumb and forefinger. I stopped to look at him, and it came into my mind, that probably the course of those fibres as they plaited in and out, over and under, was the only course of things in the whole wide world that it was left to him to understand—that his darkening intellect had narrowed down to the small cleft of light which showed him, 'This piece was twisted this way, went in here, passed under, came out there, was carried on away here to the right where I now put my finger on it, and in this progress of events, the thing was made and came to be here.' Then, I wondered whether he looked into the matting, next, to see if it could show him anything of the process through which *he* came to be there, so strangely poring over it. Then, I thought how all of us, GOD help us! in our different ways are poring over our bits of matting, blindly enough, and what confusions and mysteries we make in the pattern. I had a sadder fellow-feeling with the little dark-chinned, meagre man, by that time, and I came away."

Mr. Idle diverting the conversation to grouse, custards, and bride-cake, Mr. Goodchild followed in the same direction. The bride-cake was as bilious and indigestible as if a real Bride had cut it, and the dinner it completed was an admirable performance.

The house was a genuine old house of a very quaint description, teeming with old carvings, and beams, and panels, and having an excellent old staircase, with a gallery or upper staircase, cut off from it by a curious fence-work of old oak, or of the old Honduras Mahogany wood. It was, and is, and will be, for many a long year to come, a remarkably picturesque house; and a certain grave mystery lurking in the depth of the old mahogany panels, as if they were so many deep pools of dark water—such, indeed, as they had been much among when they were trees—gave it a very mysterious character after nightfall.

When Mr. Goodchild and Mr. Idle had first alighted at the door, and stepped into the sombre handsome old hall, they had been received by half-a-dozen noiseless old men in black, all dressed exactly alike, who glided up the stairs with the obliging landlord and waiter—but without appearing to get into their way, or to mind whether they did or no—and who had filed off to the right and left on the old staircase, as the guests entered their sitting-room. It was then broad, bright day. But, Mr. Goodchild had said, when their door was shut, "Who on earth are those old men?" And afterwards, both on going out and coming in, he had noticed that there were no old men to be seen.

Neither, had the old men, or any one of the old men, re-appeared since. The two friends had passed a night in the house, but had seen nothing more of the old men. Mr. Goodchild, in rambling about it, had looked along passages, and glanced in at doorways, but had encountered no old men; neither did it appear that any old men were, by any member of the establishment, missed or expected.

Another odd circumstance impressed itself on their attention. It was, that the door of their sitting-room was never left untouched for a quarter of an hour. It was opened with hesitation, opened with confidence, opened a little way, opened a good way,—always clapped-to again without a word of explanation. They were reading, they were writing, they were eating, they were drinking, they were talking, they were dozing; the door was always opened at an unexpected moment, and they looked towards it, and it was clapped-to again, and nobody was to be seen. When this had happened fifty times or so, Mr. Goodchild had said to his companion, jestingly: "I begin to think, Tom, there was something wrong with those six old men."

Night had come again, and they had been writing for two or three hours: writing, in short, a portion of the lazy notes from which these lazy sheets are taken. They had left off writing, and glasses were on the table between them. The house was closed and quiet. Around the head of Thomas Idle, as he lay upon his sofa, hovered light wreaths of fragrant smoke. The temples of Francis Goodchild, as he leaned back in his chair, with his two hands clasped behind his head, and his legs crossed, were similarly decorated.

They had been discussing several idle subjects of speculation, not omitting the strange old men, and were still so occupied, when Mr. Goodchild abruptly changed his attitude to wind up his watch. They were just becoming drowsy enough to be stopped in their talk by any such slight check. Thomas Idle, who was speaking at the moment, paused and said, "How goes it?"

"One," said Goodchild.

As if he had ordered One old man, and the order were promptly executed (truly, all orders were so, in that excellent hotel), the door opened, and One old man stood there.

He did not come in, but stood with the door in his hand.

"One of the six, Tom, at last!" said Mr. Goodchild, in a surprised whisper.—"Sir, your pleasure?"

"Sir, *your* pleasure?" said the One old man.

"I didn't ring."

"The bell did," said the One old man.

He said BELL, in a deep strong way, that would have expressed the church Bell.

"I had the pleasure, I believe, of seeing you, yesterday?" said Goodchild.

"I cannot undertake to say for certain," was the grim reply of the One old man.

"I think you saw me? Did you not?"

"Saw *you*?" said the old man. "O yes, I saw *you*. But, I see many who never see me."

A chilled, slow, earthy, fixed old man. A cadaverous old

man of measured speech. An old man who seemed as unable to wink, as if his eyelids had been nailed to his forehead. An old man whose eyes—two spots of fire—had no more motion than if they had been connected with the back of his skull by screws driven through it, and rivetted and bolted outside, among his grey hair.

The night had turned so cold, to Mr. Goodchild's sensations, that he shivered. He remarked lightly, and half apologetically, "I think somebody is walking over my grave."

"No," said the weird old man, "there is no one there."

Mr. Goodchild looked at Idle, but Idle lay with his head enwreathed in smoke.

"No one there?" said Goodchild.

"There is no one at your grave, I assure you," said the old man.

He had come in and shut the door, and he now sat down. He did not bend himself to sit, as other people do, but seemed to sink bolt upright, as if in water, until the chair stopped him.

"My friend, Mr. Idle," said Goodchild, extremely anxious to introduce a third person into the conversation.

"I am," said the old man, without looking at him, "at Mr. Idle's service."

"If you are an old inhabitant of this place," Francis Goodchild resumed:

"Yes."

"Perhaps you can decide a point my friend and I were in doubt upon, this morning. They hang condemned criminals at the Castle, I believe?"

"*I* believe so," said the old man.

"Are their faces turned towards that noble prospect?"

"Your face is turned," replied the old man, "to the Castle wall. When you are tied up, you see its stones expanding and contracting violently, and a similar expansion and contraction seem to take place in your own head and breast. Then, there is a rush of fire and an earthquake, and the Castle springs into the air, and you tumble down a precipice."

His cravat appeared to trouble him. He put his hand to his throat, and moved his neck from side to side. He was an old man of a swollen character of face, and his nose was immovably hitched up on one side, as if by a little hook inserted in that nostril. Mr. Goodchild felt exceedingly

B b

uncomfortable, and began to think the night was hot, and not cold.

"A strong description, Sir," he observed.

"A strong sensation," the old man rejoined.

Again, Mr. Goodchild looked to Mr. Thomas Idle; but Thomas lay on his back with his face attentively turned towards the One old man, and made no sign. At this time Mr. Goodchild believed that he saw threads of fire stretch from the old man's eyes to his own, and there attach themselves. (Mr. Goodchild writes the present account of his experience, and, with the utmost solemnity, protests that he had the strongest sensation upon him of being forced to look at the old man along those two fiery films, from that moment.)

"I must tell it to you," said the old man, with a ghastly and a stony stare.

"What?" asked Francis Goodchild.

"You know where it took place. Yonder!"

Whether he pointed to the room above, or to the room below, or to any room in that old house, or to a room in some other old house in that old town, Mr. Goodchild was not, nor is, nor ever can be, sure. He was confused by the circumstance that the right forefinger of the One old man seemed to dip itself in one of the threads of fire, light itself, and make a fiery start in the air, as it pointed somewhere. Having pointed somewhere, it went out.

"You know she was a Bride," said the old man.

"I know they still send up Bride-cake," Mr. Goodchild faltered. "This is a very oppressive air."

"She was a Bride," said the old man. "She was a fair, flaxen-haired, large-eyed girl, who had no character, no purpose. A weak, credulous, incapable, helpless nothing. Not like her mother. No, no. It was her father whose character she reflected.

"Her mother had taken care to secure everything to herself, for her own life, when the father of this girl (a child at that time) died—of sheer helplessness; no other disorder—and then He renewed the acquaintance that had once subsisted between the mother and Him. He had been put aside for the flaxen-haired, large-eyed man (or nonentity) with Money. He could overlook that for Money. He wanted compensation in Money.

"So, he returned to the side of that woman the mother,

made love to her again, danced attendance on her, and submitted himself to her whims. She wreaked upon him every whim she had, or could invent. He bore it. And the more he bore, the more he wanted compensation in Money, and the more he was resolved to have it.

"But, lo! Before he got it, she cheated him. In one of her imperious states, she froze, and never thawed again. She put her hands to her head one night, uttered a cry, stiffened, lay in that attitude certain hours, and died. And he had got no compensation from her in Money, yet. Blight and Murrain on her! Not a penny.

"He had hated her throughout that second pursuit, and had longed for retaliation on her. He now counterfeited her signature to an instrument, leaving all she had to leave, to her daughter—ten years old then—to whom the property passed absolutely, and appointing himself the daughter's Guardian. When He slid it under the pillow of the bed on which she lay, He bent down in the deaf ear of Death, and whispered: 'Mistress Pride, I have determined a long time that, dead or alive, you must make me compensation in Money.'

"So, now there were only two left. Which two were, He, and the fair flaxen-haired, large-eyed foolish daughter, who afterwards became the Bride.

"He put her to school. In a secret, dark, oppressive, ancient house, he put her to school with a watchful and unscrupulous woman. 'My worthy lady,' he said, 'here is a mind to be formed; will you help me to form it?' She accepted the trust. For which she, too, wanted compensation in Money, and had it.

"The girl was formed in the fear of him, and in the conviction, that there was no escape from him. She was taught, from the first, to regard him as her future husband—the man who must marry her—the destiny that overshadowed her—the appointed certainty that could never be evaded. The poor fool was soft white wax in their hands, and took the impression that they put upon her. It hardened with time. It became a part of herself. Inseparable from herself, and only to be torn away from her, by tearing life away from her.

"Eleven years she had lived in the dark house and its gloomy garden. He was jealous of the very light and air getting to her, and they kept her close. He stopped the wide chimneys, shaded the little windows, left the strong-stemmed ivy to wander where it would over the house-front, the moss to accumulate on the untrimmed fruit-trees in the red-walled garden, the weeds to over-run its green and yellow walks. He surrounded her with images of sorrow and desolation. He caused her to be filled with fears of the place and of the stories that were told of it, and then on pretext of correcting them, to be left in it in solitude, or made to shrink about it in the dark. When her mind was most depressed and fullest of terrors, then, he would come out of one of the hiding-places from which he overlooked her, and present himself as her sole resource.

"Thus, by being from her childhood the one embodiment her life presented to her of power to coerce and power to relieve, power to bind and power to loose, the ascendency over her weakness was secured. She was twenty-one years and twenty-one days old, when he brought her home to the gloomy house, his half-witted, frightened, and submissive Bride of three weeks.

"He had dismissed the governess by that time—what he had left to do, he could best do alone—and they came back, upon a rainy night, to the scene of her long preparation. She turned to him upon the threshold, as the rain was dripping from the porch, and said:

"'O Sir, it is the Death-watch ticking for me!'

"'Well!' he answered. 'And if it were?'

"'O Sir!' she returned to him, 'look kindly on me, and be merciful to me! I beg your pardon. I will do anything you wish, if you will only forgive me!'

"That had become the poor fool's constant song: 'I beg your pardon,' and 'Forgive me!'

"She was not worth hating; he felt nothing but contempt for her. But, she had long been in the way, and he had long been weary, and the work was near its end, and had to be worked out.

"'You fool,' he said. 'Go up the stairs!'

"She obeyed very quickly, murmuring, 'I will do any-thing you wish!' When he came into the Bride's Chamber, having been a little retarded by the heavy fastenings of the great door (for they were alone in the house, and he had arranged that the people who attended on them should come and go in the day), he found her withdrawn to the furthest corner, and there standing pressed against the panelling as if she would have shrunk through it: her flaxen hair all wild about her face, and her large eyes staring at him in vague terror.

"'What are you afraid of? Come and sit down by me.'

"'I will do anything you wish. I beg your pardon, Sir. Forgive me!' Her monotonous tune as usual.

"'Ellen, here is a writing that you must write out to-morrow, in your own hand. You may as well be seen by others, busily engaged upon it. When you have written it all fairly, and corrected all mistakes, call in any two people there may be about the house, and sign your name to it before them. Then, put it in your bosom to keep it safe, and when I sit here again to-morrow night, give it to me.'

"'I will do it all, with the greatest care. I will do anything you wish.'

"'Don't shake and tremble, then.'

"'I will try my utmost not to do it—if you will only forgive me!'

"Next day, she sat down at her desk, and did as she had been told. He often passed in and out of the room, to observe her, and always saw her slowly and laboriously writing: repeating to herself the words she copied, in appearance quite mechanically, and without caring or endeavouring to comprehend them, so that she did her task. He saw her follow the directions she had received, in all particulars; and at night, when they were alone again in the same Bride's Chamber, and he drew his chair to the hearth, she timidly approached him from her distant seat, took the paper from her bosom, and gave it into his hand.

"It secured all her possessions to him, in the event of her death. He put her before him, face to face, that he might look at her steadily; and he asked her, in so many plain words, neither fewer nor more, did she know that?

"There were spots of ink upon the bosom of her white dress, and they made her face look whiter and her eyes look larger as she nodded her head. There were spots of ink upon the hand with which she stood before him, nervously plaiting and folding her white skirts.

"He took her by the arm, and looked her, yet more closely and steadily, in the face. 'Now, die! I have done with you.'

"She shrunk, and uttered a low, suppressed cry.

"'I am not going to kill you. I will not endanger my life for yours. Die!'

"He sat before her in the gloomy Bride's Chamber, day after day, night after night, looking the word at her when he did not utter it. As often as her large unmeaning eyes were raised from the hands in which she rocked her head, to the stern figure, sitting with crossed arms and knitted forehead, in the chair, they read in it, 'Die!' When she dropped asleep in exhaustion, she was called back to shuddering consciousness, by the whisper, 'Die!' When she fell upon her old entreaty to be pardoned, she was answered, 'Die!' When she had out-watched and out-suffered the long night, and the rising sun flamed into the sombre room, she heard it hailed with, 'Another day and not dead?—Die!'

"Shut up in the deserted mansion, aloof from all mankind, and engaged alone in such a struggle without any respite, it came to this—that either he must die, or she. He knew it very well, and concentrated his strength against her feebleness. Hours upon hours he held her by the arm when her arm was black where he held it, and bade her Die!

"It was done, upon a windy morning, before sunrise. He computed the time to be half-past four; but, his forgotten watch had run down, and he could not be sure. She had broken away from him in the night, with loud and sudden cries—the first of that kind to which she had given vent—and he had had to put his hands over her mouth. Since then, she had been quiet in the corner of the panelling where she had sunk down; and he had left her, and had gone back with his folded arms and his knitted forehead to his chair.

"Paler in the pale light, more colourless than ever in the leaden dawn, he saw her coming, trailing herself along the floor towards him—a white wreck of hair, and dress, and wild eyes, pushing itself on by an irresolute and bending hand.

"'O, forgive me! I will do anything. O, Sir, pray tell me I may live!'

"'Die!'

"'Are you so resolved? Is there no hope for me?'

"'Die!'

"Her large eyes strained themselves with wonder and fear; wonder and fear changed to reproach; reproach to blank nothing. It was done. He was not at first so sure it was done, but that the morning sun was hanging jewels in her hair—he saw the diamond, emerald, and ruby, glittering among it in little points, as he stood looking down at her—when he lifted her and laid her on her bed,

"She was soon laid in the ground. And now they were all gone, and he had compensated himself well.

"He had a mind to travel. Not that he meant to waste his Money, for he was a pinching man and liked his Money dearly (liked nothing else, indeed), but, that he had grown tired of the desolate house and wished to turn his back upon it and have done with it. But, the house was worth Money, and Money must not be thrown away. He determined to sell it before he went. That it might look the less wretched and bring a better price, he hired some labourers to work in the overgrown garden ; to cut out the dead wood, trim the ivy that dropped in heavy masses over the windows and gables, and clear the walks in which the weeds were growing mid-leg high.

"He worked, himself, along with them. He worked later than they did, and, one evening at dusk, was left working alone, with his bill-hook in his hand. One autumn evening, when the Bride was five weeks dead.

"'It grows too dark to work longer,' he said to himself, 'I must give over for the night.'

"He detested the house, and was loath to enter it. He looked at the dark porch waiting for him like a tomb, and felt that it was an accursed house. Near to the porch, and near to where he stood, was a tree whose branches waved before the old bay-window of the Bride's Chamber, where it had been done. The tree swung suddenly, and made him start. It swung again, although the night was still. Looking up into it, he saw a figure among the branches.

"It was the figure of a young man. The face looked down, as his looked up ; the branches cracked and swayed ; the figure rapidly descended, and slid upon its feet before him. A slender youth of about her age, with long light brown hair.

"'What thief are you?' he said, seizing the youth by the collar.

"The young man, in shaking himself free, swung him a blow with his arm across the face and throat. They closed, but the young man got from him and stepped back, crying, with great eagerness and horror, 'Don't touch me ! I would as lieve be touched by the Devil !'

"He stood still, with his bill-hook in his hand, looking at the young man. For, the young man's look was the counterpart of her last look, and he had not expected ever to see that again.

"'I am no thief. Even if I were, I would not have a coin of your wealth, if it would buy me the Indies. You murderer!'

"'What!'

"'I climbed it,' said the young man, pointing up into the tree, "for the first time, nigh four years ago. I climbed it, to look at her. I saw her. I spoke to her. I have climbed it, many a time, to watch and listen for her. I was a boy, hidden among its leaves, when from that bay-window she gave me this!'

"He showed a tress of flaxen hair, tied with a mourning ribbon.

"'Her life,' said the young man, 'was a life of mourning. She gave me this, as a token of it, and a sign that she was dead to every one but you. If I had been older, if I had seen her sooner, I might have saved her from you. But, she was fast in the web when I first climbed the tree, and what could I do then to break it!'

"In saying those words, he burst into a fit of sobbing and crying: weakly at first, then passionately.

"'Murderer! I climbed the tree on the night when you brought her back. I heard her, from the tree, speak of the Death-watch at the door. I was three times in the tree while you were shut up with her, slowly killing her. I saw her, from the tree, lie dead upon her bed. I have watched you, from the tree, for proofs and traces of your guilt. The manner of it, is a mystery to me yet, but I will pursue you until you have rendered up your life to the hangman. You shall never, until then, be rid of me. I loved her! I can know no relenting towards you. Murderer, I loved her!'

"The youth was bareheaded, his hat having fluttered away in his descent from the tree. He moved towards the gate. He had to pass—Him—to get to it. There was breadth for two. old-fashioned carriages abreast; and the youth's abhorrence, openly expressed in every feature of his face and limb of his body, and very hard to bear, had verge enough to keep itself at a distance in. He (by which I mean the other) had not stirred hand or foot, since he had stood still to look at the boy. He faced round, now, to follow him with his eyes. As the back of the bare light-brown head was turned to him, he saw a red curve stretch from his hand to it. He knew, before he threw the bill-hook, where it had alighted—I say, had alighted, and not, would alight; for, to his clear perception the thing was done before he did it.   It cleft the head, and it remained there, and the boy lay on his face.

"He buried the body in the night, at the foot of the tree. As soon as it was light in the morning, he worked at turning up all the ground near the tree, and hacking and hewing at the neighbouring bushes and undergrowth.   When the labourers came, there was nothing suspicious, and nothing suspected.

"But, he had, in a moment, defeated all his precautions, and destroyed the triumph of the scheme he had so long concerted, and so successfully worked out.   He had got rid of the Bride, and had acquired her fortune without endangering his life; but now, for a death by which he had gained nothing, he had evermore to live with a rope around his neck.

"Beyond this, he was chained to the house of gloom and horror, which he could not endure.   Being afraid to sell it or to quit it, lest discovery should be made, he was forced to live in it.   He hired two old people, man and wife, for his servants; and dwelt in it, and dreaded it.   His great difficulty, for a long time, was the garden.   Whether he should keep it trim, whether he should suffer it to fall into its former state of neglect, what would be the least likely way of attracting attention to it?

"He took the middle course of gardening, himself, in his evening leisure, and of then calling the old serving-man to help him; but, of never letting him work there alone.   And he made himself an arbour over against the tree, where he could sit and see that it was safe.

"As the seasons changed, and the tree changed, his mind perceived dangers that were always changing.   In the leafy time, he perceived that the upper boughs were growing into the form of the young man—that they made the shape of him exactly, sitting in a forked branch swinging in the wind. In the time of the falling leaves, he perceived that they came down from the tree, forming tell-tale letters on the path, or that they had a tendency to heap themselves into a churchyard mound above the grave.   In the winter, when the tree was bare, he perceived that the boughs swung at him the ghost of the blow the young man had given, and that they threatened him openly.   In the spring, when sap was mounting in the trunk, he asked himself, were the dried-up particles of blood mounting with it: to make out more obviously this year than last, the leaf-screened figure of the young man, swinging in the wind?

"However, he turned his Money over and over, and still over. He was in the dark trade, the gold-dust trade, and most secret trades that yielded great returns. In ten years, he had turned his Money over, so many times, that the traders and shippers who had dealings with him, absolutely did not lie—for once—when they declared that he had increased his fortune, Twelve Hundred Per Cent.

"He possessed his riches one hundred years ago, when people could be lost easily. He had heard who the youth was, from hearing of the search that was made after him; but, it died away, and the youth was forgotten.

"The annual round of changes in the tree had been repeated ten times since the night of the burial at its foot, when there was a great thunder-storm over this place. It broke at midnight, and raged until morning. The first intelligence he heard from his old serving-man that morning, was, that the tree had been struck by Lightning.

"It had been riven down the stem, in a very surprising manner, and the stem lay in two blighted shafts: one resting against the house, and one against a portion of the old red garden-wall in which its fall had made a gap. The fissure went down the tree to a little above the earth, and there stopped. There was great curiosity to see the tree, and, with most of his former fears revived, he sat in his arbour -grown quite an old man—watching the people who came to see it.

"They quickly began to come, in such dangerous numbers, that he closed his garden-gate and refused to admit any more. But, there were certain men of science who travelled from a distance to examine the tree, and, in an evil hour, he let them in—Blight and Murrain on them, let them in!

"They wanted to dig up the ruin by the roots, and closely examine it, and the earth about it. Never, while he lived! They offered money for it. They! Men of science, whom he could have bought by the gross, with a scratch of his pen! He showed them the garden-gate again, and locked and barred it.

"But they were bent on doing what they wanted to do, and they bribed the old serving-man—a thankless wretch who regularly complained when he received his wages, of being underpaid—and they stole into the garden by night with their lanterns, picks, and shovels, and fell to at the tree. He was lying in a turret-room on the other side of the house (the Bride's Chamber had been unoccupied ever since), but he soon dreamed of picks and shovels, and got up.

"He came to an upper window on that side, whence he could see their lanterns, and them, and the loose earth in a heap which he had himself disturbed and put back, when it was last turned to the air. It was found! They had that minute lighted on it. They were all bending over it. One of them said, 'The skull is fractured;' and another, 'See here the bones;' and another, 'See here the clothes;' and then the first struck in again, and said, 'A rusty bill-hook!'

"He became sensible, next day, that he was already put under a strict watch, and that he could go nowhere without being followed. Before a week was out, he was taken and laid in hold. The circumstances were gradually pieced together against him, with a desperate malignity, and an appalling ingenuity. But, see the justice of men, and how it was extended to him! He was further accused of having poisoned that girl in the Bride's Chamber. He, who had carefully and expressly avoided imperilling a hair of his head for her, and who had seen her die of her own incapacity!

"There was doubt for which of the two murders he should be first tried; but, the real one was chosen, and he was found Guilty, and cast for Death. Bloodthirsty wretches! They would have made him Guilty of anything, so set they were upon having his life.

"His money could do nothing to save him, and he was hanged. *I* am He, and I was hanged at Lancaster Castle with my face to the wall, a hundred years ago!"

At this terrific announcement, Mr. Goodchild tried to rise and cry out. But, the two fiery lines extending from the old man's eyes to his own, kept him down, and he could not utter a sound. His sense of hearing, however, was acute, and he could hear the clock strike Two. No sooner had he heard the clock strike Two, than he saw before him Two old men!

Two.

The eyes of each, connected with his eyes by two films of fire: each, exactly like the other: each, addressing him at precisely one and the same instant: each, gnashing the same teeth in the same head, with the same twitched nostril above them, and the same suffused expression around it.   Two old men.   Differing in nothing, equally distinct to the sight, the copy no fainter than the original, the second as real as the first.

"At what time," said the Two old men, "did you arrive at the door below?"

"At Six."

"And there were Six old men upon the stairs!"

Mr. Goodchild having wiped the perspiration from his brow, or tried to do it, the Two old men proceeded in one voice, and in the singular number:

"I had been anatomised, but had not yet had my skeleton put together and re-hung on an iron hook, when it began to be whispered that the Bride's Chamber was haunted.   It *was* haunted, and I was there.

"*We* were there.   She and I were there.   I, in the chair upon the hearth; she, a white wreck again, trailing itself towards me on the floor.   But, I was the speaker no more, and the one word that she said to me from midnight until dawn was, 'Live!'

"The youth was there, likewise.   In the tree outside the window.   Coming and going in the moonlight, as the tree bent and gave.   He has, ever since, been there, peeping in at me in my torment; revealing to me by snatches, in the pale lights and slatey shadows where he comes and goes, bareheaded—a bill-hook, standing edgewise in his hair.

"In the Bride's Chamber, every night from midnight until dawn—one month in the year excepted, as I am going to tell you—he hides in the tree, and she comes towards me on the floor; always approaching; never coming nearer; always visible as if by moonlight, whether the moon shines or no; always saying, from midnight until dawn, her one word, 'Live!'

"But, in the month wherein I was forced out of this life —this present month of thirty days—the Bride's Chamber is empty and quiet.   Not so my old dungeon.   Not so the rooms where I was restless and afraid, ten years.   Both are fitfully haunted then.   At One in the morning, I am what you saw me when the clock struck that hour—One old man. At Two in the morning, I am Two old men.   At Three, I am Three.   By Twelve at noon, I am Twelve old men, One for every hundred per cent. of old gain.   Every one of the Twelve, with Twelve times my old power of suffering and agony.   From that hour until Twelve at night, I, Twelve old men in anguish and fearful foreboding, wait for the coming of the executioner. At Twelve at night, I, Twelve old men turned off, swing invisible outside Lancaster Castle, with Twelve faces to the wall!

"When the Bride's Chamber was first haunted, it was known to me that this punishment would never cease, until I could make its nature, and my story, known to two living men together. I waited for the coming of two living men together into the Bride's Chamber, years upon years. It was infused into my knowledge (of the means I am ignorant) that if two living men, with their eyes open, could be in the Bride's Chamber at One in the morning, they would see me sitting in my chair.

"At length, the whispers that the room was spiritually troubled, brought two men to try the adventure. I was scarcely struck upon the hearth at midnight (I come there as if the Lightning blasted me into being), when I heard them ascending the stairs. Next, I saw them enter. One of them was a bold, gay, active man, in the prime of life, some five and forty years of age; the other, a dozen years younger. They brought provisions with them in a basket, and bottles. A young woman accompanied them, with wood and coals for the lighting of the fire. When she had lighted it, the bold, gay, active man accompanied her along the gallery outside the room, to see her safely down the staircase, and came back laughing.

"He locked the door, examined the chamber, put out the contents of the basket on the table before the fire—little recking of me, in my appointed station on the hearth, close to him—and filled the glasses, and ate and drank. His companion did the same, and was as cheerful and confident as he: though he was the leader. When they had supped, they laid pistols on the table, turned to the fire, and began to smoke their pipes of foreign make.

"They had travelled together, and had been much together, and had an abundance of subjects in common. In the midst of their talking and laughing, the younger man made a reference to the leader's being always ready for any adventure; that one, or any other. He replied in these words:

"'Not quite so, Dick; if I am afraid of nothing else, I am afraid of myself.'

"His companion seeming to grow a little dull, asked him, in what sense? How?

" 'Why, thus,' he returned.   'Here is a Ghost to be dis-
proved.   Well!   I cannot answer for what my fancy might
do if I were alone here, or what tricks my senses might
play with me if they had me to themselves.   But, in
company with another man, and especially with you, Dick, I
would consent to outface all the Ghosts that were ever told
of in the universe.'

" 'I had not the vanity to suppose that I was of so much
importance to-night,' said the other.

" 'Of so much,' rejoined the leader, more seriously than he
had spoken yet, 'that I would, for the reason I have given,
on no account have undertaken to pass the night here alone.'

" It was within a few minutes of One.   The head of the
younger man had drooped when he made his last remark, and
it drooped lower now.

" 'Keep awake, Dick!' said the leader, gaily.   'The small
hours are the worst.'

" He tried, but his head drooped again.

" 'Dick!' urged the leader.   'Keep awake!'

" 'I can't,' he indistinctly muttered.   'I don't know what
strange influence is stealing over me.   I can't.'

" His companion looked at him with a sudden horror, and
I, in my different way, felt a new horror also; for, it was on
the stroke of One, and I felt that the second watcher was
yielding to me, and that the curse was upon me that I must
send him to sleep.

" 'Get up and walk, Dick!' cried the leader.   'Try!

" "It was in vain to go behind the slumberer's chair and
shake him.   One o'clock sounded, and I was present to the
elder man, and he stood transfixed before me.

" To him alone, I was obliged to relate my story, without
hope of benefit.   To him alone, I was an awful phantom
making a quite useless confession.   I foresee it will ever be
the same.   The two living men together will never come to
release me.   When I appear, the senses of one of the two
will be locked in sleep ; he will neither see nor hear me ; my
communication will ever be made to a solitary listener, and
will ever be unserviceable.   Woe!   Woe!   Woe!"

As the Two old men, with these words, wrung their hands,
it shot into Mr. Goodchild's mind that he was in the terrible
situation of being virtually alone with the spectre, and that
Mr. Idle's immovability was explained by his having been
charmed asleep at One o'clock.   In the terror of this sudden

discovery which produced an indescribable dread, he struggled so hard to get free from the four fiery threads, that he snapped them, after he had pulled them out to a great width. Being then out of bonds, he caught up Mr. Idle from the sofa and rushed downstairs with him.

"What are you about, Francis?" demanded Mr. Idle. "My bedroom is not down here. What the deuce are you carrying me at all for? I can walk with a stick now. I don't want to be carried. Put me down."

Mr. Goodchild put him down in the old hall, and looked about him wildly.

"What are you doing? Idiotically plunging at your own sex, and rescuing them or perishing in the attempt?" asked Mr. Idle, in a highly petulant state.

"The One old man!" cried Mr. Goodchild, distractedly, —"and the Two old men!"

Mr. Idle deigned no other reply than "The One old woman, I think you mean," as he began hobbling his way back up the staircase, with the assistance of its broad balustrade.

"I assure you, Tom," began Mr. Goodchild, attending at his side, "that since you fell asleep——"

"Come, I like that!" said Thomas Idle, "I haven't closed an eye!"

With the peculiar sensitiveness on the subject of the disgraceful action of going to sleep out of bed, which is the lot of all mankind, Mr. Idle persisted in this declaration. The same peculiar sensitiveness impelled Mr. Goodchild, on being taxed with the same crime, to repudiate it with honourable resentment. The settlement of the question of The One old man and The Two old men was thus presently complicated, and soon made quite impracticable. Mr. Idle said it was all Bride-cake, and fragments, newly arranged, of things seen and thought about in the day. Mr. Goodchild said how could that be, when he hadn't been asleep, and what right could Mr. Idle have to say so, who had been asleep? Mr. Idle said he had never been asleep, and never did go to sleep, and that Mr. Goodchild, as a general rule, was always asleep. They consequently parted for the rest of the night, at their bedroom doors, a little ruffled. Mr. Goodchild's last words were, that he had had, in that real and tangible old sitting-room of that real and tangible old Inn (he supposed Mr. Idle denied its existence?), every sensation and experience, the present record of which is now within a line or two of completion; and that he would write it out and print it every word. Mr. Idle returned that he might if he liked—and he did like, and has now done it.

CHAPTER V

Two of the many passengers by a certain late Sunday evening train, Mr. Thomas Idle and Mr. Francis Goodchild, yielded up their tickets at a little rotten platform (converted into artificial touchwood by smoke and ashes), deep in the manufacturing bosom of Yorkshire. A mysterious bosom it appeared, upon a damp, dark, Sunday night, dashed through in the train to the music of the whirling wheels, the panting of the engine, and the part-singing of hundreds of third-class excursionists, whose vocal efforts "bobbed arayound" from sacred to profane, from hymns, to our transatlantic sisters the Yankee Gal and Mairy Anne, in a remarkable way. There seemed to have been some large vocal gathering near to every lonely station on the line. No town was visible, no village was visible, no light was visible; but, a multitude got out singing, and a multitude got in singing, and the second multitude took up the hymns, and adopted our transatlantic sisters, and sang of their own egregious wickedness, and of their bobbing arayound, and of how the ship it was ready and the wind it was fair, and they were bayound for the sea, Mairy Anne, until they in their turn became a getting-out multitude, and were replaced by another getting-in multitude, who did the same. And at every station, the getting-in multitude, with an artistic reference to the completeness of their chorus, incessantly cried, as with one voice while scuffling into the carriages, " We mun aa' gang toogither ! "

The singing and the multitudes had trailed off as the lonely places were left and the great towns were neared, and the way had lain as silently as a train's way ever can, over the vague black streets of the great gulfs of towns, and among their branchless woods of vague black chimneys. These towns looked, in the cinderous wet, as though they had one and all been on fire and were just put out—a dreary and quenched panorama, many miles long.

Thus, Thomas and Francis got to Leeds; of which enterprising and important commercial centre it may be observed